A DICTIONARY OF

MEDIEVAL HEROES

*Characters in Medieval Narrative Traditions
and Their Afterlife in Literature,
Theatre and the Visual Arts*

Edited by Willem P. Gerritsen and
Anthony G. van Melle

Translated from the Dutch by
Tanis Guest

THE BOYDELL PRESS

Translation first published 1998
The Boydell Press, Woodbridge
Reprinted in paperback 2000

ISBN 0 85115 381 X hardback
ISBN 0 85115 780 7 paperback

Originally published 1993 as
*Van Aiol tot de Zwaanridder: Personages uit de middeleeuwse verhaalkunst
en hun voortleven in literatuur, theater en beeldende kunst*
by Uitgeverij Sun
© Sun, Nijmegen 1993

The Boydell Press is an imprint of Boydell & Brewer Ltd
PO Box 9, Woodbridge, Suffolk IP12 3DF, UK
and of Boydell & Brewer Inc.
PO Box 41026, Rochester, NY 14604-4126, USA
web site: http://www.boydell.co.uk

A catalogue record for this book is available
from the British Library

Library of Congress Catalog Card Number: 98-15872

This publication is printed on acid-free paper

CONTENTS

This translation has been supported by a grant from the
Netherlands Organisation for Scientific Research

PREFACE TO THE ENGLISH EDITION

Old stories never die. The Middle Ages left behind a large body of narratives –
epics as well as romances – which were once told and loved all over Europe.
Many of these stories lived on into later centuries, and some of them retain
some of their magic even today. Over the centuries the medieval stories
continued to inspire writers, composers and artists to renewed retellings,
reworkings, adaptations, and visual representations. This book is designed as a
guide to the narrative heritage of medieval Europe and its afterlife in various art
forms of later periods down to the present day.

The book began its life in 1993 as a volume in a series of reference books,
published by SUN at Nijmegen, on the formative traditions – classical, Judaeo-
Christian, and medieval – that contributed to the common cultural heritage of
Europe. The contributors to the volume, specialists in various domains of
medieval literature, were asked to present the leading characters of medieval
narrative fiction along with the principal works in which they figure, and to
describe the afterlife of each character in post-medieval literature and art.

As editors we take great pleasure in presenting this English version, entitled
A Dictionary of Medieval Heroes. The generous financial support of the
Netherlands Research Organisation NWO towards the translation is gratefully
acknowledged. We feel much indebted to Dr Tanis Guest for her careful and
elegant English rendering of the text. Thanks are also due to Dr Richard Barber
and his staff at Boydell & Brewer who took pains in pruning away details in the
text which would be of little interest to English readers; on the other hand the
text was enriched by a contribution on the indispensable Robin Hood. We
hope that the book will render services to anyone interested in medieval stories
and their amazing vitality.

THE EDITORS

INTRODUCTION

Every age selects its favourite characters from the stock of stories handed down to it, and provides those characters with a contemporary content. This is certainly the case with the literature of the Middle Ages; a great deal of originally medieval narrative material lives on in the literature, plastic arts and the various musical and theatrical forms of the five centuries since 1500. The object of this book is to trace the fortunes of over eighty characters from medieval narrative through time. The entries are arranged alphabetically; each begins by placing the character in the narrative context in which he – or she – first appears. There follows a survey of later medieval versions, with mention of the current state of scholarly research in that area. Where the character concerned also played a part in the work of post-medieval artists, the last section of the article is devoted to this 'afterlife'. This introduction provides the opportunity to sketch the contours of literary-historical development and briefly discuss some general aspects of medieval narrative.

We have already mentioned one feature which most of the narratives discussed in this book have in common: their retrospective nature. In other medieval narrative genres not treated here – in exempla, fabliaux and novellas, for instance – the action usually takes place in the present or in an unspecified recent past. Here, in the heroic epic, the *lai*, the romance and the various literary forms derived from them, events are usually set in a distant and splendid past. The most archaic epic narrative which has come down to us from Europe north of the Alps comes from Ireland (→ Cú Chulainn): the oldest texts date from the 9th, or possibly even from the 8th century, and depict a level of culture comparable with that of the Gauls as described by Caesar and other writers of antiquity. Not without reason did the Celtic scholar K.H. Jackson describe this Old Irish epic as 'a window on the Iron Age'. The most ancient manuscripts of Germanic heroic poetry date from around the year 1000; these poems relate to princes and heroes from the period of the migration of the tribes and the invasion of the Huns. The Gothic king → Theodoric the Great (493–526) becomes, as Dietrich von Bern, the favourite hero of 13th-century German epic. The French *chansons de geste*, written down from the 12th century on, recount events from the time of → Charlemagne (768–814), his predecessors and successors. The first Arthurian romances appear around 1160; they are set at the court of a king who, according to medieval historians, died in battle in 542. Even the story of → Floris and Blanchefleur, set mainly in an oriental world of very vague chronology, proves at the end to be firmly anchored in the past: the reunited lovers subsequently become the grandparents of Charlemagne.

The retrospective nature of many medieval tales can be explained in part by a very ancient function of narrative poetry: to perpetuate the memory of great events of the past. In an archaic society it is the poet-singer who embodies the tribe's collective memory. It is his task to provide the voice of the past when situations in the present require it. The blind Frisian bard Bernlef, who became a disciple of the evangelist St Liudger about 785, was revered by his contemporaries for his knowledge of the heroic deeds of the ancients and the wars of kings ('*antiquorum actus regumque certamina*'), of which he would sing to his own harp accompaniment. The Germanic *skop* (bard) was a highly respected figure, loved by king and people; the oldest Frisian laws specify a particular – and sizeable – compensation for injuring the hand of a harpist. In military operations, too, the bard had a significant role to play: it was he who inspired the warriors by recounting the glorious deeds of earlier heroes. The custom continued into later centuries: before the troops of William the Conqueror went into battle at Hastings in 1066, the warrior-minstrel Taillefer sang them a lay about → Roland.

Stories about the past had a contemporary function also; which explains why they were continually being adapted to different circumstances. The old stories were in fact a highly effective way of gaining acceptance for new and modern concepts or at least ensuring that they were discussed. A number of Old French *chansons de geste* tell of dynastic feuds in Carolingian times, while at the same time reflecting highly contemporary 12th-century feudal problems. What in the present was regarded as an ideal was presented as having been reality in the past. The oldest Arthurian romances provide a fine example of this. One of the 12th century's cultural ideals can be summed up in the notion of 'courtliness'. This relates to an aristocratic way of life, based on a complex of social skills which an individual must possess in order to take part in a lively social life. In the Arthurian romances – and even earlier, in the highly imaginative historical writing of Geoffrey of Monmouth – this modern cultural ideal is projected onto the (fictitious, as we now know) realm of King → Arthur, where chivalry supposedly had its finest flowering. And the new genre had a great deal more to offer than courtly example. In the hands of poets such as Chrétien de Troyes and Wolfram von Eschenbach Arthurian romance developed into *the* literary genre *par excellence* for the discussion of existential problems.

Wolfram's → Parzifal is the same as Chrétien's Perceval, and yet not the same. In adapting, expanding and completing Chrétien's unfinished romance *Perceval ou le Conte du Graal* the German poet permitted himself all kinds of deviations, among other things in his depiction of the eponymous hero. This applies even more strongly to the figure of Richard Wagner's Parsifal. This example shows that the concept of 'the character', as applied to the successive stages of a narrative tradition, is one of considerable complexity. On the one hand, there is beyond doubt a constant element: the character of Perceval with his (almost) unchanged name, and a basic pattern of events which remains broadly unchanged, are among the constants which maintain a narrative tradition and make it recognisable. But on the other hand the character can be compared to an empty hull which each new version of the story loads with a different cargo. Subtle shifts in personality are constantly appearing within the genre. A character who was at one time clearly among the public's favourites may in a later phase be treated with a hint of irony, and then at a still later stage retire to the second or third rank and make way for a new hero. A genre such as Arthurian romance assumes an intensely involved and critical public, a public which identifies with the people in the story and allows no smallest nuance to escape it.

An international public, at that. This is already the case with the very earliest literary survivals from the Germanic world. In → *Widsith*, an Old English poem from the second half of the 7th century, a *skop* enumerates the countries he has visited on his travels. He has appeared at the courts of mighty princes, before → Ermanaric, King of the Goths, before → Attila, Lord of the Huns, before Theodoric the Great, before King Alboin of the Longobards. Everywhere his art has been admired and he has been richly rewarded. In view of the fact that these princes lived in different centuries – the historical Ermanaric died in 375, Alboin in 573 – we have to regard the *skop* Widsith as a fictional figure. Nevertheless, the heroic songs he alludes to in the poem must have formed part of a single repertoire with many ramifications which was once well-known throughout north-western Europe.

Later genres also spread far beyond their lands of origin. Spanish and Italian versions have survived of a number of Old French *chansons de geste*; we also have versions in Middle Dutch (some of which were later adapted to the language of German-speaking hearers or readers) and in Old Norse. The Arthurian romances, translated into many languages (even, in one case, into Hebrew), can be considered common European cultural property. Also internationally known and translated into many languages were stories about such heroes of antiquity as → Hector, → Aeneas and → Alexander the Great, their deeds often presented in medieval narrative as examples of knightly and chivalrous behaviour. That the Low Countries more than once acted as an entrepôt in this international trade is clear, for instance, from beast epic, which spread from France to Germany and England partly via the Low Countries (→ Reynard).

In Widsith's day stories were recited or sung, accompanied by the notes of a harp. The audience listened as the singer presented the poem from memory. The *skop* carried his repertoire around with him in his head. That the Old English poem was ever set down in a manuscript is exceptional and probably more or less fortuitous; as yet writing still played little part in the creation and performance of vernacular literature. Eight hundred years later the technology of writing, perfected by the invention of printing, had totally changed the process of literary communication. In 1479 the master printer Gheraert Leeu printed a prose version of *Reynaert* in Gouda, and between 1487 and 1490 he published a *Reynaert* text in rhyme. Both books are primarily intended for individual reading (though it is not impossible that some purchaser of a copy also read aloud from it). The prose version is divided into chapters, each provided with a heading which summarises the content; a separate table of contents at the beginning of the book lists these chapter headings together with the page numbers. The rhymed incunable also has chapter headings, and this text is in addition illustrated with a number of masterly woodcuts. Both the chapter headings and the illustrations are visual aids used by Leeu to make reading easier. The eye has replaced the ear.

In the eight hundred years between *Widsith* and Gheraert Leeu narrative art distanced itself little by little from its oral origins. Following the example of Latin literature, from ancient times a literature of writers and readers, one by one the old tales in the European vernaculars were written down. The oldest narratives discussed in this book, including an epic such as → *Beowulf*, are still rooted entirely in the oral culture of the early Middle Ages. The earliest *chansons de geste*, such as the *Chanson de Roland* (→ Roland) and → *Gormond et Isambard*, also show all kinds of oral features. The performer constantly involves his audience in what is happening in his tale; enjoying a story is still a collective, social experience.

It was not only in Celtic lands that tales of King Arthur (→ Culhwch) were current; in England and France, too, travelling artists enjoyed success with narratives of the British king. That this material was popular in Italy as early as the first half of the 12th century can be seen from the famous relief over the entrance to Modena Cathedral, dating from between 1120 and 1140, which depicts an Arthurian story, and from a floor mosaic in Otranto Cathedral which shows Arthur mounted on a goat. Unfortunately, such indirect evidence is our only source of information about this oral narrative; the stories themselves have for the most part vanished for ever.

Around the middle of the 12th century *clerici* – intellectuals shaped by the study of rhetoric and Latin literature – began to devote themselves in a big way to writing works in the (French) vernacular. The earliest products of their writing-desks are the so-called classical romances, in which they adapted the 'matière de Rome', stories about Troy, → Aeneas and → Alexander the Great, to the taste of a 12th-century audience. Barely twenty years later it is the 'matière de Bretagne', the stories about King → Arthur and → Tristan, which are the focus of attention. Such writers as Chrétien de Troyes and Marie de France derive a great deal of their material from the oral tradition of the professional storytellers, but recast it in the form of a refined composition with a concealed deeper meaning, the *sen*. The same applies to some extent to Thomas, the poet of one of the earliest Tristan romances. Although the Arthurian romance in verse-form as conceived by Chrétien and his contemporaries never completely severed its links with history – after all, the action purported to take place partly at the court of King Arthur, who was regarded as a historical figure – the events recounted no longer laid claim to historical reality. The story did not have to be literally true to achieve its purpose. Through the skilful arrangement of invented elements (adventures), resulting in a truth of a higher order, the romance adds a new dimension to narrative: the dimension of fiction. This discovery of fictionality probably constitutes Arthurian romance's most significant contribution to the development of the European romance/novel.

The rise of the French prose romance in the first decades of the 13th century brought a number of important innovations. The choice of prose as the medium, rather than the traditional verse form associated with recitation, marked a further step along the road to a literature for readers. Unlike the verse romances, those in prose usually did not concentrate on the adventures of a single character but sought to recount the interlinked fortunes of a large number of characters within one complex narrative. In this way the prose romance presented itself as a chronicle, an all-embracing account that might sometimes span several decades. But things did not stop there. Lengthy prose romances were themselves amalgamated into cycles many hundreds of pages long. The best known of these is the so-called Vulgate Cycle, which consists of no fewer than six romances; the sequence of events begins in biblical times and ends with the destruction of Arthur's realm. Another work of impressive proportions is the so-called *Tristan en prose*. The same urge for completeness and synthesis manifested itself in the field of Carolingian epic in collected manuscripts and large compilations.

In the 14th century a counter-movement began to emerge; people in certain circles then evidently preferred shorter forms: independent, not-too-long romances or short stories, in verse or prose, which might or might not be contained in a framing narrative. At the same time, all over Europe much of the old epic material lived on in the form of ballads. And even outside Europe: in Sephardic Jewish communities in Morocco and Turkey, narrative songs dating from before the expulsion of the Jews from Spain in 1492 continued to be sung down to our own century.

The printing press gave medieval narrative a new lease of life and a new audience. By about 1500 it was no longer uncommon for a reasonably prosperous city-dweller to own a number of books. In order to fill the demand for reading material, the printers went in for wholesale reworking of the old knightly romances. The text was modernised: verse was replaced by prose, the narrative style was tailored to the private reader, and where necessary the message was made clearer or adapted to a bourgeois system of values. After use, the parchment manuscript which had provided the text for the printed book was often cut up and used to stiffen bindings or boiled down for bookbinder's glue. The old tales in their new form were also of use in education, particularly in the so-called 'French schools' (so called because their pupils learnt French instead of Latin). In the play *Moortje* (1615) by the Dutch playwright Bredero, a child's St Nicholas Day presents include not only a slate and a catechism but also some reading books, including the tales of 'Blanchefleur' and 'Amadis van Gauwelen'.

Slowly but surely the repertoire of stories handed down from the Middle Ages slid down the social scale. Influenced by humanism and the Renaissance, the literature of the cultural elite changed decisively. The literary ideals of the 17th-century Golden Age inexorably forced the medieval material down to the level of light reading for the lower classes. But at that humbler level the old tales of chivalry proved to be real die-hards. Reprint after reprint, in ever shabbier form, on grey paper with worn-out letters, bears witness to their stubborn durability. Some chapbooks, such as the story of the 'Vier Heemskinderen' (→ Renaut de Montauban), managed to survive until well into the 19th century.

In the 17th century, and much of the 18th, the term 'medieval' was associated almost entirely with backwardness, barbarity and superstition. In the second half of the 18th century this negative attitude quite suddenly changed to a fascinated interest in the culture of the national past, and especially the remnants of medieval literature. Not that everyone was instantly convinced of its importance. When in 1782 Christoph Heinrich Myller sent his *editio princeps* of the *Nibelungenlied*, in his view a German *Iliad*, to the Prussian king Frederick II, that monarch personally informed him that he thought the poem 'not worth a shot of gunpowder' and would not dream of including it in his palace library.

The romantic poets and writers who became active soon after 1800 found in medieval narrative a source of inspiration which, they thought, gave them a direct line to the primeval forces of human nature: feeling, imagination, creativity. The parable, in the form of a dedication to Clemens Brentano, with which Joseph Görres prefaced his survey of German chapbooks in 1807 is highly significant here. He recounts how he once wandered through the forest by night, vainly trying to decipher a message from Nature in the babbling of a brook. He encounters a monk who takes him inside a rock. There he finds the old Emperor Barbarossa, sitting at a table with his beard grown into it and surrounded by such heroes as Renaut de Montauban, Charlemagne, Siegfried, Hagen and Duke Ernst. 'What do you seek among the dead, stranger?' asks Barbarossa. 'I seek life,' is the answer, 'one must delve deep in the dry ground to find the spring.' Whereupon Barbarossa refers him to the books in which the heroic deeds of old are recorded.

Following in the tracks of Görres and other 'explorers', countless 19th-century artists 'sought life' in medieval narratives. And found it. It turned out that the old material could lend itself to the most diverse purposes – aesthetic, moral, political and ideological. The ideal of the 'gentleman' that took shape in Victorian England – the gentleman with his code of honour and service, his love of ritual, his passion for sport and games, and with his prudery – was to a considerable extent an invented tradition borrowed from the knightly world of the Middle Ages; not, of course, from the reality of knightly existence, but from the idealised literary depiction of it in the tales of Sir Thomas Malory. In 19th-century Germany the dream of the old Holy Roman Empire was constantly used to legitimise and direct political aspirations, while the genius of Richard Wagner created in Parsifal, Tristan and Siegfried figures which embodied both the ideal and the tragic elements in the 19th-century view of man. France recognised the basic idea of its 'mission civilisatrice' in Europe and beyond in the pious heroism of Charlemagne and his paladins, as hymned in the *Chanson de Roland*. One could say without much exaggeration that every 19th-century nation was busily shaping and polishing its own identity, and that in doing so each created a mythology based to a significant extent on its heritage of medieval narrative.

What has our own century produced from these well-ploughed fields? Although the medieval presence is clearly far less all-pervasive in 20th-century art than in that of the 19th century, there is still a constant stream of distinguished artists who draw on medieval narrative material in their work. The old stories can be interpreted as myths in which basic human experiences appear to be linked and combined in narrative form. It seems that major themes of 20th-century art – isolation, love and sexuality, the individual versus society – can be embodied time and again, and always differently, in such archetypal figures as Perceval and Lancelot. Often the poets and novelists are following, at a little distance, the theories of the literary historians. Thus, T.S. Eliot borrowed much of the symbolism in *The Waste Land* from Jessie Weston's *From Ritual to Romance*, a comprehensive (though rather wild) anthropological interpretation of the Grail story. The history of the reception of medieval narrative material in 20th-century art is largely still to be written. One of the surprises in compiling this book was that there turned out to be so much more than the authors had expected. Through countless adaptations, in every kind of medium, on every level, some part of the old narrative repertoire has succeeded in winning itself a place in the mental baggage of 20th-century man. This book hopes not only to help the reader find his way in the world of the medieval stories, but to make him aware of a tradition which links the narrative art of our own day with that from a far distant past.

Finally, a few words about the selection criteria used in compiling this book. Anyone seeking to give a complete picture of medieval narrative and its effects on literature and art in later ages would need to include the extensive field of hagiography, as well as a range of 'small' narrative genres such as fable, novella, exemplum and anecdote. The scope of this book did not permit such a broad approach. It confines itself principally to the two main genres of 'epic' and 'romance', each with a periphery of earlier, later or otherwise related forms. The 'High Middle Ages' (12th and 13th centuries) can be considered as the heyday of medieval narrative; works from these centuries have therefore received relatively more attention than the heroic epic of the early Middle Ages or the late medieval aftermath of epic and romance. It was necessary also to impose a geographical limitation: Western Europe, with particular attention to the Low Countries. But choosing means losing: the rich treasure of tales from Ireland and Wales is represented by only a few works; Old Norse literature, no less important, is mentioned only in passing; Southern and Eastern Europe are hardly considered at all ... But against this restriction of the field of view can be set a broadening of the horizon; an attempt has been made to chart the influence of medieval narrative material on all forms of modern art and literature.

It would have been theoretically possible to arrange the material on the basis of titles of works or authors' names (where these are known). Apart from the many practical problems involved, such an arrangement would probably have made the book awkward to use. It seemed an attractive alternative to take the name of the main character of a story or complex of stories for the head-word, though this formula too was not without its disadvantages: it appeared to reduce all other characters to the second rank. In particular, it is unfair to a number of prominent female characters, many of them quite as interesting as their male counterparts. As a small recompense, all the characters mentioned in the book are included in the index. Between them, the articles in this dictionary cover a large segment of medieval narrative; at the end of each article is a note on editions and studies listed in the bibliography. Further information, and information on characters and stories not included in the book, can be found through the reference works listed at the beginning of the bibliography.

W.P. GERRITSEN

Aeneas' fleet arriving off the coast of Italy. Limoges enamel, c.1525–1530. New York, Metropolitan Museum.

AENEAS (often spelt Eneas in the Middle Ages), son of Dardanus' descendant Anchises and the goddess Venus, husband of King Priam's daughter Creusa and father of Ascanius, is the Trojan hero who becomes the ancestor of the Roman people.

As Homer recounts in the *Iliad*, he plays a significant part in the Trojan War; his subsequent adventures are described by Virgil in the *Aeneid*. He loses Creusa in the burning of Troy. With Anchises and Ascanius he sets out for Italy at the head of a group of survivors; it is the will of the gods that he should found a city there. His wanderings take him – his father having died on the way – to Carthage, recently founded by Dido (also known as Elissa), who had fled from Tyre following the murder of her husband Sychaeus. Dido falls passionately in love with Aeneas; because of him she breaks her vow of eternal fidelity to Sychaeus, which she has kept until now. Aeneas returns her love; but their happiness is short-lived. Reminded by the gods of his mission, and despite Dido's pleas, Aeneas leaves. Humiliated, the deserted Dido kills herself. After a visit to the Underworld, where Anchises shows him the future Rome, Aeneas' journey ends at the mouth of the Tiber. There King Latinus recognises in him the stranger who, it has been foretold, will marry his daughter Lavinia. Although there is another claimant, Turnus, who is favoured by Queen Amata, the aged Latinus promises his kingdom and his daughter to Aeneas. After a violent conflict which costs the life of Pallas, the son of Aeneas' companion Euander who lives on the Palatine, Turnus is defeated and Aeneas marries Lavinia. Of this marriage Silvius is born, after Aeneas has been given a place among the gods. Aeneas' descendants become the founders of Rome.

The saga of Aeneas assumed its classical form in Virgil's heroic epic the *Aeneid* (29–19 BC), a literary masterpiece with an ideological function rooted in Olympian theology: the account of Rome's founding served to legitimise the city's position in the ancient world. Virgil constructed his image of the faithful Aeneas, who follows the will of the gods and fulfils his mission by uniting Trojans and Latins into one people, from traditions current in his day. The figure of Dido is taken from the legend of the Tyrian widow Elissa; according to the 3rd-century historian Justinus, when after the founding of Carthage her subjects tried to force her to marry the North African king Jarbas, she preferred to throw herself into the flames rather than break her vow. Ovid has a version of the story of Dido and Aeneas in the form of a farewell letter from Dido to Aeneas (*Heroides* 7).

Virgil's *Aeneid*, like Ovid's *Heroides*, was much read in the Middle Ages: as a literary model to be imitated, as a historical source for the Trojan War and the foundation of Rome, and as a story with a deeper, allegorical significance; its original ideological function now retreated into the background. The literature of Troy also contained less edifying tales of Aeneas' role in the struggle for the city, according to which Troy was taken not by a stratagem (the Trojan Horse) but through treachery by, among others, Aeneas. In antiquity stories about the traitor Aeneas were marginalised by the authority of Homer and Virgil, but they had considerable influence in the Middle Ages. Reception of both the *Aeneid* and the alternative story of Troy led to a split in the medieval image of Aeneas. At first both versions are current, as it were on different tracks; but from the 12th century on, and especially in the 13th, they begin to exercise a mutual influence. Finally, sympathy for Dido, which had in ancient times been considerable but subordinated to an understanding of Aeneas' position (St Augustine relates in his *Confessiones* that he had wept for her as a young man), told against Aeneas once the ideological justification for his behaviour was lost.

The story of the betrayal, in which Antenor is the leader but Aeneas is clearly implicated, was in circulation as early as c.400 BC. It is related at length in two late-classical prose works which claim to be eye-witness accounts of the Siege of Troy: the *Ephemeris belli Troiani*, a journal attributed to Dictys the Cretan (Latin version from the 4th century), and the narrative *De excidio Troiae historia*, supposedly by Dares the

Phrygian, a participant on the Trojan side (Latin version 5th or 6th century; more on Dictys and Dares under → Hector). In Dares, Aeneas is described as 'loyal to the Trojan cause' and acquits himself well in battle, but after Hector's death he is one of the peace party which wants to hand Helen back. He is involved in secret discussions with the Greeks and in the opening of the city gate, the Greeks having promised to spare him. He hides Polyxena (→ Hector) in Anchises' house; when this becomes known he is banished by Agamemnon. Dictys gives more detail than Dares of the betrayal, making Aeneas look even blacker. The traitors even smuggle the Palladium, the holy image which protects Troy from being conquered, into the hands of the Greeks. Moreover, Aeneas commits a second treason: once the Greeks have left he plans a coup against the Trojans' new leader, Antenor; this leaks out and the Trojans themselves force him to leave Troy. Clearly, it is not only for poetic reasons that Virgil makes the ghost of Hector appear to Aeneas just before the Greeks break into Troy and command him in the name of the gods to leave the city.

Late-classical literature takes over Virgil's picture of Aeneas. The treason remains in the background. Commentators such as Servius are aware of it. Christian writers make little play with it. Tertullian mentions it, but evidently expects readers familiar with Virgil to give it no credence; his comments are directed at the Aeneas depicted in the *Aeneid*.

In patristic literature the problems with Aeneas mainly relate to his apotheosis. This is grist to the mill of the Euhemeristic critique of the gods (so called from Euhemeros of Messene, c.340–260 BC), which supports the view that the gods are no more than men who were venerated after their deaths for their achievements. The tale of the fleeing Aeneas rescuing the gods from burning Troy is also seen as proving the impotence of the gods and the foolishness of those who look to them for aid (so says Augustine in *De civitate Dei*).

This does not mean that Aeneas is universally vilified in Christian literature. The Church fathers opposed the *Aeneid* as a heathen document. But alongside and apart from this, Virgil's epic was admired and imitated as a literary work of art by such Christian poets and rhetoricians as Claudianus, Corippus, Ennodius and Sidonius, who were to be highly influential in the Middle Ages.

The mythographer Fulgentius (*Expositio Vergilianae continentiae*, 5th century) interprets the *Aeneid* as an allegory of the life of man: a child up to the death of Anchises, an adolescent until the loss overboard of the helmsman Palinurus (just before the end of the voyage), gaining wisdom during the visit to the Underworld. This view was to exert a considerable influence on medieval interpretations. Virgil treats events from the fall of Troy up to Turnus' death in 'ordo artificialis' (artificial order): the *Aeneid* begins *in medias res*, and earlier events are recounted in flash-backs. The *Excidium Troiae* (6th century), intended as an aid to the study of the most ancient Roman history, provides a fuller, chronological survey of the Trojan War, the adventures of Aeneas (a summary of the *Aeneid*, with an additional section on his marriage to Lavinia and his apotheosis) and the foundation of Rome. The Middle Ages, with a preference for the 'ordo naturalis', gratefully seized on this useful summary.

Because of the *Aeneid*, the exemplary Aeneas was a presence in the Middle Ages from the start. Around 800 → Charlemagne, builder of a new Rome in Aachen, was portrayed in the epic *Karolus Magnus et Leo papa* as 'a second Aeneas' by means of quotations from Virgil. Until the middle of the 12th century the faithful Aeneas has the field practically to himself. According to Bernardus Sylvestris (12th century) he is a model of patient endurance (*tolerantia*), charity (*pietas*) and religious faith (*religio*). The Dido-and-Aeneas theme is still current; Ovid's *Heroides* letter is rewritten in hexameters and two of the *Carmina Burana* are laments by Dido in rhythmical stanzas. But commentators on Virgil follow Fulgentius and regard Dido as an allegory of unlawful love (Bernardus Sylvestris).

Around the mid-12th century the princely courts begin to take a great interest in antiquity. A short space of time sees the composition of the three Old French 'romans antiques' (*Thebes*, *Eneas* and *Roman de Troie*). Together they cover ancient history down to the founding of Rome, based on Latin works which serve as a source for the events rather than as literary models. Eneas becomes the hero of two early courtly romances: the *Roman d'Eneas* by an unknown author at the Anglo-Norman court (c.1150–55, over 10,000 lines) and Hendrik van Veldeke's Middle Dutch version of it, the *Eneit* (completed shortly before 1190 at the court of the Landgrave of Thüringen, almost 13,500 lines). The classical narrative material was adapted to the medieval world and its literary conventions. Eneas' adventures are recounted as though he were a knight. The role of the gods is reduced (they cannot, of course, be omitted entirely), courtly love and heroic combat take centre stage. The main characters' emotions are described in detail and expressed in monologues. They are those of chivalric culture ('anachronisme moral'), as are also their dress, domestic and military way of life, cities, palaces and fortresses ('travestie de costume'; see also → Hector).

Both these romances of Eneas devote much less time to the beginning of his journey than to his experiences in Carthage and Italy; Book III of the *Aeneid* is reduced to a few lines. The tone of the Dido episode is that of Virgil; Dido's lament, more passionate in the *Eneas* than in Veldeke with his concern for 'mâze', is still accusatory, but she forgives Eneas his unfaithfulness. From the moment Eneas lands in Italy the connection with the *Aeneid* becomes looser. Virgil determines the course of events up to the death of Turnus, though the struggle between Eneas and Turnus is narrated in much more detail: the founding of the fortress of Montauban, the heroic deeds of Pallas and of Camilla and her Amazons, Eneas' duels with Turnus. Independent of Virgil (who ends with the death of Turnus and takes little interest in Lavinia), but in line with Ovid, Veldeke and his predecessor are able to turn the developing love between Eneas and Lavinia, from the first encounter to the wedding, into a love story according to courtly conventions; in the *Eneas* this runs to some 1700 lines. It sets the seal on the image of Eneas as the landless knight from foreign parts who with a wife gains a kingdom.

Virgil and Ovid are also used as historical sources. Wace incorporates a summary of the *Aeneid* in his *Roman de* → *Brut* (1155) because a certain Brutus, a descendant of Aeneas, had been regarded ever since Nennius (9th century) as the Trojan ancestor of the Britons (→ Hector). Guido of Pisa makes room for the *Excidium Troiae* in his *Liber historiarum* (c.1118). The account of Dido and Aeneas in Alfonso el Sabio's *Crónica general* (13th century) is based on Ovid's *Heroides* letter. The compiler of the *Histoire ancienne jusqu'à César* (pre-1213–30) conflates the material of the 'romans antiques' into one survey of classical history (reminiscent of the custom of grouping them together in manuscripts). However, he bases his work not on the romances themselves but on their classical sources. Thus, the section on Eneas is derived not from the *Roman d'Eneas* but from the *Aeneid*, which the author reworks, with Servius' aid, into a chronological account of Eneas' life and adventures; confining himself to the facts, he systematically eliminates the marvels (including the journey to the Underworld) and punctuates the whole with moralisations in verse. The *Histoire ancienne* remained extremely popular down to the 15th century; almost sixty manuscripts of it survive, together with a revised version and an Italian translation from the 14th century.

Around 1165, in the years between the *Eneas* and the *Eneit*, the 'truth about Troy' as told by Dares and Dictys begins its triumphal progress with the *Roman de Troie* by Benoît de Sainte-Maure (→ Hector). In dealing with the fall of Troy Benoît follows Dictys the Cretan; as a result, Aeneas' treachery comes to feature widely in literature about Troy. Benoît, who does not describe Eneas' adventures, makes no use of Virgil's picture of the faithful Aeneas. Neither does Guido de Columpnis (*Historia destructionis Troiae*, 1272–87), though he does refer his readers to Virgil for information on Eneas after his flight from Troy. Even the author of the *Histoire ancienne jusqu'à César*, who after summarising Dictys does the the same for the *Aeneid*, ignores the issue. Not so Jacob van Maerlant, who also included a version of the *Aeneid* in his *Historie van Troyen*; he opts for Virgil's Eneas and rejects Benoît's account, because he cannot believe that God chose a rogue to be the ancestor of the Roman people. The *Historie van Troyen* takes nothing from Benoît that could reflect badly on Eneas and Antenor. This is the exception, however, and Eneas' treachery became common knowledge even outside strictly Trojan literature; for instance, in John Gower's *Confessio Amantis* (c.1390) and in *Sir Gawain and the Green Knight* (→ *Gawain*) (also late 14th century).

From the beginning of the 14th century the tale of the faithful Elissa, who would die rather than remarry, again comes to the fore. The author of the *Histoire ancienne jusqu'à César* knows the tale from Servius and modifies it: Dido does indeed throw herself into the flames to avoid marrying Jarbas, but her subjects save her in spite of herself. The Dido-and-Eneas episode à la Virgil can then follow this innovation. Boccaccio in his Dido story follows Justinus (*De casibus virorum illustrium*, 1356–60), rejecting Virgil's version as a poetic fiction.

The reception of Ovid (*Roman de la Rose*, 13th century, and *Ovide moralisé*, 1316–28) provides the final link in the chain of factors leading to the perception of Dido as a woman deceived, victim of the traitor Eneas and not of the gods – who have in any case had to surrender their role to Fortune. A whole series of writers takes up the cudgels on her behalf: Boccaccio (*Amorosa visione*, 1341–42; *De mulieribus claris*, 1361–62), Chaucer (*The House of Fame*, 1380; *The Legend of Good Women*, 1385–86), Christine de Pisan (*Epistre au Dieu d'amours*, 1399; *Livre de la Cité des Dames*, 1405), John Lydgate (*The Fall of Princes*, 1431–39) and many others. But the anti-Eneas front is not solid. In the Inferno Dante sees Eneas and Lavinia in company with → Hector, and Dido with Achilles.

Humanism was to burnish Virgil's image of Aeneas once more, and Octovien de Saint-Gelais' translation of the *Aeneid* (1500) marks the start of the period during which it became available as a literary work in the vernacular. But Troy and Dido were to dog Aeneas' heels for a long time.

Illustrations of Aeneas' adventures are to be found mainly in the many costly manuscripts of the *Aeneid* and the various versions of it made for royalty and the nobility. Illuminated manuscripts from before the mid-13th century are rare; after that date they are too numerous to mention and the *Histoire ancienne jusqu'à César* and the literature of Troy (→ Hector) are also represented. From the 15th century on, pictorial documentation includes tapestries, cassoni (bridal chests) and old printed books (such as *Le Livre des Eneydes compilé par Virgile*, Lyons 1483 at Guillaume le Roy, with 61 engravings). The commonest subjects are Dido and Aeneas, Lavinia and Aeneas (appropriate to cassoni) and, in the romances of Troy, the treachery of Aeneas.

L.J. ENGELS

Edition: Eisenhut 1958.
Studies: Semrau 1930; Boeckler 1939; Quint 1954; Scherer 1963; Leube 1969; Buchtal 1971; Cormier 1973; Lida de Malkiel 1974; Roberts-Baytop 1974; Comparetti 1981; Suerbaum 1981.

A IOL is the eponymous hero of an Old French *chanson de geste* which survives in a single 13th-century manuscript. Duke Elie, the husband of Avisse, sister to King → Louis the Pious, has been unjustly banished from France at the instigation of Makaris of Lausanne, despite the many services he had rendered to Louis in his struggle with the Saracens. Elie and his wife have taken refuge in the Landes, near Bordeaux, where they have found shelter with a hermit. There Avisse gives birth to a son who is given the name of Aiol.

When Aiol is old enough his father sends him, mounted on his old horse Marchegai and wearing his old and rusty armour, and equipped with a great deal of good advice, to Louis' court where he is to bring about his father's rehabilitation and recover his fiefdom. After a long and adventurous journey Aiol reaches Orleans, where he is ridiculed because of his horse and armour. But one of his mother's sisters, noticing his noble bearing, instructs her daughter to offer him hospitality. The girl, Lusiane, falls in love with Aiol and declares her feelings to him. Aiol rejects her because he wants to fulfil his mission first. Not until the following day, when the mother tells him that she is Avisse's sister, does Aiol realise that Lusiane is his cousin. Aiol himself does not yet tell Louis' court of his identity.

King Louis is also in Orleans. He is involved in a conflict with the Count of Bourges, who is seeking to avenge Elie's unjust banishment and recover his lands. Aiol vanquishes the Count of Bourges and delivers him to Louis, but asks mercy for him on discovering that the count is his cousin. In this way Aiol gains the favour of the king, who showers him with favours which Aiol shares with many others. Still Aiol does not reveal himself.

Aiol next travels to Pamplona where he rescues Mirabel, daughter of the Mohammedan King Mibrien, from two abductors and takes her with him. After many adventures the two reach Orleans where Aiol reveals his identity and demands his father's fiefdom as reward. When Lusiane learns that Aiol is her cousin she regretfully abandons her thoughts of marrying him.

Mirabel is baptised. Aiol recovers his father's possessions and sends messengers to his parents, who bid farewell to the hermit. Back at the royal court, Elie is reconciled with Louis. The marriage of Aiol and Mirabel is solemnised by the Archbishop of Rheims.

The wedding takes place in Langres, where Makaris attacks the festivities with thirty thousand men. He carries Aiol and Mirabel off to Lausanne and shuts them up in a dungeon. Here Mirabel gives birth to twins. Makaris promptly seizes both infants and throws them into the Rhône. The nobleman Thierry happens to be fishing by moonlight under the bridge from which Makaris throws the boys and he 'fishes' them

Thierry shows his
wife the twin sons
of Aiol and Mirabel
after saving them
from drowning.
Miniature in the
only surviving,
13th-century
manuscript of *Aiol*.
Paris, Bibliothèque
Nationale.

out of the river. Fearing reprisals from Makaris, he and his wife take the boys to Venice, where he offers his services to King Gratien. The two boys are immediately baptised and are named Manesier and Tumas.

Because of disaffection among his own people, who are threatening to defect to Louis' army, Makaris flees from Lausanne disguised as a merchant, with four servants and also Aiol and Mirabel, whom he hands over to Mirabel's father Mibrien. Mibrien throws them into prison because neither of them is willing to worship Mohammed. Bandits steal Aiol from the prison and sell him to King Gratien; Mirabel is left alone, imprisoned in Pamplona.

Aiol helps Gratien to capture the city of Thessaloniki and remains at court in the company of Gratien's two adopted sons, who remind him sadly of his own two children whom he imagines to be dead. When Aiol makes himself known for the third time, in the presence of his children and of Thierry and his wife, the latter at last give in to his grief and tell him the truth. Aiol and Gratien then ask for Louis' help in freeing Mirabel, and succeed in doing so. Makaris suffers death by quartering, Mibrien converts to Christianity, Aiol and Mirabel return to Burgundy with Elie and their two sons return to Venice.

The extant *chanson de geste*, 10,983 lines in length and dating from around 1220, was probably produced in Picardy as a reworking of an older version of c.1170. In this *Aiol* we find the traditional epic themes: knightly honour and loyalty and the restoration of honour contrasting with disloyalty, treachery and punishment by death, the holy war against the Saracens, the love of a heathen princess for a Christian hero and her conversion to Christianity.

There are two Middle Dutch versions of the Old French heroic poem, both frag-mentary: the *Limburg Aiol* and the *Flemish Aiol*. The writer of the *Limburg Aiol* seems to have attempted to reflect the Old French narrative as faithfully as possible, but his version offers a more concentrated, more swiftly moving tale.

The author of the *Flemish Aiol* took a quite different approach from that of the Limburg version; he did not directly translate the Old French work but gave a free rendering of it, cutting its length to about a third and omitting many episodes. Among other things, he cut back on the feudal elements which had received considerable emphasis in the Old French story, such as the traditional battles and duels and Aiol's recovery of his fiefdom. By contrast, he gave greater coverage to certain religious elements. For instance, he expands upon the fact that Aiol's children were saved from drowning by the will of God: it is an angel sent by God who commands Thierry to go fishing by night. The importance of the two children's baptism is stressed on two separate occasions. The writer seems to have been well acquainted with the epic narratives current in his time. He replaced certain characters in the Old French *Aiol* with well-known epic figures from other heroic tales. The motifs to be found in the added episode were also not of his own invention.

Apart from the two Middle Dutch versions of the *Aiol*, there are also two Italian versions and one Spanish. The oldest extant Italian version is a prose romance, probably written at the end of the 14th century by Andrea da Barberino and most likely based on a lost Italian verse text. The first part of this prose romance is a retelling of the Old French *Aiol*. The second part is concerned with the two sons and four grandsons of Aiol, with Aiol himself playing an insignificant role, retreating from the world as a hermit. The second, rhymed version, an adaptation of the prose romance, was printed twice at the beginning of the 16th century. The Spanish version consists of three 'romances' (epic poems) the hero of which, Montesinos, undergoes many adventures which show a marked resemblance to those of Aiol.

B. FINET-VAN DER SCHAAF

Editions: Normand/Reynaud 1877; Gysseling 1980.

ALEXANDER THE GREAT (356–23), son of King Philip II of Macedonia and Queen Olympias, subjugated Greece (336–34), crossed the Hellespont (334) and marched through Asia Minor and Syria to Egypt, where following his visit to the shrine of Ammon he was regarded as a son of Zeus/Ammon. He defeated the Persian king Darius III in three battles. Having established himself as ruler of the Persian Empire he marched east, crossed the Indus, defeated the Indian king Porus and reached the Hydaspes River. Here he was forced to turn back because his army refused to go any further. According to tradition, having conquered the East he intended to conquer the West also. He died in Babylon.

Alexander caught the medieval imagination more than any other of the great figures of antiquity. Not even the story of Troy could compete, as the 13th-century Dutch writer Jacob van Maerlant, who had written about both (→ Hector) and thus spoke from experience, remarked: 'The Trojan matter seems small indeed when Alexander's tale you read' (*Alexanders Geesten*). There was an abundance of information about Alexander, more than can be included in this survey. What was regarded as history was, however, very largely fiction; from late antiquity until the Renaissance (and in some fields even later) the image of Alexander was determined far less by genuine historiography than by the legend which had begun to emerge even in his own lifetime.

Moreover, that image lacks coherence. Built up out of heterogeneous ancient, Jewish and Arabic traditions, its reception was complicated by a comprehensive mixing of sources, fuelled by Western medieval ways of thinking, and constantly adapted to new functions and new needs. What was derived from classical and late antiquity, in addition to historiography, was above all the Alexander romance, the associated literature on the marvels of India and the philosophical critique of Alexander; the last of these lived on in, among other things, the many exempla which, originating for the most part with Cicero, Seneca and Valerius Maximus, were transmitted by Christian writers such as St Augustine and St Jerome. Biblical and Jewish traditions spread the image of Alexander as the instrument of God. In Arabic literature Alexander, having been tutored by Aristotle, survived principally as a scholar and philosopher-king. These traditions became mingled but without producing a synthesis, so that the tradition an author used remains a significant factor in his portrayal of Alexander. The traditions were also medievalised. The Alexander story of late antiquity is reworked into knightly romance, with Alexander and his companions not only carrying out heroic exploits but also paying chivalrous court to noble ladies (including the Amazons). The son of the Indian queen Candace recovers his abducted wife with the help of Alexander. Candace recognises Alexander when he tries to visit her incognito. According to the ancient story she reminds him of his mother Olympias. This is also the case in the *Strassburg Alexander* (c.1180), but here Alexander and Candace also make love (which has given rise to thoughts of Oedipus). In the *Roman d'Alexandre*, the *Basle Alexander*, Ulrich von Etzenbach's *Alexander* and the *Kyng Alisaunder* (c.1330) Candace is simply Alexander's mistress; all thought of his mother has disappeared. But in Johan Hartlieb (c.1445) Candace's feelings for her guest are strictly maternal.

Nor can we speak of a single medieval attitude to Alexander. He is viewed now favourably, now unfavourably, even by the same author or in the same work; actions and events can be regarded in widely differing ways. He is praised for his generosity, but when he gives a city to an old soldier because he wants his gifts to be on a scale befitting himself it is considered as *hubris*; and there is frequent mention of the tale of the sunbathing Diogenes: when Alexander asks Diogenes what he can do for him, and happens to be standing between him and the sun, the answer is: 'Stand out of my light.' Alexander's aerial journey in a vehicle drawn by griffins is interpreted as proof of *superbia* (pride) and *curiositas* (then still widely regarded with suspicion); but it is also explained as an exemplum of the pious soul's striving for heaven. Attempts to delineate the image of

Alexander in terms of milieu and genre (favourable in courtly secular literature, unfavour-able in works written by clerics concerned with salvation, fairly neutral in historio-graphy) or to trace a general chronological development (negative up till the 12th century, positive in the 12th and 13th centuries, less favourable thereafter) are gener-ally regarded as unsuccessful.

Alexander developed into an almost supernatural figure, with a variety of different traditions and concepts linked to his name. In Syrian literature (for example, in the homily by Jaqob of Serug, early 6th century) he is a Christian, in Hebrew a servant of Jahweh and friend of the Jews, in Arabic a follower of the Prophet, in the Christian Middle Ages a heathen who is yet in many ways admirable and, knowingly or unknowingly, an instrument of God. In the Old French epics (whose 12-syllable line, the alexandrine, owes its name to him) and romances in other vernaculars he is the chivalrous prince, and in treatises on astrology, medicine and the natural sciences he is the philosopher-king and pupil of Aristotle who searches out the secrets of Nature. He is compared now with Solomon, now with Nero. From the beginning of the 14th century he, together with Hector and Caesar, represents Antiquity among the Nine Worthies who are the types of knightly virtue and righteousness ($\rightarrow$ Hector); but people still tell of the pirate Dionides, who saw no difference between his own activities and Alexander's conquests because unlawful dominion amounts to robbery.

Of the early historical accounts of Alexander, based on eye-witness evidence and archive material, only fragments remain. Not until the 15th century did the surviving works of the later Greek historians Diodorus Siculus (1st century AD), Plutarch and Arrian (both from the first half of the 2nd century) begin to play a significant role in the West, if we disregard their reception in Latin antiquity and its continuing influence in the Middle Ages. Of the Latin texts, only that by Quintus Curtius Rufus (*Res gestae Alexandri Magni*, probably second half of the 1st century) had any real influence. His principal interest is in strange and far-off peoples, the deterioration in Alexander's enigmatic character and his alienation from his Greek-Macedonian environment and friends. Justinus' summary of the *Historiae Philippicae* of Pompeius Trogus (*Epitoma historiarum Philippicarum*, c.400), with its negative judgment of Alexander, did not become really popular until the Renaissance; in the Middle Ages the influence of the *Epitoma* itself was less than that of the first historiographer to make use of it, Paulus Orosius (*Historiae adversum paganos*).

The medieval picture of Alexander rests above all on the late-classical, pseudo-historical Greek narrative of Alexander, probably written in Alexandria towards the end of the 3rd century. Since then this text has been constantly rewritten, with new traditions continually being incorporated into it. The narrative is based on a lost historical biography, on a large number of fiction-based writings, particularly letters (for instance, from Alexander to Olympias and Aristotle about the remarkable beings, natural phenomena and events in India, the correspondence with Darius and Porus, and probably also with the Brahmins, Indian philosophers), and on oral traditions, some of them local (such as those concerning Alexander's birth). How much the author himself contributed is difficult to determine; probably the most important element is his modification of the route of Alexander's journey of conquest. The anonymous writer is known as Pseudo-Callisthenes, because in some sources the romance is ascribed to Callisthenes, peripatetic philosopher and nephew of Aristotle, who accompanied Alexander, wrote a lost account and paid with his life for criticising the honours which, in the way of the East, Alexander allowed to be paid to him as divine ruler (*proskunèsis*). Despite its limited literary quality (the author was writing for a broad Hellenistic public), the Alexander romance is one of the most widely disseminated works of world literature. It has been translated and adapted into some 35 languages, in an area stretching from England to China and Indonesia (it reached Java around 1400) and from Iceland to Ethiopia and over a period extending from the 3rd to the 20th century (the Modern Greek popular book).

The romance raises Alexander above the human scale. His appearance is remarkable: his hair is like a lion's mane, his eyes are of different colours (*heterophthalmia*) and his physical strength is greater than his modest height would suggest. He is self-confident, brave (as witness the correspondence and duels with Darius and Porus, and his incognito visits to the enemy camp) and of noble character (his treatment of Darius' women and the conversation with the dying Darius), and he also appreciates these qualities in others (such as the Persian in Macedonian disguise who almost succeeds in assassinating him). He has enjoyed the best possible education and greatly honours Aristotle, has great self-control and is just. When King Philip takes a second wife (Cleopatra), Alexander – who is devoted to his mother – is able to reconcile Olympias and her husband. He is a brilliant military planner, never at a loss for a stratagem, and is worshipped by his troops. His adventures and remarkable experiences are legion. Thus, in India he encounters the most amazing beings and natural phenomena: ichthyophagi (eaters of raw fish), cynocephali (dog-headed people), hippocentaurs (half horse, half man), a magnetic mountain, ants the size of lions and soothsaying trees; and his life is lived to an accompaniment of predictions, miraculous events and portents. Darker elements which the historian is aware of (drunkenness accompanied by unpredictable outbursts of rage and destructive urges, sexual debauchery, cruelty) are omitted or mentioned only in passing. In short, Alexander is self-evidently the *kosmokrator*; he explores the boundaries of the universe by descending into the sea in a glass ball and flying through the air in a car drawn by griffins, discovers the well-spring of life and reaches the realm of the blessed (where he is refused admittance).

The romance diverges at many points from the account given by historiography, most importantly on Alexander's birth and the route followed in his conquests. According to Pseudo-Callisthenes, Alexander was begotten on Olympias by the Egyptian sorcerer-king Nectanabus, who when confronted by superior Persian forces had fled to Macedonia and succeeded in winning the queen's confidence as an astrologer. He tells her that the Libyan god Ammon will visit her, and in Philip's absence makes his prediction come true – as she thinks – by using his magic to assume the form of Ammon and sleep with her. Nectanabus then sends Philip a dream informing him of Ammon's visit, together with miraculous signs designed to ensure the king's acquiescence in the situation and make him aware of the great future that awaits Olympias' son. He also ensures that the child is born under favourable stars and instructs the young Alexander in astrology. During a nocturnal lesson in the open air the pupil hurls his teacher into an abyss in order to prove to him that he does not know the future. But Nectanabus tells him that he had known he would die by his son's hand, confesses everything and dies. When Alexander later arrives in Egypt he is recognised, on the basis of his resemblance to a statue, as the reincarnation of Sesonchosis/Nectanabus. The founder of Alexandria has links with the country he comes so far to conquer.

The drastic changes of route in the account of Alexander's campaigns are probably intended to present him as ruler of all the known world. After Philip's death Alexander first marches west, where the Romans offer him a golden wreath in acknowledgement of his power. From there he crosses Libya and reaches Egypt. After his capture of Tyre, the beginning of his correspondence with Darius marks the commencement of his struggle with the Persians. Darius begins with a letter in which he treats Alexander as a wretched beggarly child and tells him to go home to his mother and finish his education. He sends gifts with the letter: a ball because Alexander is still young and likes to play, a whip because he needs to learn discipline, and a chest full of gold coins to pay for his journey home. The subjection of Greece comes only after the initial victories over the Persians. This is then followed by the conquest of Persia, and from there on the story generally follows the historical line.

Texts on the wonders of India like those used by Pseudo-Callisthenes also survived independently and were continually reworked; they are often found grouped together in

Alexander borne aloft by the griffins. Floor mosaic, c.1165, Otranto Cathedral.

manuscripts. One group of these so-called Indian treatises is concerned with the Brahmins or Gymnosophists. They represent ancient Utopian cultural criticism. The strange and wonderful land and the way of life of the Indian wise men (the 'naked sages' reject any interference with Nature and thus all achievements of human culture) arouse Alexander's curiosity. He makes contact with them and enters into discussion with their king Dandamis/Dindimus on the pros and cons of their view of life and his own. Conclusions are left to the reader. The two most important Indian treatises are the three-part Greek *Commonitorium Palladii* and the *Collatio Alexandri cum Dindimo*. The

Commonitorium, named for the author of its third part, Bishop Palladius of Hellenopolis (c.400), recounts an encounter with an eirenic outcome; it was translated into Latin c.600 (and, under the title *De moribus Brachmanorum*, incorrectly ascribed to Ambrosius). The *Collatio* contains the same material in the form of an exchange of letters, on Alexander's part noticeably more assertive in tone than the dialogue of the *Commonitorium*. The Greek background of the *Collatio* is obscure. The oldest Latin version dates from the end of the 4th century; later versions (10th- and 11th-century) tend to award victory to Dindimus (as does Jacob van Maerlant in his *Spiegel Historiael*). One of the later versions probably influenced Sir Thomas More's *Utopia*.

The *Epistola Alexandri Macedonis ad Aristotelem magistrum suum de itinere suo et de situ Indiae* belongs to the extensive genre of letters about the wonders of the East. It has been preserved in a 9th-century Old English translation and was reworked, together with Orosius and the *Collatio*, in the 10th-century Irish *Imthúsa Alexandair*. This letter was also used by authors of other works about distant lands, such as the *Letter of Prester John*. Conversely, Alexandrian literature also borrowed information on far-off places, strange animals and plants, human 'monsters' and natural phenomena from such writers as Solinus (*Collectanea rerum memorabilium*, 3rd century), the *Letter from Pharesmanes to Hadrian* (pre-6th century) and the so-called Aethicus Ister (*Cosmographia*, 8th century), who often derive their data from older accounts of Alexander's journey to India.

Biblical and Jewish traditions introduced the concept of Alexander as the instrument of God. In the Bible, a brief account of his conquests can be found in 1 Maccabees. In the explanation of the prophecies of Daniel (Dan. 2, 7, 8) his realm is already regarded as one of the four world-empires (a view taken in the West only since St Jerome). Alexander is usually identified with the leopard with four wings and four heads (the wings referring to the speed with which he conquered the world and the heads to the four realms of the Diadochi into which his empire split) and with the he-goat which attacks the ram (Darius) and breaks both its horns (Media and Persia). This interpretation became a commonplace in biblical exegesis and appeared in the *Glossa ordinaria* on the Bible. In Alexandrian literature it is found principally in the German language area. Petrus Comestor refers to Alexander's heterophthalmia in his influential *Historia scholastica*, forerunner of the Bible histories (c.1170).

The Daniel explication leaves it open whether Alexander was conscious of his role in the history of salvation. But the Jewish historian Flavius Josephus (1st century), who compares Alexander's army marching along the Pamphilian coast on a miraculously dry road through the sea with the Israelites crossing the Red Sea, introduces a tradition which has no doubts on the matter. He recounts that after the capture of Tyre, for which the Jews had refused to supply reinforcements, Alexander marched on Jerusalem. There he prostrated himself before the high priest, who had awaited him on foot in full regalia at the head of the frightened people, on the latter's instructions sacrificed to Jahweh in the Temple, inspected the passages in the Book of Daniel and stated that they referred to him, and finally granted the Jews the right to live according to their own laws. When his astonished retinue asked why he had honoured the high priest with a prostration he replied that he had had a dream, back in Macedonia, in which Jahweh in the shape of the high priest had promised to help him in the conquest of Persia.

There is a series of stories about Alexander as the friend of the Jews which centres around the foundation of Alexandria and clearly originated in the Jewish community there. According to Josephus, Alexander granted the Jews their own quarter in the city and, in gratitude for their help, gave them the same rights as Macedonians (Josephus actually tells of a Jewish archer, Mosollamus, who distinguished himself in Alexander's army). An interpolation in Pseudo-Epiphanius' *Vitae prophetarum* relates that Alexander brought the bones of the prophet Jeremiah to the city, and that these kept snakes and crocodiles away. In a late version of the Alexander romance, at the founding of Alexandria Alexander proclaims the one true God and proclaims all other gods nonexistent. In the West these traditions were originally received with scepticism (according to Augustine, to the heathen Alexander Jahweh was just one of the many gods to whom he sacrificed), but after their inclusion in such works as the *Historia scholastica* and the *Historia de preliis* (see below) they were generally regarded as historical. And then, there is also a letter from late classical times in which the Jew Mardochaeus tries to convert Alexander (Latin translation 12th century).

Josephus is also our oldest evidence for the tradition of the races of Gog and Magog, confined by Alexander behind a wall to protect the world from them until the coming of Antichrist. This story became widely known in the West through Pseudo-Methodius of Olympus (*Revelationes*, second half 7th century, Latin translation c.700). It is often confused with the imprisonment of the ten apostate tribes of Israel by Alexander, which is mentioned first by Pseudo-Epiphanius and achieved general currency through Petrus Comestor.

Even before AD 500 the Babylonian Talmud knows the story of Alexander's journey to the Earthly Paradise, which circulated in the West at the beginning of the 12th century in the *Alexandri Magni iter ad paradisum* ascribed to a Jewish 'didascalus Salomon'. A lengthy journey upstream along the Ganges ends in front of an enormous wall, in which there is one small hatch. When Alexander demands entry and submission, a greybeard hands him a stone through the hatch as a present. On Alexander's return to Babylon an old Jew, Papas, explains to him that if this magical stone (in some versions shaped like an eye) is placed on a scale it will outweigh any quantity of gold, but that if a little dust is sprinkled on it it becomes lighter than a feather. It is a *memento mori* and a warning against the desire for always more and more: Alexander is mighty, but all he has achieved will lose its value under the dust of death. The *Iter ad paradisum* was adapted in, among others, the *Strassburg Alexander* (c.1180), the Anglo-Norman *Roman de toute chevalerie* by Thomas of Kent (second half 12th century), the *Roman d'Alexandre* (*Voyage au Paradis terrestre*, c.1250), Jacob van Maerlant's *Alexanders Geesten* (c.1260) and *Der grosse Seelentrost* (c.1350).

Alexander's reputation as an authority on the natural sciences (attested by, among others, Albertus Magnus) did not rest solely on his letter to Aristotle about India. (Pseudo-)Aristotle maintained contact with him, in writings which often reached the West via Arabic. Here only this aspect of the very extensive Arabic literature on Al-Iskander or Dhu l-Qarnain ('he with the two horns', as he is called in Sura 18 of the Koran) will be considered.

One of the most widely disseminated medieval treatises on health is to be found in the *Epistola Aristotelis ad Alexandrum*, translated before 1150 by Johannes Hispanus from the pseudo-Aristotelian compilation *Sirr al-asrar*, which may have been in circulation even before 740. There is also a 14th-century Latin medical text attributed to Alexander himself which was repeatedly translated into German around 1400 (*Meister Alexanders Monatsregeln*). From the 13th century we have a pseudo-Aristotelian *Rhetorica ad Alexandrum*. The Arabic version (by Yuhanna Ibn el-Batrik, c.800) of an 8th-century treatise originally written in Syrian, in which Aristotle advises Alexander on the art of ruling, was several times translated into Latin under the title *Secretum secretorum* (c.1125 Johannes Hispanus, c.1225 Philippus of Tripoli, c.1257 Roger Bacon). It was subsequently translated into almost every Western European vernacular (into Middle Dutch by Jacob van Maerlant, *Heimelijkheid der heimelijkheden*, 1266). The *Secretum* is the source of the exemplum of the poison-girl sent as a gift to Alexander by the Queen of the North; she had been fed poison over a long period so that even to touch her was deadly dangerous. Aristotle protects his pupil from her lethal embrace. Apart from the *Secretum*, other advice credited to Aristotle was also in circulation (*Documenta Aristotelis ad Alexandrum*). In Johannes van Innersdorf's *Fürstenlehre* this is used as an introduction to his version of the *Secretum*, and there are also two rhymed versions from the mid-15th century.

Two books of wisdom connected with Aristotle and Alexander became available to the West via Spanish. Yehuda al-Harizi's Hebrew translation of the aphorisms of Hunayn Ibn Ishaq (809–73) was adapted in the second half of the 13th century as *Los buenos proverbios*. The section on Alexander contains among other things reflections by philosophers at Alexander's tomb, which are also known from Petrus Alfonsi's *Disciplina clericalis*. The *Bocados de oro*, a collection of brief biographies with pronouncements by philosophers including Aristotle and Alexander, was itself a translation of the *Mukhtar al-Hakim wa Mahasin al-Kalim* (1048–49) by Al-Mubashashir Ibn Fatik; it was translated into Latin towards the end of the 13th century as *Liber philosophorum moralium antiquorum*. It was extremely popular in the 15th century both in France (Guillaume de Tignonville's *Dits moraux des philosophes*) and in England (translation of the *Dits* by Stephen Crope, 1450, revised by William Worcester, 1472; *The Dictes and Sayings of the Philosophers* by Earl Rivers).

Aristotle and Alexander often appear together in exempla. The best known of these is the story of Aristotle's humiliation by Phyllis: Aristotle warns his pupil about the lady's power and wily tricks, and she takes her revenge by twisting him round her finger to such an extent that he lets her ride him piggy-back, thus making himself a laughing-stock. This theme reappears in, among others, Henri d'Andeli's *Lai d'Aristote* and the 'Schwank' (farcical tale) *Aristoteles und Phyllis* (13th century).

All these traditions come together in the Western reception of Pseudo-Callisthenes' romance of Alexander. One version was reworked in an archaic-rhetorical style around AD 310 by Julius Valerius Alexander Pomerius, consul in 338, as the *Res gestae Alexandri Macedonis*. A little later (c.350) an *Itinerarium Alexandri* was written, based on Julius Varrius and Arrian. Along with other sources, Julius Valerius' complete works were used by, among others, Albéric de Pisançon (c.1130); part of the Old French *Roman d'Alexandre* and Pfaffe Lamprecht's *Alexanderlied* are derived from his work. The influence of the *Res Gestae*, however, came mainly through an abridged version, apparently produced in the 9th century and known as the *Zacher-epitome* after its first publisher. This was used for parts of the *Roman d'Alexandre* (by Lambert li Tort, c.1170–75, and Alexandre de Bernay/Paris, c.1150–90), and was also a source for the passages on Alexander in such influential works as the *Histoire ancienne jusqu'à César* (c.1206–30; the author also uses the *Epistolam ad Aristotelem* and Orosius), the *Roman de toute chevalerie* by Thomas of Kent (second half 12th century, also influenced by the work just mentioned as well as by Justinus, Pseudo-Aethicus Ister, Flavius Josephus, Petrus Alfonsi and the *Iter ad paradisum*), and the *Speculum historiale* of Vincent van Beauvais (after 1250, to which the *Epistola ad Aristotelem*, Justinus and Orosius once again contributed, as did Quintus Curtius Rufus, Valerius Maximus and the *Collatio cum Dindimo*). Jacob van Maerlant's rhymed translation of Vincent's work, the *Spiegel historiael*, rewritten in prose and with the addition of some chapters from *Alexanders Geesten* and Petrus Comestor's *Historia scholastica*, was included in the *Bijbel van 1360*. This in turn provided the text for the *Historie van Alexander*; this work, printed in 1477 by Gheraert Leeu at Gouda, became the first secular text to be printed in the Low Countries. There is a French translation of the *Speculum historiale* dating from c.1330 (Jean de Vignay, *Miroir des histoires*).

A different version reached the West around the mid-10th century in a Latin translation by the archpriest Leo of Naples, based on a Greek manuscript he had brought from Constantinople: the *Nativitas et victoria Alexandri Magni regis*. Around 1022 a manuscript of this work reached Bamberg, where Frutolf von Michelsberg made use of it in an excursus in his *Liber chronicorum*, the *Excerptum de vita Alexandri Magni* (pre-1125). The *Excerptum* had a considerable influence on the writing of history in Germany, both in Latin (Otto von Freising's *Chronicon*, 12th century) and in the vernacular (e.g. Eike von Repgow's *Sächsische Weltchronik*, c.1230, and Jansen Enikel's *Weltchronik*, late 13th century, with its striking version of Alexander's descent into the ocean). A *Nativitas*-text now in Paris was used by the Munich scholar Johann Hartlieb in writing his *Histori von dem grossen Alexander*, printed in Augsburg in 1473 by Johannes Bämler. The Alexander text incorporated from about 1350 into the section on the tenth commandment in successive editions of *Der grosse Seelentrost* as a warning against covetousness is also taken from the *Nativitas*; the work also includes an abridged version of the *Iter ad paradisum* as well as elements from the tradition of Flavius Josephus (Alexander's visit to Jerusalem) and Pseudo-Epiphanius (the imprisoning of the ten tribes).

The most important adaptation of Leo of Naples' *Nativitas* is the *Historia de preliis Alexandri Magni*, created by interpolation before 1100. The *Historia de preliis* in its different variants contributed to, among others, the *Roman d'Alexandre en prose* (13th century), Seifrit's *Alexander* (c.1350, with added anecdotes and *Iter ad paradisum*), the Swedish *Konung Alexander* (c.1380), *I nobili fatti d'Alessandro Magno* (14th century) and Meister Babiloth's *Alexanderchronik* (printed 1472). One version had a notable influence in Italy; it begot five prose-Alexanders, an *Alessandreida in rima*, and Quilichinus of Spoleto's Latin *Alexandreis* (1236) which was rewritten in *ottava rima* by Domenico Scolari at the beginning of the 14th century and in Germany became the *Wernigerode Alexander* (late 14th century).

During a nocturnal lesson Alexander pushes his teacher, the magus-astrologer Nectanabus, into the abyss and then carries the body to the palace of his mother Olympias, where she awaits him. Illustrations in a 13th-century South Italian manuscript of the *Historia de Preliis*.

From the mid-12th century on there was a revival of interest in the historical work of Quintus Curtius Rufus. Those portions of the text of the *Res gestae Alexandri Magni* which had been lost early in its transmission were replaced with the aid of Curtius himself and other sources. Visiting Achilles' grave in Troy, Alexander had envied him his Homer; in 1178–82 he was indebted to the revived interest in Curtius for his own great poet: Walter de Châtillon, author of a Latin epic in ten books, the *Alexandreis*. This work, based mainly on Quintus Curtius but also on other sources including Julius Valerius, Justinus and Josephus, is one of the finest products of medieval Latinity. It was an immediate runaway success, as can be seen from the number of manuscripts, its use as an educational text in schools (with concomitant writing of commentaries and annotation of the text), the extent to which it was borrowed from and imitated, and the vernacular versions produced. Around the middle of the 13th century the *Alexandreis* became the major source (along with the *Historia de preliis* and the *Roman d'Alexandre*) for Gonzalez de Berceo's poem *El libro de Alexandre*. A little later, and also using additional sources, Jacob van Maerlant adapted Walter's epic as *Alexanders geesten* (c.1260; in his *Rijmbijbel* of 1271 Maerlant did no more than refer to *Alexanders geesten*, but later returned to Alexander in the *Spiegel historiael*; see above). The *Alexandreis* was translated into Icelandic around 1260 by Bishop Brandr Jónsson and into Czech by an anonymous writer around 1265; and Rudolf von Ems recast Curtius' work as a poem (c.1250). In the 15th century Curtius was repeatedly translated into the vernacular, first into Italian by Pier Candido Decembrio for Filippo Maria Visconti, Duke of Milan (1438; this was in turn translated into Spanish at least four times) and then in 1468 into French by Vasco de Lucena for Charles the Bold (*Les faitz d'Alexandre*, based on the 'Curtius interpolatus').

The rapidly increasing interest in Curtius marked the end of the primacy of the Alexander romance. Petrarch based his biography of Alexander on Curtius and other historiographers. From the 15th century Greek historical writing on Alexander again became accessible through translations of, successively, Arrian (Latin translation by Pier Paolo Vergerio c.1430; revised by Bartolomeo Facio and Giacomo Curlo c.1450–60), Plutarch (Latin, Catalan and German translations) and Diodorus (the history of Alexander and his successors translated by Claude de Seysel, *L'histoire des successeurs d'Alexandre*, early 16th century). The domain of Alexandrian romance was restricted to the chapbook, exemplum and folk-tale, where interest in the medieval Alexander dwindled, in the West in the 16th/17th centuries and in Central and Eastern Europe in the 18th/19th, while in Greece it lived on into our own century. At the end of the 15th century, at the point where romance gives way to history, and despite the support of Plutarch, Alexander has to yield pride of place to → Charlemagne: in the short humanist-academic treatise *Les trois Grands* (also translated into Latin) the three 'Greats' of history, Alexander, Pompey and → Charlemagne, dispute for the title of 'the Greatest'; it is won by → Charlemagne. As chance has it, our oldest textual evidence of *Les trois Grands* is an interpolation in *L'histoire des Neuf Preux et des Neuf Preuses* by Sebastien Mamerot: the Nine Worthies show the medieval Alexander losing ground to the classical a good century before their own disappearance (→ Hector).

Manuscripts of the Greek Alexander romance illustrated with cycles of miniatures survive from as early as the 4th century; the finest date from the 13th century. From the 13th/14th centuries on, cycles ranging from a few dozen to 150–200 illustrations are found in numerous Western manuscripts of the *Epistola ad Aristotelem*, the *Roman d'Alexandre*, the *Roman d'Alexandre en prose*, the *Voeux du Paon* (→ Hector), the *Histori von dem grossen Alexander*, *Les Faitz d'Alexandre*, the *Miroir des histoires* and the *Roman de toute chevalerie*. In the *Histoire ancienne jusqu'à César* the section on Alexander is less lavishly illustrated than the story of Troy. By far the most frequently illustrated subject is Alexander's aerial journey; it is found in manuscripts, ivory carvings, mosaic floors, sculpture (on doorways, facades and capitals), woodcarving (misericords) and tapestries. Other common themes are the snake begetting Alexander, the underwater voyage, the visits to Jerusalem and to Paradise, the magic stone, Aristotle and Phyllis, and the philosophers at Alexander's tomb.

L.J. ENGELS

Edition: Van Thiel 1974.
Studies: Anderson 1932; Cary 1956; Brummack 1966; Tubach 1969; Ross 1971; Buntz 1973; Schmelter 1977; Aerts/Hermans/Visser 1978; Frugoni 1978; Ryan/Schmitt 1982; Ross 1985; Aerts/Smits/Voorbij 1986.

AMYS AND AMELIS are the joint heroes of a legend, widespread in the Middle Ages, which also found its way into formal historical literature; Jacob van Maerlant, for instance, included it in his *Spiegel historiael*. The central theme of the story is friendship: each of two friends is severely tested and each can escape certain destruction only through extreme self-sacrifice by the other.

They were born on the same day, the sons of different parents. They are still children when they meet for the first time, in Rome, where their parents have taken them to be baptised by the Pope. As if by a miracle, they prove to be indistinguishable both in appearance and behaviour. As a mark of the bond between them they receive from the Pope two identical goblets.

The story proper begins when Amys, now grown up, is driven out of his native city. Years of searching for each other take them all over Europe. Thanks to their marvellous likeness they are eventually reunited somewhere near Paris when a pilgrim happens to meet both of them, one after the other, on the same day.

Together they travel to the court of → Charlemagne, where they win the love of the Emperor and the envy of his courtiers, led by the powerful Arderik. The latter sees his chance when Amelis succumbs to the seductive charms of Belisarde, the Emperor's daughter. Arderik betrays the lovers and to prove his innocence Amelis must submit to a trial by ordeal: a fight to the death with his accuser.

However, Amys takes his friend's place and kills Arderik. As the victor, the grateful father grants him his daughter's hand in marriage which – still impersonating his friend – he accepts. But at the same time an angel reveals to him that as punishment for his deception he will become a leper.

Meanwhile, Amelis too has assumed his friend's identity. But at night when Amys' wife becomes too importunate – thinking that it is her husband beside her – he places his naked sword between them. When Amys returns they each resume their own lives and their ways diverge.

Time passes, and the angel's prediction is fulfilled. The sick Amys is driven from his home and city by his wife. Accompanied only by two servants he begins a new wandering, with only one brief period of rest in Rome with his godfather the Pope. Eventually he arrives in his friend's city. Amelis recognises the grievously deformed Amys by the goblet the sick man uses to beg for food. He and his wife welcome the leper into their house so that they can care for him. Now the angel reappears and announces that Amys will be healed if his friend is prepared to wash him in the blood of his children. Without hesitation Amelis decapitates his two small sons and washes the leper in their blood. The disease promptly disappears and Amys stands straight again, looking exactly like Amelis, to the amazement of his wife and the assembled populace. They are even more astounded when Amelis confesses to the murder of his sons. They all hasten to the children's room to lament over the corpses. However, they find the little boys fit and well and engrossed in their play. The only reminder of the sacrifice is a red scar like a thread running round each young neck.

This marks the end of their tribulations. Amys returns home, punishes his wife and resumes control of his city. Some years later, when → Charlemagne marches against the Longobard king Diederik, his army includes Amys and Amelis. A bloody battle takes place at Mortara in Lombardy, in which Charlemagne is victorious. Among the fallen are Amys and Amelis. Out of gratitude Charlemagne has two churches built, in each of which one of the dead friends is interred. Next day, however, the two of them are found lying next to each other in the same grave.

This legend was extremely popular in the 12th and 13th centuries. It acquired a hagiographic form quite early, and the *Vita SS. Amici et Amelii* became a standard among the pilgrims' tales which were linked both to Rome and to other major centres of pilgrimage. The story can be traced back to the first decades of the 11th century. The evidence suggests that it was originally a *chanson de geste* stemming from the world of Guillaume V, Duke of Aquitaine. The story may have been partly inspired by his many pilgrimages and his friendship with his namesake Count Guillaume III of Angoulême. The oldest extant versions, however, date from the 12th century; the earliest of them has been preserved in a Latin letter written around 1100 by Radulfus Tortarius, a monk of the Benedictine house at Fleury on the Loire, which attempted to cast the story in classical-epic form.

The oldest hagiographic version dates from some decades later, and in this the main emphasis is on the salvation motif. Finally, at the end of the century, a new *chanson de geste* was written which merged French epic and the Christian doctrine of salvation. With its subtle symbolism and skilful delineation of character this *Chanson d'Ami et Amiles* is a little masterpiece.

This later *chanson de geste* soon (early 13th century) attracted a response in the form of an Anglo-Norman and a Middle English poem. Later variants followed in England: *Athelston* around 1380 and *Eger and Grime* in the 15th century. In France, the two friends' popularity is shown by their appearance in another *chanson de geste*, also early 13th-century, *La Chevalerie Ogier*, in which their death at Mortara is ascribed to → Ogier. Their story also acquired a sequel in the tale of Jourdain de Blaye, grandson of Ami.

Other characters from the story also live on in French epic. Belisarde appears as Belissent in Jean le Prier's *Mystère du roy Avennir*. Hardré, the French form of Ardericus, becomes the archtype of the traitor, on a par with Ganelon in the *Chanson de Roland*. The two of them are also depicted as being related, while Jourdain in his turn has trouble with Fromont, the descendant of Hardré.

But it was the hagiography that was to become most widely known. Not only because of its links, already mentioned, with other pilgrim tales, but also because Vincent de Beauvais (1190–1264) included it in his *Speculum historiale*. This became the basis of Jacob van Maerlant's rhymed version, which is however more colourful than his source's brief account. Jan van Boendale then took it over word for word in his *Brabantse yeesten*. It also appears as one of the exempla in *Der Sielen Troest* (1350).

In the course of the 13th century the enthusiasm for glorifying friendship seems to have cooled. The legend's influence can be clearly felt in Konrad von Würzburg's Middle High German romance *Engelhard* (c.1287), but relatively little is said of Amys and Amelis. Only in France did the story continue to nurture a literary tradition, and this was mainly based on the hagiography. Prose versions appear throughout the 13th and 14th centuries, sometimes deviating considerably from the original. Around 1400 the story was turned into a miracle play; finally, in the 15th and 16th centuries it enjoyed great popularity as a chapbook. This was a pure adventure story; it ends with the death of Girart, father of Jourdain.

In Mortara, reverence for Amys and Amelis seems to have lasted into the 19th century, although they lost their status as saints (feast-day 12 October) in the 17th century. There have been attempts to identify them with two frescos in the church of S. Lorenzo there, and until a few years ago the entrance of S. Albino was adorned with two Romanesque portraits. These have since been stolen and only the friends' supposed common tomb still remains.

Scholarly interest revived with the discovery of Radulfus Tortarius' letter in the mid-19th century. With its wealth of elements and its varied transmission the legend has given rise to endless discussions on the origins of the epic, heathen influences in the Middle Ages and the continuing influence of Antiquity.

Apart from these scholarly analyses, the legend has also borne new literary fruit. There is an anonymous Norwegian heroic poem written in the early 19th century. 1880 saw the publication of the Czech novel *On the True Friendship of the Knights Amis and Amiles* by J. Zeyers, whose work was for a long time standard reading in his country's schools. The play *Amys et Amyles* by A. Pottécher which appeared in Alsace shortly before the First World War was intended to be performed by young people as a *légende dramatique*.

W. VERBAAL

Editions: Kölbing 1884; MacLeach 1937; Mak 1954; Dembowski 1969; Vielhauer 1979.
Translation: Rosenberg/Danon 1996.
Studies: Bédier 1908–13; Calin 1966.

A POLLONIUS OF TYRE is the hero of a classical romance who has an adventurous career of alternate adversity and good fortune, in the course of which he loses his wife and daughter but is eventually reunited with them.

The original of the *History of Apollonius, King of Tyre* probably dates from the 2nd or 3rd century AD. The oldest known versions (RA and RB) of the Latin prose text *Historia Apollonii regis Tyri* (HA) were written within a short time of each other around the end of the 5th or the beginning of the 6th century. Opinion is divided as to the narrative's previous history; many scholars assume that the *Historia* goes back to a Greek original, but no evidence of this has yet been found.

The versions of the *Historia* mentioned above deal with motifs typical of its genre, Hellenistic romance. The accumulation and interweaving of motifs appears to be a hall-mark of the Apollonius romance; the number of facts and events recounted is very large.

In version RA we are told how King Antiochus has forced his beautiful daughter to commit incest, while playing the honest father seeking a husband for his daughter. He sets her suitors a riddle; failure to answer correctly means death. When the wealthy and distinguished Apollonius arrives in Antioch from Tyre the heads adorning the city gate bear witness to the danger. He solves the riddle, but Antiochus pretends he has failed and gives him thirty days to find the right answer. Returning to Tyre, after thorough consideration Apollonius reaches the conclusion that the answer he has already given is correct. Realising that his life is in danger (Antiochus' chamberlain Thaliarchus is already on his way to Tyre with evil intent), he loads his ships with grain and treasure and sets sail by night.

He goes first to Tarsus, where he learns from his fellow-Tyrian Hellenicus that Antiochus has put a price on his head. When his host Stranguilio tells him of a famine in the city Apollonius puts his grain at their disposal; the grateful citizens erect a statue to him.

Some time later, Apollonius leaves for the Pentapolis in Cyrene. His ship is wrecked

in a storm and he alone survives to reach the shore. A fisherman shares his food and clothes with him, and on his advice Apollonius tries his luck in the town. At the gymnasium where he bathes and anoints himself, but can find no athlete to match him, his skill at the ball-game and courtly manner attract the attention of King Archistrates, who invites him to dinner. He is not a cheerful guest, however, and this provokes questions from Archistrates' daughter. Apollonius tells his story, the princess tries to cheer him up with music and singing and Apollonius too demonstrates his talents in this field. He is given lodging in the palace so that he can instruct the princess in the fine arts. Soon she is pining away with unrequited love. After some mis-understanding (at first neither her father nor Apollonius realise that he is the object of her desire) the marriage is celebrated with all due splendour.

Woodcut from title page of a 1493 Delft edition of the story of Apollonius.

Shortly after this a ship from Tyre brings the news that Antiochus and his daughter have been killed in their sleep by a lightning bolt and that his kingdom has devolved on Apollonius. During the voyage to Antioch Apollonius' wife gives birth to a daughter, but herself appears to be dead. Fearing that a corpse on board will bring disaster on them, the sailors force Apollonius to put her overboard. Three days later the coffin is washed ashore in Ephesus and is found by a doctor. He is about to give the lady the last rites, but one of his pupils discovers that she is still alive and restores her to consciousness. The doctor adopts her; in accordance with her wish for a life of chastity she is taken to the priestesses of Diana.

Meanwhile, the distraught Apollonius has reached Tarsus. He names the little girl Tharsia and confides her and his wife's wet-nurse, Lycoris, to the care of Stranguilio and Dionysias. Swearing an oath not to cut his hair or nails until Tharsia is married, he leaves for distant lands, ending up in Egypt.

When Tharsia is fourteen Lycoris dies, having first told her of her parentage. Dionysias, tempted by the riches which Apollonius had left for Tharsia, and annoyed because her own daughter Philomusia cuts a poor figure alongside her foster-child, persuades her slave Theophilus to kill Tharsia. On the point of doing so, however, he hesitates; and at that moment pirates appear, overpower Tharsia and disappear with her. The slave informs his mistress that her command has been carried out, but does not receive the promised reward of freedom. The foster-parents feign mourning, as though Tharsia had succumbed to a sudden illness, and set up a monument that passes for her tomb.

Tharsia is sold at auction in Mytilene and ends up in a brothel. With the help of her first client, Athenagoras, who had also bid for her, she is able to retain her virginity. She enjoys widespread sympathy in the city and, thanks to her good education, is able to earn money for her owner as an entertainer.

Soon after Tharsia's disappearance Apollonius returns to Tarsus. Dionysias and her husband tell their story and return Tharsia's possessions to him. After visiting the tomb he retreats grieving to the fore-cabin of his ship; in despair, he decides to return to Tyre.

However, a storm drives him to Mytilene where the Festival of Neptune is in

progress. He allows his crew to take part, but himself remains where he is and will see
no one. Athenagoras, drawn into their celebrations by the crew, tries in vain to
persuade the stranger to come on deck. Then Tharsia is summoned to cheer him up.
Only at the second attempt is she seemingly successful; the stranger reacts and solves
the riddles she sets him. But when she thinks to bring him with her he brusquely rejects
her. This is too much for Tharsia. Bewailing her fate, she mentions particulars from
which Apollonius recognises his daughter. He reveals himself as her father.

Mourning and sadness give way to joy, in which the citizens of Mytilene share.
Athenagoras asks for and receives Tharsia's hand in marriage, the brothel-keeper goes
to the stake, the city is given money to repair its walls and the grateful citizens put up a
statue to father and daughter.

The two of them leave for Tyre with Athenagoras. Scarcely are they under way when
Apollonius is commanded in a dream to sail to Ephesus and report his adventures at the
temple of Diana. This they do; Apollonius' wife whom he had thought dead, now High
Priestess, recognises her husband and daughter.

One last journey takes the reunited family via Antioch, where Athenagoras becomes
king in Apollonius' place, and Tarsus, where the foster-parents are tried and stoned to
death and Theophilus receives his freedom, to Cyrene. The aged Archistrates is able
to share their happiness for one more year. The fisherman is also rewarded, as is
Hellenicus, who crosses Apollonius' path once more in Cyrene. Apollonius and his wife
produce a son and 'die peacefully and at a great age'.

This tale survived in literature from late Antiquity into modern times. As early as the
6th century Venantius Fortunatus compared his own life, which led him from Treviso to
Poitiers, with the wanderings of Apollonius, while an Apollonius ballad was in
circulation in the Cyclades in the early decades of the 20th century. In 1930 T.S. Eliot
wrote *Marina*, named for Apollonius' sea-born daughter. More than fifteen European
languages have works devoted to Apollonius. Remarkably, there are none in South
Slavonic. This is because the tale's reception was from Latin, and thus spread from the
West (in chronological order England, France, Germany, Spain, Italy) into the North
and East (with Danish and Czech, respectively, as links). Byzantium played no part in
this; the story of Apollonius came into Modern Greek via Italian.

Among the works concerning Apollonius there are of course a good many more or
less faithful translations in verse and in prose; these will be considered here only in so
far as they illuminate the route and stages of the story's reception. This was particularly
innovative in the 13th/14th and 16th/17th centuries. The 15th century is significant
for the emergence of new factors which facilitated its spread: the *Gesta Romanorum*,
which introduced the old story into a number of languages, and printing, which made
Apollonius accessible to the audience which was to remain faithful to him for longest.
In the 18th and 19th centuries chapbooks continue to reproduce older works, with or
without a degree of adaptation; for this reason, this survey will end with the 17th
century.

The romance of Apollonius does not owe its success to a single theme to which over
time successive generations reacted differently, nor to individual motifs successively
assuming a central place in its reception. HA restricts itself to facts and events, HA
does not take any specific line in its interpretation. From ancient times, the Apollonius
romance has been regarded as both an entertaining adventure story and at the same
time one with a message (a historical 'signum'). The lesson to be drawn varies: now it is
the inconstancy of Fortune, now the rewarding of good and punishing of evil
(sometimes with particular reference to chastity and faithfulness on the one hand and
to incest on the other), or again it may be the bliss that awaits us after this vale of tears.

The presence or absence of a message seems to make little difference to the telling of
the story. In both cases the central motifs are love and adventure, but the treatment,

life-style and material environment are adapted to the writer's own time and contemporary literary conventions are applied.

Although some versions themselves influenced later work, in general the reception of the Apollonius romance continued to be based on the Latin HA. About 115 extant manuscripts of this have been recorded, along with nearly 40 now lost. A number of Latin versions originate from about AD 1000 on.

The earliest vernacular translation of HA, the Old English *Apollonius of Tyre* (late 10th/early 11th century) is about the same age as the first Latin version; judging by the fragments preserved, it follows the Latin text closely. This is probably due to the Anglo-Saxon love of riddles, as well as the early date of the translation. Elsewhere, Apollonius is mentioned in vernacular works from the second half of the 12th century on (by, among others, Pfaffe Lamprecht and Chrétien de Troyes); Guerau de Cabrera (c.1150–70) sets him alongside Alexander the Great as one of the figures a troubadour ought to be familiar with. The course of the action in the second part of the *chanson de geste Jourdain de Blaye* (12th/13th century) is modelled on that in the Apollonius romance. The motif of 'seeming death at sea' appears in the Old French *Legend of Mary Magdalen* (c.1180, seeming death in childbed) and the Middle High German → *Orendel* (c.1200).

The series of versions in the vernacular begins around 1200. In the 13th-century fragment of the earliest Old French version Antiochus' daughter prays for Apollonius' success as he is about to solve the fatal riddle; HA says nothing of her feelings on the matter. The Old Spanish *Libro de Apollonio* (first half 13th century) is both a morality and a romance. The poet Christianises his material throughout: while following the outline of the story he strips it of pagan elements, inserts little homilies and parables, and adds prayers at the end. He makes the good Apollonius blame the calamities he suffers on his sins. The *Apollonius von Tyrland* by the Viennese physician Heinrich von Neustadt (c.1300, over 20,000 lines) is an example of the decline of the 'Aventiurenroman'. Heinrich follows HA up to Apollonius' departure for Egypt, uses his wide reading to supply the lack of information on Apollonius' activities over the next fourteen years, returns to HA when Apollonius returns to Tarsus to fetch Tharsia, and after the reunion of father and daughter resumes his interpolations, using all kinds of sources. Here Apollonius – among other things getting involved with a whole series of women, fighting the giants Gog and Magog, meeting the prophets Enoch and Elijah, conquering Rome and Jerusalem and inventing the Round Table – becomes the eponymous hero of an adventure story which, though the writing is not without talent, lacks plot and message and seeks to entertain by amazing the reader with an avalanche of startling occurrences. The Old Danish ballad *Kong Apollon af Tyre* (c.1300?, three versions) sets the action in the West (Apollonius is King of Naples and Antiochus' court is in Spiers), simplifies the story by omitting incidents and combining characters (there is only one princess) and introduces motifs from folklore (the sorcerer-father who brings about the shipwreck).

Of the 14th-century Apollonius texts, the so-called Brussels redaction of the Old French *Apollonius de Tyre* is notable for its moralising and biblical quotations, accompanied by the introduction of chivalrous elements. In the 15th century the so-called Vienna version (manuscript from 1459), which among other things greatly expands the Antiochus episode, is its equal in creativity. In their account of Apollonius' artistic achievements at the banquet in Cyrene these versions reflect changes in musical instruments and the entertainer's repertoire.

With the 14th century the Apollonius story moves into Italian: three prose versions (two Tuscan and one Tuscan-Venetian) and the *Cantari di Apollonio di Tiro* by the Florentine Antonio Pucci (c.1310–80). The Tuscan *Apollonio A*, a courtly text which focusses on the pathos and the explanation of events, ends somewhat surprisingly in a sermon with the moral: do not despair, God will reward and punish, here or in the hereafter. Pucci ends each section of the *Cantari* with a prayer, which does not prevent him adding a burlesque element (Apollonius wants to cook a meal for the fisherman, but can't get the stove to light). The songs have survived in numerous manuscripts and from 1486 (Venice) were often printed in chapbook form. From Italy Apollonius entered Modern Greek literature towards the end of the 14th century. The *Diegesis polupathous Apolloniou tou Turou* appears to derive from *Apollonio A*, and the 15th-century Modern Greek rhymed version, which was printed in Venice in 1525 and enjoyed three centuries of popularity, from Pucci. In the *Diegesis* Tharsia is baptised after the voyage and her mother is found in the Thecla convent in Ephesus; when Apollonius learns that his daughter is dead Nature reacts as it had to the crucifixion of Christ, and the action follows the liturgical calendar (Apollonius arrives in Mytilene on Maundy Thursday, the recognition takes place on Easter Day).

Around 1390 John Gower included a version of the Apollonius story in his *Confessio Amantis*. In book VIII the confessor Genius speaks reprovingly to the confessant Amans about the seventh deadly sin (lust) and specifically about incest. The Antiochus episode then provides an opportunity to recount the whole story of Apollonius. Godfried of Viterbo is named as the source (though he is not the only one). The framework in which the exemplum is set provides little occasion for modification, and Gower adds little of significance. The moral is explicitly stated: Apollonius is an example to all lovers, and the fate of Antiochus shows that incest is punished by God.

From the 15th century on Apollonius' fame was increased by the *Gesta Romanorum*. The success of this collection of exempla (dating from the beginning of the 14th century) had led to the production and circulation of many different collections of stories, each entitled *Gesta Romanorum*; over time HA found a place in a number of them. The reception of HA (with some, sometimes subtle, modifications) via the *Gesta Romanorum* begins in Germany with *Die hystory des Küniges Appollonii* (c.1460) by Heinrich Steinhöwel (1412–82, a doctor in Ulm), who names only Godfried of Viterbo as his (recognisable) source. This is the first printed vernacular version (1471) of HA; frequently reprinted (at least ten times before 1556, in Low German translation in 1601) it continued in chapbook form into the mid-17th century. In the Netherlands, which scored a first with the Latin HA (*editio princeps*, probably in 1474 by Ketelaer & De Leempt in Utrecht), the printing of *Die Gesten of geschienissen van Romen* (Gouda 1481) marked the introduction of the Apollonius romance, directly from the Latin, into the vernacular. It was reprinted in 1483 and 1484, also under the title *Die hystorien ghetogen uten gesten ofte croniken der Romeyen*. In 1493 the chapbook *Die schoone ende die suuerlike historie van Apollonius van Thyro* was published in Delft, with a text taken almost word for word from *Die gesten* (no known reprints). In Spain, too, the section on Apollonius from the *Gesta Romanorum* was printed in a literal translation (*Hystoria de Apolonio*, 1488); this was followed in France by *Le violier des histoires romaines* (1521), in which Apollonius is given the status of a martyr, and a separate edition of the Apollonius chapter, freely translated by Gilles Gorrozet (*Histoire du roy Apolonius prince de Thir* (1543). The *Gesta Romanorum* also contributed to the Hungarian version of the story (attributed to F.M. Bogáti, 1591), and provided the material for the Danish chapbook (c.1595, reprinted into the 19th century) which was translated into Swedish and Icelandic until the 17th century. The course of events in the Slavonic language-area is unique. The extant, fairly free Czech version of HA, *Apollon, král Tyrský* (mid-15th century) was first translated separately into Polish, then included in the Polish translation of the *Gesta Romanorum* (oldest extant printing 1543); this was translated into Russian towards the end of the 17th century.

This dispersion of the story was followed in the 16th century by a new series of adaptations. Apollonius appears in the Meistersingers' repertoire with Hans Sachs (*Der könig Apollonius im Bad*, 1553: the Pentapolis episode) and Michael Vogel (*Geschichte von Apollonius*, 1563). Extremely free adaptations are included in collections: Juan de

Timoneda (*El Patrañuelo*, 1567) changes almost all the names and adds episodes containing new adventures of Politania (= Tharsia); François de Belleforest (*Histoires Tragiques*, foreword dated 1582) provides his version, which shows an interest in humanism, with an introduction on the spread of incest since the Fall and the part played in the story by Fortune and the use of knowledge.

Reception of the Apollonius narrative reached its peak at the beginning of the 17th century in England. The way had been prepared above all by Gower and by Laurence Twine's rendering of the *Gesta Romanorum* (*The patterne of Painefull Adventures*, c.1576, reprinted 1607) which is characterised by his insertion of notes on 'the incertaintie of this world and the fickle state of mans life'. The year 1608 saw the publication of *The Painefull Adventures of Pericles Prince of Tyre* by George Wilkins, followed a year later by the première of the Shakespearian *Pericles, Prince of Tyre*.

Opinions still differ as to the relationship between these two works. Wilkins describes his romance, which shows signs of having been adapted from a stage play, as 'the true story ... as it was recently presented by the poet John Gower'. In *Pericles*, in which others beside Shakespeare seem to have had a hand (that he knew the Apollonius story is clear from the ending of *The Comedy of Errors*), Gower (one of the sources) acts as chorus; before each of the five acts he describes, accompanied by mime, events not depicted in the action. In both works the hero meets his princess when taking part in a tournament on the occasion of her birthday. They also have the new names in common, and a number of borrowings from Twine, but Wilkins stays closer to Twine. Wilkins' *Adventures* and *Pericles* introduce the Apollonius story to one last new genre. In the Netherlands we find the *Twee Tragicomedien in prosa, d'eene van Apollonius Prince van Tyro, ende d'ander van den zelven, ende van Tarsia sijn Dochter* by Pieter Bor Christiaensz (printed of 1619 and 1634) and Daniel Lingelbach's dramatic tragedy *Apollonius, Koning van Tyrus* (1662), which has nothing in common with the Apollonius story except a few names. In France the genre is represented by Bernier de la Brousse (*Les heureuses infortunes*, 1618) and Balthasar Baro (*Le prince fugitif*, 1649). Later the *Pericles* was reworked by George Lillo (*Marina*, 1738) and further new translations were published (e.g. by Antoine Louis le Brun in 1710, with a Dutch version of it printed in the same year by Isaac Trojel in Amsterdam). But the true domain of what Ben Jonson in 1631 called 'a mouldy tale' had then long been the chapbook and the popular tale.

Apart from a carving on an 11th-century draughts piece (Fürstliches Hohenzollernsches Museum, Sigmaringen), the only illustrations of the Apollonius story are to be found in manuscripts and old printed texts. Illuminated manuscripts exist of HA, the Old French prose *Apollonius de Tyr* and Heinrich von Neustadt's *Apollonius von Tyrland*. Particularly deserving of attention among the printed versions are Steinhöwel's chapbook and *Le romant de Appollin roy de Thir* (Geneva 1482); the former for the number, the latter for the liveliness, of the woodcuts they contain.

L.J. ENGELS

Editions: Archibald 1991; Kortekaas 1984; Weiske 1992.
Studies: Weitzmann 1959; Schmitt/Noll-Wiemann 1975; Archibald 1984 and 1991.

A RTHUR is the son of the British king Uther Pendragon and Ygerna. Like his brother Aurelius Ambrosius before him, Uther is embroiled in a lengthy struggle with the Saxons who invaded Britain after the Romans left. A comet with a dragon-shaped tail gave Uther his byname and his blazon. Among Uther's vassals is Duke Gorlois of Cornwall. When Gorlois brings his beautiful wife Ygerna to Uther's court the king falls in love with her. In order to possess Ygerna he makes war on Gorlois, who leaves his wife in the castle of Tintagel when he goes to do battle with Uther. By the arts of the sorcerer-prophet → Merlin Uther temporarily assumes Gorlois' appearance; thus disguised, he is able to penetrate Tintagel and beget Arthur on Ygerna. On the same night Gorlois is killed in battle. Uther marries the widowed Ygerna and they have two children: Arthur and Anna.

When Uther dies of poison the fifteen-year-old Arthur becomes king. The gallant youth, who like his father has a golden dragon as his device, inflicts a series of decisive defeats on the Saxons. With his shield Pridwen, which bears an image of the Virgin Mary, and his sword Excalibur, forged on the Isle of Avalon, Arthur is an invincible warrior. After defeating the Saxons he succeeds in subjugating also the Picts, Scots and Irish. Once peace has been restored to the whole country, among other dispositions he returns the region of Lothian to his uncle Lot, father of → Gawain and Mordred. Arthur also marries Guinevere, the most beautiful woman in all Britain. There follow twelve years of peace during which Arthur's fame spreads and his court becomes a byword for chivalry.

Now the expansion of Arthur's realm begins in earnest: he conquers Norway and Denmark and even manages to subject the whole of Gaul, where he gives Anjou to → Kay. After holding court in Paris Arthur returns to Britain, where during a court in the City of the Legions (Caerleon-upon-Usk) he renews his treaties with all his vassals. This court is the high point of Arthur's reign. Here it becomes apparent how many changes there have been; there has even been an improvement in the chastity and virtue of the ladies, since they give their love only to knights who have proved themselves at least three times in battle. The festivities are interrupted by the arrival of ambassadors from the Roman Senate demanding payment of arrears of tribute. Arthur, however, is of the opinion that Rome owes tribute to him, since two of his predecessors had conquered that city. With the support of all his vassals he decides to undertake a campaign against the Romans.

Before crossing to the Continent, Arthur appoints his nephew Mordred and Queen Guinevere as regents. Once across the Channel, and having personally made short work of the giant of Mont-Saint-Michel, Arthur sends Gawain as messenger to the Roman commander Lucius. During their discussions Gawain decapitates one of the Romans for a muttered insult, and fighting breaks out. Eventually the Romans are beaten. Arthur sends the body of Lucius to Rome with the message that this is the only tribute they will receive from Britain. He prepares to conquer Rome, but then receives the news that Mordred has set the crown entrusted to him on his own head and is now living with Guinevere, who is unfaithful to Arthur. Having returned to Britain, Arthur defeats his traitorous nephew in three battles. After Mordred's first defeat Guinevere flees to a convent and becomes a nun. In the last battle Mordred is killed, as are many of Arthur's companions. Arthur himself is mortally wounded; he is taken to the Isle of Avalon, where his wounds will be treated. He passes on his crown to his nephew Constantine in the year 542.

This biography of Arthur is taken from the *Historia regum Britannie*, the history of the Kings of Britain written around 1136 by Geoffrey of Monmouth, possibly on behalf of the Anglo-Norman dynasty which had occupied the English throne since 1066. It has been assumed that Geoffrey's work was intended as dynastic propaganda: he provides the new Anglo-Norman kings with a string of illustrious predecessors, beginning with the Trojan Brutus (→ Brutus) and with Arthur as its crowning glory. The famous Arthur, conqueror of all France and, almost, Rome itself, could serve as the English counterpart of → Charlemagne, the historical 'champion' of the French royal house. Geoffrey thus used a native, British-Celtic hero to support the foreign ruling house. He based his work on written material from chronicles and hagiographies, as well as the oral traditions which had grown up around Arthur, but he also made generous use of his own imagination. His work became the seed-bed for the Arthurian literature which began to flourish in the 12th century.

About the 'historical' Arthur little or nothing is known for certain. What information survives shows, without exception, an inextricable mix of fact and fiction. However, on the basis that there is 'no smoke without fire', the general opinion is that there is indeed a historical person hidden behind all the legend. This historical warrior would have lived in the late 5th or early 6th century and would have led the native Britons to a decisive victory over the Saxons which deterred the invaders for some time – though not permanently. According to the Arthurian specialist Geoffrey Ashe, this commander may have been the same as the British 'Riothamus' (or 'Rigotamus', supreme king) who crossed the Channel in 468 to support the Romans on the Continent against the Visigoths and was there forced by treachery to flee to Burgundy. The existence of this Riothamus is attested by reliable docu-

King Arthur; bronze figure by Peter Vischer, 1513, in the Hofkirche in Innsbruck. Arthur features as one of the Nine Worthies among the many male and female rulers who surround the tomb of Emperor Maximilian I.

ments of the time, but since no personal name is linked to the title it remains uncertain whether this was the historical Arthur. Nor is Arthur's name mentioned in Gildas' *De Excidio Britannie* (On the Destruction of Britain, 6th century), though the author does speak of a decisive victory over the Saxons in the battle of Mons Badonis (Mount Badon) in about AD 500. This battle is also mentioned in the *Historia Brittonum* (History of the Britons) written about 800 in Bangor, North Wales, and attributed to Nennius. This lists twelve battles in which Arthur fought alongside the British kings as supreme commander ('dux bellorum' in the Latin text). In the eighth battle Arthur wears an image of the Virgin Mary on his shoulders and the heathen are smashed with the aid of Christ and Mary. In the twelfth battle, at Mount Badon, Arthur himself cuts down 960 of the enemy in a single assault; this item of information shows that as early as this account legends have already begun to form around Arthur. The 10th-century

Annales Cambriae (Annals of Wales) remarks that during his successful battle at Badon (here dated c.518) Arthur bore the Cross of Christ on his shoulders for three days and nights, and also mentions under year 93 (c.539) the Battle of Camlann where Arthur and Medraut (i.e. Mordred) fell.

Legend-building around Arthur can also be found particularly in Latin hagiographies from the early Middle Ages, in which Arthur appears as a powerful, sometimes tyrannical king who is cut down to size by the saint concerned. One notable example is the biography of Gildas by Carados (1130), which relates how Gildas successfully intervenes to frustrate the abduction of Guinevere from Glastonbury by King Melwas. In secular Welsh texts of the same period the portrayal of Arthur diverges even further from the historical facts. For instance, the poem *The Spoils of Annwfn* (Annwfn is the Celtic Underworld), dating from the 10th century and erroneously ascribed to the 6th-century bard Taliesin, describes how Arthur visits the underworld in search of a magic cauldron. Such texts reflect the oral tradition of Arthurian narratives which developed over the centuries. The surviving texts are in many cases written versions of tales which had already been around for a long time. Well-known witnesses to this oral tradition are the so-called triads which summarise, always in three parts, the content of existing tales, and could be used by storytellers as a kind of register of their repertoires. Arthur features in quite a number of triads, so it is safe to assume that there were many stories about him in circulation. The story of → Culhwch and Olwen from the collection known as the *Mabinogion* dates from the 11th century and describes how the youthful Culhwch asks his uncle, Arthur, to help him in the winning of Olwen. Arthur is here a mighty king, married to Gwenhwyfar (Guinevere) and in possession of exceptional weapons such as the sword Caledfwlch (Excalibur).

Geoffrey of Monmouth used this oral tradition and the Latin sources mentioned above when writing Arthur's biography in his chronicle. His Latin *Historia regum Britannie* became accessible to lay people when the Norman poet Wace turned it into Old French verse. Wace completed this work, entitled *Brut* after the Trojan founder of a British kingdom, in 1155. He presented it to Eleanor of Aquitaine, the powerful noblewoman who had recently been divorced from the French king to marry the English King Henry II Plantagenet. Wace added certain important elements to Geoffrey's text. He informs us, for instance, that around 1150 Breton storytellers were telling stories about Arthur, and when dealing with the end of Arthur's life he says that the Bretons still hope for his return from Avalon.

This last, sometimes called the 'espoir breton', is known also from Welsh folklore, as witness the monk Hermann van Doornik who tells that when in Wales in 1113 he saw people come to blows over whether Arthur would still return. In 1191 the monks of Glastonbury Abbey discovered Arthur's grave. Most likely this discovery was instigated by remarks made by the English King Henry II, who had an interest in proving that Arthur was dead and buried and thus ending hopes of his return among the native British. However, people continued to say of various locations, from Scotland to Mount Etna in Sicily, that Arthur lay sleeping there until he should return. The idea of Arthur's return occurs in modern versions of the Arthurian story, too, in all kinds of forms.

The most important and best known of Wace's additions to his source is the Round Table, of which, he says, the Bretons tell many tales. The table was made because each of Arthur's nobles considered himself the best. Its circular shape forestalled differences of opinion on placement at table and in the hierarchy: all seats had the same status. The ideal of equality which appears here attracted little further attention in the Middle Ages, though it acquired great importance in the 19th and 20th centuries especially as a symbol for the (democratic) equality of parties to (political) discussion. In the medieval versions, in any case, King Arthur himself rarely sits at the Round Table.

Wace's *Brut* is the first of a series of texts of the same name, of which the Middle

English version by Layamon (c.1200) is the most important. Alongside this stream of historically flavoured writings we see the rise, in the second half of the 12th century, of the genre of Arthurian romance, fictitious narratives about the adventures of Arthur's knights. These texts give no account of Arthur's life but describe short episodes from his reign. Here Arthur is indeed the centre of the narrative's universe, but never the main character in the story. Thus, Marie de France describes in her *Lai de* → *Lanval* how her eponymous hero runs into difficulties because he will not respond to the adulterous advances of Arthur's wife. Somewhat comparable is the story-line of *Le Chevalier de la Charrette* by Chrétien de Troyes (c.1180): Arthur's wife is carried off by the villainous Meleagant and is eventually freed through the exertions of two knights, her lover → Lancelot and → Gawain. In earlier stories about this abduction Arthur may still have taken an active role, in view of the attacking posture in which he is portrayed in the Arthurian relief (c.1120–40) above one of the doors of Modena Cathedral, which shows the freeing of Winlogee (Guinevere?).

In the episodic Arthurian verse romances of Chrétien and his many imitators the character of Arthur shows little development, the single exception being his negative role in the romance of → Yder. He is the rather elderly king who in some texts refuses to dine before some adventure has turned up and who, in Chrétien's *Le chevalier au lion* (→ Ywain), is incapable of staying awake after the meal. He is seldom active as a knight. Indeed, this inactive Arthur has been characterised as the 'roi fainéant'; an injustice, since in these stories too everything in Arthur's realm revolves around him.

Episodic Arthurian verse romances continued to be written until well into the 13th century and from 1220 on were translated or adapted into e.g. Middle High German (Hartmann van Aue, *Erec* and *Iwein*, among others), Old Norse (*Erex saga*, *Ivens saga*, *Percevals saga*), Swedish (*Ivan Lejonriddaren*, 1303), Italian (Antonio Pucci, *Gismirante* and *Brito di Brettagna*; the anonymous *I Cantari di Carduino*) and Middle Dutch (*Perchevael*, *Ferguut*, *Die Wrake van Ragisel*). These translations give rise to original romances which follow the framework of the Old French texts in their treatment of Arthur as in other things; for instance, in Middle Dutch, the *Roman van Walewein*, → *Moriaen*, *Walewein ende Keye* and *Lanceloet en het hert met de witte voet*. One can, however, point to some German texts which take their own line in this respect. For instance, Heinrich von dem Türlin portrays Arthur in *Diu Crône* (c.1225) not as 'roi fainéant' but as an active king and knight, while Der Stricker in *Daniel von dem blühenden Tal* (1220–30) makes him into a kind of second Charlemagne.

Around 1200 a new development gets under way in France, which by combining Arthurian material with the Grail story signifies a return to Arthurian biography in the style of Geoffrey and Wace. Chrétien de Troyes introduced the Grail into the Arthurian cycle about 1190 in his *Conte du Graal ou* → *Perceval*, and soon afterwards Robert de Boron provided this holy object with a suitable history. In his verse romances → *Joseph d'Arimathie* and → *Merlin* he links the Grail – the cup from the Last Supper, in which the blood of the crucified Christ was caught – with King Arthur. He recounts that the Round Table made by Merlin for Arthur's father Uther Pendragon was the third of a series of three which began with the table of the Last Supper and continued with Joseph of Arimathea's Grail table. In his account of Merlin Robert de Boron describes how Merlin's craft was responsible for Arthur's conception. He adds that immediately after his birth Arthur was taken by Merlin to the noble Ector (who had just become the father of a son, Keu → Kay) who was to bring him up. After Uther's death, Merlin ordains that whoever can draw the sword from an anvil which stands on a great stone is the rightful king of Britain. Looking for a sword for his foster-brother Keu, Arthur pulls the sword out of the anvil; as a result he is crowned at Whitsun. Thus, Robert de Boron introduces the motif of 'the sword in the stone'.

Soon after they were written, Robert's verse texts were turned into prose and in this form were passed down in a trilogy in which Robert's *Joseph* and *Merlin* were followed by

Arthur with the crowns of the lands supposedly under his dominion. Drawing in a late 13th-century manuscript, the Chronicle of Peter Langtoft. London, British Library.

the *Didot-Perceval*, a Grail narrative possibly based on a work by Robert now lost; it ends with a brief account of Arthur's downfall which conforms with Geoffrey and Wace. The Grail story also appears in *Perlesvaus* (early 13th century), which among other things recounts the adventures of Loholt, son of Arthur and Guinevere. Loholt's death – he is murdered by Keu – causes Guinevere to die of grief. It is possible that this Loholt can be traced back to Arthur's son Llacheu who appears in Welsh poems. Robert de Boron's work provided the stimulus for the development of a very extensive cycle which inter-weaves the stories of Arthur and the Grail with the biography of → Lancelot: the Vulgate or *Lancelot en prose* cycle (1215–35). In its most extensive form this cycle covers a good five centuries: from the Cruci-fixion to the deaths of Arthur and Lancelot. After reworking Robert's *Joseph* in the *Estoire dou Saint Graal* and his *Merlin* in the first part of the *Estoire de Merlin*, the cycle gives a lengthy account of the early years of Arthur's reign, the *Suite-Vulgate du Merlin*, which forms the second part of the *Estoire de Merlin*. In this text Arthur is an uncommonly fine war-rior and an invincible hero who, with the aid of the ever-present Merlin and such young knights as Gawain and → Yvain, succeeds in overcoming the rebellious barons who contest his kingdom and thus achieves a lasting peace. He marries Guinevere, who brings as her dowry the Round Table – entrusted by Uther to her father Leodegan – back to Arthur's court.

Beside the *Suite-Vulgate*, there are two other continuations of Robert's *Merlin*: the less important *Livre d'Artus* and the so-called *Suite du Merlin* or *Huth-Merlin*. Sir Thomas Malory drew on the latter for some elements of his *Morte d'Arthur*, such as the incestuous begetting of Mordred (who in this text and in the Vulgate Cycle is no longer Arthur's nephew but his son), Arthur's attempt to drown him with all children of his age, and the episode in which, guided by Merlin, Arthur receives the sword Excalibur and a scabbard conferring invulnerability from a magical hand reaching out of a lake.

In the Vulgate Cycle, the *Suite-Vulgate* links up with the birth of → Lancelot and the account of his deeds, his relationship with Guinevere and later the adventures of → Galahad and the Grail. Arthur then becomes, as in the episodic romances, more of a background figure. He does from time to time play a leading part in connection with developments in the love-affair between Guinevere and Lancelot, for instance in the episode of his flirtation with and capture by the beautiful Scotswoman Camille and the episode of the 'False Guinevere', in which the misled Arthur rejects his wife in favour of her half-sister. In both episodes Arthur's lapses seem to function as justification for Guinevere's adultery with Lancelot.

Only in the last part of the Vulgate Cycle, the *Mort le roi Artu*, does Arthur of necessity appear as the deceived husband. Informed by Gawain's brother Agravain who succeeds in catching the lovers in the act, and by Lancelot's revealing wall-paintings in the castle of Arthur's half-sister Morgaine, he has no alternative but to condemn his wife to death by burning. When Lancelot rescues the queen and in so doing kills Arthur's nephew Gaheris, Arthur allows Gawain to persude him into seeking vengeance, a vengeance which continues after Guinevere has returned to his side on the Pope's instructions and Lancelot has left the country. Arthur himself fights bravely in the engagements with Lancelot and his men although he is, so the text informs us, 92 years old at the time. When in one battle Arthur is unhorsed and Lancelot could have killed him, he sets the king respectfully back on his horse. Following the papal intervention the struggle moves to the continent, where Arthur himself destroys the giant of Mont-Saint-Michel and the Romans become involved in the conflict and, as in the *Historia*, are defeated by Arthur. The news then reaches Arthur that the offspring of his incest, his son Mordred, has seized power. Mordred tries to take over Arthur's queen as well as his crown, but Guinevere is able to take refuge in the Tower of London and later escapes to a convent. After his return Arthur fights a fateful battle against Mordred's army on Salisbury Plain. The night before the battle Arthur dreams that he is riding the Wheel of Fortune and is cast down from its highest point. During the battle Arthur deals Mordred a fatal blow with his lance, so terrible a wound that the sun shines clear through Mordred's breast. Mordred knows that he has dealt his father a mortal wound in the head. There are very few survivors of the battle. The dying Arthur asks his confidant Griflet to throw his sword Excalibur into a pool. When he hurls the sword into the water an arm rises from it, catches Excalibur, waves it several times and then disappears with it into the pool. Griflet tells Arthur of this and then leaves. From a distance he sees the wounded king carried away on a ship containing Arthur's half-sister Morgaine le Fay. Three days later Griflet finds Arthur's grave in a chapel.

To judge from the many manuscripts and the translations and adaptations of the Lancelot cycle in Middle High German, Middle Dutch, Portuguese and even Hebrew (*Melekh Artus*, the sole manuscript dating from 1279), the *Mort le roi Artu* must have been one of the best known and best loved of Arthurian texts. This view is supported by the fact that in 1485 the printer/editor William Caxton gave the title *Morte d'Arthur* to Sir Thomas Malory's comprehensive collection of stories of the Round Table and of → Tristan (based on the *Tristan en prose*), even though this collection contains far more than just the *Mort le roi Artu* story. Malory's work can be considered as the summation of medieval Arthurian narrative, the 'matière de Bretagne', in a period when Arthur provides the main character in many more texts than can be discussed here (for instance in *Le Chevalier du Papegau*, a prose romance from the 15th century), appears as a (decorative) figure (as in the 'Wife of Bath's Tale' in Chaucer's *Canterbury Tales*), or is presented as a historical exemplar.

From the 13th century on, the tradition in texts is for richly decorated manuscripts, particularly of the prose romances, which in the *Mort le roi Artu* – to give but one example – frequently depict the scene in which Arthur studies Lancelot's wall-paintings and thus discovers Guinevere's adultery. The early prints of such texts are illustrated with large woodcuts, as in the Rouen print of the *Lancelot en prose* (1488).

Arthur is one of the Nine Worthies; together with Charlemagne and Godfrey of Bouillon he represents the Christian heroes (along with three biblical heroes and three from Antiquity). This theme, used for the first time in the *Voeux du Paon* (c.1310), contributed to Arthur's continuing appearance in all kinds of texts, and above all to his depiction on objects of various kinds, walls and tapestries. Painted statues of Arthur and the other Worthies dating from c.1325 in the Hanse room of the town hall in Cologne

attest that they early made an impression on the merchants of the Hanse. Representations of the Nine Worthies can also be found in other German town halls and in the
sheriffs' house in Mechelen. On the orders of the rich burghers Niklas and Franz
Vintler, who bought the castle in 1385, Arthur, Charlemagne and Godfrey – and,
notably, Gawain, → Perceval and → Yvain – were portrayed in frescoes on the balcony
of Castle Runkelstein near Bolzano in the Italian Tyrol. The towers of the castle of
Pierrefonds in Northern France (c.1400) bear the names of the nine heroes, with the
image of each on the appropriate tower. Louis of Orleans adorned his castle at Coucy
with the same Nine Worthies; and between 1411 and 1430 they were depicted on the
wall of the great hall of La Manta Castle in Piedmont.

Arthur can usually be recognised among the nine heroes by his coat of arms, three
golden crowns on an azure (sometimes red) field, symbolising his overlordship of
Scotland, England and Brittany. He also appeared with the other Worthies in great
processions ('joyeuses entrées'), on the first known occasion at Atrecht in 1336, but
also for instance at Henry VI of England's entry into Paris in 1431. In the late Middle
Ages Baltic towns like Danzig and Riga had so-called 'Artushofe', a kind of merchants'
guild which organised social activities such as tournaments. 'Round Tables' became part
of court or municipal festivities throughout Europe, in festive imitation of Arthur's
court. The first known instance took place in Cyprus in 1223 on the occasion of a
dubbing of knights.

The Burgundian princes Philip the Bold, Philip the Good and Jean, Duc de Berry
numbered various extremely costly tapestries of the Nine Worthies among their
possessions. A fine Arthurian tapestry once owned by the last-named now hangs in the
Cloisters Museum of the Metropolitan Museum of Art in New York; it was made around
1385 in Flanders. Similar tapestries also survive from the 15th and 16th centuries.

One striking element in this iconographic tradition is the depiction of several of
these heroes, engaged two by two in single combat and mounted on exotic beasts.
Arthur then bestrides an obstreperous camel as he fights Alexander on an elephant.
Flemish woodcuts, which were very popular as loose sheets (today we would call them
'posters'), may have originated this series, which gave rise to, among other things, a
16th-century stained glass depiction of Arthur and his camel (now in the Cloisters
Museum of the Metropolitan Museum of Art, New York) and wall-paintings of the
same period in the parish church at Dronninglund in Denmark.

In 1513 the Habsburg Maximilian I commissioned a bronze statue of Arthur after a
drawing by Albrecht Dürer; together with statues of the other Worthies it now adorns
the Hofkirche in Innsbruck.

In England the huge oak Round Table in Winchester (over 5 metres in diameter)
was made as early as the second half of the 13th century. Malory describes this table as
one of the many memorials of Arthur. In Tudor times the kings of England often
presented themselves as the new Arthur; Henry VIII had himself painted as Arthur on
the existing Winchester table, with the names of 24 knights (drawn from Malory's
Morte d'Arthur) painted round the edge – exactly the number of knights in Henry's
Order of the Garter. The centre of the table is occupied by the Tudor Rose. The royal
interest in Arthur reflected – and dictated? – the great popularity between 1520 and
1620 of decorating English houses with portrayals of Arthur. Here the most popular
theme is the Nine Worthies – with Arthur in pride of place – but there are also variants
in which Arthur is accompanied by English saints, kings and/or other national heroes.
From this period, too, dates Edmund Spenser's Faerie Queene, an allegorical poem
recounting the search of Arthur (as the symbol of magnanimity) for his dream beloved
Gloriana (the 'Faerie Queene', symbolising glory); it remained unfinished because of
Spenser's death in 1599. It is assumed that Spenser would have ended his poem by
uniting the lovers, to round out his theme that the return of Arthur in the shape of the
Tudor dynasty would restore England to its ancient glory.

In England, especially, the Arthurian tradition continued into the 17th and 18th centuries; for instance in Purcell's opera *King Arthur: or the British Worthy* (1691), to a libretto by John Dryden. In 1695 Sir Richard Blackmore wrote *Prince Arthur. An Heroick Poem in Ten Books*, based on Geoffrey of Monmouth and influenced by Virgil's *Aeneid*. Two years later he completed *King Arthur: An Heroick Poem in Twelve Books*, in which Arthur brings about a new age of peace.

With the publication of two editions of Malory's work in 1816, followed by a third in 1817, antiquarian interest in the Middle Ages provided the first stimulus for the flourishing 19th-century interest in Arthuriana. This interest developed only slowly until about 1830, after which it exploded as a result of the work of Tennyson and the Pre-Raphaelites. For a writer-antiquarian like Sir Walter Scott a 'scholarly' approach to the texts (as in his edition of *Sir Tristrem*) probably hindered the free play of his imagination, as witness the fact that he produced only one Arthurian poem: 'Lyulph's tale' in *The Bridal of Triermain* (1813). A striking Welsh-flavoured work from this period is Thomas Love Peacock's *The Misfortunes of Elphin* (1829), in which the figure of Arthur appears along with Melwas' abduction of 'Gwenyvar'.

In the 1830s and 1840s poems by Alfred Lord Tennyson, including 'The Lady of Shalott' (1832) and 'Morte d'Arthur' (1842, written 1833–34), began to circulate, inter alia in the circles of Oxford students like Edward Burne-Jones and William Morris. Stimulated by Tennyson, who published the first set of the four *Idylls of the King* in 1859, people began (again) to read Malory; and a wide variety of poems on the Arthurian material were produced by, among others, E.G. Bulwer Lytton (*King Arthur*, 1848), Matthew Arnold (*Tristram and Yseult*, 1852), William Morris (*The Defence of Guenevere and Other Poems*, 1858) and Algernon Swinburne ('Queen Yseult', 'Lancelot' and 'Joyeuse Garde').

Tennyson has been well described as 'the painter's poet', and so it is not surprising that the Arthurian material also surfaced in the plastic arts, particularly in the work of those artists known as the Pre-Raphaelites. Another powerful influence was the painter William Dyce, who worked from 1849 until his death in 1864 on a series of frescoes after Malory in the Queen's Robing Room in the new Palace of Westminster. In 1852 he completed 'Generosity: King Arthur unhorsed, spared by Sir Lancelot'. Between 1867 and 1870 the same room was also adorned with wood carvings by Henry Hugh Armstead; ten of the eighteen oak panels depict scenes from the life of King Arthur.

As far as the painters are concerned, the most important Arthurian subject is the king's death as described in Malory's *Mort le roi Artu* and Tennyson's *Morte d'Arthur*: after the sword Excalibur has been thrown into the lake and the hand has caught it, Arthur lies badly wounded on the shore, sometimes surrounded by his sister Morgaine and her ladies, as the boat approaches which will carry him to Avalon. Thus Arthur Hughes painted 'Arthur carried away to Avalon and the sword thrown back into the lake' as his part of the Oxford Union Murals (1857). In the same series John Pollen showed how Arthur acquired Excalibur. In 1860 James Archer painted the picture 'La Mort d'Arthur' (City of Manchester Art Galleries), while Joseph Noël Paton (1862), E.H. Corbould (1864), F. Dicksee (1889) and Edward Burne-Jones (1881–98) also devoted canvasses to this theme.

Arthur's passing was also the subject of book illustrations, as for instance in Edward Moxon's edition of Tennyson's *Poems* (1857), in which Daniel Maclise portrayed both the giving back of Excalibur and Arthur's departure for Avalon. In the same book a woodcut by Dante Gabriel Rossetti depicts Arthur asleep in Avalon, surrounded by weeping queens. An 1874 edition of Tennyson's *Idylls* is illustrated with twelve very early photographs by Julia Margaret Cameron, including 'So like a shattered column lay the King.' Editions of Malory, in particular, provide a constant stream of Arthurian illustrations by such artists as Gustave Doré, Aubrey Beardsley, Arthur Rackham, Charles Gere, Walter Crane and Howard Pyle. Jean Cocteau made sketches for his *Les*

The dying Arthur's sword Excalibur, thrown into a pool by Bedivere, is caught by an arm rising from the water. Illustration by Aubrey Beardsley in an 1894 edition of Malory's *Le Morte d'Arthur*.

chevaliers de la Table Ronde (1937) and in 1941 produced his *Dessins en marge du texte des Chevaliers de la Table Ronde*. Trevor Stubley illustrated T.H. White's *The Book of Merlyn* (1977). Children's books, especially, about Arthur are still illustrated in the 20th century; drawings by Shirley Felt illustrate Rosemary Sutcliff's stories. Natural extensions of these are comic-strip books about Arthur such as the American *Camelot 3000* series by M.W. Barr and B. Bolland (1982–84), the Dutch strip cartoon *Ridders van de Tafelronde* by Frank Herzen (1983), the pop-up book *The Legend of King Arthur and the Round Table* (1987) by Nick Williams and Geraldine McGaughrean and also the photo book *Arthur* (1985) in which Hubert Lampo retells the story of Arthur as accompaniment to Pieter Paul Koster's atmospheric nature-photographs. Pictures of Arthur with no textual context have been rare in the 20th century. The few exceptions include the wood mosaics of Arthur, Gawain and Lancelot created by Josef Engelhart in 1904 and the painting 'King Arthur' by Charles Ernest Butler (1903).

It is above all in literature and on film that Arthur continues to flourish. While the 19th century was primarily concerned with the emotional high points of Arthur's life, elaborated in poems or paintings, in the 20th century the biographical framework has become more important. There is a great deal of Arthurian poetry – we will mention only Ernest Rhys, *Lays of the Round Table* (1905); G.K. Chesterton, 'The Grave of Arthur' (1930); Charles Williams, *Taliessin Through Logres* (1938) and *The Region of the Summer Stars* (1944). Sometimes the biographical aspect enters into the poetry, as in John Masefield, *Midsummer Night and Other Tales in Verse* (1928). But by far the largest group is the prose works – often very lengthy, sometimes trilogies – which recount Arthur's whole history from conception to death or describe significant portions of his life.

A fine example here is the five-volume series of novels by T.H. White, *The Once and Future King* (the first four volumes 1944; *The Book of Merlyn* appeared posthumously in 1977), which devotes considerable attention to the nerve-wracking education provided by Merlin for the young Arthur. As early as 1938 this first part of the cycle was adapted as a radio play by Marianne Helwig, with music by Benjamin Britten. Walt Disney turned the story into a full-length cartoon film (THE SWORD IN THE STONE, 1963); a version in book form and a video were also produced. White's work also formed the basis for the musical *Camelot* (1960) by Frederick Loewe to the libretto of Alan Jay Lerner, which was filmed in 1967. Although this first volume – the most accessible and comic of the cycle – has provoked the most adaptations, the other volumes – *The Queen of Air and Darkness* (which deals among other things with the conception of Mordred), *The Ill-Made Knight* (about Lancelot) and *The Candle in the Wind* (the discovery of Guinevere's adultery and the downfall of Arthur) – are well worth reading for the way in which White (concerned about Fascism, Communism and the Second World War) demonstrates how despite all efforts Right fails to triumph over Might. Just before the fatal blow, he introduces Thomas Malory as Arthur's page who will pass the tale on to later generations, so that Arthur shall also be the 'future king'.

Malory's work often provides the starting-point for English-language retellings of Arthur's story. This allows authors to stay close to Malory, as did John Steinbeck in his unfinished *The Acts of King Arthur and Noble Knights* (published posthumously by C. Horton in 1976) and Rosemary Sutcliff in *The Sword and the Circle* (1981), *The Light Beyond the Forest: The Quest for the Holy Grail* (1979) and *The Road to Camlann* (1981); it also allows them to make use of Malory in telling stories all their own, as Sutcliff did in *Sword at Sunset* (1963). Thomas Berger in his *Arthur Rex. A Legendary Novel* (1978) makes effective use of a Malory-type style in presenting his richly ironic compilation of Arthurian tales.

In modern Arthurian novels the events surrounding Arthur are usually related from the viewpoint of a single personage: Arthur's foster-brother Bedivere in Catherine Christian's *The Pendragon: Variations on a Theme of Sir Thomas Malory* (1979, also published as *The Sword and the Flame*, 1978), Merlin in Mary Stewart's trilogy (*The Crystal Cave*, 1970; *The Hollow Hills*, 1973 and *The Last Enchantment*, 1979, later followed by *The Wicked Day*, 1983, where Mordred is the central character) and Kay in John Gloag's *Artorius Rex* (1977), Phyllis Ann Karr's *Idylls of the Queen* (1982), Cary James's *King and Raven* (1995) and the *Squire – Trilogy* by Peter Telep (1995–96). Narratives told from Guinevere's point of view include *In Winter's Shadow* (1982), the last part of Gillian Bradshaw's trilogy *Down the Long Wind* (volume 1: *Hawk of May*, volume 2: *Kingdom of Summer*) and the Guinevere novels of Persia Woolley (*Child of the Northern Spring*, 1987, and *Queen of the Summer Stars*, 1990) and Sharan Newman (*Guinevere*, 1981; *The Chessboard Queen*, 1984; *Guinevere Evermore*, 1985. The best-known example of such a new and surprising perspective is *The Mists of Avalon* (1982) by Marion Bradley, where events are recounted from the standpoint of Morgaine (Morgan le Fay), who as a representative of the old matriarchal religion tries to prevent Arthur being won over by Christianity in the form of the sanctimonious Guinevere.

Other modern versions of the King Arthur story include (the list does not claim to be complete): Edward Frankland, *The Bear of Britain* (1944); John Masefield, *Badon Parchments* (1947); Henry Treece, *The Great Captains* (1956); Marshall Edison, *The Pagan King* (1959); Walter O'Meara, *The Duke of War* (1966); G.E. Turton, *The Emperor Arthur* (1967); Victor Canning, *The Crimson Chalice* (trilogy, 1980); Kane Gil and John Jakes, *Excalibur!* (1980); Parke Godwin, *Firelord* (1980) and *Beloved Exile* (1984); David Drake, *The Dragon Lord* (1982); Joy Chant, *The High Kings* (1983); Stephen Lawhead, *The Pendragon Cycle* (*Taliesin*, *Merlin*, *Arthur Pendragon* and *Grail*, 1989–96); Joan Wolf, *The Road to Avalon* (1989); Patricia Kennealy, *The Hawk's Gray Feather* (1991); Courtway Jones, *In the Shadow of the Oak King* (1991); Molly Cochran and Warren Murphy, *The Forever King* (1992); A.A. Attanasio, *The Dragon and the Unicorn* (1994) and *Arthur* (1995); Helen Hollick, *The King-making* (1994) and *Pendragon's Banner* (1995); Bernard Cornwell, *The Winter King* (1995) and *Enemy of God* (1996).

Among these novels, a separate category is formed by those in which different historical periods are brought in contact with each other, for instance by Arthur's return in the 20th century (as in Martyn Skinner's *Merlin; or the Return of Arthur*, 1951) or by transporting a modern character to Arthur's time. The latter was done first by Mark Twain, who in his novel *A Connecticut Yankee at King Arthur's Court* (splendidly illustrated by Daniel Beard) sends the rationalist Hank Morgan back to Arthur's time, where he causes total chaos with his modern ideas. Twain uses the Middle Ages to criticise abuses in his own time. Following a silent film version in 1921 the book was twice adapted as a musical: in 1927 by Richard Rogers and Lorenz Hart and in 1947 as a film with Bing Crosby. A separate case is the retelling of the Arthur story in *Yarns for Boy Scouts Told Around the Camp Fire* (1909) in which Lord Baden Powell presents Arthur as the real founder of the Scouts – in his eyes, modern knights in search of the Grail. In his trilogy *The Fionavar Tapestry* (1984: *The Summer Tree*, 1986: *The Wandering Fire*, 1986: *The Darkest Road*) Guy Gavriel Kay transports five Canadian students to another world, where one of them is revealed as a new Guinevere and where Arthur and Lancelot are recalled from the dead for the battle against evil. Other works of the same kind are: John Cooper Powys, *A Glastonbury Romance* (1932); Sanders Anne Laubenthal, *Excalibur* (1973); Roger Zelazny's story 'The Last Defender of Camelot' (1979); Joan Aiken, *The Stolen Lake* (1981); C.J. Cherryh, *Port Eternity* (1982); Diana Norman, *King of the Last Days* (1982); John M. Ford, *The Dragon Waiting* (1983); Peter Hanratty, *The Last Knight of Albion: The Quest for Mordred* (1986) and *The Book of Mordred* (1988); Peter David, *Knight Life* (1987); Robert Holdstock, *Mythago Wood* (1984), *Lavondyss* (1988), *The Hollowing* (1994) and *Merlin's Wood* (1994); Anthony Burgess, *Any Old Iron* (1989); Michael Coney, *Fang, the Gnome* (1988) and *King of the Scepter'd Isle* (1989); Donald Barthelme, *The King* (1990) and Deepak Chopra, *The*

Return of Merlin (1995). A number of these can be classified as 'fantasy'. In this genre, extremely popular since Tolkien's *Lord of the Rings*, full-blooded Arthurian motifs recur: the quest, the Otherworld, magical objects which can be used only by the elect, and so on. The romance of sword and steed lives on in these works, passionate and undimmed. There are even fantasy-type role-plays about Arthur, such as *King Arthur Pendragon* (1985) by Greg Stafford, *Grailquest. The Castle of Darkness* (1984) by J.H. Brennan and the French game *La Table Ronde*; and there are also Arthurian computer games such as *Excalibur* (Atari Program Exchange, 1983); *Merlin's Apprentice* (Funhouse/Philips Media, 1995) and *Chronicles of the Sword* (Psygnosis, 1996).

Compared with the enormous popularity of Arthurian material in Great Britain and the US, which also spread (via translations) to Western Europe, there are relatively few versions in languages other than English. Works about Arthur in French include: Jacques Boulanger, *Les romans de la Table Ronde* (1922–23); René Guénon, *Le roi du Monde* (1925); Pierre d'Espezel, *Les romans de la Table Ronde* (1960); Xavier de Langlais, *Le roman du Roi Arthur* (completed in 1971); Michel Cosem, *La Chasse Artus* (1974); Romain Weingarten, *Le Roman de la Table Ronde, ou le livre de Blaise* (1983); Jacques Roubaud, *Le Roi Arthur au temps des chevaliers et des enchanteurs* (1983). German works include *Artussagen neu erzählt* (1978) by Ulla Leippe and *König Artus: die Geschichte von König Artus, seinem geheimnisvollen Ratgeber Merlin und den Rittern der Tafelrunde* (1985) by Auguste Lechner.

The Arthurian material has also exercised a great attraction on opera, theatre, ballet, television and film, again especially among artists from the Anglo-Saxon world. There are operas by Edgar Fawcette (*The New King Arthur: An Opera without music*, 1885); Joseph Parry (*King Arthur*, 1897); Isaac Albeniz (the trilogy *King Arthur*, 1897–1906); Ernest Chausson (*Le roi Arthur*, 1903) and Laurence Binyon (*Arthur: A Tragedy*, 1923, to music by Edward Elgar). Rutland Boughton was engaged from 1920 until his death in 1960 on a cycle of operas about Arthur, the individual parts being *The Birth of Arthur*, *The Round Table*, *The Lily Maid*, *Galahad* and *Avalon*. Elinor Remick Warren's oratorio *The Passing of Arthur* had its première in Los Angeles in 1940. In 1912 Guy Ropartz wrote his musical composition *La Chasse du Prince Arthur*. In 1975 the pop musician Rick Wakeman recorded *The Myths and Legends of King Arthur and the Knights of the Round Table*. In 1990 the Flemish Royal Ballet produced the ballet *Camelot*, inspired by Malory, with choreography by S. Sebastian.

Among the stage plays based on Arthur are: Wilfred Campbell, *Mordred* (1893); Ralph Cram, *Excalibur: An Arthurian Drama* (1893); Sir Henry Newbolt, *Mordred: A Tragedy* (1895); J. Comyns Carr, *King Arthur: A Drama in a Prologue and Four Acts* (1895); Richard Hovey, *The Marriage of Guinevere* (1898); F. Lienhart, *König Arthur* (1900); Morley Steynor, *Lancelot and Guenevere* (1904); Graham Hill, *Guinevere* (1906); Arthur Dillon, *King Arthur Pendragon* (1906); Stark Young, *Guenevere* (1906); Francis Coutts, *Romance of King Arthur* (lyric drama, 1907); Laurence Binyon, *Arthur: A Tragedy* (1923); Jean Cocteau, *Les chevaliers de la Table Ronde* (1937); John Arden and Margaretta d'Arcy, *The Island of the Mighty* (1973) and Chr. Hein, *Die Ritter der Tafelrunde, eine Komödie* (1989). In France, Florence Delay and Jacques Roubaud have been working since 1977 on a ten-part play cycle called *Graal théâtre*. In 1991 Rock-en-Rolstoel-produkties of Arnhem produced the musical *Avalon* with thirteen players, seven of them in *rolstoelen* (wheelchairs), while an adaptation of Malory's *Morte* was recently staged at the Lyric Theatre, Hammersmith.

The story of Arthur has also been transferred to the cinema screen and to television. In the 1970s there were English television productions: ARTHUR OF THE BRITONS (also shown in the Netherlands) and THE LEGEND OF KING ARTHUR (BBC, 1979, script by Andrew Davies). Hubert Lampo wrote the script for the documentary IN DE VOETSPOREN VAN KONING ARTHUR (1981). As for the films – several have already been mentioned – John Boorman's impressive EXCALIBUR (1981) rates as one of the most successful productions, while for lovers of zany humour MONTY PYTHON AND THE HOLY GRAIL (1975) takes the palm. Also worth mentioning are KNIGHTS OF THE ROUND TABLE (1953, directed by Richard Thorpe), SWORD OF LANCELOT (also called LANCELOT AND GUENEVERE, 1962, Cornell Wilde), SIEGE OF THE SAXONS (1963, Nathan Juran), CAMELOT (Joshua Logan, 1967), KING ARTHUR, THE YOUNG WARLORD (1975), the comedy UNIDENTIFIED FLYING ODDBALL based on Mark Twain's novel (Disney Studios 1979, also called KING ARTHUR AND THE SPACEMAN), ARTHUR THE KING (CBS, 1982) and a British film version of Malory: THE MORTE D'ARTHUR (1984). As in the fantasy novels, Arthurian themes alo work their way into films such as STAR WARS.

Arthur's *Nachleben* has been exceptionally extensive and many-facetted, even outside literature, music and the plastic arts. Just one example, to conclude this survey: keywords from Arthurian legend such as Avalon, the Round Table and Camelot crop up everywhere. The same goes for the name of Arthur's sword: Excalibur. In the *Suite-Vulgate du Merlin* Excalibur is the sword in the stone. However, Arthur later captures the magic sword Malmiadores from King Rioen and then gives Excalibur to Gawain. In Malory it is the Lady of the Lake who gives Excalibur and its scabbard of invulnerability to Arthur, after the sword has been broken out of the stone. In our own time the name 'Excalibur' has been borne by, among other things, an English custom-made sports car, an association of history students in Nijmegen, a sex-club on the quays of Amsterdam, a gambling palace in Las Vegas and a hamburger in a restaurant in Amherst, Massachusetts. There is an enterprise which makes and sells a modern version of Excalibur, and also a chess set depicting Arthur's knights. Not to mention Guinevere bath-salts and King Arthur ironware ...

FRANK BRANDSMA

Edition: Cowen 1969.
Translations: Thorpe 1966; Cable 1971.
Studies: Morris 1982; Taylor/Brewer 1983; Thompson 1985; Lacy/Ashe 1988; Ashe 1990; Barber 1990; Simpson 1990; Whitaker 1990; Gamerschlag 1991; Lacy et al. 1996.

ATTILA (Atli, Etzel), King of the Huns, is the protagonist of two Old Norse *Edda* songs and a major character in many Scandinavian and German heroic lays and epics, in Latin chronicles and in a Middle Dutch legend. The 10th-century Latin epic → *Waltharius* states that Attila had subjugated the Burgundians and Aquitanians (i.e. the Visigoths). The subject peoples had provided hostages; these were, however, well treated at Attila's court, and even attained distinguished positions. This apart, Attila plays no part in the epic. When Waltharius, one of the hostages, escapes he takes no action. The Old High German *Hildebrandslied*, which was written down at the beginning of the 9th century but probably originated as early as the 7th century, also speaks of a King of the Huns at whose court a German prince was living in exile; however, it does not mention the name Attila.

The second half of the *Nibelungenlied* (→ Siegfried) is set at Attila's court; here he appears under the German name Etzel. He is the son of Botelunc and has a brother called Bloedelin. His immense wealth and enormous power are apparent from the large number of kings to be found at his court. This text tells of him requesting the hand of Siegfried's widow Kriemhild after the death of his first wife, Helche. It also says that he is a heathen, but makes no difficulties for Christians and may possibly convert to Christianity if Kriemhild wishes it. In one of the manuscripts and in *Die Klage*, a kind of sequel to the *Nibelungenlied*, it is explicitly stated that he did indeed convert for his wife's sake, but lapsed again after her death. He lets Kriemhild persuade him to invite her family to court so that she can take vengeance on her brothers and their vassals, who were responsible for the murder of her first husband. Etzel then sees a disaster taking place before his eyes but does nothing to prevent it. At the end he, along with Dietrich (→ Theodoric) and Hildebrand, is one of the few survivors. Etzel plays the same role in *Dietrichs Flucht* and *Rabenschlacht*, the two most important epics about Dietrich von Bern's attempts to recover his land of Italy. Etzel supports Dietrich with money and troops, but himself never leaves his residence. The latter epic also relates how Etzel's two sons, Scharpfe and Orte, are killed because of Dietrich's negligence, but Etzel and Helche forgive him. In another epic, *Rosengarten*, Etzel accompanies Dietrich to Worms, where the latter enters the lists against Siegfried in a rose-garden; Etzel, however, takes no part in the fighting. Only in the epic *Biterolf* does he appear as a military commander; here his sons are called Erpfe and Orte. Etzel is also mentioned, but plays no significant role, in a few other texts from the 13th century (*Dietrich und Wenezlau*, *Der Wunderer*, *Walther und Hildegunde*, fragments from a German version of *Waltharius*).

Quite different is the description of Etzel/Attila in the legend of *Sint Servaes* by Hendrik van Veldeke. This work tells how the holy Servatius falls into the hands of the Huns when on his way from Rome to Tongres. In this legend, in contrast to all the texts so far discussed, the portrayal of the Huns and their king, Attila son of Bodelingh, is remarkably negative. They are depicted as vicious, cruel warriors who have a particular animus against Christians and massacred eleven thousand virgins in Cologne (the St Ursula legend). True, Servaes does succeed in converting Attila; but this text too says that he very soon became apostate. In a number of later texts Etzel or Attila is mentioned but takes no part in the action: in Wolfram van Eschenbach's *Willehalm* he is said to be a great warrior; in the Carolingian romance *Karlmeinet* (→ Charlemagne) he finds a treasure buried by Etzelin; the poet of the didactic poem *Seifrid Helbling* knows him from the *Nibelungenlied* and a song by the minnesinger Frauenlob calls him a king of ancient times. His name also appears in two Old English texts: in the *Waldere* fragments, a version of the well-known *Waltharius* story, and in → *Widsith*, which mentions him as ruler of the Huns.

The Old Norse tradition speaks of a grasping, cruel King Atli, who is married to Gudrún (the Kriemhild of the *Nibelungenlied*). He invites his brothers-in-law Gunnarr (Gunther) and Högni (Hagen) to court in order to gain possession of a treasure. When they refuse to reveal where the treasure is hidden he first kills Högni, then cuts the still beating heart from his body and shows it to Gunnarr. Gunnarr is now the only one who knows the secret. When he still refuses to talk Atli throws him into a snakepit. Gudrún kills her two children Erpr and Eitil in revenge and feeds their hearts to Atli. She then kills him and sets fire to the hall. This is in outline the content of a number of old *Edda* songs ('Atlakviða', 'Atlamál', 'Guðrúnarkviða' etc.).

Scholars have always wondered at the existence of three so very different images of Attila. The starting point for all three must have been the historical Attila, King of the Huns. This warlike race of horsemen had settled in what is now Hungary in the 4th century and from there mounted campaigns against other peoples. In 434 Attila succeeded his father Mundzucus, becoming king jointly with his brother Bleda (Bloedelin in the *Nibelungenlied*). In 445 he murdered his brother and became sole ruler. At the height of his power his empire stretched from the Baltic to the Alps and from the Caspian to the Rhine. In 443 and 447 he cut a swathe of destruction through the Eastern Roman Empire, which eventually agreed to pay tribute. When his request for the hand of Honoria, the sister of Emperor Valentinianus III, was rejected, together with his demand for half the Western Roman Empire as dowry, he invaded Gaul. In 451 he

Kriemhild is escorted to Etzel. Drawing in the 15th-century Hundeshagen *Nibelungen* manuscript. Berlin, Staatsbibliothek Preussischer Kulturbesitz.

encountered his first defeat, at the hands of an army led by the Roman general Aëtius and which included Visigoth troops. In this battle of the Catalaunic Fields (near Troyes) Ostrogoths fought on the side of the Huns. A year later he invaded Italy and destroyed Aquileia. In 453 he married a Germanic woman, Hildico. During the wedding night he choked to death on his own blood. His sons (from previous marriages) were defeated by rebellious Germans at the battle on the Nedao (454), in which his eldest son Ellac was killed. The subjugated Germanic tribes, including the Ostrogoths, seized their independence.

The Byzantine ambassador Priskos, who spent some time at his court and met Attila and his wife Kreka (Helche in the *Nibelungenlied*), wrote an account of him. A century later the Ostrogoth historian Jordanes paints a remarkably positive picture of the Hunnish King: his court is a refuge for exiles and he himself a loyal friend to all who seek his protection. The same mighty but exceedingly humane king features in the *Nibelungenlied* and the tales of Dietrich von Bern. This image of Attila probably originated among the Ostrogoths at a time when they were still allied to the Huns, and then reached the Bavarians either directly or via the Langobards. Both the *Nibelungenlied* and the Dietrich epics have their origins in Bavaria or Austria.

Attila's image in Western Europe is completely different. Ever since Isidore of Seville (7th century) Attila has been known as the 'Scourge of God'. This same negative image is apparent in innumerable local legends describing his behaviour towards holy men, for instance during the taking of Metz or the siege of Orleans, or when he threatened Rome but was induced to withdraw by the fearless stance of Pope Leo I. It is this view of Attila that we find not only in the *Kaiserchronik* of around 1150 and in Jacob van Maerlant's *Spiegel historiael*, but also in the *Sint Servaes*, though there it is tempered by Attila's short-lived conversion. In later chronicles we find constant attempts to harmonise the two images of Attila. Thus, the annals of Quedlinburg say not only that Attila ravaged Gaul, but also that he helped Theodoric (Dietrich) to reconquer his country. This ambiguous picture of Attila is a recurring feature in the late Middle Ages. Harder to explain is his totally negative image in Scandinavian literature. Some think that it originated among those Germanic tribes who successfully resisted subjection by the Huns and were forced to form an alliance. These tribes would have retained contacts with their original homelands in Scandinavia. However, it is also possible that a less positive image of Attila developed in Western oral tradition, among the Burgundians and Franks, as a result of the defeats these peoples suffered in their struggle against the Huns in the first half of the 5th century. This negative perception, bolstered by the Church's negative attitude to Attila, would then have reached Scandinavia via North Germany. The *Thidrekssaga* is, broadly speaking, based on the *Nibelungenlied*, though its view of Attila is less positive; at the end he is locked up until he dies of starvation.

Attila himself has inspired few artists. On the north side of the Palais Bourbon in Paris Delacroix painted a cycle on the protectors and menacers of the arts and sciences (1838–47) in which he included a scene of 'Attila trampling on Italy and the Arts'. Verdi's opera *Attila*, first performed in Venice in 1846, was based on a play by Zacharius Werner. Under the name of Etzel Attila is inextricably bound up with the *Nibelungenlied* and Dietrich von Bern, and so he often crops up where scenes and motifs from this material have inspired writers, painters or composers – though he does not appear at all in Richard Wagner's *Ring des Nibelungen*. In addition to his role in film versions of the *Nibelungenlied* he is the main character in the film ATILLA, FLAGELLO DI DIO (1953) by Pietro Francisci. In Hungary, where he was regarded as a national hero as early as the Middle Ages (Simon Kéza, *Chronica Hungarorum*, 1282–90), children's and young people's book have been written about him; however, these are practically unknown outside Hungary.

N.TH.J. VOORWINDEN

Studies: De Boor 1932; Gillespie 1973.

B ARLAAM & JOSAPHAT, a hermit and a prince, are the main characters of a legend set in India, an 'edifying tale' as the superscription has it. India is ruled by King Abenner, who cruelly persecutes Christians. At a feast to celebrate the birth of his son Josaphat it is foretold that the latter will become a Christian. To prevent this he has the child brought up in a splendid palace by trusted guardians and with excellent tutors, but completely isolated from the world outside. The boy is not allowed to come into contact with old age and death, sickness and poverty, or with Christianity.

Josaphat grows in knowledge and wisdom but frets at his isolation. He gains his father's permission to make trips outside the palace, and thus, despite all the precautions, becomes acquainted with want, sickness and old age. He begins to ask questions about the meaning of life, questions to which his entourage has no answers. He falls into a brooding melancholy.

The man in the abyss who, pursued by a unicorn, manages to hold on to a branch.
Engraving by Boetius a Bolswerth, c.1625.

Guided by Heaven and disguised as a merchant, the hermit Barlaam succeeds in gaining access to the prince on the pretext of showing him a costly jewel. In a series of conversations he instructs Josaphat in Christian doctrine, which provides the answers to all his questions, and persuades him to become a Christian and renounce the world. The prince is baptised. When those around him become concerned and consider informing the king Barlaam leaves. Josaphat reluctantly stays behind, and Barlaam leaves him his hermit's hair-shirt as a memento and a symbol of hope.

Josaphat's changed way of life leads his chief guardian to inform King Abenner. With his counsellor Araches the king devises a plan to reclaim Josaphat for heathendom: either Barlaam must be forced to recant, or the astrologer Nachor, who strongly resembles him, must pass himself off as Barlaam and take part in a public debate in which he will argue the Christian case and allow himself to be persuaded of his error. The real Barlaam proves impossible to find. Abenner tries to persuade his son to change his views. When this fails, he proposes the debate on the truth of their two religions, the result to be binding on both. Josaphat, warned of Nachor in a dream, agrees. Like a second Balaam (see Numbers 22–24) the pseudo-Barlaam Nachor defends Christianity in a disquisition to which the heathens have no answer. After a discussion with Josaphat he converts and retires into the desert.

On the advice of the magus Theudas, lust replaces reason as the weapon against Josaphat. The men in his entourage are replaced by strikingly beautiful women. He almost succumbs to one of them, but is saved by a vision of the splendours of Paradise and the pains of Hell. Eventually Theudas himself, in Abenner's presence, undertakes a debate with Josaphat. He, too, is unable to withstand the prince's arguments and is converted.

In desparation, Abenner now gives Josaphat half of his kingdom to rule as he will. This Christian realm becomes exceedingly prosperous, while Abenner's heathen lands fall into decline. Now Abenner too is converted; he abdicates in favour of Josaphat, withdraws from the world and dies after doing penance.

Once Christianity is firmly established throughout the reunited kingdom Josaphat abdicates and, at long last, retreats into the desert. After years of searching he finds Barlaam again, and they are parted only by the latter's death. Strengthened by a vision of the reward of the righteous (including his father Abenner) in the Hereafter, he continues his life of prayer and mortification alone until, at the age of sixty and 35 years after 'leaving the world', he dies. A hermit directed by an angel buries him next to Barlaam, but Josaphat's successor transfers both sets of remains to the church Josaphat had built in his kingdom. Many miracles take place both during the journey and later at the tomb.

The Greek, Russian and Roman Catholic Churches honour Barlaam and Josaphat as saints, with feast-days on 26 August, 19 and 27 November respectively. From the 11th century on, their legend spread from the Byzantine world throughout Europe and, via colonialism and missionary activity, far beyond. As early as 1446 a copyist of Marco Polo's travel narrative commented on the similarities between the Christian legend and oriental traditions. Since the mid-19th century Indian, Old Turkish, Islamic-Arabic, Georgian and Persian texts have been discovered, and on the basis of these it is now established that the legend is a Christian reworking of ancient Buddhist traditions.

Opinions are still divided as to the route by which the story reached the Greek world, and also on the identity of the author of the most widespread Greek version (oldest known manuscript, 1021). For a long time the theologian John of Damascus (c.650–750) was generally regarded as the author; however, since the early modern period the work has been ascribed to any number of others. Apart from John of Damascus, the Georgian Abbot Euthumios (d.1028) of the Iviron monastery on Mount Athos is the most serious candidate for the authorship.

The first Latin translation was produced in Byzantium in 1048–49 by a visitor from the West. The legend owes its wide dissemination, however, to translations made in the 12th and later centuries. Jacobus de Voragine subsequently included it, in a highly abbreviated form, in his *Legenda Aurea* (c.1260–67), thus making the legend accessible to a broader public and some new language areas, and assuring it of a regular place in other hagiographic collections and devotional works.

The influential history of the world by Vincent of Beauvais, the *Speculum historiale* (c.1245), contains the Latin legend in almost complete form. Among the oldest instances of the reception of this intermediary is Philip Utenbroeke's supplement to Jacob van Maerlant's *Spiegel historiael* (c.1300). In other literatures, too, the relevant part of the *Speculum historiale* provided the basis for versions of the legend (among others, Neri di Landocchio's *Cantari*, c.1350–93, and the Old Spanish *Estoria del rey Anemur e de Josaphat e de Barlaam*).

The Christian legend is in essence an edifying tale of conversion, stuffed full with biblical quotations and reminiscences, which makes a plea for renouncing the world. It is in addition a catechesis, an apologia and a pastoral work. The conversations systematically expound Christian teaching, using the tried and tested question-and-answer form. All kinds of questions relating to the Christian life are raised, such as the veneration of relics and images of saints. Nachor's great speech, which is borrowed word for word from the *Apologia* of Aristides of Athens (2nd century), offers a comparison of Christian doctrine with ancient and Jewish ideas. Josaphat practises the cure of souls when he gives encouragement to Theudas, who despairs of forgiveness for his grave sins. On top of all this, the story is set in India, land of wonders *par excellence*, its naked sages contrasting with its luxurious palace culture. And finally, the lessons are illustrated not only with biblical parables and exempla but also with oriental 'vanitas' parables and fables. For example, when immediately after his baptism Josaphat wants to accompany Barlaam into the desert the latter tells him the legend of the 'tame gazelle', which by running off every morning and returning in the evening set her keepers on the trail of the herd of wild gazelles with which she so loved to spend the day, with disastrous consequences. All this explains the vast reception of the legend, in translations and adaptations both in prose and in verse, and in a whole range of genres: hagiography, mystery play, Jesuit drama, baroque theatre and popular plays, works on rank and hierarchy (the earliest Spanish version of the story, Juan Manuel's *Libro de los estados*, c.1330), moral tale, fairy tale and folksong.

The first vernacular versions, written in the period of missionary zeal following the crusades and scholastic delight in disputation, usually still contain a marked dogmatic element. The Middle English prose version (12th century), the Laubach *Barlaam* by Bishop Otto II of Freising and the anonymous Old French version in verse (both c.1200) follow their source faithfully. More free versions intended for a court audience also allow plenty of scope to the theological discussion alongside the adventures. Gui de Cambrai's *Balaham et Josaphas* (1209–20) gives the debate on the two religions an important place. In 1800 lines the conflicting parties are described in detail and the argument is dramatised into a real disputation. Gui also adds reflections on, among other things, free will. Rudolf of Ems (*Barlaam und Josaphat*, c.1225) stays closer to his source, but he too devotes considerable space to Nachor's speech (over 2000 lines).

From the 13th century, the fables and 'vanitas' parables were included in collections such as Odo of Cheriton's *Fabulae* (first half of the 13th century), the *Gesta Romanorum*, and the *Summa predicantium* by John Bromyard (c.1390). It was mainly from these collections that they found their way into sermons and moralising works, and also into other genres. Thus, the parable of the 'three friends', of whom only the least valued stands by a man in need, is recognisably the forerunner of *Elkerlijc*, *Everyman* and *Jedermann*.

The most famous parable was that of the 'man in the abyss'; alongside the *Physiologus* tradition in which the unicorn, since it becomes docile in the lap of a virgin, is seen as a symbol of the incarnate Christ, this introduces the unicorn as an emblem of death. Fleeing from a unicorn, a man falls into a ravine. He manages to grab hold of a bush (life) and finds a protuberance which offers some support to his feet. Beneath him he sees a fire-breathing dragon with gaping jaws (Hell), four adders emerge near the protuberance (the four elements of which the human body is composed), and the roots of the bush are being gnawed by a white and a black mouse (day and night, the rapid passage of time). Some honey drips onto him from the bush; enjoying it, the man forgets his awkward situation. This exemplum found its way into almost all the influential collections. It survives in individually circulated versions such as *Le dit de l'Unicorne* (more than ten manuscripts from the 13th–16th centuries) and *Vanden Eenhoren* by the poet Lodewike, who identifies the unicorn with the devil.

The parable of the unicorn was also more than any other the part of the legend that inspired visual artists. The oldest illustrations are to be found in Byzantine manuscripts of the legend (11th-century manuscript in the Holy Cross monastery in Jerusalem) and in psalters (manuscript dated 1066 in the British Library in London, at Psalm 144.4 ('Man is like to vanity, his days are as a shadow that passeth away'). Slavic psalters, in particular, continue this tradition (but so does the Amiens Psalter, c.1300, in the Holford Collection, London). In the West, illustrations appear from about 1300, particularly in books of hours and in manuscripts of vernacular versions (*Miracles de Nostre Dame*, *Le dit de l'Unicorne* and, relatively often, *Der Renner*). From 1476 the parable is depicted in woodcuts in the chapbook. It is found in monumental art from about 1200, particularly at the entrances to churches, in the East in wall-paintings in the narthex, in the West on facades, such as the tympanum of the Baptistry at Parma (1196, by Benedetto Antelami). In the 14th century it also appears in other places with a didactic or edifying function (pulpit relief in Ferrara Cathedral [now cathedral-museum], window medallion in Saint-Ouen in Rouen, wall-painting in the choir at Bischoffingen). The theme occurs incidentally in funerary art (tomb of Adelaide of Champagne in Joigny, c.1250; a miniature of Death triumphant mounted on a unicorn at the office for the dead in the *Très riches heures du Duc de Berry*, 1485–86). The iconography of the exemplum shows some variation. Sometimes the man is eating fruit instead of honey. Often he is climbing or sitting in a tree. The dragon and the mice take all kinds of forms. A ladder may point to the possibility of salvation with God's help. In an etching which became a model for imitators the 'Meister mit den Bandrollen' (1450–1500, Westphalia or Lower Rhine) integrated elements of the parable into a 'memento mori' with a tree of life and wheel of Fortune.

From the 14th to the 18th century the legend was adapted for the stage. The oldest plays, a *Miracle de Nostre Dame* (14th century) in which Mary hastens to Josaphat's aid when he is danger of succumbing to the woman, and *sacre rappresentazioni* by Bernardo Pulci (1433–88) and Socci Peretano (late 16th century) are short. The genre lends itself to dramatisation of the religious debate; usually the discussion centres on one or two questions of dogma (Christ's dual nature, the meaning of the Incarnation and Crucifixion, the Trinity). The *Mystère du roy Avennir* by Jean le Prier (mid-15th century) reflects prevailing conventions in its scale (some 120 dramatis personae, estimated duration three days), its epic expansiveness and augmented content. Josaphat's erotic adventure, for instance, is provided with some background: Bellissent, the almost successful beauty, had previously rejected a count who in revenge took up arms against her father, who was then supported by Josaphat's father Abenner. The number of disputations is increased, but the author is here not concerned with the dogmatic content but with the dramatic portrayal of their effect on the participants. Nachor does not dispute, he bears witness.

In the 16th century Barlaam and Josaphat becomes a favourite theme of Jesuit drama in Latin, probably at first in Germany (an anonymous play of 1573, followed by others

including those by J. Bidermann, 1619, and J. Masen, 1647); nineteen productions of
such works are known from before 1649. Spain, too, is prominent here. The series of
plays begins with *Tanisdoro*, which survives in incomplete form (late 16th century,
Jesuit circles in Seville, Spanish with Latin monologues), one of the few versions in
which the names have been changed. The great disputation is enlivened by the
unmasking of Polemio (Nachor), which enables Josaphat (Tanisdoro) himself to appear
as intercessor for Christianity, and by the dramatic depiction of the conversions. The
high-point of the legend's reception in Spanish baroque theatre is Lope de Vega's *Barlán
y Josafá* (1610–11), in which Josaphat is a melancholic type who is already inclining
towards Christian ideas before Barlaam appears. Here, too, greater space is devoted to
gallantry: the great debate is attended by Leucippe, the woman who almost brings about
Josaphat's downfall, and the ladies of the court. The discussion is influenced by current
events: the apologia is preceded by a missionary sermon and ends with a confession of
faith which seems to be influenced by the Council of Trent. About 1760, Spanish
Counter Reformation dramatic literature on Barlaam and Josaphat (which produced
among other things three more works from the school of Lope de Vega) ends with *Los
dos luceros de Oriente* (the second piece of this title), a free adaptation in which among
other things Barlaam is also a physician and Josaphat is baptised during a garden party.
One of the three main themes of the religious debate is predestination.

From about 1600 the writers of these stage pieces usually take the legend from the
Vitae et res gestae ss. Barlaam et Josaphat (1577) by Jacques de Billy. Billy's new
translation was itself repeatedly translated, into French, Dutch (Frans van Hoogstraten,
Het leven en bedryf van Barlaäm den heremyt en Josaphat koning van Indien, 1672) and
Polish among other languages.

Finally, in the 18th and 19th centuries it is popular culture and popular literature,
continuing the tradition begun in the 15th century (first chapbook printed in Germany
c.1476, in Italy c.1480), that become the vehicle for the legend's survival.

In the visual arts, a particularly favoured theme was the parable of the man in the
abyss, or tree (see above). Also typical are scenes of conversions (for instance, a 13th-
century manuscript in Düsseldorf) and Barlaam and Josaphat incorporated in surveys of
the tradition of the desert fathers (principally in East European wall-paintings; in the
West among others a miniature in the Breviary of the Duke of Bedford, 1424–35, and an
engraving in J. Sadeler's hermits series, c.1597–1600, after Maarten de Vos). Manuscripts
of the Greek legend contain cycles of miniatures, ranging from 23 to 211 in number,
illustrating the conversion story and the parables. A 17th-century manuscript of a
Christian-Arabic version contains 36 miniatures. In the West, where only one illustrated
manuscript (from 1311) is known, nothing comparable appears until the emergence of
the chapbook. Günther Zainer's print (Augsburg c.1376) contains 64 woodcuts; the *Vita
di san Giosaphat convertito da Barlaam* (17th century) has 16.

L.J. ENGELS

Edition: Hirsch 1986.
Studies: Sonet 1949–52; Williams-Krapp 1986; Aguirre 1988.

B AUDOUIN DE SEBOURC is the principal character of the Old French courtly
romance which bears his name, and which was written down by an anonymous poet
from Hainault around 1350. A good deal of late medieval vernacular literature is
characterised by complicated plots in which the most remarkable adventures are mixed
and mingled with gay abandon. *Baudouin de Sebourc* is no exception: stereotyped
narrative elements are linked in an episodic structure which obscures our view of the
plot as a whole.

The story – it is impossible to summarise it briefly – is set in Europe (the Low
Countries, Germany, France, Norway), the Orient, the Earthly Paradise and at the
entrance to Hell. It begins when Baudouin's father, King Ernoul of Nimaie (Nijmegen),
leaves for the East where he hopes to rescue his brother Baudouin of Beauvais from
captivity among the Saracens. This gives Ernoul's seneschal, the villainous Gaufroi de
Frise (Friesland), the opportunity to rid himself of his lord. For Gaufroi is in love with
Rose, Ernoul's wife, and by disposing of Ernoul – Gaufroi treacherously delivers him
into the hands of Rouge-Lion, Sultan of Abilant – he is able to take Ernoul's place both
as Rose's husband and as king of Nimaie.

But Ernoul and Rose have four sons: Esmeré, Gloriant, Alexander and Baudouin.
Gaufroi therefore decides to dispose of them too. Realising that Gaufroi is up to no
good, Rose sends the three eldest boys to her family in Boulogne. She keeps the
youngest, Baudouin, then two years old, with her. But when the toddler disrupts
Gaufroi's coronation he too has to leave Nimaie. The servant who is supposed to take
him to Boulogne dies on the way and Baudouin is given shelter by the Lord of Sebourc.
Thus the whole royal family is split up. The romance then recounts in detail all the
vicissitudes that befall them in their attempts to find each other again, recover their
heritage and punish the treacherous Gaufroi.

All the characters have a long road to travel before this is accomplished. Along the
way Gloriant marries the daughter of the King of Cyprus and Alexander the Queen of
Scotland. Esmeré and Eliénor, daughter of Rouge-Lion of Abilant, fall in love and
secretly marry, but are discovered and thrown in a dungeon. The three brothers make
an alliance with Eustatius of Boulogne (the brother of → Godfrey of Bouillon) and
together besiege Gaufroi in Nimaie, but without success. However, the romance
devotes most attention to Baudouin de Sebourc. At a youthful age he sires 31 bastards,
including one by Marie, the daughter of his patron. At a tournament at Valenciennes
Baudouin falls in love with Blanche, the sister of Count Robert of Flanders.

Only then do his wanderings really begin. He almost loses Blanche to a scoundrelly
and lecherous priest, but they manage to escape and reach the county of Cleves, where
Baudouin becomes involved in a conflict between the Counts of Cleves and of the
Mark. From there they head for the Orient. On their way they deal with Gaufroi's cruel
tax-gatherers at Luzarches (Leeuwarden); learning of this, Gaufroi leads an army against
Luzarches, which falls to him by treachery. Blanche, now Baudouin's lawful wife, is
captured by Gaufroi. Baudouin escapes and heads for the East alone.

Here he has the most bizarre adventures, several times escaping death by the skin of
his teeth. For instance: Baudouin and a companion, Polibant, arrive in Baghdad. The
city's previous Caliph had been highly sympathetic towards Christians, even building
them a church, but his young successor persecutes them and does all he can to make
their lives difficult. One of the new Caliph's courtesans advises him to demand the
return of the stone, donated by the old Caliph, on which the whole structure of the
church rests. This command is transmitted to Pastor Thomas who, with the assembled
Christians, is unable to think of anything to do but lament. At that moment Baudouin
and Polibant arrive. Baudouin advises them all to make their confessions and to pray.
At the end of the third day the stone removes itself unaided and the pillar whose base it
had formed remains in place, resting on thin air. This miracle only makes the Caliph
more savage; he has Polibant thrown in a dungeon. Baudouin is then suddenly struck

down by a mysterious illness. Soon he is covered all over with stinking sores, so that everyone turns away from him and he has to beg for his bread. Only a humble cobbler, like the Good Samaritan, takes pity on him and invites him into his house. There he recovers from his sickness, ready for further events in Baghdad.

After a series of such adventures Baudouin finds his family again and together they are able to defeat and punish Gaufroi, who even has the nerve to poison his confederate, the King of France. Baudouin then spends a winter in Nimaie, but remembers that he has promised the King of Jerusalem to return there to fight the Saracens. In the East he is reunited with all his 31 bastard sons and together they enter the service of the ruler of Jerusalem.

The Old French *Baudouin de Sebourc* (almost 26,000 lines) has been preserved in two manuscripts, one of which dates from the middle of the 14th century and is thus chronologically close to the period in which the text itself originated. Like many late medieval romances the *Baudouin* is a patchwork of allusions to and borrowings from other works, such as *Les Chétifs* and the continuations of *La Conquête de Jérusalem*. At various points the writer presents his work as a 'school for love', and some moralistic-didactic intent cannot be denied. However, contemporary history can also be recognised in the text, if in a disguised form. Thus, the figure of Baudouin is recognisably a compound of two kings of the Christian kingdom of Jerusalem: Baldwin II of Bourg (ruled 1118–31) and Guy de Lusignan (ruled 1186–87). However, the hero's name derives from the village of Sebourc near Valenciennes; it was, then, in this area that the story was written. From another reflection of contemporary history in the narrative we can deduce that whoever commissioned it must have been close to the ruling house of the counties of Hainault and Holland. The principal antagonist, Gaufroi le Senescal, is a Friesian, as are a number of other villains. This is a unique feature in Old French literature, but is found on a number of occasions in Dutch literature. The animosity between Holland and Friesland was a not uncommon topic, particularly in works circulating in Holland, as a result of the claims which the Counts of Holland made to Friesland. It appears that these claims were taken over by the Counts of Hainault when they became Counts of Holland in 1299.

The small number of copies surviving may be taken to indicate a rapid decline in the popularity of *Baudouin de Sebourc*, and it had little influence on other works. What is important about the text, which was translated into Middle Dutch, is that it is one of the sources for the 'abele spelen' *Esmoreit* and *Gloriant*, two of the four Middle Dutch 'clever plays', which are the earliest complete secular dramas surviving in any Western European vernacular. The author of these plays probably borrowed from the *Baudouin*, or its Middle Dutch translation, not only the names of his main characters but also motifs and elements of the plots.

The figure of Baudouin de Sebourc has left no traces in the visual arts.

G.H.M. CLAASSENS

Edition: Claassens 1993.
Studies: Labande 1940; Claassens 1993.

BEOWULF is an Old English epic about the heroic deeds of Beowulf, nephew of King Hygelac of the Geats in Southern Sweden and subsequently himself king. It is the most important poetic work in Old English literature (and, at 3182 lines, also the longest); it was written by an unknown cleric, probably between about 675 and 850, and is therefore the earliest surviving Germanic heroic poem, preserved in a single manuscript from around the year 1000 (British Library, London).

The story, which has two parts, begins by recalling the heroic deeds of Scyld, King of the Danes, and his descendants. We are expressly told that Scyld was a good king; when he dies he is placed with all his possessions in a ship which is then entrusted to the waves, a form of burial also known to have been practised in the time of the Vikings. Scyld is succeeded by his son Beowulf (not the Beowulf of the title) and he by his son Healfdene. After Healfdene comes his son Hrothgar, and with him the story proper begins.

Hrothgar has a splendid royal hall built on the Danish island of Sjælland, which he calls Heorot ('Hart'). Hrothgar's brave followers gather in the hall for a banquet. The sound of their feasting carries to the water-monster Grendel, which lives in a lake not far from Heorot. Enraged by the din, Grendel goes to the hall by night and finds Hrothgar's men fast asleep there. He devours thirty of them and returns to his lair, happy with his slaughter. Next morning Grendel's activities are discovered and the festive mood turns to loud lamenting. Hrothgar's men retreat to the outbuildings and no longer attend the royal hall. From that day on Grendel is sovereign; for twelve years he visits Heorot every night, the king's hall stands empty, the King of the Danes is deeply humiliated.

In south-western Sweden Hygelac rules over the Geats. One of his men, Beowulf, hears of the sorry state of affairs in Denmark; he decides to go to King Hrothgar, with fourteen brave men to aid him, and offer his assistance in the fight against the monster. Hrothgar gratefully accepts his help and the mood at Hrothgar's court takes a turn for the better. Briefly it seems that things may miscarry when one of Hrothgar's followers, a certain Unferth, tries to belittle Beowulf because he is afraid that Beowulf will gain more glory than himself. Unferth brings up the story of a swimming contest between Beowulf and another hero, Breca. Seven days that contest had lasted, and eventually Breca won. That, says Unferth, does not bode well for Beowulf's battle with Grendel. But Beowulf has another explanation for his defeat: on the way he had had to do battle with no fewer than nine sea-monsters. If Unferth and Hrothgar's other retainers had shown similar boldness, says Beowulf, Grendel could not have carried out such a slaughter in Heorot. He promises that before the sun rises anyone who wishes will be able to enter Heorot again without fear. Hrothgar is delighted with this promise and gives a banquet for his guests.

Once everyone has gone to bed Beowulf and his fourteen men keep watch in the hall. That night Grendel comes again to Heorot. On seeing that the hall is once more full of men he thinks gleefully of the feast he will soon enjoy. He grabs a man, cracks his bones, sucks the blood from his veins and then swallows him whole. Then he makes for Beowulf, tries to get hold of him, but at once discovers that he has never encountered anyone with such very strong arms. A mighty duel takes place, shaking Heorot to its foundations. Beowulf's companions try to kill Grendel with their swords, but cannot pierce the monster's thick skin. When Grendel makes a last desperate effort to escape Beowulf's iron hold the monster's shoulder is torn from his body – so powerful is Beowulf's grip on him. Mortally wounded, Grendel returns to his lair. Beowulf has triumphed, and as a mark of his victory he places Grendel's hand, arm and shoulder under the roof of Heorot.

Morning comes, and everyone can see that Beowulf has defeated the monster. Young and old, they follow the trail of blood left by Grendel in his flight, which leads to the lake where the water-monsters live. Back in Heorot one of Hrothgar's followers sings the lay of Sigemund who vanquished a dragon. Hrothgar is deeply impressed by Beowulf's heroic deed and says that by it he has won everlasting renown, which is the greatest honour one can give a hero. He commands that Heorot shall be restored to its original splendour. Beowulf and his men are richly rewarded and at a feast Hrothgar's court poet sings the tragic tale of Finn, Hildeburth and Hnaef.

After the feast they all settle to sleep with a feeling of security. But next morning it appears that one of Heorot's inhabitants has failed to survive the night. Evidently another monster has sought to avenge Grendel's defeat. Hrothgar is devastated, for the victim is his beloved counsellor Ashhere. Beowulf is summoned (he had spent the night in another part of Heorot, far from the scene of the disaster) and Hrothgar tells him of Ashhere's death. He has been told by his retainers that they had seen two bloodthirsty monsters in a marshy area near a lake whose waters were red with blood. One looked like a woman, the other like a man. Beowulf instantly decides to go there, girds on his sword Hrunting, sets off and on reaching the lake dives straight in without hesitating. The female monster – Grendel's mother – realises at once that a human being has penetrated her domain and she immediately attacks. She slashes at Beowulf with her talons, but his mail-shirt is proof against them. She drags him to her den, where the water no longer hinders him and where a fire is burning. Beowulf strikes at her with his sword, but although Hrunting has never before let him down it can make no impression on the monster's thick hide; he throws the useless thing away. Now a wrestling match begins, Beowulf finds himself underneath, she tries to kill him with a knife, but the knife will not go through his mail-shirt. Beowulf manages to regain his feet, he sees a huge sword lying there, made by giants and so large that no man could lift it, and with a single blow of this he cuts off her head. Then he goes looking for Grendel and finds him, maimed and mortally wounded, lying on a bed; him too he decapitates with one blow of the giant sword.

Beside the lake Hrothgar and his people, together with Beowulf's companions, are awaiting his return. When they suddenly see yet more blood welling up through the water they fear that Beowulf has paid for his boldness with his life. Sadly Hrothgar and his men return to Heorot, only the Geats still wait and hope. Some time later Beowulf does indeed reappear above the water, with as proof of his victory the head of Grendel and the hilt of the giant's sword; the rest of it has melted in the monsters' blood.

Beowulf's men escort him back to Heorot in triumph; Grendel's head is dragged in by the hair. After a great feast Beowulf and his companions return to Geatland, where Beowulf reports on his Danish adventures to his king, Hygelac.

The second part of the story deals with the kingship of Beowulf, who has succeeded Hygelac's son Heardred as King of the Geats. For fifty years Beowulf reigns over his country, a time of peace and prosperity. But then he is forced into a new adventure, which is to cost him his life. On an island off the coast lives a dragon, guarding a treasure in a grave-mound. Someone has stolen a goblet from the hoard while the dragon was sleeping, and the mainland has to pay for the island's loss. The dragon spreads destruction and dismay among the people there, burning everything and everyone. It moves ever further inland. Even Beowulf's house, the royal hall of the Geats, is burned to the ground. Then Beowulf resolves, despite his advanced age, to fight this monster also. He commands a shield all of iron to be made, realising that a wooden shield could not withstand the dragon's fiery breath. With twelve loyal companions he goes to where the dragon is lurking. One of the twelve is the individual who had stolen the golden goblet, and he has to show Beowulf the way. Beowulf bids his men farewell and goes forward alone; he is anxious and heavy-hearted, for he knows that he too is now under the dragon's curse.

When he reaches the dragon's lair Beowulf shouts his challenge to the monster, so loudly that the earth shakes. The dragon recognises a human voice and emerges from its den in a rage. The iron shield protects Beowulf from the fire-breathing monster, but his sword is ineffective; it glances off the monster's scaly hide, merely infuriating it the more. Beowulf is pressed harder and harder, things look bad for him, particularly since his companions have fled into the forest away from the terrible battle. One of them, the youthful Wiglaf, accuses the others of cowardice and comes to his lord's aid – the only one to do so. Undaunted he approaches the dragon, his shield is burnt away in the fire and his breastplate offers little protection. Quickly he ducks behind his lord's iron

shield. Then Beowulf attacks the
dragon with all his strength and hits it
squarely on the head with his sword,
but the sword snaps. The dragon
attacks again, and bites Beowulf in the
neck so the blood pours out. Wiglaf
now stabs his sword into the belly of
the dragon; his hand is badly burnt,
but the dragon is mortally wounded.
The fire immediately slackens, allowing Beowulf to rip open the monster's
belly with his knife. So Beowulf and
Wiglaf together overcome the dragon.

Beowulf's wounds begin to burn
and swell up. He realises that a deadly
poison has entered his body and is
eating him away inside. His strength
quickly fails. He asks Wiglaf to fetch
the dragon's treasure so that he may
see all those splendid things before he
dies. When Wiglaf shows him the
hoard, Beowulf is glad to have given
his life in return for a treasure which
will now belong to his people. His last
wish is that when his body has been
burned on a coastal clifftop a great
barrow shall be raised over his ashes as
a beacon for passing seamen, and that

The Sutton Hoo Helmet, 7th century. London,
British Museum.

this beacon shall be known as 'Beowulf's Hill'. Then he dies. The story ends with
Wiglaf rebuking the dishonourable men who had hidden in the forest and with the
burning of Beowulf's body and the raising of his barrow, in which the treasures from the
dragon's hoard are buried. Twelve princes praise Beowulf's heroic deeds: of all kings he
was the gentlest, the most amiable, the kindest to his people and the most eager for fame.

So the story ends as it began, with the death and burial of a good king: Scyld at the
beginning, Beowulf at the end. Thus the circle is closed; and there is a cyclical pattern
in the story itself, of which more later.

Since the studies of Klaeber and especially of Tolkien, the theme of *Beowulf* has been
thought to be the conflict between good and evil, with the monsters (Grendel,
Grendel's mother, the dragon) symbolising evil and Beowulf, combatting this evil,
representing good. Previously, at the end of the last century, a mythological
interpretation had been put forward, particularly by German scholars. Thus, the
monsters are seen as the hostile North Sea and Beowulf as a kind of sun-god, beating off
the sea's repeated assaults on the low-lying coastal regions every spring (in this view
Grendel's mother is the deep ocean); Beowulf's kingship, characterised by a long period
of peace, represents the summer calms; in fighting the dragon he is resisting the autumn
storms; in winter he dies. Since the adherents of this mythological interpretation never
wondered just why the monsters should symbolise the North Sea, later scholars,
including Chambers, contested their interpretation. Klaeber saw Beowulf's battles with
the monsters as a struggle between the forces of good and evil and produced a Christian
interpretation: according to him Beowulf displays 'features of a Christian Saviour', 'the
destroyer of hellish devils, the brave and gentle warrior, irreproachable in word and
deed, the king who dies for his people'. Other critics thought that Klaeber's view went

too far; they pointed out that Christ's name is never mentioned in the poem and that it contains much that is irreconcilable with Christian teaching, such as Beowulf's statement that it is better to avenge one's friend than to grieve much for him, or the fact that his last thoughts are of the earthly treasure he has won, the grave-mound which is to keep his memory alive, and of his ancestors. Nor is Beowulf as gentle as all that; he avenges Hygelac by killing Daeghrefn, Hygelac's slayer and Beowulf's only human opponent, with his bare hands. Some see an explanation of Beowulf's name in the fact that he crushes his opponents to death in his grasp: it is the technique used by a bear, and so the name Beowulf would mean 'bear', a compound of *beo* (bee) and *wulf* (wolf, wild animal); and the bear is a wild animal which dotes on what bees produce.

Tolkien returned the monsters to a central place in the poem, as incarnations of death and ineradicable evil. He regarded the poem as a myth which in its original form belonged to Old Norse popular literature, including the threefold repetition of battles with almost indistinguishable monsters. It is the virtue of the *Beowulf* poet that he has introduced variation between them: the monsters which attack Heorot genuinely differ from the dragon guarding its hoard. Moreover, this distinction is reflected in the two parts of the poem, the two stages in Beowulf's career: his rise and his eventual fall. The poet deliberately contrasts Beowulf's glorious youth with his inevitable decline and death in old age. But this division does not mean that the poem is broken in the middle, as some critics think. Tolkien has shown that the two halves of the poem are just as much a whole as the two halves of the Old English line of verse, with its central caesura and the alliteration that binds the two halves of the line together. Because the poem's structure is thematic, rather than a continuous narrative, that structure is as rhythmic and complete as the rhythm of the line: just as the line contains unstressed metrical elements, so the poem contains a large number of tales in which the poet seems to diverge from his real story; but in each case it can be shown that these stories actually form part of the whole in that, however subordinate to the central theme, they do in fact illustrate, clarify or emphasise that theme.

One such story is the account of King Scyld and his funeral at the beginning of the poem: although it seems to have no direct connection with the story proper, it still has a significant function in it. Just as the very first word of the poem, *Hwæt!* (Listen!) is hypermetric – i.e. has no metrical place in the line – so the tale of King Scyld functions as a kind of advance information: without this awareness of the glorious deeds of the Danish king it might have been thought that the Danes were cowards because they could do nothing to counter Grendel's attacks. But it is precisely the courage of the Danish people that this picture of Scyld reminds us of. However, there is another reason why the poet begins with this story: it foreshadows the tragic ending, and there are many such anticipatory references throughout the story. When he tells of Heorot's building, he immediately adds that this royal hall will later be consumed by fire; the same fate befalls Beowulf's hall. The story of Finn, Hildeburth and Hnaef has a similar predictive function: it concerns just such a blood vengeance as King Hrothgar's daughter will encounter in her marriage to → Ingeld. The song of Sigemund's victory over the dragon again serves the same purpose: it looks forward to Beowulf's last fight.

The events of the poem have a characteristic cyclical pattern: a king's hall is built (Heorot); that hall is attacked by a monster and Beowulf does battle with the monster and overcomes it. This pattern is repeated twice more, with certain subtle changes. Alexander (1973) has suggested that in this context we should take the royal hall as a symbol of the community in the kingdoms of Hrothgar and Beowulf; by his victory over Grendel and Grendel's mother Beowulf twice saves a society from destruction, and although he overcomes the dragon also this victory happens only after the dragon has destroyed Beowulf's hall and mortally wounded Beowulf himself. This view thus adds an extra dimension to the tragic ending, since the destruction of the king's hall and the death of the king imply the end of the Geat nation. Historically this seems to fit, for in the sixth century the Geats were overrun by their arch-enemies the Swedes; in this context it is worth noting that the only person who helps Beowulf in his struggle with the dragon is a Swede, the young Wiglaf. It is as though the poet wants to say that not one of the Geat people had the courage to tackle the dragon in the king's place, as Beowulf in his youth had come to Hrothgar's aid and taken his place in fighting the monsters.

Beowulf is the work of a Christian poet writing about the Germanic past, but it cannot be termed a Christian poem. Apart from the references to God there is little in it that is really Christian; it deals in fact with the values of pagan Germanic society: loyalty unto death to the chosen leaders, the sacredness of the ties of blood-kinship and the duty to avenge a dead leader. Nevertheless, the poet has succeeded in expressing these Germanic values in a way acceptable to a Christian audience.

In 1939 a great treasure was found at Sutton Hoo, not far from Ipswich in Eastern England; it had been placed in a ship entombed in a barrow. This discovery contributed to a better understanding of certain elements of *Beowulf*, such as the account of King Scyld and his funeral: the dead Scyld had been placed with his possessions in a ship which was then entrusted to the waves. The Sutton Hoo burial is almost certainly that of a king, and it lies only four miles from the residence of the rulers of the Anglo-Saxon kingdom of Essex. Among the most striking objects from the grave are a sword, a shield, a helmet, a battle flag, a harp (probably intended to accompany the recitation of such poems as *Beowulf*) and gold coins from the period 650–670. The helmet dug up there corresponds very closely to the description of a helmet given to Beowulf by Hrothgar. The motifs and decoration on both helmet and shield also show close similarities with recent discoveries in Sweden, pointing to very early contacts between England and Southern Sweden; which may explain how a story set in Denmark and Southern Sweden became the most important literary work of Anglo-Saxon England.

The *Beowulf* material is still alive in the 20th century, as witness the publication in 1966 of Henry Treece's *The Green Man*, in 1971 of John Gardner's *Grendel* (which tells the story from the monster's point of view), and in 1976 of Michael Crichton's *Eaters of the Dead*. The names of Victor Davies and Betty Jane Wylie are attached to the rock opera *Beowulf* (1974). Michael Alexander has translated the work in alliterative verse in the tradition of Old English narrative (1973), and Kevin Crossley-Holland has produced a modern translation in rhythmic prose (1987).

HENK AERTSEN

Edition: Klaeber 1922.
Translations: Alexander 1973; Crossley-Holland 1987.
Studies: Chambers 1921; Tolkien 1936; Newton 1993.

BERTE AUX GRANDS PIEDS is the main character of a legend in which her place as bride to Pepin the Short is usurped by an imposter. Eventually the treason is uncovered and Berte is restored to her rightful position. More than twenty medieval versions of this legend have survived; here we shall follow the oldest of them, that of the *Chronique saintongeaise* (c.1225).

On the advice of his counsellors Pepin requests the hand of Berte, daughter of King Floris of Hungary. Berte travels to Paris. But by trickery her old nurse arranges that it is her own daughter who spends the wedding night with the king. She then orders two servants to murder Berte, but they allow her to escape. Berte finds refuge with Pepin's cowherd and his wife Constansa and for four years she is their servant. King Pepin and the nurse's daughter produce two sons, Remfré and Andri.

Hearing how detested the Queen of France has made herself, Berte's mother journeys to France. The false queen keeps to a darkened room, feigning illness; but despite this she is unmasked by Berte's mother. The old nurse is burned; nothing more is heard of her daughter. Shortly after this Pepin goes hunting and spends the night with his cowherd. He does not recognise Berte, but feels strongly attracted to her. The cowherd tells him how he found her and gives Pepin permission to sleep with her that night. A bed is prepared on a cart. Berte reveals her identity and recounts her adventures. The news that she has been found is received with great joy.

Some elements of this chronicle are also found elsewhere, often with Pepin's bastard sons and the false bride playing an active role. In the *Mainet* (an Old French poem from the 13th century which tells of → Charlemagne's youth in Spain under the name of Mainet) and in the Franco-Italian versions of the Berte legend they later poison Pepin and Berte, and the young Charlemagne also has reason to fear them. The cart on which Pepin and Berte sleep also receives several mentions, to explain Charles' name: on that cart he was conceived. The etymology in Latin and French texts is *carrus/Carolus* or *char/Charles*.

The central element of the intrigue, the motif of the substituted bride, is a widespread folk-tale motif with many variants; it apppears, for instance, in *The Goose Girl*, one of the folk-tales collected by the brothers Grimm. In the folk-tales a – usually anonymous – king's daughter loses her mother's talisman while on the way to her bridegroom. This puts her in the power of her waiting-woman, who makes her exchange clothes and identities with her. The real princess is compelled to silence by an oath, mutilation or threats, and has to do humiliating work. Eventually the imposter is unmasked and the princess regains her rightful position, either with the aid of animal helpers or through magical powers.

It is difficult to establish just when and how the historical mother of Charlemagne, who was called Bertrada and was the daughter of Charibert of Laon, became entangled in this story. Of course, the descent and birth of a hero ought to be special. And conflicting, more or less historical facts about Charles Martel, such as his illegitimacy, could readily be transferred to Charlemagne. The mention of 'Berte aus granz pies' in *Floire et Blancheflor* (c.1160; → Floris and Blanchefleur) as the daughter of the title characters and mother of Charlemagne indicates that the tale was already current at this time. For Berte's large feet play a part in the discovery of the imposture, particularly in the Romance versions of the legend, where the exchange takes place only after the wedding. In these versions the false queen is Berte's double, except for her feet. Historical and epic personages quite often have nicknames referring to physical peculiarities, as with Pepin the Short. In the past Berte's big feet led to her being linked with a mythical Germanic spinner, Perchta. However, the treadle-driven spinning-wheel, the reason for Perchta's flat feet, was not invented until the 15th century.

The most extensive and influential treatment of the Berte material is that of Adenet le Roi, who was active at the courts of Brabant and, later, Flanders. He wrote his *Berte as grans piés* around 1275. The work is in the form of a *chanson de geste*, but its content is much more that of a courtly romance. The positive characters are strongly idealised. Berte is presented as the innocent victim of a mean deception, who acquiesces in her fate with exemplary piety. While in the forest she even swears of her own accord that if she survives these privations she will not reveal her true identity unless her virginity is threatened. In the house of her foster parents, Symon and Constance, she makes herself beloved for her great beauty, virtue, piety, and skill in embroidery. During a visit to Paris Berte's mother Blanchefleur discovers the deception perpetrated by Berte's old nurse Margiste and her daughter Aliste, who is passing as Queen Berte. Some time later Pepin loses his way while out hunting and encounters Berte. They do not recognise each other, but to prevent Pepin raping her Berte reveals that she is the Queen. Pepin vainly seeks an explanation from Berte's foster parents; once safe, Berte withdraws her statement. Pepin, greatly confused, asks Berte's parents to come and identify her. So everything turns out well in the end.

Adenet's source has not survived; details from his work do appear in older versions, but never all together. Adenet claims to have read the true story in Saint-Denis but this, like his choice of form, is probably mainly intended to give his work greater authority. He appears to be in conflict with current traditions.

Adenet's *Berte* was the direct source for, among others, the stage adaptation *Le miracle de Berte* (c.1375) and the 15th century prose romance *Histoire de la reyne Berte et du roy Pepin*. Girard d'Amiens' *Charlemagne* (c.1300) forms a kind of sequel to Adenet's work.

Other works not dependent on Adenet paint a totally different picture. In the Franco-Italian versions it is Berte herself who asks another girl to take her place in the marriage bed. In Andrea da Barberino's *I Reali di Francia* (late 14th century), for example, she finds Pepin repulsive and too old; in *Berta da li gran pié* (c.1400) she is

Berthe's old nurse and her daughter Alise dismayed at the announcement of Blanchefleur's arrival. Engraving, illustration in Pieter Pijpers' *Adélaïde van Hongarije*, 1793.

saddle-sore from the long journey. Her replacement, in both cases the daughter of the Count of Mainz, then wants to continue as queen and tries to have Berte murdered. In Rafael Marmora's prose romance *Aquilon di Baviera* (1407) the false queen's name is Gaiete and she is the grandmother of → Roland; she disposes of Berta after Pepin himself lets her see his interest in her.

The German versions differ from the Romance in several respects. The oldest of them is to be found in *Karl der Grosse* (pre-1230) by Der Stricker. Here the exchange takes place before the wedding, as it does also in the *Chronicon Weihenstephanense* (second quarter 15th century) and the *Chronica Bremensis* (1463) by Heinrich Wolter; in these works Berte is not reinstated in her rightful place until some time after Charles' birth. A prose version of 1475 and Ulrich Fuetrer in 1478, like the first-mentioned chronicle, include an astrologer who tells Pepin when he is far from home that that night he will beget a mighty son. Pepin is determined not to miss such a chance and so embraces the first miller's daughter he comes upon, who later turns out to be Berte.

The Berte story remained popular for a long time. Antonio de Esclava's *Noches de Invierno* has a version which links up with the Franco-Italian texts. Here Berte takes the initiative in a definitive exchange of roles with a girl from Mainz, her reason being that Pepin is old and worn out and that she is in love with someone else.

C.-J. Dorat (1734–80) three times adapted the material for the stage, once in prose and twice in verse, under the titles *Adélaïde de Hongrie* and *Les deux reines*. In 1774 R.T. Regnard de Pleinchesne wrote *Berthe*, a pastoral 'comédie en vers libre'. Three years earlier Peter Pijpers' tragedy *Adélaïde van Hongarije* (1793) had appeared under the title

Pepyn, koning der Franschen. Pijpers drew his inspiration from Dorat's various stage versions and he, too, rechristens Berte as Adélaïde. In Pijpers' piece the real leading character and tragic heroine is the fraudulent queen Alise. Her ideal marriage with Pepijn is overshadowed by remorse; in the end she commits suicide. Political and moralistic ideas play a significant part in this lachrymose piece.

We are indebted to German Romanticism for further versions. F. de la Motte Fouqué adapted the material in his poem *Karl des Grossen Geburt und Jugendjahre* (1816); K. Simrock wrote *Berthe die Spinnerin* (1845) and O.F. Gruppe the epic verse trilogy *Kaiser Karl* (1848) of which the first part, *Königin Bertha, ein romantisches Epos*, is derived from Wolter's *Chronica Bremensis*. Here Pepin's court is located in Aachen. In 1878 the composer Victorin (de) Joncières (F.L. Rossignol) staged his opera *La Reine Berthe* in Paris; it won him no public acclaim.

'La Reine Pedauque', the queen with the goose's foot depicted on French churches and cathedrals (Saint-Bénigne in Dijon, also in Nevers, Saint-Pourcain, Nesle), has been identified with Berte of the big feet. Most likely, however, she represents the Queen of Sheba.

ANNELIES VAN GIJSEN

Edition: Henry 1951– 63.
Study: Colliot 1970.

BEVIS OF HAMPTON (Beuve de Hantone) is the hero of a widespread and very popular adventure story in which he is the son of Count Gui of Hantone (= Southampton), who is married to a woman much younger than himself. When he is ten years old his father is murdered by his mother and her lover, the German emperor Doon. Beuve himself escapes death thanks to the faithful counsellor Sabot but is sold as a slave to Saracen merchants who make a present of him to King Hermine of Egypt.

Beuve distinguishes himself at the Egyptian court; after some years he is made a knight and given the magic horse Arondel. King Bradmond of Damascus wants to marry Hermine's daughter Josiane but is rejected and declares war. Beuve defeats him. Josiane is in love with Beuve, but he dare not respond to her love because of his much lower social position and she is married off to Yvori of Montbrant. Because of her love for Beuve she uses magic to retain her virginity. Beuve carries her off, subdues the giant Escopart and flees with the two of them to Cologne, whose bishop is his uncle.

Beuve leaves for England, intending with the aid of the ever-loyal Sabot to avenge his father's death. Meanwhile Josiane has to endure the unwelcome attentions of a count who forces her to marry him. On their wedding night she kills him. She is condemned to death by burning but Beuve, warned by Escopart, arrives in the nick of time and rescues her. They marry and return to England where Beuve defeats and kills Doon. His mother commits suicide.

Beuve is now Count of Hantone, but a new difficulty arises; the son of his overlord, the King of England, tries to take the horse Arondel from him and is killed. Beuve is banished and separated from his wife. Josiane gives birth to twins whom she entrusts to foster parents while she herself, disguised as a *jongleur*, goes in search of her husband. It takes seven years of wandering before she finds him, just in time: under pressure, he is about to marry again. They are reunited with their two sons and hasten to the aid of Josiane's father Hermine, who is being besieged by Yvori of Montbrant. Yvori is defeated, Beuve becomes King of Montbrant, one of his sons succeeds Hermine and the other the King of England. Finally Beuve, Josiane and Arondel all die on the same day. The earliest known version of this story dates from the late 12th or early 13th century.

It is written in Anglo-Norman, the dialect of French used in England, and is in the form of a *chanson de geste*. This version is the basis for the English verse work *Sir Beues of Hamtoun* (14th century), which survives in manuscripts and early prints. The Welsh and Norwegian prose versions, *Bown o Hamtwn* (13th century) and *Bevers saga* (14th century), also derive from the Anglo-Norman. The English and Norwegian texts contain many additions, but the story remains basically unchanged. The English translation provides the model for the Irish prose version *Bibuis o Hamtuir* (15th century). The Faroese ballad *Bevusar taettir*, probably late medieval in origin and later set down from oral tradition, recounts in stanzaic form an episode from the Norwegian version.

Alongside this off-shore tradition, from the beginning of the 13th century we also find a 'continental' version of the story; the earliest representative of this is also in the form of a *chanson de geste*. This French text is longer; certain scenes are expanded and on occasion motifs are repeated. The author shows a considerable predilection for the supernatural, and consequently gives a greater role to the giant, here called Acopart, and the horse Arondel. Seven manuscripts of this epic have been preserved.

Both types, insular and continental, must descend from a common ancestor; the differences are too marked for us to assume that one was the model for the other. The story must have been popular in Southern France as early as the middle of the 12th century, as is clear from references in Occitanian lyric of the period and in the Occitanian *chanson de geste Daurel et Beton* (pre-1168). A 15th-century prose version in French also survives in two contemporary manuscripts and in prints by Antoine Vérard (pre-1500), Michel Lenoir (1502), and a few others of later date.

In Italy, too, the story was extremely popular. We know of a number of Italian texts, most of them in verse. The most important are a Franco-Italian fragment which formed part of a cycle based on French epic works, the *Reali di Francia*, and a Tuscan version in *ottava rima* (an eight-line stanza rhyming abababcc). Compared with the French source, the Italian *Buovo d'Antona* shows a great many changes and expansions; for example, the giant Escopart becomes the monster Pulicane, half man and half dog, and the merchants who buy the young Buovo as a slave play a major part. The Italian texts differ among themselves not only in form and dialect but also in approach. The Tuscan version is a straightforward adventure story, while that from Northern Italy has a strong anti-feudal political tone. Tomasso Traetta's opera *Buovo d'Antona*, to a libretto by Carlo Goldoni, was premièred in Venice in 1758.

The Tuscan poem was translated into Yiddish in Venice in 1501 by the Jewish humanist Elia Levita. His *Bovo-* or *Baba-boek*, also in ottava rima, first appeared in print in 1547 and was regularly reprinted throughout Central and Eastern Europe until well into the 19th century. The Yiddish version was translated into Romanian by M. Aziel and published in 1881, together with two other medieval narratives, under the title *O mie si una de zile* (A thousand and one days).

A Russian version dates from the 16th century. This chapbook, which was frequently reprinted and remained popular into the 19th century, derives from the Tuscan version; it is uncertain, however, whether it is a direct translation. Some specialists are of the opinion that the Russian author used the Yiddish *Baba-boek*, others posit a lost Serbian version as intermediary.

The French, continental, tradition also includes the Middle Dutch *Buevijn van Austoen*. Only a small fragment of the verse text survives, but we have a number of prints of a prose adaptation. The two oldest, both from Antwerp, date from 1504 and 1511.

In Spain, too, the story of Beuve touched a chord. The Sephardic Jews, who left the Iberian peninsula after 1492 and settled in other countries around the Mediterranean, preserved many traditions from their former homeland in their everyday language, Ladino, which was based on Spanish. Thus it was that on Rhodes, in the 18th and 19th centuries, Sephardic ballads were being sung and written down which had as their subjects episodes from the story of Beuve. The source for these was a Spanish ballad, *Celinos y la adúltera*, which itself goes back to the French *Beuve*.

To sum up: we find stories about Beuve being written from the 13th century to the 19th in the form of full-length epics, ballads dealing with only a single episode and popular chapbooks in prose, over an area extending from the Faroes to Russia and from Scandinavia to Rhodes.

C. HOGETOORN

Edition: Stimming 1899.
Studies: Doutrepont 1939; Debaene 1951; De Riquer 1956².

BRENDAN, the abbot of a large monastery in Ireland, is reading a book which describes marvellous things and places, including a variety of paradises and heavens; he throws the book in the fire in disbelief and then hears the voice of an angel commanding him to put to sea. He builds a ship on the model of Noah's ark and sets sail with eighty fellow-voyagers. A gigantic deathshead washed up on a beach provides the occasion for the first remarkable conversation. The head declines both Brendan's offer to intercede for its return to life and his offer of baptism. A new life as a baptised mortal would be too risky; the punishment for sin would be more severe and the thought of dying a second time is too much. After watching a remarkable duel between a chimera and a flying stag the voyagers land on an island which turns out to be a fish. Following a confrontation with a mermaid they visit an island where Brendan is able to give temporary relief from their torments to the souls of venal stewards. Successfully avoiding the perils of the Liver Sea and the dangerous magnetic rocks, they then visit a monastery of perfect monks. The next encounter is with the former King of Pamphilia and Cappadocia, now a hermit doing penance in grim conditions for his sins of incest and homicide. At the entrance to Hell Brendan sees the souls of unjust rulers and corrupt officials; for these he can do nothing, however, excluded as they are from God's grace.

After an enforced rest in total darkness Brendan's company finds itself in the first citadel of paradise, a place of exotic delights. One of the chaplains loses his self-control and at the Devil's instigation steals a valuable bridle. Awaiting the monks is a yet more imposing castle, its entrance guarded by an angel with a flaming sword. St Michael seizes one of the monks, grasping him by his habit. The sea-bottom here proves to be of gold. Next, devils carry off the chaplain who stole the bridle; but Brendan's intercession eventually persuades God to relent and the Devil is forced to return him, scorched and blackened by his brief sojourn in Hell. The enchantment of a singing siren lulls the entire company, except for Brendan, into a deep sleep. There follows a further encounter with the Devil near a burning mountain. The scorched chaplain is beside himself with terror. Devils send a hail of red-hot stones and fire-arrows down upon the ship, but God prevents them scoring any direct hits. Brendan has a vision in which he is shown the heavenly paradise, and has the ship hove to while he writes down all its wonders. When he wants to turn back a storm drives them into the Liver Sea, which swarms with sea-monsters. They see a hermit on a floating clod of earth; he has been there for 99 years and is part of a whole community of pious floaters. A fresh storm gets up and Brendan comes face to face with Judas, who is exposed to conflicting hardships. Brendan's intercession succeeds in adding Mondays to his weekends off, but the devils' assault then becomes even more violent. Again the voyagers pass an entrance to Hell, but they then come to 'Multum Bona Terra', where dwell those angels who remained neutral in Lucifer's rebellion against God. As punishment they have a monstrous appearance; but their place of exile is the loveliest spot on earth, with a splendid castle on the mountain Mons Syone. Brendan has a lengthy discussion with the spokesman of the neutral angels, in which he is compared to the Apostle Thomas. Why does the abbot refuse to believe what he cannot understand?

After his encounter with the fallen angels Brendan comes upon a little man floating on a leaf in the sea. He is busy measuring the volume of the ocean. When Brendan reproaches him for attempting an impossible task he answers that to behold all God's wonders is no less impossible. A sea-serpent surrounds the ship, then suddenly disappears. They lie becalmed for weeks, hearing noises from beneath the surface of the sea. The water turns out to be very shallow. Discovering that his logbook is full, Brendan gives orders to make sail and cut the anchor cable. An easy voyage brings them all safe home. Brendan dies soon afterwards; the Archangel Michael himself comes to fetch his soul.

Thus the account of Brendan's adventures in the most romantic version of his story, the Middle Dutch *De reis van Sinte Brandaan*, whose antecedents will be discussed later. The historical Brendan came from somewhere near Tralee in County Kerry, in the south-west of Ireland. He is generally thought to have been born in 484, though the sources are not unanimous on this point. A descendant of the Kings of Munster, he shares his aristocratic origins with other Irish saints of the period. He is thought to have been the founder of a number of monastic houses, the most famous being that of Clonfert, whose associated school had at one time as many as 300 pupils. His name lives on in Ireland in various geographical names containing the element Brandon.

Like his literary descendants, the historical Brendan had a reputation as a voyager. He is recorded as having been *Orcadum et Scotiarum insularum apostulus*, which may refer to his journeys to the Orkneys and Shetlands; possibly he also travelled to the Faroes. He visited St Columba on Iona. He was appointed abbot of the monastery of Llanaervon in South Wales in the early 6th century. The *Vita Sancti Brendani* indicates that he may also have visited Brittany. Brendan probably died at Annaghdown in County Galway and was buried in Clonfert Abbey. According to the *Vita* he died on 16 May 576.

Narratives about seafarers made up a significant part of Old Irish literature, and one of these, 'The Voyage of Mael Duin', dating from the 8th or 9th century, contains various motifs which correspond with what on the Continent would later develop into the Brendan story. Mael Duin, offspring of the rape of an abbess, seeks to avenge the death of his father when the latter is killed by pirates. Three foster-brothers volunteer at the last moment for the voyage to track down the perpetrators; by taking them on board Mael Duin infringes his magical obligations, with the result that the forces of nature are hostile to him and he is condemned to wander the oceans. Only when the three foster-brothers are deleted from the muster-roll is Mael Duin able to approach the object of his voyage, the pirate ships, and avenge his father's death.

This work must have had an influence on the *Navigatio Sancti Brendani* which was written, almost certainly in the Trier area, in the late 9th or early 10th century. On the advice of a certain Barinthus, Abbot Brendanus of Clonfert goes in search of a paradisiacal island; this involves him in a cyclical journey lasting seven years. His crew consists of twice seven monks, plus three latecomers. One of these dies after stealing a precious bridle, one goes to the Devil and the third joins some singers. Thus the motif of the three supernumeraries recurs in this text, which is otherwise notably ascetic and liturgical in character. It is a real *peregrinatio pro deo*, a pilgrimage for God. Seven times they celebrate Easter on the back of the sea-monster Jasconius. Seven evokes the image of the seven *aetates*, the seven periods into which St Augustine divided world history; the sea-monster represents Christ's victory over Hell. Another motif from the *Immram Mael Duin* which reappears in the *Navigatio Sancti Brendani* is that of the column rising out of the sea, shrouded in a curtain; a niche contains a paten and a chalice, attributes of the Holy Sacrament. On the other hand, the work has a strongly mimetic character. The ship's construction resembles that of the Irish *curragh*, while the encounters during the voyage relate to a variant on the desert ideal from the early history of Christianity: in these northern regions anchorites retired to inhospitable rocky peaks and hermits inhabited the small islets off the Irish and Scottish coasts. For the people of the time, the realistic description of the life of monastic communities on remote islands must have enhanced the story's credibility, and thus its exemplaristic function. In consequence the *Navigatio Sancti Brendani* enjoyed great popularity; at least 116 manuscripts of it are known. An Anglo-Norman adaptation of it into French was produced in the first quarter of the 12th century and, moreover, in circles close to King Henry I. This *Voyage de saint Brandan* was the work of one Benedeit, who wrote in French but lived in England. His narrative has survived, in whole or in part, in six manuscripts.

The German-Dutch complex of the so-called *Reis* version dates from the 12th and 13th centuries. The original version, now lost, must have been written around 1150 on the banks of the Rhine in a Rhineland-Middle Frankish dialect; from it developed the versions in Middle High German (shortened, 13th or 14th century) and Middle Low German (15th century). A richly illustrated codex of 1460 contains a Middle High German prose version of the story. Apart from the so-called Krumauer Bildercodex of the *Navigatio*, this is the only illustrated version of the Brendan story. The Rhineland text must have been translated into Middle Dutch in the 12th or early 13th century. This Middle Dutch version has been preserved in two manuscripts, the Comburg manuscript (c.1370) and the Van Hulthem manuscript (c.1410). In the second of these the text is incomplete, the first 323 lines being missing.

At many points this *Reis* version of the story diverges considerably from its Latin predecessor. Brendan's voyage is a punishment for his lack of faith: he burns a book which enumerates the marvellous signs of God's creative hand. It tells of two paradises and three heavens; a world beneath our world; a whole forest growing on a fish's back; Judas enjoying relief from his punishment every Saturday evening. All this is too much for Brendan the doubting Thomas; nine years of voyaging are needed to change his view. He is to see God's wonders with his own eyes and gain insight into the workings of God's mercy. There are strong indications that these versions link up with developments in thinking on Purgatory around 1170. St Augustine's fourfold classification of mankind – entirely good, not entirely good, not entirely bad, entirely bad – is reflected in the categories of sinners Brendan meets in his travels.

Of more significance is the omission from the Middle Dutch of the motif of the world under this world, which may have been prompted by the fear of heresy: if there were other people under the earth these would be excluded from the redemption brought by Christ. The theory of the antipodes had proved theologically risky as early as c.748, though Macrobius' commentary (400) on the *Somnium Scipionis* had offered a model in which the earth was divided into five zones, thus catering for life south of the equator. This commentary on a text by Cicero enjoyed such authority as a source of cosmological knowledge that the Church too accepted this proposition. But the Middle Dutch author's handling of this episode may indicate self-censorship; he skirted around the old question of the antipodes. An equally contentious text was the apocryphal *Visio Sancti Pauli*, originally written in Greek (Egypt, 3rd century), which, despite Augustine's opposition to it, was translated into Latin by Duns Scotus Eriugena in the 9th century. The Middle Ages read this vision of St Paul's as a guide-book to the Hereafter, in which there was room for intermission of the punishments of Hell. The Judas episode in the *Reis van Sinte Brandaan* should also be seen against this background: at the intercession of Paul and his guide, the Archangel Michael, Christ grants the souls in Hell relief from their torments from Saturday morning until Monday evening!

Was Brendan a forerunner of Columbus? In the view of Tim Severin this possibility should certainly not be ruled out. Severin had a medieval curragh built following the description in the *Navigatio Sancti Brendani*, and during the summers of 1976 and 1977 he sailed it by the North Atlantic route to Newfoundland, wintering in Iceland. His experiences confirmed a number of remarkable details in the Latin work, some of which also appear in the Middle Dutch versions: the behaviour of whales, the pillar/column and curtain motif as descriptive of an iceberg, the gates of Hell as volcanic islets. Moreover, it proved possible to reach America in a craft made of tanned ox-hide with a draught of only twelve inches. Severin thus concluded that it was entirely possible that Irish monks discovered America 'by accident' between AD 500 and 600 – long before the Vikings set foot in the New World around the year 1000.

What we read in the *Navigatio Sancti Brendani* would then be the sedimentary remains of such an expedition, though no trace of any Irish settlement has been found on the north-east coast of America. However, the works mentioned above should not be regarded as a documentary account of the Great Crossing. They are a product of medieval spirituality and should be read as such. This is not to deny that empirical observations found their way into the narrative. Although Brendan's voyage cannot be charted on a medieval map, although it is set in the world of the medieval imagination, much of what Brendan experiences formed part of current belief in the 12th century; while at the same time the story continues a narrative tradition going back to the 9th century.

Not long after the invention of printing, editions entitled *Die wunderbare Meerfahrt des heiligen Brandan* appear in Germany. Here we may mention the print published by Anton Sorg (Augsburg 1476) and that produced by Konrad Hist (Spiers 1496), both of which are lavishly illustrated with woodcuts. The same title was used by Michael Furter (Basel 1491) and Matthis Hüpfuff (Strassburg 1499); these too are both illustrated.

Brendan's popularity as a patron saint seems to be concentrated mainly in three areas: Britanny, the upper Rhine and along the North Sea and Baltic coasts. In Bruges, traces of the veneration of Brendan can be seen from as early as 1359: the church of the hospital of O.L. Vrouwe ter Potterie contains an altar dedicated to St Anne and St Brandanus. Devotions here were intended to avert house-fires. The same function must be attributed to the fresco in Sint-Jan in 's-Hertogenbosch. The island of Terschelling probably served as a link between the North Sea and the Baltic; the present Brandaris lighthouse there was built in 1594 on the site of a dilapidated chapel of St Brandarius. In North Germany, too, one finds signs of the Brendan cult, with the saint invariably linked to fire. One could mention here such places as Güstrow, Schwerin, Wittenburg, Malchin, Wittstock, Parchim, Eixen and Zierzow, where in the 16th century the saint was depicted with a torch or a candle. In Lübeck there was a link with the smiths' guild, in Stralsund the brewers too had masses said for Brendan. Popular etymology will have played a part in this association, though awareness of Brendan's experiences with fire cannot be ruled out.

A separate issue is the Brendan's Island which appears as early as c.1300 on such famous maps as the Mappa Mundi in Hereford and the Erbstorf World Map. Columbus was convinced of the existence of such an island, and until the 18th century it was thought to lie somewhere near the Canaries, which has proved to be in the most literal sense a mirage.

The novel published by Michael Scott and Gloria Gaghan in 1988 under the title *Navigator, The Voyage of Saint Brendan*, is based directly on the *Navigatio Sancti Brendani*. In some episodes the story follows the *Navigatio* closely; in others the authors' imagination has freer rein, as for instance in the description of the island of Ailbe, who is here a heathen priest of the God of the Sea. Many familiar motifs are retained, but the fairy-tale element is strengthened and the voyage romanticised.

Abbot Brendan relates the story in the first person; he is the Great Navigator but also has moments of doubt, while his relationships with some of his companions give the events added emotional value.

A.G. VAN MELLE

Editions: Short/Merrilees 1984; Sollbach 1987.
Studies: Severin 1978; Strijbosch 1994 and 1995.

BRUTUS, legendary grandson of → Aeneas, was regarded as the first king of Britain. He is the eponymous hero of two romances on the history of Britain: the Old French *Roman de Brut* by the poet Wace, completed in 1155, and the Middle English *Brut* (between 1190 and 1216), a translation and adaptation of Wace's work by Layamon.

Brutus, the Italian-born grandson of the Trojan Eneas, is fifteen when he accidentally kills his father while out hunting and is consequently driven out by his countrymen. He flees to Greece, where he becomes the leader of a group of Trojans who had been taken there as slaves after the fall of Troy. Under Brutus's leadership the Trojans free themselves from slavery; Brutus even marries Innogene, the daughter of the Greek king.

He takes ship and leaves Greece with his men, having no desire to remain there; too much blood has been shed in the war for them to be able to live permanently in peace with the Greeks. Looking for somewhere to settle, after three days' sailing they reach an island called Loegres. They find it unpopulated, though there are signs of previous habitation including a temple to the goddess Diana. They ask her counsel and she advises Brutus and his followers to continue to the island of Albion. Twenty days later they reach the mainland of Europe. There they find a man, Corin by name, who is also of Trojan descent; he joins their ranks. When they reach the mouth of the Loire in Aquitaine the country's king, Goffar, becomes concerned at the Trojan presence; he

Brutus landing in England. Part of a tapestry from a workshop in Doornik, c.1475. Zaragoza Cathedral.

decides to attack them, aided by eleven other kings, because they are plundering the country and laying it waste. Brutus succeeds in defeating Goffar's much larger army and then leaves for Albion. They find the island, as they had been told, inhabited only by a band of giants. One day they are attacked by thirty of these; although they initially kill the same number of Trojans, Brutus's little army manages to slaughter all of them save one, Gogemagog. This last surviving giant is overpowered by Corin, who hurls him from the cliffs.

Corin is given part of the country; he names it Cornoalle (Cornwall) after himself and builds houses and towns. He founds the city of 'Nouvelle Troye' on the Thames; this later becomes London. Brutus names the whole country Britannia and divides it among his followers. He and his wife have three sons: Locrin, Albanac and Camber. Albanac receives an area in the north of Britannia which he names Albanie, later known as Escoce (Scotland). Another, more westerly, region is given to Camber, who calls it Gales (Wales). After Brutus's death Locrin becomes king of all Britannia. Brutus is the founder of a line from which King → Arthur will be born and to which Wace's patron King Henry II also belongs.

Wace adapted Geoffrey of Monmouth's pseudo-historical 'chronicle' *Historia regum Britannie* (History of the Kings of Britain, completed 1136). The figure of Brutus also appears in Nennius' chronicle *Historia Brittonum*, which had been used by Geoffrey. Both in Wace and in Layamon the eponymous hero appears only in the first chapter; the reign of King Arthur, in particular, is described in much more detail. The continuing interest in the romances of Wace and Layamon is due mainly to this section on Arthur, which draws not only on Geoffrey but also on oral traditions. Wace is the first writer to mention Arthur's Round Table. The work probably took its title from the figure of Brutus because according to tradition Britain was named after him.

In addition to Wace's 14,866-line work and Layamon's *Brut* we have various other chronicles both in verse and in prose, written between the late 13th and late 15th centuries; these include Robert of Gloucester's verse chronicle, the Anglo-Norman prose *Brut* and the English prose *Brut*. This last was printed by Caxton in 1480 under the title *The Cronicles of England*; it was extremely popular and was reprinted many times. There are also Norwegian, Spanish and Portuguese chronicles in which Brutus appears as the ancestor of the British kings.

Brutus' 'survival' is confined to the above-mentioned medieval works. Even later versions of the *Aeneid* lack any sequel describing Brutus' killing of his father and consequent exile. In the cathedral of La Seo in Zaragoza there is a tapestry which depicts the hero's landing in England; it was made at Doornik in the Southern Netherlands around 1475.

ADA POSTMA

Edition: Esty 1978.
Translations: Thorpe 1966; Bzdyi 1989.
Study: Esty 1978.

CHARLEMAGNE or Charles the Great (Latin: Carolus Magnus) is the central figure in the epic world of Carolingian narrative. Stories set in the empire he rules have come down to us in manuscripts from the 12th century on. Earliest are the French *chansons de geste* (literally: songs of heroic deeds), but the genre soon spread to the surrounding language areas. At a later stage cycles develop as the existing works are expanded to include earlier or later events or grouped into more or less coherent complexes. One well-known example is the Old Norse *Karlamagnús saga*, an extensive prose cycle of Charlemagne stories which dates from the end of the 13th century. Though there is still a clear division into ten sections (*branches*), the whole is presented as a biography of the great emperor: it begins with an account of the early years of his reign and ends with his death. A summary of this saga provides a good impression of the content of Carolingian epic.

The first branch draws on a variety of sources and deals with the beginning of Charlemagne's reign. After the death of King Pepin of France his son and successor, Charles, is warned by God of a conspiracy against him. He is instructed to go out stealing with the thief Basin. For this nocturnal excursion Charles uses the pseudonym 'Magnus', later to become his established byname. With God's help the conspirators are unmasked and Charles can be crowned by the Pope. On his return to Aachen the young ruler begets a child on his sister. He confesses his sin and is commanded by God to give the mother-to-be in marriage to Milo. Seven months later → Roland is born. The youth performs his first heroic deeds during the war against the disloyal vassal → Girart de Vienne. He comes up against Oliver in single combat. The duel ends indecisively and from that moment on Oliver is his loyal comrade in arms; Roland promises to marry Oliver's sister, the beautiful Aude.

Charles then learns that the Saxons under King → Widukind are in revolt. He hastens to meet them, but is checked by the Rhine. His men start building a bridge, but progress is slow until Roland and Oliver arrive; they quickly complete the bridge. The Saxons are defeated and their king slain. One day Charles sees on the Rhine a boat drawn by a swan. In the boat is a knight who is unable to speak. The → Swan Knight becomes a member of the court and is given the king's sister as his wife.

After the birth of his son → Louis, Charles decides to make a pilgrimage to Jerusalem. On his way home he assists the King of Constantinople in his struggle against the heathen. He is rewarded with relics which he brings back with him to the West. Then the Angel Gabriel informs him that he must do battle with the heathen in Spain. Early in the war Roland is sent back to France to deal with various matters for Charles. While he is there the wife of Charles' vassal Ganelon succeeds in seducing him, and this is the origin of the hatred between Roland and Ganelon – a hatred clearly to be seen in the *Chanson de Roland* (in which Ganelon is Roland's stepfather). On Roland's return to the army preparations are made to pursue the war against the heathen. Charles knights → Ogier and presents horses and arms to Ogier, → Turpin and Roland. He then selects twelve knights to be his commanders.

The second branch, entitled *Olif en Landres*, derives from a Middle English narrative brought to Norway from Scotland in 1287 by the Norwegian noble Bjarni Erlingsson. It concerns Olif, a daughter of the Frankish king Pepin, and her son Landres. Olif is married to King Hugon, but by cunning and sorcery the wicked courtier Milon brings about her disgrace; she is walled up in a dungeon with snakes and toads. Seven years later Landres finds his mother and rescues her. Olif's brother Charles, who has succeeded his father in the meantime, ensures that she is restored to her position and the villain dies in the same dungeon in which the falsely accused queen had miraculously survived for so long. Olif goes into a nunnery, Hugon dies and Landres succeeds him as king.

The third branch is closely related to the first part (the 'Enfances') of the well known Old French *chanson de geste La Chevalerie d'Ogier de Danemarche* (c.1200). Ogier is the son of the King of Denmark and a hostage at Charlemagne's court. When the army marches to Italy to fight the Saracens Ogier goes with them and performs his first deeds of heroism. As a result of his actions the heathen are defeated. During the war Ogier strikes up a friendship with the noble Saracens Karvel and Glorionde.

The fourth branch is named after the enemy king *Agulandus* and is based on two sources: the Latin *Historia Karoli Magni et Rotholandi* or 'Chronicle of pseudo-Turpin' (see below) and the 12th-century *Chanson d'Aspremont*. King Agulandus is an African ruler who has invaded Spain. Charles fights a lengthy war against him. The theological discussions that take place during pauses in the fighting between Charles and Agulandus and between Roland and the giant Ferrakut have become well known. Jamund, Agulandus' son, is the leading warrior among the Saracens. He has even Charlemagne in difficulties on the battlefield, but Roland comes to his aid in the nick of time. He kills Jamund and is rewarded with the latter's sword Dyrumdali and his horn Oliphant. When Agulandus learns that his son has fallen there is a last fierce battle, in which the heathen are decisively beaten and Agulandus is killed.

The fifth branch, *Guitalin*, is closely related to the *Chanson de Saisnes* by Jehan Bodel (c.1200). It describes Charles' war with the Saxon king Guitalin (→ Widukind). Guitalin has captured Cologne while Charles and his Franks were besieging the city of Nobilis in Spain. Charles leaves Roland to continue the siege and marches to Cologne. Through his own recklessness Charles finds himself encircled by Guitalin's forces in Saxon territory. He sends for aid to Roland, who first captures Nobilis and then rescues Charles. A lengthy conflict ensues. To defeat the Saxons it is necessary to build a bridge over the Rhine, a difficult undertaking with many setbacks. Not until this bridge is completed do the Franks win the war. Guitalin is brought to trial and dies soon after in captivity.

The sixth branch is named *Otuel* for its protagonist, and is closely related to the *chanson de geste Otinel*. Having captured Rome, the heathen king Garcia sends his son Otuel to Paris to demand Charles' surrender. A duel is arranged between Roland and Otuel; however, it remains undecided because the Holy Ghost suddenly appears in the form of a dove and commands Otuel to yield. This miracle decides Otuel to convert to Christianity; in gratitude Charles promises him his daughter Belesent. The army then marches on Rome, where the heathen are defeated thanks to the aid of their own, now Christian, general. Otuel marries Belesent and becomes governor of Lombardy.

The seventh branch corresponds closely with the Old French *Voyage de Charlemagne à Jerusalem et à Constantinople*. Once when Charles was meeting with his council under an olive-tree he suddenly asked the queen if she knew of any king whose crown so befitted him as himself. When she then mentions the Emperor of Miklagard (Constantinople) Charles becomes angry and decides to go and discover the truth for himself. He first travels to Jerusalem, where he and his paladins sit in the seats used by Jesus and his disciples at the Last Supper. A chance passer-by takes Charlemagne for God and warns the patriarch, who presents Charles with a nail from the Cross, a fragment of the crown of thorns and many other relics. The company then travels on to Miklagard, where they are received by Hugon (in this text an emperor). They are greatly impressed by the riches of the palace, but once on their own in their bedroom they start boasting of the mighty deeds they are capable of. Roland brags that with one blast on his horn he could open every door in the palace and strip the Emperor of his beard and clothes. Oliver claims to be able to make love to the Emperor's daughter at least a hundred times, and each of them makes a similar drunken boast. The Emperor hears of all this from a servant; next day he demands that they should make good their boasts. The Franks are saved from this tricky situation by God's help and a white lie from the Emperor's pretty daughter. At a formal gathering it is apparent to all that Charles cuts a far more kingly figure than Hugon. Laden with relics, the Franks return home. The queen is forgiven her incautious remark.

The eighth branch is a version of the *Chanson de Roland* (→ Roland) about the defeat of the Frankish rearguard in the war against the Saracens in Spain. The first part of the text is very close to the 'Oxford Version' of this *chanson de geste*; later in the story the differences increase. The third episode of the *Chanson de Roland*, that of Balingant, is completely lacking in the saga.

The ninth branch, *Vilhjalm Korneis*, corresponds with the Old French *Moniage*

Guillaume, which concerns the final period in the life of → Guillaume d'Orange. Roland's death at the battle of Roncevaux left Guillaume as the greatest champion among the Franks. Charles gave him a newly-captured town together with the widow of its defeated ruler. One day the lady discovers a grey hair on her new husband's head and teases him about it; he promptly leaves her and enters a monastery. He hangs up his weapons in the monastery church and performs his religious duties meticulously; the worldly inclinations of the other monks attract his strong disapproval. Attacked by robbers on a dangerous mission outside the monastery, he manages to save himself; but the monks refuse to let him back in. Guillaume forces the gate, takes his revenge on the monks and abbot and leaves the monastery. Not long afterwards the Franks are assisted in their fight against the heathen Madul by an unknown warrior, who even decapitates the enemy leader. Years later, the body of the unknown is discovered through a miracle in an odour of sanctity. It turns out to be Guillaume, who has spent his remaining years as a hermit living in a cave. The body is interred with great honour and Charlemagne has a church built on the site.

The tenth branch contains narrative material from a variety of historiographical texts, including the 'Chronicle of pseudo-Turpin'. The branch treats of the relics brought back by Charlemagne from the East and the wonders and signs connected with his death. The great Emperor died in Aachen, where he was buried with splendid ceremonial. The text ends with a prayer for a blessing on the writer of the work, the one who commissioned it, the one who recited it and those who listened to it.

For a long time this *Karlamagnús saga* determined the image of Charlemagne in the Scandinavian countries. Its textual history is extremely complex; the extant manuscripts date from a period extending from the 13th into the 17th century. The cycle seems to have been meant as a biography, but – as is clear from the above summary – it is very far from being a coherent entity. There are many conflicting details. For instance, the first branch says that Roland's famous sword Durendal was forged by the mythical smith → Weland, and Roland was given it by Charles, who had in turn received it from a grateful citizen of Vienne. But the fourth branch tells how Roland won it from the heathen general Jamund. The atmosphere of the branches varies, too: we find the robust epic of the battle of Roncevaux, but also the fairy-tale setting of the second branch about the falsely accused queen Olif. All of which gives the modern reader a good impression of the diversity of Carolingian narrative.

What holds the saga together, as it does the whole genre of the *chansons de geste*, is the figure of Charlemagne, in European history the most important ruler of the early Middle Ages. The historical Charlemagne was born in 742, the son of Pepin III, the Short, and Bertrada. He succeeded his father in 768, jointly with his brother Carloman; on Carloman's death in 771 he became sole ruler of the Franks. On Christmas Day of the year 800 he was crowned Holy Roman Emperor by Pope Leo III in Rome. He died on 24 January 814 and lies buried in the chapel he himself built (now part of the cathedral) in Aachen.

The principal source for our knowledge of Charles and his rule is the *Vita Karoli Magni Imperatoris* by Einhart, who as a member of the court knew the Emperor personally. He describes him as the prince of order and justice, defender of the Church and protector of learning and culture. He gives a detailed account of Charles' almost endless wars against the Langobards, the Saxons, the Avars and many other enemies as he sought to expand and consolidate his empire. This eventually stretched from the Pyrenees and Central Italy to the North Sea and from the Atlantic to the Elbe. Charlemagne had a very good relationship with the Pope, whom he repeatedly protected, and maintained friendly relations with the Eastern Empire and with the Islamic Caliph Haroun al-Rashid, from whom he received the gift of an elephant. His reign was also a period in which culture flourished. The Emperor attached great

OLVSORAVIOTMESICVTOADISTAVOCAVITJACOBV

Charlemagne's Spanish campaign: the walls of Pamplona miraculously collapse during his siege of the city. Metal relief on the reliquary of Charlemagne, early 13th century, in Aachen Cathedral.

importance to education and scholarship and gathered learned men around him from here, there and everywhere. Einhart relates that at mealtimes he would listen to readings from heroic stories and that he gave instructions for the mighty deeds of kings from the past to be written down. Another early biography is the more anecdotal *Gesta Karoli Magni* by Notker Balbulus, a monk of St Gallen (c.884).

The mighty commander and world-ruler described by Einhart and Notker, or occasionally one of his predecessors or successors, is the king of the epic world in which the Carolingian tales are set. The genre originated in France as oral narrative. Just how those early oral stories sounded, and how they developed out of the historical events they dealt with, is something that cannot now be established, even though research into the *chansons de geste*, and particularly the *Chanson de Roland*, has for a long time focused on these questions. At present most researchers assume that the first texts were written down around 1100, having previously existed in oral tradition. Approximately eighty *chansons de geste* still survive in French. Sometimes they are subdivided into *laisses* (stanzas) of unequal length, composed of lines of ten syllables with assonant rhyme or, in the later texts, of twelve-syllable lines with pure rhyme. It is highly probable that these narratives were originally performed by bards to the accompaniment of some simple musical instrument.

In line with what Bertrand de Bar-sur-Aube says in the prologue to his *Girart de Vienne* (c.1180), modern literary historians divide Carolingian epic into three groups (*gestes* or cycles) according to whether the protagonist is the king himself or belongs to the house of Garin de Monglane or that of Doon de Mayence. The first group (the 'Cycle du roi') consists of those narratives in which Charles himself, or his relations, play a significant part. Adenet le Roi's *Berte aus grans piés*, for example, is about Charles' mother → Berte, daughter of → Floris and Blanchefleur, who is compelled by her maid's trickery to spend years in exile before her husband Pepin finds her again by chance; soon afterwards their son Charles is born. The *Mainet* deals with Charles' youth in Toledo at the court of the Saracen prince Galafre, where he performs his first heroic deeds and has his first love-affair. This is a short, episodic tale in which at God's command Charles goes out stealing with the disgraced Duke Elegast and so discovers to his astonishment that his brother-in-law Eggeric intends to rob him of his throne. Other narratives in this royal cycle are the *Voyage de Charlemagne*, the *Chanson de Saisnes* by Jean Bodel, the *Chanson de Roland* and the *Chanson de la Reine Sebile* (→ Sibilla).

The second group (the 'Cycle de Garin' or 'Cycle de Guillaume') concerns the family founded by Garin de Monglane. The outstanding hero of this house, though, is → Guillaume d'Orange. The cycle includes, among others works, *Girart de Vienne*, *Le couronnement de Louis*, *Le charroi de Nîmes*, *La Prise d'Orange* and the *Moniage Guillaume*. This is the most coherent of the three groups; already in the 14th century the *chansons de geste* concerning the house of Garin were collected and arranged in correct order of events in so-called *manuscrits cycliques*.

The 'Cycle de Doon de Mayence' brings together the *chansons de geste* about vassals who rebelled against the king. These tales usually revolve around a conflict of loyalty. Thus, → Ogier is forced into a feud with Charles when Charles' son kills Ogier's son for beating him at chess. In such a situation family loyalty, which obliges Ogier to avenge his son, inevitably leads to disloyalty to the feudal lord; but the narrator's sympathy usually lies with the rebellious vassal. As well as the *Chevalerie d'Ogier de Danemarche* this cycle includes → *Gormont et Isembart*, → *Raoul de Cambrai* and → *Renaut de Montauban*.

The treatment of the epic ruler Charlemagne is not the same in every story. The texts offer a wide range of portraits of him, which can broadly be divided into the positive and the negative. The positive image, for which Einhart had laid the foundation, predominates in the early narratives of the 'Cycle du roi'. Here Charles is the devout warrior for God who at need, like a new David, does battle with the heathen in person; as in his duel with Baligant, stirringly described in the *Chanson de Roland*. With God's help he establishes and maintains order and justice on earth. The fact is that around 1100 the French kings were weak; it is therefore assumed that the early *chansons de geste*, and especially the *Chanson de Roland*, are presenting an ideal: a king should be, like Charlemagne, a strong ruler who fights against the heathen as a crusader. This high ideal is treated with gentle irony in the *Voyage de Charlemagne à Jerusalem et à Constantinople*, in which Charles and his paladins occupy the seats of Jesus and his disciples and their heroic deeds are reduced to mere braggadocio.

The negative image of Charlemagne appears mainly in the *chansons de geste* about the rebellious vassals, which date from the end of the 12th century. They portray him as a king who allows himself to be influenced by bad counsellors and who alienates his loyal vassals, such as Ogier and Renaut, by unjust treatment. These stories may well reflect the views of the great feudal lords in France during the last decades of the 12th century. In their distant lands they felt themselves belittled by the ever-increasing power of the king and his court. This would also explain the paradox of such figures as Renaut and Ogier, who are at odds with the king but whose conduct is otherwise beyond reproach and who receive sympathetic treatment from the narrator.

Carolingian epic probably spread from France to other language areas while still in its oral phase. In any event, written versions in other languages have survived from as early as the 12th century, including the German *Ruolandes liet* of Pfaffe Konrad (c.1170) and the Middle Dutch → *Aiol* from the end of the 12th century. Surviving remnants of other Dutch texts include, among others, the *Roelantslied*, *Willem van Oringen*, *Renout van Montalbaen*, *Ogier van Denemarken*, the *Roman der Lorreinen* (→ ?Lorraine) and the *Floovent*. *Karel ende Elegast* may possibly be an original Dutch Carolingian work.

The epic tradition also profoundly influenced Carolingian historiography. The *Historia Karoli Magni et Rotholandi* or 'Chronicle of pseudo-Turpin', written in France as early as the first half of the 12th century, contains an account of Charles' Spanish campaigns which is based almost entirely on epic material. This chronicle is extremely important for our perception of Charlemagne in the Middle Ages. It forms the basis of the *Vita Sancti Karoli*, compiled in 1165 when the great emperor was canonised. This event also led to the inclusion of a chapter on Charles in Jacobus de Voragine's *Legenda aurea* (c. 1270), a work of extraordinary influence in the Middle Ages.

Another interesting development in the history of this material is the formation of cycles. The Old Norse *Karlamagnús saga* discussed above is one result of this process. Other cycles with compilations of Carolingian material are the *Chronique rimée* by Philippe Mousket (mid-13th century), the *Roman de Charlemagne* by Girard d'Amiens (c.1300), the *Myreur des histors* by Jean d'Outremeuse from Liège (late 14th century) and the *Croniques et conquestes de Charlemaine*, a prose cycle commissioned by the Burgundian duke Philip the Good and compiled in 1458 by David Aubert. From the 13th century there is a Welsh compilation entitled *Campeu Charlyamen* and from the 14th the German *Karlmeinet*. Andrea da Barberino's late 14th-century Italian cycle *I Reali di Francia* became extremely influential.

Everywhere in Europe in the 15th century the verse narratives were reworked as prose romances, which in printed form soon reached ever wider audiences. Interestingly enough, *Karel ende Elegast* was *not* turned into prose; the text continued to be printed from the 15th century to the second half of the 16th, but always in the original verse form. Almost all these printers texts were produced in Brabant, which may tie up with the great interest taken by that duchy's rulers in Charlemagne. Already the Dukes of Brabant and Burgundy were making much of the fact that they were descended from Charles and on these grounds they laid claim to the inheritance of Charles' grandson Lothar, the Heartland of Lorraine. The Habsburg Charles V also regarded himself as the successor to his great medieval namesake.

The memory of the great Emperor was kept alive in the Middle Ages not only by stories, but also by portraits and other material objects. The most important representative of this last category is the Palatine Chapel in Aachen. Built during Charles' lifetime as part of his palace, and modelled after the Byzantine Church of San Vitale in Ravenna, it now forms part of the great cathedral of Aachen dedicated to the Virgin Mary.

There is nothing we can point to with certainty as an accurate, contemporary portrait of Charlemagne. Einhard says of the Emperor's appearance that he was broad and powerfully built, tall of stature, with a round, amiable face and lively eyes. Of course, we have no way of knowing how close this description was to the reality; but it is striking that the 'tall stature' is confirmed by Charles' skeleton, which still exists and shows that he must have been about 6 feet 5 inches in height. Portraits on coins and a famous little equestrian statue (originally in Metz Cathedral, now in the Louvre in Paris; it is not entirely sure that it is of Charlemagne) show an Emperor who corresponds with Einhart's description.

The selection which follows will give some impression of the rich iconographic tradition which grew up around the figure of Charlemagne during the Middle Ages. First of all we must mention the reliquary in which Charles' bones repose in Aachen. The casket was created at the beginning of the 13th century at the urging of Emperor Frederick I Barbarossa as a result of Charles' canonisation; it is ornamented with reliefs depicting scenes from the 'Chronicle of pseudo-Turpin'. In France a stained glass window was made for Chartres Cathedral during the same period, to demonstrate the kinship of the French kings with Charles. The window depicts scenes from the battle of Roncevaux, inspired by a text closely related to this same pseudo-Turpin. A reliquary in the form of a bust of Charles in Aachen Cathedral dates from the middle of the 14th century. It was commissioned by Charles' namesake, the emperor Charles IV, out of admiration for his great predecessor.

Of the very many illustrations in manuscripts and old prints of works about Charlemagne only a few can be mentioned here. Many manuscripts of the *Grandes chroniques de France*, a vernacular history of the French kings, originally 13th century but with many later additions, contain fine illuminated miniatures which include various illustrations of the history of Charlemagne. In 1493 the text was printed by Antoine Vérard in Paris. The book was illustrated with woodcuts, but in the two copies intended for Charles VIII the woodcuts were replaced by miniatures (Bibliothèque Nationale, Paris). A manuscript of the *Chronique de Hainaut* by Jean Wauquelin (mid-15th century) contains a very fine scene by the Utrecht miniaturist Willem Vrelant. It shows the passage from from the pseudo-Turpin in which the traitor Ganelon returns from his visit to Marsile with rich treasures and beautiful women (Koninklijke Bibliotheek, Brussels).

Charlemagne is one of the Neuf Preux or Nine Worthies, the group of exemplary kings and war-leaders from classical, Jewish and Christian history, and he is frequently depicted in this role, especially in the late Middle Ages; for instance on the fragments of a tapestry of 1470–90 (Historisches Museum, Basel). A tapestry probably inspired by the pseudo-Turpin and produced c.1470 can be found in the Musée des Beaux-Arts in Dijon. Finally, two works by Albrecht Dürer deserve a mention. The first is a pen drawing from 1510 which shows the emperor in full regalia (Österreichische Nationalbibliothek, Vienna), the second an oil-painting of the same subject from 1512 (Germanisches Nationalmuseum, Nuremberg).

Even after the end of the Middle Ages Charlemagne continued to appeal to the imagination and the stories about him lived on. An early example of this is Raphaël's fresco *Le couronnement de Charlemagne* in the Vatican (early 16th century). Classical Spanish theatre has some thirty plays based on Carolingian material; Lope de Vega alone was responsible for eleven of them (including *Los Palacios de Galiana*, based on the *Mainet*). The other pieces are the work of, among others, Calderón, Cervantes, Baltasar Diaz, Moreto and Mira de Amescua. The Spanish authors allowed themselves a free hand with their material; they show Charles' knights as gallant adventurers, Charles himself as a weak and risible prince.

A number of writers were inspired by the story of Charles' love for a dead woman, a tale which already appears in the German *Karlmeinet*. A bishop removed a magic stone from this woman's mouth and threw it into a spring near Aachen, which from that moment on became Charles' favourite place. This episode, which also appears in Petrarch (1333), was turned into a romance by Southey (1797). N. Vogt included it in his *Rheinische Geschichten und Sagen* (1817), linking it with Charles' wife Fastrada. In the 19th century the same theme inspired ballads by Friedrich Schlegel, W. Müller, Karl Simrock and H. Lingg. It is found yet again in G. Hauptmann's drama *Kaiser Karls Geisel* (1908). In his *Karolingisches Heldenbuch* (1847) Simrock brought together ballads and romances by his contemporaries; worthy of mention are the ballads by Uhland and Geibel's *Rheinsage* (1836).

Napoleon's interest in Charlemagne is well known; he regarded himself as Charles' successor and in 1802 had himself anointed by the Pope in Notre Dame de Paris, after which he himself set the imperial crown on his head. Napoleon greatly admired Népomucène Lemercier's tragedy *Charlemagne*; but because the writer was not prepared to modify his text to make Charles' history better express Napoleon's ideals the play could not be produced in Paris until 1816. The opera *Charlemagne empereur d'Occident* by H. Montol de Sérigny (1808) is a product of French national consciousness.

A well-known series of frescos was designed by Alfred Rethel for the Kaisersaal in Aachen Town Hall (1839–53); after four scenes the project was continued by Joseph Kehren. The frescos were restored by Franz Stiewi after suffering serious damage in 1943–44. Also from the 19th century are the painting *Charlemagne traversant les Alpes* by Paul Delaroche (1847) in the Musée de Versailles and the proud equestrian statue of Charlemagne by M. de Rochet (1867). They bear witness to the powerful national feelings evoked in France by the figure of the great emperor. The same feelings are responsible for much of the scholarly interest in the *chansons de geste* and in Charlemagne which developed at this time. The introduction to L. Gautier's sumptuous edition of the *Chanson de Roland* (Tours 1872) has the heading 'Histoire d'un poème national'. In the same period the memory of the great emperor was used to give historical legitimacy to the unification of Germany.

A number of prose romances in simple chapbook form ('blue books') were regularly reprinted until well on in the 19th century. This happened in the Netherlands, for example, with the *Historie van de vier Heemskinderen* and the *Schoone*

Charlemagne in full regalia with crown, sword and orb, painting by Albrecht Dürer, 1512. Nuremberg, Germanisches Nationalmuseum.

historie van den ridder Maleghijs. At the same time the Carolingian stories were kept alive by Sicilian puppeteers, but also in the puppet theatres of such cities as Antwerp, Brussels and Liège. The Belgian puppet plays have a comic element, achieved partly by the inclusion of numerous anachronisms; thus in one Brussels theatre Charlemagne was given the voice of the French president Charles De Gaulle. An unusual case is the opera *El retabolo de Maese Pedro* (Master Pedro's Puppet Show) by Manuel de Falla (1923). The opera is set in 17th-century Spain, with a libretto based on Cervantes' *Don Quijote*. In it Don Quijote and Sancho Panza attend a puppet play in which Don Gaiferos is sent by Charlemagne to rescue a beautiful maiden from the hands of the Moors.

The Carolingian material is still being reworked today. *Karel ende Elegast* is staged in special performances for schoolchildren and a version of the text for young children has been produced. And where political-cultural matters are concerned, in the 20th century Charles has become more and more the symbol of a united Europe; a vision crowned by the impressive exhibition *Karel der Grosse – Werk und Wirkung* held in Aachen in 1965 under the auspices of the Council of Europe.

H. VAN DIJK

Translation: Hieatt 1975–80.
Studies: De Riquer 1956²; *Karl der Grosse* 1965; Geith 1977.

CHÂTELAINE DE VERGY is the niece of the Duke of Burgundy and a welcome visitor to his court. In secret the châtelaine is the mistress of a knight who also visits the court frequently. The duke's wife falls in love with the knight and suggests to him that it might be to his advantage to have a lady of high rank as his 'friend'. At first the knight pretends not to understand what the duchess is hinting at, but when she expresses herself more plainly he rejects her, firmly but politely. The lady feels slighted and plots revenge. She tells her husband that the knight has made dishonourable advances to her. The duke, who is otherwise on good terms with the knight, speaks privately with him and insists on being told the truth of the matter. The knight, desperate, wonders what to do: if he keeps silent and is banished from the country he will never see his beloved again; but if he tells the duke of his love he is afraid he will lose the châtelaine. For had not secrecy been an absolute condition of their love? The duke swears to keep what the knight tells him confidential. The latter then reveals his love for the châtelaine. The rest of the story is not hard to guess. The duke, reassured (particularly after he has witnessed a nocturnal meeting of the two lovers), is once more on good terms with the knight and thus brings upon himself the wrath of his duchess, who succeeds in worming the knight's secret out of him.

Some time later, during a Whitsun banquet to which the châtelaine is invited, the duchess takes her revenge. By a remark about the châtelaine's pet dog, which had played the part of *postillon d'amour*, the duchess lets her know that she is aware of her secret love. The châtelaine believes that her beloved has betrayed her and dies of grief. The knight finds her (just too late!), learns from a waiting-woman of the châtelaine's dying lament, and decides that he is guilty of her death since he had betrayed their secret to the duke. He stabs himself and falls dead on the corpse of his beloved. The duke is then alerted by the distressed waiting-woman; he finds the dead lovers, realises that his wife had failed to keep her mouth shut, and kills her with the knight's sword. He then explains the whole thing to his assembled guests and departs for the Holy Land.

The original Old French text was written around 1240, when courtly literature was already past its peak. The *Châtelaine de Vergy* is almost universally regarded as a work of exceptional quality. It is not a *lai* (the fairy-tale element is lacking), but rather an early attempt at the later *nouvelle*. Some manuscripts, however, set it among all kinds of *fabliaux* (humorous verse narratives), while in others it appears alongside the *Roman de la Rose*. It is not difficult to recognise in this short narrative of 948 lines a number of motifs which also appear in various *lais* (→ Lanval), in *Piramus et Tisbé* and in tales about Tristan (the châtelaine herself mentions → Tristan and Yseut [Isoude] in her lengthy lament). A stanza from a known crusader song about the Châtelain de Coucy is also quoted, as a comment by the author on the knight's state of mind when the duke gives him the choice 'tell or go'. All these works are courtly in content and date from the second half of the 12th or the early 13th centuries. Although there is no account of the winning of the beloved (this is disposed of in two lines, before the beginning of the action) and there are no heroic deeds to be recounted, the *Châtelaine de Vergy* is usually also regarded as a courtly work. Love is taken for granted, and it must be kept secret; both foreword and epilogue emphasise this. In the middle of the tale it is again specifically stated that this kind of love is reserved for, and can only be understood by, initiates. This being so, it is not clear just why such a love must remain secret. There have been years of debate as to whether or not the châtelaine was married, but the one line in the text that might tell us something about this is ambiguous: the 'signor' mentioned by the châtelaine could be either her overlord (the duke) or her husband. In the epilogue the work is presented as an exemplum, with the moral that you must not make your love public.

The story was extremely well known: about twenty medieval manuscripts are still extant and we know of some ten quotations from it in French literature of the 14th and

Scenes from the story of the Châtelaine de Vergy. Lid and back of a 14th-century ivory casket. Paris, Musée du Louvre.

15th centuries (which often portray the châtelaine as the model of a faithful mistress). The Old French text was twice translated into Middle Dutch, and was still in circulation in the 16th century. It was translated into Italian in the 14th century. Several adaptations of the old rhyming text were produced in France from the late 15th century on (prose and stage versions, in some of which the châtelaine is magically transformed into a virtuous widow who is secretly married to her admirer!). In the 18th century a 'Gabrielle de Vergy' is the protagonist of a reworking of the late 13th-century romance *Le Châtelain de Coucy et la Dame de Fayel*. Plays with a Vergy as main character continue to appear down to the 19th century.

The tale's great popularity is also evidenced by the fact that we still have nine ivory caskets (complete or fragmentary) carved with highlights from the story. These date from the first half of the 14th century and were probably made in Paris. Such caskets were often given as wedding presents and used as jewel cases or make-up boxes. The story is also depicted in the bridal chamber of the Palazzo Davanzati in Florence (c.1395).

R.E.V. STUIP

Editions: Dufournet and Dulac 1994; Stuip 1985.
Study: Resoort 1988.

CID (El Cid), or more accurately Mio Cid (My lord, from Arabic *Sayyidí*), and Campeador (warrior, victor in battle) are the bynames earned by Rodrigo Díaz de Vivar, a Castilian warrior of the minor nobility (infanzón). King Fernando I (1035–65) divided the kingdoms he had united among his sons: Castile went to Sancho, the eldest; Léon to Alfonso; Galicia to García. The Cid, who was Sancho's right-hand man in his defeat of Alfonso, became the symbol of Castile's struggle for Spanish hegemony. In 1094 he captured Valencia, where he died in 1099 at the age of 56. (Valencia fell to the Moors again in 1102.)

His deeds were celebrated, in mingled fact and fiction, in the Castilian heroic epic *Poema de Mio Cid*; this probably dates from the first years of the 13th century, though there is still support in Spain for an earlier date of c.1140. One of the very few survivals of Spanish epic, it has been preserved in only one, incomplete, 14th-century manuscript, discovered in the municipal archive at Vivar in the 16th century. The first folio is missing; the second begins with the hero weeping as he looks back at his house and blames malicious enemies for his banishment. The people of Burgos come out to watch him pass and sigh 'God, what a good vassal, if only he had a good lord.' He must be out of Alfonso's realm in nine days. No one in Burgos dares shelter him, for harsh penalties await any who help him. His possessions, and those of all who accompany him, are forfeit to the king. To acquire funds he has to resort to deception: he leaves two chests which look splendid but are filled with sand as security for a loan of six hundred marks. He places his wife, doña Jimena, and his two small daughters in a convent in Cardeña.

The Cid then has a three days' journey to the borders of his lord Alfonso's territory. On the last night he dreams that the Archangel Gabriel promises him success. Meanwhile, he has been joined by mounted warriors from the whole area. He had ridden through Burgos with sixty men; when he leaves Alfonso's lands and enters those of the Moors he has three hundred. The taking of Castejón marks the start of his first campaign, along the Henares; it is followed by others along the Jalón and the Jiloca, one in the eastern coastal area, and finally by the siege and capture of Valencia. An attack on the city by the Emir of Seville is beaten off. The Cid appoints a Cluniac monk, Jérôme de Périgord, as Bishop of Valencia.

Now his family is able to join him; their reunion forms the emotional high point of the poem, together with the victory over the Moorish king Yúsuf which follows. Once again the Cid sends a princely gift to his king. After only three weeks of exile he had sent him thirty horses, and later a hundred; now he presents his lord with two hundred horses. Alfonso makes his peace with the Cid and next day asks him to give his daughters in marriage to the two young lords of Carrión; whereupon the Cid, with a presentiment of evil, gives his daughters to the king to marry to whomever he will. The double wedding takes place in Valencia, with festivities lasting two weeks.

When the Cid's pet lion escapes from its cage the terror of his sons-in-law attracts the ridicule of the Cid's men, but he takes them under his protection. When they show fear in the battle against King Búcar it is kept secret from the Cid; but the young lords still think themselves underrated and plot revenge. They ask leave to go to Carrión with their wives. Their plan to murder their Moorish host in Molina is discovered in time; Avengalvón, a good friend of the Cid, gives them a good dressing-down but lets them go 'for the Cid's sake'. The company spends the next night in a clearing in the wild oak forest of Corpes. In the morning the young lords send the rest of the company on ahead, themselves remaining behind with their wives. They tear off the ladies' outer garments, thrash them with leather straps and leave them unconscious. If the two women had not quickly been found by a cousin who became anxious and returned covertly, they would have fallen prey to wild beasts. The Cid demands satisfaction. Alfonso calls his vassals together in Toledo to pronounce his royal judgment. The Cid first demands the return of his swords Colada and Tizón, which he had given to his sons-in-law (he now gives them to two of his men); then the dowry of three thousand marks he had given his daughters on their departure; and finally the restoration of his honour in single combat. The formal charges are laid by the Cid; three of his men challenge the two young lords and their elder brother.

Messengers from the North arrive for the king, requesting the Cid's daughters as brides for their lords; with their father's consent King Alfonso gives Doña Elvira and Doña Sul in marriage to the Princes of Navarre and Aragon. Before leaving for Valencia the Cid demonstrates his speedy warhorse Babieca and offers it to the king – a gift which the latter naturally declines. In the duels three weeks later the Cid's men defeat their opponents, the swords Tizón and Colada striking appropriate terror into the ne'er-do-wells. Following discussions with King Alfonso the Princes of Navarre and Aragon marry Doña Elvira and Doña Sul.

As we have already said, the *Poema de Mio Cid* mixes historical fact (even minor characters turn out to have really existed) with a great deal of fictitious material. The historical Cid was banished twice (1081–87 and 1089–92); the exile in the *Poema* is plainly the second, but the reasons given apply to the first. The poem omits the fact that the Cid entered the service of the Moorish ruler of Zaragoza; while Alvar Fáñez, his right-hand man in the poem, was actually one of King Alfonso's warriors. That the Cid found sanctuary for his family in the convent at Cardeña is not historically certain (but he was buried there, though the poem does not mention this). In real life his daughters' names were Cristina and María; his son Diego is not mentioned in the poem. Non-historical, too, are the daughters' marriages to the young Lords of Carrión, their mistreatment in Corpes and the judicial duels: the whole second strand of the story.

The first strand runs from the hero's unjust banishment to his rehabilitation through his own efforts and the renewed bond with his king. The poet interweaves with this a strand which runs from loss of honour for the Cid's family (and also for the king, who had chosen the daughters' husbands) to restoration of honour for the king and for the Cid and his men. With these two main strands the poet clearly means to demonstrate that correct relations between vassal and lord result in honour and prosperity for them and their successors. The *Poema's* division into three cantos of roughly equal length, probably with a view to performance, is independent of this binary structure.

The poet portrays his hero as a pious Christian, a devoted husband and father, a loyal vassal, a skilful commander and fearless fighter, who knows and respects what is right and treats his defeated opponents with generosity, a shrewd man of mature judgment and courtly manners. This hero also symbolises the Castile of his day, with its eyes on the south where there was land to be conquered, honour to be won, fortunes to be made. At a time when the Christian kingdoms in Spain were recovering from their crushing defeat at Alarcos (1195) and girding themselves for the great southern offensive which began with the victory of Las Navas de Tolosa in 1212 this poem may well have been a powerful aid to recruitment.

When the *Poema* was published in 1779 by T.A. Sánchez it received a lukewarm reception in Spain. Thirty years later its first romantic admirers, the Scotsmen Southey and Hallam, rated it as on a par with Homer and Dante; Friedrich Schlegel hailed it as the Spanish national epic (1811) and Ferdinand Wolf devoted an exhaustive study to it (1831). In 1830 the Venezuelan Andrés Bello compared it in general terms with the French *chansons de geste* and following the publication of the *Chanson de Roland* in 1837 Damas Hinard wrote a comparative study which came down in favour of the Spanish work (1858). Milá (1874) set it in the context of a previously unkown Castilian epic literature. In 1893 the young philologist Ramón Menéndez Pidal (1869–1968) won a competition organised by the Spanish Academy with an edition and detailed study of the *Poema*, a revised and improved version of which was eventually published in four volumes (*Cantar de Mio Cid*, 1908–11). Aided by the intellectual climate around 1900 and the enthusiastic reaction of the critic Menéndez y Pelayo, it became a source of inspiration for writers and poets.

If the *Poema* itself probably dates, as we have said, from the early 13th century, there are some half-dozen texts attesting to the Cid's 12th-century fame. The *Carmen Campidoctoris* is a celebration of the Campeador written some time after his death. It tells of his youthful courage, his close relationship with Sancho, his break with Alfonso, his defeat of Count García in single combat at Cabra, and then breaks off after 129 lines. The *Historia Roderici* of c.1144–47 is one of the few sources for the Cid's genealogy and the events leading to his exile. The last part of the *Chronica Adefonsi Imperatoris*, completed around 1148, relates in hexameters the siege of Almería in 1147; this *Poema de Almería* mentions the Cid as someone who is 'sung of' as invincible. The *Crónica Najerense* is a Latin text compiled in the 1150s in Santa María de Nájera (La Rioja). This chronicle, the first general history of León and Castile not written under the auspices of the royal court, draws on a multiplicity of sources and displays a lively interest in heroic legends. In its most detailed narrative, thought to derive from a lost epic of Sancho II and the siege of Zamora, the Cid appears three times. Here he is already a famous hero who is introduced without further ado simply as 'Rodericus Campidoctus'. The title *Liber Regum* refers to a Castilian text, the oldest surviving historical work in any Spanish dialect, which dates from the last years of the 12th century and describes the genealogies of the ruling royal houses of Asturias, Castile, Navarre, Aragon and France. Finally there is the *Linaje del Cid*, which contains information on the Cid's lineage not included in the *Historia Roderici*.

Two Latin chronicles completed a few decades after the writing of the *Poema* contain no evidence that their authors knew it. Lucas, Bishop of Tuy ('el Tudense') completed his *Chronicon Mundi* in, or shortly after, 1236; and Rodrigo Ximénez de Rada, Archbishop of Toledo ('el Toledano') finished his *De Rebus Hispaniae* in 1243. Both are mainly interested in the civil war between Sancho and Alfonso. Lucas is the first to recount that Rodrigo Díaz, in the name of the Castilian nobility, let Alfonso swear a solemn oath that he had had no part in the murder of Sancho – an episode which reappears in all later chronicles.

Writers of chronicles in Spanish under Alfonso the Wise and later often reworked parts of heroic poems. Cid episodes too were rewritten in prose and the *Crónica de Veinte Reyes* (c.1350) made use of a Cid song which can have differed but little from the *Poema*.

The other extant Cid epic is a work of c.1360 discovered in 1840 by F. Michel in the Bibliothèque Nationale in Paris: the *Mocedades de Rodrigo* (Youth of Rodrigo; also known as *Crónica rimada* or *Cantar de Rodrigo*). It is a new version of a lost song which had been retold as early as c.1300 in the *Crónica de los reyes de Castilla*. Rodrigo kills his father's enemy; King Ferdinand commands him to marry the dead man's daughter Ximena; the hero refuses to see her again until he has won five battles. The fabulous story breaks off when Rodrigo and his king are besieging Paris. The poem is of historical importance, since episodes from it lived on in ballads (*romances* in Spanish).

Orally transmitted songs, composed soon after the events they describe, are known from as early as the 1320s; in the conflict between King Pedro (1350–69) and his half-brother Enrique of Trastámara they were used as propaganda by both sides, and in the 15th century border ballads told of skirmishes with the Moors. Most of these were not written down until the 16th century. Alongside adventure ballads belonging to the international folktale heritage there were also romances on epic subjects; however, most of these did not derive from epics, as the traditionalists would have it, but were based on written sources. The most extensive cycle is a corpus of 205 ballads about Rodrigo Díaz, the so-called *Romancero del Cid*. The figure of the Cid takes on a variety of forms in the romances, which are the work of many poets. One of the last of them recounts how the Cid's men take their dead lord's body into battle with them, bound to Babieca's saddle, and thus put a large Moorish army to flight.

Wherever an oral tradition exists, ballads live on in the memory. When the Jews were expelled from Spain in 1492 they took them along; four centuries later there was not a Jewess in Tangier who could not sing the romance in which Jimena demands justice. The ballads' enormous popularity ensured that the romance developed into a literary poetic form (*romancero nuovo*); it also led to the use of traditional ballads in the polymetric Spanish *comedia*. In 1579 Juan de la Cueva produced plays on no fewer than four historical subjects, including *La muerte del rey don Sancho*, into which he worked more than twenty Cid ballads as well as quoting a number of well-known lines.

Guillén de Castro used over forty romances in his two Cid plays, *Las mocedades del Cid* and *Las hazañas del Cid* (the Youth and the Heroic Deeds of the Cid, respectively; earliest known print 1612/13). These two comedias together make up a fascinating 'dramatised Romancero' (Menéndez Pidal), the ballad quotations providing the audience with the pleasure of the familiar. But Castro is also a master of natural, realistic dialogue. The first of the two pieces acquires a strong dramatic unity from the conflict between

Gérard Philipe in the title role of Corneille's play *Le Cid* in Avignon in 1951. This production contributed greatly to the worldwide reputation of the actor and of the Théâtre National Populaire under its director Jean Vilar.

love and honour – it was Castro's idea to have Rodrigo and Jimena already in love with each other before the action begins. Count Lozano, the father of Jimena, strikes Rodrigo's father, the aged Diego Laínez, in the king's presence. To avenge his father's honour the young Rodrigo kills the Count, knowing that this will lose him Jimena's favour. Jimena demands satisfaction from the king, who banishes Rodrigo. His military successes restore the young hero to the favour of the king, who decrees that his nickname 'Cid' shall become his official title but for Jimena's sake banishes him once more. To deny the admission of her love extracted from her by guile, Jimena calls on all knights to avenge her. Rodrigo shares his meal with a leprous beggar: St Lazarus, who promises him St James' aid in all he undertakes. In a single combat between Castile and Aragon he defeats Jimena's champion and she consents to marry him.

It was this piece that Pierre Corneille reworked along classical lines into his *Le Cid*; while following his model closely in part, he simplified the action so as to bring out the dramatic conflict more clearly. His tragicomedy, the basic facts of which corresponded to current events in France (the war with Spain, the ban on duels, the relations between king and nobility) was enormously successful right from its première in January

1637. Jealous colleagues embroiled Corneille in a bitter debate (the 'Querelle du Cid') in which, on Richelieu's instructions, the Academy also involved itself. The success of *Le Cid* was never in danger, but for a long time every critic was expected to pronounce on the relative merits of the French and the Spanish piece. The most even-handed verdict: 'Corneille produced a masterpiece which he derived from another masterpiece' (A. Gassier, 1898).

El honrador de su padre (The son who honoured his father) by J.B. Diamante (thought by Voltaire to be Corneille's model) is a 1657 adaptation of the French piece with a markedly different dénouement in the final act. There are some ten other 17th-century plays on the Cid, among them Lope de Vega's *Las almenas de Toro*, which we have no space to discuss here. The 19th century brought historical dramas by Bréton de los Herreros (*Bellido Dolfos*, 1839), Hartzenbusch (*La jura en Santa Gadea*, 1845) and García Gutiérrez (*Doña Urraca de Castilla*, 1872). *Las hijas del Cid* by E. Marquinas is based directly on the *Poema*; while the daughters and sons-in-law are credible characters, the figure of the Cid himself is weak. In a play by Antonio Gala from the last years of Franco's rule, *Anillos para una dama* (1973), Jimena has to reconcile herself to the fact that as the Cid's widow she must stay on her historical pedestal and cannot just be herself. There are verse narratives by J.G. Herder (*Der Cid*, 1802) and J. Zorilla (*Leyenda del Cid*, 1882); a lyrical prose romance by the Chilean V. Huidobro (*Mio Cid Campeador*, 1929); Cid operas by H. Neeb (Frankfurt 1857), Peter Cornelius (Weimar 1865) and Jules Massenet (Paris 1885); a 'musical trilogy' by Manrique de Lara; and a spectacular American film (EL CID, 1961) with Charlton Heston and Sofia Loren.

Since Spain lost its last colonies in 1898 (the same year in which Pidal published his first edition of the *Poema*) poets and thinkers have treated the Cid as the symbol of Castille, of Spain as a whole and of the Spanish spirit. During the political debate on the Spanish-American War Joaquín Costa warned that Spain 'should double-bolt the Cid's tomb, to prevent him riding out once more'. Two poets recreated specifically non-military episodes from the Cid legend. The founder of Modernismo, Rubén Darío, grafted his *Cosas del Cid* (written in Spain in 1899) onto a poem by Barbey d'Aurevilly which reshaped the encounter with the leprous beggar, but Rubén takes the story further: immediately afterwards an innocent girl appears and gives the hero a rosebud and a laurel branch. In *Castilla* (in the collection *Alma*, 1902) Manuel Machado recreated an episode from the beginning of the *Poema* (which had also influenced Darío) in which 'a little girl of nine' begs the Cid to move on so as not to endanger her family. The same volume also includes 'Alvar-Fáñez', a portrait of the man who, having fought at the Cid's side, refuses any reward and later goes and tells the king 'The Cid has taken Valencia, my lord, and presents it to you as a gift.'

H. DE VRIES

Edition: Hamilton/Perry 1975.

CLIGÈS is the hero of a romance of that name written around 1176 by Chrétien de Troyes. The Emperor of Greece and Constantinople has two sons, Alixandre and Alis. Alixandre, the elder, decides to visit Britain with a retinue of young nobles in order to learn the use of arms at → Arthur's court and become a knight. He reaches Arthur's realm, is made welcome at his court and immediately distinguishes himself by his generosity. He accompanies Arthur when the latter has to visit Brittany. During the voyage Alixandre and the young noblewoman Soredamor, sister of Gauvain (→ Gawain), fall in love with each other. Their musings on love, their doubt and indecision, their sorrow because neither dares to believe his/her love is returned, form an episode hundreds of lines in length. Before ever they have declared their love, a messenger arrives from England and informs Arthur that his regent, Count Angrès of Windsor, has treacherously seized power. Arthur knights Alixandre and his followers. The queen marks the occasion by presenting Alixandre with a silken shirt made by Soredamor; into it she has woven one of her hairs, which gleams more beautifully than gold thread. During the siege of Windsor Alixandre performs his first heroic deed. He then spends an ecstatic night gazing at the blonde hair, whose origin has been revealed to him by the queen. Next day he succeeds in entering the town by a ruse and capturing the traitor. The queen now brings the lovers together; they marry and produce a son, Cligès.

Messengers are sent from Constantinople requesting Alixandre to return home as his father is close to death. Their ship sinks; the one survivor returns to Constantinople, claiming that Alixandre has perished in the shipwreck. Alis is crowned Emperor. News of his coronation reaches Alixandre in Britain; with his wife and child he returns to Greece to claim his rights. The brothers come to an agreement: Alis will keep the throne, but Alixandre will wield power behind the scenes. Alis also promises not to marry, so that Cligès shall succeed him. Then Alixandre and Soredamor both die within a short time of each other.

Years later, Alis yields to the demands of his courtiers and decides to marry the young Princess Fenice, daughter of the Emperor of Germany and already betrothed to the Duke of Saxony. Alis travels to Cologne; his entourage includes the young knight Cligès, who distinguishes himself by defeating the Duke of Saxony's envoy in a tournament. Cligès and Fenice fall in love, but Fenice marries Alis. However, she has no intention of becoming a 'second Isoude', giving her body to a man who does not have her heart. So her old nurse, Thessala, brews a magic potion. Alis drinks it after the wedding feast; as a result, he goes straight to sleep each evening and dreams that he possesses his wife. On waking he is unable to distinguish the dream from reality.

The Duke of Saxony tries to abduct Fenice, but Cligès rescues her. He decides not to return with his uncle but, like his father, to spend some time at Arthur's court. Here he excels in courage and knightly virtue, defeats Sagremor, → Lancelot and → Perceval in a tournament and shows himself the equal of his uncle Gauvain. However, his love for Fenice drives him to return home. The Empress and her nephew by marriage confess their love to each other. Fenice tells him of the magic potion and its effect. But she refuses to become Cligès' mistress or to allow him to abduct her. Again she declines to follow Isoude's example, and again Thessala finds the solution: a second magic potion brings about Fenice's seeming death. She is laid in a burial vault from where Cligès carries her away.

He takes Fenice to a castle built by his loyal helper Jean, the entrance to which can be found only by those in the know. Within the castle walls is a beautiful garden. For more than fifteen months Fenice lives in concealment here, while Cligès spends all the time he can with her. One day a knight searching for his hawk climbs over the wall and discovers the lovers sleeping naked in the shade of a tree. A pear falls from the tree and wakes Fenice. She sees the knight and screams. Cligès wakes, seizes his sword and hacks a leg off the fleeing knight. Despite this, he manages to reach the court; the lovers are forced to flee. Alis is so furious, however, that he dies of rage. Now Cligès is recalled to court to succeed him. He marries Fenice and they are crowned Emperor and Empress.

Chrétien's *Cligès* can be seen as a response to the → Tristan story, in which adulterous love is central, and uses the same structure. *Cligès*, too, begins by recounting the history of the hero's parents; here, too, the main character is his lord's nephew and designated successor and plays a decisive part in winning his uncle's bride. Other motifs such as the use of magic potions, the role of confidants (Thessala, Jean), the golden hair evoking feelings of love, and the discovery of the sleeping lovers also point to the *Tristan*, but they are employed to different and often contrasting effect. Chrétien's disapproving attitude to the *Tristan* material is expressed principally through the words and actions of Fenice, who twice explicitly rejects Isoude's behaviour. The happy ending of *Cligès* contrasts strongly with the tragic denouement of the tale of Tristan and Isoude.

The romance, which is ironic in tone, enjoyed a fair measure of success in the century following its appearance. It is referred to in Old French narratives (among others *Les merveilles de Rigomer*, *Blancandin et l'Orgueilleuse d'Amour* and *Meraugis de Portlesguez*), in Occitanian romances (→ *Flamenca*, *Jaufre*), and in Wolfram von Eschenbach's *Parzival*. Traces of German versions survive in the form of quotations or allusions in other texts: Konrad Fleck (active around 1230) and Ulrich von Türheim (mid-13th century) each seem to have written a *Clîes*. An anonymous French (Burgundian) prose version dates from 1454. Since the revival of interest in medieval literature in the 19th century the *Cligès* has been overshadowed by Chrétien's other romances and those about Tristan. Its geographical setting makes it more of an oriental than an Arthurian romance; consequently, Cligès and Fenice have played no part in recent Arthurian literature.

C. HOGETOORN

Edition: Foerster 1884.
Translation: Kibler 1991.
Study: Frappier 1968.

C Ú CHULAINN is the Achilles or Siegfried of the Ulster Cycle, the group of heroic narratives whose background is the Kingdom of Ulster and its conflict with the rest of Ireland led by Connacht. His mother is Deichtine (or Deichtire), sister of King Conchobar of Ulster, whose seat is at Emain Macha. His father is Sualdam mac Roich; but he is also regarded as the son of the Celtic god Lug. At his birth he was given the name Sétanta; he earned the name Cú Chulainn (Hound of Culann) at the age of six with his first heroic deed: killing the watchdog of the smith Culann. The name also points to what will be his task in life: the protection of Ulster.

His initiation as a warrior takes place outside Ireland (in the ancient homeland of his race?). Cú Chulainn goes to the female warrior Scáthach, who can be seen as the personification of the warrior's art, and concludes a holy marriage with her. There are magical elements to his heroism. When he goes into a heroic frenzy this manifests itself in the abnormal heat of his body. He is able to call on extra strength by falling into a kind of trance; his byname, 'the Twisted One of Emain', derives from the physical contortions which accompany this. Though small of stature, he is handsome; and, as befits a Celtic hero, he combines martial and intellectual qualities. His wife Emer is his match in beauty, intelligence, education and birth. His charioteer is Laeg mac Riangabra, his horses are called Liath Macha (the Grey One of Macha) and Dubb Sainglenn (the Black One of Sainglenn).

The various parts of Cú Chulainn's heroic biography are spread over a large number of tales (*scéla*, singular *scél* from different centuries. The 8th-century *Compert Con Culainn* (The Begetting of Cú Chulainn) belongs to the oldest stratum. It tells how Conchobar, Deichtine (who in this one text is his daughter) and some of his nobles are lured away from Emain Macha by a flock of birds (i.e. supernatural beings in bird form). After a fruitless hunt he spends the night in 'a new house'. During this night his hostess gives birth to a son; in front of the house a mare produces twin foals. The visitors from Ulster agree to foster the newborn infant, and their host gives him the foals as the 'son's portion'. When the visitors wake next morning they are alone in the wilderness with no house and no birds, but with the baby boy and the foals. (This motif of supernatural beings 'conjuring' a building into existence for a short time so as to bring about a specific encounter – in this case enabling one of them to gain entrance to the human world – reappears later in Chrétien's → *Perceval*.) A couple of years later the little boy dies. The god Lug then appears to Deichtine in a dream and tells her that it was he who had lured her into the wilderness and the boy was his son, that he is now in her womb and is to be called Sétanta. Conchobar gives Deichtine, whose pregnancy is a mystery to everyone, to Sualdam mac Roich as his bride. However, she is ashamed to marry while pregnant with another man's child and induces a miscarriage. Immediately after the wedding she becomes pregnant again and bears a son. Thus Sétanta comes into the world as it were in three stages: first as the son of supernatural parents, then of a supernatural father and a human mother, and finally of a human couple.

The 'Macgnímartha', the heroic deeds performed by Cú Chulainn from his fifth to his seventh year – including the killing of Culann's dog – form part of the *Táin Bó Cúailnge* (The Cattle Raid of Cuailnge), the longest and most authoritative work in the Ulster cycle. The central theme of the *Táin*, which has a historical core, is a campaign against Ulster by the rulers of Connacht, Ailill and his wife Medb, backed by the rest of Ireland. Their army also includes a number of exiled Ulstermen. The real opponents are Medb, the driving force on the Connacht side, and Cú Chulainn, who at first has to defend Ulster on his own because his countrymen are under a curse which strikes them with weakness as soon as they are attacked. Partly by the use of magic, partly by waging a kind of one-man guerilla war, he induces the enemy to agree to send one warrior each day to meet him in single combat; if Cú Chulainn is victorious they will march no further that day. When the first (chance) encounter costs a couple of Connachtmen their heads, Ailill asks the Ulster exiles for more information on their seventeen-year-old opponent; Cú Chulainn's boyhood deeds are now recounted in a kind of flashback. After three weeks of constant fighting Cú Chulainn is near to exhaustion; Lug then appears on the scene and stands guard over him for three days to enable him to recover. However, Lug takes no part in the conflict; he is concerned only with his son. The tragic climax of the war, which Ulster eventually wins, is the duel between Cú Chulainn and Fer Diad. The latter is Cú Chulainn's foster brother, for they had studied the arts of war together under Scáthach.

Fer Diad is not the only sacrifice Cú Chulainn has to make for his compatriots during this time. In *Aided Óenfhir Aífe* (The Death of Aífe's Only Son) he is compelled to kill the son he had begotten on the warlike Aífe during his studies with Scáthach. At their parting he had instructed Aífe to send the boy to him at the proper time. He had also imposed strict rules of warrior conduct on the unborn child: never to reveal his name to one man alone and never to refuse combat to, or step aside for, one man alone. The result is that when the seven-year-old boy arrives in Ireland he is unable to identify himself, for the same warriors' code bars the Ulstermen from acceding to his request that they send two warriors to him instead of one; to do so would be to show themselves his inferiors. Each time he refuses to give his name there is a duel, which he wins. In the end Cú Chulainn has no alternative but to face the boy, who he can guess is his son. He defeats him and lays the mortally wounded Conle before his countrymen with the words: 'Here is my son for you, men of Ulster.'

Cú Chulainn also has to do battle with beings with supernatural attributes. The oldest text of this type is early 8th-century and consists almost entirely of a poem in an archaic and obscure style. This is *Forfess Fer Falgae* (The Night Attack on the Fir Falgae), in which Cú Chulainn fights the Fomore, who can be seen as personifications of untamed Nature.

Cú Chulainn has two rivals in the contest to be first among the heroes of Ulster: Conall Cernach and Laegaire Búadach. The narrative that establishes his superiority beyond doubt is *Fled Bricrenn* (The Feast of Bricriu). In a whole series of tests, one after the other – with Conall Cerdach and Laeghaire always doubtful as to the outcome –

The dying Cú Chulainn, bronze statue by Oliver Sheppard, 1911–12. Later placed in the General Post Office in Dublin as a memorial to the victims of the Easter Rising of 1916.

they have to do battle with, among others, monstrous beasts and giants. The judges are at first Ailill and Medb and then Cú Roi mac Dáiri, a semi-demonic creature with magical powers who lives in the south-west of Ireland. In the final, decisive test (which later provides the beginning and end of the Middle English Arthurian romance *Sir → Gawain and the Green Knight*) Cú Roi appears at Emain Macha in a terrifying disguise and makes an offer to the assembled heroes: he will decapitate one of them, and the victim may then do the same to him the following evening. Having managed to reverse the order of events, the Ulster heroes agree. Each time the challenger's head is struck off he gets up and leaves, carrying the severed head in his arms, so that the hero concerned never fulfils the second part of the bargain. The sole exception is Cú Chulainn; having cut off the stranger's head, he returns the following evening and lays his own head on the block. The stranger raises the axe to the roof-tree, but lowers the back of it to Cú Chulainn's neck. In the presence of all the nobles he then proclaims Cú Chulainn chief of all the heroes of Ulster and Ireland. Cú Roi is in the Ulster cycle a universally feared and respected outsider. Even Cú Chulainn can only kill this mighty sorcerer, who has an external soul, by a ruse; this happens in *Aided Con Roi* (The Death of Cú Roi).

Some of Cú Chulainn's adventures are set in the Otherworld. In *Serglige Con Culainn ocus Óenét Emire* (The Sickbed of Cú Chulainn and Emer's Only Jealousy) supernatural beings persuade him to visit their country by the sea and do battle with their enemies; his reward is to be Fann, wife of the sea-god Manannán, who has fallen in love with him. So it befalls. When Cú Chulainn eventually takes leave of Fann he arranges to meet her again in Ireland. On his return he tells his wife Emer of this. She goes to the appointed place on the day of the meeting, and there she reminds her husband of the love between them. He says that he will love her as long as she lives, but begs her to allow him this one other love. For Emer's sake, however, Fann decides to return to Manannán, who shakes his cloak between her and Cú Chulainn so that they shall never meet again. There is nothing pathetic or ridiculous about the noble Emer in her role of jealous spouse.

In *Tochmarc Emire* (The Courting of Emer [by Cú Chulainn]), thought to date from the Middle Irish period (925–1200), Emer embodies a new type in Irish epic literature.

Previously there had been warlike women, and women such as prophetesses who had magical talents; but here Emer is the attractive young princess who has used the new freedoms to develop her many gifts.

Already at his ritual assumption of arms (at the age of seven) Cú Chulainn's early death had been foretold. In *Aided Con Culainn* (The Death of Cú Chulainn), the latest of the *scéla* mentioned so far (the oldest version is 12th-century), Cú Chulainn's enemies, including Cú Roí's son Lugaid, take their revenge on the Ulster hero. Again the Ulstermen are stricken with weakness, again Cú Chulainn stands alone. As is usual in Irish epic, his approaching doom is signalled by him being forced to break his *geissi* (singular *geis*), the strict list of things he must or must not do, any infringement of which brings disaster. Thus, on his way to meet his enemies he passes three sorceresses roasting a lapdog, though it is *geis* (forbidden) for him both to pass a cooking-place without tasting the food and to eat the flesh of his namesake, the dog. When in the long battle against overwhelming odds Cú Chulainn finally receives his death-wound, he ties himself to a boundary stone so that he can die on his feet; and the horse Liath Macha comes and stands over him to protect him while he still lives. Only when a crow lands on his shoulder, a sign that he is really dead, do his opponents dare come closer; then Lugaid cuts his head off. When the men of Ulster recover from their weakness they set out to avenge Cú Chulainn's death. During their absence the dead hero appears to the noble ladies of Emain Macha in a ghostly chariot, tells how he and his charioteer Laeg met their deaths and predicts the coming of Christianity. This posthumous appearance of Cú Chulainn is also the subject of the independent *Síaburcharpat Con Culainn* (The Ghost-Chariot of Cú Chulainn),in which St Patrick recalls Cú Chulainn from the dead to persuade King Laegaire of Tara to accept the new religion.

The *Táin*'s place in Irish epic tradition is comparable with that of the *Iliad* in Greek literature, and it poses similar problems for researchers. In both works the narrative background belongs to an older period than the literary text. The *Táin* dates from the 9th century, in part possibly from the 8th century, except for a few additions which are not only philologically but also stylistically later. But though the kingdom of Ulster seems to have lost ground to the (originally Connacht) Uí Néill dynasty from the late 5th century, in the *Táin* it is still at the height of its power; the heroic life-style described in the work evokes associations with that of the continental Celts as revealed by the notes of classical writers and archeological material, and the Christian element is confined to a number of loanwords. This implies a measure of continuity between the writing phase and the earlier oral tradition, facilitated by the fact that the antagonism between Ulster and the rest of Ireland, which goes back to the prehistoric period, continued into historical times. One powerful aid to memory was the *dinnshenchas* tradition, a system of place-names in which the location where an event occurred seems to derive its name from the event itself. For instance, in the *Táin* Fer Diad's death is said to have taken place at Áth Fhir Diad (Death of Fer Diad), now Ardee in County Louth. Although the *Táin* is rooted in historical reality, a recent reconstruction of that reality based on some 7th-century texts suggests that the figure of Cú Chulainn is an inno-vation, possibly intended as a heroic embodiment of Ulster's resistance.

The *Táin* has survived in a number of versions and redactions, the most recent of which dates from the 15th century (the manuscript tradition continued even into the 19th century). This is not to say that the literary appeal of the Ulster cycle did not decline towards the end of the Middle Ages. It did, however, retain its value as history. Quite early on, Irish monastic scholars began to fit events and personages from their illustrious past into the chronological scheme of the late-classical world chronicles, in the process dating the Ulster cycle to around the beginning of the Christian era. This 'pseudo-history' resulted in the 11th- and 12th-century *Lebor Gabála Érenn* (Book of the Conquests of Ireland); through Geoffrey Keating's *Foras Feasa ar Érinn* (1634), an

Irish-language history of Ireland from the Creation to the coming of the Normans which was translated into English in 1811, it determined the image of Irish history down to the beginning of the present century.

In the second half of the 19th century the Irish struggle for political independence led to a renewed interest in the figure of Cú Chulainn. Inspired by the work of Eugene O'Curry, from 1854 Professor of Irish History at the newly founded Catholic University of Ireland, Standish James O'Grady published his *History of Ireland: Heroic Period* in 1878. It was largely due to this romanticised recreation of the Irish heroic past, with Cú Chulainn in a central role, that the old symbol of Ireland, a female personification of (the fertility of) the land with which the king enters into a marriage – which had gradually dwindled to a sad and pathetic girl sighing for a bridegroom – was displaced by the new symbol of the heroic warrior. In the later 1880s John O'Leary (1830–1907), who devoted his life to the cause of Irish independence, aroused the enthusiasm of the young W.B. Yeats (1865–1939) for an Irish national literature in English. Yeats began to immerse himself in the cultural heritage of Celtic Ireland, but since he knew no Irish was restricted to what was then available in English. In 1898 he began his collaboration with Lady Augusta Gregory, which was also of great benefit to the Irish stage (1904 saw the opening of the Abbey Theatre). The first of Lady Gregory's English-language versions of Irish heroic tales was *Cuchulain of Muirthemne*, published in 1902. The hero has a significant place in that part of Yeats' work devoted to Irish themes. *Aided Óenfhir Aífe* provides the basis for both the 1892 poem *The Death of Cuchulain* (later changed to *Cuchulain's Fight with the Sea*) and the 1904 play *On Baile's Strand*. The poem shows how little Yeats still knew of older Irish literature: here Conle is the son of Emer, who out of jealousy commands him to kill his father. The play is based on Lady Gregory's version of the story, which appeared before the publication of the Old Irish *scél* with its tense atmosphere of destiny. The 1908 farce *The Golden Helmet* (in 1910 retitled *The Green Helmet*) takes *Fled Bricrenn* as its starting point. As regards the other three plays, *The Only Jealousy of Emer* (1919) is based on *Serglige Con Culainn* and *The Death of Cuchulainn* (1939) on *Aided Con Culainn*. *At the Hawk's Well* (1917), which has Cú Chulainn among the *dramatis personae* but seems strongly influenced in its symbolism by Japanese Nōh plays, appears to have an autobiographical significance, as does the poem *Cuchulainn Comforted* (on the hero's death) with its image of souls changing into birds, which Yeats wrote shortly before his death. The dramatic ballet *Fighting the Waves* (1929) can in some sense also be included in Yeats' Cú Chulainn repertoire.

To remain with Cú Chulainn as symbol of the new Ireland: the bilingual (Irish-English) St Enda's College near Dublin, founded in 1908 by Patrick Pierce (1879–1916; leader of the 1916 Easter Rising against English rule), apparently had a wall-painting of Cú Chulainn which depicted the hero arming himself for battle. In 1911–12 Oliver Sheppard (1865–1941) made a bronze statue of the dying Cú Chulainn; it now stands in the General Post Office in Dublin as a memorial to the Easter Rising.

D.R. EDEL

Study: Thurneysen 1921.

CULHWCH AND OLWEN are the eponymous hero and heroine of a Welsh prose narrative. Culhwch's mother is the sister of → Arthur's mother; she dies when Culhwch is still a child. Seven years later his father Cilydd acquires a new wife by attacking a king, stealing his wife and daughter and annexing his kingdom. When the new wife learns that Cilydd has a son by his first marriage she has the youngster, who in accordance with Celtic custom was being raised by foster parents, brought to court. She wants him to marry her daughter, but he gets out of it by pleading his youth. Thereupon she lays a doom upon him: he will never have a wife unless he succeeds in winning Olwen, daughter of Ysbaddaden Penncawr (First among Warriors or First among Giants). The lad is at once filled with love for the unknown girl; his father advises him to seek help from Arthur, who is after all his cousin. (The description of the young man's departure and the dialogue with Arthur's gatekeeper which immediately follows are stereotypical elements of the British-Celtic tradition.)

Contrary to court protocol, Culhwch seeks admittance while Arthur and his court are at table; the ruler agrees, against the advice of his chief hero Cei (→ Kay): 'So long as people seek us out we have respect. The greater our generosity, the greater our fame and honour.' Culhwch then rides his horse into the hall (a motif later found in Chrétien's *Perceval*) and asks Arthur for Olwen's hand, invoking his warriors as witnesses and sureties. (The list begins with Cei and Bedwyr and contains some 220 names, many of which belong to the heroic tradition of Celtic Britain.) For a full year Arthur's messengers search for the girl, without success. When this failure begins to endanger Arthur's honour, Cei volunteers to accompany Culhwch until either Olwen is found or Culhwch admits that she does not exist. Arthur orders Bedwyr to go with them, together with the guide Cynddylig, the interpreter Gwrhyr, the magician Menw and Gwalchmai son of Gwyar.

How this band reaches Ysbaddaden's country is not related. Once there, the heroes are given hospitality by the shepherd Custennin and his wife, who again proves to be a sister of Arthur's mother. Because of Custennin's wife Ysbaddaden has already killed 23 of the couple's sons. Cei takes the last survivor, who will subsequently earn the heroic name Goreu ('the Best'), under his protection: 'Let him come with me, and they will have to kill us both together.' Culhwch's aunt arranges for him to meet Olwen; she tells him that he will have to ask her father for her hand and agree to all his demands. The description of the girl's beauty is again a stereotyped element of the British-Celtic narrative tradition.

Ysbaddaden sets Culhwch a great many tasks; the young man must provide him with a number of necessities for the wedding feast, including a famous cauldron and an equally famous drinking horn for the banquet as well as a comb, scissors and razor for his personal use. These last three objects require the tusks of two wild boars which can be hunted down only with the aid of a number of picked heroes, horses and hounds. There are in all 39 *anoetheu* (singular: *anoeth*) or things hard to come by; we are told of the acquisition of fourteen of them, sixteen already belong to Arthur's court, and nine appear only in Ysbaddaden's list of tasks (at least, in this story; elsewhere they occur in various learned lists from the British-Celtic tradition). It is notable that Culhwch does not appear in any of these 'collection tales', not even the first, which takes place on the return journey from Ysbaddaden's land to Arthur's court and earns Goreu his heroic name. The real protagonist is Arthur, 'the first among the princes of the island of Britain', together with his warriors. When informed of Ysbaddaden's demands it is he who decides each time which of the *anoetheu* shall be next. There are prisoners to be freed, challengers of Arthur's peace to be defeated, destructive beasts to be hunted, overseas campaigns to be undertaken. The high point is the hunting of the boar Trwyth, which begins in Ireland and leads right across Wales to the furthest point of Cornwall, where this bringer of death and destruction is chased into the sea. The heroic deeds are performed partly by the individual heroes, notably Cei, partly by Arthur as commander of the forces of Britain. One combat is undertaken by Arthur in person: that with the demonic female warrior Gorddu, a figure reminiscent of Scáthach, → Cú Chulainn's instructress in heroism.

When this last task also is completed Culhwch, together with Goreu, returns with the *anoetheu* to Ysbaddaden. Culhwch marries Olwen and Goreu takes his revenge on Ysbaddaden by beheading him and taking possession of his land and fortress. The story ends with the return of Arthur's troops, each to his own land.

Medieval manuscripts from Wales contain many indications that the oral tradition of Celtic Britain was comparable with that of Celtic Ireland, but that it entered the written culture to a much smaller extent – and, as regards the narrative tradition, at a consistently later stage in its development. *Culhwch ac Olwen* belongs to a period of transition from oral to written culture. One indication of a still incompletely developed written culture is that while the first part of the narrative is fairly detailed, it then goes over to a resumé style. Oral narrative technique still survives in the many stereotyped narrative elements (descriptions, lists, dialogues).

The extant redaction of *Culhwch ac Olwen* dates from around 1100 or a little earlier. It is the oldest of the eleven surviving Welsh prose narratives published by Lady Charlotte Guest in the middle of the last century under the (inaccurate) title *Mabinogion*. It is included in fragmentary form in the White Book of Rhydderch (c.1350, National Library of Wales); the Red Book of Hergest (1382–c.1410, Bodleian Library, Oxford) contains the complete text. The central role played by Arthur and his heroes makes this a true Arthurian tale. As the only Arthurian narrative that can be dated with certainty to before the publication of Geoffrey of Monmouth's *Historia Regum Britannie* it is of great importance for the early development of Arthurian material.

Because the framing story with the courtship theme is so much more expansive in style than the Arthurian adventures of the collecting of the *anoetheu*, and because research into British and Irish Celtic narrative tradition was strongly influenced by folktale research with its emphasis on story types and motifs, for a long time there was little interest in the epic-heroic aspects of *Culhwch ac Olwen*; it was generally approached as a collection of folktales. As a result the two long lists, of Arthur's warriors and Ysbaddaden's demands, which together make up a good quarter of the text, attracted far more attention than the events of the story. However, in the context of the Celtic narrative tradition of the British Isles, the Arthur of *Culhwch ac Olwen* is a traditional Celtic chieftain. Most of the Arthurian adventures in this work have parallels in Irish epic-heroic tradition and here, as there, events are set in actual locations (*dinnshenchas*; → Cú Chulainn). As 'first among the princes of Britain' Arthur is the leader of a coalition, and as such he frequently appears as peacemaker between two parties; his court includes (under)kings and warriors from all over Britain and from overseas (Ireland, the Continent). The magic-heroic qualities of his principal hero Cei are comparable with those of the Irish Cú Chulainn; for instance, in both the heroic frenzy is expressed in heating of their bodies. But there are also later characteristics. The fact that halfway through the 'difficult tasks' Arthur comes into conflict with Cei, leading to Cei breaking with him, may be an early indication of the decline of this Celtic hero seen in the continental Arthurian texts (→ Kay). Gwalchmei, the Welsh Gauvain or → Gawain, who is mentioned once in *Culhwch ac Olwen* but takes no further part in the story, is probably a later addition. The inclusion of the originally independent Arthurian adventures in the courtship story brought about a mutual influence: on the one hand a romanticising of the heroic deeds of Arthur and his warriors, partly through a shift of emphasis from the heroic deed itself to the *anoeth* involved, on the other an 'Arthurianising' of the courtship, partly by making Ysbaddaden Arthur's opponent. Ysbaddaden appears as a challenger of Arthur's rule, not only for killing Goreu's brothers but because in his list of demands he is made to claim that Arthur is 'under his hand' (subject to his authority).

The development of a British-Celtic legend of Arthur first becomes apparent in the 9th century, both in Latin historical writings and in vernacular heroic poetry. The *Historia Brittonum* (c.830) and the slightly later Welsh Annals name Arthur as commander against the advancing Germans; the ancient core of the elegiac poem *Gododdin*, attributed to the North British poet Aneurin, speaks of him as an outstanding warrior. The *Mirabilia*, a list of the sights of Britain appended to the *Historia Brittonum* in the 10th century, calls him 'miles' (soldier); along with the oldest mention of his hunting of the boar Troit it tells of him killing a son (in the British-Celtic tradition Arthur has a number of sons).

As in *Culhwch ac Olwen*, Arthur and his warriors also do battle with non-historical opponents in the poems *Pa gur yw porthawr* (Who is the Gatekeeper?) and *Preiddeu Annwfn* (The Plundering of the Otherworld) which date from the same period as *Culhwch ac Olwen* and are closely related to it in content. This theme may be connected with the political prophecies, very popular in Wales, about the liberation of Britain from its foreign overlords: the Angles and Saxons, the Vikings and the Normans successively. In this genre, which also appears first in the 9th century, Arthur becomes over time one of the predicted liberators of the island.

The 12th-century narrative *Breudwyt Ronabwy* (The Dream of Rhonabwy), with its nostalgic looking back to Arthur and his world, should also be seen as part of the British-Celtic tradition. In the *Trioedd Ynys Prydein* (Triads of the Island of Britain), which provided Welsh poets with a survey of the narrative traditions of Celtic Britain, Arthur is the heroic leader and protector of the island. The Triads also lay the basis for the link with the Tristan material, likewise British-Celtic in origin.

Although the three romantic Arthurian tales *Owein* or *The Lady of the Fountain*, *Peredur vab Evrawg* and *Gereint vab Erbin* contain a number of insular-Celtic (stylistic) elements, in a sense they represent the 'afterlife' of insular-Celtic Arthurian tradition. In these stories, as in continental Arthurian literature, Arthur is reduced to a more or less passive central figure and the adventures are set not in concrete locations but in an ideal (dream)world.

Something of the 'historical' approach to Arthur which characterises the British-Celtic tradition survived in Geoffrey's *Historia Regum Britannie*, however limited its author's knowledge of that tradition; and from there it influenced the English Arthurian tradition.

D.R. EDEL

Translation: Jones/Jones 1949.
Studies: Jones 1964; Edel 1980.

D EOR is a Germanic poet whom we know only from the Old English poem of the same name. The poem, forty lines in length, has been preserved in a 10th-century manuscript. Deor is the first-person narrator. He gives six examples of suffering endured by human beings, taken from the world of the Germanic sagas; each episode ends with the line: 'þæes ofereode; þisses swa mæg' (that passed; so may this also). The first two instances centre around → Wieland and Beaduhild (the princess raped by Wieland). The otherwise unknown Mæþhild and Geat provide the third example, which is probably a tragic love story. The fourth example quoted is Deodrik (→ Theodoric the Great or the Frankish king Theodoric, Wolfdietrich, Dietrich), the fifth is Eormenric (the Gothic king → Ermanaric). The sixth and final instance of misfortune is Deor's own story. For a long time he was '*skop*', bard, to the Heodenings, but has been displaced by his rival Heorrenda. This Heorrenda is the most famous bard of Germanic antiquity, the Hôrant of the Middle High German epic → *Kudrun* and the Yiddish *Dukus Horant*, and the Hjarrandi of Old Norse sources.

Although the name Deor does occur a few times in Old English, here we are probably dealing with a fictitious character set in a heroic context. The poem is an elegy and probably originated in the 8th or 9th century. The author was clearly quite at home with the heroic sagas: even the Heodenings whom Deor served are known from other sources as the Hjadningar of Old Norse and the Hetelings of Middle High German literature.

A. QUAK

Edition: Malone 1977.

ELIDUC is the male protagonist of the *lai* (short verse narrative) of the same name by Marie de France. There is in Brittany a brave and courtly knight called Eliduc. He has a wife, Guildeluëc. When Eliduc falls victim to slander he decides to leave and seek refuge in England; there he enters the service of an elderly king whose only daughter, Guilliadun, is coveted by a number of violent barons. Guilliadun and Eliduc fall in love, but Eliduc does not mention his marriage.

When the King of Brittany suddenly finds himself in difficulties Eliduc hastens to his aid. On parting from Guilliadun he promises her that he will return. Having restored order in Brittany he secretly returns to his beloved and elopes with her. During their voyage to Brittany a raging storm gets up; the captain wants to throw Guilliadun overboard but Eliduc opposes his suggestion. From this exchange Guilliadun realises that Eliduc is married; she is so distraught that she faints and does not regain consciousness. Eliduc lays her lifeless body on the altar in a chapel where he visits her every day. His wife, curious as to where her husband goes each day, follows him and discovers her rival's body. As she stands there looking a weasel creeps from under the altar. A servant kills it. Another weasel puts a small red flower in the mouth of the murdered animal, whereupon it returns to life. Guildeluëc gets hold of the flower and puts it in Guilliadun's mouth. Guilliadun recovers and at once tells her rival the whole story. Guildeluëc enters a convent and Eliduc is thus able to marry Guilliadun.

The oldest known version of Eliduc – of which only one manuscript survives – is a *lai* of 1184 lines, ascribed to Marie de France (c.1130–c.1200; → Yonec).

In 1974 John Fowles included a translation of this *lai* in *The Ebony Tower*. In 'A personal note' which precedes this translation Fowles says: 'The working title of this collection of stories was *Variations*, by which I meant to suggest variations both on certain themes in previous books of mine and in methods of narrative presentation.' On closer inspection it is clear that the title story is a variation on the story of Eliduc.

Eliduc is the story of a man who is deprived of the presence of his beloved and who then – more or less against his better judgment – enters into a relationship with another woman (cf. the marriage of → Tristan with Yseult-of-the-White-Hands). With the exception of the storm at sea (cf. the Book of Jonah in the Bible), the seeming death (cf. the Sleeping Beauty and Snow White) and the restoration to life by means of a 'magic herb' there are no folklore elements in this story.

LUDO JONGEN

Edition: Burgess/Busby 1986.

EREC AND ENIDE are the hero and heroine of the first French Arthurian romance, written about 1165–70 by the poet Chrétien de Troyes. Erec, the son of King Lac, is a young knight at the court of King → Arthur. One day he leaves the court to avenge an insult by another knight, → Yder, to Queen Guenièvre and himself. Soon he encounters Enide, the very lovely and extremely wise daughter of an impoverished minor vassal. Next day a sparrowhawk is offered as prize for the most beautiful lady; Erec wins the sparrowhawk for Enide in a combat with Yder, at the same time avenging the shameful insult. He requests Enide's hand in marriage and takes her with him to Arthur's court, where they are married with full courtly ceremony. They then leave for the court of King Lac.

Here Erec seems completely absorbed by love for his wife. The knights in his retinue complain of the shameful way he neglects his knightly duty. Enide learns of this and is ashamed, feeling herself responsible for her husband's dishonour. One morning Erec is woken by her tears and demands to know the reason for her sorrow. He appears to take her explanation as criticism of himself and resolves to leave court, accompanied only by Enide; he forbids her to speak to him. Four times Enide defies this ban: she warns Erec first of three, then of five robber knights, of a count they lodge with one night who means to kill Erec so as to possess Enide, and finally of a dwarfish knight, Guivret le Petit, who is about to attack Erec. Each time Erec averts the danger and reproaches Enide for her disobedience. After defeating Guivret and then granting him his life, the two men become friends. After an encounter with Arthur and his train, out hunting in the forest, Erec rescues a knight waylaid by two giants. He is so exhausted by his exertions in this battle that he falls from his horse, apparently dead. A count who happens to be passing falls in love with Enide and decides to take them both with him, intending to bury Erec and marry Enide. As Erec lies on his bier the count tries to force Enide to accept him. When she persists in her refusal he hits her in the face, she screams and Erec rouses from his swoon. This revival of the seeming corpse causes great confusion, and Erec and Enide take advantage of it to escape.

They are now reconciled, with all their differences and misunderstandings forgotten. They meet Guivret again, and he takes them to his castle to rest and recover. There follows one last adventure, the 'Joie de la Cour' (Joy of the Court). In a fairy-tale garden lives the knight Maboagrain with his beloved. Maboagrain kills every knight who dares to enter the garden and sets his victims' heads on sharp stakes. Erec defeats Maboagrain, thus releasing him from the promise he had made to his mistress: to remain with her in the garden until he should be defeated. The garden no longer poses a threat to the surrounding area and the lovers can return to normal life. Erec's victory has restored harmony and Enide manages to convince Maboagrain's beloved that she will be happier outside the garden. Erec and Enide now return to Arthur's court. Shortly after this King Lac dies, and Erec and Enide are crowned King and Queen in Nantes.

This story, older versions of which were according to the poet in circulation, rightly bears the names of both male and female protagonists. Enide is a fascinating character: a courtly but shy girl who, in a development expressed in the repeated conflict between obedience and loving concern, grows to become the equal of Erec – an equality which is symbolised in their joint coronation. Erec undergoes a parallel development which leads to a balanced solution to his conflict between love and knightly duty.

Chrétien's romance was translated into various languages during the Middle Ages. Hartmann von Aue's *Erec* (c.1190) is the first Arthurian romance in German. Hartmann follows Chrétien in broad outline, but often diverges from him in details. Because he expands on his source and provides explanations, his version is half as long again as the original. For instance, he gives a much fuller description of Enide's despair at Erec's supposed death. Comparison of the structure of Hartmann's text with Chrétien's alerted German scholars to a structure frequently found in Arthurian romances (the 'Doppel-wegstruktur'): in the course of his early adventures the hero finds a beloved and enjoys a fragile bliss, then there is a crisis which initiates a second, more serious sequence of adventures leading to lasting happiness. The same structure occurs in, for example, Chrétien's romance about → Yvain and Marie de France's *Lai de* → *Lanval*.

Like the German work, the Welsh version bears the name of the male protagonist only: *Gereint ab Erbin* (Gereint, son of Erbin). This anonymous prose narrative forms part of the *Mabinogion* (→ Culhwch) and probably dates from the early 13th century. Its relationship to the French text is not entirely clear; although it seems certain that the Welsh author was familiar with Chrétien's version, he also used material from other, Welsh, sources, particularly where names and family relationships are concerned. The story also differs in some details; for example, the estrangement between the couple is explained by jealousy on Gereint's part.

Around 1230 the Old Norse *Erex saga* was written as a shorter prose version of Chrétien's romance; the abridgment mainly results from the omission of descriptive material and does not affect the action. A French prose version of Chrétien's verse romance was written in the 15th century by someone close to the Burgundian court; its content is the same as its model.

Another French prose narrative of Erec appears in two manuscripts of the *Tristan en prose* and, in incomplete form, in a Spanish and a Portuguese translation of it. The story probably dates from the 14th century. As well as the name of Erec's father, Lac, it gives that of his mother: Crisea, or, in one French source, Ocise. He also has a sister, but there is no mention of Enide. In this story Erec has the reputation of being the most trustworthy of all the knights. He has taken an oath never to break his word – an oath which proves fatal to him. As a knight errant with several adventures to his credit, one day he encounters a young noblewoman who promises to tell him about the fate of his father, who had been defeated in a duel, on condition that he later does whatever she asks of him. This Erec promises. His father proves to be lying wounded in a monastery, and his honour has already been avenged by Hestor of Mares, half-brother to →

'The brave Geraint' or 'Geraint and Enid', painting by Arthur Hughes, 1860.
Private collection.

Lancelot. What the lady later requires of Erec is the head of his own sister. To avoid breaking his oath he cuts off his sister's head. As punishment for this deed Erec dies a dishonourable death at the hands of Gauvain (→ Gawain).

In the 19th century an Arthurian knight called Geraint appears as a bard in the Welsh-oriented short story 'The Enchanted Shield' in the collection *Stories of Chivalry* by Henry Davies. The Welsh version of the story of Erec and Enide, as translated and published by Lady Charlotte Guest in 1840, provided Alfred Lord Tennyson with the inspiration for one of the earliest poems in the cycle *Idylls of the King*. In the short cycle *The True and the False: Four Idylls of the King*, published in 1859, the first poem is entitled 'Enid'. In 1870 Tennyson changed the title to 'Geraint and Enid' and in 1873 the poem was divided in two: 'The Marriage of Geraint' and 'Geraint and Enid'. Tennyson faithfully follows events as described in his source; his contribution is in the structure and the poetic language. As regards the structure, he begins the story *in medias res*, at the point where Geraint and Enid are leaving Arthur's court after their marriage. Then we are told of Geraint's all-absorbing love, his followers' grumbling, Enid's concern and Geraint's jealousy which leads him to command Enid to go with him in search of adventures. There then follows a retrospective account of their whole story from the beginning. The break between 'The Marriage of Geraint' and 'Geraint and Enid' comes when this 'flashback' reaches the point at which it started.

In 1868 an edition of *The True and the False: Four Idylls of the King* appeared with illustrations by Gustave Doré; nine of Doré's engravings relate to 'Enid'. Around 1860 Tennyson inspired the Pre-Raphaelite painter Arthur Hughes to paint his 'The Brave Geraint' (also known as 'Geraint and Enid', now the property of Lady Anne Tennant). Because of her devoted love for her husband, 19th-century artists saw in Enid(e) a foil to adulterous wives such as Guinevere and Yseult. She was portrayed many times by, among others, J. Hallyar (1860), J.B. Bedford (1862), F.M. Miller (1866), E.H. Corbould (1873), H.M. Paget (1879), G.F. Watts (1879), Mrs Samuel Nicholl (1880), Alice M. Scott (1881), Helen Blackburn (1885), F. Sydney Muschamp (1885) and Madeline M. McDonald (1896). One of the tapestries in the 'Court of Arthur' series commissioned from the Windsor Tapestry Works by the MP Coleridge Kennard in 1876 showed Geraint bowing to Enid and her parents in front of a ruined castle. In 1895–96 George James Frampton, an artist of the New Sculpture Movement who was influenced by the Pre-Raphaelites, depicted Enid on one of the ten silver-gilt panels which still hang in Astor House, Temple Place, Westminster. He also produced a bust of 'Enid the Fair' (1908). In 1908 Ernest Rhys used the story of Geraint and his beloved in his *Enid: A Lyric Play*, for which Vincent Thomas wrote the music.

C. HOGETOORN

Editions and translations: Foerster 1884; Jones/Jones 1949; Cramer 1972; Kibler 1991.
Studies: Loomis 1959; Schmolke-Hasselmann 1980; Whitaker 1990.

ERMANARIC was King of the Ostrogoths; according to the Roman historian Ammianus Marcellinus, his contemporary, he committed suicide in 375 when the Huns overran his kingdom. The Gothic historian Jordanes (6th century) tells us that 'Hermanaricus' belonged to the Amelung family, which also produced → Theodoric the Great (Dietrich von Bern). According to him, this Hermanaricus established a great empire. When the Rosomon tribe went over to the Huns, he reacted to this treachery by having Sunilda, a Rosomon woman, torn to pieces by wild horses. In revenge her brothers Sarus and Ammius seriously wounded Ermanaric. Prevented by this injury from leading his people's resistance to the Huns he died, aged 110.

Ermanaric is one of the earliest historical characters in Germanic heroic epic. However, there are considerable differences in the way the historical facts are treated in the various traditions. As a character in heroic epic, Ermanaric features in a number of saga complexes.

Firstly, there is the *Svanhild* saga, found in its complete form only in Scandinavia. The principal source for this is the poem 'Hamdismál' in the *Edda*. In this tradition Svanhild is a daughter of Sigurd (→ Siegfried) and the wife of King 'Jörmunrekk' (Ermanaric). Jörmunrekk has her trampled to death by wild horses because he suspects her of being unfaithful to him with his son Randvér. Randvér is hanged. Svanhild's brothers Sörli and Hamdir want to avenge her, but refuse the help of her half-brother Erpr; they go so far as to kill him during their journey to Jörmunrekk. Hamdir hacks off Jörmunrekk's feet and Sörli his hands. Because Erpr is not there to cut off his head he is able to shout for help and instruct his guards to stone the brothers, since metal cannot harm them. The Danish historian Saxo Grammaticus (c.1200) is also aware of this story. In his version, however, 'Iarmerik' is King of Denmark. The false counsellor Bikki accuses Broder, the King's son, of adultery with Queen Svanhild. She is trampled to death by horses; Broder is pardoned at the last moment when his father realises that he has no other heir. Svanhild's brothers try to avenge her, but succeed only in seriously wounding Iarmerik.

A second complex, the *Harlung* saga, concerns two brothers of questionable historicity, nephews of Ermanaric, who appear in Middle High German Dietrich epic (e.g. in *Biterolf*) and in the Old Norse *Thidrekssaga* which was translated from German. According to these sources the Harlungs Imbreke and Fritele were slandered by the wicked counsellor Sibecke and subsequently hanged. The *Thidrekssaga* even says that they had cast lustful eyes on Queen Svanhild. Despite the precautions of the loyal Eckart they were arrested and hanged. Saxo Grammaticus also relates that two nephews of King Iarmerik of Denmark rebelled against him, and that after their defeat he had them hanged. It is clear from the Old English → *Widsith* that the story was also known in England: the poet relates that he had visited the court of 'Eormanric' and met the 'Herelingen' Emerca and Fridia. The Middle High German epic *Dietrichs Flucht* informs us that Ermenrich had gained possession of the gold of the Harlungs. Here, therefore, lust for gold provides an additional motive for the murder of kinsmen.

Thirdly, there is the *Dietrich* saga. In medieval German heroic epic Ermenrich's main role is as the opponent of Dietrich von Bern (= Theodoric the Great). The various narratives tell how Dietrich was driven out of Italy by his uncle Ermenrich. Dietrich makes several attempts to recover his kingdom, but despite his victories is always forced back into exile with King → Attila (Etzel) of the Huns. In these works Ermenrich has assumed the role of the historical Odoacer; the Old High German *Hildebrantslied* makes it clear that Odoacer was Dietrich's original antagonist, in the epic as in real life. Most likely Ermenrich, being well-known from the other epic works (see above), took the place of the forgotten historical opponent.

A. QUAK

Edition: Bertelsen 1908–11.
Translation: Fisher/Davidson 1979–80.
Studies: Boer 1910; Brady 1943; Zink 1950; Wisniewski 1986.

ERNST is the hero of a Middle High German epic which, like → *Salman* and *König* → *Rother*, is classified among the so-called 'Spielmannslyrik'. The original was probably written around 1170 and survives only in some three fragments. The earliest extant form of the complete story is a rather later rhymed version which appeared in the early 13th century. Our retelling of the story is based on this redaction.

Duke Ernst of Bavaria receives an excellent upbringing and becomes an exemplary ruler of his country. His mother, after years of widowhood, marries Otto, ruler of Saxony and Holy Roman Emperor. Ernst renders his stepfather Otto valuable service as an advisor and administrator and becomes a much respected figure at his court. As a result, the influence of his rival the Palatine Heinrich is diminished. Jealous of Ernst's power, he falsely tells the Emperor that his stepson has designs on his throne. Emperor Otto believes his lies and invades Bavaria with a great army to oust Ernst from his dukedom.

Duke Ernst flees with some thousand of his knights and crosses the Balkans to Constantinople. With the core of his army he boards a great ship; they are also joined by many Greeks. Thus a great crusader army is formed and under the duke's leadership prepares to liberate the Holy Land. Soon after the fleet sets sail a violent storm gets up. Many ships are lost, the duke's vessel becomes separated and is driven out to sea by the gale. After months wandering the ocean they at last sight land and drop anchor in an unknown port.

It turns out to be the town of Grippia which, strangely enough, is totally deserted. Duke Ernst and his trusty comrade-in-arms Count Wetzel set out to investigate; they witness the return of the inhabitants. They are escorting their king home in triumph, together with the heiress to the kingdom of India who has been brought there against her will. The people of Grippia prove to be monsters, people with the heads of cranes. Duke Ernst fights them in an attempt to rescue the princess, but her abductors stab her to death before she can be saved.

Again the duke puts to sea. A new adventure follows: the ship is drawn into the field of the 'Magnetic Mountain' (→ Kudrun), from which it is impossible to escape. The ship is held fast. The food runs out. The situation is hopeless. The seafarers begin to die of starvation, and terrible birds of prey called griffins snatch their corpses from the deck and carry them away to feed their young in the nests on the mainland. Count Wetzel has a bright idea: the survivors sew themselves into animal-skins and so are borne away to the mainland by the predatory birds. But their adventurous journey is not yet over. On reaching the mainland Duke Ernst and his companions are captured by a monstrous one-eyed people, the inhabitants of Arismaspi. The German knights take service with their king and ensure his victory in a battle against another monstrous race, this time with huge duck's feet. The duke is rewarded with a dukedom, which he has to defend against a repulsive people with big ears. Next he frees the dwarves of the neighbouring country of Prechami from a plague of cranes. Finally he defeats an army of giants who had been trying to make his royal overlord pay tribute to them.

After spending six years in the country Ernst and his men begin their homeward journey on a merchantman from Moorland (= Ethiopia). He brings his treasure as a memento, together with – among others – a giant and two dwarves. On the way he assists in the defence of Christian Moorland against the Sultan of Babylonia (= Cairo in Egypt). He then makes himself useful defending Christian Jerusalem against heathen enemies. Meanwhile, Emperor Otto has realised that he acted unjustly in forcing Ernst from his lands; consequently, on his return Ernst is able to resume his honoured place at court. The monstrous folk he has brought with him now join the Emperor's retinue; only the giant continues in Duke Ernst's service.

Strange though it may seem, the story of Duke Ernst is not all fiction. The beginning and end of the work, which describe the conflict between Duke Ernst and the Emperor Otto, probably have a historical background. Two historical events appear to have become merged. It is known that in 953 Duke Liudulf of Swabia rebelled against his father, Emperor Otto the Great. Otto besieged and captured Regensburg, after which his son pleaded for pardon. In 1027 Duke Ernst II of Swabia rebelled against his stepfather, King Konrad II. His rebellion failed. However, his mother Gisela was able to bring about a reconciliation between the two.

The most important part of the narrative, Ernst's travels in the Orient, has no historical basis; it derives from Arabic sources such as the tales of Sinbad the Sailor in the *Thousand and One Nights*. The geographical details to be found in the story are of great interest, since they reflect the geographical knowledge of an educated Western European of the 12th and 13th centuries. The earth is not thought of as flat, but as a sphere. Part of it is surrounded by a broad belt of water called *Oceanus*. This watery girdle encircles that part of the earth inhabited by men, which is itself divided into three continents: Europe, Africa and Asia. This view had come down from Antiquity. The unknown poet of *Herzog Ernst* happily makes use of this tradition, and has no hesitation in adding his own fabrications. But some of what he includes seems to be reminiscent of Oriental reality: for example, the palace gardens in Grippia and the Grippians' way of fighting using mounted archers. The geography of *Herzog Ernst*, in which Far East ('India') and Far North ('Magnetic Mountain') meet, is vague in the extreme. The duke's homeward journey, in which he visits all kinds of exotic regions, presents no problems. A merchant from 'Ethiopia' arrives in Arismaspian waters and transports the duke to his home port. From there he travels via Cairo and Jerusalem, and we can follow his route on medieval maps.

The remarkable story of Duke Ernst must have been extremely popular, judging by the fact that versions of it appear throughout the Middle Ages, both in verse and in prose. There was a highly successful early 15th-century prose version which in turn, in abridged form, provided the text for a printed version (from Anton Sorg's printing house in Augsburg, c.1476). This chapbook, entitled *Ain hüpsche liepliche Historie ains edeln fürsten herczog Ernst von bairn vnd von österich*, was illustrated with fine woodcuts and for a long time was in great demand. The book continued to be extremely popular; it was reprinted at least twenty times down to the early 19th century. As well as the German texts there were also versions in Latin such as Hartmann Schedel's of 1471. The theme of the noble rebel also became a favourite in late-medieval art. A tapestry from the second half of the 14th century, of which, sadly, only fragments survive, depicts the history of Duke Ernst in twelve scenes (Städtisches Museum, Brunswick).

The early years of Romanticism gave new life to the old story. It was reworked many times in the early 19th century, often with the intention of restoring to the German people something of their national literature. In particular Ludwig Uhland's dramatised version, a tragedy in five acts entitled *Ernst, Herzog von Schwaben* (1818), was extremely successful. In 1953 P. Hack wrote a dramatised version entitled *Volksbuch vom Herzog Ernst oder: Der Held und sein Gefolge*, in which he ridiculed the idealising tendency of the romantic retellings.

J.H. WINKELMAN

Edition: Sowinski 1970.

FERGUS is the hero of the Old French romance of that name, which was translated/adapted into Middle Dutch as *Ferguut*. The outline that follows is that of the Old French version. Fergus is the eldest son of Soumilloit, a well-to-do peasant married to a noblewoman, whose wealth allows him to live in a castle. After holding court on St John's Day at Karadigan (Cardigan) in Wales, King → Arthur decides to go and hunt the white hart that lives in the forest of Carduel. Only → Perceval is able to keep up with the animal. The chase takes them as far as barbarous Ingeval, where Perceval's hound kills the hart. The journey back to civilisation takes them past the field where Fergus is busy ploughing – for Soumilloit made his sons work! At first the lad is terrified, but fear gives way to curiosity when he sees a squire bringing up the rear and asks him what is going on. The squire tells him that those he has just seen riding by are King Arthur and his knights of the Round Table (of whom his mother has so often told him). In high excitement the youngster unyokes his beasts, picks up the ploughshare, runs home and asks his father for arms and leave to go to Arthur's court. Soumilloit is furious, berates him for a whoreson and is about to take his stick to him. Fortunately, his mother intervenes; understanding his longing, she pretends to take the insult literally. Soumilloit has no option but to grant his eldest son's wish. Wearing his father's rusty armour the young man sets out for Arthur's court, unskillfully dispatching a couple of robber knights on the way.

His arrival at court proves a disillusionment when the 'seneschal' Ke (→ Kay) makes fun of him, hailing him with mock relief as the long-awaited knight who will rid the land of the Black Knight. However, Gauvain (→ Gawain) is annoyed at Ke's sarcasm and takes Fergus under his wing. After proclaiming a feud between himself and Ke the young man leaves the court, expecting to find lodging in the town. But nobody invites him in, and he has to shelter from the rain under a projecting window. The daughter of Arthur's chamberlain sees him there and lets him in. Later the chamberlain returns home; he manages to persuade Fergus to lay aside his old clothes and accept knighthood from Arthur. Fergus spends the night there and next day, unrecognisable in the new clothes which accentuate his beauty, he returns to court with his host. Never had any strange knight been shown more honour than Fergus when he is knighted by Arthur, Gauvain, → Yvain, Perceval and his host. But celebration turns to sadness when Fergus proves determined to seek out the Black Knight and fight him.

On his way to the Black Crag, home of the Black Knight, Fergus spends a night at Castle Lidel, where the castellan's niece, Galiene, is also staying. As soon as she sets eyes on Fergus' beauty, she falls head over heels in love with him – so much so that after great inner conflict she goes to his room that night and wakes him by laying her hand on his heart. Fergus, still quite ignorant of such love and totally absorbed in his knighthood, asks her to postpone matters until after the duel.

Next day Fergus defeats the Black Knight, sends him to Arthur's court with a greeting for the King and a threat for Ke, and returns to Lidel. But he discovers that Galiene has left, overcome by shame, and no one knows where she has gone. Fergus' joy turns to sorrow as he realises what has happened. Now it is his turn to fall passionately in love. With hindsight he understands how offensive his behaviour of the previous night had been; from now on the object of his quest will be to find Galiene again.

Fergus falls into a depression. He has a trio of adventures which bring him no closer to his goal, though he shows himself a protector of courtly order and sends defeated opponents to Arthur, but then spends a whole year riding around aimlessly. He recovers from his melancholia after drinking from a miraculous spring. A dwarf who lives there tells him that to find Galiene again he must first win the Shield Beautiful, which lies in the castle of Dunostre guarded by a giantess and a dragon. This he successfully achieves. Then he learns from some shepherds that Galiene is being besieged by a king in the town of Rocebourc in her land of Lodien (Lothian). On his way there Fergus becomes lost and so comes face to face with the giant of Mont Dolerous, who recognises him by his shield as the murderer of his wife. Fergus disposes of him too, but only after a considerable struggle in which his horse dies. In the giant's castle he finds two ladies who welcome him as their saviour, a giant-child which he drowns in the moat, and, in the cellar, a miraculous horse. The ladies tend his injuries and three days later he is recovered. He tames the horse with a single blow.

From the tower of his new castle Fergus can see Rocebourc in the distance. For a week, in his new persona as Knight of the Shield Beautiful, he wreaks havoc among the besiegers as though he were a hero from the Otherworld, returning to his castle each evening without revealing his identity. The king holds a council of war; as a result his arrogant nephew Artofilaus goes to Galiene and in an insulting manner demands her

surrender. This upsets Galiene; without consulting her council she impulsively offers a
duel of one against two, a decision she immediately regrets. None of her knights is
willing to volunteer. So her maid Arondele goes to Arthur and asks him for a
champion, but all his knights are away looking for Fergus. Lamenting loudly she sets out
for home, and her way takes her past Fergus' castle. He speaks to her, learns of the duel
which is to take place next day, and discovers that Galiene still loves him.

With the king and his nephew claiming victory in default of any opponent, and
Galiene on the point of hurling herself from a tower, Fergus appears. He kills Artofilaus,
defeats the king and sends him via Galiene to Arthur with a vengeful message for Ke.
From what the king says about his conqueror Galiene realises that it was Fergus who
had saved her, but that he still dares not hope for her love.

The king's arrival increases Arthur's regret at Fergus' absence. The search for him
having failed, on Gauvain's advice Arthur decides to organise a great tournament at
Gedeorde around Ascension Day, with a marriage as first prize, in order to lure Fergus
into the open. This ploy proves successful.

As usual Ke insists on having first joust. Fergus easily unhorses him and thus avenges
the indignity inflicted on him. At the end of the day he retreats to his castle. On
subsequent days the other knights of the Round Table fare no better. One by one Fergus
defeats them, all but Perceval. As the tournament is nearing its end Galiene arrives;
with her council's approval she has come to ask Arthur for a husband – the Knight of
the Shield Beautiful. Arthur hesitates; he does not know who this knight is, and
moreover he is avoiding Arthur's court.

Gauvain now arms himself, speaks to Fergus and asks him to go with him to the
king. Fergus is willing, but in exchange asks the other for his name. On learning that he
is dealing with Gauvain Fergus also reveals himself and is then reunited with Arthur.
The latter asks him if he wishes to take Galiene for his wife and become King of Lodien.
Only if it is her own wish, answers Ferguut, whereupon Arthur gives her to him in
marriage. The wedding takes place on the same date as the story had begun, 24 June,
the feast of St John, and they live together long and happily.

We know almost nothing of the author of Le Chevalier au Bel Escu, alias Fergus, save
that in the epilogue he calls himself Guillaume le Clerc. On the basis of his dialect and
his use of the place-names Namur and Dinant he most likely came from the north of
France (Picardy), not far from Wallonia. Certainly he was familiar with the works of
Chrétien de Troyes (d. c.1185). The date of the Fergus can be established only
approximately. The romance was inspired by Chrétien's Conte du Graal, but takes
nothing from the Continuations written by various poets (→ Perceval); for this reason a
date somewhere around 1200 seems justified.

The Fergus is a non-historical Arthurian verse romance written in the style of
Chrétien de Troyes, and thus has a two-phase structure. There are two main themes: 1.
natura-nutritura (nature-nurture) and 2. amour-chevalerie (love-knighthood). The first
concerns Fergus' origins and background. He comes from the backwoods and has been
raised by his father as a 'yokel'. Despite this, the noble nature inherited from his mother
triumphs in the end and he succeeds in becoming the best knight in the world. The
second theme concerns the interaction between love and knighthood: Galiene sees
ahead of time that Fergus is a true knight and falls in love with him, and for love of
Galiene Fergus does indeed become a true knight.

While the Fergus is a very readable work in its own right, it is in essence a literary
reaction to Chrétien's Conte du Graal. This is clear above all from the fact that Fergus'
path to perfect knighthood is analogous to that of Perceval in the Conte du Graal. After
an amorous start to his career, Perceval followed a spiritual road which would
eventually lead him to the mystery of the Grail. Fergus completes what Perceval had
started, save that the object of his quest is profane: a fusion of love and knighthood

which results in marriage and the possession of earthly goods. Guillaume was able to do this because the *Conte du Graal* had remained unfinished. He made Perceval the forerunner of Fergus and presented his *Fergus* as the uncompleted second phase of the *Conte du Graal*. This is why *Fergus* has no prologue but begins on the feast of St John, precursor of Christ, with an episode in which Perceval plays the main part. Guillaume's intention in this was ironic, to outdo his model; he clearly did not care for the spiritual path which Chrétien himself had taken in the *Conte du Graal*.

A further feature of Guillaume's work is the use he makes of Scotland as the setting for his nature/nurture theme. The names of the main character and his father, and of the places involved, are taken from reality; it is possible to follow Fergus' quest on the map. For this reason it was long thought that the *Fergus* was an ancestral romance based on one Fergus of Galloway (d. 1161); but this Scottish thesis has now been rejected. The actualities are all part of Guillaume's literary game. Escoce is not so much Scotland as Escu-land: Shieldland. In this way Guillaume could portray Fergus as a pseudo-historical hero from the sagas.

There are two extant manuscripts of the *Fergus*, both of which date from around 1300. The only literary text in Old French which borrows directly from the *Fergus* is → *Huon de Bordeaux*.

There is a single foreign translation, the Middle Dutch *Ferguut*, which to judge from its language was written in East Flanders, probably in or near the town of Oudenaarde on the Scheldt. On the basis of borrowings from other Old French literary works the *Ferguut* can be dated to around 1250. One curious feature is that Gauvain is here translated as Gawein rather than the usual Walewein. The *Ferguut* has been preserved in a West Brabant manuscript of about 1340 (now in Leiden University Library). A striking feature of this manuscript is that it contains some 250 emendations in a 14th-century hand; the purpose of these is not to correct actual errors, but to give the romance a face-lift – it was, after all, a century old.

One mystery is that the *Ferguut* follows the *Fergus* faithfully up to line 2590, but thereafter takes its own, creative line while retaining the actual plot. For a long time this break was explained by assuming that the translator had written the so-called second part from memory. However, in view of the translator's *ad hoc* approach and the significant differences in language, style and vocabulary, a likelier assumption seems to be that there were two authors: a translator and an adaptor.

WILLEM KUIPER

Editions: De Haan 1974; Rombauts/De Paepe/De Haan 1982; Frescoln 1983.
Translations: Wolf-Bonvin 1990; Owen 1991.
Studies: Kuiper 1989; Zemel 1991.

FIERABRAS is the eponymous hero of a *chanson de geste* written around 1170 which was extremely popular both during the Middle Ages and later. A prologue (a longer version of which also exists as an independent text, *La Destruction de Rome*) relates how Balan, Emir of Spain, and his son Fierabras, King of Alexandria, conquer Rome, kill the Pope and carry off the holy relics – the Crown of Thorns, the nails from the Cross and the board with the inscription, together with the oil with which Christ was anointed. → Charlemagne then comes to Rome's aid. There is a battle between the twelve paladins and the Emir's men, in which Oliver distinguishes himself but is seriously wounded. The paladins have to be rescued by Charlemagne and the older knights. Charles finds this vastly amusing; → Roland in particular is the butt of his mockery, and feels gravely insulted. The Saracens escape to Spain with the relics.

Fierabras slices an opponent in two. Engraving by Gustave Doré, illustration in an 1857 edition of *Fierabras, légende nationale*, translated by M. Mary-Lafon.

The *Fierabras* proper begins with the Saracens back in Spain, pursued by Charles and his army. Fierabras, fifteen feet tall and with a giant's strength, challenges the French: let their boldest man came and fight him. Nobody dares accept; even Roland refuses, because he still feels himself unfairly treated. Eventually the wounded Oliver volunteers. Fierabras sees that his opponent, who does not at first give his name, is in a bad way. The two take a liking to each other, but the fight goes ahead. After a long, hard struggle Oliver is victorious. Fierabras promises to become a Christian. He manages to reach the French camp, but Oliver is captured by Balan. Assorted skirmishes result in the capture of a number of other French prisoners.

The prisoners are locked up together in a tower; there they are helped by Floripas, Balan's daughter and Fierabras' sister, because she is in love with one of them, Gui de Bourgogne. She manages to protect the captives until Charlemagne arrives to release them, at the same time recovering the relics. Balan is defeated. Despite his son's passionate urging, he refuses to accept Christianity and pays for his stubbornness with his life. Floripas is baptised and marries Gui de Bourgogne. Gui and Fierabras are each given half of Spain. Charlemagne returns to France and presents the relics to the abbey of Saint-Denis.

No historical event can be identified with any certainty as the basis for the story of Balan and Fierabras. Historians have mentioned both the siege of Rome by the Saracens in 847 and the battles between Belisarius and the Goths in 537. The story is precisely located within the framework of the 'poetic history of Charlemagne' provided by the *chansons de geste*: the French text twice states that the 'treachery of Roncevaux' occurred three years later. The narrative's most important function is to guarantee the provenance of the relics in the abbey of Saint-Denis.

The story's popularity is evident from the many translations and adaptations of it.

From the 12th century we have a French and an Occitanian *chanson de geste*, which probably go back to a common source. An English version in rhyme, *Sir Ferumbras*, dates from the end of the 14th century. The Italian *Cantare di Fierabraccia e Ulivieri*, in thirteen cantos, survives in an incunable from the late 15th century. A Middle Dutch fragment (13th or 14th century), in which Fierabras is mentioned by name, describes how he, in company with Elegast and Roland's father Milon, resists a large Saracen force. Elegast is possessed of magical powers. It is uncertain, however, whether this is a version of a Fierabras story.

A few French chronicles use the *Chanson de Fierabras* as source material; the most important of these are the *Chronique rimée* by Philippe Mousket (mid-13th century) and David Aubert's *Croniques et conquestes de Charlemaine* (1458). The author of the Dutch chapbook *Den droefliken strijt van Roncevale* must also have made use of the *Fierabras*.

There are two other French prose versions as well as David Aubert's: one in a 15th-century manuscript which is anonymous and one by Jean Bagnyon of Lausanne, the oldest print of which is an incunable of 1489. A German chapbook of 1533, *Eyn schoene kurtzweilige histori von eym maechtigen Riesen auss Hispanien, Fierrabras genannt [...]*, was reprinted as late as 1809 and may have been the source for Schubert's 1823 opera *Fierrabras* (libretto by Josef Kupelwieser) which through the efforts of Claudio Abbado had its world première in Vienna in 1988.

In Spain the story does not appear until fairly late. Around 1528 Nicola of Piamonte included it in his *Historia del emperador Carlomagno y de los doce pares de Francia*, a prose rendering of several French epic texts. Cervantes alludes to the Fierabras episode in this text in *Don Quixote*, and it provided Calderon de la Barca with the material for his play *La Puenta de Mantible* (1635). Here the emphasis is on the love-affair between Floripas and Gui; all reference to Rome and the relics is omitted, and the fight in which Fierabras is defeated and welcomed by the French takes place only at the end of the piece. In the 18th century the Spanish popular poet Juan José Lopez used the material in some *romances* (ballads). The story still survives today, in a modified form, in puppet theatres in Wallonia.

In 1857 Gustave Doré produced twelve engravings as illustrations to *Fierabras, légende nationale*, a translation of the Occitanian *chanson de geste* by M. Mary-Lafon.

C. HOGETOORN

Edition: Kroeber/Servois 1860.
Studies: Bédier 1908–13; Doutrepont 1939.

FLAMENCA, 'the flaming one', is the heroine of an anonymous Occitanian verse romance of the 13th century. She is the remarkably beautiful and highly cultured daughter of the Count of Nemours. The narrative begins with her marriage to Archambaut of Bourbon, celebrated with brilliant festivities first in her home city and then at Archambaut's court. The attention which the King of France shows the bride out of courtesy provokes the queen's jealousy; and she in turn kindles Archambaut's suspicions. Archambaut turns into the awful example of the jealous husband; he locks up his wife and loses all care for himself. From a courtly nobleman he becomes a wild man with ungroomed hair and beard, long dirty nails and filthy clothing. Flamenca is allowed to leave their residence only to attend church, where she has to sit in an enclosed gallery, or to visit the bath-house, where her husband checks the room before and after her bath and stands guard outside the closed door while she bathes. Her only solace is the companionship of her maids Alis and Marguerite, who share her confinement.

Flamenca's cruel fate comes to the ears of the young nobleman Guilhem of Nevers. He falls in love with Flamenca without ever having set eyes on her and devises a stratagem for making contact with her. An intelligent lad, he possesses the qualities not only of a good knight but also of a cleric. He presents himself in Bourbon in the guise of an acolyte. During Mass every Sunday and holy day it is then his duty to offer 'pax' to Flamenca in her box, i.e. to proffer her the Holy Book to kiss. During this brief procedure it is possible for just one of them to speak a few words. On 7 May Guilhem begins the conversation with the one word 'Alas'. A week later Flamenca asks him 'Why the lament?' Over the course of twenty Masses Guilhem succeeds in declaring his love for Flamenca, winning her for himself and arranging an assignation with her. Meanwhile, he has rented a room in the building which also houses the public bath and has had a secret tunnel dug from it to the room where Flamenca bathes. Thus he is able to meet his beloved.

In her happiness Flamenca's attitude to her husband changes: she treats him with contempt. When he asks the reason for this, she tells him that since their wedding he has changed from a courtly, universally respected man into a common boor. Archambaud realises that his wife is right and that he must change his behaviour. At his request she promises that if released she will comport herself as well as she had done when confined. This 'sophistry', as the poet calls it, leaves her free to continue her liaison with Guilhem. Yet she asks Guilhem to go away and make a name for himself competing in tournaments. This he does, with the result that Archambaud, who has also resumed a knightly way of life, encounters Guilhem and becomes friendly with him. The last episode we have of the romance describes a tourney at Bourbon, at which Guilhem and Flamenca find the opportunity to continue their covert liaison.

The romance is in accordance with the code of courtly love, with such motifs as 'amour lointain' (falling in love with somebody one has never met), the ridiculing of marital jealousy and exaltation of courtly qualities, particularly those which spring from intelligence and tact. The author was well up in the literature of his day; he made use of, among other things, the first part of the *Roman de la Rose* (the part written by Guillaume de Lorris). There is, however, nothing to indicate that his story exercised any influence in its turn. Only one manuscript of it has survived, of which the beginning and the end are missing, as are a few pages in the middle. It may have been because of the frivolous use of the Mass to promote an adulterous love that this story, despite its considerable merits, elicited no greater response in a Southern France then dominated by the Inquisition; while the language in which it was written, Occitanian, would have been an obstacle to any possible success elsewhere.

C. HOGETOORN

Editions: Lavaud/Nelli 1960; Hubert/Porter 1962.

FLORIS AND BLANCHEFLEUR (in Old French: Floire & Blancheflor) are the hero and heroine of a little love story written around the middle of the 12th century by an unknown Old French poet, probably somewhere in the Loire valley. The tale must have become popular quite early on: the Provençal countess Beatrix de Dia, who probably died before 1171, wrote a love-song in which she compared her feelings for her beloved, Count Raimbaut, with Blancheflor's for her Floire.

The oldest extant version of the story, the so-called 'version aristocratique', goes as follows. The Mohammedan King of Spain attacks a group of French pilgrims on a penitential pilgrimage to the shrine of Santiago de Compostela in Northern Spain.

Among his captives is an extremely pregnant Christian noblewoman; he gives her as a companion to his consort, who is also expecting. Both women have their babies on the same day. The infidel queen gives birth to a son, the Christian lady to a daughter. Because they were born on the Christian festival of Palm Sunday (Old French *pasques florie*) the children are given the names of flowers. The Moslem prince is called Floire (Floris) after the best-loved flower of all, the rose. For the Christian slave-child they choose the name Blancheflor (Blanchefleur), meaning 'white flower' (lily).

The children grow up together, are educated together and from their earliest youth they are devoted to each other, to the great displeasure of Floire's father, who for reasons of rank and religion has no intention of letting his son marry the girl. He sends Floire away to a school in far-off Montoire (Montoro in Andalusia?) and sells the beautiful Blancheflor to slave dealers who take her to Babylon. There she is sold to the emir for his harem. Separated from his sweetheart, Floire pines away; eventually he returns to the parental palace. His parents lie to him, saying that his darling has died while he was away. To give verisimilitude to this story the king has had a splendid tomb constructed for Blancheflor. When in utter despair Floire threatens to kill himself, they at last tell him the truth. Young Floire resolves to go, unarmed and with only a few retainers, and rescue his beloved from the emir's harem.

After a trouble-free voyage Floire, passing as a merchant, reaches the port of Baudas (Baghdad?). Here he finds lodging in the home of a sympathetic citizen, with whom Blancheflor had also stayed on her way to Babylon. Floire now knows that he is on the right track and after a brief stop in Monfelix he too reaches Babylon. The city's amiable bridgekeeper, Darius by name, offers him a temporary home. He provides Floire, who knows nothing of local conditions, with more information about the harem tower where Blancheflor is held. Rescuing her will not be easy, for the entrance to the harem is guarded by heavily armed soldiers. Darius also tells the astonished Floire about the strange ways of the Oriental despot who has his lady-love in hold. Each year he chooses a new wife, but only after subjecting the ladies of the harem to a chastity test. One by one they have to walk along by a stream, which remains clear if the lady concerned is virtuous. But if one of them has behaved unchastely, the placid stream undergoes a change. It is as though its surface is whipped up by an unseen hand. The guilty lady is thus exposed and is ruthlessly hurled into the flames. To his horror Floire discovers that this year the emir has selected Blancheflor as his consort.

The bridge-keeper suggests a stratagem which will enable Floire to outwit the guardian of the harem. Floire is to attract the guard's attention by taking measurements of the harem tower. He must pretend to be a Western architect who wishes to build a similar tower when he returns to his own country. Floire must also ask the guard if he feels like a game of chess. The stake should be a quantity of gold which Floire, even if he wins, should give to the grasping Oriental. The trick works perfectly. The guard's head is turned by the large sums pressed on him by our hero even though he lost the game, and he is happy to become Floire's vassal. It is now his duty to assist the young man, his new lord. He arranges for Floire to enter the harem unobserved, hidden in a basket of flowers. There is a brief panic when the porters deliver the basket to the wrong room, but Blancheflor's friend, the faithful Claris, realises what has happened and ensures that Floire reaches his beloved undiscovered. In Blancheflor's room Floire finds a congenial and – at first – safe refuge.

For some weeks Floire lives secretly in the Babylon harem-tower, happily reunited with his love. Then one day Blancheflor oversleeps in her lover's arms and fails to perform her domestic duties. One of the emir's men goes to investigate and discovers the two young people together in bed. Informed of this treachery, the emir is furious. The intruder Floire is sentenced to death. But during their trial, and in the face of death, the lovers demonstrate their love. Each seeks to sacrifice him/herself for the other. At the sight of such unselfish loyalty the emir at the last moment allows mercy to

Floire plays chess with the guard. Pen drawing from the studio of Diebolt Lauber at Hagenau (Alsace), 1430–1440, in a 15th-century German manuscript of the romance by Konrad Fleck. Heidelberg, University Library.

prevail over justice. Floire is even allowed to marry Blancheflor (the emir himself takes Blancheflor's friend Claris to wife). The young couple return to Spain, where Floire converts to Christianity. Our hero becomes King of Spain. Floire and Blancheflor have a daughter called Berta (→ Berte), later to be the mother of Charlemagne. And they lived happily ever after.

Thus the earliest version of the romance (the 'version aristocratique'), of which only three complete manuscripts and one fragment survive; an adaptation of it written in France around 1200 has become known as the 'popular' version. In this version the idyllic naïvety of the original redaction is played down. There is more scope for knightly combat and feats of gallantry and strength. For example, in Babylon Floire is able to save himself from death at the stake by a victory in the lists.

Yet the material became known in Northern Europe mainly through the older redaction, which was translated into many languages within a short time of its composition. The oldest foreign-language version (written around 1170) comes from the Maasland area, probably from somewhere around Roermond. This redaction would thus have been produced by an early contemporary and fellow-countryman of the renowned Hendrik van Veldeke; alas, only 368 badly mutilated lines of it survive. Despite this, the fragments of this version, known as the *Trierse Floyris* after its present home (the Municipal Library in Trier), are of great importance. They prove that the Limburg cultural area played a significant role in the early reception of French narrative material. It is noteworthy that this version mentions a certain 'greve bernhard' who does not appear in the French redaction. Since this count plays a positive part in freeing the children, was the poet here inserting a reference to his patron? We may also wonder whether such interest in a story about the lives of Charlemagne's grandparents, in an area so close to Aachen, might be connected with the fact that the Emperor Charles was canonised in 1165.

The 13th century saw the appearance not only of the *Trierse Floyris*, but of many other West European versions in, among others, Middle High German (Konrad Fleck, c.1220), Middle Dutch (Diederic van Assenede, c.1250), Middle English (*Floris and Blauncheflur*, c.1250) and Old Norse (*Flóres Saga ok Blankiflúr*, c.1300). The 'popular' version of the Floris story proved particularly successful in Southern Europe, where we find Spanish, Italian and even Byzantine versions. Boccaccio, too, rewrote the story in his *Filocolo*, which then became the (indirect) source for the comedy *Florio mit der Bianceffora* (1551) by the German 'Meistersänger' Hans Sachs. In Yiddish narrative tradition the tale of Floris is known as *Flere Blankeflere*. When we consider that the Floris material was heard (and read) from the far North of Europe (Scandinavia) to the far South (Greece), it may fairly be described as a medieval best-seller.

Naturally, scholars have wondered where the poet of the oldest, 'idyllic' version found his material. There are two views on this, which could be termed the 'eastern' and 'western' theories. According to supporters of the former, the Floris material would be of oriental, more specifically of 'Arabian' origin. Many motifs in our story seem explicable only in terms of an Arab background: the harem tower is called *tor as puceles* (maidens' tower), there are armed eunuchs in Babylon, each lady in the harem has her own room – all details then unknown in the West. The emir's cruel custom of killing his wife every year is strongly reminiscent of the framing story of the *Thousand and One Nights*. But medieval Arab literature contains no story which, taken as a whole, seems a plausible candidate for the source of the Floris narrative. We may note, however, that the Floris romance displays a structure (shared youth, separation, reunion) which is also a regular feature of late Hellenistic narratives.

Supporters of the 'western' theory, on the other hand, regard the correspondences between our tale and the East as too superficial to indicate a direct descent. They regard the Floris romance as an original French creation, composed using contemporary literary and eschatological material. The oriental elements which are indubitably present would have been added to the tale to provide 'local colour'.

One may wonder what function the Floris romance fulfilled at the time it was written (1150–60). One striking fact is that the story is set against the background of a political situation which would be instantly recognisable to the French audience of the day. At that time, after all, most of Spain was in Arab hands. Only in Northern Spain could small Christian border states survive, which then expanded southwards – taking advantage of disputes among the Arab princes – over the course of the Middle Ages. While the Christian *Reconquista* (Reconquest) was in reality still going on progress, the Floris story provided the struggle with a ready-made 'fictional' legitimation. For Floire, son of the Moslem King of Spain, had already converted to Christianity; and therefore Charlemagne, his grandson, had a legitimate claim to the Spanish throne.

In the late Middle Ages, the Floris story attracted interest. The invention of printing made it possible to reach a broader public, and to satisfy the demand for entertaining reading the printers began to bring out prose versions of the old medieval verse narratives. The oldest known Floris chapbook from the Low Countries was published by the printer Jan van Doesburg, probably around 1517. The tale of Floris and his beloved continued to be extremely popular in the Low Countries, despite the fact that the religious authorities took exception to, in particular, the 'immoral' bed scene.

The tenor of the story chang+ed completely over time. While in the Middle Ages it had been the true love of Floris and Blanchefleur that was esteemed, now the central theme is not the worldly love of the youthful protagonists, but the love of God; thus we read in the prologue to the chapbook published in 1642 by Ot Barentsz. Smient of Amsterdam: 'Therefore you young people, whether men or women, take instruction from this, and let yourselves be drawn to this moral tale, and be receptive to the affection and love of God which will endure eternally [...].' In Germany we know of chapbooks which offered a prose form of Konrad Fleck's version of the Floris story. In the early 19th century, a period characterised by a great interest in medieval themes, there was a brief revival of interest in Floris and Blanchefleur, particularly in Germany. In 1822 F. Koreff reworked the story into a (little-known) opera. August von Platen even made a play of it which he entitled *Treue um Treue*, but which quickly fell into oblivion. From the turn of the twentieth century dates a symphonic poem by the Swedish composer Wilhelm Stenhammer, inspired by a text by Oscar Levertin: *Florez och Blanzeflor* (*Edition:* Mak 1965).

J.H. WINKELMAN

Translation: Leclanche 1986.
Studies: Winkelman 1977; Grieve 1997.

GALAHAD is the Grail knight *par excellence* of Arthurian literature, the shining example of knighthood in the service of God as preached in, most notably, the *Queste del Saint Graal* (1215–35). The Grail was introduced into the Arthurian cycle by Chrétien de Troyes, who in his unfinished *Conte du Graal ou Perceval* makes his eponymous hero → Perceval the first of Arthur's knights to behold the Grail. After Chrétien the Grail was incorporated into the Christian redemption story by Robert de Boron; according to him the Grail is the cup from the Last Supper, in which also the blood of the crucified Christ was caught by → Joseph of Arimathea. In this respect the *Queste del Saint Graal* follows Robert de Boron. Faced with the existing Grail knight Perceval, the author of the *Queste* decided to introduce a new Grail hero: Galahad, the perfect knight who outdoes Perceval in chastity, piety and unfailing achievement.

Galahad – whose name is a mystical designation of Christ taken from the Bible (Numbers 26, 29) – is the offspring of → Lancelot's extramarital relations with the daughter of the Grail-King Pelles; on his mother's side he is descended from Joseph of Arimathea and King David. Even at his conception a great future is predicted for him. Galahad is brought up in the Grail Castle until he is old enough to undertake the Grail quest recounted in the *Queste del Saint Graal*. The exceptionally comely youth is dubbed knight by his father Lancelot shortly before he arrives at Arthur's court at Whitsuntide in the year 450 after Christ's Resurrection. His arrival is accompanied by numerous portents. A sign on the 'Siege Perilous' at the Round Table, a seat reminiscent of that vacated by Judas at the Last Supper, declares that Galahad will sit there, while a stone with a sword in it drifts by with the message that only the best knight will be able to pull the sword out. Galahad draws the sword from the stone and takes his place in the Siege Perilous. At a subsequent gathering of the Round Table the Holy Grail suddenly floats into the hall. Those present are not granted a clear view of the holy object – it is covered with a white cloth – but it does provide them all with the most marvellous food. When it then vanishes again Gauvain (→ Gawain) calls on everyone there to go in search of it: the Quest of the Holy Grail has begun.

Although all 150 members of the Round Table take part in the quest, only three of them, chaste and pious knights, are successful: Galahad, Lancelot's youngest cousin Bohort (Bors) and Perceval. The latter two have a few moments of weakness, for instance in the matter of chastity; they are thus tested much more severely than the spotless Galahad, who sails effortlessly through the adventures which have been awaiting him since the days of Joseph of Arimathea and the coming of the Grail to Britain. For example, Galahad acquires a white shield with a red cross marked on it in the blood of Josephé, the son of Joseph of Arimathea. Josephé himself had foretold that the shield would belong to Galahad, who like his father Lancelot would be a descendant of Nascien, one of Josephé's companions. Galahad also proves to be the chosen one who will take up the sword which lies in a ship built by King Solomon on a special bed made from the wood of the Tree of Life which grew in Eden.

Eventually Bohort and Perceval, together with Galahad, discover the Grail at Corbenic. There they acquire the companionship of nine other knights and of Josephé, who is transported to the Grail Castle by angels. Josephé leads the twelve Elect in a mass which seems to be a repetition of the Last Supper. The Grail appears uncovered and the companions behold the miracle of transsubstantiation. In addition, a figure with wounds on its hands, feet and body (Christ with the stigmata?) appears from the holy dish and commands Galahad to take Perceval, Bohort and the Grail and sail to the city of Sarras in Solomon's ship. In Sarras Galahad is granted full understanding of the mystery of the Grail. After beholding this indescribable wonder he asks God to take him up into Heaven, and his soul is carried thither by angels. The Grail then immediately floats away to Heaven, never to return. Perceval decides to become a hermit. After Perceval's death Bohort, the only remaining Grail knight, returns to Arthur's court to report these marvellous events.

In the *Queste* Galahad is described as the long-awaited saviour, the new Christ in knightly form. The many adventures connected with the Grail, already attempted in vain by many knights, are successfully completed by him and the other two Grail knights, so that what is left at the beginning of the *Mort le roi Artu* is an Arthurian world empty of adventures. And with Galahad the ideal of the 'divine' knight also disappears from Arthur's world, which will be destroyed by its own, earthly shortcomings (such as the Queen's adultery). In the *Lancelot-Queste-Mort Artu* the new ideal does not lead to a new and lasting meaning to knighthood, as one might have expected if the text had been intended as a stimulus to, for instance, the crusade mentality. Religious ideas, especially those of the Cistercians, certainly influenced the text and the ideal of the chaste warrior of God put forward in it, but it is not (yet) entirely clear to what extent the work was intended to provide a model for its noble, knightly audience.

As the bearer of an ideal, the character of Galahad in the *Queste* is infallible. He is the virgin Christian knight, the perfect chosen one who effortlessly succeeds in all his predestined adventures. Full of (self)confidence he relies on God's hand to direct him on his road to the Grail castle and to Sarras. He seems to be

'Sir Galahad', painting by George Frederick Watts, 1862. Cambridge, Mass., Fogg Art Museum.

without doubt or fear, and for the modern reader this makes him in some respects less interesting as a character. Because of this lack of development and of any tragic element Galahad has been described as 'a cardboard saint'.

While the narrative tradition regarding the Grail-hero Perceval contains all kinds of differing versions, throughout the Middle Ages the tale of Galahad and the Grail always adheres closely to the account in the *Queste*; as, for instance, in Sir Thomas Malory's *Tale of the Sangrail* (books XIII–XVII of his *Morte d'Arthur*, published by William Caxton in 1485). Through Malory the Galahad material was also taken up from time to time in later centuries, among others by Tennyson (e.g. in the poem 'Sir Galahad', which in the 1830s greatly influenced such artists as Edward Burne-Jones). In Tennyson's 'The Holy Grail' (1869, later included in the *Idylls of the King*) the hermit Sir Percivale tells of the Grail quest which he undertook in company with Galahad. In this text too Galahad is the shining example, but the poet seems to be more interested in the more dramatic adventures of Sir Percivale and Sir Lancelot. In William Wordsworth's 'The Egyptian Maid; or The Romance of the Water Lily' (begun 1828, published 1835) Galahad's touch rouses the eponymous heroine from death. Wiliam Morris gives Galahad a leading role in his poems 'Sir Galahad: A Christmas Mystery' and 'The Chapel in Lyonesse' in the volume *King Arthur's Tomb* (1858). In the 20th century, too, there have been poems about Galahad, including 'The Coming of Sir Galahad and a Vision of the Grail' (1917) by Alfred Graves, 'Galahad, Knight who Perished' (1923) by Vachel Lindsay and 'Galahad in the Castle of Maidens' (1911) by Sara Teasdale.

From the second half of the 19th century there have been many paintings of Galahad as the pure and exalted knight, particularly by Pre-Raphaelites such as Dante Gabriel Rossetti, who painted 'Sir Galahad at the Ruined Chapel' (1859, City Museum and Art Gallery, Birmingham) and 'How Sir Galahad, Sir Bors and Sir Percival Were Fed with the Sanc Grael' (1864, Tate Gallery, London), and Arthur Hughes, who painted 'Sir Galahad: The Quest of the Holy Grail' (1870, Walker Art Gallery, Liverpool). Around 1880 Sir Joseph Noel Paton depicted 'Sir Galahad's Vision of the Sangreal' (private collection, England) under a sky full of Victorian angels. George Frederick Watts repeatedly took Galahad as his subject between 1862 and 1903; his finest 'Sir Galahad' is the one in Harvard University's Fogg Art Museum in Cambridge (Mass.) The same museum now houses Edward Burne-Jones' 'Sir Galahad', painted in 1858. Burne-Jones designed stained glass windows on the Grail quest, and in 1891–94 he chose 'The Arrival of Sir Galahad to take his place in the Siege Perilous' as the subject of one of the tapestries woven in the workshops of William Morris for Stanmore Hall and now in the Duke of Westminster's collection. Galahad is the central figure in a series of wall-paintings in Boston Public Library, painted between 1890 and 1901 by Edwin Austin and furnished with an accompanying text by S. Baxter (*The Legend of the Holy Grail*, 1904).

The paintings and carved panels based on Malory's work in the Queen's Robing Room in the Palace of Westminster can be seen as foreshadowing the work of the Pre-Raphaelites. Among William Dyce's contributions there is the fresco 'Religion: The Vision of Sir Galahad and his Company' (1851), while H.H. Armstead's carvings include 'Sir Galahad's Soul Borne to Heaven'.

Mainly in and through the work of the Pre-Raphaelites, Galahad became a symbol of intense, dedicated striving and sacrifice for a lofty ideal. For instance, a stained glass window designed by Veronica Whall in 1931 depicts just such an exalted-looking Galahad. In 1905 E.W. Keyser used the figure of Galahad to symbolise self-sacrifice in the statue of a man who drowned while trying to rescue a girl; the statue was erected in Wellington Street in Ottawa. In the same way Galahad also appears on memorials to the dead of the two World Wars. In Charles Williams' 1938 poetry cycle *Taliessin Through Logres* Galahad is the purest of knights, a symbol of the new man. In modern versions of Galahad's story the Grail may still be a religious symbol, as in Williams, but it may also represent the heart's desire of the main character, whatever that may be. In the adventure film INDIANA JONES AND THE LAST CRUSADE (Steven Spielberg, 1988) the Grail bestows eternal life, while the hero of Terry Gilliam's film THE FISHER KING (1991) finds through the Grail a new love and earthly happiness. Even the cup awarded for the men's singles championship at Wimbledon is known as 'the Grail'. We find the same idea in *The Grail: A Novel* (1963) by Babs H. Deal, where the Grail stands for a perfect season in American college football, and the film KID GALAHAD (US 1937, directed by Michael Curtiz with Edward G. Robinson, Humphrey Bogart and Bette Davis), in which the eponymous hero is a young boxer.

In the 20th century we also find Galahad in retellings of Malory such as the children's book *The Light Beyond the Forest. The Quest for the Holy Grail* (1979) by Rosemary Sutcliff, and in novels such as *Galahad: Enough of His Life to Explain His Reputation* (1926) by John Erskine and *Galahad, Knight Errant* (1907) by Mary E. Southworth. A special case is *Too Bad Galahad* by Matt Cohen, a novel in which Galahad is a failure: he is a failed schoolmaster, a dragon-slayer who is gobbled up by the dragon and a Grail knight who does not recognise the Grail until just before he dies. There are plays devoted to Galahad – *The Birth of Galahad* (1898) by Richard Hovey, and Gerhart

Hauptmann's *Galahad* (unfinished, 1908–1914) – as well as an opera (Rutland Boughton, *Galahad*). In 1985 the British Post Office issued four stamps designed by Yvonne Gilbert depicting scenes from the Arthurian legends. The highest denomination stamp (34p) shows Sir Galahad kneeling, looking up in adoration at a beam of light.
FRANK BRANDSMA

Translation: Matarasso 1969.
Studies: Lot-Borodine 1979; Whitaker 1990; Lacy et al. 1996.

G AWAIN, eldest son of King Lot of Orkney, King → Arthur's nephew and, with → Lancelot, the most important knight of Arthur's Round Table, also appears in medieval literature as Gauvain, Gawein, Gawan, Walwanus, Walewein and Gwalchmai. He is the hero of one of the finest medieval Arthurian romances, the *Walewein*, written by the Flemish poets Penninc and Pieter Vostaert in the middle years of the 13th century. The plot of the romance derives from a well-known folktale (the Golden Bird). King Arthur promises his realm to the knight who brings back to him a magical flying chessboard which had floated into the hall but had flown away shortly afterwards. Walewein, riding out after it, has to achieve a series of interlocking quests in order to obtain it. In the end he returns to the court with the chess-board and the beautiful princess Ysabele. Pieter Vostaert, who completed Penninc's unfinished text, refuses to offer an opinion on whether Walewein married Ysabele and eventually became King Arthur's successor.

The poets see Walewein as a hero without parallel for courtesy and valour. The same positive judgment is also apparent in the epithet he is given in some Middle Dutch Arthurian romances: 'father of adventures'. This epithet probably originated in very early, still purely oral, Low Countries Arthurian literature. Even at this early date he must have been an admirable knight, as witness the fact that we find Flemish nobles bearing his name – and that of Ywein (→ Yvain) – from the beginning of the 12th century.

Gawain's predecessor in Welsh literature, Gwalchmai, appears in the extant version of → *Culhwch ac Olwen*; like Cei (→ Kay) he is one of Culhwch's highly talented helpers in his efforts to win Olwen. Of Gwalchmai it is said that he is Arthur's nephew, and never returns home without having completed a quest; he is also the best runner and horseman. Elsewhere in Welsh literature he has the nickname 'dafod aur' (the golden-tongued), a reference to his skill with words. In line with this, in the great majority of medieval Arthurian romances the king's nephew expresses himself in extremely courtly language. The curious name of his trusty steed, Gringalet, also seems to come from the Welsh tradition, where Gwalchmai's horse is called Kein Calet (hard back).

Around 1136 Geoffrey of Monmouth completed his *Historia regum Britannie* (History of the Kings of Britain), one of the most influential books of the Middle Ages. In this Latin chronicle Arthur's nephew is called Gualguanus; he is one of the king's chief counsellors and also commands his army. According to Geoffrey he was killed in Arthur's war with Mordred. An earlier Latin chronicle, William of Malmesbury's *Gesta regum Anglorum* (Deeds of the Kings of the English, c.1125), relates that the grave of Arthur's nephew Walwen was discovered during the reign of William the Conqueror.

In Old French Arthurian literature the character of Gauvain is progressively deval-ued. In Chrétien de Troyes' first verse romance, → *Erec et Enide* (c.1165), Gauvain is portrayed as positively as in Geoffrey of Monmouth. He first appears in the romance as Arthur's wise counsellor, and it is stressed throughout the work that he is the embodi-ment of many virtues, such as valour and courtesy. In the *Chevalier de la Charrette* (c.1180, → Lancelot) he is again an admirable knight, though here he is surpassed by

Gawain (Walewein) pursuing the chessboard. Miniature in the *Walewein*
manuscript, 1350. Leiden, Universiteitsbibliotheek.

Lancelot, with whom he is searching for the kidnapped queen. While Lancelot, spurred
on by his love for Arthur's wife, succeeds in crossing the terrible Sword Bridge, Gauvain
fails at the rather less dangerous Underwater Bridge and is barely saved from drowning.
Lancelot thus appears superior to Gauvain; but this is explained by his love for the
queen, which makes him incomparably brave. Nowhere in the romance is any doubt
cast on Gauvain's qualities.

The hero of Chrétien's → *Yvain* (c.1180) is also compared with Gauvain who, as in the foregoing romances, is a friend of the protagonist. In the course of the work it becomes apparent that Gauvain's character is not entirely faultless. For instance, his advice to Yvain to leave his young wife for a while to attend tournaments says little for his wisdom; Yvain's absence costs him dear. On top of this, at the end of the romance Gauvain fights a judicial duel with Yvain on behalf of a lady who is patently in the wrong. Gauvain's role on these occasions seems to foreshadow his performance in Chrétien's last work, the → *Perceval* (c.1190). In this unfinished romance the comparison between Gauvain and Perceval, the yokel who wants to become a knight, initially favours Arthur's nephew, the great knight who knows exactly how things should be done. But Perceval learns quickly, and when later in the work Gauvain leads him with courteous words to Arthur's camp Perceval – now a powerful knight engrossed in thoughts of love – is aware of the rules of the game; the two knights now seem to be equals. In the last part of the story Gauvain goes downhill: while Perceval, who learns to understand and appreciate spiritual values, heads for success in his search for the Grail, it looks as if Gauvain will fail in a series of adventures which lack any logical sequence and have all manner of negative consequences for him. True, he passes the test of the perilous magic bed, and so saves a castle, but then he can no longer leave that castle. Gauvain, the representative of the courtly Arthurian world, has to cede pride of place to Perceval, the outsider who is alive to spiritual values.

For some medieval poets the unfinished *Perceval* posed an irresistible challenge: within a fairly short time the romance acquired four sequels, each following on the other. Each of these continuations gives a different picture of Gauvain. In the first and second, both written before 1200, the portrayal of Arthur's nephew conforms with that in Chrétien: he is an outstanding knight, but with limitations, and when it comes to the Grail Quest he fails. A new element is his activity as a skirt-chaser – an aspect of his character which receives a fair amount of attention in the third continuation, written around 1230 by Gerbert de Montreuil. In the fourth and last continuation, also c.1230, the poet Manessier takes a softer line than Gerbert with Gauvain: although the Grail is not for him, he is again Arthur's finest knight and the paragon of many virtues.

Of the other post-Chrétien Arthurian verse romances in Old French, most take a critical view of Gauvain. In some of them the writers play on his reputation as a lover. A good example is the romance *Le chevalier à l'épée*, written shortly before 1200, in which Gauvain stays overnight with a nobleman who orders his daughter to share the hero's bed. Although both would dearly like to make love, a magic sword hanging above them makes it impossible – as soon as Gauvain tries to touch the girl the sword strikes him. Thus we see the great lover hopelessly frustrated, unable to indulge his desires. There is a similar situation in *Le chevalier aux deux épées*, also known as *Mériadeuc*, a romance written in the second quarter of the 13th century. In this work Gauvain finds himself at one point in bed with a girl who is so impressed by Gauvain's reputation that she will make love with no one else. Alas for our hero, she rejects his advances because, never having met him before, she refuses to believe that her bedmate really is Gauvain.

Raoul, the poet of *La Vengeance Raguidel* (c.1220), goes a step further and writes a real anti-Gauvain romance. Here Arthur's nephew is made to look ridiculous as a knight when he sallies forth to avenge Raguidel's death but forgets to take with him the lance-head he had taken from the dead man's body, an item vital to his purpose, and has to return empty-handed to Arthur's court half-way through the tale in order to collect it. His reputation as a lover also suffers in the *Vengeance Raguidel*. He meets the beautiful Ydain and promptly falls in love with her. Ydain, however, seems not over-impressed by his expertise as a lover. When at a particular moment she has to choose between Gauvain and an unknown knight whom they encounter while he is urinating against a hedge, she chooses the stranger – because, the narrator suggests, she had caught a glimpse of his noble parts.

While the poets of Old French Arthurian verse romances rarely do more than explore Gauvain's comic possibilities, those who write such romances in prose often take a sternly critical line with him. The author of the *Suite-Vulgate du Merlin* (c.1230), a romance translated into Middle Dutch by Lodewijk van Velthem (the *Merlijn* continuation of 1326), is an exception: he gives an markedly favourable account of the youthful deeds of Gauvain and his brothers in support of the newly-crowned Arthur. In contrast, the prose cycle *Lancelot en prose – Queste del Saint Graal – Mort le roi Artu* (1215–35) condemns him as the leading representative of worldly norms and values, which are viewed as reprehensible when set against the background of a chivalry based on religious values; here Gauvain is an unrepentant sinner who fails in the Grail Quest. Thus he and Hector are barred from entering a perilous churchyard; the adventure that awaits there is for → Lancelot alone. Moreover, in the course of his quest he kills many other knights of the Round Table. In *Mort le roi Artu* his vindictiveness even drives him to enter the lists against Lancelot, once his closest friend. In the *Tristan en prose* (c.1230) Gauvain's degradation is complete: he is portrayed as an unprincipled rogue who does not shrink from murder and rape.

English literature of the medieval period can boast one truly outstanding Gawain romance: *Sir Gawain and the Green Knight*, a gem of medieval narrative which was probably written in the last quarter of the 14th century. The story begins with a strange, gigantic knight, dressed all in green, turning up at a feast at Arthur's court. He issues a challenge to the Round Table: one of those present may smite him with an axe, provided that the Green Knight may return the compliment in a year's time. Gawain shows himself the bravest of Arthur's knights. He accepts the challenge and strikes off the Green Knight's head. To the court's amazement, the knight does not fall dead; he picks up his head, mounts his horse and tells Gawain to meet him in a year's time at the Green Chapel.

When the year is nearly up Gawain sets out, leaving the court bewailing the loss of the world's finest knight. After a long and perilous journey he comes to a splendid castle, where he is made welcome by a nobleman, his beautiful wife and an old lady. Gawain learns that he can stay at the castle until the appointed day, for his host tells him that the Green Chapel lies close by. The nobleman then makes a proposal: he will give Gawain whatever game he kills next day if in return Gawain gives him anything he has come by that day in the castle. Gawain agrees. Next morning, while the host is out hunting, his wife comes to Gawain's bedchamber and tries to seduce him. Gawain deflects her advances with courtly phrases, and finally she kisses him and leaves. When the nobleman returns from hunting he and Gawain exchange their booty: Gawain gets some venison and gives the nobleman a kiss. They agree to continue the arrangement.

Next morning the same thing happens: the nobleman goes hunting and his wife attempts to seduce Gawain. At the end of the day Gawain receives the flesh of a wild boar, killed with great difficulty, and gives the nobleman two kisses received from his would-be seductress. On the third day the nobleman catches a fox; his wife gives Gawain three kisses and a girdle of green silk which makes its wearer invulnerable. At the exchange Gawain keeps the girdle, contrary to the agreement, thinking it could save his life when he meets the Green Knight.

On the following day a guide takes Gawain, wearing the girdle, to the Green Chapel, where the Green Knight has an enormous axe ready honed. Gawain offers him his neck. Twice the Green Knight swings the axe but checks his stroke at the last moment; the third time he gives Gawain only a slight cut. The Green Knight, who turns out to be Gawain's host, then explains the reason for the three blows. They reflect the way in which Gawain had kept his agreement with the nobleman: twice entirely honourably, the third time less so. Gawain is deeply ashamed. The Green Knight introduces himself as Bertilak de Hautdesert and explains that he was acting on the instructions of Morgan la Fay (the old lady in the castle), who had learned magical arts from her former lover, the magician → Merlin. Morgan, Arthur's half-sister and Gawain's aunt, had wanted to test the reputation of Arthur's court by means of the Green Knight's challenge. Gawain returns to court, where he gives an accurate account of his adventure. He is joyfully received, with no complaints at his slight lapse in honour.

It is evident from the many romances devoted to him that Gawain was an exceptionally popular figure in Middle English literature. In these narratives Gawain, like the Middle Dutch Walewein, is almost always the faultless hero. One exception to this rule is Sir Thomas Malory's *Morte d'Arthur* (c.1470). Malory follows certain of his sources, the Old French prose romances, in giving a portrait of Gawain which is not invariably positive: we are constantly reminded that even an influential and valiant knight is far from perfect and is capable of failing.

Sir Gawain and the Green Knight is not the only English Gawain text to contain a trial by decapitation. It is found, for example, in three short tales of about 550 lines each, all written about 1500: *The Carle off Carlile* (a later version of *Syre Gawene and the Carle of Carlyle*, c.1400), *The Turke and Gowin* and *The Grene Knight* (a shortened version of *Sir Gawain and the Green Knight*). In other texts, such as *The Wedding of Sir Gawain and Dame Ragnell*, Gawain meets a lady who because of a spell is of repulsive appearance, whom he must marry if she answers correctly when asked what women most desire (namely, dominion over men). In *The Wedding of Sir Gawain and Dame Ragnell*, a work of 855 lines thought to date from c.1450 and attributed to Malory, Gawain's brand-new spouse faces him with a difficult choice: apparently she can either be beautiful by day and ugly by night or the other way round. Gawain is unable to decide. He leaves the choice to his wife and so accepts her dominion, which breaks the spell. The 15th-century ballad *The Marriage of Sir Gawain* tells almost the same story. In the *Canterbury Tales* (1392–94) Chaucer uses a variant on this, with an unnamed knight in place of Gawain, in the 'Wife of Bath's Tale'. In his version the hero can choose between an ugly, faithful wife or one who is beautiful but unfaithful.

In German romances, as in English and Dutch, the treatment of Gawan/Gawein is usually positive. This is already the case in Wolfram von Eschenbach's *Parzival* (1200–1210); Wolfram diverges from his source, Chrétien's *Perceval*, in stressing that Arthur's nephew is a perfect knight. A similar picture is found in Wirnt von Grafenberg's *Wigalois* (c.1220). Here Gawein is portrayed as the ideal representative of Arthur's court and an eminently suitable father to → Wigalois, a son who from his first appearance is clearly a superior knight. The most favourable portrayal of Gawein in German literature is that given by Heinrich von dem Türlin in *Diu Crone* (c.1225). This extensive work can justifiably be termed a Gawein romance, even though it begins with the story of Arthur's youth and marriage. In a whole series of exploits Gawein is the ideal hero; he shows himself the greatest knight of all, capable of successfully completing any adventure – even, it appears, the Grail Quest.

While Gawain certainly inspired far fewer visual artists than → Perceval, → Lancelot or → Tristan, representations of him do exist. Among the best-known is the full-page miniature in the Leiden *Walewein* manuscript (1350), which shows Arthur's nephew riding after the floating chessboard. An English manuscript of 1390–1400 contains four drawings of scenes from *Sir Gawain and the Green Knight* (the headless Green Knight, Gawain's seduction by his hostess, Gawain at the Green Chapel, Gawain's return to court). From the second quarter of the 14th century dates a portion of a tapestry from the Heilig-Kreuz monastery in Brunswick which shows Gawain in company with Lady Orgeluse, from Wolfram's tale. A capital made in the mid-14th century for Saint-Pierre in Caen depicts Gauvain in the Perilous Bed (and Lancelot on the Sword Bridge). The same scenes are found on Parisian ivory caskets from the first half of the 14th century, which were popular as gifts for ladies. The last medieval representation we will mention here can be admired in Runkelstein Castle, north of Bolzano in Italy. The 13th-century castle was bought in 1385 by the brothers Niklaus and Franz Vintler, who had the walls embellished with paintings. In the summer-house, added before 1413, are portrayals of scenes and characters from Arthurian romance, including one of Gawain as one of the three best Arthurian knights (with Parzival and Iwein [→ Yvain]). The frescos were renovated in the early 16th century on the orders of the castle's new owner, Emperor Maximilian I.

In post-medieval literature it is mainly in the English tradition that we have to look for Arthur's nephew. Malory's work, the incomparable *Sir Gawain and the Green Knight* and the tale of Gawain's marriage to the Loathly Lady clearly provided later authors with a major source of inspiration. One good example from the early 19th century is the unfinished *Fragments of the Masque of Gwendolen* (written 1816, published 1830) by Reginald Heber, in which Merlin casts a spell on Gwendolen when she refuses to marry him. As an ugly woman she succeeds in answering Gawain's question as to what women most desire: power. Edward Bulwer-Lytton's *King Arthur*, a long narrative poem of 1848, gives a comic account of Gawain's amorous adventures. The events recounted accord with those in such works as *The Carle off Carlile*, the *Vengeance Raguidel* and *Le chevalier à l'épée*. A similar picture of Gawain emerges from two sonnets by Richard Hovey, *Launcelot and Gawaine* (written 1888, published 1898) and *The Last Love of Gawaine* (written 1898, published 1908). In these poems Arthur's nephew is a textbook example of unreliability.

We find a negative portrayal of Gawain also in the work of Tennyson, who took an active part in the revival of interest in the Arthurian tales in Victorian England. His most important work, *Idylls of the King*, was written over a period of years: in 1859 he published four idylls under this title, in 1870 he added four more, and the final revised edition of 1886 contains twelve. Tennyson's Gawain, to some extent following Malory, is in many respects a deplorable character. He lacks integrity, is not true to Arthur's ideals, a poor specimen of chivalry and incapable of genuine worldly or religious love.

The American poet Edward Arlington Robinson, who wrote three long poems on Arthurian subjects, also follows Malory. In the second of these, *Lancelot* (1920) he succeeds in giving the character of Gawain greater psychological subtlety and depth. The third and last work, *Tristram* (1927), gives a similar picture of Gawain to Tennyson's, but makes him rather less of a scoundrel. Some years earlier, in 1921, the New York poet Arthur Guiterman published a number of ballads, among them *Gawaine's Choice*. Like Robinson, in this poem (in which Gawain with two other knights has to choose between three ladies each offering a quest) Guiterman makes use of Malory's work.

Not surprisingly, *Sir Gawain and the Green Knight* has proved an important source for later authors. In 1903 Charlton M. Lewis published a comic retelling in verse of the medieval work under the title *Gawayne and the Green Knight: A Fairy Tale*. Here Gawain has a sweetheart, the fairy Elfinhart, whose foster-mother is responsible for the knight's testing; she wants to find out if he is worthy of her daughter's love. In contrast, John Hartington Cox stayed close to the medieval story in a 1913 version for young people. In 1952 the material was reworked by Yvor Winters in a short poem.

Vera Chapman's *The Green Knight*, published in 1975, tells the story from the point of view of the (strong) woman in the tale, here called Vivien. In this work Chapman also makes use of the tale of Gawain and the repulsive lady, as does Joanna Troughton in *Sir Gawain and the Loathly Damsel* (1972), a version for young readers of *The Wedding of Sir Gawain and Dame Ragnell*. In 1985 Selina Hastings published *Sir Gawain and the Loathly Lady*. Another work for young people which includes both the tale of Gawain's marriage and his adventure with the Green Knight is *The Tale of Sir Gawain* (1987), a collection of stories by Neil Philip. He puts the tales into the mouth of the dying Gawain as he tells his squire about his life.

In 1979 Y.R. Ponsar published a modern prose version of *Sir Gawain and the Green Knight*. Two years later Rosemary Sutcliff included a version of the medieval tale in one of her Arthurian children's books, *The Sword and the Circle* (1981), which is based on Malory. A few years before, in 1978, Thomas Berger had published one of the most important of modern Arthurian novels, *Arthur Rex*, in which he too reworked *Sir Gawain and the Green Knight*. Berger's work is an ironic, comic version of Malory, augmented with a plethora of other material including the story of Gawain's marriage to the Loathly Lady.

Some 20th-century works about Arthur's nephew deliberately avoid the standard literary tradition as represented by Malory, *Sir Gawain and the Green Knight* and the texts on Gawain's marriage. One such is the 1921 short story by Heywood Broun, *The Fifty-first Dragon*. Gawain is here the least promising student in a school for knights. The school's crafty headmaster makes him fight dragons with an axe, helped by a magic word which is supposed to protect the timid Gawain from the monsters. In the course of his fiftieth fight Gawain discovers that speaking this word has no magical effect, and he then becomes easy prey for the fifty-first dragon.

There are other modern works in which the influence of the tradition is fairly limited; for example, *The Wraith of Gawain* (1948), a long poem in eight books by Ervin H. Tax which contains powerful echoes of the horrors of the Second World War. *Gawain*, a 1971 poem by the American John Wheatcroft, has the dying hero looking back on his youth. In *Parsival: Or a Knight's Tale* (1977) another American, Richard Monaco, depicts Gawain as a soldier with a taste for rape and pillage. Gillian Bradshaw's Arthurian trilogy *Down the Long Wind* from 1980–82 gives a far more positive picture of Arthur's nephew. The first part, *The Hawk of May*, is narrated by Gwalchmai. As a fourteen-year-old boy he flees in horror when his mother Morgawse, the Queen of Darkness, tries to draw him into her world. In the second part, *Kingdom of Summer*, Gwalchmai's servant Rhys ap Sion tells of the struggle between his master, the champion of the Light, and Morgawse. The third part, *In Winter's Shadow*, concerns Gwalchmai's quest for vengeance when Bedwyr, the lover of Arthur's wife Gwynhwyfar, accidentally kills his son Gwynn.

Looking at the post-medieval appearances of Arthur's nephew outside the domain of literature, it is immediately apparent that he did not escape the attention of the dramatists. In 1901 the German author Eduard Stucken published the play *Gawan*, which enjoyed Europe-wide success in the years that followed. Ten years later James Yeames based *Sir Gawain and the Green Knight: a Play in Five Acts* (1911) on the jewel of English medieval literature. A production for children is the work of Marguerite Merington; her play *The Testing of Sir Gawayne*, a version of the tale of Gawain's marriage to the Loathly Lady, appeared in 1913. In 1931 *Sir Gawain and the Green Knight* was adapted for radio by William Ford Manley. In 1979 the Movingstage Marionette Company of London produced a successful puppet version of the same romance.

Sir Gawain and the Green Knight provided Tim Porter with the inspiration for a musical (1970). Two operas have also been based on the work: one by Richard Blackford (1978–79), the other by Harrison Birtwistle (1991). Blackford has also written an opera based an the story of Gawain's marriage to the Loathly Lady: *Gawain and Ragnell* (1984).

Victorian artists as well as writers produced representations of Gawain. In 1848 William Dyce was commissioned to design a cycle of seven frescos for the Queen's Robing Room in the new Palace of Westminster. Based on Malory, they depict Arthur and his companions as models of the Victorian virtues. In 1854 Dyce completed *Mercy: Sir Gawaine Swearing to Be Merciful and Never Be Against Ladies*. A few years later, in 1857, a group of artists led by Dante Gabriel Rossetti began work on a different project: ten wall-paintings for the Debating Hall in the Oxford Union's new building. Rossetti based his designs on Malory's work. Rodham Spencer Stanhope was to have been responsible for *Sir Gawain Meets Three Ladies at the Well*, but like most of the other artists he never completed his assignment. In 1891 Edward Burne-Jones, who was also involved in Rossetti's project and who did finish his painting, designed a series of six tapestries for the dining room of Stanmore Hall near Uxbridge (now in the collection of the Duke of Westminster). The tapestries were made by the Merton Abbey Tapestry Works, a company belonging to the poet and designer William Morris. One of the series, which was completed in 1894, shows *The Failure of Sir Gawain*: an angel forbids Gawain, who is accompanied by Ywain, to enter a chapel in the wilderness.

Film-makers have shown no great interest in Arthur's nephew. We can mention only the English director Stephen Weeks, who made the low-budget film GAWAIN AND THE GREEN KNIGHT in 1973; a decade later and with greatly increased funding he remade it as THE SWORD OF THE VALIANT (1985).

BART BESAMUSCA

Editions: Van Es 1957; Gerritsen 1963; Barron 1988; Johnson 1992.
Studies: Busby 1980; Taylor/Brewer 1983; Whitaker 1990; Lacy et al. 1996; Brewer/ Gibson 1997.

GIRART DE ROUSSILLON first appears in a text of 10,000 rhyming decameters written in an Occitanian heavily flavoured with forms from Poitou, dating most likely from 1170 and certainly between 1155 and 1180. In gratitude for their defence of Rome against the heathen, the Emperor of Constantinople has promised his two daughters to Charles Martel and his vassal Girart. The intention is that Berte should marry Charles and Elissent Girart. However, Charles Martel falls for the younger daughter and makes Girart marry Berte; in return he has to release Girart from his feudal

Girart de Roussillon returns to the French court after his wanderings. Miniature from the *Histoire de Charles Martel*, 14th century. Brussels, Bibliothèque Royale.

duties. Girart's fiefdom thus becomes independent of the French crown (though Charles can still hunt there). On parting, Elissent gives Girart a ring in token of her love.

Later, when Charles is hunting in Girart's territory, he is piqued to see the splendour of Roussillon (which in this story is neither the region in Southern France nor the town in Vaucluse but a place near Pothières, now in ruins) and he lays siege to Girart. A traitor delivers Roussillon into his hands and Girart flees to Avignon. There he gathers an army and recaptures Roussillon. He seeks a reconciliation with the King, but Charles prefers to settle the matter in battle, at Vaubeton. After a long fight God sends a miracle and the two of them reach an agreement. Girart founds a number of churches and monasteries.

The text could have ended there, but a second war breaks out. Initially Charles and Girart fight side by side against the Saracens and the Frisians, but the murder of Charles' nephew by Girart's brother poisons their relationship. After a few victories by the king, including one at Vaucouleurs, Girart successfully avoids battle for five years; but then Charles succeeds in taking Roussillon and defeats Girart on the nearby plain. Girart and Berte then head for Hungary, where she should still have relatives; but a pilgrim in the Ardennes informs them that these are now dead.

The couple then spend some twenty years in the Ardennes, where Girart makes his living as a charcoal-burner and Berte works as a seamstress. Eventually he returns to France in disguise and – with the help of the queen and the ring she had given him – makes his peace with Charles in Orleans; after further quarrels, he finally submits and builds the church at Vézelay and the monastery at Pothières (near Vaubeton). With angelic assistence Berte works secretly by night on the building of Vézelay, as Girart discovers when he tries to catch her in extramarital activities. The body of Mary Magdalen is brought from heathen parts to rest in Vézelay.

The historical figure on whom Girart de Roussillon was based also provided the model for → Girart de Vienne and for Girart d'Eufrate (or de Fraite) in the *Chanson d'Aspremont*. They represent three legendary aspects of a 9th-century Baron Gerardus, but it is also possible that Girard de Roussillon is derived rather from one Duke Bozo, the father of a certain Girart II who died in 878. If so, the Charles Martel of the text has taken the place of Charles the Bald. According to Rita Lejeune, however, the *chanson* has no connection with a legend from Vienne: she takes 'Rousillon' to be the historical 'Castell-Rosello' in Southern France. As evidence she points to the many Catalan placenames in the text (and the first documented use of the word 'Catalan') and to the fact that in the South it was Charles Martel who was the hated occupier. Whatever the literary archaeology, the extant version is already markedly Burgundian; the Girart story had a clear function in the 12th century, illustrating such contemporary problems as the transition from free inheritance to royal fiefdom and the legitimacy of resisting unjust actions on the part of the king.

A Girart de Roussillon already features in the oldest heroic epics, as one of Charlemagne's paladins. The development of legend around Girart has been the subject of detailed research by R. Louis. In his view, the story of Girart de Roussillon as we now have it evolved in stages; a writer from Poitou would have merged all the versions of it known in his time into a single narrative. According to Louis, that same writer added the second war and the courtly intrigue of the love between Girart and the queen. Also, Girart had already founded monasteries following the battle of Vaubeton, and Pothières and Vézelay lie close to Vaubeton. Moreover, the account of the second war is a sometimes literal imitation of the first. The affair of the two princesses has no functional role in the quarrel between Girart and Charles; it appears mainly at the very beginning and after each of the two wars, as a kind of courtly cement for a martial epic. What we can say with certainty is that the extant versions show a courtly influence which is suggestive of the circle around Eleanor of Aquitaine (some scholars recognise

Eleanor and Louis VII in Elissent and Charles). At the same time the text makes a clear contrast between the submissiveness of Berte and Girart's recklessness; it also displays an enthusiasm for Constantinople (probably influenced by the Second Crusade). Berte and Aëlis, in the story daughters of the eastern Emperor, were in reality the daughters of Hugo the Coward from Tours. Despite the flaws in the narrative's content, its author was a great poet, one who knew his psalms and must have had a direct connection with Vézelay. He was thus most likely a cleric, not a *jongleur*. His version was probably produced in the north of the Occitanian language area.

Alongside the long heroic epic there is also a Latin *Vita Gerardi* dating from the 12th century; probably written in Pothières, it was quickly translated into French. Louis has convincingly demonstrated that this text does not derive from an earlier monastic tradition but is simply a version of the *Girart de Roussillon*. It is notable, however, that the *Vita* tells of only one great battle and that it is historically more accurate than the *chanson*. Here the story is set in the time of Charles the Bald, not of Charles Martel. Moreover, Girart's birthplace is here given as Avignon. In this fine text we find, among other things, etymological explanations of 'Roussillon' – from *ro* (master) and *sillon* (counsellor) – from 'rossignol' (nightingale), *rosée* (dew) etc.

A significant next stage in the Girart legend is the Girart romance in alexandrines written in French in the 14th century. For this work the author drew on a *romant* and a Latin *cronique*, and comments that the *romant* contains much that is incorrect according to the Latin; we are also told that the Latin text was read out at meals in Pothières and Vézelay as though it were a hagiography. This version in alexandrines was written for Johanna of Burgundy, wife of Philip VI of Valois, and Robert de Tonnerre (in Burgundy). Here again it is Charles the Bald, not Charles Martel, who is Girart's opponent. This French text makes extensive use of local material and local saints. A characteristic feature is the picture of the devoted Queen of France (Elissent), who tries to restore Girart to favour. Here the two girls are the daughters of Hugo of Sens, and Girart and Berte are eventually canonised. The work consequently ends with the miracles performed by Girart and Berte after their deaths.

Sometime around 1300 a Low German (probably Eastphalian) prose translation was produced, probably based on the French *chanson de geste*; but only one double page of this has been preserved. This version is closest to the Poitevin text, though the German translator may have had access to an older, lost, 12th-century version. This *Gerart van Rossiliun* has a place of its own in German literary history as regards both its content, since the French material did not become popular in Germany until about 1450, and its form, since prose was not again used for secular literature until later. It is also somewhat curious that such strongly 'local' material was apparently able to function internationally.

In June 1447 Jean Wauquelin completed a prose version of the *Girart* for Philip the Good, of which five finely illuminated manuscripts, typical of the splendour of Burgundian book production, survive. A striking feature of Wauquelin's work is the Burgundian colouring of the story, particularly the numerous references to local legends of saints. One of Wauquelin's concerns was, of course, to curry favour with his patron by laying maximum stress on Burgundy's independence with regard to the French crown, a thought which must have greatly gratified Philip the Good – he was, after all, the duke responsible for the development of the Burgundian realm. Wauquelin's version probably derives from the *Girart* in alexandrines, of which Philip the Good possessed a manuscript (now in Brussels).

Later texts mainly provide a summary of Wauquelin's version, as in David Aubert's compilation from 1448, the *Histoire de Charles Martel*. It is striking that here the girls are the daughters of the King of Hungary, the more so when we recall that Hungary had played a part in the exile episode in the oldest *Girart*. Also derived from Wauquelin's prose is the *Fleur des Histoires*, a compilation by Jean Mansel. This text became the

standard version for printed popular literature; prints of it were produced by Michel le
Noir in Paris in 1520 and Olivier Arnouillet in Lyons in about 1547.

J. KOOPMANS

Editions: Ham 1939; Hackett 1953–55.
Studies: Louis 1947; Bumke 1967; Guerrand/Thomas/Zink 1990.

G IRART DE VIENNE is the main character in a narrative of which the best
  known version is that by Bertrand de Bar-sur-Aube. Around 1180 this poet wrote
a *chanson de geste* entitled *Girart de Vienne*, which runs as follows.

As a lad Girart enters the service of → Charlemagne. When Charles one day
receives a message that the Duke of Burgundy has died, he promises Girart his lands and
the duchess' hand in marriage. He then dubs Girart knight. But as soon as Charles has
informed the duchess that she is to marry the young and gallant Girart he is struck by
her beauty. Going back on his earlier decision, he proposes himself as her new husband.
She, however, prefers a marriage with the young knight, asks for time to consider, sends
for Girart and asks him straight out to marry her. Girart is flabbergasted. A woman
proposing to a man! He tells her that he has no immediate intention of marrying and
she should look elsewhere for a husband. The duchess feels deeply offended, but next
day she again requests Girart's presence. He haughtily asks for a fortnight's delay,
whereupon the duchess marries Charlemagne. Girart has thus lost his chance of
Burgundy. As compensation, on the advice of his barons the king grants him Vienne, a
prosperous city on the Rhône. Girart kneels to kiss the king's foot in gratitude. Charles
is in bed at the time. His wife, lying beside him, sees her chance of revenge; she puts her
foot out from under the sheet and Girart unwittingly kisses that instead of the king's.
The following day he leaves for Vienne, where within the year he marries Guibourc.

One day Aymeri, the son of Girart's brother Hernaut, goes to Charlemagne with the
intention of asking for arms. The queen, painfully reminded by Aymeri's coming of her
rejection by his uncle, triumphantly and publicly recounts the tale of her splendid revenge
on Girart. Aymeri explodes. The assembled knights restrain him from killing her, beat
him up and throw him out of the hall. He gallops straight to Vienne, where he tells Girart
the whole story. Girart summons his kinsmen, who all hasten to his side: his brothers
Hernaut de Beaulande, Milon de Pouille and Renier de Ganvres and his father Garin de
Monglane. The clan rides to the king's court, they ask Charles for satisfaction and demand
the queen's head. Charles for his part demands satisfaction from Girart for failing in his
feudal duties: he has now held Vienne in fee for years without doing anything in return.

The clan's confrontation with the king and his men ends in fisticuffs. Years of war
then follow. Charles lays siege to Vienne and there is vicious fighting. In Charles' army is
his nephew → Roland. He gets to know Renier's son Olivier (Oliver), whose valour fills
him with admiration. The beauty of Olivier's sister Aude sets his heart aflame; Aude,
too, looks on him with favour. One day Olivier and Roland meet in single combat. If
Olivier wins, Charles will withdraw his forces; if Roland wins, Girart will give up
Vienne. The fight ends without a decision when God sends down a cloud between the
combatants. An angel commands them to bear arms no longer against each other, but
against the heathen in Spain. They swear friendship and Olivier promises Roland his
sister's hand in marriage. Roland tries to persuade Charles to be reconciled with Girart,
but in vain. Not until Charles is captured one day by Girart and his people is he prepared
to make peace. Roland and Aude are betrothed. Then messengers bring news of a
heathen invasion and Charlemagne and his men set out for Spain.

At the beginning of the *Girart* Bertrand tells us that it is possible to distinguish three

Charles meets Girart de Vienne before the walls of Vienne; on the right Aude, on horseback. Grisaille, c.1460, by Jean le Tavernier in a manuscript of David Aubert's Croniques et conquestes de Charlemaine. Brussels, Bibliothèque Royale.

gestes, or epic cycles: those of the king, of Doon de Mayence and of Garin de Monglane. *Girart de Vienne* belongs to the last of these (also known as the 'Cycle de Guillaume d'Orange'), that of the vassals loyal to the king; though it can equally well be regarded as part of the 'Cycle des barons révoltés', the cycle of the rebellious barons (*Geste de Doon de Mayence*). The *Girart*'s composition may possibly be linked to the marriage of Scholastique, daughter of Henri le Libéral, Count of Champagne, and his wife Marie, to Guillaume, son of Girart I of Vienne. Marie was for some time part of a coalition against Philip II Augustus, and between 1181 and 1183 it was very much in the interest of the House of Champagne to ally itself with Girart, a fervent opponent of the king.

The historical core of the *Girart* is the siege of Vienne by Charles the Bald in 870; Count Girart, governor of Vienne, refused to surrender the city. To these historical facts were then added traditional literary motifs, local legends and episodes from *chansons de geste*. Shifting the story's setting to Provence (pre-Bertrand) led to the development of the narrative about the arrogant, hot-tempered and in reality unlikeable Girart de Fraite (in the *Chanson d'Aspremont*), while relocating it to the Pyrenees and thence to Burgundy resulted in the *Girart de Roussillon*.

In the original narrative the conflict must have been purely feudal in nature, with Girart as a vassal who did not have right on his side and failed to fulfil his feudal obligations. A shortened form of this old version of the story has survived in the Old Norse *Karlamagnús saga* (1230–50) and in Philippe Mousket's *Chronique rimée* (mid-13th century). In Bertrand's version, however, Girart has good reason to rebel, since the king (already guilty of other injustices) denies him satisfaction for the queen's offence. Bertrand may have introduced the foot-kissing into his story to justify Girart's actions. It would also have been Bertrand who allied Girart to Aymeri's family, which was loyal to the king. Bertrand's treatment of Girart is in accordance with the way in which the literary *barons révoltés* were presented in the time of Philip II Augustus.

In *La Geste de Monglane* (a 14th-century verse adaptation), as in the text of the 15th-century manuscript (mostly in prose) in the Bibliothèque de l'Arsenal in Paris and the 15th- and 16th-century printed texts, the story is broadly the same as in Bertrand's *chanson*. This late-medieval version, however, devotes more attention to the love of Roland and Aude, among other things. In 1458 David Aubert, one of the principal copyists of the Burgundian dukes, completed his *Croniques et conquestes de Charlemaine*. Here the story of Girart de Vienne (in its late-medieval form) is linked with that of Girart de Fraite preserved in the *Chanson d'Aspremont*. The foot-kiss is omitted; the reason for the war is Girart's refusal to acknowledge Charles as his overlord. A kind of excerpt from Aubert's chronicle is to be found in the *Histoire de Charlemagne* (manuscript in Dresden, late 15th century).

Only two fragments now survive of a Middle Dutch *Gheraert van Viane*; from a (West Flemish?) manuscript of c.1320, they together comprise 192 lines. The poet must have based his work on the French tradition and knew a version which included the foot-kiss. Viane is a variant of Vienne; though it is not impossible that the Middle Dutch poem may relate to the village of Viane near Geraardsbergen in East Flanders; in the 13th and 14th centuries the (influential) Lords of Viane were called Gérard.

In the 18th century De la Vergne de Tressan included a summary of the story, in a modernised form, in his 'Bibliothèque universelle des dames' and 'Corps d'extraits de romans de chevalerie' under the title *Guérin de Montglave* (the title invariably found in the printed texts). This is also the title of a puppet play in which part of the material, freely adapted for children from the text in the 'Bibliothèque bleu' (a series of chapbooks), is still performed in Liège. In the 19th century the duel between Roland and Oliver provided Victor Hugo with the inspiration for his romantic poem 'Le mariage de Roland' (in *La légende des siècles*), in which Oliver is Lord of Vienne and Girart's son. In the plastic arts, the grisailles with which Jean le Tavernier illustrated the *Croniques et conquestes de Charlemaine* are of particular interest. Two of the surviving manuscripts of Bertrand's *Girart* contain miniatures. Sculptures depicting two battling knights being separated by a priestly figure can be found in various places in Northern Spain, for example on San Salvador in Fruniz (12th century). These may represent the beginning of the friendship between Roland and Oliver; it is equally possible, however, that they had a more general meaning, being intended as a warning to the Christians to abandon their mutual strife so that they could better prosecute the war against the heathen. The Benedictine abbey church of Saint-Faron in Meaux at one time contained a mausoleum of → Ogier (c.1280); Mabillon included an engraving of this (now destroyed) monument in his *Acta sanctorum ordinis sancti Benedicti* (1704). On one side of Ogier's supposed tomb stand Roland and Aude with Oliver, who is offering Roland his friendship and his sister's hand. On the other side are a man and a woman who have been taken for Girart and Guibourc, but who are now generally thought to represent Charlemagne and his consort. In this monument the Benedictines will have sought to express their ideal: peace among Christians in the interests of the service of God.

I. SPIJKER

Editions: Guiette 1940–51; Dougherty/Barnes 1966; Van Emden 1977.
Translation: Hieatt 1975–80.
Studies: Louis 1947; Lejeune/Stiennon 1971.

GODFREY OF BOUILLON was born about 1060, the second son of Eustace II of Boulogne (d. c.1090) and Ida of Lower Lorraine (d. 1113). History knows him as the crusader *par excellence*; as 'Defender of the Holy Sepulchre' he became the first ruler of the Kingdom of Jerusalem established by the crusaders in 1099 in what was then Palestine. He died in 1100. His life and works were celebrated – in an idealised and to some extent fictionalised form – in several branches of the Old French 'Cycle de la Croisade' produced between 1100 and 1300 in Northern France and the Duchy of Brabant. The opening parts of this cycle are devoted to the → Swan Knight, Godfrey's legendary grandfather; his own biography begins in the fourth branch, the *Enfances Godefroi*.

Here Godfrey's birth is presented as the fulfilment of a prophecy according to which his mother would bring three remarkable sons into the world – a king, a duke and a count. Godfrey's brother Eustace succeeds their father as Count of Boulogne; the youngest brother, Baldwin, becomes King of Jerusalem. On receiving knighthood Godfrey himself – here the eldest of the three – journeys to the court of the German Emperor Otto and requests the Duchy of Bouillon in fee, the previous duke, his uncle Godfrey the Hunchback, having died without issue. At the Emperor's court he becomes involved in a dispute about an inheritance: the daughter of Count Yvon sees her inheritance threatened by Gui de Montfaucon. Godfrey enters the lists on her behalf (as his grandfather the Swan Knight had once defended the rights of the Duchess of Bouillon) and defeats Gui in single combat.

Godfrey is duly invested with the Dukedom of Bouillon; while this is being celebrated in Nijmegen, another significant event is taking place in the East, in 'Mec' (Mecca?). There Calabre prophesies to her son, King Corbaran of Jerusalem, and her grandson Cornumarant, that Nicaea, Antioch and the Temple of Solomon will fall to the Christians. Thereupon Cornumarant decides to travel to the West, to assess the strength of the Christians on their home ground. On reaching the Abbey of Saint Trudo he is recognised by Abbot Gerard, who had met the Moslem during a pilgrimage to Jerusalem. Gerard challenges Cornumarant and is thus able to ascertain his purpose. He at once informs Godfrey of Cornumarant's plans, and Godfrey then decides to lead the spy up the garden path. At a military review he marches a number of detachments of his army past Cornumarant several times; the spy is flabbergasted. Disconcerted at Godfrey's strength, he reveals his identity to the duke. In the ensuing discussion Cornumarant is granted safe passage back to Jerusalem. But Godfrey also gives him a warning: within five years the Christians will march East under Godfrey's leadership.

The next branch, *Le Retour de Cornumarant*, centres on Cornumarant's experiences on the journey and after his return home. Godfrey does not reappear on the scene until the branch after this, *La Chanson d'Antioche*. Godfrey is now one of the leaders of the First Crusade (1096–99). The crusader army crosses Europe to Constantinople, where it sets out on a perilous march through Asia Minor, captures the cities of Nicaea and Dorylaeum, besieges Antioch, takes that city also and then heads for Jerusalem. Godfrey's part in this is no more prominent than that of the other commanders, though remarkable feats of arms are ascribed to him. For instance, at the siege of Antioch he is said to have cloven a mounted Saracen in two with one blow of his sword, half of his victim falling to the ground while the other half, still on horseback, sowed fear and dismay among the besieged. With Antioch firmly in the crusaders' hands the 'common folk' insist on continuing their march to Jerusalem. This episode from the literary history of the *expeditio crucis* forms the subject of *La Conquête de Jérusalem*. After a harsh siege the crusader army takes Jerusalem by storm and the city's defenders are put to the sword wholesale. The crusaders proclaim Godfrey king, but he refuses the crown, as does each of the other nobles to whom it is then offered. They decide to hold a vigil in Solomon's Temple and beg God to send them a sign. When during this vigil Godfrey's candle miraculously ignites of itself he realises that he cannot decline the responsibility of the kingship. However, he flatly refuses to wear a golden crown in the place where Christ had had to endure a crown of thorns.

The young kingdom is immediately attacked by the Saracens, and in this struggle Godfrey proves his leadership qualities. But he also makes enemies among his own people. *La Mort Godefroi* describes how the envious Eracles, Patriarch of Jerusalem, murders Godfrey by poison because the latter had sent certain holy relics to his mother Ida by his brother Eustace. Godfrey's death leads to a dangerous and bloody division in the crusader camp, heralding the eventual destruction of the Kingdom of Jerusalem.

Godfrey's literary biography is inextricably interwoven with the vernacular history of the early Crusades as recorded in the Old French 'Cycle de la Croisade'. This cycle, created over the course of two centuries, is a heterogeneous whole which mixes fantastic fairy-tales with more historically flavoured *chansons de geste*. The way in which the cycle developed explains the imbalance in the account of Godfrey's life. In the oldest sections, the *Chanson d'Antioche* (c.1100), *La Conquête de Jérusalem* (c.1135) and *Les Chétifs* (c.1149), Godfrey's role is not particularly significant. This can be explained by their North French/Flemish background: other nobles such as Robert of Flanders, Hugo of St Pol and Thomas of Marle receive roughly the same attention as Godfrey of Bouillon. The only version we have of these three branches is that by Graindor de Douay (late 12th century), though the name of Richard le Pélerin has also been linked with the authorship of the *Chanson d'Antioche*. Godfrey is given a more prominent position in the cycle between 1170 and 1220 when the so-called *épopées intermédiaires* (the Swan Knight branches and the *Enfances Godefroi*) are added to the older pieces by one or more poets whose identity remains unknown. This linking of the Swan Knight narrative with the history of the Crusade is interesting. The man behind it was probably Duke Henry I of Brabant (d. 1235), who was thus able to slot the growing cycle into the literature on the origins of the Brabant dynasty. Godfrey of Bouillon retrospectively becomes a Brabanter, and the emphasis of the whole cycle shifts from an account of the crusade itself to a dynastic-genealogical history of the crusader Godfrey of Bouillon. Episodes added even later, and also anonymous, such as *La Mort Godefroi* and the *Chanson des Rois Baudouin* (c.1250–1300), still contain a strong dynastic component, but at the same time they display a new historiographic approach; the fairy-tale and fantasy elements typical of the *épopées intermédiaires* are here considerably reduced.

Godfrey of Bouillon's literary 'afterlife' is (in contrast to the scholarly-historiographic interest in him and the Crusades) more limited than that of his grandfather the Swan Knight. Around 1350 the material of the 'Cycle de la Croisade' was reworked by an anonymous (Hainault?) poet. In this work, *Le Chevalier au Cygne et Godefroi de Bouillon*, the original narrative is shortened and the poet also emphasises its fantastic elements. For instance, he makes Godfrey marry Florie, the sister of his former Moslem opponent Corbaran. Even before this, Godfrey had been included in the ranks of the Neuf Preux, or Nine Worthies, in a poem known throughout Europe which presented the public with nine exemplary heroes as role-models: Hector, Alexander, Julius Caesar, Joshua, King David, Judas Maccabeus, King Arthur, Charlemagne and Godfrey. Godfrey is the last of these, and 'never since then has the world seen a better knight, nor one his equal', as the poet of the Middle Dutch version *Van den IX Besten* (early 14th century) put it. Torquato Tasso's *La Gerusalemme liberata ovvero Il Goffredo* (1575), a long poem which includes fantastic and supernaturally controlled events in what is specifically intended to be a historically reliable setting, makes Godfrey the undisputed leader of the crusade.

In his crusader role he also stands by the tomb of Emperor Maximilian in Innsbrück; the statue is by Stefan Godl and dates from 1532. As one of the Nine Worthies he is portrayed on Brussels tapestries of the 16th century and appears on a tapestry made at Felletin in the second half of the 16th century, now in the Kulturhistoriska Museet, Lund. In 1688 Willem van Waha's *Labores Herculis christiani Godefridi Bullonii* was published in Liège; here Godfrey's deeds are described as the labours of Hercules.

In Handel's opera *Rinaldo* (London, 1711) Goffredo is the leading role in a libretto

The crusaders Godfrey of Bouillon and Peter of Amiens at the Holy Sepulchre in Jerusalem.
Part of the series of frescos after Torquato Tasso's *Gerusalemme Liberata* painted by Friedrich
Overbeck between 1818 and 1828 in the Tasso Room of the Casino Massimo in Rome.

about the First Crusade which derives from Tasso. Between 1818 and 1828 Friedrich Overbeck painted a series of frescos illustrating Tasso's poem in the Tasso Room of the Casino Masimo in Rome.

More recent is the play *Godefroid de Bouillon* by Herman Closson (Marseilles 1933), in which Godfrey is portrayed as a far from saintly figure. A serious biographical study of Godfrey of Bouillon is J.C. Anderson's *The Ancestry and Life of Godfrey of Bouillon* (Bloomington 1947).

G.H.M. CLAASSENS

Editions: Duparc-Quioc 1976–78; Grillo 1984–87; Thorp 1992; Michel 1993.
Studies: Anderssohn 1947; Cook 1980; Claassens 1993.

G ORMONT AND ISEMBART are the principal characters in a French *chanson de geste* of about 1130, only one fragment of which, of 661 lines, survives. This fragment contains an account of a battle near Cayou (possibly Cayeux-sur-Mer) between the French king Louis and the pagan Gormont, lord of Cirencester. Gormont's military commander is the renegade Isembart, son of the Frenchman Bernart who is fighting on Louis' side.

At first the battle goes well for Gormont and his men. Large numbers of the French are killed, with Gormont wreaking the greatest havoc. Among the dead are Hues, Louis' standard-bearer, and his squire Gontier. In the end Louis himself attacks Gormont and succeeds in killing him. Out of admiration for his opponent he allows him to lie in state alongside Hues and Gontier. Gormont's death causes a panic among the heathen, but Isembart manages to restore order and continue the battle. This leads to a duel between him and his father, whom he does not recognise. He does not kill his father, but does take his horse. Hungry and exhausted, Isembart's men eventually take to their heels; he himself fights on until he is mortally wounded. As he lies dying he calls on the Virgin Mary and prays God for forgiveness.

As well as the account of the battle the fragment also contains references to episodes earlier and later in the story. Thus we know that Hues and Gontier had visited Gormont before the battle as Louis' ambassadors and played some strange tricks on him. Louis' death is also foreshadowed; within a month of his fight with Gormont he succumbs to internal injuries received at the time.

Three other medieval texts provide versions of this tale, one fictional and two historical. The former is the German prose romance *Loher und Maller*, which has come down to us in a number of late-medieval manuscripts and a printed text of 1514. The last part deals with the death of Gormont. This text goes back to a lost French original, *Lohier et Mallart*. There was also a Middle Dutch verse romance *Loyhier ende Mallaert*, of which a couple of short fragments survive.

The historical texts are a Latin chronicle written c.1100 by the monk Hariulf in the Abbey of Saint-Riquier and the mid-13th-century French *Chronique rimée* by Philippe Mousket. Brief references to the narrative occur in a fair number of historical and epic works during the Middle Ages. Most important are those in Geoffrey of Monmouth's *Historia Regum Britannie* (c.1135) and its vernacular versions, the French *Roman de Brut* by Wace and Layamon's English translation of this, the *Brut*, and the Welsh *Brut Tysilio*. In Geoffrey's account, Gormundus is King of the Africans in Ireland and Isembardus is nephew to Lodewicus, King of the Franks. The Welsh version is the first to tell how Gormont took Cirencester by making sparrows carrying burning straw fly over the town. Later English texts took over this incident.

There are various theories as to the historical events behind the story. The most widely accepted is based on Hariulf's chronicle, which derives from an older version of the *chanson de geste* than that to which the extant fragment belongs. According to this hypothesis the narrative relates to the Battle of Saucourt in 881, in which Louis III defeated the Norsemen. In that case Gormont is a Viking: either Wermund, King of the Angles, or Godrum, leader of the Danes. Isembart is either an unidentifed nobleman from the Ponthieu area in Northern France or a figment of the poet's imagination.

An alternative hypothesis sees the epic as an echo of Clovis' struggle with the Vandals in 511. The name Clovis is etymologically the same as the name Louis. Gormont would then be the younger son of a North African Vandal prince who subdued first Ireland, then part of England. According to this theory Isembart is the apostate son of Clovis' sister.

C. HOGETOORN

Edition: Bayot 1914.
Translation: Thorpe 1966.
Studies: Bédier 1908–13; Calin 1962.

G REGORIUS is the main character of a small epic, highly religious in tone, written around 1190 somewhere near Lake Constance (Eglisau, west of Schaffhausen?) by the great Middle High German poet Hartmann von Aue. Hartmann was probably working from a French source, an account of the life of Pope Gregory known to romance scholars as *La Vie de Saint Grégoire*. The German poet followed the so-called Version B of the Old French verse legend, which survives in a manuscript in London.

After a lengthy prologue in which Hartmann addresses the theme of human sinfulness and divine mercy with reference to specific examples (Adam, Abel, the parable of the Good Shepherd), and in which he expressly warns against *desperatio*, despair, as the mortal sin which obstructs God's grace, the narrative proper begins. This is divided into two sections: an introduction describing the lives of Gregory's parents and the main part which relates the vicissitudes of their son's life.

In the land of Aquitaine there live two noble children, twins, boy and girl. Their mother had died when they were born, their father dies when they are ten years old. On his deathbed the father charges his son to lead a chivalrous life and, above all, to care for his sister. Prompted by the devil, the boy seduces his sister and she becomes pregnant. The young man is in despair; a wise vassal advises him to make a pilgrimage to the Holy Sepulchre. The unhappy youth dies on the way, consumed by love for his adored sister. The girl is advised to put the child, with a memorial telling in veiled terms of its incestuous origin, in a little boat and then entrust it, like a second Moses, to the whim of the waves (and to the will of God!). When the child, a well-formed son, is born, the mother follows this advice. She herself withdraws from court life to devote herself to God.

After three days adrift the boat and the helpless infant are found by a fisherman. He takes the baby to the abbot of the local monastery. The abbot baptises the foundling, names him Gregorius and entrusts him to the fisherman's wife, instructing her to care for him as his foster-mother. By chance Gregorius discovers that he is a foreigner and thus does not belong with the fisher couple. He had been destined for the Church; but he now abandons his training. His mind is made up; Gregorius wants to be a knight and go in search of his parents. Ignoring the emphatic warnings of the abbot, who now reveals to him his true origins, the young Gregorius sets out on his travels.

After many and various wanderings he comes to a city whose queen is in danger from a besieger with evil intentions. Gregorius enthusiastically performs the basic duty of a knight, to aid ladies in distress, not realising that this noble deed will lead to a new catastrophe. He defeats the enemy and marries the queen, unaware that he, himself the fruit of incest, is entering on a new incestuous relationship. For the unknown queen is none other than his mother! Gregorius' unusual behaviour (he prays daily for his parents and weeps for his fate) brings the painful truth to light: his mother eventually recognises her son in her young husband.

Once more Gregorius sets forth. Laying aside his knightly dress, he covers himself in the wretched garb of a sinner. A fisherman takes the young man to a rock in the ocean, where he binds him with chains and throws the key of his shackles into the sea. Gregorius spends seventeen years on this lonely rock, supplied miraculously, if sparingly, with food. Then the Pope dies. In a vision two high dignitaries of the Church are divinely commanded to seek out 'the sinner on the rock'. And they do ... A further miracle takes place: the key to Gregorius' fetters is found in the belly of a fish. The sinner is saved. Gregorius is called to the highest office of all: he becomes God's new Viceroy in Rome. The miracle is made manifest three days before he ever reaches the city, when all the church bells in Rome begin to ring of themselves. Gregorius' mother learns of the new Pope and confesses her sins to him. The Pope, recognising the lady as his mother and wife, absolves her of her sin. Hartmann sums up the moral of his story in an epilogue: even the greatest sinner will, if he genuinely repents and does penance, partake of God's grace.

Hartmann's *Gregorius* displays the hallmarks of a legend about the miraculous elevation of a sinner to sainthood. The issues it addresses can be summarised in the basic question of sinful man: 'How do I live with my guilt?' Gregorius, bearing the brand of a double incest, confronts the two paths open to the sinner: despair on the one hand, repentance and penance on the other. And what happens to the 'good' sinner Gregorius, 'the chosen one', provides a mirror image of the life of Judas, 'the accursed', which ends in despair and suicide.

However, the question of Gregorius' actual guilt is far from simple. For God does not visit the sins of the parents upon the children! Moreover, medieval theology links 'guilt' to the subjective will of the sinner and his conscious decision to sin; but when the unwitting Gregorius marries his mother there is no such 'will'. Even so, the general medieval view was that the child born of incest partakes of the sin of its parents. Does Gregorius make a crucial error in turning away from his religious vocation (and from God) and seeking to become a knight? After all, it is this decisive step which brings the new disaster upon him. Of greater significance than theoretical arguments about Gregorius' guilt, however, is Gregorius' own acceptance of this guilt and desire to do penance for it.

Rarely has a poem with such striking parallels to the Oedipus story enjoyed such popularity as Hartmann von Aue's *Gregorius*. Soon after it was written, Duke Wilhelm of Braunschweig-Lüneberg commissioned a Latin translation of it by Arnold von Lübeck. The prose version from the second half of the 14th century also deserves a mention since, as part of a collection of legends (*Der Heiligen Leben*), it proved highly influential in later generations. The story has been told and retold down to modern times. There is, for instance, R. Henz's dramatised version of 1956, entitled *Der Büsser*. But the undoubted high point in the history of the reception of Hartmann's poem is Thomas Mann's novel *The Holy Sinner* (*Der Erwählte*, 1951). Mann became acquainted with the Gregorius story through a prose translation by Samuel Singer while working on his novel *Doktor Faustus*. He incorporated the basic facts in his account of Leverkühn's puppet opera. In outline, *Der Erwählte* follows Hartmann's narrative. By introducing a 'narrator', the monk Clemens, Mann was able to maintain an ironic distance from his material which results in some hilarious scenes. If Hartmann, the medieval man, adopted a markedly Christian perspective showing man as the Devil's plaything, Thomas Mann 'humanises' events and (clearly influenced by Freud's psycho-analytical studies) looks for the causes of wrong-doing within the individual. The incest between brother and sister has its roots in an inherited animal-erotic tendency, com-bined with a powerful aesthetic sense, in both of them; as a result of this, the beautiful twin children are irresistibly drawn to each other. The incestuous brother-sister relation-ship, consciously desired by both, is no longer seen as a disaster; Mann 'lightens' and makes of it a blissful submerging of each self in the other, which (for the twins) is the self. The marriage of Gregorius (in Mann, Grigorss) and his mother is reshaped into a conscious act, the result of an 'unknowing-knowing', a 'recognition' of oneself in the other. The high point of Mann's grotesque narration is the description of the penitent on the rock. As a result of his physical asceticism Grigorss shrivels into something like a cross between a hedgehog and a marmot, an animal thing with no human features. It keeps itself alive by means of an indefinable primeval soup, 'earthmilk', and only resumes its human form when called on to be Pope. Thanks to this masterpiece by Thomas Mann, the *Gregorius* is among the most widely known of medieval tales in our own day.

J.H. WINKELMAN

Editions: Neumann 1958; Kippenberg 1959.
Studies: Wolf 1967; Ohly 1976; Mertens 1978.

GUILLAUME D'ORANGE is the central figure of twenty-four *chansons de geste* which together make up the 'Cycle de Guillaume d'Orange', most of which were written during the 13th century. In the late 13th and early 14th centuries scribes col-lected them into huge cyclic manuscripts with a genealogical-biographical basis; that is, they contained, in chronological order, all the *chansons* concerning members of Guillaume's family. A few late *chansons* never found their way into the collections, and the oldest of them all, the 11th-century *Chanson de Guillaume*, also remained outside the traditional cycle.

The twenty-four *chansons* of the 'Cycle de Guillaume d'Orange' fall into three groups: 1. those about Garin de Monglane, Guillaume's great-grandfather (at one time the 'Cycle de Guillaume d'Orange' was known as the 'Geste de Garin de Monglane'); 2. those about Aymeri de Narbonne, Guillaume's father, including → *Girart de Vienne*, *Les Narbonnais* and *La Mort Aymeri de Narbonne*; 3. those about Guillaume d'Orange, including the *Enfances Guillaume*, *Couronnement de Louis*, *Charroi de Nîmes*, *Chanson de Guillaume*, *Aliscans*, *Moniage Guillaume*, *Enfances Vivien* and *Chevalerie Vivien* (= *Covenant Vivien*).

The *Chanson de Guillaume* (whose content parallels parts of the *Chevalerie Vivien* and *Aliscans*) describes the great battle of Archamp between the Saracen forces of King Deramed and the Franks under Tiébaut de Bourges, his nephew Esturmi and Guillaume's nephew Vivien. Tiébaut and Esturmi want to fight the battle without Guillaume (here called Guillaume Short-Nose); they are afraid he will claim the honour of their victory. But finding themselves vastly outnumbered by the Saracens, whose invasion force numbered twenty thousand ships, Tiébaut, Esturmi and their army take to their heels; only Vivien remains, at the head of a much reduced Frankish force. He is joined by his cousin Girart, who has taken Tiébaut's weapons. Their losses are high; only twenty men are left to face some five hundred thousand Saracens. In the hope that Guillaume (here called Guillaume Fierebrace) will come to the aid of himself and his comrades, Vivien sends Girart to ask his help. While Girart is on his way Vivien fights the Saracens. They savage him with their spears so that his intestines fall out. But he fights on gallantly until he receives a head wound that spills his brains; then he dies.

At the time Guillaume is in Barcelona. He is reluctant to respond to Girart's plea, having only just returned from a battle near Bordeaux. His wife Guibourc persuades him that he must go to Archamp. He gathers an army and sets out, accompanied by Girart and Guibourc's nephew Guischart, a converted Saracen. The infidels kill Girart and wound Guischart, who dies after repudiating the Christian faith. Guillaume is on his own. With Guischart's body before him on his saddle he returns to Barcelona, where Guibourc has raised a new army. Guibourc comes out of the city to meet her downcast and exhausted husband. When they return she tells her knights – to avoid discouraging them – that her husband has defeated the Saracens and they must make ready to ride to the battlefield to collect the spoils. She offers them the prospect of a sizeable reward in the form of land and pretty young girls.

Next day Guillaume leaves with his troops, accompanied by Gui, a brother of Vivien. The battle lasts two days; only Guillaume and Gui survive, exhausted and starving, and Guillaume is on the point of collapse. However, Gui finds fresh courage and rescues him. Guillaume has won the battle. By a little stream he and Gui find Vivien, who briefly regains consciousness and dies a Christian death in his uncle's arms. Then the Saracens attack once more, capture Gui and chase after Guillaume as he carries the corpse of Vivien back to Orange. At the gates of Orange Guibourc refuses to believe that Guillaume is her husband; she thinks he is a Saracen. To prove his identity she demands that he defeat his seven thousand pursuers, free their prisoners and show her the scar on his nose (hence his nickname). In this way Guillaume enters Orange, where he and his wife weep for his defeat and the loss of his nephews.

The following day Guillaume leaves for Laon to seek assistance from King → Louis, while Guibourc takes over the defence of the city. He is poorly received in Laon: Louis initially refuses to give him any help, but in the end yields to the threats of Guillaume and his kinsmen. They muster an army of twenty thousand men. Among them is the giant Rainouart, a kitchen hand of enormous strength whose weapon is a massive club. The other cooks often get him drunk and torment him. Next day the great army sets out for Archamp. Rainouart plays a major role: he destroys the Saracens' ships, frees the prisoners and himself accounts for more than three thousand heathen. The Christians win the battle and return to Orange. They celebrate, and Guillaume rewards his knights. Rainouart, who had at first been overlooked, is loaded with gifts and given Ermintrude as his wife. He turns out to be Guibourc's brother, who had been stolen as a child and sold into slavery in Paris, where he worked as a kitchen boy for seven years.

Only one manuscript of the *Chanson de Guillaume* has come down to us. This dates from c.1225, while the *chanson* itself is from about 1150. Its author is unknown; he may have come from Normandy.

The main character in the 'Cycle de Guillaume d'Orange' is an epic hero who has become identified with a historical figure, St Guillaume of Toulouse, Count of Aquitaine. This Guillaume of Toulouse was born in 752, the son of Theodoric, Count of Autun, and Aude, daughter of Charles Martel; he was thus the grandson of Charles Martel and cousin of → Charlemagne. He was installed as Count of Toulouse around 790. His position was an important one: he had to defend the Frankish borders against incursions from Saracen Spain and advise and support the thirteen-year-old Louis. When Emir Hixem I invaded Southern France the two forces met on the River Orbieu. Guillaume had to break off the engagement when some of his troops fled the field. However, the invaders' losses were such that they abandoned the campaign and retreated to Spain with their booty. In 795 the Franks established the Spanish March as a defence against Saracen incursions. From here they often mounted campaigns in the border areas; Guillaume and his family played a major part in, for instance, the North Spanish campaign of 801–803, in which Barcelona and Cordoba were taken.

Following his wife's death, in 804 Guillaume came into contact with the monk

Capital, c.1200, from the Abbey of Saint-Guilhem-le-Désert, now in The Cloisters
(Metropolitan Museum), New York. Once assumed to represent Daniel in the lions' den, it
is now thought to depict Guillaume d'Orange with the lion that appears in his coat of arms.

Benoît (the Visigoth Witiza), founder of the Benedictine abbey at Aniane. Under his
influence Guillaume withdrew from the world and became a monk in Aniane. Some
time later he himself founded an abbey in Gellone, which soon acquired the name
Saint-Guilhem-le-Désert after him. He died on 28 May 812. In 1066 he was canonised,
his feast-day being 28 May. The monks of Gellone wrote an account of his life in the
Vita Sancti Wilhelmi.

After Guillaume's death fiction and reality became confused: the North French epic
hero Guillaume d'Orange (the warrior captain of the *chansons de geste* in whom were
concentrated the heroic deeds of sixteen different Guillaumes) became identified with
the (historical) Saint Guillaume de Toulouse who took part in the conquest of Catalonia and whose life was recounted in the aforementioned *Vita*. The three oldest *chansons*
featuring this composite epic hero were combined in a collected manuscript with
chansons about other heroes who had fought the Saracens: Beuve de Barbastre, Hernout
de Gerone and Garin d'Anseüne. These war heroes from other, older songs were then
metamorphosed into his kinsmen.

One of the four main pilgrim routes to Santiago de Compostela was the Via
Aegidiana or Via Tolosana. The starting-point in Paris was at the church of Saint-
Jacques-du-Haut-Pas near the present Rue de la Tombe Issoire, which held the tomb of
Ysoré of the *Moniage Guillaume* (a wall in the catacombs still bears the inscription
'Tombe Issoire'); from there pilgrims travelled to the church at Brioude, where
Guillaume's shield and Rainouart's club were preserved. Their route then took them
through Clermont-Ferrand and Le Puy and along the Via Regordane to Nîmes and
Saint-Gilles; here they could make a detour via Arles and visit the battlefield of
Aliscamps (= Archamp; the Roman tombs were taken for those of the fallen heroes)

and Guillaume's grave in Gellone. The principal shrines along this route were the monasteries at Aniane, where Guillaume became a monk, and Gellone (= Saint-Guilhem-le-Désert), which Guillaume had founded and where he died in 812. It was here the *jongleurs* found their material. The *Chronique d'Aniane* gave them Guillaume's struggle against the Saracens (793), the Battle of Barcelona (801) and the name of one of Guillaume's wives, Guibourc (Witburgis). There was an element of reciprocity between the monastic houses and the creation of the *chansons* about Guillaume. The *jongleurs* for their part found the material for the *Moniage Guillaume* in the monasteries of Aniane and Gellone; while the influence of the Guillaume story as a whole worked the other way – when the time was right, and under the influence of the Crusades, the monks linked the tales of the gallant warrior Guillaume to their own saintly Guillaume so as to attract pilgrims to their monasteries. Most likely, spiritual and knightly narrative traditions evolved in parallel and later became fused together.

The *Moniage Guillaume* tells how Guillaume, 'le marchis au cort nés', travels to Aniane to become a monk there, leaving his shield on the altar of the church of Saint Julien in Brioude. In the monastery he leads a life of piety, but is often drunk and terrorises the other monks. They for their part make fun of him. The abbot and monks devise a crafty plan to be rid of him: they will send him to the coast to buy supplies, in the hope that he will be killed by brigands on the way. Guillaume is made to promise that he will not defend himself unless they try to rob him of his drawers. But he sees through their plan and has a costly girdle made for this garment. On the return journey he lures the brigands to him and as soon as their chief tries to pull the girdle free Guillaume strikes him dead. When they see him returning the monks are frightened; with good reason, for Guillaume gives them a good hiding. They beg for mercy and make their peace with him. An angel instructs him to become a hermit in the wild country near Montpellier; the monks are delighted to see him go. Guillaume builds himself a hermitage and a chapel. Meanwhile, the Saracen king Synagon has discovered his whereabouts. The great wars are over now, all his old enemies save Guillaume are dead. Synagon has Guillaume taken captive; he is taken into Spain, to Palerne. Seven years later Landri li Timonier, a nephew of Guillaume's, discovers by chance that he is being held by Synagon and assembles a great army to release him. A terrible conflict ensues. Synagon is killed and the Saracens take to their heels. Landri is given Palerne in fee and Guillaume returns to his hermit's cell. When King Louis is besieged in Paris by a heathen king, Ysoré de Coninbre, Guillaume is called on for help. He kills Ysoré in single combat, and then returns to his cell in the wilderness. After rebuilding it he starts to build a bridge over the mountain torrent that runs nearby; but every night the devil tears down what Guillaume has built during the day. Guillaume manages to catch the devil and hurls him into the chasm, from which ever since a roaring noise can be heard; many pilgrims travelling that way have heard it. Guillaume finishes the bridge and a short time later he dies.

Only the fight with the robbers and the Synagon episode now survive of the Middle Dutch *Willem van Oringen*, an adaptation of the *Moniage Guillaume* by Clays Verbrechten (= Nicolaas Persijn?) of Haarlem. His version is mentioned by Jacob van Maerlant (*Spiegel historiael*) and Jan van Boendale (*Brabantse yeesten*).

Guillaume's popularity is evidenced by three adaptations of the *Chanson de Guillaume*: the epic *Willehalm* by Wolfram von Eschenbach, from the early 13th century (14,000 lines, 13 extant manuscripts and 53 fragments); a 15th-century prose romance, *Guillaume d'Orange*, of which two manuscripts survive, and an Italian version by Andrea da Barberino, *I Nerbonesi*, from the early 15th century. Dante, too, was familiar with the story of Guillaume d'Orange (*Divina Commedia*, Paradiso, Canto XVIII). At the end of the 13th century, Ulrich von den Türlin wrote an account of the events preceding those in the *Willehalm* and Ulrich of Türheim provided Wolfram's work with a conclusion some 36,000 lines long entitled *Der starke Rennewart*. These three works were later combined in a German prose romance. In Middle Dutch there are extant fragments of *Garijn van Montglavie, Gheraert van Viaene* and *Fierabras*, in addition to the fragment of *Willem van Oringen*. The *Geste de Monglane* (= *Galien le Restoré*) was adapted as a prose romance, of which there are two known manuscripts. The incunable *L'histoire du vaillant et preux chevalier Galien Rethoré* appeared in 1500; at least ten editions are known of this, from the 16th and 17th centuries. In the Low Countries, 17th-century censureship lists refer to a chapbook, sadly now lost: *De historie van den vromen Galien Rhetore*, printed by Paulus Stroobant in Antwerp. This Dutch prose romance may have been derived from the French one.

A monastery still stands on the site of Guillaume's hermitage in Saint-Guilhem-le-Désert. Because of Guillaume's widespread fame (and encouraged by a 12th-century *Guide du Pèlerin*), thousands of pilgrims on their way to Santiago de Compostela visited it to venerate a fragment of the True Cross presented to Guillaume by Charlemagne. The choir contains two magnificent marble tombs. In the first (7th century) lie the bones of two of Guillaume's sisters (Alane and Bertrane); the second (c.1140) holds the remains of Guillaume himself, transferred to the choir from the crypt in 1138 (his arm was preserved as a relic in the church of Saint-Sernin in Toulouse). Most of the sculptures from the monastery are now in 'The Cloisters' (Metropolitan Museum of Art) in New York; one of them probably represents Guillaume. The Hérault River is spanned by an ancient bridge, built for the pilgrims around 1025 by the monks of Aniane and Saint-Guilhem-le-Désert. This 'Pont du Diable' recalls the bridge in the *Moniage Guillaume* where a devil destroyed Guillaume's work each night until vanquished by Guillaume.

A 17th-century chronicle of the abbots of the monastery of Saint-Guilhem-le-Désert, *Chronologica abbatum Sancti Guillelmi de Desertis* (1700) by Jean Magnan, mentions Guillaume's heraldic shield with its device of a lion. Guillaume's shield had previously been displayed on the altar in Saint-Julien at Briaude. The *Couronnement de Louis* also speaks of Guillaume's shield with its lion.

A 15th-century seal preserved in Montpellier depicts Guillaume d'Orange on horseback with a hunting-horn and shield. An even older seal shows him on one side as a monk; on the other he is mounted, holding a lance with a pennon on it and with his hunting-horn on his back. The hunting-horn does not fit with a warrior knight, but it may be an heraldic attribute such as is found in connection with the Princes of Orange. This horn reminds us of Guillaume's nickname: *al corb nes* (with the short nose). This should then be: *al cor nier* (with the black hunting-horn). There is another possible interpretation of this nickname: in the *Chanson de Guillaume* Guillaume has to prove his identity to Guibourc by showing her his nose. After all, he has been famous for his short nose ever since the giant Corsolt cut off the tip of it in the *Couronnement de Louis* (Guillaume *al cort nes*). Alternatively, Guillaume is sometimes described as 'with the crooked or hooked nose' (*courb nes*). Both nicknames are to be found in the *Chanson de Guillaume*.

A 13th-century fresco in the Tour Ferrande at Pernes-les-Fontaines, south of Carpentras, depicts the battle between Guillaume and the giant Ysoré under the walls of Paris (from the *Moniage Guillaume*). This, too, shows the shield with the lion. Guillaume's life is also portrayed on a number of tapestries from the 14th or 15th and the 16th centuries. Finally, a Dutch heraldic work of 1911 contains two illustrations of Guillaume d'Orange. This is no coincidence; as early as the 19th century there were attempts to link Guillaume d'Orange with the Dutch royal house whose founder, William the Silent, had inherited the principality of Orange.

TH. BROERS

Editions: Dunn 1903; Tyler 1919; MacMillan 1949–50; Iseley 1961; Wathelet-Willem 1975; Suard 1991.
Studies: Doutrepont 1909 and 1939; Frappier 1955; Tyssens 1967; Klooke 1972; Debaene 1977; Gibbs/Johnson 1984.

H AVELOK's story has come down to us in an anonymous Middle English poem of about 3000 lines which was written down early in the 14th century. On his deathbed the King of England, Athelwold, entrusts his only daughter Goldeboru to Godrich, Count of Cornwall, charging him to bring her up and marry her to the handsomest, strongest and best man in all England. At the same time, on the the the other side of the North Sea the King of Denmark, Birkabein, is also dying; he too confides to a count, Godard, the care of his children, his son Havelok and his two daughters. As soon as Birkabein is dead Godard kills the two girls before Havelok's eyes. Havelok is handed over to a poor fisherman, Grim, with instructions to drown him at sea. But that night Grim sees the royal flame issuing from Havelok's mouth. This sign, togeth-

Grim flanked by Havelok and Goldeboru. Seal of the town of Grimsby, mid-13th century.

er with the kingly mark on his shoulder – evidently a shining golden cross – tells Grim that the boy is the future king of Denmark.

Grim takes the child and his family and flees Denmark. He reaches England, where he founds the town of Grimsby at the mouth of the Humber. Havelok grows up, becomes servant to the cook in Count Godrich's household and acquires a great reputation for his physical strength and good looks, his work for the cook and his success in stone-throwing at the Lincoln games. Hearing of this, Godrich announces that Havelok meets the dying king's specification and forces Goldeboru into a marriage with the youth, hoping thereby to disparage the princess and acquire all England for himself.

The young couple move to Grimsby. Grim is now dead, but his children treat Havelok as a lord. Goldeboru, though, is not exactly reconciled to her new life; happily, as she lies awake one night brooding over her unhappy situation she sees the marvellous flame coming from the mouth of the sleeping Havelok. She also sees a gleaming cross of red gold on his shoulder. An angel appears and confirms her hopes, telling her that Havelok is of royal blood and prophesying that they will rule together over Denmark and England. They now travel to Denmark, with Grim's three sons as their loyal followers, where they receive the protection of the powerful Count Ubbe. To Ubbe, too, the marks of Havelok's royal descent are revealed, and he then recognises Havelok as king. Together they capture the usurper Godard; he is condemned to death by hanging and Havelok is crowned king. He then returns to England with the Danish army, landing at Grimsby. Godrich is defeated and taken captive. Goldeboru now appears on the battlefield to claim the throne of England and the English nobles acknowledge her as their new queen. Godrich's execution is followed by the coronation of Goldeboru and Havelok.

The above is the story according to the early 14th-century Middle English version mentioned above. The oldest known version of the tale is that found in the *Histoire des Engleis*, a chronicle by the Anglo-French writer Geffrey Gaimar (c.1150); another Anglo-French version is the anonymous *Lai d'Haveloc*, also from the middle years of the 12th century. As we shall see, there are notable differences between this *Lai* and the Middle English version.

The Middle English poet has given his narrative a clearly-defined structure, determined in part by the parallel developments in England and Denmark at the beginning of the tale and the changes in location that follow. The poet has taken pains to make these changes intelligible to his audience: every time the action shifts from England to Denmark or vice versa he interpolates some comment of his own, most often calling for a glass of beer. In view of these pauses at natural breaks in the narrative, it is likely that the tale would not have been told in its entirety at one sitting.

The poet's call for a beer indicates another significant aspect of the poem: we are not dealing here with a courtly work or one intended for a courtly audience, but rather with one performed in an inn, probably by a travelling minstrel, before an audience of ordinary people. Among the arguments for the non-courtly character of the *Havelok* are the facts that Grim is here a simple fisherman, while in the Anglo-French *Lai d'Haveloc* (a courtly romance) he is a baron, and that during the parliament called by Godrich at Lincoln there is no knightly tournament but games for the common folk.

The first two episodes in *Havelok* concern two similar events in England and Denmark; here mention is made on two occasions of misery and misfortune, emphasising the contrast between the helplessness of the children (Goldeboru, Havelok) and the power of the adults (Godrich, Godard). This contrast points directly to two major elements in the plot: the development from loss to recovery of what was lost and the development from immaturity to maturity. By linking young people to loss twice in rapid succession at the beginning of his story the poet not only indicates the theme of his tale but also how it will develop. The development from loss to recovery of what was lost is marked in the text by two almost identical lines. When the wicked Count Godard has murdered Havelok's two sisters and is about to kill Havelok too, the boy falls to his knees and begs for mercy with the words 'My Lord, I pledge you my troth.' He is referring to the fealty owed under the feudal system by a vassal to his lord. By acknowledging Godard as his lord Havelock abdicates his own position as overlord and thus loses his social identity as heir to the Danish crown, which leads to the loss of his personal identity when he leaves Denmark to grow up as a fisherman's son in England. This line thus marks the low point in the story. It occurs again later on: the Danish Count Ubbe, a loyal friend of Havelok's father King Birkabein, addresses the same words to Havelok when, having seen the signs of Havelok's royal descent (the flame and the golden cross), he concludes that Havelok is Birkabein's son and thus the rightful heir. At this point Ubbe and his men kneel and swear fealty to Havelok, which symbolises the moment when what had been lost is recovered. Notably, the recovery of the losses takes place in exact reverse order to their original loss: Havelok regains first his personal identity, then his social identity and finally his position as overlord. With the repetition of this line and the inverted order of the stages of loss and recovery the poet demonstrates that he is a great story-teller, who well knows how to tailor his plot to a narrative structure. The result, though it was meant not for the court but for the common people, is a literary masterpiece.

HENK AERTSEN

Editions: Aertsen 1988; Smithers 1987.
Study: Hanning 1967.

HECTOR, the son of Priam and Hecuba, husband of Andromache and father of Astyanax/Scamandrius and Laodamas, is – as Homer's *Iliad* relates – commander of the Trojans in their struggle with the Greeks who are besieging Troy in order to recover Helen; his death in a duel with Achilles heralds the city's destruction. Established as a noble hero by Homer, he was also widely renowned during the Middle Ages. Here, though, it rests largely on late-classical traditions which deviate from the classical view and tarnish the image of Achilles and → Aeneas. Among the Neuf Preux or Nine Worthies, the flower of chivalry, Hector, represents the mythical heroes of Antiquity. His image is determined by Christian interpretations, by the tradition according to which the Trojans who emigrated after the city's fall became the ancestors of many Western peoples, and by drastic medievalisation of the narrative material. It is significant, for example, that in the medieval romances of Troy Hector is not defeated by Achilles in fair fight; the Greek can dispose of him only by taking advantage of an unguarded moment on the Trojan's part. Here Achilles reveals himself as a coward, and later in the story he shows his lack of self-control when he is hamstrung by his love for the Trojan Polyxena; a love which eventually leads to his rather ignominious death from an arrow fired by Paris.

For some thousand years after about AD 500 nobody in the West read the *Iliad* and the *Odyssey* in the original, because nobody knew Greek. Medieval readers were dependent on a greatly abridged Latin version of the *Iliad* in hexameters, the *Ilias latina* (1st century AD), and reworkings of the classical tradition by such authors as Virgil (*Aeneid*) and Ovid (*Metamorphoses* and the *Heroides*, letters from famous women to their lovers). These poets, and the early Christian writers, wrote for a public which was familiar with the stories about Troy and needed no more than a word or an allusion. The same could not be said of their medieval readers. They sought enlightenment from commentators (Servius, 4th century) and mythographers (Hyginus of the 2nd and Fulgentius of the 5th century). Or they resorted to a work intended as a study-guide to the earliest Roman history, the *Excidium Troiae* (6th century), which provides a chronological survey from the Trojan War down to the foundation of Rome (including the youth of Paris and Achilles). This contains information not found in other sources available to the Middle Ages. Here, for instance, Priam does not ransom Hector's body, as Homer relates, during a visit to Achilles in the Greek camp. While the Greeks are dragging the corpse behind a chariot, watched from the walls by Priam, Hecuba and his youngest daughter Polyxena, Achilles agrees to Priam's offer to ransom it for its weight in gold. Scales are lowered from the wall and when all the gold collected is not quite enough Polyxena throws her ornaments on the pile. Smitten by her beauty, Achilles will happily relinquish Hector's body and all the gold just to possess her. So it is arranged. But once they are married Polyxena shows herself a second Delilah; she worms from Achilles the secret of his heel, so that Paris knows where to strike him.

Medieval readers consulted two late-classical prose sources in particular: the *Ephemeris belli Troiani*, a journal attributed to Dictys Cretensis, companion to King Idomeneus (Greek original, mostly lost, from the 1st or 2nd century AD; Latin version 4th century), and the *De excidio Troiae historia*, an account purportedly by Dares Phrygius, a participant on the Trojan side (the Latin version dates from the 5th or 6th century and may also derive from a Greek original). Both *pseudepigrapha* come with covering letters explaining how they have remained unknown for so long. In reality they play neatly to the doubts about Homer's reliability which existed in Antiquity: after all, there were other tales about Troy in circulation, he was writing centuries after the event, he wrote in poetry and was thus suspected of serving up fabrications (as witness the part played by the gods in his account); and Dictys is not devoid of anti-Roman sentiments. The 'truth about Troy' (see also → Aeneas and → Troilus) looks quite different from the view favoured by classical tradition, and the cry 'Homer lied!' rings through the Middle

Ages. Dictys, the better stylist of the two, describes events from the abduction of Helen to the homecoming of the Greeks, claiming that he was informed about adventures on the return journey by heroes who called at Crete, including Ulixes (Odysseus) and Menelaus with Helen. He cleverly combines the various traditions, including the Homeric, into a new whole. Dares begins with the voyage of the Argonauts and ends with the departure of those Trojans who are seeking a future elsewhere. He relies for credibility on a simple journal style, concentrating on facts (numbers of ships and of the fallen, duration of truces, portraits of the main players). Every word of both was believed down to the 17th century. Dictys influenced the Byzantine image of Troy until the 12th century; in the West he was used, together with the classical authors, as a supplement to Dares. Dares had no influence at all in the Greek East, but set his stamp on the Western vision of Troy more powerfully than any other source – a fact which ties up with the pro-Trojan attitude of the West.

Around AD 400 the Latin Church father St Jerome established the practice of recording the fall of Troy in chronicles of world history as a historical fact; he included it in his version of Eusebius' *Chronicle*. Augustine, Orosius and Fulgentius set the tone for the medieval lesson to be drawn from this history: to trust in the heathen gods is to build upon sand; worldly power is transitory (*vanitas*-motif); there were disasters a-plenty in pre-Christian times too; lust (personified by Achilles as early as Fulgentius), adultery (Maerlant speaks of the 'whoredom' of Paris and Helen), ambition (Palamedes), intrigue (Hecuba) etc. are punished.

Troy acquired an additional function from the 7th century on when, starting with the Franks, more and more peoples, cities and noble families of Western and Northern Europe began to claim Trojan descent in imitation of Rome (→ Aeneas) and with the same object: to gain prestige and legitimise their power and pretensions. Their alleged progenitors were Trojans who emigrated after the fall of Troy (Aeneas and Antenor, but also less familiar figures like Phorcys, founder of Pforzheim) or their imaginary descendents whose names either recall Troy (Priam, Paris, Anchises) or are selected with their supposed posterity in mind (Francio/Francus for the Franks, → Brut/Brutus for the Britons, Torquotus/Turcus for the Turks, Colonius as founder of Cologne). From the 12th century until well into early modern times the whole West was one New Troy. The consequences for politics and intellectual history of this genealogical belief were considerable; relinquishing these legendary genealogies – which began in the 15th century – was a long and difficult process. Francis I of France (1515–47) knew himself to be 64th in line of descent from Hector, and as late as 1656 Abraham Kemp snappishly disposes of the Trojan origins of the lords of Arkel: 'Troy is a sow with many farrow.' Troy is part of medieval national or dynastic history, and because of Troy the West harboured a grudge against Byzantium. Conquests of Constantinople (1204, 1453) were seen in the West as a delayed revenge.

In the 12th century, when Latin Troy poetry also reaches a peak with the anonymous *Historia Troyana Daretis Frigii*, Joseph of Exeter's *Frigii Daretis Ylias* and the *Ilias* of Simon Chèvre d'Or, which is based mainly on the classical tradition, Troy becomes an important theme for princes and the nobility. The 'matière de Troie' moves into vernacular literature. Troy comes to be seen as an exemplary prefiguration, cradle and mirror of courtly chivalric culture, the story of a class and a way of life. Benoît de Sainte-Maure, a poet at the Anglo-Norman court, sets the trend with his *Roman de Troie* (c.1165, over 30,000 lines). This work directly influenced writers of courtly romances down to the 14th century: among others, Herbort von Fritzlar, *Liet von Troie* (1210–17), Segher Diengotgaf (c.1250), Jacob van Maerlant, *Historie van Troyen* (1261–66, incorporating Segher's work), and Konrad von Würzburg, *Trojanerkrieg* (late 13th century, unfinished, with a later continuation based on Dictys). Prose versions of it were also produced (the *Roman de Troie en prose*, mid-13th century; others in Italian, Modern Greek and Spanish). Benoît's influence continued, indirectly and unrecognised, from the early 14th into the

17th century through a Latin prose version, the *Historia destructionis Troiae* (1272–87) by Guido de Columpnis of Messina (probably not the same as the Sicilian poet Guido delle Colonne), who names Dares and Dictys as his sources but actually rewrites the *Roman de Troie* (a fact not discovered until the 19th century).

Ever since Benoît the story of Troy has opened (thanks to Dares) with Jason's voyage, which provoked Hercules' punitive expedition in which Troy was destroyed for the first time, Priam's father Laomedon was killed and his sister Hesiona taken as booty by Telamon. (With this Dares laid the foundation for the establishment in 1430 of the Burgundian Order of the Golden Fleece.) The story ends with the death of Ulixes at the hand of Telegonus, his son by Circe; in Dictys, Benoît's supplementary source, this is the final episode in the tales of the returning Greek heroes after the second destruction of Troy. Benoît also used classical source material, and for the sake of maximum completeness later authors follow him in this. For example, Maerlant and Konrad von Würzburg include the story of the youth of Achilles, based on Statius' *Achilleis*. Maerlant

The death of Hector. Illustration in a French manuscript dating from 1264 of Benoît de Sainte-Maure's *Roman de Troie*. 's-Heerenberg, Huis Bergh.

adds the adventures of Aeneas, based on Virgil's *Aeneid*, to Benoît's narrative; he may have got the idea from the *Excidium Troiae*. Conflict between sources gives rise to tensions or even contradictions in the Trojan romances and to (intertextual) debate.

Central to the Trojan romances are the themes of war and of love. The clothes, weapons, military and other conduct, the thoughts and feelings of the heroes are those of chivalry. The women are noble ladies who admire their knights and discuss their deeds of arms among themselves, who inspire the heroes, pray for their well-being, welcome and cosset them after battle, engage in courtly dalliance with them and grant them their love when the weapons are laid by. Here, too, the Trojans have the advantage, for in the Greek camp the women are almost exclusively trophies of war. Courtly love plays a greater part in Benoît than in the *Roman d'Alexandre* and the *Roman de Thèbes*. It is embodied in traditional pairings such as Medea and Jason, Polyxena and Achilles, or in lovers brought together only in the Middle Ages: in Benoît and his successors → Troilus and Criseide, in Maerlant Penthesileia and Pollites. And in conversations about love, such as those in Segher's *Tprieel van Troyen* between Helen and Polidamas, Polyxena and Mennoen, Andromache and Menfloers. Everything is described in detail and often with a parade of learning, with particular attention paid to splendid clothing and glittering interiors, fine edifices and tombs (such as Hector's in the Temple of Apollo), and above all to products of exotic refinement. Councils, conversations, exchanges on the battlefield, funeral orations are reproduced at length. The course of the conflict is also, as usual in knightly romances, influenced by treachery, low cunning and cowardice; Dares and Dictys had put forward Antenor, → Aeneas, Hecuba and Achilles as candidates for such roles.

In the *Roman de Troie* Hector as commander of the Trojans is the model of knightly valour and 'corteisie'. The flaws in his beauty, all too familiar since Dares' depiction of him (he lisps and has a slight cast in one eye), are totally overshadowed in Benoît's account by his knightly deeds. So long as the great Hector, astride his warhorse Galathee and with the lion, symbol of kingly courage, on his shield, is involved in the conflict, the parties are at least evenly balanced. His feats of arms are legion. His grave will bear for all to see the names of the seventeen princes (give or take two) slain by him; to say nothing of the more than three hundred others of the second rank. His contributions in council are testimony to his wisdom. His moments of weakness are rare; on one occasion when he is wounded and feels like taking things easy he sees the ladies watching the battle from the walls and the thought of his honour lends him new energy. He is chivalrous in his encounter with his cousin Ajax, son of Telamon and Hesiona, though here he makes a strategic error: he agrees to cease fighting for the day, even though a Trojan victory seems there for the taking. Of course this mistake does not escape the expert audience, and for centuries he will be censured for it: at this point Hector – was it Chance or the will of God? – let final victory slip from his grasp. He is courtly in his conversation with Helen when he tells her of the encounter between Paris and Menelaus. Hector is in no way inferior to his great adversary Achilles.

By contrast, the medieval image of Achilles, Hector's opponent, is less favourable than the classical. He is still the great warrior whose actions are governed by passion, but to his valour and hot temper, easily aroused and leading him to harbour grudges, has been added sexual passion. His greatest feats of arms are tarnished by unknightly conduct and his unworthy death is the direct result of his love for Polyxena. In the pro-Trojan West Achilles' star declines, while that of Hector is in the ascendant.

Initially Achilles fulfils expectations as champion of the Greek cause. He leads a successful expedition into Mysia, returning just in time to turn the tide of the first great battle in the Greek favour. Next day Hector kills Patroclus. Achilles is naturally deeply grieved and looks for vengeance. He does not achieve this at once, as in Homer, but only much later. Many encounters between Hector and Achilles remain undecided. Meeting during a truce, they decide to fight in single combat, but those around them try to prevent this: the Greeks have learned to fear Hector, while in Troy only Priam is confident of his son's victory.

The drama surrounding Hector's end is quite different from Homer's account. Andromache has an ominous dream and tries to keep her husband from the battlefield. Hector thinks it dishonourable to heed a woman's fancies but is prevented by Priam, Hecuba and his brothers from taking part in the coming battle. He dons his armour but remains, chafing, within the city. Until, with the Trojans in difficulties and yet another victim being carried from the field, he can stand it no longer. He hurls himself into the battle. Achilles, wounded, has to give ground before him but awaits his opportunity. The way in which he finally disposes of Hector is hardly knightly; he takes cowardly advantage when Hector, occupied with another adversary, for a moment neglects to guard himself. According to Maerlant he even attacks Hector from behind, like a knight unheeding of honour, a 'vicious blade'; had he looked Hector in the face the outcome would have been different. Hector's death is a blot on Achilles' escutcheon; that of → Troilus will be another.

The dishonourable Achilles is an innovation of Benoît's; Achilles the lover is not. The Middle Ages were aware from classical sources of Achilles' relations with Deidamia, Briseis/Hippodamia, Polyxena, Iphigeneia, Penthesileia and Patroclus. In Trojan romance Polyxena is Achilles' great love. Dares' account was sufficient to determine Achilles' image because the hero's love for Polyxena changes him so radically in ways crucial to the knightly code. Love does not inspire him to noble deeds. It cripples him as a warrior: from the second he first sets eyes on Polyxena during a truce (according to Dares, at Hector's grave during the ceremonies on the anniversary of his death) and her

Achilles sees Polyxena at Hector's funeral. Illustration by Jean Miélot in a 1461 manuscript of Christine de Pisan's *Epistre d'Othéa*.

parents insist that there can be no discussions while there is no peace, he argues for the departure of the Greeks. He betrays his honour and his duty by absenting himself from the field of battle, even when he is told that the Greeks are in difficulties. Weighty delegations, Ulixes, Nestor and Diomedes, and eventually Agamemnon himself, fail to change his mind (Benoît has him playing chess). Not until Troilus wreaks havoc among his Myrmidons does rage get the better of love. He joins the battle and kills Troilus. Immediately afterwards, blinded by love, he walks into the trap set for him by Hecuba: she lures him to the Temple of Apollo to discuss Polyxena. There Paris slays him; despite his brave resistance, an inglorious end. Authors and audiences alike of Trojan romances pondered on Achilles' dilemma, caught between *amor* and *militia*, and Polyxena's reactions to it, looking both for guilt and for excuses. Benoît compares Achilles with Samson, David and Solomon; the author of the *Roman de Troie en prose* adds Adam, Holofernes, → Merlin and Virgil to the list. Around 1300 Guido makes of Achilles the man who chooses life above honour and fame, the conqueror defeated by love and, morally, also by Hector. Dante's *Inferno* places him in the second circle of Hell, among the sinners against the flesh who pursued passion against all reason. There is sympathy for Polyxena: Benoît himself tells how concerned she is for Achilles when he returns to the battle, how she heaps reproaches on Hecuba for the ambush and how her grieving image adorns Achilles' grave. Herbort's Polyxena writes Achilles a letter which shows her understanding for his resumption of arms. Classicist drama, influenced by Euripides and Seneca, for the most part treated Polyxena's death as a sacrifice required by the shade of Achilles. But had Goethe completed his *Achilleis* the medieval Polyxena would have been back: in 1797 he borrowed an edition of Dares and Dictys.

The various reworkings of the *Roman de Troie* also show how closely Hector's image is linked to that of Achilles. Herbort van Fritzlar develops the contrast between character and duty: Achilles acts according to his temperament, while for Hector knightly ideals come before all else. This contrast gives added depth to the conflict between them. Their confrontations, in Benoît a series of incidents which do little to increase the tension, form a continuous thread running through the story. Maerlant's picture of Achilles is more negative than Benoît's. Additional details mean that Hector's chivalry and his equality with Achilles receive rather more emphasis in the *Historie van Troyen* than in the *Roman de Troie*. Ajax and Hector exchange gifts which will play a tragic role: Ajax receives the sword on which he will later fall, Hector the girdle by which his corpse will be dragged. In the discussion about the duel Achilles' rancour against Hector is sharpened, and the Greek's cowardice and murderous nature are stressed. Konrad von Würzburg's unfinished *Trojanerkrieg* runs to over 40,000 lines, but he never reached the final encounter between the two. His Hector is Troy's salvation incarnate, the saviour, helper and comforter of the Trojans, seemingly an allegory of Christ. Reflecting on the breaking off of the battle just when final victory seems within the Trojans' grasp, Konrad concludes that Achilles' triumph is 'gotes wille'.

With Guido de Columpnis the tale of Troy returns to the domain of history. In his *Historia destructionis Troiae* Guido presents 'the past as though one had been there' in a mostly rather hurried style (with strongly rhetorical passages which betray that the author was capable of better). He stresses Dares' reliability and takes a dim view of the poets (especially Homer and Ovid; Virgil he respects). Benoît's poem is again reduced to a factual chronicle embellished with moralising commentary or naively rational-ising explanation.

This had no serious consequences for the image of Hector as chivalrous hero. But it did affect the further dissemination of that image. The *Historia* displaced the *Roman de Troie*, but opened up the Trojan saga to a wide public. It was translated and adapted – often at the request of princes and aristocrats – into many languages, including Italian (Filippo Ceffi, 1324), German (Hans Mair's *Buch von Troja*, 1391, followed before 1600 by some ten other translations), English (successively, between c.1300 and 1426, *Gest Hystoriale of the Destruction of Troy*, *Laud Troy Book* and John Lydgate's *Troy Book*), Spanish (Pedro de Chencilla, 1443), French (Raoul Lefèvre, *Recueil des Histoires de Troie*, 1464, preceded in 1450–52 by Jacques Milet's drama *Istoire de la destruction de Troye la Grant*) and Dutch (*Historie van Troyen als si bescreven is bi den rechter Guidonem vander Columnen*, 1479, printed in Gouda by Gheraert Leeu, which also includes a prose adaptation of Maerlant's version of the *Aeneid*). Two versions of Guido's *Historia* also became highly successful chapbooks. In 1474 Joh. Bämler of Augsburg printed a compilation of Mair and a 14th-century *Buch von Troja* (which combined a prose version of Konrad von Würzburg with a translation of Guido as continuation). Lefèvre's *Recueil* was printed in Bruges in 1475 by William Caxton. Caxton's translation of Lefèvre (*The Recuyell of the Historyes of Troye*, 1468–71, reworked as late as 1609 by the poet Thomas Heywood) was the first book to be printed in English (Bruges 1474). In 1485 Jac. Bellaert of Haarlem published the *Vergaderinge der Historien van Troyen door Roelof die Smit* (= Raoul Lefèvre).

Dante (*Inferno*) and his contemporaries show Hector as the ideal hero, regrettably unbaptised. His status as the supreme figure of the milieu regarded as the source of all chivalry (*translatio militiae*) is confirmed when he is included among the Nine Worthies (Neuf Preux, Neun Gute Helden), of whom three each are drawn from heathendom (Hector, → Alexander the Great and Julius Caesar), Jewry (Joshua, David and Judas Maccabeus) and Christendom (→ Charlemagne, → Arthur and → Godfrey of Bouillon). From the 14th into the 16th century these embody the aristocratic ideal. They appear first in a romance of Alexander (*Les voeux du Paon* by the Lorrainer Jacques de Longuyon, 1312–14, so called from the oaths sworn by the heroes on a peacock served at a banquet). They soon became extremely popular in the West European literature and culture of chivalry, at the courts and in the towns. Originally they embody *prouesse* above all, the knight's fighting spirit, and also, when portrayed in council chambers and courts of law, wisdom and justice, and eventually civic virtue. They also illustrate *vanitas*, the transitoriness of earthly things. A whole literature on the Nine Worthies comes into being. They are joined by Nine Worthy Women. Their coats of arms are included in the books of heraldry (Hector usually displays the lion, either one or two, as already in Benoît). They are portrayed in sculpture (for example in the Hansa Hall in the Rathaus in Cologne, c.1325), on tapestries, in precious manuscripts particularly of the 15th century, in wall-paintings (of both sexes by Jacques d'Yverni in La Manta Castle near Saluzzo, c.1420), in windows (the Gerichtslaube in Lüneburg Town Hall, c.1420), on everyday objects (French playing-cards, 1450–1500, and faience stoves from e.g. Salzburg 1548), woodcuts (Jacob Cornelisz. van Oostsanen, 16th century) and etchings (Virgil Solis, 1525–50). At court banquets people dress up as one of the Nine, on state occasions (coronations, marriages, formal entries into cities) they appear on triumphal arches and in *tableaux vivants*. Many a ruling prince is honoured with the title of 'the Tenth Worthy'. Quite early on they find their way into instructional literature.

Hector's place among the Nine was never contested. As the oldest he seems also to be *primus inter pares*. In representations of the Nine Worthies he is sometimes shown gesturing as though he is their spokesman. A fresco in the Weberstube in Augsburg (1457) shows Emperor Frederik III and the seven Electors together with Hector; the number 9 and the presence of the hero of Troy convey the message. Christine de Pisan speaks of Hector as the pattern of 'la droicte chevalerie de la vie humaine' in a letter meant for her eldest son, Jean de Castel (1383–1426) from Othéa, goddess of wisdom, which contains a hundred lessons in life for the fifteen-year-old Hector (*Epistre d'Othéa*, c.1400). This splendidly produced work (the text forms an accompaniment to one hundred miniatures) enjoyed great success at French-speaking courts and also (judging by three translations) in England. The extant copies include one intended for Jean Duc de Berry and an illuminated copy of the version by Jean Miélot (1461).

In the course of the 16th century the Nine Worthies are reduced to the level of village festivities; here and there in literature they have already become objects of mirth (Shakespeare, *Love's Labours Lost*, 1596). In serious literature and in art the medieval view of Troy and of Hector has largely given way to the humanist reception of the classical tradition.

Hector fascinated princes and the aristocracy. From the mid-13th century he is frequently found depicted, independently of the Nine Worthies, in richly illustrated manuscripts of, among others, the *Roman de Troie*, the *Histoire ancienne jusqu'à César* and the *Historia destructionis Troiae*. Documentary sources mention numerous wall-hangings with depictions of Hector; but only a few, from the 15th century, survive.

I.J. ENGELS

Edition: Gorra 1887.
Studies: Gorra 1887; Rey/García Solalinde 1942; Scherer 1963; Buchthal 1971; Schroeder, H. 1971; Knapp 1974; Benson 1980; Radin 1981; Eisenhut 1983; Ehrhart 1987.

HELMBRECHT is the eponymous hero of a Middle High German epic poem composed between 1250 and 1280. The son of a prosperous peasant farmer, he has no intention of spending his whole life in arduous toil on the land. He would much rather devote himself to the pleasures of this world. He dresses elegantly, in defiance of medieval law, in the colourful rich man's garb of the nobility. Among his favourite items of attire is a splendid bonnet, beautifully embroidered with famous figures from medieval literature; but the fate of these figures provides food for thought! The bonnet depicts, among other things, the cruel end of the disobedient sons of King → Attila (→ Theodoric).

Splendidly turned out, with beautiful long wavy blond hair, our charmer cuts a fine dash with the peasant girls who flock around him. His father tries to persuade the lad to make a life for himself within his own class. He advises him to marry the daughter of the farmer Ruobrecht. But Helmbrecht forcefully rejects this suggestion. With an allusion to → Erec, the Arthurian knight who neglected his knightly duties because he would rather spend the time in bed with his pretty wife, he replies that he has no desire to spend his life in bed because of a woman. Quite the reverse; the farmer's son has grandiose ideas, he wants to break through the class barrier and himself become a knight. His father's ominous dreams foreshadowing the boy's ruin cannot divert him from his plan.

Helmbrecht leaves the parental farmstead and joins a band of robber knights, the scourge of the country and the rural population. He travels round plundering until, a year later, he wants to go home. The much-travelled son, laden with (stolen) gifts, is received with great honour. He graciously accepts the welcome and responds to the astonished questions of the stay-at-homes in a variety of foreign languages. The boastful puppy addresses his sister in a sort of Flemish, his father in Old French, and greets his mother in Czech. This linguistic marvel attracts universal admiration.

But Helmbrecht doesn't stick it out at home for long, particularly when his father reproaches him with making up all his tales. For a second time he ignores his father's advice and sets out again, this time accompanied by his sister Gotelinde whom he thus drags down with him. He intends to marry her to a comrade of his whose nickname is 'Lemberslinde' (lamb-devourer). There is a great wedding-feast, but it is rudely interrupted. The sheriff appears with his men and arrests the whole robber band. Nine of them are hanged without mercy, but in accordance with medieval custom Helmbrecht – who happens to be the tenth – is spared. He is punished 'only' by mutilation: his eyes are put out. His sister too suffers a cruel fate: if we understand the poet aright, she is raped by the soldiers.

The blind Helmbrecht returns home once more. And although he swears that he is the son of the house, nobody there wants anything to do with him. His father scornfully sends him packing. The handicapped rogue, now totally alone, soon falls into the hands of his former victims, the peasants he had so cruelly mistreated when he was a robber knight. They remember his misdeeds only too well. First they extract a confession by putting earth in his mouth; then they string him up from a tall tree. His 'status symbol', the beautiful bonnet, lies trampled on the ground. In an epilogue the poet spells out the wise lesson concealed in his tale: should there be other self-willed children who go their own way and refuse to heed the fourth Commandment, let this example be a warning to them.

The poem was written by one Wernher der Gartenare, probably in the southernmost part of the German language area, possibly in the 'Innviertel' in Austria. Little is known of the poet himself. One suggested explanation of his striking last name is that it is geographical and that he came from the South Tyrol, with 'Gartenare' meaning 'the man from Garda'. But it is more likely that it should be seen as a typical nickname for a travelling professional poet: 'Wernher the Gardener'.

The work has come down to us in two manuscripts, one of them the famous compilation from Ambras Castle commissioned by Emperor Maximilian I, which also includes the Arthurian romance → Erec and the heroic epic → Kudrun. In this manuscript the title refers to Helmbrecht's father; it runs: *Das puech ist von dem Mayr Helmprechte* (The book is about Farmer Helmbrecht). Because of this the work was at one time known as *Meier Helmbrecht*.

This tale of the rebellious peasant boy Helmbrecht has to be read in the context of the time (second half of the 13th century) in which it was written. The social order of the feudal period, with its rigid division into three classes (nobility, clergy and peasants) was falling into decay. This 'divinely decreed' *ordo* was no longer accepted without question; the peasantry began to rebel (initially in vain) against the nobles who oppressed them.

Helmbrecht is an exponent of this rebellion. He wants to break through the limitations of his class, and does so openly by assuming, if only outwardly, the manner and appearance of a knight. This brings him into conflict with his father, who represents the old hierarchical relationships. With the typical intermingling of religious and secular rules – it was, after all, God himself who issued the Commandments – by rebelling against the social order Helmbrecht also infringes the divine law bidding him honour his parents. Given this background, it is not surprising that scholars studying the *Helmbrecht* thought they could detect in it the influence of the parable of the Prodigal Son – albeit with a negative outcome.

The *Helmbrecht* shows the remarkable 'two-phase' structure which is also typical of Arthurian romance. Twice Helmbrecht leaves his parents' farm, twice he returns. But where the Arthurian romance usually ends in happiness and harmony, with the triumph of the adventure-seeking knight, the *Helmbrecht* by contrast ends in a clear anticlimax: after his eyes are put out as punishment, the peasant's son drags out a desolate existence and ends on the gallows. The piece has been called, tellingly, a counterpoint to Arthurian romance. The veiled allusions to Arthurian stories also point in that direction. The upstart's discomfiture makes the message of the narrative crystal clear: a peasant boy who tries to make a career for himself at the expense of his own class will come to a bad end.

Interest in the material continued into the 20th century. At the beginning of the century, especially, a number of plays were based on the medieval *Helmbrecht*. Worthy of mention is the one-act play by K. Felner (1905) which begins with Helmbrecht's return. At the end of the play, in punishment for his sins, the good-for-nothing is struck by lightning. A positive treatment of the peasant's son is to be found in the opera *Der junge Helmbrecht* by E.A. Reinhardt and J. Zaiczek-Blankenau, written around 1906. Here Helmbrecht's social deterioration is blamed on his love for a girl of dubious background. F. Feldigl's stage version (written in 1925) pins the blame for Helmbrecht's ruin on his ambitious father. E. Ortner, in his dramatised treatment of the tale, also attempts to restore Helmbrecht's image by presenting him as a flawed idealist. Finally, there is a novel by H. Rieder, published in 1936, which is particularly concerned with the social abuses which form the background to the *Helmbrecht*. H. Brackert, W. Frey and D. Seitz have produced a highly readable Modern German translation of the original (1972).

J.H. WINKELMAN

Editions: Panzer/Ruh 1968; Brackert/Frey/Seitz 1972.
Translation: Ninck 1962.
Study: Grosse/Rautenberg 1989.

H ENGEST AND HORSA are two brothers who supposedly led the Saxon invasion
of England around the middle of the 5th century. Geoffrey of Monmouth gives a
detailed account of their story in his *Historia Regum Britannie* (History of the Kings of
Britain, c.1136).

According to Geoffrey, Hengest and Horsa commanded a band of men which landed
in Kent from three great ships during the reign of King Vortigern. Explaining that Fate
has compelled them to leave their homeland, Saxony, because of imminent over-
population, they offer their services to the king. They make themselves useful defending the country against the Picts. In payment Hengest asks for a piece of land, as much
as can be spanned by an ox-hide. The king agrees, whereupon Hengest cuts the hide
into such a thin strip that he is able to mark out a considerable area of land. He builds a
castle on it, sends for his family and invites the king to visit him. The latter is smitten
by the beauty of Hengest's daughter Ronwen and asks for her hand in marriage. In
return Hengest receives the duchy of Kent.

However, when more and more Saxons cross to England tensions arise, leading to
four battles. In the second of these Horsa and Catigern, Vortigern's son by a former
marriage, kill each other. Another of Vortigern's sons then seizes power and the Saxons
are forced to leave the country. However, Ronwen poisons this rebellious son and
Hengest is able to return.

Geoffrey's account provided the source for later poets such as Wace, who includes the
story in his *Roman de → Brut*, completed in 1155, as does Layamon in his Middle
English verse chronicle *Brut* of about 1200. Finally, the tale of Hengest and Horsa also
features in Jacob van Maerlant's *Spiegel historiael*. Several centuries before Geoffrey, the
Venerable Bede (673–735) tells the same story in his *Historia ecclesiastica gentis
Anglorum* (Ecclesiastical History of the English People), though his account is much
shorter and he takes a far more negative view of the heathen Saxons. Bede dates the
coming of Hengest and Horsa to the year 449.

The Fight at Finnsburg, an Old English epic of which only a fragment survives,
contains an account of a battle in which Hengest is involved, in this case as a Danish
warrior fighting the Frisians under their leader Finn. In this scene, however, the reason
for the war is not apparent. That is revealed in a passage in the Old English epic
Beowulf describing a feast during which a bard performs a song about the Danish-Frisian
conflict. The situation is this: the Frisians and the Jutes are allies, the Frisian leader
Finn is married to a Danish princess, but the Jutes and the Danes are enemies. The
Danish war-leader Hnaef is murdered by the Jutes in Finn's stronghold, though Finn
himself is not involved. Hengest succeeds Hnaef and avenges his predecessor by killing
Finn who, though he had taken no part in the crime, was responsible as host for the
safety of his guests.

Although the names Hengest and Horsa have been linked with the Saxon invasion
of England since the 7th century, it is not certain that they actually were leaders of the
Germanic tribes which came to England around 450. That invasion appears to have
started much earlier. It is also not certain that they were Saxons, unless that term was
also used for other tribes. It is known that Jutes settled in Kent during this period, and
both epic sources name them as allies of the Frisians. They, however, speak of Hengest
as a Danish war-leader. Finally, it has also been suggested that we are here dealing with
a mythical pair of brothers, an interpretation which was of course prompted by the
names Hengest and Horsa, meaning Stallion and Horse.

N.TH.J VOORWINDEN

Translation: Thorpe 1966.

H UON OF BORDEAUX, a knight of that city, is one of three principal characters
in *Huon de Bordeaux*, a 13th-century *chanson de geste*, the others being his feudal
overlord → Charlemagne and his protector the elf-king Auberon (Oberon). Though set
in the time of Charlemagne, the *chanson* has no historical basis. *Huon de Bordeaux* is a
fictional narrative, made up of motifs from a variety of sources, in which adventures and
marvels play a large part. The work is anonymous, probably written in Picardy, and
became popular in Northern France, Flanders and England.

The story is as follows. At a meeting of his court in Paris Charlemagne abdicates the
throne in favour of his son Karlot. A villainous knight, Amauri de Viés Mes, uses the
occasion to accuse Huon of Bordeaux and his brother Gérart of neglect of duty because
of their absence from the court. The king summons the brothers to Paris, but on the
way they run into an ambush set by Amauri and Karlot; Amauri had persuaded Karlot
to join him in taking revenge on the brothers, claiming that they had injured him
(Amauri). Karlot wounds Gérart. Huon in turn kills the prince, not recognising him
because he had covered his shield.

Huon resumes his journey with his wounded brother. In Paris Charlemagne promises
Huon that he will certainly punish whoever wounded Gérart so badly if he can be found.
When a little later Amauri brings in Karlot's corpse Charlemagne forgets his promise
and Huon is charged with murder. Huon's kinsmen plead his case, but Charles is deaf to
reason. Huon has to prove his innocence in a judicial duel with Amauri. Although Huon
emerges the victor, Charles still refuses to be reconciled with his vassal. He intends to
banish Huon, because Amauri had not publicly admitted his guilt before dying. Charles
withdraws his sentence when the *pairs* leave court in protest, but he attaches a condition
to the reconciliation: Huon must go to Babylon to the Emir Gaudisse, decapitate the first
man he comes upon at the emir's table, kiss Gaudisse's daughter Esclarmonde three times
and, lastly, collect the emir's beard and his four eye-teeth.

Huon sets out, accompanied by eleven knights. Two others join the company along
the way: Garin de Saint-Omer and Geriaume, both of them good friends of Huon's
father. During his adventurous journey the hero is helped by King Auberon, an
uncanny individual he meets in a forest which lies between Jerusalem and the Red Sea.
Auberon gives him two things: a goblet which provides unlimited wine to whoever is
without sin and an ivory horn with which in time of need Huon can summon
Auberon's army to his aid. The king urges Huon to behave in an upright way and not to
transgress against his code. As soon as Huon tells a lie or commits a sin he will forfeit
Auberon's protection. Some time later the knights reach the city of Tormont, where
they come into conflict with Oede, the lord of the place, who hates Christians and
turns out to be an uncle of Huon's. With the help of Auberon and his army the conflict
is decided on Huon's favour. The knights then arrive at Castle Dunostre, where dwells
the giant Orgueilleux. Huon successfully penetrates the castle and kills the giant. He
thus acquires a suit of armour which makes its wearer invulnerable to wounds and frees
the damsel imprisoned there. Huon leaves his fellow-knights with the damsel and
travels on alone to Babylon to carry out his task. One of Auberon's servants, Malebron,
transports him across the Red Sea to Babylon.

In a series of adventures Huon successfully completes his mission and in addition wins
the love of Esclarmonde. Meanwhile his knights, who had become anxious, also arrive in
Babylon, so that they can begin their homeward journey together. Before they leave,
Auberon forbids Huon to have anything to do with Esclarmonde until they have been
married in Rome. Hardly has their ship left harbour when Huon breaks this command. A
tremendous thunderstorm breaks out, the ship is wrecked and the company scattered.
After many complications they all meet up again in the city of Aufalerne.

From there Huon, Esclarmonde and the knights set sail on a Frankish ship. They
travel via Brindisi to Rome, where Esclarmonde is baptised and she and Huon are
married. Returning to France, Huon again finds himself the victim of a conspiracy.

During his absence his brother Gérart has married the daughter of a scoundrel; he fears that now Huon is back he will have to give up the power he has acquired. With his treacherous father-in-law Gibouart he lures Huon's company into an ambush; the knights are killed and Huon, Esclarmonde and Geriaume are taken to Bordeaux as prisoners. The villains then ride to Paris to inform Charlemagne that Huon is in Bordeaux. The king is furious; he had forbidden Huon to return to Bordeaux before reporting back to Paris and proving that he had carried out his task. He goes to Bordeaux with his barons to bring Huon to trial. Things look black for our hero, for the barons can see no chance of saving him from the death penalty. They suspect treachery, but can prove nothing. Only one person can do this: Auberon. The elf-king appears unexpectedly in the hall. He proves Huon's innocence and has Gérart and Gibouart hanged. Charles is now reconciled with Huon, who recovers all his old honours. Auberon names Huon as his heir; in three years time he will be crowned and Auberon will die. With these words Auberon leaves for his fairy kingdom and Charlemagne returns to Paris.

This adventurous *chanson de geste*, written in decasyllabic lines, has been preserved in three almost complete and two fragmentary manuscripts. All of them, save for one of the fragmentary manuscripts, go back to the same copy of the text. The date of the work is disputed; most handbooks date it to c.1225, but there are those who argue for a later date, around 1260. Although a great part of the narrative concerns Huon's adventurous journey the work can still be called a genuine *chanson de geste*, since that journey results from the juridical conflict between the authoritarian Charlemagne and his vassal. Though initially the youthful Huon can certainly not be acquitted of negligence and recklessness, as the story progresses he becomes an ever better knight.

The oldest manuscript, from the mid-13th century, contains only the tale of Huon's banishment. The later manuscripts include not only *Huon de Bordeaux* itself but also other of Huon's adventures. For in the second half of the 13th century new poems were written which tell of the further adventures of Huon and Esclarmonde and their descendants, and the original poem evolved into an extensive cycle. The tale of the youth of Auberon the elf-king (*Le Roman d'Auberon*) functioned as a prologue to the cycle, which has been preserved in its most complete form (a good 32,000 lines) in a manuscript of 1311.

In this redaction *Huon de Bordeaux* continued to exert an influence until well into the 19th century. In the 15th century a prose version was made of part of the cycle. No manuscript survives of this prose version (which dates, according to the colophon of the oldest print, from 1454), but we know that Philip the Good, Duke of Burgundy, had a copy in his library. The prose version was reprinted in the 16th century, and new prints and reprints continued to appear until far into the 19th century (at least 32). In the 18th century Count Tressan, editor of the *Bibliothèque Universelle des Romans*, reworked the prose text for that series. He changed the emphasis here and there in his version, giving greater prominence to the love story.

This is also the case with a 15th-century version in alexandrines. The story remained essentially the same, but the text contained many small variants compared to the decasyllabic redactions; it was also shortened. Moreover, the adaptor inserted two lengthy interpolations into the *Huon* text (*Huon et Callisse* and *Combat contre les géants*) and linked the *Huon* text harmoniously with certain continuations from the cycle. In another 15th-century manuscript, by contrast, the continuations are independent of *Huon de Bordeaux* both graphically and in content.

England became familiar with the *Huon de Bordeaux* through the translation by John Berners, Lord Bouchier (c.1525), which was printed about 1534. The English text is a faithful rendering of the early 16th-century French prose romance. It was through Berners' translation that Oberon entered English literature. We meet the elf-king in

Edmund Spenser's *Faerie Queene* (1590–96), where he can be identified with Henry VIII, in Robert Greene's drama *James IV* (c.1591), in Ben Jonson's *Oberon, the Fairy Prince* (1610) and in Shakespeare's *A Midsummer Night's Dream* (between 1594 and 1596). It was in this last play that the elf-king and his consort Titania made the greatest hit.

Various references indicate that the *chanson de geste* itself was also produced as a play. We learn from the diary of Philip Henslowe, a man with many contacts in the theatrical world, that the Earl of Sussex's company performed a play entitled *Huon of Burdeux* in London in 1593–94; however, the piece has not survived. In France, too, a stage version of the *chanson de geste* must have been performed. It appears that on 14 December 1557 Parliament was petitioned for permission to produce the play, which had evidently been banned. In 1660 Molière's company gave three performances of the *Jeu de Huon de Bordeaux*; sadly, this play too has failed to survive. These references to stage versions of *Huon de Bordeaux* are quite remarkable, since the French theatre made little or no use of medieval epic material. *Huon de Bordeaux* is still performed in the puppet theatres of Liège, which date from the 19th century. In these theatres the epic tradition remains alive; the players base their work on texts from the 'Bibliothèque bleue'. Also of interest is the opera *Holger Danske* by F.L.A. Kunzen first performed in Copenhagen in 1789, with a text by I. Baggesen after Christoph Martin Wieland's *Oberon*. The librettist replaced Huon with Holger Danske (Ogier the Dane) as Charlemagne's paladin; otherwise he kept to the standard Oberon-and-Titania material.

In the 19th century the story of Oberon proved a source of inspiration for romantic composers. Best known is the opera by Weber, first performed on 12 April 1826 at Covent Garden in London. The librettist, Planché, based his text on Wieland's *Oberon*. For his 1780 verse narrative in fourteen cantos (later reduced to twelve) Wieland used Tressan's shortened version and made a number of changes in the story. Huon has to acquire the eye-teeth and beard of the Caliph of Baghdad and kiss the latter's daughter Rezia three times. As in the *chanson de geste*, he is helped by Oberon; here, however, Oberon quarrels with Titania because she has taken an adulterous woman under her protection. He refuses to be reconciled with her until a human couple has achieved the ideal of pure and steadfast love, a task to be accomplished by Huon and Rezia. Wieland borrowed the Oberon-Titania situation from Shakespeare and tied it in with the Old French poem, thus showing Huon's mission in a different light. Wieland's *Oberon* provided inspiration for the Swiss artist Füssli. In 1804 and 1805 he painted 'Huon Freeing Angela with the Magic Ring' (private collection, Zürich) and 'Huon and Rezia Throwing Themselves into the Sea / United' (private collection, Wädenswill).

M. LENS

Editions: Guessard/Grandmaison 1860; Ruelle 1960.
Studies: Doutrepont 1939; Rossi 1975.

I NGELD is the principal character in the *Ingeldlied*, a poem which has been preserved only in a Latin work, the *History of the Danes* by the Danish historiographer Saxo Grammaticus (c.1200). In this text 'Ingellus' is the son of King Frodi of Denmark. Frodi is killed during a feast at the court of King Swerting of Saxony. Instead of avenging his father Ingeld makes friends with Swerting's sons; he even marries their sister. During a feast the hero Starkad violently reproaches the king for leading a life of luxury and idleness while his father is still unavenged. Ingellus thereupon kills his Saxon brothers-in-law and repudiates his wife.

The material was also known in England. In 797 Alcuin even used Ingeld as a warning: 'Quid Hinieldus cum Christo?' (What has Ingeld to do with Christ?).

Evidently the monks would rather listen to heroic poetry of this kind than to the church fathers. The Old English epic → *Beowulf* tells how the Danes made war on the Headubards, and during this war the Headubard king, Froda, was slain. The Danish king, Hrothgar, fears that eventually Froda's son Ingeld and a new generation of warriors will try to avenge his father's death. To forestall this he plans to marry his daughter Freawaru to Ingeld. He succeeds in this, but Freawaru arrives at the court of the Headubards with the Danes in her company bearing the arms of Froda and the other fallen and an old warrior heaps reproaches on Ingeld. He then breaks off the peace. Here the story breaks off, but from comments in *Beowulf* and → *Widsith* one gathers that the Danish royal stronghold of Heorot is destroyed during Ingeld's campaign, and he himself is killed.

The story as found in Saxo thus differs considerably from that in *Beowulf*, though the motif of vengeance for a father's death remains the same. Most likely Saxo made changes here and there. It is even possible that the words attributed to Starkad are to a great extent the product of Saxo's pen. The reproaches about the opulence of life at the Danish court are strongly reminiscent of Latin satirical verses, while the relocation of the action to Saxony may have been prompted by the historical situation around 1200.

A. QUAK

Translation: Fisher/Davidson 1978.

JOSEPH OF ARIMATHEA is a character of biblical origin who features mainly in Arthurian romances connected with the Grail. In the four gospels his role is confined to burying Jesus after the Crucifixion, but in the apocryphal gospel of Nicodemus, and specifically in the section known as the *Gesta Pilati*, he plays a significant part in the stories surrounding Jesus' death and resurrection. Joseph is here a prominent member of the Jewish High Council. After Jesus' death, with Pilate's permission and assisted by Nicodemus, he removes Jesus' body from the cross, wraps it in cloth and buries it in a new tomb. When the Jews discover that Joseph, with a few others, had also pleaded with Pilate on Jesus' behalf, they are furious. Joseph is arrested and imprisoned in an isolated, heavily guarded building. On the day after the sabbath the door is opened again, but Joseph has vanished. Some time later he is found in Arimathea, his birthplace. He says that Jesus appeared to him in the night and released him. He suddenly found himself in Arimathea, with no idea how he had got there.

The first writer to devote an entire work to the life of Joseph of Arimathea was Robert de Boron. This Burgundian poet probably produced his verse romance *Joseph d'Arimathie*, also known as *Le Roman de l'Estoire dou Graal*, shortly before the year 1200. His work is of great importance, for in it he was the first to make a connection between the dish used at the Last Supper and the mysterious Grail of Chrétien's → *Perceval*, and thus between sacred history and the Arthurian world. The *Joseph d'Arimathie* was enormously influential, particularly because the verse romance was followed within a short time of its appearance by a prose version. The *Prose Joseph d'Arimathie* was translated into many languages, and also forms the basis for *L'Estoire del Saint Graal*, the romance which serves as an introduction to the Old French prose cycle *Lancelot en prose – Queste del Saint Graal – Mort le roi Artu* (→ Lancelot). Around 1260 Jacob van Maerlant completed a Middle Dutch verse translation of the *Prose Joseph* entitled *Die historie vanden Grale*.

The author of the prose romance begins with a prologue summarising the history of salvation up to the Passion, and then recounts the events surrounding Jesus' death. Joseph, one of Pilate's soldiers and a secret follower of Jesus, receives from Pilate the dish used by Jesus at the Last Supper. The reason is that Pilate wants nothing in his possession that had belonged to Jesus, for fear of being taken for one of his followers. Once Jesus is dead, Pilate gives Joseph permission to bury his body. When he is taken from the cross Jesus' wounds begin to bleed again. Joseph catches the blood in the dish. After the burial Joseph is arrested by the Jews and loses the dish. The Jews decide to starve him to death in a remote prison, but the resurrected Christ visits him and returns the dish. He reveals its mysteries to him, but not its name. Years go by and Joseph is utterly forgotten. More than forty years later Vespasian, the son of the Roman Emperor, comes to Jerusalem seeking vengeance on the Jews. For Vespasian was a leper, and had discovered that the Jews had killed the prophet who could have cured him. Eventually, however, he is healed by the handkerchief with which St Veronica had wiped Jesus' face. In Jerusalem Vespasian hears about Joseph and goes to see the place where he had been imprisoned. To general astonishment, he finds Joseph alive and well. He has been miraculously kept alive by the Grail and thinks that only three days have passed.

Joseph, his sister Enygeus and her husband Hebron (or Bron) leave Judea and travel with a few followers to a distant land. When one misfortune follows another and the company is starving, Joseph, inspired by the Holy Ghost, prepares a table to celebrate the service of the Grail, in commem-

'Joseph of Arimathea among the rocks of Albion'. Engraving by William Blake, 1773, based on a drawing by Salviati after Michaelangelo.

oration of the Last Supper. One seat at this table is left empty because of Judas' betrayal; at some time in the future it will be occupied by a descendant of Bron. The Grail is placed on the table and Bron is asked to catch a fish, which is put on the table next to the Grail. When everything is ready the followers can take their places. Only those unspotted by sin are allowed to sit there. Their hearts are filled with such bliss as they had never known. Here the name 'Grail' is used for the first time, supposedly derived from the Old French 'agreer': to experience delight. Moyses, one of the sinners, attempts to take his place at the table despite Joseph's warning. As soon as he sits on the empty chair the earth opens and swallows him up.

Enygeus and Bron have twelve sons, the last of whom, Alain, leads a life dedicated to God. He is destined to lead his brothers to the West and bring the Gospel there. A descendant of this Alain will later become the third and last owner of the Grail (i.e. Perceval). Until that time the Grail will be kept by Bron, who since catching the fish is known as 'le Riche Pescheor'. He, too, journeys to the West with the others. Towards the end of his life Joseph returns to Arimathea and dies there.

The tale of Joseph of Arimathea and the Grail was extremely popular in England, partly because it ties up with a legend which makes Joseph the founder of Glastonbury Abbey. The first mention of Joseph's presence in England occurs in a manuscript of William of Malmesbury's *De Antiquitate Glastoniensis*. This particular manuscript was written around 1250 in Glastonbury Abbey itself; the story of Joseph being the abbey's founder was added to William's text to attract pilgrims. According to this account Joseph, with twelve followers, was sent to England from France by the apostle Philip. A heathen king granted him a piece of land to live on at what is now Glastonbury. The 'missionaries' built a church there in honour of the Virgin Mary, and on his death Joseph was buried near Glastonbury.

According to a later legend Joseph crossed the Mediterranean by ship, accompanied by Lazarus and his sisters Martha and Mary, and landed in Marseilles. From there France, Spain and finally England were converted to Christianity. New legends continued to develop even after the Reformation, especially around Glastonbury. When Joseph stuck his staff in the ground at Glastonbury it turned into a thorn tree which blossomed each year at Christmas; today that tree's descendants still flower in December. Another legend portrays him as Mary's uncle, who on one occasion brought the child Jesus with him to Britain.

Joseph's popularity in England resulted in two Middle English translations/ adaptations of the *Estoire del Saint Graal*: the *Joseph of Arimathie* (c.1375) and *The History of the Holy Grail* (c.1450) by Henry Lovelich.

In 1585 Joseph was officially declared a saint. Even outside the realm of legend the figure of Joseph of Arimathea exerted a considerable and continuing influence, most notably in painting and sculpture but also in other fields. In the 19th century Tennyson linked Joseph the Grail-bearer and Joseph the founder of Glastonbury in his *Idylls of the King*. In pictorial art Joseph is often shown taking Jesus from the cross or laying him in his tomb, either with or without Nicodemus. Joseph can always be identified by his white hair and beard; often he is wearing the crown of thorns, or holding the nails which had pinned Jesus to the cross, a pair of pincers, the shroud or a pot of ointment. He is also regularly found with the Grail, e.g. on the 17th-century altar of Göttweig monastery and in the Church of the Holy Cross in Landau. Michelangelo depicted himself as Joseph of Arimathea in a Descent from the Cross intended for his own tomb.

ADA POSTMA

Editions: Treharne 1967; Sodmann 1980; Cerquiglini 1981; O'Gorman 1995.
Study: Sandkühler 1958.

K AY, or Keu, is King Arthur's sarcastic chamberlain; he appears in almost all the Arthurian romances, though he never achieves a leading role. His omnipresence is due to his function: Sir Kay is the official responsible for the management of Arthur's household. In that capacity he is much in the king's presence, ensuring that things run smoothly (especially at banquets).

Kay's character was largely determined by the Old French poet Chrétien de Troyes, who in the second half of the 12th century wrote the earliest Arthurian romances (in rhyming couplets). In the first of these, → *Erec et Enide* (c.1165–70), Kay (here Keu) features in a scene which was to be much imitated. His behaviour on meeting Erec is so boorish that a duel becomes inevitable; his angry opponent then knocks him off his horse quite easily. Clearly, he is a born loser.

Chrétien's → *Yvain* draws attention for the first time to Keu's sarcastic nature. The narrator characterises him as a spiteful, unpleasant, fault-finding, sharp-tongued individual. At the beginning of the story Keu ridicules Calogrenant when he shows his respect for the queen by leaping to his feet more quickly than anyone else. In Chrétien's last and unfinished romance, → *Perceval* (c.1190), Keu's taste for derision in part determines the action. In the first part of the work Keu makes fun of the naive young Perceval, who has come to court to win his knighthood. When a lady declares that Perceval will become the best knight in the world Keu strikes her; a jester who backs up the lady's prediction receives the same treatment. Perceval resolves to pay Keu back for his behaviour, and later in the story he does just that: he knocks Keu, who is trying – rudely, as always – to escort him to Arthur, off his horse; the chamberlain breaks his right arm and collar-bone, just as the jester had predicted.

Unpleasant though Keu is, King Arthur seems very attached to him. Not only does he continue to tolerate his presence, he cannot manage without him. So much is clear from Chrétien's → *Lancelot* (c.1175), in which the king is close to despair when Keu announces that he wishes to leave the court. Arthur will do anything to keep him, with the result that on his queen's advice he agrees to Keu's request for an unspecified favour. With far-reaching consequences, for Keu the bungler asks permission to escort the queen as sole representative of the court in response to a challenge by the wicked Meleagant. Of course Keu is beaten, and Meleagant then carries off the queen.

Chrétien's chamberlain is a far cry from his literary predecessor Cei, who in Celtic literature is a mighty hero. In the Welsh narrative → *Culhwch ac Olwen*, for instance, Cei is Arthur's foremost and most trusted hero. In this tale, probably first written down around the middle of the 11th century, Cei appears to possess extraordinary qualities: he can remain under water for nine days and nights, can make himself bigger than the tallest tree and radiates an intense heat. When he wounds someone with his terrible sword no cure is possible. It was probably Cei's magical powers that made him unsuitable for a role in the 12th-century Arthurian romances, reflecting as they did the chivalrous and courtly ideals of their own time and culture. Consequently, when the world of the Celtic heroes gave way to that of the romance Cei changed his nature but retained his connection with Arthur through his role of chamberlain. It is highly probable that much of this transformation should be ascribed to Chrétien.

The depiction of Keu in Chrétien's romances forms the starting-point for the character's development in medieval literature. As one might expect, many writers sought to pick up where Chrétien left off. Thus Keu often appears as a scoffer. Knights in many romances are afraid of his sharp tongue and time and again it is he who ridicules newcomers to Arthur's court. Another frequently recurring feature is the ease with which he can be defeated. The *Lancelot en prose* (c.1225), an Old French prose romance, makes pleasant play with this idea of Keu as the eternal loser. At one point the outstanding knight Lancelot is going around in Keu's armour. In this guise he overcomes many knights who, sure that they are facing the easily vanquished Keu, find theselves sadly deceived.

In some works Keu's image differs from that to be found in Chrétien. Strikingly, some authors take a more favourable view of his behaviour. In the *Lancelot en prose*, for example, Keu's role is on occasion decidedly positive. In his *Parzival* (c.1200–10) the German poet Wolfram von Eschenbach rejects the negative image: his Keu is a brave and loyal vassal, who treats other knights with honour.

In other works Keu's character is far more negative than in Chrétien. While Chrétien's Keu likes to ridicule others, he is no coward; by contrast, the authors of two Old French romances, the prose *Perlesvaus* (early 13th century) and the verse *Yder*, portray him as a markedly malicious, treacherous, cowardly and cruel individual. In *Perlesvaus* he kills Arthur's son Loholt after the latter has killed a giant. With the giant's severed head as proof Keu then presents himself at Arthur's court as the giant-killer. When his deception is uncovered he flees. In *Yder* Keu uses his lance during a battle to strike the gallant Yder from the side in a most cowardly way. Later in the story he offers Yder a poisoned drink when that hero is thirsty from fighting two giants. Keu's crimes bring down on him the wrath of Arthur's knights; Arthur himself, who cuts a notably poor figure in the *Yder*, does his best to protect his chamberlain.

Arthur's remarkable patience with Keu is brilliantly explained by the Old French poet Robert de Boron in his *Merlin* (c.1200). In this tale the wizard Merlin entrusts the orphaned infant Arthur to the care of Keu's parents. Keu's mother, a high-born lady, suckles Arthur herself, while her own son Keu is nourished by a wet-nurse of humble origins. This explains not only the bad qualities in Keu's character, but also Arthur's attitude to his foster-brother. For when later in the story Arthur becomes king, Keu's father Antor asks that in recompense for his fosterage he should make Keu his court chamberlain and stand by him under all circumstances. Arthur, who feels guilty towards Keu, grants his request.

In the Middle Dutch Arthurian romance *Walewein ende Keye* (→ Gawain), from the second half of the 13th century, Arthur, surprisingly, has had enough. In this romance Keye accuses Walewein of bragging: he is supposed to have said that in one year he would have more adventures than all the other knights of the Round Table put together. Furious, Walewein leaves court and performs one heroic deed after another, making it clear that even if Keye's accusation were just there could be no question of bragging. Although Arthur is concerned at Keye's plight (he begs his knights not to handle his chamberlain too roughly) at the end of the romance he banishes Keye, who has by then admitted his misdeeds, from court.

Kay's biography is rounded off in, among others, the Old French prose romance *Mort le roi Artu* (c.1230) by his death at the hand of the Roman Emperor during a great battle against the Romans. Arthur at once avenges his death, taking the Emperor's life with one terrible blow. The last gap in the story of Kay's life, his childhood and youth, was filled in only in the 20th century, by T.H. White, author of the inimitable *The Once and Future King* (1958). The first part of the book, *The Sword in the Stone*, which appeared in 1938, consists of a splendid account of the youth of Arthur and Kay, who is characterised as follows: 'He was not at all an unpleasant person really, but clever, quick, proud, passionate and ambitious. He was one of those people who would be neither a follower nor a leader, but only an aspiring heart, impatient in the failing body which imprisoned it.'

BART BESAMUSCA

Study: Gowans 1988.

KUDRUN (also: Gudrun, Chutrun, Chautrun) is the eponymous heroine of a Middle High German epic in stanzaic form, written in the first half of the 13th century (probably around 1230–40) somewhere in Bavaria or Austria. The city of Regensburg has been suggested as its birthplace. As usual with heroic epic, no author's name has come down to us. The work falls into three sections which focus on the lives of three successive generations of the same heroic family. The first part, a kind of prelude, recounts the life of Kudrun's grandfather Hagen, the second (the 'Hilde section') is devoted to the adventures of her mother Hilde, the third and final part tells the story of Kudrun herself.

Sigeband, King of Ireland, wins the hand of a Norwegian princess. A son is born of this union and is named Hagen. During a tournament the seven-year-old boy is carried off by a griffin and taken to its nest on a faraway island. One of the young griffins pulls him out of the nest and drops him. Little Hagen runs to a cave where he is brought up by three princesses from India, Portugal and Iceland. The blood of a 'gabiloen' (a dragon-like monster) which he kills gives him superhuman powers. A dead crusader is washed up on the island; using this unfortunate's arms and armour Hagen succeeds in killing the griffin. A pilgrim ship takes him and the three princesses safely back to Ireland. Hagen marries one of his three foster-mothers, Princess Hilde of India, and succeeds his father as King of Ireland. The couple have a daughter whom they name Hilde after her mother.

When the young Hilde is twelve years old many foreign princes compete for her hand, but Hagen has the wooers' emissaries hanged; he will not marry his daughter to a man weaker than himself. Hetel, King of the Hegelings, is the ruler of a coastal realm which includes Ortland, Nifland and Tenemarke (Denmark); his counsellors recommend the beautiful Hilde as a suitable consort. He sends the famous bard Hôrant and the wild man Wate to Ireland to secure her as his bride. They pass themselves off as wealthy merchants who have been driven from Hetel's court; but for a military option they have armed knights hidden below decks. The supposed refugees manage to win the favour of the king and queen with costly gifts. Young Hilde, too, is eager to meet the visitors, so her father Hagen invites them to his court. The strangers make a great impression. Wate defeats Hagen in a mock duel while Hôrant, like a second Orpheus, secretly wins Hilde's heart for Hetel with his wonderful singing. Just before leaving they lure Hilde on board their vessel and sail away to Hegelingland with the young beauty before the eyes of her father and mother. Fuming with rage Hagen sets sail in pursuit. In an inconclusive battle both Hagen and Hetel are wounded. Finally, with Hetel's help, young Hilde manages to separate the still-fighting Hagen and Wate. Hagen agrees to his daughter marrying the Hegeling king and returns to Ireland.

Hetel and Hilde have two children: a son Ortwin and a daughter Kudrun. The princess grows up into a remarkably beautiful young woman; many suitors seek her hand, but all are rejected. After all manner of complications she is finally betrothed to Herwig of Seeland, but is to spend one more year with her parents before marrying him. One of the rejected suitors, Siegfried of Morland, is jealous and invades Seeland. Kudrun's father Hetel hastens to the aid of his future son-in-law. Another rejected lover, Hartmut of Ormania, seizes on Hetel's absence to raid Hegelingland, robbing and plundering and abducting the lovely Kudrun and other maidens. A wild chase after the abductors now begins. A bloody battle takes place on Curlew Sands and Kudrun's father Hetel is killed. In the darkness of the night Hartmut manages to escape with his captives (Kudrun and sixty other girls).

When they reach Ormania Hartmut's mother, the cruel and ambitious Gerlind (the epic calls her 'she-devil') tries to persuade Kudrun to marry her son. But Kudrun refuses and remains faithful to her betrothed, Herwig. Gerlind is furious and compels the royal lady to perform tasks far beneath her station; she has to make the fire, spin thread, carry water, etc. Gerlind then humiliates her still more by making her act as washerwoman. For years she and her faithful maid have to do the washing on the beach in all weathers. All this Kudrun endures steadfastly and with resignation.

Thirteen years after her abduction a great fleet sails for Ormania to rescue Kudrun and her maidens. Having overcome numerous difficulties on the voyage (magnetic rocks, calms, fog) it reaches Hartmut's country. Her betrothed Herwig and her brother Ortwin find Kudrun and a friend, Hildburg, on the snow-covered beach, shivering with cold as they wash Gerlind's clothes. Their position seems hopeless, but the previous day an angel in the shape of a bird had foretold that their misery would soon be at an end. A touching reunion follows. The men promise to return very soon and rescue Kudrun and her companions from their unpleasant situation. The women throw the laundry into the sea. When the cruel Gerlind sees them return empty-handed she is about to have them flogged; however, Kudrun pretends that she is willing to marry Hartmut after all. She is bathed and given splendid clothes. That night the rescuers' army attacks the castle. A savage battle ensues, in which the wild man Wate fights particularly ferociously. He cuts off Gerlind's head and does not spare even the babes in the cradle. The ships then depart laden with rich booty, bearing with them in triumph not only Kudrun and her maidens but also the old enemies Hartmut and his sister.

On reaching Ireland the returned voyagers are welcomed by Hilde. There follows a general reconciliation of the formerly hostile families, with a number of marriages between the two sides. The high point of the festivities is of course Kudrun's wedding to Herwig of Seeland. They had endured no less than thirteen years of separation and humiliation, but here too the old saying applies: all's well that ends well.

The epic of Kudrun and her family is a work full of enigmas. We have only one late manuscript of it, known as the Ambras manuscript from Ambras Castle, its former home. This compilation was produced in Bolzano between 1502 and 1515 by the court official Hans Ried on the instructions of Emperor Maximilian, who had a great admiration for the ideals of courtly chivalry. As well as the *Kudrun* the manuscript contains many other Middle High German works, including the *Erec* and *Iwein* of Hartmann von Aue. Hans Ried adapted the language of the 13th-century original to that of his own time and place; for example, instead of 'Kudrun' he wrote 'Chautrun'.

Research into the origins and development of the story has concentrated mainly on the Hilde and Kudrun sections. The Hilde section in particular shows clear links to the past, since related material has been found in old sources. The Danish chronicler Saxo Grammaticus (c.1150–1220) in his *History of the Danes* and the Icelander Snorri Sturluson (1179–1241) in his prose *Edda* between them provide so much information that we can reconstruct an early form of the Hilde saga from them. The main points of the old story are: 1. Hilde's abduction by Hetel (known in the North as Hedinn); 2. the pursuit by Hilde's father Hagen; 3. a battle on an island between abductors and pursuers. In Snorri Sturluson it becomes a mythic, unending struggle, because every morning Hilde restores to life the warriors who had died during the night. In this developmental phase of the Hilde legend we can recognise an old Viking song about bride-stealing.

In the Old Norse *Edda* this type of Germanic hero-song is represented by the so-called *Helgi songs*; the relationship is clear not only from the content but also the names (Hedinn = Hetel, Högni = Hagen). The names Hagen, Heoden and Wada (Hagen, Hetel and Wate) also appear in the Anglo-Saxon poem → *Widsith*, written in the 8th century. Time and again, Middle High German verse epics of the 12th century allude to the Hilde saga; this is so in, for instance, the *Rolandslied* (→ Roland) and → *Salman und Morolf*. It is notable that over the centuries the setting has shifted from the Baltic to the North Sea; in the more recent version the site of the great battle, 'Curlew Sands', is located in the Scheldt estuary.

In 1896 an incomplete text was discovered in a Cairo synagogue; this so-called *Dukus Horant* shows striking similarities with the Hilde section of the *Kudrun*. The poem probably originated around 1300 in a German-speaking area somewhere on the Rhine. The manuscript, in Hebrew script, dates from 1382; it is now in Cambridge. The relationship between the two works is as yet unclear. Was the *Dukus Horant* composed by a Jewish man of letters, using motifs familiar to him from Middle High German works, or are we justified in assuming, in view of the observed differences between it and the *Kudrun*, that the *Dukus Horant* represents an independent Yiddish tradition?

The evolution of the Kudrun section of our epic is less clear than that of the Hilde section. Because of their similarities it has been supposed that the Kudrun section developed out of that of Hilde; but today scholars are once more stressing the differences between the two which, they think, indicate an independent origin for the Kudrun story. The basic elements of the Kudrun section are thought to be: 1. the winning of the bride; 2. the abduction; 3. captivity and 4. release. These narrative elements are frequently combined in medieval literature. In such stories the female protagonist is often called Hildburg and people sometimes speak of the 'Hildburg/ Kudrun legend'. A Hildburg tale of this type can be found in the Old English → *Beowulf* (8th century); it is probably derived from an Old Frisian heroic lay. This early form of the Kudrun legend probably originated along the North Sea coast.

So what did the 13th-century poet (or whoever provided his model) do with the material handed down to him? The similarities between the Hilde and Kudrun sections clearly demonstrate that an exchange of motifs took place. It is also evident that the author was a master of the art of repetition with variation – an important artistic principle in the Middle Ages. In each of the three sections he is concerned with the winning of a bride, but the obstacles to success are such as to make it increasingly difficult to bring about the actual marriage.

Here we also have to ask ourselves: is the *Kudrun* really a heroic epic like, for instance, the *Nibelungenlied*? In general one can say that a Middle High German heroic epic is about the 'persistence of the moral personality in a situation inescapable because predestined, in which the last resort, staking one's own life, is not avoided' (H. de Boor). In the *Kudrun* the heroic element lies in a woman's refusal to give up her personal dignity on any terms whatever. As a queen she is willing to undertake the most menial of tasks rather than gain material benefit through a dishonourable surrender. Moreover, Kudrun demonstrates that she is capable of respecting her enemies, forgiving them and being reconciled with them. She thus embodies the Christian ideals of forgiveness and love for one's enemies. The concept of vengeance found in the early Germanic system of justice, embodied in the *Nibelungenlied* (c.1200), is represented by the figure of Wate; but here it has clearly been pushed into the background. The work reflects the courtly environment with its service of ladies, its feasts and tourneys, its court ceremonial. The ideals of the courtly period, moderation, self-discipline, steadfastness and loyalty, combined with Christian charity, are represented in the figure of Kudrun. For this reason Kudrun, who was able to break the mechanism of injustice and vengeance, is one of the most striking female characters in Middle High German heroic epic.

Comparatively few traces of the *Kudrun* epic are to be found in later literature. At most one can point to a certain kinship with the so-called *Südeli* ballads (the rediscovered sister) and the *Meererin* ballads (the washerwoman by the sea) recorded in the second half of the 19th century in Spain, Scandinavia, Germany, the Netherlands and Russia, which show striking correspondences of detail with the *Kudrun*. The Olimpia episode in a late edition of the Italian work *Orlando furioso* by Ariosto (1474–1533) also shows the influence of the Middle High German *Kudrun*; and the second, Hilde, section lives on in folktales and ballads. In this connection one can point to *Faithful John* from the fairy-tales of the Brothers Grimm, which tells of the abduction by trickery of a king's daughter on a merchant vessel – the same thing that happened to Hilde. It is not clear, however, how far this is dependent on the *Kudrun*. The drama *Gudrun* by the Flemish poet G. Rodenbach (1855–98) combines the steadfast Kudrun with historical motifs that are Flemish Nationalist in tone. Less well known German-speaking writers also made use of the material. In the last century C.L.A. Mangold wrote a *Kudrun* opera (1849) which rightly failed to become widely known. E. Hardt in 1911 and G. Schumann in 1949 adapted the material for the stage. In 1922 W. Jansen wrote a version, quite popular in its time, entitled *Das Buch der Liebe: Gudrun-Roman*.

F. VAN DER RHEE

Editions: Symons/Boesch 1964[4]; Simrock 1978.
Study: Wisniewski 1969[2].

L ANCELOT is the lover of Guenièvre (Guinevere), King → Arthur's wife. He is the son of King Ban of Benoyc and his baptismal name is Galaad (Galahad); so we are told at the beginning of the *Lancelot en prose*, an Old French Arthurian romance written between 1215 and 1235. When Ban is besieged by King Claudas he flees with his wife and young son. A last look back at his burning castle kills him. As everyone crowds around the dead man a fairy carries off the child and takes him to the magic lake in which she, the 'Lady of the Lake', lives with her followers. In this magical realm she brings up the boy, together with his younger cousins Bohort (Bors) and Lionel. Although he is called 'Prince', Ban's son remains ignorant of his name and origins.

At the age of eighteen the Lady of the Lake takes him to King Arthur's court, having provided him with extremely detailed instructions on knightly behaviour. On the eve of his knighting the handsome youth meets Queen Guenièvre and is at once smitten with love for her. Her presence robs him of speech, but as he leaves court next day he manages to find words to tell her that henceforth he will regard himself as her knight. The link between his knighthood and his love for the queen is reinforced by the fact that she gives him a sword and thus completes the ceremony of knighthood. The young knight establishes his reputation in numerous adventures, while the court tries to discover his identity by means of various quests by, among others, Gauvain (→ Gawain). The mysteries that surround this subject are very gradually resolved, in part when during the adventure of the 'Doloreuse Garde' he himself reads on the underside of a tomb lid that he is Lancelot du Lac, son of Ban of Benoyc.

Lancelot sends every opponent he defeats in his adventures to Guenièvre. When in a revealing conversation she presses him about his feats of arms he confesses his love for her. After this conversation Lancelot's bosom friend Galehot arranges for the queen to kiss Lancelot in proof of her love. Like Galehot, the Lady of the Lake also encourages their relationship. She sends Guenièvre a shield on which are depicted a knight and a lady divided by a crack in the shield, symbolising her unconsummated relationship with Lancelot. When Arthur is seduced by the Scottish sorceress Camille and spends the night with her, Lancelot sleeps with Guenièvre and the crack in the shield closes up. Camille imprisons Arthur and, soon after, Gauvain, Galehot and Lancelot as well. When Lancelot loses his mind in prison he is released. The Lady of the Lake and Guenièvre manage to cure him with the aid of the shield; Lancelot then frees the king and the other captives.

Contrasting with the helpful attitude of Galehot and the Lady of the Lake are various other figures who seek to destroy the lovers, chief among them the arch-intriguer Morgaine, Arthur's half-sister. She successfully filches from Lancelot a ring given him by Guenièvre and later, at court, confronts the queen with this compromising object. Guenièvre manages to avert the danger in diplomatic fashion, saying that as queen she is bound to feel courtly love for the best knight in the world.

The all-consuming nature of Lancelot's love leads Galehot to realise that it will eventually mean the end of their friendship. When Arthur temporarily rejects his wife in favour of the 'false Guenièvre' Lancelot, Guenièvre and Galehot are still able to live together as brothers and sister; but in the end Lancelot's heart chooses his lady. The friends come to a parting of the ways. Lancelot seeks out and frees the abducted Gauvain while Galehot stays behind, tormented by dreams of his ruin. A wise man who expounds Galehot's dreams tells him also that Lancelot lost his baptismal name of Galaad as a sign that his love for Guenièvre will bar him from successfully completing the quest for the Grail. When Galehot is told (erroneously) that Lancelot is dead, he dies.

The hypothetical 'non-cyclic' version of the *Lancelot en prose* ends with Galehot's death. In the cyclic version the story continues with the episode known as the 'Charrette'. This episode revolves around the ancient theme of the (voluntary) abduction of the queen (also known as *aithed*) and is a slightly modified prose version of Chrétien de Troyes' *Le chevalier de la Charrette* (c.1180), the first romance to depict Lancelot as the lover of Guenièvre.

According to this tale Guenièvre, together with Keu (→ Kay), is carried off by the knight Meleagant to Gorre, the country of his father Baudemagu, where a great many of Arthur's subjects are already held captive. Gauvain immediately sets out in search of the queen; he is joined in his quest by an unknown knight (Lancelot). They encounter a cart driven by a monstrous dwarf who promises them information if they are willing to ride in his cart. Just for a moment, the dishonourable nature of such transport deters the unknown knight. Then he climbs aboard the cart of shame. The dwarf takes him and Gauvain to a stronghold from which they see the queen's train in the distance. Giving chase, the knights are faced with a choice between two ways into Gorre. Gauvain chooses the underwater bridge, Lancelot (who reveals himself to his companion when they part) the sword bridge. On his way to this bridge Lancelot comes to a churchyard where he raises the lid of a tomb, thus learning that he will bring the prisoners safely out of Gorre. Lancelot's failure at a second tomb signifies – so a voice from the grave tells him – that because of his love for Guenièvre he can no longer complete the Grail quest. By crawling along the sharp blade of an enormous sword, not without considerable injury to himself, Lancelot manages to enter the land of Gorre where Meleagant is waiting for him. Their first duel, in which Lancelot is so distracted by the sight of Guenièvre that he is almost beaten, is halted by Baudemagu when Lancelot regains the upper hand. When he is subsequently taken to the queen her reaction is extremely chilly; mainly, it emerges when they talk things out, because of the episode of the compromising ring.

Lancelot spends the next night with Guenièvre in the room she shares with the injured Keu. In removing the bars from her window he injures himself and leaves bloody marks on the bed. Meleagant discovers the bloodstains and accuses Guenièvre of adultery with Keu. Lancelot proves her innocence in a judicial duel; again he comes close to defeating Meleagant. However, at the queen's behest Baudemagu once more intervenes.

They decide to go in search of Gauvain. On the way Lancelot is captured by Meleagant's men and taken to an isolated tower. The others find Gauvain, still frantically trying to cross the underwater bridge. He is pulled out of the water and later returns to Arthur's court with the queen and the other prisoners. In the meantime Lancelot's cousin Bohort has arrived there, seated in the cart of shame. He persuades the king and queen, Gauvain and all the other knights to take their places on the cart, thus erasing the stigma of Lancelot's ride in the demeaning vehicle. Eventually Lancelot too returns to court, released from his long imprisonment by Meleagant's sister. At Arthur's court he fights Guenièvre's abductor for the third time. This time Meleagant is killed.

Bohort plays a major role in those parts of the text which follow the 'Charrette'. At the beginning of the 'Préparation à la Queste', the final part of the *Lancelot en prose*, he is duped into promising to abduct the queen, which he attempts to do incognito. Lancelot manages to prevent the abduction by defeating Bohort, but – though gravely wounded – is at once taken away from Guenièvre and the court by an old woman. The court fears for his life and a great search is organised, in the course of which Gauvain, Lancelot, Bohort, → Perceval and Lancelot's half-brother Hector behold the Holy Grail. From his encounter with the Grail it is again evident that Lancelot can no longer be the chosen Grail hero, in contrast to Bohort, who like Perceval will be one of the three knights to complete the Grail quest. This section points out that there is not only a positive, but also a distinctly negative side to Lancelot's love for Guenièvre; for example, in the episode of Lancelot's imprisonment by Morgaine. His love inspires him to create magnificent wall-paintings telling the story of their relationship; but Morgaine will later use those very paintings to enlighten Arthur. Lancelot's adventures are dominated by his loyalty to Guenièvre. There are all kinds of attempts to induce him to break faith with her, but in vain. Yet he is in fact unfaithful, albeit unknowingly. During his visit to the Grail castle he is deceived into believing that Guenièvre is awaiting him in a nearby castle. Confused by a drugged drink, he thinks he is bedding his beloved; but he is actually making love to the daughter of the Grail-King Pelles. On her he begets Galaad (→ Galahad), the future Grail hero, whose virginity enables him to bear the name Galaad which Lancelot had lost. Towards the end of the work, at Arthur's court, Lancelot is again lured into the bed of Pelles' daughter. This time, however, Guenièvre catches him. Her reprimand and his own guilt drive Lancelot into a recurrence of his love-madness, for which the Grail proves to be the only cure. It turns out that the inspirational love which had made Lancelot the best knight in the world can also lead to disaster. Coupled with the rise of Bohort and Perceval, who show themselves Lancelot's equals in knightly qualities, what happens to Lancelot in the 'Préparation à la Queste' indicates that worldly knighthood is about to be overshadowed by religious knighthood and the service of the Grail.

The *Queste del Saint Graal* relates how all the knights of the Round Table set out in search of the Grail but only three are successful. In the end it is given only to Galaad, the chosen one, to look directly into the Grail cup; after which he is immediately taken up into Heaven. Perceval will eventually die a hermit, and Bohort is the only Grail hero to return and report the miraculous events. In this text worldly knights such as Gauvain, Hector and Lionel are 'unmasked' as hardened sinners and murderers. Lancelot, as a repentant sinner, stands somewhere between the two. As father of the Grail hero he is allowed to spend some time with his son and also on two occasions to witness the Grail procession. He abjures his love for the queen when charged to do so by a hermit and does penance for his voluptuous life (*luxure*) by becoming a strict ascetic.

Lancelot's rejection of Guenièvre does not last long, however, for the *Mort le roi Artu*, the final part of the Lancelot trilogy, tells how the lovers resume their relationship a month after the end of the Grail quest. For a while there is a coolness between them when the queen mistakenly suspects Lancelot of an affair with the Lady of Escalot; the matter is cleared up when a boat brings the body of the lady, dead of unrequited love for Lancelot, to court. The lovers' carelessness leads to their discovery. Arthur, who has already been informed by Morgaine by means of Lancelot's wall-paintings, is forced to act. His consort, caught in the act, is sentenced to be burnt at the stake but is saved at the last moment by Lancelot, who had managed to evade capture. In rescuing the queen Lancelot accidentally kills his friend Gaheret (Gareth), Gauvain's youngest brother. Gauvain is determined to avenge Gaheret's death – and that of his other brothers Agravain and Guerrehet (Gaheris) – at any cost. Even after Guenièvre has returned to Arthur's side on the intervention of the Pope Gauvain continues to insist on war with Lancelot, who has retreated to his lands on the continent. Arthur marches out to battle, leaving his country in the hands of his bastard son Mordred. The conflict reaches its climax in a duel between Lancelot and Gauvain in which Lancelot deals his former friend a head-wound which eventually proves fatal, but spares his life.

After this battle Arthur's forces become involved in a war with the Romans. On top of this, Arthur is informed that Mordred has seized power and is now besieging Guenièvre, whom he intends to marry. Arthur returns to Britain, but refuses – despite ominous dreams and the pleas of the dying and remorseful Gauvain – to summon Lancelot to his aid. In the battle that follows Arthur and Mordred mortally wound each other and the dying Arthur is taken to Avalon. Mordred's sons then try to take power. On hearing the result of the battle Guenièvre decides to take the veil. Lancelot returns; just before settling accounts with Mordred's sons he learns that his beloved has died. He ensures that Arthur's crown is in good hands and then joins Bohort and Hector as a hermit. Four years later he dies. One of his companions has a dream in which he sees him being carried up into Heaven by angels. Lancelot is buried beside Galehot in the tomb in which he had read, long ago, who he was.

The Old French Lancelot trilogy provides the complete biography of the world's greatest knight, but it is not the first text in which he appears. In all probability, a

Lancelot legend existed in the second half of the 12th century as part of the oral tradition of tales about King Arthur and his knights, a legend which portrayed him as a great lover and a great knight. The Middle High German *Lanzelet*, written c.1200 by Ulrich von Zatzikhoven, goes back to a lost Anglo-Norman Lancelot text which uses elements from this oral tradition. The *Lanzelet* tells of a hero who is carried off and raised by a water-sprite, learns his name from a tomb only after becoming a knight and is involved as one of Arthur's knights in the rescue of the kidnapped queen Guinevere. There is extensive coverage of Lanzelet's amorous adventures with various ladies, but no mention of any relationship with the queen. The work ends with an account of the extremely fruitful marriage of Lancelot and Yblis.

The Anglo-Norman source of the *Lanzelet* probably also formed an important source for Chrétien de Troyes' *Le chevalier de la Charrette* (c.1180). The content of this verse romance was later included in the *Lancelot en prose* and is thus included in the summary above. Chrétien's romance portrays Lancelot for the first time as Queen Guinevere's lover – possibly on the instructions of Countess Marie de Champagne, for whom the work was written. Now Arthur's consort had already shown extramarital aspirations in earlier texts; in the *Lai de* → *Lanval*, for instance, she tries to seduce the eponymous hero, while the chronicles of Arthur's decline suggest a relationship between her and Mordred. True, the 'ladies' man' Lancelot of the *Lanzelet's* source does not appear in the Arthurian chronicles; but he does seem eminently suited to fill the vacant post of Guinevere's lover. One consequence was a radical reworking of the relationship between Guinevere and Mordred in later works on Arthur's death such as the *Mort le roi Artu* summarised above. Once brought together, the characters of Lancelot and Guinevere become as inseparable as → Tristan and Yseult.

Chrétien's *Charrette* establishes Lancelot's name as a lover, but also as an outstanding knight. He is even given a Saviour's role, as the predicted liberator of the prisoners in Gorre; but the idea of allowing him, as a reflection of the Messiah, to find the Holy Grail was rejected as early as the prose romance *Perlesvaus* (1200–10). In this work Lancelot fails in the Grail quest because of his love for Guinevere. The *Lancelot en prose* cycle takes over this line of thought but shifts the Messiah aspect to Lancelot's son → Galahad, who in the *Queste del Saint Graal* is expressly presented as the 'new Christ'. In the hypothetical non-cyclic prose *Lancelot*, probably written about the same time as the *Perlesvaus*, all attention is focused on the development of the courtly love, stimulus to valour, between Lancelot and the queen. The expansion of this text into the *Lancelot* trilogy seems to result in some contradiction between the exaltation of secular love in the first part and its condemnation in, particularly, the Grail quest. However, this apparent contradiction proves to be an apparent contrast, also known as 'double esprit', if secular knighthood is regarded as a preliminary phase of the divine knighthood represented by Galahad. Not for nothing is Lancelot, greatest of worldly knights, the father of Galahad, the culmination of 'chevalerie célestielle'. From this perspective, religious knighthood in the service of the Grail constitutes the highest ideal. Once the source of inspiration, the Grail, has vanished again into Heaven, the Arthurian world of the *Mort Artu* is left with only the old, now exposed, ideal of secular knighthood and is then destroyed by the human failings of the king, his wife, and his closest companions.

Although the Lancelot portrayed in the *Lancelot en prose* cycle is far from infallible, either as lover or as knight, he never loses his brilliance or his tragic fascination. The cycle was extraordinarily popular; around a hundred manuscripts of it have survived, as have some early prints (including one of 1488 from Rouen). To a great extent, therefore, the cycle provides the context for Lancelot's entrance into other vernacular literatures. Exceptions to this are the *Lanzelet* mentioned above and another Middle High German romance, *Diu Crône*, written around 1225 by Heinrich von dem Türlin. This text gives an idealised picture of Gawein (→ Gawain), even allowing him to achieve success in a Grail quest in which he compares favourably with Lancelot, who

Lancelot learning archery. Illumination in a manuscript of c.1325. Oxford, Bodleian Library

Lancelot on the sword bridge. 13th-century capital in the Church of St Pierre, Caen.

misses his chance in the Grail adventure by falling asleep. Heinrich tarnishes Lancelot's reputation on another occasion: while seeking the kidnapped queen Lancelot got into the cart less because of the promised information than because he was tired and the wood was so very thorny. These texts were followed around 1250 by an anonymous German prose translation of the *Lancelot en prose*, which was abridged by Ulrich Fuetrer about 1467 as his *Prosaroman von Lanzelot*, which he later again reworked and expanded to produce the second part of his *Buch der Abenteuer*.

Through the *Tristan en prose*, an Old French work from the mid-13th century which uses the friendship between Lancelot and Tristan to fuse the Tristan story with that of Arthur and the Grail, Lancelot also appears in Italian literature in, among others, the *Tristano Riccardiano* (late 13th century) and the *Tavola Ritonda* cycle (second quarter of the 14th century). He also entered Spanish and Portuguese literature via translations of the *Lancelot en prose* and the Old French texts which followed it, such as the *Tristan en prose* and the so-called Post-Vulgate Cycle. In fact this last work, which relegates the character of Lancelot to the background in favour of Arthur, can be reconstructed only from its Portuguese and Spanish translations. A late Catalan representative of the Vulgate texts is the incunable *Tragèdia de Lançalot*, a version of the *Mort Artu* of which only fragments now survive; its author was the poet Mossèn Gras.

The Lancelot story was much in demand in Middle Dutch, as witness at least three translations of the *Lancelot en prose* in the space of barely half a century. The so-called Lancelot compilation is a manuscript from the early 14th century in which the three parts of the *Lancelot* cycle are interspersed with seven Arthurian romances. One of the seven, the → *Moriaen*, contains a striking Lancelot episode, and the inserted texts also include a short Lancelot romance, *Lanceloet en het hert met de witte voet*. This romance is an original work by a Middle Dutch poet, but was clearly influenced both by the dragon-slayer episode from the Tristan material and by the *Lai de Tyolet*. When Keye (Kay) returns empty-handed from the quest for the hart with a white foot, Lancelot undertakes the task. A beautiful princess has resolved that she will marry only the man who brings her the white foot. The hart is guarded by seven lions, but after a bitter struggle Lancelot manages to acquire the foot. Since he is exhausted and injured, he asks a passing knight to take the foot to the princess's court and bring help. But the knight turns out to be a scoundrel: he takes the foot and then strikes Lancelot a terrible blow with his sword. The princess is horrified when he – a notoriously evil and ugly knight – arrives at her court with the intention of claiming her as his bride. Meanwhile Walewein (Gawain) has found the injured Lancelot and discovered what had happened. He takes Lancelot to a doctor and prevents the villain's marriage to the princess by defeating him in a judicial duel. When it becomes clear that Lancelot had won the white foot the princess wants to marry him. However, the marriage is postponed indefinitely because Lancelot loves only the queen. This creation of a new Lancelot story is exceptional and can be seen as indicative of the character's popularity in the Middle Dutch language area.

In medieval England, on the other hand, Lancelot seems to have made little impression. While several romances were written about Gawain, not one English romance was devoted to Lancelot. The *Lancelot en prose* had not even been translated until Malory's version of the cycle and the late 15th-century Scottish fragment *Sir Lancelot of the Laik*. Lancelot does of course play a major part in an English text on Arthur's end, the stanzaic *Le morte Arthur* (c.1350); this is modelled on the Old French *Mort le roi Artu* but includes an additional episode in which Lancelot and Guinevere meet for one last time after Lancelot's return. They confess their common guilt – the exposure of their relationship marked the beginning of the end for Arthur – and promise to devote themselves to God in penance. Guinevere even refuses Lancelot a final kiss. This dramatic scene reappears in the last book of Sir Thomas Malory's *Morte d'Arthur* (1485: first printing of a version by William Caxton), the work which formed the keystone of the medieval treatment of the Arthurian material and also laid the foundation for by far the greatest part of the story's *Nachleben* in the centuries that followed. Taking the Lancelot and Tristan romances as his guide, Malory collected the disparate Arthurian material into twenty books. From Book VI on, Lancelot is one of the main characters in his tale.

The great diversity and wide dissemination of Lancelot texts means that scholarly interest in Lancelot also extends into many areas. That Lancelot has no place in the oldest stratum of Arthurian material, that he is not mentioned in such chronicles as Geoffrey of Monmouth's *Historia regum Britannie* nor in the old story of → Culhwch and Olwen, has not prevented scholars from searching for the character's Celtic roots and claiming, for instance, that Lancelot derives from the god Lug of Irish mythology. More significant is research into the 'abducted queen' (or *aithed*) theme, which has been found to be widespread in European literature and also turns up in, for example, an early 12th-century stone relief in Modena Cathedral.

With regard to the Old French texts, research has centred on Chrétien's *Charrette* and the *Lancelot en prose*. Major topics of discussion concerning Chrétien's work are its place in his oeuvre and the poet's own ideas. Chrétien says in his prologue that the work was commissioned by Marie, Countess of Champagne, and states emphatically that it was she who provided the 'matière' (narrative material) and the 'san' (tenor, moral of the story) and that he contributed only his narrative skill. Since Chrétien did not himself complete the romance (from the start of Lancelot's captivity in Meleagant's tower it is the work of Godefroy de Leigni), and since the *Charrette* shows no thematic links with his *Erec et Enide* and *Yvain*, it has been suggested that in fact Chrétien found the tone of the Lancelot romance uncongenial. While his tales of → Erec and → Yvain advocate courtly love within marriage and social knighthood in the service of the Arthurian community, this romance concerns an adulterous love which can stimulate Lancelot's knighthood but also cripple it, and which seems to be possible only outside court circles (in Gorre).

Though Chrétien may have written the story with reluctance and did not finish it, the *Charrette* elicited a far greater literary response than his earlier romances – exactly as happened with the also unfinished *Conte du Graal* (→ Perceval). According to Elspeth Kennedy, an original version of the biography of Lancelot as it now exists in the *Lancelot en prose* would have taken the story summarised above only as far as the beginning of the *Charrette*. The existence of this 'non-cyclic' *Lancelot* is somewhat controversial, even though Kennedy has in the meantime produced an edition and a study in which she adduces forceful arguments for the version's right to exist. Following the non-cyclic stage the Lancelot biography would have been combined with a prose version of the *Charrette* and then expanded into a trilogy by the addition of the *Queste del Saint Graal*, the *Mort le roi Artu* and some linking passages such as the 'Préparation à la Queste'. At a later stage the previous history of the Grail and the story of → Merlin were slotted in at the beginning. During this process of amalgamation the *Charrette* was not only turned into prose, it also underwent various modifications to tie the text into the new, massive whole. Thus, in the prose text Guenièvre's coolness to Lancelot in Gorre is attributed to a long-ago unfortunate incident with a ring, while in Chrétien's verse romance she is angry with Lancelot because he had for a moment been reluctant to get into the demeaning cart.

With regard to the *Lancelot en prose* cycle, a major focus of discussion is the question of the trilogy's authorship. In view of the already mentioned 'double esprit' – the ideological differences between the *Queste* and the other two parts – it was considered impossible that a single author could be responsible for the whole trilogy. It was thought that different authors could be distinguished even within the *Lancelot en prose* itself – a view refuted by F. Lot, who demonstrated the degree of thematic unity within the *Lancelot* text and explained the working of the narrative's confusing structure, which he termed 'entrelacement'. Since then most scholars have gone along with J. Frappier's suggestion that a number of authors worked on the text under the guidance of an 'architect' who was responsible for the trilogy's ideology and structure.

The most contentious issue relating to the *Lancelot en prose* arises from the manuscript tradition. At the beginning of this century H.O. Sommer produced an edition based on a manuscript in London; it then became apparent that there existed – notably in the Bibliothèque Nationale in Paris – *Lancelot en prose* manuscripts which gave a much more extensive version of the story. The issue of which version – short/London or long/Paris – is the more original has occupied minds considerably. The most authoritative scholar in this field, A. Micha, is of the opinion that the shorter version derives from the longer. Possibly the most important outcome of this debate is that Micha has charted the extremely complex transmission of the roughly one hundred manuscripts. Moreover, he has produced an edition of the long version (with variants), so that both versions are now available; this is of great importance for research into translation and narrative techniques in the translations of the *Lancelot en prose*, for instance in the Utrecht Lancelot project, which is concerned with the study and editing of the Middle Dutch Lancelot texts.

The 'afterlife' of the Lancelot material really begins as early as the *Divina Commedia* of Dante Alighieri (begun c.1308). During his visit to the second circle of Hell, that of the lascivious ones, whose denizens include Paris and Tristan, the protagonist converses in one of the book's most famous passages with Francesca da Rimini (*La Divina Commedia*, Inferno, Canto V). She tells him how she and her lover Paolo succumbed to their love when reading together about Lancelot and Guinevere, with 'Galeotto' (Galehot) as pander.

Given Lancelot's prominent role in medieval narrative, one would expect that he would have won himself a place alongside Tristan as the ideal (or not) lover. But this happened only to a limited extent. For instance, the story of Lancelot rarely appears on everyday objects, while Tristan is a favourite subject in this context. An Italian painted tray of c.1400 shows Lancelot and Tristan worshipping Venus, in company with Achilles (→ Hector), Samson, Paris and → Troilus, all heroes who were destroyed by their love. Like Tristan, Lancelot is at his peak in the second half of the 19th century, the time of the English Pre-Raphaelites. Before then we find only occasional works about Lancelot, such as the chapbook *Lançarote do Lago* of 1746, for which António da Silva ('mestre de Gramàtica') borrowed motifs and passages from Cervantes' *Don Quixote*, or the ballad 'Sir Lancelot of the Lake' written in 1765 by Bishop Percy and based on Malory's *Morte d'Arthur*. A relatively early play about Lancelot is Chr.J. Riethmüller's *Launcelot of the Lake* (1843).

For the artists and poets who displayed a renewed interest in Arthurian material in the Victorian England of the second half of the 19th century, Lancelot came to represent the ideal of the gentleman, of noble manliness. However, their portrayals of Lancelot and the Grail show that they were also well aware of his tragic side. Their principal source was Malory's *Morte d'Arthur*, but the influence of their contemporary, the poet Tennyson (*Idylls of the King*), can also be seen. These works were published in many editions, leading to numerous illustrations portraying Lancelot and others. The Moxon edition of Tennyson's *Poems* (1857), for instance, contained illustrations by Dante Gabriel Rossetti, Holman Hunt and Millais, among others; Aubrey Beardsley illustrated an edition of Malory published by Dent in 1893; and in 1917 Arthur Rackham did the drawings for A.W. Pollard's edition of the *Morte d'Arthur*. Rossetti was one of the pioneers of the Pre-Raphaelite movement. In 1857 he produced a design for the Oxford Union murals entitled 'Lancelot's Vision of the Sangreal' which shows Guinevere in an apple tree, placed like a second Eve between Lancelot/Adam and the Grail. In the same year he did a painting of the discovery of Lancelot and Guinevere, 'Sir Launcelot in the Queen's Chamber' (Birmingham City Museum and Art Gallery).

'The Lady of Shalott', engraving by William Holman Hunt, 1857.

In 1894 Sir Edward Burne-Jones designed a series of tapestries for Stanmore Hall, one of which is entitled 'Lancelot's Failure' (now in the Duke of Westminster's collection). The tapestries were made in the workshops set up by William Morris ('The Defence of Guinevere', 1858) to manufacture 'medieval' arts and crafts. Burne-Jones' 1896 painting 'The Dream of Sir Lancelot at the Chapel of the San Graal' hangs in Southampton Art Gallery. He had previously designed some stained glass windows for his home (again made by Morris), with such scenes as 'How Lancelot sought the sangreal and might not see it because his eyes were blinded by such love as dwelleth in Kings' houses'. These windows were installed in the kitchen over the sink, which, like the fondness for murals, shows how much these images of Arthur and the Grail formed part of the artist's daily lives. W.E. Reynolds-Stephens made sculptures in Pre-Raphaelite style, including 'Sir Lancelot and the Nestling' (1899).

Precursors of the Pre-Raphaelite wall decorations are the paintings of scenes from Malory in the Queen's Robing Room in the Palace of Westminster, painted by William Dyce in the 1850s. One of them depicts 'Generosity: King Arthur unhorsed, spared by Sir Lancelot' (1852). The same chamber was furnished with oak reliefs by H.H. Armstead, who produced mainly episodes from Arthur's life and the Grail quest. Contrasting with Rossetti and his ilk there is Sir John Gilbert, whose 'Sir Launcelot du Lake: She brought him to a river then' (1886; now in the Guildhall Art Gallery in London) is an action-packed representation of a duel between Lancelot and Sir Tarquin.

Sir Lancelot is an important though sometimes invisible element in the subject most frequently depicted during this period: Elaine, 'the Lily Maid of Astolat'. Well-known from the Old French *Mort le roi Artu*, from Malory and from Tennyson's 'Lady of Shalott' (1832) and 'Lancelot and Elaine' (in *Idylls of the King*, 1859), the maiden who dies of unrequited love for Lancelot came to symbolise the Victorian view of womanhood: young, beautiful, innocent and sacrificing herself to male dominance. She is often portrayed in the tower room to which she retreated with Lancelot's shield, observing the world outside in a mirror and weaving what she sees into a tapestry; but the commonest image in the dozens of pictures of her from this time is that of her – or, in many cases, her corpse – travelling by boat to Camelot. J.W. Waterhouse painted her no less than seven times (an 1888 version hangs in the Tate Gallery in London) and Holman Hunt also produced several depictions of her: a drawing of 1850 is now in the National Gallery of Victoria in Melbourne, his 1886 'The Lady of Shalott' is in

Manchester's City Art Gallery and the 1906 version is in the Wadsworth Athenaeum in Hartford, Connecticut. An early 'Lady of Shalott' is William Maw Egley's painting of 1858, now in the Sheffield City Art Galleries. As late as 1981 Shelah Horvitz drew 'My Lady of Shalott', complete with loom and mirror. Elaine even has a Japanese poem devoted to her: Natsume Soseki's *Kairo-kō: A Dirge* (1905).

In the late 19th and early 20th centuries a number of stage pieces were written about Lancelot, including Richard Henry's burlesque *Lancelot the Lovely* (1889), Anton Averkamp's symphonic ballad *Elaine and Lancelot* (1901), Francis Coutts' lyric drama *Launcelot du Lake* (1907), Eduard Stucken's *Lanzelot* (1909), H.H. Ewers' *Das Mädchen von Shalott* (1921) and James Bridie's *Lancelot* (1939). The opera *Lancelot du Lac* by Victorin Joncières had its première – to little acclaim – in Paris in 1900. Between 1911 and 1945 Rutland Boughton wrote a cycle of Arthurian oratorios which included *The Lily Maid* (on Elaine and Lancelot). In 1953 Boris Vian continued this tradition with his *Le chevalier de neige*, an open-air play with ballet and music (composed in 1957 by Georges de la Rue) which is mainly concerned with the pure nature of Lancelot's adulterous love. In 1920 Edward Arlington Robinson wrote his *Lancelot: A poem*, which deals with the last days of Arthur; here Lancelot's love for Guinevere is portrayed as beginning the decline which with the broken friendship of Lancelot and Gawain becomes inevitable ruin. Alongside such traditional treatments as *Launcelot and the Ladies* (1927) by Will Bradley, *The Ballad of Elaine* (1926) and *The Riding of Lancelot* (1929) by Sidney Fowler Wright, *The Little Wench* (1935) by Philip Lindsay, *Lancelot, my Brother* (1954) by Dorothy Roberts, *Lancelot und Ginevra, ein Liebesroman am Artushof* (1961) by Ruth Schirmer-Imhoff and *Le Chevalier de la Charrette* (1985) by Claude Duneton and Monique Baile, there is the occasional work in which Lancelot is an object of ridicule: in Lord Ernest Hamilton's *Launcelot: a Romance of the Court of King Arthur* (1926) the hero is married to Elaine and Guinevere is a sex-mad seductress who entices him into her bed. The character is also given an ironic twist in two recent novels. In his 1978 novel *Lancelot* Peter Vansittart gives a picture of the collapse of Roman Britain, represented by Lancelot, which is hardly romantic; while serving under Aurelius Ambrosius Lancelot encounters the prostitute Gwenhever. Walker Percy in his *Lancelot*, published in the same year, set the themes of lust and consequent ruin in the contemporary film world. His hero, Lancelot Lamar, sees himself as the 'Knight of the Unholy Grail'. And where the big screen is concerned, apart from the obligatory American spectaculars such as FIRST KNIGHT (Jerry Zucker, 1995), starring Richard Gere as Lancelot, Lancelot has also been the subject of French films of a more artistic nature, such as Robert Bresson's LANCELOT DU LAC (1974), in which following his failure in the Grail quest Lancelot is torn between his promise to God not to resume his relationship with Guinevere and his unremitting love for her.

As a leading character in the many modern retellings of the Arthur story which have appeared – usually as trilogies – in recent decades, Lancelot has an established place in modern novel-writing. Authors who draw on Malory for such works find it impossible to avoid him; but he takes on a variety of forms. T.H. White in his *The Ill-made Knight* (1940; third part of the cycle *The Once and Future King*) gave his protagonist Lancelot a particularly ugly appearance, contrasting with his inner striving for purity. He cherishes a pure love for Guinevere, but loses his virginity to Elaine, in this novel the Grail princess. In Marion Bradley's *The Mists of Avalon* (1982) Lancelot oscillates between the bigoted Guinevere and her Christian faith on one side and Morgaine and her old pagan, matriarchal world on the other. Most modern romances about Guinevere, such as Sharan Newman's trilogy (*Guinevere*, 1981; *The Chessboard Queen*, 1984; *Guinevere Evermore*, 1985), also reserve a leading role for her lover. Some novels, however, omit the character of Lancelot because he does not feature in the Celtic origins of the Arthurian legend. In such cases his role as lover of the queen (here usually called Gwenhwyfar), which appears to be indispensable on narrative-technical grounds, is taken over by Bedwyr/Bedivere with his suitably Celtic roots. Examples of this are: Rosemary Sutcliff, *Sword at Sunset* (1963), Mary Stewart, *The Last Enchantment* (1979) and Gillian Bradshaw, *In Winter's Shadow* (1982). Despite this trend, there seems to be little danger of Lancelot soon losing his prominent position in Arthurian narrative.

FRANK BRANDSMA

Editions and translations: Matarasso 1969; Micha 1978–83; Cable 1971; Gerritsen 1987; Lie 1987; Besamusca 1991; Kibler 1991; Brandsma 1992; Lacy 1992–96; Besamusca/ Postma 1997.
Studies: Lot 1954; Haug 1978; Van Oostrom 1981; Kennedy 1986; Whitaker 1990; Lacy et al. 1996.

L ANVAL is the protagonist in the *lai* of the same name by Marie de France. One day King Arthur distributes gifts with a lavish hand to his assembled Court; only Lanval receives nothing. Disappointed, he goes for a ride beside a river. There he is approached by two remarkably beautiful damsels who ask him to accompany them to their mistress. The lady, who is even more beautiful than her two maids, tells Lanval that she has been waiting for him and offers him her love: he will be able to see her whenever he wishes, and in return she will provide him with money and goods in abundance. On one condition, though: he must never under any circumstances say a word about her. Lanval and the lady spend a wonderful afternoon together, and for a while he continues to visit her.

One day Arthur's knights are in a garden talking. The queen notices the handsome Lanval. She joins the knights, draws Lanval aside and offers him her love. Lanval rejects the offer. When the queen persists, Lanval tells her that he loves another, a lady far more beautiful, courtly and wise than she. Mortified, the queen withdraws. When Arthur returns from hunting, she accuses Lanval of trying to seduce her and insulting her. The king summons Lanval, who denies the accusation but still maintains that his lady is much more beautiful. Lanval is ordered to prove, in the presence of all the king's vassals, that his lady is indeed more beautiful than the queen.

On the appointed day Lanval is unable to produce his lady. Just as Arthur's vassals are about to pass sentence on him two lovely damsels come riding up, followed a little later by two more; finally Lanval's mistress arrives; she exceeds in beauty all the other ladies. After Lanval's acquittal he leaves with his lady for the Isle of Avalon. Nothing is ever heard of him again.

The earliest version of *Lanval* – of which four manuscripts survive – is a *lai* of 646 lines ascribed to Marie de France (c.1130–c.1200; → Yonec). In the first half of the 13th century a translation of this was included in the Old Norse *Strengleikar* (→ Yonec). In the prologue to the Middle Dutch *Spiegel historiael* (written between 1280 and 1288) Jacob van Maerlant refers to 'that nonsense about Lenvale'. Because of this reference it is thought that there must have been a Middle Dutch version of the *Lanval*, but as yet no trace of it has been found. Between 1350 and 1400 the English poet Thomas Chestre reworked the story as a stanzaic poem of 1044 lines: *Sir Launfal*.

In 1848 Marie de France's *lai* provided the poet James Russell Lowell with one source of inspiration for his *The Vision of Sir Launfal*. Between 1901 and 1924 the German Eduard Stucken (1865–1936) wrote eight dramas on Arthurian themes, which he collected under the title *Der Gral, ein dramatisches Epos*; the second in the series is the story of Lanval (1903). The material was also adapted for the stage by Paul Ernst in *Ritter Lanval* (1906) and Thomas Ellis in *Lanval* (1908).

Like almost every other lai, the Lanval story has a fairy-tale quality. It is one of the many versions of the so-called *fée-maîtresse* story. In many cases the hero is lured away while out hunting by a magical beast (hart, wild boar) to a world where time seems to stand still; a single day there can last for decades in the normal world. The queen offers the hero her love; after a few days the hero wants to return to the ordinary world; his mistress warns him to eat no food; the hero of course disobeys, and as a result ages rapidly, but is saved at the last moment by his lady. Such stories were very popular in the Middle Ages; the tales attached to such characters as Désiré, Graelent, Guigemar, Guingamor, Tyolet and → Parthenopeus of Blois are examples of the type.

While it is true that there is no hunting-party in *Lanval* (he sets out of his own accord), the beautiful lady is unquestionably of fairy origin: she comes to the river specifically for Lanval, she loads him with gifts and she forbids him to speak of her. Of course the hero breaks the taboo, though the way in which this happens is unusual: the attempted seduction and subsequent revenge by Arthur's wife is a motif familiar from the biblical story of Potiphar's wife, which appears also in other medieval narratives (for example, in the → *Châtelaine de Vergy* and *Graelent*).

LUDO JONGEN

Translation: Burgess/Busby 1986.

L ORRAINE: narratives about the Loherains or Lotharingians are found in two literatures, French and Dutch. French has a 'Geste des Loherains' made up of five *chansons de geste*, while in Middle Dutch fragments survive of what is traditionally called the *Roman der Lorreinen*. The main theme is simple: the conflict between the Dukes of Lorraine and the Counts of Bordeaux, with their respective followers, who are caught up, generation after generation, in an irreconcilable feud. Between them stands the King of France, who must try to reconcile Lorrainers and Bordelais.

At the core of the complex is a pair of Old French *chansons de geste*, *Garin le Loherain* and *Gerbert de Mez*. Though not written at the same time – *Garin* is definitely 12th-century, *Gerbert* late 12th or early 13th – they are inseparable and are invariably placed together in the manuscripts. Around this central pair are grouped the French cycle and the Middle Dutch epic. The story of *Garin-Gerbert* can be summarised as follows.

Garin le Loherain (over 16,000 lines) tells how the feud between the Loherains and their enemies originated. At first all is peace and light. Four boys are being brought up at the court of King Pepin: Garin le Loherain and his brother Begon from Lorraine, Fromont de Lenz and his brother Guillaume de Monclin from Bordeaux. The first shadow on their friendship appears when the king knights all four at the same time and makes Begon, his favourite, Duke of Gascony. Fromont's jealousy is appeased with the promise that the next vacant fiefdom will be his. That Garin first acquires the lordship of Lorraine is a matter of course: he succeeds his father.

Garin is among the many Frenchmen who march south to where the Saracens have invaded the land of Maurienne. That country's king, the aged Thierry, asks on his deathbed whether Garin will marry his daughter Blanchefleur. Garin is willing and asks King Pepin for permission, which is granted. Then Fromont protests: if Garin marries Blanchefleur he automatically becomes Lord of Maurienne, while the first vacant fiefdom had been promised to himself. Tempers become inflamed. Garin strikes the enraged Fromont in the face and thus begins a feud that will have no end.

King Pepin's role in the story is not always above reproach. Although Blanchefleur is Garin's promised bride, the king decides to keep the girl for himself. To this end he organises some false testimony: two monks swear on reliquaries that Garin and

Blanchefleur are related and thus forbidden to marry. Garin is furious, but has enough sense to accept the situation; with the result that Blanchefleur becomes the Loherains' loyal advocate at court. And they have need of her, for Pepin is not always impartial; for instance, he does not scruple to accept bribes from the Bordelais.

A famous scene from *Garin le Loherain* is that of Begon's death. On his way to Metz to visit his brother Garin, he decides to pursue an extremely formidable wild boar in a wood belonging to Fromont. There he is killed by Fromont's men, who are unaware of his identity. But Fromont recognises him and is greatly grieved at the death of his former antagonist. This does not prevent hostilities flaring up again, though – hostilities in which eventually Garin too is killed.

In the second *chanson* of the pair, *Gerbert de Mez* (almost 15,000 lines), the sons take their fathers' places: here the protagonists are Garin's son Gerbert for Lorraine and Fromont's son Fromondin for Bordeaux. Otherwise the narrative continues along the same lines: Queen Blanchefleur energetically promotes the interests of Lorraine, King Pepin continues unpredictable, conflict and reconciliation alternate with each other, the Saracens pose a constant threat. Eventually Fromondin is persuaded by a hermit to turn his back on the world. He retires to a hermitage at Pampelune, but has still an old score to settle with the Loherains: Gerbert had had the skull of his father Fromont mounted in a golden goblet which had been set before Fromondin at a banquet. When he is visited in his hermitage by Gerbert and some companions he tries to kill the Loherains. They, however, are aware of his intentions and put an end to Fromondin.

This evidently successful story lent itself to expansion by the addition of both earlier and later events. The earlier history (with as yet no mention of a feud) is called *Hervis de Mez* (over 10,000 lines). Its eponymous hero appears in *Garin le Loherain* as the aged father of Garin and Begon; *Hervis* recounts how in his youth he manages to become Duke of Lorraine. At first such an achievement seems highly improbable, for Hervis is of bourgeois origins and destined by his father for a career as a merchant. But the son has no taste for such a life; he would rather perform knightly deeds and through his valour – not to mention his father's money – he succeeds in winning the hand of the daughter of the King of Hungary. The dukedom is then his for the taking. There are actually two French continuations of the *Garin-Gerbert: Anseys de Mez* and *Yon ou la Venjance Fromondin*. Both probably date from the 12th century, and in both Gerbert is slain in revenge for Fromondin's death.

More interesting, however, is the way in which a Brabant poet continued the story. The *Roman der Lorreinen* consists of two, or possibly three, books. The first of these is a translation of the central core of the French cycle, the *Garin-Gerbert*. In the second book the poet moves away from his French source: as in the French, Gyrbeert (Gerbert) is killed; but otherwise the story undergoes a remarkable metamorphosis. The King of France is no longer Pepin but Charlemagne. The villain's part, which had been assigned more or less to the leader of the Bordelais, is taken over by Gelloen (Ganelon), the scoundrel from the *Chanson de Roland*. The new leader of the Lorraine faction is King Yoen of Gascony, later supported by his son Ritsart. The action takes place in many more locations simultaneously (Africa, Jerusalem, Scythia, the Caucasus, Norway) and the structure thus becomes more complicated, with various narrative threads intertwined.

The most important of these are: 1. events in and around France, the main setting for the conflict, where Charlemagne from time to time intervenes between the parties; 2. the activities of Gelloen; sometimes he is in France, sometimes in exile roaming from place to place, with disastrous consequences; 3. the Saracen incursions under their leader Agulant; 4. the activities of a competing group of Saracens led by Gelloen's sons Beligant and Marcilijs; 5. events in Scythia, one of King Yoen's possessions and under constant threat from Gelloen's daughter Yrene, now Queen of Greece; 6. the vicissitudes of King Yoen following his abduction of Helene and escape to Hoog-Goten, far away in Asia.

The skill of the Brabant poet lies in the way he brings all these threads together at the end of the second book, and ties everything up in a decisive battle at – where else? – Roncevaux. This part of the story has not been preserved, but Gelloen, Yrene and the other villains must have met their fate there.

About halfway through his narrative the poet tells us that there is yet a third book to follow, which will continue the feud down to the 12th or 13th century. It is not entirely certain that this book was ever written; at any event, no fragments of it have survived.

The *Roman der Lorreinen* lays even more stress on the truth of the story than had the French texts. It is much more like a 'history' than a 'romance'; with its division into 'books' which are again subdivided into 'parts' its author was clearly aiming at something on a par with the *Spiegel historiael*, Jacob van Maerlant's great history of the world. Its length and scope are in accordance with this aim: the whole thing probably ran to some 150,000 lines.

The work was very likely written c.1275 and commissioned by the court of Brabant. These two hypotheses go together; in the second half of the 13th century the Dukes of Brabant were fascinated by their own history. They saw themselves as descendants and rightful successors of Charlemagne; they even commissioned the writing of Latin chronicles to prove this. In formal documents they styled themselves 'Duke of Lorraine' among other titles; good grounds for suspecting that a Brabant 'Epic of Lorraine' would have suited their dynastic aspirations extremely well.

The Loherains must have left something of a mark; at least in the case of Garin. It is likely that the name of the Swan Knight Lohengrin goes back via *Loherengrin* to *Li Loheren Garin*. And Huizinga mentions in his great work *The Waning of the Middle Ages* (London 1924) that the Burgundian princes had in their treasury a number of romantic relics of heroes, including a tusk from Garin le Loherain's boar. These may indicate the existence of a non-literary, oral Garin tradition; but here we can do no more than speculate.

J.B. VAN DER HAVE

Editions: Mitchneck 1935; Green 1939; Overdiep 1939; Vallerie 1947.
Translations: Walter 1984; Guidot 1986 and 1988.
Studies: Van der Have 1990; Suard 1992.

L OUIS THE PIOUS, son of → Charlemagne, in fact appears in medieval literature in two forms. Some epic texts depict him as the great hero who defeated the Norsemen at Saucourt; and it is this image of Louis that we find in the French *chanson* → *Gormont et Isembart*. Dating from about 1130, the work survives only in a 661-line fragment now in the Koninklijke Bibliotheek in Brussels; but it is possible to reconstruct the story with the aid of the late epic *Lohier et Mallart*. This text simply appends *Gormont et Isembart* to its own, complete, narrative of the friends Lohier and Mallart.

However, we see Louis far less often as hero than as anti-hero, as a bad or weak king. Specific accusations against him are his lack of drive and ungracious treatment of his vassals. Most of the *chansons* of the 'Cycle de → Guillaume d'Orange' portray him either as so weak that he has to be defended by the ultra-strong Guillaume or as unjust, neglecting his most faithful vassals when allocating fiefdoms. Within this cycle the image of Louis as a weak ruler is most apparent around 1135 in *Le couronnement de Louis*, a *chanson* of 2695 assonant decameters which falls into five parts. It opens with the, now aged, Charlemagne wishing to crown his young son Louis as king. When Louis proves reluctant, however, a traitor proposes himself as regent; but then Guillaume d'Orange turns up, kills the traitor and crowns Louis. The second part is concerned with Guillaume: he defends the Pope against heathen attacks on Rome and overcomes the giant Corsolt in single combat. In the third part, however, he again has to hasten to Louis' aid following the death of Charlemagne, for a rebellion has broken out, led by the Norseman Acelin. In the fourth part Louis and Guillaume together liberate Rome, which had been captured by Gui of Germany. Guillaume crowns Louis King of Italy in St Peter's. In the fifth and final part Guillaume yet again has to come to Louis' aid, this time against rebellious barons. He forces them to submit to the king, and at the end Louis marries Guillaume's sister. In the last line of the *Couronnement* Louis shows himself devoid of gratitude.

Strikingly, in the highly archaic *Willalme* epic from the mid-12th century (the *Chanson de Guillaume*) Louis appears simply as the king, with no negative connotations. In early biographies of kings, too, such as those by l'Astronome Limousin and Ermold the Black (9th century), Louis does not come off badly. Ermold goes so far as to say that everyone praises his deeds, the people even more than the poets.

In *Lohier et Mallart*, which clearly represents Louis as a great hero, the friends Gormont and Isembart function as a matching pair to the friends Lohier and Mallart. Lohier is Lothar, son of King Charles (the Simple), who unsuccessfully rebels against his brother Louis III: a detail of some importance. For the historical hero of the battle of Saucourt in 881 was in fact not Louis I, the Pious (as *Gormont et Isembart* and the Gormont section of *Lohier et Mallart* have it), but Louis III. In the *Ludwigslied*, a 9th-century Old German heroic lay written in Northern France in a Frankish dialect, the hero of this battle is indeed Louis III, but there is no direct connection with Gormont and Isembart; the *Ludwigslied* is an independent praise-song. Later historiographers variously ascribe the battle of Saucourt to Louis I the Pious, Louis II the Stutterer, Louis III or Louis IV d'Outremer.

Nothing has survived of the French original of *Lohier et Mallart*, but Dutch (14th century, fragmentary) and German (1437) versions of it are extant. In 1405 Marguerite de Joinville commissioned a French prose *Lohier et Mallart*, which in all probability also included the Gormont-and-Isembart story; sadly, this text also has been lost, save for a fragment of 160 lines. The German version is a translation of the French original by Elisabeth of Nassau-Saarbrücken, née de Lorraine, daughter of Marguerite de Joinville; there are five known manuscripts of it and three prints. This version was reworked by the German writer Karl Simrock (1868) on the basis of a 1514 print. In France the tale of Gormont and Isembart remained popular; we find it in the chronicles of Hariulf and Philippe Mousket. It also occurs in Geoffrey of Monmouth's *Historia regum Britannie*; though (because he was British?) he omits the end of the story (the death of Gormont).

The five episodes of the *Couronnement*, with their negative image of Louis, probably derive from five separate *chansons*; yet a measure of unity can be discerned in the work as a whole. The coronation scene in the first part relates to 12th-century political history: to ensure a hereditary succession, not yet established by law, in 1131 Louis VI (the Fat) had his still young son crowned as Louis VII (the Younger). Louis the Pious did in fact need protection from a malevolent regent on becoming King of Aquitaine while still a child; but at the time of his coronation as Charlemagne's successor he was already in his thirties and the historical Guillaume (Count of Aquitaine) was dead. Guillaume never went to fight the heathen in Italy (the first Roman episode); that was Louis II, in 873. And it was Louis IV (d'Outremer) who did battle with the Normans. Something of a propaganda text, then, with a pot-pourri of historical deeds by an assortment of Louis. The *Couronnement*'s unity lies in its treatment of a number of important themes such as the obligations of a monarch, the obligations of a vassal, hereditary kingship and the French claim to the imperial crown. This last features specifically in the fourth episode, the coronation in Rome; it probably echoes the attack launched in 1124 by Henry V of Germany on Louis VI because of his support for the

Pope. In the 15th century the crowning of Louis became a standard feature of the great cyclic Guillaume manuscripts in prose.

The ingratitude shown by Louis in the last line of the *Couronnement* looks forward in narrative terms to another text in the 'Cycle de Guillaume d'Orange': *Le charroi de Nîmes* (c.1140). This text too clearly projects the image of the unjust Louis. Louis overlooks Guillaume when distributing fiefs and Guillaume then conquers his own fiefdom of Nîmes by some such stratagem as that of the Breda peat-barge in 1590 (here a cartload of wine). This is followed by the taking of Orange in the *Prise d'Orange* (mid-12th century). In → *Raoul de Cambrai* (late 12th century) Louis is again the ungrateful lord who refuses to grant the young Raoul his father's fiefdom. The question of hereditary fiefdoms was a major issue in the 12th century; Louis the Pious became a literary stereotype illustrating this political problem. In the already-mentioned cyclic prose-manuscripts from the late Middle Ages, every aspect of Louis' image underwent readjustment; the writers attempted to burnish the royal reputation and reduce the conflicts to some extent. They were not, however, entirely successful.

J. KOOPMANS

Edition: Lepage 1978.

MAUGIS is a sorcerer-knight who makes his first appearance in *Renaut de Montauban*, a French *chanson de geste*. When → Renaut and his brothers are in danger of coming off worst in their struggle against the unjust king → Charlemagne, Maugis enters the lists in support of his kin. Whenever his military prowess proves inadequate he calls on his magic powers to save himself, but primarily also his kinsmen. The actions of the sorcerer-knight thus acquire a political justification which must have been well understood by the medieval audience; for *Renaut de Montauban*, an epic about rebels, was written at a time when the monarchy was increasing its power at the expense of the nobility.

Maugis undergoes a striking development both within the text of the *Renaut* and in its textual history. Over the course of the *chanson* he evolves from a marginal figure to an influential personage. He even assumes a key position in the conflict between Charlemagne and Renaut: Charles will be reconciled with Renaut and his brothers only if Maugis is rendered harmless. Alongside this, the various redactions of the narrative also show a development in Maugis' role: in later versions the magical element becomes more and more prominent. At the same time, in these redactions the episodes which centre on Maugis' ingenuity and magic acquire a comic cast.

The mysterious sorcerer's undoubted popular success inspired an unknown poet to construct a new epic around him: *Maugis d'Aigremont*. In it he sought to elucidate a number of points which had remained obscure in the original epic, *Renaut de Montauban*, such as Maugis' origins and his relationship with Renaut and his brothers and the magic horse Bayart. Maugis' magic powers, which had already become increasingly important in the *Renaut*, are strengthened still more in the *Maugis*; they are employed primarily to bring about the moral humiliation of the king. This tale, in which the knight-sorcerer Maugis takes centre stage, has survived in three differing versions: one in French and two in Dutch. If we take what is common to the three versions as the basic story, it goes as follows.

At the court of Duke Beuve d'Aigremont twins are born, at the precise moment when heathen forces storm the town. In the chaos one of the infants is kidnapped and taken to heathen Monbrant. A lady of the court tries to take the other child to safety. On the way she is torn to pieces by wild beasts, but thanks to a magic earring the child

Comment maulgis duchemont endormi char
lemeine et ses barons par nigremance et si
emporta leurs espees en montauban

Y dist listoire que quant lemperur
eut fait lier maulgis a ung pillier
et ainsi eut soupe Il fist lors ses barons venir

Having sent Charlemagne and his knights to sleep by his magic arts, Maugis steals their swords. Miniature by Loyset Liédet, c.1460, in a manuscript of *Renaut de Montauban*. Paris, Bibliothèque de l'Arsenal.

is unharmed. It is found by the fairy Oriande of Rocheflor, who names the boy Maugis. At an early age the foundling is initiated by Oriande's brother Baudris into the black art of necromancy.

At the same time his brother Vivien is growing up in Monbrant, where a passionate love blossoms between him and the heathen queen Esclarmonde. When King Sorgalant of Monbrant finds out about this Vivien has to flee. He joins the retinue of the Spanish king Antenor, who is on his way to Rocheflor to win Oriande as his bride. Not far from Rocheflor is an island where the magic horse Bayart is held prisoner by devils and dragons. Aided by his magic and after a lengthy struggle Maugis manages to capture and tame Bayart. While Maugis is fighting for the horse, Antenor is besieging Rocheflor; Vivien distinguishes himself in action with the Spanish forces. Luckily Maugis returns – with Bayart – in time to intervene successfully in the battle. The brothers engage each other in violent combat, which ends inconclusively. They discover their true identity and are reconciled; Vivien follows his brother into the Christian camp and the Christian faith. During the feast that celebrates their reconciliation Maugis and Vivien resolve to go in search of their parents.

Meanwhile, Charlemagne has laid siege to Montpellier. Maugis manages to save the town, however, and takes advantage of the confusion in the royal camp to release his father Beuve from prison in Paris. Partly because of this, Charles agrees to a recon-ciliation. Sorgalant of Monbrant, meanwhile, has besieged Aigremont; but the town is saved by Maugis and Vivien and the enemy punished. The marriage of Vivien and Esclarmonde is crowned by a great feast, after which everyone returns to his own place.

The Old French *chanson de geste* *Maugis d'Aigremont* was probably written in the first half of the 13th century in the region of Beauvais in Northern France. There are three extant verse redactions of the French version and three in prose, all of which agree closely with each other. Additionally, some fourteen prints of the prose narrative can be traced, dating from the 16th and 17th centuries. The 'Bibliothèque des Romans' (1778) also included an extract from the romance.

Around 1300 the French *chanson* was translated into Middle Dutch. The wealth of surviving manuscripts of the *Madelghijs* – of no other Carolingian work are there so many known manuscripts – shows just how popular the material was in the Low Countries. The Middle Dutch prose romance exists in two versions, a shorter and a longer. The shorter version devotes particular attention to Maugis' magical arts and the love between Oriande and Maugis. The longer version is found in three (fragmentary) verse redactions and in the prose romance. The author of this version took the shorter version as his starting point and expanded it with new episodes, some of them distinctly legendary in content.

Outside the French and Dutch language areas the story of Maugis was completely overshadowed by that of Renaut; not one Italian, Scandinavian or English version of the tale is known. Large parts of it do appear, however, in the Italian *Rinaldo da Monte Albano*, including the birth of the twins Maugis and Vivien, their separation and eventual reunion, and also the winning of Bayart. Although its title suggests otherwise, the Scandinavian *Mágus saga* very largely corresponds to the Dutch *Renout van Montalbaen*. Those events specific to the *Maugis d'Aigremont* and the *Madelghijs* are not to be found in it.

Even in the 20th century the story of *Malegijs en Vivien* was still performed in the puppet theatres. Maugis is remembered in many local legends, particularly in the Belgian and French Ardennes. Aigremont-le-Duc had a Tour Maugis, and the Table Maugis could be found near 'Château-Regnault'. A 17th-century map marks a Pont de Maugy near Sedan. Belgian Bévercé at one time boasted the Château Magis and the Moulin Magis. The Château d'Aigremont (at Awirs) also has links with Maugis. The town of Ypres in West Flanders and its surroundings were the setting for the legend of

the 'Peerdeken Malegijs', a huge horse that carried several people – in this case three
young girls – on its back. It is uncertain whether this legend has any closer connection
with Maugis than the association of an outsize horse with the name of the sorcerer from
the epic tale who won himself such a steed.

B.W.TH. DUIJVESTIJN

Edition: Duijvestijn 1989.
Study: Spijker 1990.

MERLIN (Latin: Merlinus) is an enchanter and prophet who features in numerous
Arthurian romances. The earliest coherent account of his birth and his dealings
with the British kings Vortigern, Ambrosius and Uther Pendragon is to be found in
Geoffrey of Monmouth's *Historia regum Britannie* (History of the Kings of Britain) of
c.1136. Some years earlier Geoffrey had published a long series of prophecies attributed
to Merlin, the *Prophetiae Merlini*, which he incorporated in its entirety into his *Historia*.
Around 1150 he completed the *Vita Merlini*, a biography in 1539 hexameters in which
he delved more deeply into Merlin's origins. With these three works Geoffrey created a
character which has continued to fascinate novelists and poets, and artists and scholars
as well, down the centuries. First, let us summarise what Geoffrey says about Merlin in
the *Historia regum Britannie*.

King Vortigern has seized the crown by unlawful means. He is unable to maintain his
position without the help of the Angles and Saxons, who have established themselves
on British soil under their leaders → Hengest and Horsa. Vortigern becomes more and
more a tool of the pagan intruders, particularly after he marries Hengest's daughter
Renwein. During negotiations about the admission of a new contingent of German
immigrants Hengest and his followers seize their chance and massacre the British
aristocracy. Vortigern manages to save his skin by fleeing into Wales. There he summons his magicians (Geoffrey's word is *magi*, which can also be translated 'astrologers')
to advise him. Their advice is to build a mighty tower as a defensible refuge. Vortigern
selects a site for the tower on Mount Erith (Snowdon). Masons begin laying the foundations, but each morning they find that the earth has swallowed the previous day's work.
Again Vortigern consults his magicians. They tell him that the foundations must be
sprinkled with the blood of a boy who has no father. Vortigern sends out searchers to
track down this fatherless lad. One day they come to a town where boys are playing
near the gate and quarrelling. They hear one of the boys, Dinabutius, taunting another,
whose name proves to be Merlin, that nobody knows who he is because he doesn't have
a father. The searchers question the bystanders and learn that the boy's father is indeed
unknown; his mother, who has entered a convent, is a daughter of the King of Demetia.
The boy and his mother are sent to King Vortigern. The lady swears that she never had
sexual relations with any man of flesh and blood. But she had indeed repeatedly been
visited in her chamber by someone with the form of a handsome youth, who used to
embrace and kiss her and then become invisible. While invisible he had made love to
her and as a result Merlin was born. Vortigern puts the case to a learned man, who explains
that this must be an *incubus*, a demon who combines the qualities of man and angel.

Confronted with Vortigern's magicians, the young Merlin (who according to
Geoffrey is also called Ambrosius) exposes their ignorance. Following his directions, an
underground lake is discovered beneath the foundations. Asked what is at the bottom
of the lake, the magicians are again unable to answer. Merlin declares that they will find
there two hollow stones, in each of which is a sleeping dragon. The lake is drained and
the stones are found. The two dragons – one red and one white – emerge and start

fighting each other. Merlin predicts the victory of the white dragon, which symbolises the Saxons; the red dragon's defeat means that the Britons will be enslaved until the Boar of Cornwall (Arthur) shall crush the invaders. Merlin also foretells Vortigern's end: besieged in his tower by Aurelius Ambrosius and Uther Pendragon, the sons of King Constantine whom Vortigern had betrayed, he dies in the flames.

Aurelius Ambrosius is crowned king, and after a bloody war succeeds in subjecting the Saxons. He decides to erect a monument in honour of the fallen Britons. Only Merlin is considered capable of creating such a memorial. He proposes to Ambrosius to bring the Giants' Ring, a massive stone circle, from Ireland to the battlefield. By supernatural means Merlin succesfully raises the stones from their places, ships them to Britain and then re-erects them on Mount Ambrius near Salisbury. When Aurelius Ambrosius dies shortly afterwards of Saxon poison he is buried within the Giants' Ring, which is now called Stonehenge. He is succeeded by his brother Uther Pendragon.

Uther Pendragon also has trouble with the rebellious Saxons. Helped by strategic advice from Gorlois, Duke of Cornwall, he is able to break their resistance. At a feast to celebrate the victory Uther's eye is caught by Gorlois' wife Ygerna, the most beautiful woman in Britain. Consumed with desire, he lavishes attentions upon her. Gorlois leaves court in a rage and with Uther on his heels retreats to Cornwall, where he lodges Ygerna in the castle of Tintagel; he himself takes up a position in a nearby fort. While laying siege to this fort Uther's longing for Ygerna becomes too much for him. Fearing a breakdown, on the advice of one of his nobles he decides to summon Merlin. Merlin then transforms Uther into the spitting image of Gorlois. Uther's friend Ulfin and Merlin himself also change their appearance. The guard, thinking that his master has come home, admits the three of them to Tintagel. The unsuspecting Ygerna welcomes Uther into her bed and satisfies all his desires. That night Arthur is conceived. Meanwhile the besieged Gorlois and his garrison have made a reckless sortie, in which Gorlois is the first to fall. When messengers bring the news of his death to Tintagel they are dumbfounded to see their master sitting large as life next to his duchess. The supposed Gorlois tells them that he will go to King Uther and make peace. He then returns as himself and takes possesion both of Tintagel and of Ygerna. From that day on Uther and Ygerna live as man and wife, united in their great love for each other. They have two children, Arthur and Anna.

Geoffrey's *Historia* mentions Merlin only once more after this, in a reference to one of his prophecies.

A great deal of research has been devoted to the question of the source or sources on which Geoffrey drew for his stories of Merlin. He himself states that he translated his *Historia* from 'a very ancient book in the British language', but nowadays hardly anyone still believes this claim. Geoffrey did, though, make use of Welsh oral traditions as well as of a sizeable number of Latin historiographic and literary sources. With regard to Merlin, he must have been aware of the existence of a tradition concerning a British seer called Myrddin who was supposed to have lived in early medieval times. Welsh literature still has a number of poems supposedly spoken by this Myrddin. One of these is *Afalennau* (Apple-trees), dated to between 850 and 1150, in which Myrddin, living in a deranged state in the Caledonian Forest, laments his sad fate. In another Welsh poem, *Hoianau* (Goodbye, piglet), Myrddin addresses the piglet that is the sole companion of his loneliness and draws a connection between his sleeplessness and the death in battle fifty years before of Gwenddolau, the great king from the North. By combining references in various sources it has been possible to reconstruct the outlines of a tradition: at the battle of Arfderydd, which according to tradition took place in 573 and in which Gwenddolau was defeated by King Rhydderch of Dumbarton, Myrddin King of Dyfed lost three brothers; he then fell into a deep depression and withdrew into the Caledonian Forest in Southern Scotland. In the figure of Myrddin at least two literary types have coalesced: the asocial wild man of the woods (*homo silvester*) who understands the language of animals, and the seer, mad and wise at the same time, who at one time babbles nonsense and at another proves to know the future.

When he wrote the *Historia* Geoffrey probably knew little more of Myrddin than that he was a British seer or prophet from the distant past, who lived in the forest and possessed supernatural gifts. He took the story of the fatherless boy very largely from Nennius' *Historia Brittonum* (early 9th century), in which the young seer is called Ambrosius. The account of the deceiving of Ygerna and the begetting of Arthur seems to have been inspired by the classical myth of the conception of Heracles, in which the god Zeus assumed the form of Alcmene's husband Amphitryon. With his French-speaking readers in mind Geoffrey would have latinised the Welsh name Myrddin as Merlinus to avoid unfortunate associations with the word *merde* (shit). After completing his *Historia* he must have discovered more about his character's legendary history. In the *Vita Merlini*, written some fifteen years after the *Historia*, he shows himself aware of, for instance, the traditions concerning the battle of Arfderydd; he also mentions other details of Celtic (Welsh) origin, some of which found their way into later Merlin literature.

We are indebted to the French poet Robert de Boron (late 12th century) for a significant deepening and broadening of the Merlin theme. He created a three-part romance cycle, a single grandiose design which linked the biblical story of → Joseph of Arimathea, via Merlin, to an early version of the Grail story (→ *Perceval*). Of Robert's *Merlin* – the central part of the trilogy – only the beginning survives in its original verse form; however, it was in prose that the romance enjoyed its greatest success. The story opens with an assembly in Hell. The devils discuss how to thwart Christ's work of salvation and decide on a kind of mockery of the Incarnation: a child shall be born of a relationship between a virgin and a devil. One of them readies himself to carry out the plan and selects a young girl as victim. Having first consigned her father and two of her sisters to perdition, he then has intercourse with her while she is sleeping. But the devils' plan miscarries because of the girl's piety. She confides in her confessor, and he gives her absolution. Nine months later she gives birth to a son who is baptised with her father's name, Merlin. The child is covered in shaggy hair and strikes fear into everyone, including his mother. From his demonic father Merlin derives his knowledge of all that has happened in the past; as counterbalance God has given him the power to know also the future. Before he is a year old he is a sufficiently accomplished advocate to save his mother from the stake; he also has his mother's confessor, here called Blaise, record the history of the Grail (as recounted in the first part of Robert's trilogy) and the story of his own birth.

Robert de Boron follows Geoffrey's account of Vortigern's tower and the raising of Stonehenge, albeit with considerable divergences. According to Robert, Uther has the Round Table constructed on Merlin's advice to commemorate two earlier tables, the table of the Last Supper and the Grail table made for Joseph of Arimathea in its memory. The empty place at the Round Table will, so Merlin prophesies, be occupied only in the reign of Uther's successor by a knight who will successfully complete the Grail quest. Robert's account of the begetting of Arthur also shows a variation which determined the later development of the narrative. According to Geoffrey, Uther married Ygerna immediately after the death of Gorlois and the birth of their child thus occasioned no surprise. In Robert the wedding does not take place until two months after Gorlois' death; consequently, Arthur's birth has to be kept secret to prevent a scandal. On Merlin's advice the child is entrusted to a guardian, Antor (also called Auctor or Ector), who brings him up with his own son Keu (→ Kay). Fifteen years later Uther dies. Again Merlin assumes control of events. The new king will reveal himself by drawing a sword out of an anvil fixed to a block of stone. Antor knights his son so that he can try his luck. For a moment it even seems that Keu is the chosen one: he shows Antor the sword and claims the kingship. But it was his unknown foster brother who had drawn the sword effortlessly from the anvil. The prose version of Robert de Boron's *Merlin* ends with the crowning of Arthur.

The romance acquired a number of sequels by various writers. Best known is the so-called *Suite-Vulgate du Merlin*, which relates how Arthur established his rule in a series of wars. The prose *Merlin* and this continuation together form the second part of the five-part Vulgate cycle (→ Lancelot) which covers the whole history of Arthur's rule. The *Merlin* was translated into Middle Dutch c.1260 by Jacob van Maerlant; in 1326 Lodewijk van Velthem added to this a translation of the *Suite-Vulgate*. Alongside this chronicle-like *Suite-Vulgate du Merlin* there also exists a more 'romantic' version of the story, the *Suite du Merlin*, previously known as the *Huth-Merlin*. This text too forms part of a cycle, the so-called Post-Vulgate Cycle, which later became the source for the first four books of Malory's *Morte d'Arthur*; Spanish and Portuguese versions of it are also known.

Both versions of the *Suite* show Merlin as the mastermind who controls events, counsellor to the young king Arthur, interpreter of dreams, and increasingly as a whimsical magician with a taste for ironic situations. Thus, he appears before the imperial court in Rome in the shape of a wild man; by interpreting a dream of the Emperor's he unmasks twelve of the Empress' ladies-in-waiting as young men, with whom the Empress secretly indulges in lewd conduct. A striking motif, already present in Geoffrey, is Merlin's laughter whenever he foresees how his opponents' expectations will be thwarted by future events. The account of Arthur's military exploits is inter-woven with the story of Merlin's unhappy love-affair. He becomes infatuated to the point of madness with a young girl, Viviane (forms such as Niniane, Nivienne, Nimue and Nymenche are also found). In return for her favour she persuades him to instruct her in magic. In this way she learns a spell by which a person can be confined indefin-itely, and another by which she induces in him the illusion of making love to her. Quite deliberately (for of course he knows what will happen) Merlin puts himself in Viviane's power. She shuts him up in a thicket in the depths of the forest of Brocéliande. All the adventures that follow Lancelot's arrival at Arthur's court take place in Merlin's absence. Years later, Gauvain (→ Gawain) is crossing the forest of Brocéliande. He hears a voice lamenting that everyone has forgotten him. It is Merlin, still in the thicket and invisible to Gauvain. Gauvain is (at least in this version) the last mortal to hear the great enchanter's voice.

By his submission to Viviane Merlin joins Solomon, Aristotle and Virgil in the ranks of illustrious sages brought low by the wiles of women, a theme which was to become exceedingly popular in the didactic literature of the later Middle Ages.

That Merlin retained his place in early British history even after the Middle Ages is evident from, for instance, the drama *The Birth of Merlin, or the Childe Hath Found His Father* (1662), which was at one time attributed to Shakespeare. Merlin's prophecies, expressed in oracular language and full of obscure allegories, were taken seriously until well on in the 18th century. In 1641 Thomas Heywood published a history of England based on Merlin's predictions: *The Life of Merlin, Surnamed Ambrosius, His Prophecies and Predictions Interpreted, and Their Truth Made Good by Our English Annals*. In his *A Famous Prediction of Merlin, the British Wizard, Written Above a Thousand Years Ago and Relating to the Present Year 1709* Jonathan Swift poked fun at the habit of ascribing predictions of the future to Merlin. Until well into the 19th century almanacs and horoscopes appeared in England under such titles as *The Philosophical Merlin*, *Merlin's Almanach and Prognostications* and *The Madmerry Merlin*. The influence of Merlin's prophecies can be seen on the Continent, too, at least until the Council of Trente (1545) placed *Merlini Angli liber obscurarum praedictionum* (The book of obscure predictions of the English Merlin) on the Index of forbidden books.

At the end of the 18th century interest in Merlin as seer and prophet gave way to a fascination with his role as bard and enchanter. Symptomatic of this is that, as early as

1804, the German romantic philosopher Friedrich Schlegel published a *Geschichte des Zauberers Merlin* (History of Merlin the Magician). The poet Ludwig Tieck translated the English drama *The Birth of Merlin* as *Die Geburt des Merlin* (1829). Heinrich Heine felt himself, like Merlin, 'festgebannt in die eigenen Zauberkreise'. The play *Merlin, eine Mythe* by Karl Leberecht Immermann (1832) was regarded by a contemporary as 'a second *Faust*'. In England, Tennyson took Merlin's tragic love as the subject for his poem *Vivien* (1859), which in turn inspired Edward Burne-Jones to paint his 'The Beguiling of Merlin' (1877, Lady Lever Art Gallery, Port Sunlight). In his 24-book epic *Merlin l'Enchanteur* (1860) the French writer Edgar Quinet sought to give the story the status of a French national myth ('Merlin, le premier patron de la France, est devenu le mien') and cast Emperor Napoleon III, whom he detested, in the role of → Hengest. Regional patriotism inspired the Breton writer La Villemarqué to produce a fantastic hotchpotch of scholarship and absurdity: *Myrddin ou Merlin l'Enchanteur* (1862). The United States, too, contributed in characteristic style: in Mark Twain's satire *A Connecticut Yankee in King Arthur's Court* (1889) Merlin's old-fashioned magic proves no match for superior modern technology.

On several occasions elements from the old story have provided material for opera, as in Karl Goldmark's *Merlin* (Vienna 1886, revised version Frankfurt 1904) and works of the same name by Felix Draeseke (première Gotha 1913) and Isaac Albeniz (1900). The 19th-century Italian repertoire included such operas as *Merlino (la Grotta del Mago)* by Amiconi and *La Tomba di Merlino* by Astaritta.

The 20th century recognised in Merlin the archtype of the poet-seer who stands outside society. Guillaume Apollinaire published his obscure *L'Enchanteur pourrissant* in 1909, Eduard Stucken his *Merlins Geburt* in 1912 and *Die Zauberer Merlin* in 1924, two parts of his eight-part dramatic Grail cycle; Jean Cocteau has a malevolent Merlin in his play *Les Chevaliers de la Table Ronde* (1927). Elements from the Merlin stories also find a place in John Cooper Powys' novels *A Glastonbury Romance* (1932), *Morwyn* (1937) and *Porius* (1951).

1938 saw the appearance of T.H. White's *The Sword in the Stone*, a book that powerfully influenced most later writers' depictions of Merlin. White's Merlin is a half-serious, half-comic figure, attuned to both nature and culture, at once magician and absent-minded professor. He is the young Arthur's mentor while he is growing up at his guardian's castle and has his pupil take on the form of various animals, one after the other, to prepare him for his future task as ruler. White later rewrote the book (which was also made into a Walt Disney film) and combined it with three other novels, also based on Malory, in the tetralogy *The Once and Future King* (1958). A fifth work, *The Book of Merlyn*, a testament to White's negative view of humanity and his wrestling with pacifist ideals, was published only after his death, in 1977.

From 1938 on the Dutch composer Willem Pijper and his compatriot the novelist Simon Vestdijk worked together on an opera, *Merlijn*, based on astrological principles; Pijper's death in 1947 meant that it was never finished.

The influence of the Second World War is clearly to be felt in C.S. Lewis' book for young readers *That Hideous Strength* (1945), in which Merlin returns to thwart a sinister bid for world power. The writer Mary Stewart devoted a trilogy of novels to Merlin, *The Crystal Cave* (1970), *The Hollow Hills* (1973) and *The Last Enchantment* (1979), in which she gave a psychologically convincing interpretation of the data derived from medieval sources. In France the same topic received a completely different treatment in the novel *L'Enchanteur* (1984) by René Barjavel. In his drama *Merlin oder das wüste Land* (1981), which in its unabridged form runs to over a hundred scenes, Tancred Dorst gives a pessimistic view of the utopia of the Round Table. An intriguing contribution to the literature of Merlin is Willem Brakman's story 'Artorius' in the volume *Een familiedrama* (1984). The American children's writer Jane Yolen addressed an adult audience in *Merlin's Booke* (1986), a collection of thirteen stories and poems;

'The Beguiling of Merlin', painting by Edward Burne-Jones, 1877. Port Sunlight, Lady Lever Art Gallery (National Museums and Galleries on Merseyside).

the German Maria Christiane Benning used much the same material in *Merlin der Zauberer und König Artus* (1958, reprinted 1980).

The Merlin material also proved amenable to use in science fiction. In *Merlin's Mirror* (1975) the American Andre Norton made Merlin the son of an extraterrestrial being; and in such books as *Merlin's Ring* (1974) and *Merlin's Godson* (1976) H. Warner Munn has him taking part in an expedition to the New World after the destruction of Arthur's realm. The motif of Merlin's devilish begetting stimulated Robert Nye to write a scabrous version with a satanic-hedonistic perspective, *Merlin* (1978), recommended on the jacket as 'a feast of flesh and flagellation'.

It was to be expected that the figure of Merlin would exercise a powerful attraction for the unravellers of esoteric mysteries. After Walter Johannes Stein had set the prophet in an anthroposophical context (*Der Tod Merlins*, Dornach 1984) the first 'Merlin Conference' was held in London in 1986. The participants received 'clear indications of transpersonal powers of consciousness'. A second conference, a year later, had as its theme 'Merlin and Woman'. Since 1988 it has been possible under the banner of 'Images, Insight and Wisdom from the Age of Merlin' to form a picture of the future with the aid of *The Merlin Tarot*. So in the end the old seer could not escape the forces of pseudo-science, occultism and trivialisation. The question is: did he foresee this, too?

W.P. GERRITSEN

Editions: Clarke 1973; Micha 1979; Cerquiglini 1981; Vielhauer 1985.
Translation: Thorpe 1966.
Studies: Zumthor 1943; Tolstoy 1990; Brugger-Hackett 1991.

M ORIAEN is the (black) protagonist of a Middle Dutch Arthurian romance of that name written in the second half of the 13th century. The knights → Lancelot and Walewein (→ Gawain) leave Arthur's court in search of Perchevael (→ Perceval). They encounter Moriaen, a knight as black as a raven. Moriaen's boorish behaviour forces Lancelot to fight a duel with him; it ends inconclusively when Walewein intervenes. Moriaen tells them that he is looking for his father, Acglavael, who had begotten him 24 years before in the land of Moriane but left immediately after and never returned. When it turns out that Walewein and Lancelot are also looking for Acglavael, Perchevael's brother, the three knights decide to join forces. A hermit living near a crossroads on the borders of Arthur's realm tells them that he has indeed seen the two knights they are seeking, but does not know which way they went. So the three of them take a road each: Lancelot chooses the right-hand way, which leads to a land plagued by a ferocious beast, Walewein goes straight ahead to the 'land of unreason', Moriaen takes the road to the left which leads to the sea.

Walewein rescues a lady from a knight who is mistreating her. When the knight refuses to amend his unchivalrous behaviour, Walewein kills him. Walewein and the lady seek lodging in a castle for the night. That evening the knight's body is brought in; he proves to be their host's son. When his wounds spontaneously begin to bleed again it becomes apparent that Walewein is his killer. His host is reluctant to break the rules of hospitality, but neither will he leave the death of his son unavenged. Next day Walewein is lured into an ambush and taken to the crossroads to be broken on the wheel.

Moriaen reaches the sea, but is unable to cross it because the sailors run away when they see his black skin. He returns to the crossroads without achieving his purpose, arriving just in time to rescue Walewein. Next day Walewein's youngest brother, Gariët, arrives with the news that Arthur has been captured by the Saxons and the King of Ireland has invaded Britain. Only the return of Walewein, Lancelot and Perchevael can save Arthur's realm. Gariët also tells them that Perchevael has become a hermit and that he and the wounded Acglavael are staying with their uncle in a hermitage on the far side of the sea. Walewein decides to go in search of Lancelot. Moriaen and Gariët continue their quest for Perchevael and Acglavael and reach the hermitage. Acglavael acknowledges Moriaen as his son; as soon as he is recovered he will return with him to Moriane and marry his mother.

In the land of the ferocious beast Lancelot hears that the country's queen will marry the knight who slays the monster. Lancelot kills the animal, but is then badly wounded by a treacherous knight. In the nick of time Walewein arrives and manages to prevent the villain carrying off the prize. Walewein and Lancelot return to the crossroads, where they are soon joined by Perchevael, Gariët and Moriaen. Under their leadership the Irish king is defeated and Arthur is freed. The Arthurian knights then accompany Moriaen and Acglavael back to Moriane. The rebellious knights of that country are crushed and Acglavael and Moriaen's mother are married. After the wedding Walewein, Lancelot and Perchevael return to Arthur's court.

The *Moriaen* is a fascinating Arthurian romance, composed in Middle Dutch, and is highly regarded for its readability, composition and characterisation. The romance has been preserved in the so-called 'Lancelot compilation' (early 14th century). This is a manuscript from Brabant containing ten Middle Dutch Arthurian verse romances, several of which were adapted by the compiler to fit his compilation. It is not impossible that the *Moriaen*, which on the evidence of a few fragments of the original text was written in Flanders, was also adapted in this way; the section on Lancelot, in particular, has been the subject of debate in this connection. The *Moriaen's* position in the compilation – before the Grail quest – is determined by the overall composition; for one thing, Perchevael dies soon after completing the Grail quest. The compiler used references to earlier and later events to anchor the text securely in his collection.

Acglavael's appearance in the story has given rise to the most intriguing question about the *Moriaen*: just who is the father of Moriaen? The prologue tells us that while some books state that Perchevael is Moriaen's father, others give that honour to Acglavael. It cannot have been Perchevael, so says the prologue, because as a future Grail-knight he had to preserve his virginity. This has not prevented a number of scholars from claiming Perchevael as the original father, partly on the grounds of inconsistencies in the text. It would then be the compiler who attributed paternity to Acglavael. On the other hand, there are those who maintain that Acglavael was Moriaen's father in the original romance. They argue, for one thing, that at the time when the original *Moriaen* was written a paternal role for Perchevael was already almost unthinkable, since the Old French *Queste del Saint Graal* (1215–35) had by then been in circulation for some time.

This brings us to another question: the date of the *Moriaen*. If the text was at one time labelled 'early 13th century', or even 'late 12th century', the prevailing opinion now is that it dates from the second half of the 13th century. Much of the evidence for this comes from the work's textual relationships with other Arthurian romances and the dating of these. Influence of the *Walewein* on *Moriaen* can be seen in Walewein's fight with the unchivalrous knight in the 'land of unreason' and the subsequent episode of the breach of hospitality. Another argument is the close correspondence between *Lantsloot vander Haghedochte* (a Middle Dutch version of the *Lancelot en prose*), the *Riddere metter mouwen* and the *Moriaen*. If *Lantsloot* dates from c.1250 and *Walewein* from shortly after, an acceptable date for the *Moriaen* is after 1260. This dating is supported by the fact that 'post-chivalric middle-class attitudes' can be discerned in the romance: for example, the behaviour of King Arthur, who tears his hair at the absence of Perchevael, Walewein and Lancelot because he is helpless without them.

In recent years discussion has concentrated mainly on intertextuality. There is demonstrable influence of the *Lancelot en prose* and (the Middle Dutch translation of) Chrétien de Troyes' *Conte du Graal*. The Lancelot-episode in the *Moriaen* is a conflation and adaptation of (the Middle Dutch translation of) Thomas' *Tristan* and the *Lanceloet en het hert met de witte voet*.

As a main character Moriaen is unique because of his black skin. He has been compared with Feirefiz, Parzival's half-brother in Wolfram von Eschenbach's *Parzival* (c.1210), who also undertakes a quest for his father. But Feirefiz, like Moriaen the son of a Moorish woman and a white knight, has the coloration of a magpie: black and white.

In 1901 Jessie L. Weston produced an English prose translation of the *Moriaen*.

R. STUFKENS

Edition: Paardekooper-Van Buuren/Gijsseling 1971.
Study: Besamusca 1991a.

OGIER THE DANE (French: Ogier le Danois) features in Carolingian narrative as one of → Charlemagne's most outstanding knights. His Danish origin has been disputed: the name 'le Danois' may be a corruption of 'l'Ardennois'. He is the chief character in *La Chevalerie d'Ogier de Danemarche*, a *chanson de geste* which in the form we now have it was probably composed c.1200, possibly by the poet Raimbert de Paris. Its content can be divided into five branches. The first of these ('Enfances') tells of Ogier's youth. He is the son of the Duke of Denmark and a hostage at Charlemagne's court. When his father neglects his obligations to his overlord Ogier is imprisoned in the fortress of Saint-Omer, where he falls in love with the daughter of the castellan and begets his son Baudouinet on her. When Charles sets out for Italy to do battle with the heathen who have captured Rome Ogier goes with him. The Franks cross the Alps and soon encounter the Saracen army. Young Ogier performs his first heroic deeds in this battle and is consequently knighted by Charles. After this he again distinguishes himself in duels with the chivalrous Karaheu and with Brunamont, in the course of which he wins his sword Courtain and his trusty steed Broiefort. Helped by Gloriande, daughter of the heathen general Corsubles and Karaheu's betrothed, Ogier overcomes all difficulties. Eventually the defeated heathen retreat to their own country; Karaheu and Gloriande refuse to convert to Christianity and go with their people.

The second branch ('The Chess-game') is set some years later at Charlemagne's court in Laon. Ogier's son Baudouinet is now a young man; he plays chess with Charles' son Charlot and wins. Enraged, Charlot strikes his opponent with the chessboard and kills him. When Ogier then tries to kill Charlot to avenge his son Charlemagne banishes him. He takes refuge with Desiderius, King of the Lombards in Pavia, who grants him Castelfort in fee.

The third branch ('Battle against the Lombards') deals with Charles' war against King Desiderius in Northern Italy. Ogier is in command of the Lombard army and loses the battle. When he falls asleep from exhaustion and is in danger of being discovered by the pursuing Franks, his horse Broiefort wakes him. He flees to Pavia, but Desiderius refuses to open its gates to him. Our hero then retreats to Castelfort.

The fourth branch ('Castelfort') tells how Charles besieges Castelfort for seven years. At the end of this time all Ogier's men are dead. Left alone, he carves figures out of wood to look like armed warriors and sets them on the castle's battlements. He leaves Castelfort by night. In the enemy camp he seeks out Charlot's tent and hurls his lance into it, but Charles' son escapes death because he is sleeping in another bed. Ogier continues his flight, but one day he is discovered asleep in a wood by Archbishop Turpin. The good bishop arrests him out of loyalty to the king, but reluctantly, and

Monumental tomb of Ogier and his comrade Benoît in the monastery church of Saint-Faron in Meaux, pre-1180, now vanished; engraving, 1704. The figures on either side of the tomb represent characters from Carolingian epic: from left to right Bishop Turpin, a woman and a man (probably Charlemagne and his consort), Oliver, Aude and Roland.

takes him in a cart to Rheims. He promises Charles that he will give the hero, who is renowned for his large appetite, no more than a quarter of a loaf and one beaker of watered wine a day. Turpin keeps his promise, but every day he has a huge loaf baked; a quarter of this is given to Ogier, together with an enormous beaker of wine, so that the hero does not perish from hunger and thirst in his captivity.

The fifth and last branch ('Battle against the Saxons') begins with the threat posed by the heathen giant Brahier, who has invaded Charles' realm at the head of a great army of Africans and Saxons. The Franks realise that only Ogier can save them and demand his recall, despite the king's ban on mentioning his name. Under pressure of circumstances Charles releases Ogier, but the latter is implacable; he insists that Charlot, the murderer of his son, should first be surrendered to him. Charles agrees to this also, sacrificing his own son to save the kingdom. But with Ogier about to decapitate his arch-enemy, God intervenes. St Michael informs him that he must content himself with giving Charlot a box on the ears. This done, nothing prevents the hero from turning his might on the heathen. These he overcomes by killing the giant Brahier in single combat. He then rescues a girl from the clutches of five villainous

Turks. She turns out to be the daughter of the King of England, and the story ends with the marriage of Ogier and this princess. Charlemagne gives Ogier Hainault and Brabant in fee. The hero is buried in Meaux.

Long before the *Chevalerie* existed in this form Ogier was already to be found in historical, legendary and epic sources. The historical core of the narrative is concealed in the third branch. Ogier's behaviour here corresponds closely with that of the Frank Autcharius who fled to Desiderius following the death of Charlemagne's brother Carloman in 771. When Charles crossed the Alps in 773 to support the Pope against Desiderius, it was Autcharius who commanded the Lombard army. This third branch narrative was then extended, first by addition of the fourth branch, about Castelfort, which reflects the gallant resistance of the city of Pavia in the war with Charlemagne.

An example of an old legend is the *Conversio Othgerii militis*, which relates how at the end of his life Ogier retired to the monastery of Saint-Faron in Meaux. A tomb in the monastery church, dating from before 1180, depicted Ogier together with his comrade Benoît. The tomb was flanked by other figures from Carolingian epic. The oldest literary source in which Ogier appears is the *Chanson de Roland* (c.1100), in which he commands Charlemagne's vanguard and later, in the battle with Baligant, leads the Bavarian army.

To the historically-based material of the third and fourth branches was then added the completely unhistorical second branch about the chess-game, the object being to explain the hero's disloyalty to his overlord. The fifth branch was necessary to bring about the reconciliation between Charles and Ogier, and the first was added to provide an account of the youth of a hero who had become a favourite. An alternative view of how this *chanson de geste* developed, which regards branches II–V as a later continuation of the 'Enfances', seems less convincing.

Ogier was an exceptionally popular figure, both in the Middle Ages and later. The *Chevalerie*'s version of the story was expanded with new adventures in the Holy Land and the Far East (*Roman d'Ogier en alexandrins*, c.1335). Around 1275 the poet Adenet le Roi presented an independent version of the first branch, *Les enfances Ogier*, to Maria of Brabant, Queen of France. In 1498 the story was published by Vérard in Paris in a prose adaptation which was reissued many times in the 16th century.

Outside the French language area, too, Ogier was well known. In Southern Europe parts of the material have been preserved in Italian epic (e.g. *Uggeri il Danese*, c.1455) and in Catalan *romanceros* (15th and 16th century). But Ogier achieved his greatest popularity in Northern Europe. There our hero became known quite early on through the inclusion of his story in the late 13th-century Old Norse compilation of Carolingian narratives known as the *Karlamagnús saga*. In the 19th century, after a long evolution, Ogier became the symbol of the Danish people. According to Andersen's famous fairy-tale *Holger Danske* he is to be found in the cellars of Kronborg Castle near Elsinore. He is asleep, his beard has grown into a marble table-top, but one day, when Denmark is in danger, he will rouse himself and save his country.

H. VAN DIJK

Edition: Eusebi 1962.
Studies: De Riquer 1956²; Togeby 1969.

ORENDEL is the hero of a German heroic legend describing how the Holy Mantle of Christ came to Trier. The story, whish probably originated in the 12th century, has been preserved in two printed texts from the 16th century and an 18th-century copy of a burned manuscript of 1477.

Orendel, son of King Ougel of Trier, decides to seek the hand of Bride, Queen of Jerusalem. He puts to sea with a mighty fleet, but his ship is wrecked. Orendel is rescued by a fisherman and with God's help discovers the Grey Mantle of Christ in the belly of a whale. From then on he wears this cloak like a kind of monk's habit as his sole protection. He succeeds in winning Bride's love and with her survives a great many battles against the heathen. At the end of the poem the Mantle is brought to Trier.

This last fact probably tells us something about the time when the legend originated, for on 1 May 1196 the Mantle, together with other relics, was solemnly transferred to the new altar of St Peter's in Trier.

The appendix to the Strassburg Heldenbuch (15th century) names King 'Erentheil' of Trier as the earliest of the heroes. Saxo Grammaticus in his *Gesta Danorum* (c.1200) mentions one 'Horwendillus' as the father of 'Amlethus' (= Hamlet). The name is also found as a personal name among the Lombards ('Auriwandalo') and in Old High German ('Orentil'). Partly because of this, it has been thought that there must have existed an older epic about a hero called Orendel. The king's name has been linked to the Old English word 'earendel' (daybreak, morning star, beam of light) and with the Old Norse 'Aurvandill', the name of a semi-mythical figure. This, however, is extremely problematic. It is even questionable whether a heroic lay about Orendel – that is, without the Holy Mantle legend – ever existed. It seems more likely that the legend of the Holy Mantle was expanded using motifs current at the time ($\rightarrow$ Oswald and $\rightarrow$ Rother).

A. QUAK

Edition: Schröder 1976.
Study: Curschmann 1968.

OSWALD is a historical-legendary figure, the hero of a Middle High German epic. The name comes from an English king, Oswald of Northumbria (635–642); in his *Historia ecclesiastica Anglorum* the Venerable Bede (673–735) says that Oswald was responsible for the spread of Christianity in England and that he was killed in a war against the heathen king Penda. He became famous in the Middle Ages through the *Vita Sancti Oswaldi regis et martyris* (1165) by the English monk Reginald.

In Germany Oswald became the main character of a so-called minstrel epic, which set the saint in the rather more profane context of his search for a bride and of the crusades. Here Oswald is a powerful King of England. In order to secure the succession he is looking for a suitable wife. The pilgrim Warmunt tells him about Princess Pamige, daughter of the heathen king Aron. The latter has sworn to chop off the heads of all his daughter's admirers because, his wife being dead, he wants to marry her himself. Oswald manages to make contact with Pamige, who has secretly embraced Christianity, by means of a talking raven which takes her a ring. He fits out a great fleet to go and fetch his bride.

When they reach the heathen country Oswald and a number of his followers disguise themselves as goldsmiths, a stratagem which gains them admittance to the king's castle. A golden hart lures Aron's servants out of the fortress, and Pamige and a few other women are able to escape and join Oswald. Her father pursues them with a fleet. A battle ensues; the heathen are defeated and King Aron captured. After seeing Oswald perform several miracles he converts to Christianity. On their return to England a great feast is held.

But Oswald is now tested by God himself, who in the guise of a pilgrim demands more and more of him, even including his wife. Oswald passes the test, and it is then foretold that he has only two years to live, but that he will become one of those saints who can be called on for aid in time of need. Oswald and Pamige live together without physical contact and on their death are taken up into Heaven.

The epic's religious ending is in sharp contrast to the motif of the hard-to-win bride usually found in heroic epic (cf. → Orendel and → Rother). The cult of St Oswald probably reached the continent and Germany as early as the 11th century; his popularity was greatest in Southern Germany and in Austria. In pictorial art we initially find only portrayals relating to the Latin *Vita*; but from the 14th century on traces of the epic can be found in Germany. Thus we find Oswald depicted with the raven, which often has a ring in its beak; examples are a sandstone figure c.1370 at Regensburg and a painting by Andrea Belunello of about 1480. A wall-painting c.1420 in the Sankt-Vigil in Bolzano shows Oswald handing over his wife to a Christ disguised as a beggar.

A. QUAK

Edition: Schröder 1976.
Study: Curschmann 1968.

PARTHONOPEUS OF BLOIS, nephew of the King of France, loses his way while hunting in the Ardennes. He eventually finds himself on the coast, where an unmanned ship is lying at anchor. Parthonopeus boards the ship, which then mysteriously transports him to a splendid but totally deserted city. The young man goes to reconnoitre and enters a most beautiful castle, which is likewise completely deserted. Although somewhat ill at ease, Parthonopeus sits down at the lavishly spread table and allows himself to enjoy the food served to him by unseen hands. After the meal two floating candlesticks guide him to his bed, where after a while – once the light is out – he has company. Using his sense of touch Parthonopeus discovers that he has a young lady lying beside him and tries, rather clumsily, to seduce her. The lady struggles a little at first, but in the end the youth has his way and the two of them abandon themselves – both for the first time – to lovemaking.

Afterwards the lady – it turns out that her name is Melior and she is a powerful queen – explains that her behaviour had not been merely wanton. At her barons' insistence she had been looking for a suitable husband and had finally selected Parthonopeus of Blois. With her magic arts – for it was she who had sent the magic ship – she had successfully lured him to her realm. Only he had not been meant to end up in her bed straightaway, for the planned wedding cannot take place for another two and a half years. Melior promises to visit her young lover every night, but until they are married the youth must make no attempt to look at his beloved. He can spend the waiting time leading a life of luxury in the prosperous city (Chief d'Oire); though, as on the first evening, he will never see a soul there.

This arrangement suits Parthonopeus very well, but after a while he feels like paying a visit to his parents. After a second stay in France Parthonopeus breaks his promise to Melior – using an inextinguishable lamp given him by his mother – and sees that his beloved is a most beautiful woman. Melior is furious at Parthonopeus' disobedience and throws her lover out. In any case, their relationship can no longer remain secret; his action has broken the spell and Parthonopeus is now visible to all.

Mad with grief, Parthonopeus goes to live like a wild man in the forest, where Urake, Melior's sister, eventually manages to track him down. She takes him with her and cares for him. In Chief d'Oire, meanwhile, preparations are under way for a great tournament with Melior's hand as the prize. With Urake's help Parthonopeus is able to take part in the contest without Melior being aware of his presence. Of course Parthonopeus is proclaimed the victor and the lovers find each other again. The romance ends with a magnificent wedding, but in the closing lines the author announces a sequel. In this the country of Parthonopeus and Melior is invaded by Margarijs, Sultan of Persia. The Sultan finds his failure to win Melior's hand at the tournament intolerable and now he is out for revenge. This second part is totally dominated by battles between Christian and infidel.

This is the story of Parthonopeus as found in the Old French *Partonopeu de Blois* and the Middle Dutch *Parthonopeus van Bloys*. Anyone wishing to study the Middle Dutch version is compelled to refer to the Old French original (late 12th century), if only to follow the story; for the Middle Dutch romance has survived only in fragmentary form. The known fragments come from five different manuscripts, preserved in libraries spread across the whole of Europe. The standard edition of *Parthonopeus van Bloys* was published as long ago as 1871 by the Liège professor J.-H. Bormans; not only is it almost impossible to find, it also has so many shortcomings that it is certainly not to be regarded as a reliable tool. Moreover, twelve new fragments have been discovered since 1871.

Parthonopeus – unlike King → Arthur or → Gawain or → Lancelot – is not a figure who still appeals to our imagination. Yet this narrative material must have been extremely popular. The many translations and versions of the Old French work bear witness to that: we know of versions not only in Middle High German, Middle Dutch and Middle English, but also in Italian, Old Icelandic and Danish. During the 16th and 17th centuries it appeared in chapbook form in various language areas. In the Romantic period the Parthonopeus story was dusted off once again; a number of English and French writers were inspired by the material.

In the Dutch language area, too, the *Parthonopeus* left its mark. We do not know how many Middle Dutch manuscripts were in circulation – there were at least five – but the romance is mentioned repeatedly in a variety of works. Jacob van Maerlant mentions both Parthonopeus and Melior in *Alexanders geesten* (c.1260). In his later *Spiegel historiael* (c.1285) Maerlant inveighs against non-historical figures from romance such as Parthonopeus.

VEERLE UYTTERSPROT

Edition: Uri 1962.
Study: Kienhorst 1988.

P ERCEVAL is the hero of *Le conte du Graal* (c.1182), an Arthurian romance in verse by the French poet Chrétien de Troyes. It tells of a widow who lives with her son Perceval in a castle in a wasteland known as the Gaste Forest. Her husband had died of grief when their two eldest sons fell in battle, and to protect Perceval from a similar fate she keeps him far from the world of chivalry. Her plan misfires when a group of King → Arthur's knights lose their way in the forest. Perceval bombards their leader with questions about the various items of their equipment, all of which are new to him. As a result the lad sets his heart on going to Arthur's court and becoming a knight. He is dressed as a peasant and his only weapon is a javelin. His mother supplements this with some wise advice. When Perceval leaves she collapses as if dead; but he takes no notice and rides away.

On his journey he enters a tent where a lady is sleeping and follows his mother's instructions on the treatment of ladies, but in an absurd way. He forces a kiss on the girl and pulls off her ring. He then helps himself to the available food and drink, quite unconcerned at the girl's distress, and leaves again. Later her friend Orguelleus de la Lande arrives, and refuses to believe that she had been kissed against her will. As punishment she has to follow him in a state of wretchedness, which is to continue until he has killed the miscreant.

Perceval's behaviour on reaching Arthur's court is equally ridiculous. Outside he sees the Red Knight, who has seized Arthur's golden goblet and is demanding dominion over the country. Perceval takes a fancy to his arms and armour. He rides his horse into the hall and asks for it. Keu (→ Kay), the ill-natured chamberlain, challenges him to go and get it. A girl smiles at Perceval, saying that he will become the best knight in the world; the court fool was wont to say of her that she would never smile until she saw the best knight. Irritated by her words, Keu knocks the girl down and kicks the fool into the fire. Perceval goes outside and runs his javelin through the Red Knight's head. He has no idea how to remove the armour and has to be helped by Yvonet, a squire at the court. He sends Yvonet to return Arthur's goblet, and also to promise the girl that he will avenge Keu's outrageous act. When the message is delivered the fool predicts that Keu will be punished by the hero.

After this Perceval lodges at a castle belonging to Gornemant, who teaches him to fight like a knight. He also gets Perceval out of his peasant garb, gives him new clothes and dubs him knight. Perceval wants to go home and see how his mother is. But his road takes him to Beaurepaire, the castle of the beautiful Blancheflor. That night the maiden comes to Perceval's bed and tells him of her wretched situation: the castle is being besieged by Clamadeus des Isles and his marshal Engygeron. She expects the castle to surrender next day; then she will kill herself with a knife. Perceval keeps Blancheflor with him that night and then takes up the fight for her lands. First he defeats Engygeron and later Clamadeus. He spares them both and sends them to the court of King Arthur.

Perceval leaves Blancheflor because he again wants to go and look for his mother. Now he is led to the castle of the invalid Fisher King. There he is given a remarkable sword. During dinner he sees a servant carrying a lance, from the point of which blood is constantly dripping. He is followed by a girl with a 'grail' – a dish – which radiates a clear light. Perceval asks no questions about lance or Grail. He intends to do so next morning, but then he finds the castle deserted. Close by he comes upon a girl weeping for her slain lover. She is Perceval's cousin and tells him that his silence in the Grail castle will have destructive consequences.

Perceval goes in search of the knight who killed his cousin's lover. This is our old acquaintance Orguelleus de la Lande, who kills everyone who speaks to his mistress. He means to continue doing so until he has avenged himself on whoever had made love to his lady in the tent. Perceval puts an end to her misery by defeating Orguelleus. Him, too, he sends to Arthur's court. When Orguelleus arrives there the fool again foretells the punishment awaiting Keu. The king and all his court then set out in search of Perceval.

One morning Perceval arrives in the vicinity of Arthur's camp. For hours he stares in a trance at three drops of blood in the snow; they come from a goose attacked by a falcon. In them he discerns the face of his beloved Blancheflor. First Saigremor and then Keu make aggressive attempts to get him to the court, which costs Keu a broken arm and a dislocated collar-bone. King Arthur's nephew Gauvain (→ Gawain) employs courtly diplomacy, and with him Perceval returns to court. Arthur takes Perceval with him to Carlion, where his return is celebrated with three days of feasting.

The festivities are interrupted by the arrival of a hideously ugly, deformed young woman who greets everyone except Perceval. Him she condemns for his behaviour at the Grail castle. Had he questioned what he saw the Fisher King would have been cured and able to rule his country in peace. Now, because of his silence, the world will suffer great misfortune. Perceval reacts by deciding to undertake a quest to find the secret of the Grail and the bleeding lance. One episode of this quest is recounted, set among the adventures of the other hero, Gauvain. The narrator then skips five years. During that time Perceval has vanquished sixty knights and sent them to Arthur's court. But he has forgotten God and is not an inch nearer his goal. It is Good Friday when he meets some penitents in a wasteland and questions them. They remind him of Christ's work of redemption and direct him to a hermit. Perceval sees the error of his ways and makes his confession to the hermit, who turns out to be his uncle. He tells Perceval that his silence in the Fisher King's hall was the result of his sin against his mother, who had died of grief when he left. He also tells him about the mystery of the Grail. The Grail is a holy object which contains a Host which keeps the Fisher King's father alive. Perceval receives instruction from the hermit, who propounds the idea of a knighthood founded on the love of God. Perceval stays with the hermit for two days, sharing his simple food in penance. The last the narrator tells us of Perceval is that at Easter he takes Communion.

The rest of the romance is devoted to Gawain. Having pronounced judgment on Perceval, the Loathly Lady mentions a couple of 'adventures' in which Arthur's knights can distinguish themselves. One of these concerns the rescue of a maiden. Gawain wants to take this on, but is thwarted by the arrival of Guigambresil, who accuses him of killing the King of Escavalon in an unknightly manner. Gauvain now heads for Escavalon to clear himself of this charge; but subsequent adventures lead him ever further from that goal. His conduct is described with consistent irony. Finally in a castle he passes the test of the magic bed; the inhabitants then welcome him as their lord and saviour. This adventure forms a counterpart to Perceval's visit to the Grail castle, with Gauvain apparently succeeding where Perceval had failed. But we see nothing of any salvation. Moreover, Gauvain becomes the prisoner of his own deed, for he is not allowed to leave the castle even though he is given a day's leave. It appears that his mother and Arthur's live there, ladies who in the real world are long dead. It is as though Gauvain has entered a realm of the dead, as though Chrétien is entombing Arthur's leading knight in a mausoleum for a defunct Arthurian world.

The *Conte du Graal* is Chrétien de Troyes' last work, and in many respects it offers something new. If Chrétien's previous romances had been concerned with 'amour' and 'chevalerie', here the Graal hero Perceval is shown the beckoning perspective of a Christian knighthood. This new direction probably has to do with the man who commissioned the work. Chrétien wrote the *Conte du Graal* for Philip of Alsace, Count of Flanders (1142–91). Philip and his family maintained close links with the Holy Land; he was an active crusader and was killed while taking part in the siege of Acre during the Third Crusade.

Chrétien structured the tale of Perceval as a process of development. The romance begins with an introductory phase, tracing its hero's route to the world of chivalry. At this stage Perceval acts like an ignorant fool. However, it is already clear that a high destiny awaits him. For he disposes of the Red Knight, a redoubtable foe to Arthur's court. A new phase begins with Perceval's stay with Gornemant. He becomes a knight, and from then on behaves as the ideal chivalrous knight when he relieves Blancheflor's castle. In this episode his 'chevalerie' is enriched by 'amour'. What follows, however, reveals the existence of a still higher ethos to which the hero must conform. He has not reached that point yet, for when he sees the Grail and the lance Perceval remains silent. This first phase of his knightly career ends with his return to Arthur's court. A peak of achievement turns into a crisis when he is condemned by the Loathly Lady.

This marks the beginning of the second stage, the quest for the Grail. A period of fruitless searching is followed by a turning point, the penitential sacrament, which for Perceval effects the transition from sin to grace. In this thematic structure secular chivalry is gradually surpassed by a religious chivalry; and as part of this Arthur's court has to relinquish its role as Perceval's intended goal to the other world of the Grail.

The narrative's development is tied up with the theme of decline and recovery. There are various representations of a 'waste land' (in modern times a controlling theme in T.S. Eliot's poem of that name), for instance in the Blancheflor episode. The buildings in her fortress-city are laid waste and the inhabitants wretched. It is Perceval who saves her. Perceval's next stopping-place also has elements of a waste land through the figure of the injured Fisher King, who is unable to govern his country. Here Perceval remains silent, so that there is as yet no salvation for the Grail castle. This is because Perceval himself is, spiritually speaking, in a waste land. He is in need of healing and rebirth, which he will later receive on Good Friday.

Coupled with the 'waste land' theme is a distanced attitude to 'chevalerie'. The *Conte du Graal* reveals the darker side of chivalry: a world of 'vaine gloire', empty renown, of destruction and violence. The tone is set at the beginning of the romance with the tragic tale of Perceval's mother. Her husband's land had been devastated, and they then fled to the Gaste Forest; Perceval's brothers, having achieved knighthood, met their death by weapons. When he encounters knights for the first time Perceval thinks them devils, because of the din they make; then angels, because of their glittering arms and armour. He thus unwittingly expresses a deeper truth about the appearance and reality of knighthood. Perceval himself seeks to become a knight. But his departure from the Gaste Forest is presented as sinful because of his failure in 'carité' to his mother – which leads to his setback at the Grail castle. On the other hand, and this is the paradox, the knight Perceval is the intended saviour of the Grail world. In order to achieve this he eventually opts for 'carité', love of God.

This new road of Perceval's is thrown into extra relief by the comparison with Gauvain, the other hero. In the middle of the romance comes the crucial moment when Perceval resolves to go in search of the Grail. At that point Gauvain opts for 'vaine gloire'. His deeds serve no spiritual end whatsoever. Gauvain is a static hero, who gradually becomes locked into his own adventures. With this contrast between Perceval and Gauvain the romance seems to be testifying to a knightly ideal in which earthly glory must give place to Christian humility.

Symbol of the ideal and of Perceval's destiny is the Grail. There is a certain ambiguity here between pagan and Christian. At first, during Perceval's stay with the Fisher King, we have 'a dish' surrounded by an aura of magic, with nothing discernibly Christian about it. Much later, the hermit gives the Grail a Christian, spiritual interpretation. This ambiguity is typical of the romance's stylistic approach, which is one of mystification and the enigmatic. This is enhanced by the fact that the narrative is incomplete. There are no simple explanations. The essence of the story lies in what Perceval has to do – namely, ask questions. The primary concern is with the literary dimension of the romance. Chrétien created a fantastic world of words, open to many interpretations and rich in meaning, thus reserving a creative task for those who listened to the story. And that story is packed from beginning to end with fascinating scenes, related with sparkling humour and irony.

In scholarly research Chrétien's Grail romance has given rise to numerous studies of its structure, themes, meaning and interpretation. In the past a great deal has been written about Chrétien's description of the Grail castle, leading to various theories as to its source. Very probably Chrétien looked to Celtic literature for his ideas. According to some scholars, the model for the Grail is to be found in Celtic tales of food-producing talismans in the Otherworld, which represent sovereignty. Other motifs connected with the Grail, such as the magic lance, the invalid king and the sterile land which awaits

Perceval, still a rustic youth, confronted by the troop of knights. Ivory casket from a Paris studio, c.1400. Paris, Musée du Louvre.

The Grail Knights around the Grail Table. A scene from Richard Wagner's opera *Parsifal* (Act 1) in a production by Wieland Wagner (Bayreuth Festival, 1951). George London in the part of Amfortas.

the coming of a hero to make it bloom, have also been linked to Celtic sources. Chrétien combined these motifs with images from Christian liturgy and so created the most magical myth in Western literature.

The *Conte du Graal* exercised medieval minds, too. The mysterious and unfinished nature of the story led to attempts at continuation, completion and explanation. In France four continuations of Chrétien's romance appeared in the early decades of the 13th century, along with new Grail romances. These show a Christianisation of the theme, with the Grail traced back to the Last Supper and the death of Christ. In the Second Continuation – the First is about Gauvain (→ Gawain) – Perceval is the hero of a long string of adventures. His way brings him in the end to the castle of the Fisher King. During the meal he sees two girls carrying the Holy Grail and the bleeding lance. They are followed by a servant who bears the two pieces of a broken sword. Perceval now inquires about these objects. The Fisher King tells him only about the sword. Perceval manages to reunite the pieces, but a small crack can still be seen, suggesting that his success is not yet complete. This unsatisfying conclusion stimulated two authors to write new continuations. One was Gerbert de Montreuil, the other Manessier, author of the Third Continuation which he dedicated to Countess Johanna of Flanders. Perceval learns that Partinal had used the sword kept in the Grail castle to kill the Fisher King's brother. Whoever is able to unite the pieces of the sword will avenge the murder and also cure the Fisher King. Perceval takes the duty of vengeance upon himself and after a series of adventures is successful. When the Fisher King dies Perceval succeeds him. He rules the country for seven years in peace and prosperity. Eventually he withdraws from the world and leads a life of service to God as hermit and priest. On his death the Grail is taken up into Heaven.

The theme of vengeance also plays a part in the Welsh version of the Perceval story, *Peredur*. In an uncle's castle Peredur sees a salver bearing a blood-soaked head. Years later, after many adventures, he learns that it was the head of his cousin, killed by the witches of Caer Loyw – a deed which will be avenged by Peredur. Vengeance is also a major theme in the French prose romance *Perlesvaus*, another sequel to Chrétien's *Conte du Graal*. Of the three heroes engaged in the quest it is Perceval, here called Perlesvaus, who is the chosen Grail Knight. He wreaks vengeance on a variety of miscreants, as when he frees the Grail castle, symbolising Jerusalem, from the rule of the King of Chastel Mortel, the Fisher King's destructive brother. Here the spiritual and mystical Grail adventure serves a militant crusade ethic. Perceval is the ideal representative of a knighthood defending Christ's New Law in the struggle with the infidel.

In his → *Joseph d'Arimathie* and → *Merlin* Robert de Boron wrote about the Grail's biblical prehistory and the years leading up to Arthur's coronation. His account was later expanded into a cycle by the addition of the *Perceval en prose*. This work offers a revised and completed version of Chrétien's Perceval story, closing with an account of the end of the Arthurian world. A subsequent, culminating stage in the evolution of the quasi-historical Arthurian romance is the trilogy *Lancelot en prose* – *Queste del Saint Graal* – *Mort le roi Artu*. The Grail quest in the central section has the character of an initiation into the mystical life, with a monastic tone. The principal Grail knight is now Lancelot's son Galaad (→ Galahad); Perceval is second and Bohort third. The quest ends in the spiritual city of Sarras, where it is given to Galaad to behold the divine mysteries of the Grail. The picture of Perceval in this romance is in accordance with our last sight of him in Chrétien, when he is staying with the hermit; here his 'simplece' and humility verge on saintliness. While Perceval is living on a rocky island he withstands a temptation sent by the devil. A ship sails in bearing a most beautiful woman, who is on the point of seducing him. But his eye falls on the red cross on the pommel of his sword and he crosses himself, thus banishing the temptress. A voice proclaims that Perceval is saved, and he is then ready to join the two others who have been selected to complete the Grail quest. Perceval's biography ends with his death as a hermit, a year after Galaad's passing. A version of this narrative also appears in *Le Morte d'Arthur*, Malory's 15th-century treatment of the Arthurian material, which in its turn greatly influenced 19th-century Arthurian literature in English.

Meanwhile, Chrétien's romance had also attracted attention outside France. In the first half of the 13th century it was translated into Middle Dutch as *Perchevael* (of which only fragments survive) and into Old Norse as *Parcevals saga*. This latter work, probably written for the court of King Hákon Hákonarson, follows Chrétien's text as far as the episode with the hermit (the remainder was translated in *Valvens páttr*, the story of Gauvain); we are then told in conclusion that Parceval returns to Blankiflúr and marries her. *Sir Perceval of Galles* is a short Middle English version of Chrétien's *Perceval* dating from the early 14th century, in which the Grail quest plays no part; instead Perceval finds his mother again.

Middle Dutch provided Chrétien's Perceval with a descendant. This happened in the → *Moriaen* (Flanders, second half 13th century), which links up with the Perceval of the *Conte du Graal*. Here too Perceval is searching for the Grail, but without success. Meanwhile – at least, this must have been the case in the original version of the story – he had begotten a son, Moriaen, on a Moorish princess. This son then goes in search of his father and along the way develops from a rough-hewn into an exemplary knight. Once he has found his father he plays a major role in the struggle to liberate Arthur's realm. In this 'neo-Perceval' the son outshines his father.

The most impressive Perceval romance after Chrétien's *Conte du Graal* was written by the German poet Wolfram von Eschenbach. His *Parzival* (c.1210) is a free, expanded version of Chrétien's Grail romance which includes prior events and a completion. It begins with the adventures of Gahmuret. Twice his brilliant performance as a knight wins this hero a beautiful queen for his bride: the Moorish Belacane in the East, Herzeloyde in the West. By the former he begets Feirefiz, who has a black and white piebald skin, and by the latter Parzival. After Gahmuret's death Herzeloyde retreats with Parzival into the wilderness. From there Parzival, dressed in motley, sets out on his knightly career. Up to the meeting with the hermit he follows much the same route as Perceval in the *Conte du Graal*; though Wolfram does introduce all manner of modifications, including the use of new and different names. For instance, Parzival's beloved and bride, whose castle he relieves, is called Condwiramurs. The Grail King is Anfortas and his castle is Munsalvaesche. The ugly maiden who curses Parzifal is called Cundrie and the hermit who teaches him to reconsider his way of life is Trevrizent. The hermit expatiates at length on the mysteries of the Grail, which itself differs from Chrétien's. Wolfram's Grail is an exotic gemstone with miraculous qualities around which has gathered a brotherhood of chaste knights known as the 'templeise', a name reminiscent of the religious military order of the Templars. During a love-adventure Anfortas had fought and been wounded by an infidel. The Grail keeps him alive, but he is in constant pain. They now await the coming of a knight who by posing a question will release Anfortas from his suffering and himself become the new Grail King.

From this point Wolfram continues the story of Perceval left unfinished in the *Conte du Graal* and also rounds off the story of Gauvain (here Gawan). Their two paths meet after Gawan's adventure at Schastel Marveil, the castle with the magic bed. The inhabitants were being held captive by the vengeful sorcerer Clinschor; Gawan releases them. There then follows a reunion between Parzival and Arthur's court. After this the author takes up the thread of the earlier history again with a confrontation between Parzival and his Eastern half-brother Feirefiz. Once more Cundrie appears at court. This time she bestows a blessing on Parzival in connection with the Grail. Accompanied by Feirefiz, Parzival rides to Munsalvaesche, where he asks the question that heals Anfortas. Feirefiz becomes enamoured of Repanse de Schoye, the maiden who carries the Grail. He is baptised, marries her and returns to the East. One of the two sons of Parzival, the new Grail King, is Loherangrin, the later → Swan Knight.

The main theme of the romance is 'triuwe' (faithfulness); it forms the basis for a way of life which the hero embraces after a period of rebellion against God. Parzival's road to the Grail, unlike that of Chrétien's Perceval, is bound up with love. When Parzival moves on after Cundrie's curse, his mind is set both on the Grail *and* on Condwiramurs. And once Parzival has completed the Grail adventure Condwiramurs comes to join him. Parzival also retains his bond with Arthur. The company of the Grail does indeed represent a higher plane than the Arthurian world, but through Parzival the two are integrated. The struggle for harmony eventually leads to a Grail-kingship of worldly allure in which East and West come together. Wolfram's recreation of Chrétien's romance is founded on a grandiose conception. In a complex literary world he brings before us all kinds of characters who illuminate various forms of existence. What gives the *Parzival* its fascination is Wolfram's role as narrator, commenting with humour and irony on his story and thus involving his hearers in the action.

The most famous version of the Perceval story in modern times is Richard Wagner's musical drama *Parsifal*, his last work, which was completed in 1882 and had its first performance at Bayreuth in the same year. Wagner's principal source was Wolfram's *Parzival*. To give it dramatic form he designed the work in three acts and reduced the number of characters to five main roles: Kundry, Amfortas, Klingsor, Parsifal and the narrator Gurnemanz. The drama concerns the opposition between the kingdom of the Grail and that of Klingsor. The conflict is symbolised by the holy spear, which belongs with the Grail but has fallen into the hands of Klingsor. An innovation in Wagner's version is the role of Kundry. She is a woman with two faces. As seductress she is the tool of Klingsor, but she also longs to expiate her sin in the service of the Grail. She can be saved only by someone who resists her. Her opposite number Parsifal is a hero who becomes a saviour through a 'compassion' that brings awareness. In the first act he is still ignorant, watching the liturgy of the Holy Grail in silence. When he penetrates Klingsor's magic castle in the second act he withstands Kundry's seductive wiles. He feels Amfortas' suffering within himself and thus becomes 'welthellsichtig'. This awareness leads to the act of redemption in the third act, when as saviour he returns the spear to its rightful place with the Grail. Ideas from Schopenhauer's philosophy find expression in the drama. Wagner's interpretation of the Grail myth transmutes religion into art. It is art which reveals the deeper truth of the mythic symbols of religion. Wagner called his creation a 'Bühnenweihfestspiele', a play to consecrate a theatre. What was to be consecrated was first and foremost his own temple of the arts, the Festival Opera House in Bayreuth. Until thirty years after his death the work was allowed to be performed nowhere else.

Following Wagner's recreation of Wolfram's romance the Grail hero appears many times in German-language literature of the early decades of the 20th century, for example in the cycle *Parcival* (1902) by Karl Vollmöller, a Jugendstil poet from the circle of Stefan George. The poem's hero seeks the lost realm of the childhood to which he longs to return. Gerhart Hauptmann wrote a children's novel, *Parsival* (1914), for his twelve-year-old son. In this version there is a conflict between father and son. The object of Parsival's quest is to take vengeance on whoever was responsible for the suffering of his mother Herzeleide; it turns out to be his father, the Grail King Amfortas. Albrecht Schaeffer published a volume of poetry entitled *Parzival* in 1922. In 1928 Peter Macholin wrote a drama, *Parsifal*. In the Netherlands Marie Koenen wrote the novel *Parcival*, a neo-romantic, Catholic version of Wolfram's romance.

Modern German literature also has a place for Perceval, as in the dramatic spectacle *Merlin oder das wüste Land* by Tancred Dorst (1981). Here the Arthurian material is recast as a parable showing that it is precisely those who dream most passionately of a better world who destroy that dream. In a few scenes derived from Wolfram Parzival is looking naively for a higher way of life, but as he sets out to find the Grail he disappears from the scene. Dorst brings him back again in *Der nackte Mann* (1986). Here Parzival follows a huge naked man to his mud hut. The naked one is a former farmer now living in harmony with nature in paradisial surroundings. Copying his interlocutor, Parzival throws away his sword and armour and adopts a holy life. But this utopia is an illusion, as becomes apparent when the naked man's wife arrives pushing a barrow with two dead children in it. They had died from lack of food after their father left them. Parzival leaves the naked man; looking back, he sees a fish he had previously rescued coming over the ground towards him. He goes on his way, accompanied by the fish. Does this symbolic ending hint at some kind of alternative to the failed utopia of the *Merlin* play? Dorst's interest in the Grail hero is apparent in other works of his, such as the scenario *Parzival* (1990) which includes the text of *Parzival: Auf der anderen Seite des Sees*. Here Parzival's quest is set against a montage of mysterious images and ends in a void. Another reworking of the Arthurian material is to be found in the play *Die Ritter der Tafelrunde* (1989) by Christoph Hein, a parable of conflict between generations in which the old holders of power are confronted with the fiasco of their governance. Here Parzival is the publisher of a critical journal; he no longer believes in the Grail. The piece was written just before the end of the DDR.

In PARZIVAL (1980) Richard Blank used Wolfram's romance in a screenplay for a television film, updating and commenting on the medieval tale. *Flechtungen – der Fall Partzifall* is the title of of an experimental play by Werkhaus Moosach (1978), in which fragments of Wolfram's Parzival story are interwoven with the case history of a psychiatric patient. The medieval Parzival appears as the 'Unnormale', the fantasist who tries to understand the nature of things. Nathalie Harder brought the Parzival story from Wolfram's romance to life in puppet-theatre form: *Recht mitten durch* (1982), with an interpretation in line with the tenets of depth psychology. Frido Mann's novel *Professor Parsifal* (1985) concerns the quest of a young man from the protest generation of 1968. A central motif from the medieval romance was given a modernistic treatment as the main theme of the dramatic work *Das Spiel von Fragen oder die Reise zum sonoren Land* (1989) by Peter Handke, with Parzival as the protagonist. Adolf Muschg is the author of *Der Rote Ritter. Eine Geschichte von Parzivâl* (1993). This lengthy novel is a new *Parzival*, in which Wolfram's tale is adapted to a new age's view of humanity. Parzival becomes a contemporary for whom the Grail no longer has any purpose. Muschg adds a new twist to the history of interpretations of the Grail: he makes it disappear. And Parzival ends as a bourgeois, for whom the great lies in the realisation of the small.

Also worth mentioning are PARSIFAL, Hans-Jürgen Syberberg's film of Wagner's opera (1981–82), and Konrad Becker's total theatre *Parzival* (1984), 'rituelle Oper nach Wolfram von Eschenbach'. A musical composition on an ambitious scale, to be performed by, among others, symphony orchestra, jazz ensemble and choirs, is *Parzival* by Chris Hinze, to a text by James Batton (première: Holland Festival 1976).

English-language literature of the 19th and 20th centuries, too, is interested in Perceval. He features prominently in 'The Holy Grail', an episode in Tennyson's poetic cycle *Idylls of the King*. Among the Grail-seekers is Percivale, who also narrates the story. He abandons his intended goal in life to pursue a quest for the spiritual, something reserved not for him but for Galahad. A Grail novel with a modern setting is *The Secret Glory* (1922) by Arthur Machen. The main character shows similarities to Perceval. As a child he had seen the Grail when with an old farmer in Wales; as a result he lives in a visionary world which contrasts with the reality around him: an ugly industrial town and a wretched existence at boarding-school. In Bernard Malamud's *The Natural* (1952) elements of the Perceval story are transplanted to the world of sport. The hero is a naive individual who owns a remarkable bat with which he comes to the aid of Pop Fischer's baseball team, the New York Knights. Thomas Berger's *Arthur Rex: A Legendary Novel* (1978) offers an ironic fantasy based on Arthurian material. Here Percival's purity brings about a temporary renewal of the ideals of the Arthurian world. His career has a farcical beginning: he is brought up as a girl. A version of the Perceval component of Chrétien's romance is *Percival and the Presence of God* (1978) by Jim Hunter. The story is set in a dream world in which Percival tells of his unfinished quest. His thoughts are occupied with an attempt to understand the existential questions about God and man.

Richard Monaco wrote a series of novels about the Grail. The first, *Parsifal: or A Knight's Tale* (1977), which draws on Wolfram's *Parzival*, deals with Parsival's route to knighthood and the quest of the Grail. The diabolic opponent of the Arthurian world is Clinschor, who like a second Hitler is out to conquer the world. *The Grail War* (1979) describes a new assault by Clinschor on Arthur's realm. *The Final Quest* (1980) tells of the fate of the survivors and Parsival's quest for his son Lohengrin. An anti-climax follows in *Blood and Dreams* (1985). These novels with their shocking accounts of horror and violence give a discouraging view of the world. Amid this chaos Parsival strains towards the illusion of a better life. In John Boorman's film EXCALIBUR (1981) Parzival has become Lancelot's assistant, who discovers the Grail and alone survives the final massacre, the end of the Arthurian world. A Perceval and a Loathly Lady (→ Gawain) also appear in *The Fisher King* (1987) by Anthony Powell, a novel about a crippled photographer on a cruise ship. In Peter Vansittart's novel *Parsifal* (1988) Parsifal turns up in various periods of history: we encounter him at the court of the Duke of Burgundy and, lastly, during the collapse of the Third Reich.

In France Paul Verlaine, forerunner of the symbolists, wrote the sonnet 'Parsifal', published in the *Revue Wagnérienne* for 1886. The poem speaks of the temptations overcome by Wagner's hero Parsifal in order to become king and priest of the Grail. Wagnerian themes later play a part in the works of Julien Gracq, such as his play *Le Roi Pêcheur* (1945–49) which provides a new and, in view of the ending, striking version of the Grail myth. Here it is Anfortas, not Perceval, who holds centre stage; and this Grail King has no desire for release. He does not wish to relinquish his position as king. His wound is his link to Montsalvage, the shadow realm. He regards the Grail as the world's dream, and wants to keep it hidden so that the dream shall not be destroyed. In this he is successful, for his actions result in the failure of Perceval's quest.

Pierre Benoit's novel *Montsalvat* (1957) sets the Grail quest in France during the German occupation. This modern Perceval is a lecturer in medieval history at the University of Montpellier and the heroine is a Cathar student. They go in search of the Grail, a relic of the treasure of the Cathars; their quest leads them to Montsalvy, Montségur and to Montserrat in Catalonia, the setting of Wagner's Grail castle. Two German officers engaged in the same search are killed. Though the lecturer loses his beloved, he does become Keeper of the Grail, which he takes back to the Holy Land, its original home. Florence Delay and Jacques Roubaud are the authors of *Graal Théâtre*, designed as a ten-part play cycle on the world of Arthur and the Grail from the beginning to the final destruction. Chrétien's hero appears in the fifth part, 'Perceval le Gallois' (1977). After the encounter with the hermit his quest ends in obscurity; the action then continues with the coming of Galaad. PERCEVAL LE GALLOIS (1979) is also the title of a splendid film version of the *Conte du Graal* by Eric Rohmer, with settings reminiscent of medieval miniatures. The film follows Chrétien's romance as far as Perceval's meeting with the hermit; it then ends with a kind of passion-scene with Perceval as the Christ-figure.

In medieval pictorial art Chrétien's Perceval appears in miniatures in manuscripts containing the *Conte du Graal*. Those of greatest artistic value are in an early 14th-century manuscript in the Bibliothèque Nationale in Paris. One of them illustrates Perceval's stay with the Fisher King. On the left we see the young knight receiving the sword; on the right the Grail and the lance are being carried round. The portrayal typifies the process of christianisation undergone by the material, for the Grail has the form of a ciborium. From the same period dates an ivory casket with illustrations of Perceval (Louvre, Paris). In a kind of strip-cartoon it shows scenes from the early, rustic stage of Perceval's career.

Portrayals of Wolfram's Parzival can be found in a manuscript of c.1240 in the Bayerische Staatsbibliothek in Munich. Each of the four pages of a double fold contains three illustrations arranged vertically. They represent scenes from the last part of the romance, such as Parzival, Feirefiz and Cundry arriving at the Grail castle and Parzival's reunion with Condwiramurs. In 1929 the demolition of a house in Lübeck revealed the battered remnants of a Parzival cycle in the form of a mural painted around the middle of the 14th century. Some 15th-century manuscripts of Wolfram's *Parzival* contain illustrations, coloured pen drawings in a style akin to the new art of the wood-cut.

In 19th-century England the revival of Arthurian literature again provided a source of inspiration for artists, including such Pre-Raphaelites as Dante Gabriel Rossetti and Edward Burne-Jones. Rossetti's works include the watercolour 'How Sir Galahad, Sir Bors and Sir Percival were fed with the Sanc Grael' (1864, Tate Gallery, London). Burne-Jones designed the tapestries in Stanmore Hall; Perceval appears on the panel 'The attainment: the vision of the Holy Grail' (the Duke of Westminster's collection). Against a background of flowers and angels Galahad, Bors and Percival approach the chapel containing the Grail. Three angels bar the way to Perceval and Bors, so that they are able to view the Grail only from afar. 'Sir Percival' is the subject of a painting by George Frederick Watts (The Astley Cheetham Art Gallery, Stalybridge). The expression of the knight in the forest suggests a falling-short in the spiritual quest for the Grail which accords with Tennyson's work. Füssli based his 'Parsifal freeing Belisane' (1783; Tate Gallery, London) on Wolfram. An earlier painting (1782) of the same figures is now in Berlin.

Wagner's friend and patron was Ludwig II, King of Bavaria, whose decorative scheme turned his dream castle of Neuschwanstein into a medieval temple to the Grail. There Parzival is the hero of the Sängersaal. Fifteen wall-paintings executed in 1883 represent in idealistic-romantic style scenes from Wolfram's *Parzival*. In France Odilon Redon was in contact with Wagner and symbolism, as his portrait of the Grail-hero in the lithograph 'Parsifal' of 1892 (Bibliothèque Nationale, Paris) bears witness. He shows Parsifal bearing the lance which, in Wagner's version, he restores to the Grail castle. Another symbolist portrayal is Jean Delville's 'Parsifal' (1890), which shows a face rapt in contemplation under the light of the Grail. Jan Toorop drew 'Kundry and Parsifal' (c.1895). The scene is Klingsor's magic garden; the naked Parsifal is resisting the seductress Kundry when he catches sight of the Grail, depicted as a chalice bearing the emblem of the Rosicrucians. Germany has seen some references to Wagner in modern art, for instance in the painting 'Parsifal' by Anselm Kiefer (the fourth of a series, 1977; Kunsthaus, Zürich). The characters have vanished from the picture. The scene is a 'waste land' in the shape of a bare attic. But there is a hint of betterment in what is written above a chair on which a washbowl represents the Grail: 'Höchsten Heiles Wunder! / Erlösung dem Erlöser!' They are the final words of Wagner's *Parsifal*.

R.M.T. ZEMEL

Editions: Roach 1959; Weber 1977; Busby 1993; Kühn and Nellmann 1995.
Translations: Hatto 1986; Kibler 1991; Bryant 1992
Studies: Loomis/Hibbard Loomis 1938; *Grundriss* 1978; Frappier 1979; Beckett 1981; Topsfield 1981; Taylor/Brewer 1983; Wynn 1984; Thompson 1985; Müller/Wapnewski 1986; Lacy/Ashe 1988; Bumke 1990; Whitaker 1990; Bumke 1991[6]; Lacy et al. 1996.

R AOUL DE CAMBRAI comes into the world as the son of Taillefer of Cambrai, who dies shortly before his birth, and Taillefer's young widow Aalais, sister of King Louis. Soon after, King Louis decides to give the fiefdom of Cambrai, complete with the widow, to Gibouin of Le Mans. Guerri the Red (le Sor), Lord of Arras and the dead man's brother, lets it be known that he will fight for his little nephew's rights; he ought, after all, to inherit his father's fiefdom! Years pass; Raoul is about sixteen and is knighted by the king. When he asks for his father's former fiefdom the king refuses; as compensation he is promised the first fief to become vacant. Just over a year later Herbert de Vermandois dies; although he has left four sons, the king is obliged to transfer the fief to Raoul. However, Raoul's mother asks her son not to accept it; she wants no quarrel with a family with whom they are on friendly terms. When Raoul flatly refuses she curses him. The first violent encounter between Raoul and the sons of Herbert de Vermandois leads to the destruction of the abbey at Origny; all the nuns there perish in the flames, including the mother of Bernier, Raoul's loyal vassal and companion. Bernier, abused and struck by his lord, publicly renounces his fealty and joins the opposing side, which is led by his father Ybert de Ribemont. In a subsequent battle Raoul is mortally wounded by Bernier. Hostilities then cease.

Some years later the conflict resumes. Now it is Raoul's nephew, Gautier, who confronts Bernier and his people. Eventually the king orders the two parties to make peace. They agree. When a few days later the king tells Ybert de Ribemont that after his death he will give his lands to someone else, Ybert is angry; he has already given them to his son Bernier. The northern barons now unite in rebelling against the king, who is blamed for starting all these wars through his own stupidity. The whole of Paris is burned to the ground, after which the northern forces withdraw.

To seal the reconciliation between the former enemies Bernier is to marry the daughter of Guerri the Red. Before the wedding Bernier and his men are still fighting the king's troops; Gibouin is among those killed and so Raoul is avenged. Bernier then stops fighting. However, immediately after the wedding Bernier and his wife Beatrix are ambushed by the king's men. Beatrix is seized and promised by the king to Herchambaut de Ponthieu. Bernier recovers his bride. Eventually all parties are reconciled. During a pilgrimage to Saint-Gilles Beatrix gives birth to a son, Julien. The town is attacked by Saracens, Bernier is captured and his son stolen; his wife returns home. With Bernier assumed dead, Beatrix is (again) given to Herchambaut de Ponthieu. With the aid of a magic herb, however, she manages to fend off his amorous advances. Meanwhile, Bernier has done his Saracen lord a great service; he returns home laden with gifts and, disguised as a pilgrim, succeeds in freeing his wife. Years later, he finds his son Julien again. A second son, Henri, is born. Later again, Bernier makes a pilgrimage to Santiago de Compostela with his father-in-law Guerri the Red. On the way back they pass Origny, where Raoul had been slain, and old grudges are resurrected. Guerri strikes Bernier dead with a stirrup-iron. The war flares up again; Bernier's two sons lay siege to Arras, but Guerri escapes from the beleaguered city under cover of darkness. Here the story ends. Julien becomes Lord of Saint-Gilles, Henri inherits Ribemont from his father.

Raoul de Cambrai has had a significant role in the debate on the origins of *chanson de geste*; for the oldest part of the text speaks of a certain Bertolai who supposedly sang of the conflict. According to past scholars, this meant that we were here dealing with the eye-witness testimony of one Bertolai, a 10th-century 'soldat-trouvère', whose account would subsequently have been reworked. This was in accordance with the ideas of the traditionalists, who maintained that the *chansons de geste* ultimately derived from a kind of 'chants lyrico-épiques' composed immediately after the events they described. Modern scholars take the view that a number of events of the 9th and 10th centuries have become clustered around a legendary Raoul; none of the four known Raouls of the period answers to the description in the text. Philological and literary analysis shows that the text as we now have it developed in various stages between c.1180 and 1225. The oldest and most dramatic section (Ia) was (probably) originally written in assonant *laisses* (stanzas of irregular length). A reviser then put this into rhyme and added a section (Ib) written directly in rhyming *laisses*. A subsequent adaptor then added part II, in assonant *laisses*. Each adaptor drew on existing material on Raoul de Cambrai, but also made use of other epic matter, so that there are connections between *Raoul de Cambrai* and other *chansons* from the 'Cycle des Lorrains' and the 'Cycle de Saint-Gilles'.

Raoul de Cambrai clearly belongs to the 'Cycle des barons révoltés', the epics about rebellious vassals. Very sharply brought out are the problems resulting from the king's arbitrary disposal of a vassal's fief after his death without regard to his heirs. This was very much a live issue during the reign of King Philip II Augustus (1180–1223). The various disputes among the barons are painted in lurid colours; Raoul's cruel and inconstant character comes out very strongly in, for example, the scene in which Origny Abbey is destroyed and all the nuns burnt to death. *Raoul de Cambrai* is widely regarded as among the most violent of the *chansons de geste*.

The contrast between Raoul and his companion Bernier also seems to be part of the narrative's central theme: Raoul, the king's nephew but headstrong, vengeful and foul-mouthed, is raised by his mother together with Bernier, the illegitimate son of Ybert de Ribemont and grandson of Herbert de Vermandois; but this bastard is level-headed and peaceable by nature. That Raoul is eventually mortally wounded by Bernier is in part due to the fact that Raoul had been cursed by his mother.

Stories about Raoul de Cambrai were fairly widespread in the 12th and 13th centuries; Sarah Kay in her edition lists some sixteen works (in Latin, Occitanian and Old French) in which Raoul is mentioned in greater or less detail or a work about him is quoted. From this, too, it is clear that the history of the evolution of *Raoul de Cambrai* is extremely complicated. The text has come down to us in one complete 13th-century manuscript, what is known as a 'manuscrit de *jongleur*' (a simply-produced manuscript of small format, 14 x 18cm) and in 13th-century fragments which reveal a slightly different version. Lastly, there is a 16th-century transcription of about 250 lines by the hand of Claude Fauchet.

Only since the end of the 19th century has there been a revival of interest in the work, evidenced by its publication and by rewritings and translations. It appears to have inspired no other artistic works.

R.E.V. STUIP

Edition: Kay 1992.
Translation: Berger/Suard 1986.

R ENAUT DE MONTAUBAN is the leading character in a story set in the time of → Charlemagne. It is to France that we must look for the origins of the story. There are various versions of the French *Renaut de Montauban*; most widespread is the 'traditional' version, which survives both as a *chanson de geste* and as a prose romance. In the oldest manuscript (13th century) to preserve this (verse) version, the story is as follows.

Charlemagne is holding court, and all the great lords have come to Paris. All except Charles' vassal Beuve d'Aigremont. He had also failed to turn up when Charles went to war with the Saxons. Furious, the king sends his son Lohier (Lotharius) to Aigremont to order Beuve to come and do service to Charles. Lohier threatens Beuve with severe punishment if he refuses. The vassal is not to be overawed; he threatens Lohier in his turn. Feelings run so high that he orders his men to seize the royal messenger. Lohier and his men defend themselves, and in the struggle Beuve kills the prince. Meanwhile, Charles is becoming concerned. He swears to take vengeance if Beuve harms Lohier. Aymon, Beuve's brother, entirely agrees with the king. He offers him the support of his sons: Renaut, Aalart, Richart and Guischart. The four young men are brought to Charlemagne and knighted. To mark the occasion Renaut is given Bayart, a magic horse which is exceptionally fast and so strong that it can carry all four of them together. Soon after this Lohier's body is brought to Paris. At the insistence of Renaut, who fears (not without reason) that they will have to pay for the reckless act of their kinsman Beuve, Aymon and his sons return to their castle at Dordonne in the Ardennes. They do not join the army raised by Charles to march on Aigremont, but intend to support Beuve. Charles gives Beuve one last chance: if he does homage to the king and serves him he will be forgiven. Beuve accepts. He is granted safe-conduct and journeys to Paris. But there is a treacherous family which is constantly plotting and executing base plans and also encourages the king to act unjustly; members of this family set an ambush, with Charles' approval, and murder Beuve. His son → Maugis resolves on vengeance. With the aid of his uncles, → Girart de Roussillon and Doon de Nanteuil, he invades Charles' lands. However, they are no match for the king's military might; they therefore submit and make their peace with Charles.

Charlemagne's return to Paris is celebrated with extravagant festivities. Aymon, his sons and Maugis are present at court. Renaut plays chess with the king's nephew Bertelai. They quarrel and Bertelai kicks Renaut, who is so furious that he demands satisfaction from Charles for the murder of his uncle Beuve. The king refuses. Renaut then picks up the chessboard and hits Bertelai with it so hard that he falls dead. This starts a fight between Renaut's kinsmen and the rest. The four brothers manage to escape to their father's castle of Dordonne. Their father is forced to repudiate them and also leaves for Dordonne. True to his sworn oath, he throws his sons out.

They then build a castle of their own in the Ardennes. As soon as Charles discovers where they are he leads an army against their hiding-place. His men get into the castle by a ruse and set it on fire. Renaut and his brothers manage to escape. For a long time they wander the Ardennes; eventually they return to Dordonne, ragged and unrecognisable from the privations they have endured, to visit their mother. She is very happy to see her sons again; but Aymon berates them soundly and tells them what he thinks of them with heavy irony. Renaut defends himself against his father's remarks, telling him that he ought to help his own sons. Aymon then gives them permission to take whatever they need from Dordonne. Mindful of his oath of repudiation, he retreats to the orchard meanwhile; if he does not see what they are doing he is not forsworn.

Clean, and provided with new clothes and other valuable items, Renaut and his brothers leave Dordonne; their cousin Maugis goes with them. The five of them travel to Gascony. Here Aymon's sons enter the service of King Yon and help him to vanquish his Saracen enemies. One day they come upon a place which seems to them eminently suitable for a castle. Having gained Yon's permission they build the castle of Montauban. Yon also gives Renaut his sister's hand in marriage. One fine day Charlemagne, returning from a pilgrimage to Santiago de Compostela, happens upon Montauban. He sends a summons to Yon to deliver up Aymon's sons to him. Yon refuses. Renaut, who is present at the time, says that he is willing to make his peace with the king, but the king will not hear of it. Back in Paris, the king announces an immediate campaign against Gascony. He is advised, however, to let his men rest a little first after all their fighting. Also, the city of Cologne happens to be in urgent need of assistance, having been attacked by the heathen. Charles' young nephew → Roland, who has just joined him, takes on this task and wins a glorious victory. If only he had a good horse, Charles is told, Roland would be the best knight in the world and overcome any foe. To find such a horse Charles organises a race, intending to buy the winning beast. At the finish is a glittering array of valuables, including his golden crown. Renaut, who has heard of this from a messenger, is among those competing. So that he and Bayart shall not be recognised Maugis, who is skilled in magic, has changed their appearance. Renaut reaches the winning-post ahead of all the rest. He seizes the crown, mockingly refuses to let Charles buy it back, and disappears with it back to Montauban. Now Charles marches south. He makes camp not far from Montauban and again commands Yon to hand over Aymon's sons. This time Yon agrees. He tells the four brothers that he has made their peace with Charles and arranges for them to ride on muleback to the plain of Vaucouleurs. There Charles' men are waiting for them. They defend themselves heroically for a long time, but eventually it seems that they will be able to hold out no longer against the superior numbers. Then Maugis comes galloping to their aid on Bayart, followed by a large troop of warriors. This saves them; some time later they arrive safely back in Montauban. Even before they reach there Yon has fled. He is captured by Roland, but Renaut, to whom Yon sends a messenger begging for his help, relieves Roland of the traitor. After a number of other exciting incidents, including the capture and rescue of Renaut's brother Richart, and after Renaut has vainly attempted to settle their differences, Charles lays siege to Montauban. With a view to forcing a reconciliation Maugis transports the king to Montauban in his sleep; he then leaves his kinsfolk to become a hermit. Even now, with Charles totally in the power of Aymon's sons, it proves impossible to reach an agreement. Renaut releases him and the war continues. In vain do Charles' barons urge him to make peace. Food supplies in Montauban run out. When the besieged are starving and at their wits' end an old greybeard draws their attention to an underground passage which leads into the woods. The castle's inhabitants and Bayart escape from Montauban through this passage.

They now go to Dortmund, which belongs to Aymon's sons. As soon as Charles learns of this he follows them there. In vain does Renaut appeal for mercy, the war goes on. An eminent French knight is captured. Then Maugis pops up again and transports Charles' son Charlot to Dortmund before returning to his hermit's cell. Not until Renaut is about to hang his two captives is Charles prepared to make peace. True, he reneges on this a little later; but when his finest knights threaten to walk out on him he no longer persists in his stubbornness. Renaut is made to undertake a pilgrimage to the Holy Tomb. His brothers are enrolled among Charlemagne's leading knights, his sons too are to enter the king's service and Dortmund is given to his wife. But Bayart must be surrendered and destroyed. The poor beast is thrown into the Rhine with a millstone tied round its neck. However, it manages to shatter the stone and reach land. In the forest it finds its way back to Maugis.

After confessing to the Pope in Rome Renaut travels to the Holy Land; there he is reunited with Maugis, who has also become a pilgrim. They discover that Jerusalem has been captured by the Sultan of Persia. Renaut and Maugis enthusiastically join the battle with the infidel and through their efforts the city is recaptured. They visit the holy places, Renaut is offered the kingship of Jerusalem but declines, and they return to Europe. Then Maugis goes back to his cell while Renaut returns to court, where he learns that his wife has died while he was away. Having seen his sons vanquish two members of the treacherous family in a double duel, and disposed of his possessions, Renaut leaves court again. First he lives for a long time in the forest; then he works as a labourer building St Peter's in Cologne, where he turns in a superhuman performance. Jealous, and fearing for their jobs, his fellow-workers murder him and throw his body in the Rhine. Then miracles begin to happen. When the body is taken from the water and laid on a cart ready for burial, the cart drives itself to Dortmund. The city's bishop recognises the corpse as that of Renaut de Montauban. His mortal remains are interred in Dortmund and God performs miracles in honour of the man known in those parts as Saint Renaut.

Renaut as St Reinoldus, early 14th-century statue in the Reinoldi-Kirche in Dortmund.

The traditional version of *Renaut de Montauban* summarised above must have come into being around the end of the 12th century. The *chanson de geste Renaut de Montauban* is regarded as belonging to the so-called 'Cycle des barons révoltés', the cycle of the rebellious vassals. These *chansons de geste* have to be seen against the background of the political situation in France at the time. During the reign of Philip II Augustus (1180–1223) the great vassals were faced with a powerful king who was pursuing a strong policy of centralisation, a policy which threatened their independence. And the *chansons de geste* which comprise this particular cycle are about essentially loyal vassals who take up arms against an extremely powerful, unjust, cruel King Charles who fails to carry out his feudal obligations. The relationship between king and vassal is at the heart of these works. In *Renaut de Montauban* it is stressed more than once that it is Renaut, not Charles, who has right on his side. These *chansons* are a literary discussion on the topical question of the proper attitude to be taken to the ever-increasing power of the king; they gave form and justification to the vassals' resistance to the growing power of the Capet king. It has to be borne in mind that the Capet propaganda machine lauded Philip Augustus as not just the successor but also the descendant of Charlemagne. Consequently, a negative portrayal of Charlemagne in the literature will also have reflected on the prestige of the real-life 12th-century monarch.

Time and time again the story was written down in French. As already mentioned, we have the traditional version both in verse and in prose. The *chanson de geste* has been preserved in a number of manuscripts, the prose romance based on it in several manuscripts and numerous prints. In the redaction from which the above summary is taken (the so-called redaction D) the *chanson* runs to over 14,000 lines; other traditional redactions are even longer. Just how all these redactions hang together is not yet entirely clear; in any case no two verse redactions are exactly the same. As well as the traditional version there are two other known versions in French. The earlier of these, in verse, initially corresponds with the traditional version but later goes its own way: Renaut and Charles are reconciled soon after the battle of Vaucouleurs, Renaut does not visit the Holy Land, nor does he die a holy martyr. This version is known only from one early 13th-century manuscript. The more recent French version, dated (at latest) to the second half of the 14th century, is a modernised reworking of the traditional one. It has been preserved in the form of a *chanson de geste* of over 28,000 lines and as a prose text. This version expands considerably on Renaut's adventures in the East. Not only does he conquer Jerusalem (without Maugis' aid), he also makes himself master of Angorie and thus comes into possession of the relics of the Passion. When he opens the shrine containing them – something permitted only to someone without sin – a miracle happens: as Renaut reverently lifts out the crown of thorns it leaps in his hands and the bystanders see that they are bleeding. Renaut's sons marry Eastern beauties. One of them becomes King of Angorie, the other King of Jerusalem. That such a favourite story should have found its way into large compilations goes almost without saying. It was included in, for instance, Phillippe Mousket's *Chronique rimée* (mid-13th century), *Ly Myreur des histors* (late 14th century) by the Liège writer Jean d'Outremeuse and the *Croniques et conquestes de Charlemaine* (1458), copied and possibly also compiled by David Aubert.

The tale of Renaut was not confined to French; there are Renaut texts in Dutch, German, English, Old Norse and Italian, and his deeds were also recorded in Spanish. A couple of Latin texts are devoted to St Renaut. The Middle Dutch verse *Renout van Montalbaen*, most likely written in Flanders, probably dates from as early as the first quarter of the 13th century. The poet must have known the traditional French version, with which the *Renout* very largely agrees. It also shows striking differences, however, of which we will mention the most important. Instead of opening with the story of Renaut's uncle Beuve, the Middle Dutch version begins with Renaut's father: for many years Aymijn has been in feud with Charlemagne, ever since the latter killed a nephew of Aymijn's. Later, Renaut decapitates Charles' son Lodewijk (→ Louis) when Lodewijk strikes one of Renaut's brothers with a chessboard. This is the cause of the feud between Charles and the four brothers, who in the Dutch tradition are known as the 'Vier Heemskinderen' (the four sons of Aymijn). They live successively in Spain, where they are in the service of a heathen king, in Gascony and in the Ardennes. In contrast to the French version, Charles does succeed in drowning Beyaert (Bayart) when the horse is handed over to him after the reconciliation. Malegijs (Maugis) falls in battle in the Holy Land. The Middle Dutch *Renout* also differs from the traditional French *Renaut* in tone: the *Renout* is less weighty. This is partly because the serious political issue which permeates the *Renaut* receives much less emphasis in the Middle Dutch work. We are not constantly reminded that the 'Heemskinderen' are in the right and Charles in the wrong. Charles also inspires less fear and respect in his vassals than in the *Renaut*. The question of how to behave towards a king who does not have right on his side plays a much smaller part. In the French text we are continually being told that Charles, however unjust his behaviour, is the king and overlord, to whom there is a duty of respect. In the *Renout* both the 'Heemskinderen' and the paladins find their relations with the king far less problematic. This ties in with the fact that the *Renout* was written later and in a different area; the topical political question reflected in the French work will not have been a live issue for the Middle Dutch poet and his audience. The main concern of this Middle Dutch writer seems to have been to offer his audience an exciting, entertaining story, dynamic and action-packed.

The oldest extant complete printed text in Dutch dates from 1508. Produced by the Leiden printer Jan Seversoen, it bears the title *Dit is de historie vanden Vier Heemskinderen*. For centuries the prose version could bask in its exceptional popularity. Over a period of four centuries it was reprinted at least 25 times. At the time of the Counter-Reformation it was censored in the Southern Netherlands. Whole passages, regarded as offensive because they conflicted with morality or with the teaching of the Roman Catholic Church, and including a number of comic episodes involving Malegijs, were scrapped. Thus there came into being an expurgated southern version, which received official approval in 1619.

The German Renout tradition is closely bound up with the Dutch. The Middle Dutch verse *Renout van Montalbaen* was translated very faithfully into German (Rhine-

Frankish). This verse translation, *Reinolt von Montelban*, would have been made for the Countess Palatine Mechtild. Two complete manuscripts of the work have survived. The older of these, given by Mechtild to her son Eberhard V im Bart von Württemberg on his marriage in 1474, may be the autograph manuscript or a first copy of it. There was a Middle Low German verse translation of the *Renout*, of which only a fragment survives (14th century). The Dutch prose text was also translated into German: once in Ripuarian (the printed text dates from 1493), once (via this Ripuarian translation?) by Paul van der Aelst into Early Modern High German (first printed 1604). Van der Aelst also made use of the *Historie van sent Reinolt*, a short prose work of c.1447 which was itself based on the Middle Dutch *Renout* and the Latin works. Two other German prose works (one preserved in a 16th-century manuscript now in Aarau, the other in a printed text published in Simmern in 1535) are based on the printed French prose, which also provided the basis for the English *Historie of the Foure sonnes of Aymon* (translated and printed by William Caxton, c.1489).

It was probably via England and Norway that the Renaut material reached Iceland, where the *Mágus saga jarls* was composed. This saga, which in its present form cannot date from before c.1250, is a compilation of originally independent texts. It exists in a long and a short version. In the sections based on *Renaut de Montauban* the writer handled his material very much in his own way. The events are set in Germany, and not under Charlemagne but his grandson Louis (in the shorter version: Emperor Jatmund) and Louis' son Charles.

From France the Renaut story also reached Italy. We have both a verse and a prose version of *Rinaldo da Monte Albano*. The oldest extant verse text will have been composed around the middle of the 14th century. Along with the *Renaut* the Italian poet also used other texts. The Renaut material may have found its way to Spain via Italy.

Long after the end of the Middle Ages the story of Aymon's Sons remained extremely popular in large parts of Europe, and in some places still is. The Dutch and French prose romances were reprinted many times up to the end of the 19th century. The Flemish writer Hendrik Conscience tells in his *Geschiedenis mijner jeugd* (Story of my Youth, 1888) that as a boy he spent all his money in the shop of the Antwerp printer and publisher Thys buying 'blue books' (cheap editions with blue covers) like *De Vier Aymonskinderen*. In France, too, the tale of the Four Sons of Aymon was included in the 'Bibliothèque bleue'. The Dutch prose text has repeatedly been reworked or retold, among others by J.A. Alberdingk Thijm (1851) and Felix Timmermans (1922). In 1972 A. Lechner published a free adaptation of *Reinolt von Montelban*, and this was translated into Dutch by Tadema Sporry (1975). A version for young people by F. Herzen appeared in 1983. As early as the 16th century the prose romance was being read by schoolchildren, something described as undesirable in a little book on proper behaviour for children (*Goede manierlijcke seden*, 1546). In the preface to an edition of the French chivalric romance *Amadis de Gaule* (1561) the Antwerp printer and publisher Plantijn expresses his disapproval of the use of such books as the *Quatre fils Aymon* in education (in French). Once the Dutch prose romance had been purged of all things unsuitable at the time of the Counter-Reformation it was, according to the official licence, 'very pleasant and fitting to be learnt by the Youth in the Schools'. In the 20th century the tale has again been adapted specifically for use in schools.

In the south of Europe, too, the Renaut story lived on after the Middle Ages. Renaut is mentioned in Cervantes' *Don Quijote* (1605–15); in 1685 Domínguez published his *Libro de Don Reynaldos*. In Italian literature of the 15th century we meet 'Rinaldo' in Pulci (*Il Morgante, Il Morgante maggiore*) and Boiardo (*Orlando innamorato*); in the 16th century Ariosto gives him a role in *Orlando Furioso*. Boiardo and Ariosto present Rinaldo's sister Bradamante and her husband Ruggiero as the founders of the d'Este family, in whose service both poets were. Tasso's *Rinaldo* appeared in 1562. In Italian literature, where knights and their adventures are for the most part treated with irony

and comic exaggeration, Rinaldo is the counterpart to Orlando (Roland). Much
attention is devoted to his amorous adventures and those of his relations. The
adventures of his son Rinaldino are recounted in the *Storia di Rinaldino da Montalbano*,
and one of Rinaldo's brothers is the central character in Civeri's *Ricciardetto innamorato*
(1595) and Forteguerri's *Il Ricciardetto* (published in 1738). In 19th-century Naples
there were still storytellers who regaled their hearers mainly with tales of Rinaldo and
were consequently themselves known as 'Rinaldi'.

Aymon's sons also appeared on stage on more than one occasion. About 1604 the
Spanish author Lope de Vega wrote *Las pobrezas de Reynaldos*. The piece was imitated or
otherwise used by other Spanish and Italian writers. In the early 17th century an
English company in Amsterdam performed a stage version of the Renaut story; a stage
adaption by J.A. Gleich dates from 1809. A Breton play was performed in the second
half of the 19th century. In Belgium *Le jeu des Quatre fils Aymon*, by H. Closson, was
staged in 1941; its text was published in 1943.

The attention lavished by Italian literature on the amorous adventures of Rinaldo
and his kinsmen ensured that later centuries took grateful advantage of this literature
for operas, ballets etc. Ariosto's *Orlando furioso* provided the basis for the text for
Caccini's ballet *La liberazione di Ruggiero dall'isola d'Alcina* (1625) and the opera *Ruggiero
ovvero L'eroica gratitudine* by Hasse (1771). A great many other operas and ballets (Lully
1686, Handel 1711, Gluck 1778, Haydn 1783, among others) took as their subject the
love-story of Rinaldo and the sorceress Armida; the material derives from Tasso's *La
Gerusalemme liberata ovvero Il Goffredo* (printed in 1581). In this epic Rinaldo, an
excellent knight, goes to fight the infidel in the train of → Godfrey of Bouillon. The
association with Rinaldo da Montalbano seems obvious, but it is dangerous simply to
assume that the two knights are the same. The Rinaldo of the *Gerusalemme liberata* is
the son of Sofia and Bertoldo and is presented as the founder of the d'Este family; the
work is dedicated to Tasso's patron Alfonso II d'Este.

The story of the Four Sons of Aymon entered the puppeteers' repertoire quite early,
in Germany by the 16th century. Even today it is still performed in Belgian puppet
theatres and by puppeteers in Sicily. The puppet plays lend themselves extremely well
to the introduction of comic anachronisms linking the material with current events; as,
for instance, in *Les Quatre fils Aymon* by Géal and Closson, produced in the Brussels
theatre Toone. The material has also been adapted for children's performances.

The story is still alive today in oral tradition. The written precipitate of this oral
tradition can be found in books of legends and folktales. Sometimes different Renaut
traditions have become merged in transmission. Fairy-tale elements became mingled
with the epic narrative material. For the people of the Ardennes the 'Heemskinderen',
those fighters against tyranny, came to symbolise all freedom-fighters. The partisans
who fought the Germans were compared with them. But it was Bayart above all, Bayart
who in the traditional French version smashed the millstone, escaped into the
Ardennes and could neither be killed nor captured, who came to symbolise freedom.
According to folklore he is still galloping round in the Ardennes. On St John's Day (24
June) he can be heard running through the woods. Near Dinant one can see the Rocher
Bayard, supposedly cloven by Bayart's hoof. At Robertville (Reinhardstein, Renastène)
and elsewhere in the Ardennes they show (ruined) castles said to have belonged to the
Heemskinderen. Even in the 20th century, in West Flemish dialect an 'Eemszeune' is a
person of exceptional qualities.

Many artists, too, have been inspired by the Renaut material. In the Middle Ages
Aymon's sons and Bayart featured in miniatures in manuscripts, woodcuts in prints and
on tapestries. One such tapestry was supplied to the Duke of Orleans by Nicolas Bataille
between 1389 and 1396. The painting 'Children's Games' of 1560 by Pieter Bruegel the
Elder (Kunsthistorisches Museum, Vienna) shows among other things four children
standing one behind the other while a fifth pushes a stick between their legs. This has

been identified with a game which must represent the four brothers riding Bayart and which was still played in Flanders in the twentieth century. At snow festivals the brothers were carved out of snow (Atrecht 1434, Mechelen 1571). Unusual is a portrayal of the four of them on Bayart on the seal on a Middle Dutch legal document of 1313. After the Middle Ages the brothers (usually all four together mounted on Bayart) were depicted not only in prints as book illustrations and in paintings (even by Saenredam in his 'Interior of the Buurkerk in Utrecht') but also on signboards, stone tablets on buildings (still to be seen in, for instance, Amsterdam, Haarlem and Maastricht), lantern-brackets (Utrecht), decorative ceramics on buildings, coloured glassware, postage stamps and biscuit moulds. In 1824 the Dutch writer Bilderdijk tells us of the useful purpose served in his childhood by the edible 'Heemskinderen': 'Their images in biscuit-dough invariably formed part of the children's St Nicholas gifts, and their grandparents, parents, nurses, or nursemaids, did not neglect to instil in them, by elucidating this and other such images, something of the courage, dauntlessness and resignation to the Will of God of the knights of old.' Bayart and the Sons of Aymon have many times been immortalised in statues. Between 1960 and 1976 alone, six such statues were erected in the Netherlands. Some of them are in schools (Haarlem, Nijmegen) and these, in line with their location, show the four brothers as young children. In Belgium statues can be found in Ghent and Dendermonde, among other places. Streets, houses, cafés, hotels and restaurants have been called after the Heems-kinderen or their steed.

Ever since medieval times Bayart has taken part in processions. In Dendermonde they still hold the 'Ros-Beiaard procession'. Scenes from the Dutch version of the story are shown, culminating in a tour by a colossal Bayart on which are seated four Dendermonde boys from the same family. Reminiscent of the Dendermonde folklore is the well-known song 'Ros Beyaert doet syn Ronde', so often sung by the 'little ones' in the nuns' school in Hugo Claus' novel *The Sorrow of Belgium* (*Het verdriet van België*, 1983). The song as we now know it is the work of Prudens van Duyse. Using old material he put together a song of seven verses and a refrain which he published in 1835. The jealousy of the people of Aalst mentioned in the song, which in 1952 even led them to attempt to kidnap the Dendermonde steed, has inspired them to produce a number of parodies of this popular song. The popularity of Beyaert and the 'Vier Heemskinderen' has given rise to various musical compositions, some of them meant for performance during the Ros Beyaert procession. The procession has been painted by a number of artists, including Verhas and De Beul.

Since Renaut is also revered as a saint he has churches dedicated to him. Dortmund, Düsseldorf and Gdansk each has its St Reinoldus Church. The one in Dortmund has, in addition to a 14th-century statue, also an 'Iron Reinoldus' made in 1915: a proud knight with an impressive sword. By contrast, the main entrance of the St Mauritius Church in Cologne shows the saint with plank and hammer. There are also devotional pictures of Renaut. One such, distributed in Utrecht in 1948, shows the saint at work with hammer and chisel. In 1918 the Roman Catholic Hanzebond, the employers' organisation of the interior decoration and furnishing industries, chose St Reinoldus as their patron saint. In 1922 Dortmund printed emergency money showing scenes from Renaut's life. In fact, Renaut's whole story is told on these notes: one of them shows him mounted on Bayart, together with his three brothers, while others show him as 'der eiserne Reinoldus', as church-builder and as protector of the city. This last ties up with the legend according to which after his death he appeared on the walls of Dortmund to protect the city from the enemy.

I. SPIJKER

Editions: Castets 1909; Overdiep 1931; Thomas 1989.
Studies: Bender 1967; Spijker 1990.

R EYNARD THE FOX is one of the few characters from medieval narrative who is
still alive and kicking today. Throughout the Middle Ages countless tales were told
about him, ranging from the very short to the extremely long. The oldest surviving
Reynard stories in the vernacular are in French, together they are known as the *Roman
de Renart*. It is clear, however, that this *Roman de Renart* could not have existed without
the Latin *Ysengrimus*, the true starting-point of European beast-epic (which is, in fact,
fox-epic). *Roman de Renart* is a collective name for a whole series of anecdotes and
'novellas', called branches, in which the fox Renart plays a part; each manuscript containing this type of material makes its own selection from the mass of stories available.
The various tales came into being between 1170 and 1230. There are arguments for
assuming that the oldest surviving Renart narrative is a combination of branches II and
Va (the numbering is that of the first scholarly edition of the *Renart*; it is not chronological but follows the sequence of the tales in the manuscript used).

Branch II opens with the tale of Renart and the cock Chantecler. Renart's smooth
tongue enables him to catch Chantecler, but as he is running away from a horde of
pursuers with the cock in his mouth the latter manages to convince him that he ought
to refute the insults hurled after him by his pursuers. When he opens his mouth to do so
the cock escapes. The trickster has himself been tricked.

Renart then encounters a titmouse. He offers her the kiss of peace, and when she is
suspicious tells her that she has no need to fear him because Noble the lion, the King of
Beasts, has proclaimed a universal peace. The tit is still not convinced, so Renart offers
to kiss her with his eyes closed. The tit then agrees, but slyly touches his whiskers with
some moss and thus unmasks his treacherous intentions. Renart tries twice more and
then makes himself scarce; he can see a hunter approaching with his dogs. The tit calls
to him to stay, after all he has nothing to fear. Renart answers that he is not sure that
the dogs have heard about the king's peace and so he is leaving just in case. (These two
stories are variants on the fox-and-cock story from the *Ysengrimus*.)

Next Renart meets Tibert the tomcat. They agree a mutual assistance pact. To pass
the time they decide to race against each other. During the race Renart tries – contrary
to his promise of help – to lead Tibert into a trap he has recently discovered. At the last
moment Tibert realises his evil intentions and avoids the trap. Renart tries again, again
without success. Then two dogs appear and chase the cat and the fox. Both have to pass
the trap again and this time Tibert gives Renart a shove so that he is caught. The dogs'
owner, meaning to beat Renart to death, accidentally hits the trap, which springs open.
Renart is injured, but manages to escape in the nick of time. He then meets the raven
Tiécelin. The bird has stolen a cheese and is holding it between his foot and the branch
he is sitting on. Renart persuades him to sing and spurs him to ever greater efforts. As a
result the raven loses hold of the cheese and it falls to the ground. Renart pretends he
can't stand the smell of it and asks Tiécelin please to remove it. When he tries Renart
goes for him, but Tiécelin escapes. However, Renart retains the cheese as booty.

After these adventures Renart accidentally finds himself in the den of Ysengrin the
wolf. The master of the house is away, but his wife Hersent and her young cubs are at
home. Renart is afraid, but when Hersent teases him and asks why he doesn't visit them
more often he says that it's not his fault but Ysengrin's. He has been telling everyone
that Renart is Hersent's lover, and has even promised a reward to anyone who captures
him. The she-wolf is furious at this false accusation of her husband's (which Renart has
actually made up). 'Come here', she tells Renart, 'if my husband says you're my lover,
then my lover you shall be.' No sooner said than done. When Ysengrin comes home the
cubs tell him what has happened. He forgives Hersent, though, when she promises to
treat Renart henceforth as her enemy. A few days later the two wolves see Renart and
chase him, with Hersent in the lead. Renart dashes into his earth and Hersent, going
too fast to stop, follows him, but gets stuck in the entrance. Renart emerges through
another exit and rapes her, almost before the eyes of the lagging Ysengrin. Branch Va

then relates how the wolf and his wife bring their complaint to the king. Some of the courtiers defend Renart – he had, after all, acted out of love – but he is made to come and swear his innocence. This he must do on the teeth of the dog Roonel, who is playing dead; and Roonel has arranged with Ysengrin that he will bite off Renart's foot. Just in time the fox spots their plan and escapes to his den, pursued by the entire court.

Branch IV tells how Renart lands up in a well, stuck in one of two buckets linked by a rope. The well is on land belonging to an abbey. When Ysengrin comes by and finds Renart, the latter makes him believe that he is dead and in the earthly paradise, surrounded by an abundance of the most delicious food. Ysengrin wants to be in that paradise too. 'No problem,' says Renart, 'just get in that bucket.' Ysengrin does so, and his greater weight pulls him down into the well and Renart up and out. Next morning the monks pull Ysengrin out of the well and before he can escape they give him a good thrashing.

A number of branches have variations on tales from the *Ysengrimus*. Thus, in branch III Ysengrin tries to become a monk. This branch also includes the use of the tail as a fishing-line. Branch V tells of the theft and division of the ham, branch X of the illness of King Lion and how Renart cures him.

The *Roman de Renart* was a very influential work. In France it gave rise to a number of major Renart stories, the most important of which are *Renard le bestourné* by the Paris trouvère Rutebeuf (1260–70), the anonymous *Couronnement de Renard* (after 1251), *Renard le nouvel* by Jacquemard Gielée of Lille (c.1288) and, also anonymous, *Renard le contrefait* (1319–42). In each of the first three the plot centres on the power-struggle between Renart and King Noble, with Renart always victorious. A striking feature of these stories is the negative role of the mendicant orders (the Franciscans and Dominicans). *Renard le contrefait* is the longest Renart narrative we know of. It runs to over 40,000 lines and contains innumerable stories – not just about Renart but also about, among other things, the earthly paradise and Troy. The narrative reads like a travesty of the medieval taste for cramming the maximum possible information into encyclopedic texts.

In other countries, too, the *Roman de Renart* continued to exert an influence. In Germany Heinrich der Glîchezâre wrote his *Reinhart Fuchs* towards the end of the 12th century, basing it on the oldest branches. The narrative is in three parts. The first describes the fox's encounters with, successively, the cock, tit, cat and raven (cf. branch II). In the second part Reinhart is apparently in the wolf's service, but in fact doing him harm. Among the incidents included here are the tail-fishing, the well and the rape of the she-wolf. The third part tells how King Lion falls ill; Reinhart comes to court and at first cures the king but then poisons him. In the process he does extremely well for himself and his assistants but plunges the kingdom into chaos.

Around the middle of the 13th century, in the Low Countries, branch I (the most famous and most popular branch of the *Roman de Renart*) provided the basis for the genre's finest achievement: *Van den vos Reynaerde*. The story goes as follows: Nobel the lion, the King of Beasts, has proclaimed a meeting of his court. Here Reynaert the fox is accused by Ysengrim of raping the she-wolf, by the dog Courtois of theft and by Pancer the beaver of the attempted murder of the hare Cuwaert and breach of the king's peace. The charges are refuted by Grimbeert the badger, a nephew of Reynaert's. But the arrival of the corpse of the hen Coppe, murdered by Reynaert, demonstrates his guilt beyond a shadow of a doubt. Three times he is summoned to appear before the court. The first two messengers, Bruun the bear and Tibeert the tomcat, he successfully entraps by playing on their greed. (The former is seduced by honey, the latter by mice.) The third, his nephew Grimbeert, he accompanies to court where he is sentenced to death.

Thus far the story broadly follows the plot of branch I. In that branch Renart then falls at King Noble's feet and says that he wishes to atone for his sins by a pilgrimage to the Holy Land. Noble forgives him and provides him with the equipment for his pilgrimage. After leaving court Renart meets Coart the hare, who had thrown stones at him during the sentencing. In revenge Renart now seizes him as food for his young. Climbing on a high rock, he mocks the king and the court by wiping his backside with his pilgrim's cross and throwing it to the king. In the meantime Coart escapes. Enraged, the whole court, led by Tardif the snail (!), sets off in pursuit. But by the skin of his teeth Renart manages to reach the safety of his castle of Malpertuis.

While this part of the story is related with a good deal of pace and verve and is clearly satirical in tone, to the modern reader Noble's volte-face seems surprising. The narrative gives no hint as to why he should suddenly abandon his hostility to Renart. It would seem that Willem, the author of *Van den vos Reynaerde*, was also unhappy about this. At any event, from this point on he deviates from his source and begins to tell his own story.

After being convicted Reynaert asks the king's permission to make a public confession, and in the course of this he casually mentions a treasure supposedly in his possession. The king then releases him in exchange for this treasure. To avoid having to accompany the king to the spot where the fictional treasure is buried, Reynaert announces that he is excommunicate and has to go to Rome to have the ban lifted.

Bruin the Bear, looking for honey at the fox's instigation, gets his head wedged in a log and is thrashed by villagers; Reynard the Fox looks on. Wood relief, misericord from 1520 in the choir of Bristol Cathedral.

After that he intends to travel on to the Holy Land in penance for his sins. With the queen's help he manages to acquire a pilgrim's scrip cut from Bruun's hide as well as four shoes which cost Ysengrim and Hersint the skin of two paws apiece. Reynaert leaves court with Bellijn the ram and Cuwaert the hare. Back in his earth he murders the latter and sends his head back to court by Bellijn. He himself leaves for the wilderness with his wife and children. When he discovers he has been tricked the king is greatly distressed. On the advice of the leopard Firapeel he makes his peace with Bruun and Ysengrim and offers them Bellijn and all his kind in compensation. On the surface, at least, peace has been restored.

Van den vos Reynaerde was itself reworked towards the end of the 14th century. This new work is usually known as Reynaerts historie. It follows the story-line of Van den vos Reynaerde meticulously, though with changes to small details throughout. The ending of Van den vos Reynaerde, however, is modified. Reynaert does indeed mean to retreat to the wilderness, but he gives up the idea at his wife's insistence. A new section begins when the king extends the court sitting to make up for his unjust treatment of Bruun and Ysengrim and to do them honour. During this extension further charges are brought against Reynaert. Lapeel the rabbit complains that Reynaert attacked him and he escaped only at the cost of one of his ears. Corbout the rook charges Reynaert with having gobbled up his wife 'feathers and all'. The king decides to arrest Reynaert. Grimbeert informs him of this and Reynaert returns to court. In a new verbal confrontation with the king Reynaert again emerges the victor (albeit with the help of his aunt, the ape Rukenau) by means of another treasure story, this time about three precious objects (a ring, a comb and a mirror) which he claims to have sent to court instead of Cuwaert's head which actually arrived there. Ysengrim is the only one not to be taken in by Reynaert's spiel; but even he is no match for Reynaert in a battle of words. He therefore challenges him to a duel. Reynaert wins and the king gives him high office. In the epilogue the narrator tells us that ever since then Reynaert has had an established place at every court. All over Europe, from the end of the Middle Ages until well into the 19th century, this was *the* standard Reynard story.

In these beast stories plot is usually relatively unimportant. They derive their character and attraction from the way they are told. The narrative technique is characterised by two connected aspects: repetition and use of language. Firstly, internal repetition is found within beast stories. This can be clearly seen in, for example, the first part of branch II, where Renart's successive encounters with the cock, titmouse, cat and raven all follow the same pattern. Renart attempts to trick the other animal. Each time he makes several attempts, using the same stratagem, but they all fail. Then outside intervention changes the situation and the other animal strikes back. Reynard's trickery brings himself into difficulties. The various encounters are deliberately structured in such a way that the audience eagerly awaits the return of the pattern. Then, suddenly, the last episode ends rather differently: Renart may not catch the raven, but at least he gets a cheese for his trouble.

Such repetitions also occur between beast stories. This is apparent, for instance, in the branch I – Van den vos Reynaerde – Reynaerts historie trinity. All three centre on court proceedings which to some extent follow the same course. Branch I itself provides a variation on the trial in branch II – Va, which in French led to imitations in branches VI, X and XXIII. A characteristic feature of this repetition of stories is that new tales are constantly developing through a combination of imitation and originality. Thus, in branch I only the wolf Ysengrin brings a complaint against Renart. In Van den vos Reynaerde there are three charges, including the attempted murder of Cuwaert. This reappears at the end, when Reynaert does in fact kill Cuwaert and uses his head to show the court that it has been fooled. This is a variation on and an elaboration of Renart's mistreatment of Coart at the end of branch I. And Corbout's complaint in Reynaerts *historie* is a variation on the death of Coppe in *Van den vos Reynaerde*. In both cases Reynaert kills a bird. In the first, the body can be displayed to the court, which leads to Reynaert being summonsed. In the second, the crime is committed with far greater expertise. Only a few feathers are left, and they prove nothing. Reynaert consequently has no difficulty in brushing aside Corbout's accusation.

These parallels between stories imply that the audience was assumed to know the tradition. The object was not to tell a completely new story, but to present a familiar one in a new way. This applies to the *Roman de Renart* to a greater extent than to such stories as *Reinhart Fuchs* and *Van den vos Reynaerde*, but in these too there are references to incidents which are not connected but are assumed to be familiar from the tradition.

The use of language is on the one hand a comic factor, on the other a central theme of this type of story. One illustration of the deliberately comic use of language is the encounter between Renart and Tybert in branch II. The two of them run a race. The account of this uses many images related to riding, employed in a deliberately confusing way. The result is that at the beginning and end of this section it is clear that we are dealing with two animals running on four feet. The central part, however, seems rather to relate to two riders on horseback. This paradoxical combination produces a comic effect. Something similar occurs when Renart meets Hersent. Having resolved to take him as her lover she tells him to come and embrace her. Renart joyfully does so. All this is recounted in terms used in other stories to describe the behaviour of courtly lovers. But the next line says: 'Hersent lifted her leg.' With this the characters instantly change from human to animal, the situation from exalted to commonplace.

These two examples not only demonstrate the role of descriptive language-use and the dual perspective on the characters (which are represented both as human and as animal), they also show why these techniques were employed: as a vehicle for criticism. Renart and Tibert are presented as knights. Their encounter begins with them swearing loyalty to each other. Such an oath was supposed to be kept at all costs; but these two make every effort to frustrate each other, and in this way the knightly oath is put in perspective. At several points in the branch Renart and Hersent are portrayed as courtly lovers, often with allusions to the story of → Tristan and Yseult. At other times their behaviour is animal, crude or even reprehensible – indirectly suggesting that the love of Tristan and Yseult and, in broader terms, courtly love itself is less exalted than it is made out to be. In this respect beast stories reflect other medieval and/or ideological concepts such as courtly love.

Thus far we have focused on the role of the narrator's language. But it is a distinguishing feature of beast stories that their characters are animals who talk. In real life animals do not talk; only humans do that. But in this stories it is essential that the animals should speak; they are used to represent the human world and without speech this would be impossible. In the Middle Ages, though, this phenomenon carries a particular charge. For it was then thought that humans were distinguished from animals not only by the use of language but above all by the possession of reason (language being the medium through which reason is expressed). That faculty of reason was given to man to enable him to lead a just and righteous life, and thus eventually come to God. If he disregards his reason and follows his urges for sex, food, worldly goods and the like, he debases himself to the level of an animal. Quite simply, he is no longer a man. This is the fundamental background to the medieval beast stories. They show the bestial element in mankind.

For the animals invariably use language in a negative way. On the one hand it is a weapon, or a means of achieving some end: Renart flatters the raven to get hold of his cheese and if possible himself; Reynaert tells the king lies about a treasure to save his skin; he lures Cuwaert into his den in order to eat him. On the other hand language is used to camouflage bad behaviour: when Renart is defending himself against the charge of raping the she-wolf, he says that he was only trying to pull her out of the hole she was stuck in; it was Ysengrin's malice that interpreted this as rape. This attention to the linguistic behaviour of the animal characters not only determines the themes of the various stories, it also influences their specific formal and structural qualities. Some examples of this have already been given.

Until now we have described the qualities of beast stories. A question with broader implications is why these stories have these qualities and for whom they were intended. To begin with the latter, in general the Reynard stories portray an aristocratic society. Very often their setting is the realm of King Noble; the wolf (in the *Ysengrimus* an abbot or bishop) is in the *Roman de Renart* 'connétable' (commander-in-chief); Reynaert has a castle; and so on. Because this aristocratic society is made an object of ridicule, in the past nearly all scholars assumed that these stories were intended for the bourgeoisie, providing it with an outlet for its criticism of the nobility. Nowadays, however, it is generally thought that the nobility itself was the principal audience. What concrete information we have about the origins of these texts and the original owners of the manuscripts (which is very scanty) all points in that direction. A real appreciation of the beast stories requires so much knowledge of the aristocratic way of life and of aristocratic literature that it makes any other primary audience than the aristocracy extremely unlikely. There is some evidence, though, that in late medieval times the Reynard stories were also known to or owned by prominent bourgeois.

In no case do we know the original audience of any Reynard story. We do however have a string of data, all of which point to a single geographical area. The *Ysengrimus* was written in Ghent. Almost all the oldest branches of the *Roman de Renart* come from the northern part of France, some of them possibly from Flanders. *Le Couronnement de Renard* is dedicated to the memory of William of Dampierre, Count of Flanders. *Renard le nouvel* comes from Lille, very close to Flanders. The two Dutch Reynaert stories are almost certainly from Flanders. That region thus played a decisive part in the evolution of the beast epic.

Beast stories had a dual purpose – to criticise and to entertain. In this respect we can see a parallel with modern politically involved cabaret: this too seeks to make people laugh at things which are at bottom taken very seriously. What the animal stories show is that courtly aristocratic society does not by any means always live up to its ideals, that courtly love is sometimes no more than a cloak for sexual lust, that knightly honour can be taken as a licence for selfish behaviour, that fine words and outward conduct are all too often a cover for ambition, abuse of power, aggression and malice. But no names are mentioned and the criticism is expressed indirectly. So everyone can think that it refers not to him but to the others, and the criticism can be extremely vehement. Because it is mixed with humour and is usually positive in tone (being voiced in the hope that the situation will improve) it is easily swallowed. In any case, the ratio of edification to entertainment is not always the same. In the later branches of the *Roman de Renart* the comic element predominates and the tales seem to be reduced to a literary game. In late medieval versions such as *Reynaerts historie* the didactic element is dominant, though they are not devoid of humour.

The development of a uniform Reynard story and the triumphal progress of *Reynaerts historie* began with two printed editions of *Reynaerts historie* by Gheraert Leeu (Gouda 1479 and Antwerp c.1490). These initiated a Dutch tradition which continued into the mid-19th century. One of the Leeu texts (1479) was translated and published in English by William Caxton (1481). This marked the beginning of an English tradition which lasted to the end of the 18th century and also left its mark in Ireland. The other Leeu text (1490) was translated in an adapted form into Low German. This translation appeared in Lübeck in 1498 and began a German Reynaert tradition. Prints of the Low German text are known up until 1660. In 1544 a High German version appeared, and within a century this was reprinted more than twenty times. Moreover, this High German version was translated into Latin by Hartmann Schopper in 1567,

Bruin, Ysengrim and Tybert prepare for Reynard's execution, which he thwarts by his talk of a treasure. Illustration by Wilhelm von Kaulbach in an 1846 edition of Goethe's *Reineke Fuchs*.

leading to a string of 16th- and 17th-century Latin prints. The High German translation too was translated into English in 1706, so that since then English has had two related but distinct Reynard traditions. The Low German text was translated into Danish in 1555, and Swedish and Icelandic versions based on this were also produced. And finally, the Low German text led, via a number of intermediate stages, to *Reineke Fuchs* by Goethe (1794), a version of the tale written in hexameters. Goethe's work (as part of his total oeuvre) established a tradition of its own; it was translated into French, English, Dutch, Hungarian, Russian and Japanese among other languages.

Throughout this entire tradition the story remains virtually unchanged. Minor simplifications are made and some scenes are modified – usually for reasons of prudishness – but anyone familiar with one version has the gist of them all. That is not to say that all the texts are identical. Modifications are made, but they relate to the

presentation and interpretation of the tale. For instance, each branch of the tradition
has its own division into chapters and/or books. Many versions contain explicit
moralisations, and these can vary fundamentally. The Low German tradition provides a
fine example of this. The oldest printed text comes from the Catholic camp, and its
added moral contains many exhortations to remain true to the faith and respect its
priests. In 1539 a printed text appeared with a Protestant commentary; and now
suddenly all kinds of elements in the same story are proof of the absurdity of the
Catholic faith and the shadiness of its priesthood. Another example is the Reynaert
version from the Southern Netherlands which, under pressure from the Inquisition, was
thoroughly expurgated and stripped of pronouncements which might give offence. A
final difference between the various versions lies in the production of the books
themselves. There are luxury editions with splendid illustrations, but also little books
produced as cheaply as possible with third-rate plates on poor-quality paper.

Until the 19th century the tradition in each country remained fairly consistent.
Then, however, there was a broadening of interest. Firstly, that century saw an increase
in scholarly interest in the Middle Ages and the resultant publication of a string of
editions of the medieval beast stories. In the Netherlands *Van den vos Reynaerde* was
rediscovered and hailed as a masterpiece. In consequence, interest in *Reynaerts historie*
and its tradition declined, in the 20th century almost to vanishing-point. At the same
time there have been more and more new versions. These fall into two groups, with
different objectives. First there are the culturally-minded laymen, for whom retellings
in modern language, often also in rhyme, are produced. Many of these are bibliophile
editions. Secondly, there are versions of the story for children. These show far more
divergences from the original. There is more censorship and the moral is brought out
more strongly. The illustrations are for the most part simpler, though since the Second
World War this trend has diminished. In the Netherlands it is usually *Van den vos
Reynaerde* that is reworked: the 19th and 20th centuries have yielded at least 110
versions of the Reynaert story in Dutch, including works by Stijn Streuvels, Karel
Jonckheere, Arjaan van Nimwegen, Paul Biegel and Ernst van Altena. In Germany it is
mainly Goethe's work that provides the model. In the last decade children's versions of
parts of the *Roman de Renart* have been cropping up all over Europe.

What is striking about the post-medieval Reynard tradition is on the one hand its
extent and on the other its stability. As already mentioned, divergences in a text are
usually a matter of specific interpretation and presentation. Works in which the story is
changed or a new story is told are rare. In the Netherlands the tale has several times
been adapted for the stage, e.g. by Paul de Mont (1924) and Jan Walch (1935).
Similarly, this century has also seen a number of musical versions of the story, most
recently the musical *Dear Fox* by Stuer and Ditmar (1990) and the Reynaert opera by
the Stichting Kameropera Nederland (Van Altena and Bos, 1991).

In 1941 R. van Genechten published a story which was called *Van den vos Reynaerde*
but which contained a new plot set after the death of Nobel. The story is indirect Nazi
propaganda, notable particularly for the introduction of a new and highly negative
character: the rhino Jodocus (Jood = Jew). Louis Paul Boon made use of the entire
Reynaert tradition in his *Wapenbroeders* ('Comrades in Arms', 1955), using the beast
story to criticise the Communist Party and the Catholic Church.

In England two continuations were written in the 17th century. The first, *A
continuation or second part of Reynard the Fox* (1672), tells of Reynard's life from his
victory over the court to his death. The second, *The shifts of Reynardine the son of
Reynard* (1684) recounts the life of his son.

In Germany several adaptations were produced in the 18th century. *Hennynk de Han*
(Sparre 1732) gives Reynke's biography up to his death. In form it closely follows the
Reynke de vos tradition. *Reineke Fuchs am Ende des philosophischen Jahrhunderts* (1797) is
a retelling of the standard narrative, but with all manner of changes and additions. The

tale is a cutting satire on monarchy, and specifically on the Danish ruling house of the day. The 20th century has seen an increase in the number of creative treatments of the material. Two recent reshapings are those by Liebchen (1989) who, dissatisfied with Goethe's version, produced a revised version with numerous additions drawn from fables, and by Steinberg (1989), who retells Goethe in hexameters with crossed rhyme, adapting the abuses he tells of to the present day.

Also deserving of mention is Stravinsky's opera *Renard, histoire burlesque chantée et jouée* (1917, first performed 1922). The piece is a variation on the fox-and-cock story for four voices.

So far as the visual arts are concerned, the Reynard story has yielded mainly book illustrations. A number of *Renart* manuscripts do contain miniatures, but the illustrative tradition really only gets under way with the printed versions. The oldest cycle of illustrations was also one of the most influential. It was created for the Leeu print of c.1490 by an anonymous artist known as the Haarlem Master. Only three, partially damaged, illustrations from this series survive, but it can be shown that imitations of it were used in the Netherlands, Germany and England. The influence of the series can be traced down to the 18th century. The most extensive series (which in Germany also enjoyed a long period of success) was produced by Jost Amman for the second edition of the Latin translation of the High German *Reynke* (1574/75). Goethe's version ensured the dissemination of two interesting sets of illustrations. The first consists of a series of etchings by Allard van Everdingen (1621–75), apparently produced in the first instance for a collector rather than for a book edition. These etchings came into Goethe's possession by a circuitous route and were then used for a number of reprints of his *Reineke Fuchs*. They are notable for their black-and-white treatment. This is the only major cycle which depicts the animals purely as animals. The illustrations *par excellence* to Goethe's *Reineke Fuchs* are, however, those by Wilhelm von Kaulbach, in his day one of the most famous painters in Europe. For the second edition of *Reineke Fuchs* (1841) he made 36 drawings from which steel engravings were prepared, a series which has been the most influential of the last two centuries and has been very widely imitated. Kaulbach's drawings are striking for their satirical attitude to the Establishment and the many comic details they contain.

Apart from the books, the Reynard story has given rise to penny prints, bookplates, luxury furniture with scenes in pewter, watercolours, stained-glass windows, statues, etc. They come from the whole period of its existence and from all over Europe. The range of material is enormous and no coherent account of it all has ever been produced. So there we shall have to leave it.

P. WACKERS

Editions: Hellinga 1952; Blake 1970; Göttert 1980; Goossens 1983a; Lulofs 1983; Dufournet/Méline 1985; *Van den vos reynaerde* 1991.
Studies: Jauss 1959; Flinn 1963; Varty 1967; Rombauts/Welkenhuysen 1975; Goossens/ Sodmann 1980; Goossens 1983b; Wackers 1986; Goossens 1988; Varty 1988–91; Scheidegger 1989; Bouwman 1991; Varty 1999.

R OBERT THE DEVIL derives his name from his behaviour, and that is bound up with the circumstances of his birth. Under pressure from his barons, who are concerned for the succession, Duke Aubert of Normandy marries a daughter of the Duke of Burgundy. Seventeen years later, though, the desired result has still not been achieved, despite the many hours spent in prayer by the pious couple. When the duchess in despair promises her offspring to the Devil, the latter is not about to miss such a chance and he makes sure that the duchess becomes pregnant. After a difficult confinement and in hellish weather conditions Robert (in this text: Robrecht) is born. He outstrips all his contemporaries in size and strength and behaves so aggressively that he is soon universally known as Robert the Devil. When he is about seven years old they try to get him to buckle down to learning – in vain, for he strikes his tutor dead. Ten years later he is knighted, but this makes no difference either: at the tournament held to celebrate his knighthood he behaves like a wild beast.

For many years he engages in wholesale rape, murder and plunder and nobody can do a thing about it. The men sent by his father to capture him return with their eyes put out. After the appalling murder of seven hermits he suddenly sees the error of his ways while at Arques Castle and wonders how he had come to such a pass. When his mother tells him that she had given him to the devil at his conception Robrecht decides to make his confession to the Pope. The Pope hears his confession, but sends him to a

Robert murders the seven hermits. Title page of Robrecht de duivele, published in Antwerp in 1516 by the printer Michiel van Hoogstraten

hermit for penance. As punishment the hermit orders him to act as a fool, never to speak and to eat and sleep with the dogs. He spends a long time as fool at the imperial court in Rome.

The court chamberlain, who has been vainly seeking the hand of the Emperor's daughter, secretly makes an agreement with the Saracens and they attack the city. Three times Robrecht – incognito, in white armour and mounted on a white horse provided by an angel – saves the Emperor from defeat. Only the Emperor's daughter – who is dumb – knows that this white knight is Robrecht. After the third battle some of the Emperor's knights waylay Robrecht to ask who he is. Escaping from them, he is wounded in the thigh by a spear-point. When the Emperor then promises his daughter to whoever can show the injured leg and the spear-point, the chamberlain shows a self-inflicted wound and claims to be the white knight. Meanwhile, an angel has commanded the hermit to go to Rome and tell Robrecht that his penance is over. Just as the chamberlain is about to marry the princess God gives her the power of speech. She accuses the chamberlain of deceit and points to Robrecht as the true wounded saviour. He however maintains his fool's role until the hermit gives him God's message. At first the hermit forbids him to accept the offered marriage to the princess; but after he has left Rome an angel instructs him to return and marry her after all. After the wedding they leave for Rouen, where he succeeds his deceased father as lord. When Rome is again attacked by the chamberlain and the Saracens Robrecht hastens to the city's aid and avenges the (already slain) Emperor on the chamberlain. He then leads a long and virtuous life and his wife bears him a son, Rijckaert (Richard), who will perform great deeds in the service of → Charlemagne.

Although the story itself is a great deal older (see below), it was this late-15th-century printed version that was most widely known and provided the basis for new versions from the 16th century on.

Narratives about a married couple who eventually manage to produce a child with a stranger's help, on condition that the child is returned after a certain time, occur in a number of fairy-tales: the Grindkopff (sore-headed), the male Cinderella and the Goldenermärchen. The story of Robert the Devil can be regarded as a Christianised variant on such tales. As such it shows similarities to the Old Irish story of Conall the Red from the *Immram Húi Corra* (11th century). Conall is a great landowner whose offspring all die in childhood, leaving him without an heir. Here too the couple appeal to the Devil for help. He gives them triplets; these, however, show devilish qualities only when they learn of their origins. Here too heart-searching, repentance and penance follow. The role of the devil as helper should be seen as a Christianisation of older fairy-tales.

The oldest narrative in which the child is named Robert (or rather Robertus) is a Latin exemplum by the Dominican Etienne de Bourbon (first half 13th century). That this oldest version already contains almost every element of the penance is no surprise, since the object of this exemplum, according to two superscriptions, was precisely to stress the importance of doing penance. Here the account of Robert's misdeeds is not yet so extensive. Compared with the printed version it lacks his misbehaviour at the tournament, the putting out of eyes and the murder of the hermits. The emphasis is strongly on the period of penance. The Emperor's opponents are here not the chamberlain and the Saracens but 'barbarians', while Robert's identity is revealed after the second, not the third, battle. An important difference is the ascetic ending: while in Etienne de Bourbon Robert is also offered the hand of the Emperor's daughter, he is forbidden by the hermit to accept and spends the rest of his life as a hermit.

The *Roman de Robert le diable* (second half 13th century) is the earliest French version in verse form (c.5000 lines), and the first to specify where the events took place: in Normandy and Rome. This version introduces his supernatural birth and his crimes, and the Saracens and the chamberlain also make their appearance. Here Robert repents of his own accord, and the ending is again ascetic. Also from the 13th century is the *Chronique de Normandie* (preserved in numerous manuscripts and after 1487 also in prints) containing the first prose version, which diverges somewhat at several points. For instance, it omits Robert's supernatural birth, the tournament after his knighting, the putting out of eyes and the conflict with the Saracens. The *Chronique* also gives a quite different motivation for Robert's repentance: badly wounded, he finds a hermit who cares for and converts him and sends him to the Pope. This version too has an ascetic end: after his stay in Rome Robert spends the remainder of his life as a hermit in Jerusalem.

Of these three versions with the ascetic ending the *Roman* gives the most powerful portrait of Robert as a grave sinner with an essentially strong character, who reforms his life of his own accord. His submissiveness and heroism make sympathy and admiration for him understandable. It is therefore not surprising that this particular version of the story should have played a part in the development of later versions.

In the 14th century the material was reworked in the short narrative genre fashionable at the time, the *dit*. This *Dit de Robert le diable*, composed of 254 four-line stanzas, forms the principal link to the later versions. The content too undergoes some modification, with the events removed from their purely religious setting to accord with what laymen expected of a bachelor: at the end Robert no longer opts for the ascetic life as a hermit but marries the Emperor's daughter. He also avenges the Emperor on the chamberlain who had treacherously claimed the liberator's role, and he returns to his native country. Based on this *Dit* an unknown author (probably the printer) wrote *La vie du terrible Robert le dyable*, published in Lyons in 1496. The story was apparently still popular, for only a year later two editions appeared in Paris, and these also contained a sequel: *Le Roman de Richart, filz de Robert le diable qui fut duc de Normandie*.

Outside France, too, the work quickly found a response. Editions of the story based on the French prints appeared in England (c.1500), Spain (Burgos 1508) and the Low Countries (Antwerp 1516). In England especially it clearly aroused interest; here an edition in verse appeared in addition to the prose text. Two 15th-century manuscripts preserve the story in *romance* form under the title *Sir Gowther*, mentioning an otherwise unknown Breton *lai* as source. After 1591 the material became even more widely known through the printed version by the jurist, physician and man of letters Thomas Lodge. Shakespeare made use of this version in *King Lear*.

In Germany the story was at first much less widely disseminated, though two 15th-century manuscripts from Bavaria are known. The texts differ fairly considerably from the known French versions, so that we must think of oral sources. Not until Georg Rudolf Widmann's edition of *Faust* (Hamburg 1599) did the story become accessible in print in Germany for the first time; it includes a version derived from the *Chronique*, but greatly abridged and modified.

In France, Spain and the Low Countries the books were reprinted into the 19th century. Along with the romances *Pierre de Provence*, *La belle Hélène de Constantinople*, *Richard sans peur*, *Jean de Paris* and *Jean de Calais*, the French *Robert le diable* was among the best-selling volumes in the 'Bibliothèque bleu'; all except *Jean de Calais* were also available in Dutch-language prints. In the mid-18th century the French text was radically revised.

A *Ballet de Robert le Diable* was danced in Paris as early as 1652, but it is in Spain that we find the earliest dramatisations. In an anonymous *El loco en la penitencia* (c.1700) Robert is induced to repent by a letter fixed to a tree, while F. Viceno in his *Roberto el Diablo* (1751) uses the power of a portrait of the Emperor's daughter. Transformations and magical effects feature largely in *Robert le diable ou le criminal repentant*, a 'vaudeville' by M. Franconi from 1815. A little later the material was used for a horror story, *The friend of Normandy or the repentant criminal* (1821), while two years later A. le Flaguais made a serious ballade out of it, *Le château de Robert le diable*.

Modifications and additional motifs are also found in other works from the 19th century, such as the *Romanzen von Robert dem Teufel* by Schwab, in which Robert is induced to repent by the sight of his reflection. K. von Holteis used the same motif in his drama. In 1831 Meyerbeer's opera *Robert le Diable*, with a libretto by G. Delavigne and A. Scribe, had its first performance in Paris. Here remorse, confession and penance feature not at all. Robert's devilish father Bertram has to deliver him over to Hell and for this reason persuades him into sinful deeds. Robert goes along with this in order to win the love of Princess Isabella. Before a pact seals his fate he is saved by his mother's warning, brought to him by the girl Alice, his good angel. The opera was extremely successful and led to increased interest in the tale. The work was seen as a link between Weber's *Der Freischütz* and Wagner's *Der fliegende Holländer*. As well as a parody by Nestroy, *Robert der Teuxel* (1833), new stage versions appeared. In 1834 Raupach tried to equal Meyerbeer's opera by piling up fantastic motifs without straying too far from the traditional treatment. In Paris on 27 March 1841 Franz Liszt played his *Réminiscences de Robert le Diable*, one of the opera fantasies for which he was famous. A month later the audience insisted that he repeat this triumph during a Beethoven concert conducted by Hector Berlioz. Among those present was Richard Wagner; according to him, Liszt would have to play his request item yet again, before the assembled angels.

E. Jourdain's monster drama *La Comédie Normande* includes both traditional and newly devised motifs. A verse epic provides a treatment in line with the chapbook, while twelve songs by V. von Strauss (1854) emphasise the religious undertone. In A. Wilbrandt's drama *Der Herzog* (1898) Robert chooses his own penance and also discharges himself from it; he then reconquers his lands from a ruler who has neglected his duties.

Apart from reworkings of the material in new literary creations, the familiarity and popularity of Robert's story are also evident in innumerable references to it in other works such as Goncharov's *Oblomov* and Robert Nye's *Falstaff*. The remains of Robert the Devil's castle can be found at Moulineaux on the banks of the Seine.

R.J. RESOORT

Edition: Resoort 1980.

T HE BEST and earliest version of the story of ROBIN HOOD is *A Gest of Robyn Hode*, a deliberate attempt to make up a complete version of his career from different sources. The three main tales are: Robin Hood and the poor knight, Little John and the Sheriff of Nottingham, and Robin Hood and the king. The poem ends with a brief account of his death.

The poem opens with Robin Hood in Barnsdale, surrounded by his men. He outlines the code which he makes his followers obey: they are not to harm peasants and yeomen, or even knights and squires who will play their game, but their targets are to be bishops and archbishops, and, in particular, the Sheriff of Nottingham. Robin declares that he will not dine until he has a suitable guest (a parody of Arthurian romances, where the king will not dine on a feastday until a suitable adventure has begun). So he sends Much, William Scarlocke and Little John up to the Saylis, where they see an unkempt knight coming along a forest path. They invite him to dine with Robin Hood, which he does cheerfully enough. But when Robin asks him to pay for his dinner, on the grounds that a yeoman should not pay for a knight's meal, he explains that he only has ten shillings. Little John searches him and confirms this, and Robin asks how he has come down in the world so badly. He explains that his son went to a tournament and killed a knight, and to save him he has had to pledge his lands to St Mary's Abbey in York to raise £400. He pledges his word by the Virgin Mary that he will repay Robin if he lends him the money, which is now due for repayment, and Robin agrees. Little John says that such a knight deserves better clothing, and he is given a suit, and a horse and palfrey as well. As he has no squire, Little John goes with him as his servant.

The next day the knight goes to find the abbot, who has given him up as a forlorn hope, and is already looking forward to taking over the knight's lands. At first the knight pretends to have no money, and asks for an extension of the time-limit; the abbot curses him and says that the lands are now his. But the knight produces the money, and says that the abbot has forfeited any gift he might have given him by way of interest. He rides home and is greeted by his lady, who thinks that all is lost: but he tells her that thanks to Robin Hood the day has been saved. He stays at home until he has amassed £400, and then sets out, with a splendid retinue, to meet Robin Hood on the day appointed. But on the way he comes across a country wrestling match, which a stranger has won. The local people are furious, and are about to kill the stranger; the knight intervenes, 'for love of Robyn Hode', to give the stranger the prizes due to him.

The story now changes to the exploits of Little John, who goes to an archery match at Nottingham, where he always succeeds in splitting the 'wand', a stick stripped of its bark and used end-on as a target. The sheriff notices him and hires him as one of his retinue, which is as Little John planned, for he intends to be the worst servant the sheriff ever had. One day when the sheriff goes hunting and leaves him behind, Little John demands dinner of the butler, who refuses to serve him until his lord has come back. Little John knocks him down, raids the buttery for drink, and then goes to seek his dinner from the cook. But the cook is an expert swordsman and holds him at bay, until Little John proposes that they should become friends and go to join Robin Hood. The cook agrees, and after breaking into the sheriff's treasury, they set out for the forest, where they present Robin Hood with the proceeds: £300 in cash and all the sheriff's silver dishes. Little John then thinks of another trick: he goes to find the sheriff while he is out hunting, and tells him that he has just seen the finest stag he could imagine, and 140 deer following him – meaning of course, Robin Hood and his company. The sheriff takes his words literally, and follows him. Robin Hood makes the sheriff dine off his own silver, and then has him dressed in the same green livery as the others. The sheriff spends a wretched night sleeping in the open, and complains the next day that Robin Hood's 'order' is stricter than that of any monk or friar, saying that he would rather be beheaded than spend another such night. Robin Hood makes the sheriff swear an oath never to harm any of his men, but if he should come across them, to help them as best he could.

It is now time for the knight to repay his loan, and Robin Hood refuses to dine until the money is found. His men go in search of guests for dinner: Robin says that if they are messengers, poor men or minstrels, he will give them something. However, the first travellers are two monks in black with seven packhorses and an escort of 52 men. Little John says that three of them will take the monks to dinner with Robin Hood, and at their appearance the whole of the escort take to their heels. One of the monks and the packhorses are led off to Robin Hood. It turns out that the monk is none other than the high cellarer of St Mary's Abbey, on his way to London to bring a lawsuit against the knight. He claims to have only 20 marks with him: 'if that is the case', says Robin Hood, 'I won't touch the money, as you will need it for the journey – indeed I will lend you some more'. Little John is sent to search the monk's baggage, and finds in his trunk no less than £800. Robin says that Our Lady has kept her word – more, she has doubled his outlay – and has sent a monk from her own abbey to deliver it. The monk does not wait for Little John to search the next horse, but spurs off, saying he could have dined much more cheaply at Blyth or Doncaster. Robin tells him to ask the abbot to send such a monk to dinner with him every day.

The knight now appears, and explains why he is late. Robin applauds his action, and says that the debt is already repaid, because Our Lady has sent her high cellarer with the money, and he cannot take it twice. The knight gives him a present of bows and arrows, and Robin returns the compliment by giving him the extra £400 that the monk had brought him. The knight, delighted at the outcome, takes his leave and rides off.

We now return to the Sheriff of Nottingham, who announces an archery contest in the forest, the prize to be a gold and silver arrow. Robin Hood says that he will go to the contest, and sets out with 140 men. Only six are to shoot with him in the contest; the rest are to be ready armed in case of treason. All six of Robin's men acquit themselves well, but Robin Hood shoots best of all. Just as the arrow is being given to him, he is recognised, and the sheriff's men attack him. Robin Hood reproaches the sheriff for breaking his word, and his men let fly. In the ensuing battle, Robin's men drive off the sheriff's forces, but Little John is crippled by an arrow in his knee. He begs Robin Hood to kill him rather than let him fall into the sheriff's hands, but Robin carries him away to the castle of the knight whom he had helped, Sir Richard at the Lee, which is only a little way off. Sir Richard welcomes them, pulls up the drawbridge, and swears that they shall stay with him for forty days.

Soon afterwards the sheriff and his men arrive, and lay siege to the castle, demanding that Sir Richard should hand over Robin Hood: but Sir Richard refuses to do anything until he knows what the king wishes to be done. So the sheriff goes to London and puts the matter to the king, who vows that he will be at Nottingham in a fortnight and take both Sir Richard and Robin Hood. Meanwhile, Robin Hood and Little John return to the forest, and evade all the sheriff's attempts to catch them; but Sir Richard is captured while out hawking and carried off to Nottingham prison. Robin Hood hears of it before the sheriff has gone more than three miles, and swears he will release him. They catch up with the sheriff in Nottingham itself: the sheriff is killed and his men driven off, and Robin takes Sir Richard to shelter in the forest until he can win pardon from King Edward.

The king now arrives in Nottingham, and finds not only the sheriff dead but all the deer in his forests killed. He declares that Sir Richard's lands are forfeit, and that he will give them to anyone who kills the knight. But although he spends six months in the region, he cannot find Robin Hood until a cunning forester suggests a way in which to do it. The king is to dress as a monk, and take only five knights with him, similarly dressed; the forester will lead him through the greenwood, and before they get to Nottingham they will meet Robin Hood. The king does so, disguising himself as an abbot, and before they have gone far, Robin and his archers stop them. Robin says that they are forest yeomen, whose only resources are the king's deer: the abbot must have many churches and lands, so he asks him for charity's sake to give them money. The 'abbot' says that he has been at the royal court for a fortnight, and it has been an expensive business: he has only £40 left, but Robin is welcome to that. Robin takes the money and divides it: he gives half to his men, and returns the rest to the abbot, who thanks him, and says that King Edward has sent his seal as a token that he should come and be his guest at Nottingham. The abbot then produces the royal seal; Robin kneels out of respect, and says that the abbot must dine with him, since he brings a message from the king.

Dinner is served, and then Robin's men hold an archery contest. The king thinks that the targets have been set up fifty yards too far off. Many of Robin's men miss the target; the penalty is to forfeit their equipment and to be given a blow on the head by Robin himself. Robin twice splits the wand in the centre, but at the third shot he too misses the garland. He says that he will take his punishment from the abbot, who at first refuses, but then gives him a blow that nearly fells him to the ground. As Robin recovers, he recognises the king; the king asks for mercy for himself and his men, but Robin answers by asking the same for himself and his followers. The king pardons them, on condition that they leave the forest and come to court. Before they leave, the king and his followers are all given Lincoln green liveries to wear, and they ride off together to Nottingham. The king and Robin play 'pluck buffet' as they go, each shooting in turn; the king always loses and has to take a blow from Robin as penalty, and declares that he could shoot for a year without beating him.

When they reach the town, there is panic, because all that can be seen are green cloaks, and everyone thinks that the king has been killed. But the king reveals himself, and order is restored. Sir Richard is summoned, and given a full pardon, and Robin tries to settle down to life at court. However, in a little more than a year, he has spent all his money on entertaining and on gifts to knights and squires, and only two of his men, Little John and Scathelock, are left with him. Robin longs to go back to the greenwood, and begs leave of the king to go on pilgrimage to a little chapel in Barnsdale that he had built. Once he gets there, he returns to his old ways. He shoots a deer, and summons his band of outlaws by blowing his horn. For all his respect for the king, he never goes back to court, but lives in the forest for twenty-two years.

At this point the author of *A Gest of Robyn Hode* tells very briefly of Robin Hood's death, naming the Prioress of Kirklees and Sir Roger of Doncaster as responsible for killing him. We only know the full story from a much later but defective poem. It opens with Robin Hood declaring that he must go to Kirklees to be let blood, a common cure for illness. Will Scarlett says that there is bound to be fighting if he goes there, and he must take fifty men with him, but he refuses to take anyone except Little John. On the way, they come across an old woman cursing Robin Hood, kneeling on a plank over a ditch; here half a page is missing, and the next verse contains a warning from an unknown speaker, who is weeping for Robin Hood because he must undergo blood-letting that day. Robin Hood declares that the prioress is his first cousin, and will not harm him, and he and Little John go on to Kirklees. Robin gives the prioress £20 and she begins the bloodletting; but once the thick blood is out, she lets the blood run on, and Robin Hood knows he has been betrayed. Again half a page is missing, and Robin Hood is next seen fighting with Red Rogers (probably Sir Roger of Doncaster from the *Gest*), whom he kills, but he himself is mortally wounded. Little John wants to burn down the priory, but Robin Hood will not let him: instead, he is to carry Robin into the street, and dig a grave 'of gravel and grit', where he is to bury him with his weapons. Here the manuscript has another half-page missing.

Still later, in the mid-18th century, a chapbook printer at York produced a complete version, which includes the two most famous episodes of Robin Hood's death. As he feels that he is dying, he summons Little John by three blasts of his horn, a theme possibly borrowed from other medieval romances such as that of Roland. When Little John comes, Robin chooses his burial place by firing an arrow out of the window.

A Gest of Robyn Hode is not a 'definitive' account of Robin's career; it was clearly made up from separate ballads, as the sudden changes of scene and characters show. Some of the episodes are found in other poems and had evidently become stock themes of the story: in *Robin Hood and the Monk*, for example, Robin refuses to take anyone except Little John with him to Nottingham when he wants to hear mass, and is of course betrayed when he is in the church. The tell-tale is a monk, who, like the cellarer of St Mary' in the *Gest*, has been robbed by Robin and his men. The sheriff is duly summoned and Robin is captured. But, with the usual prayer to Our Lady, Little John sets out to free him, which he does by tricking both the sheriff and the king. Once again, it is Little John who finds his way into the sheriff's favour and steals the keys to the cell where Robin is imprisoned.

Yet the legend did change and develop as time went on. The early outlaw ballads – not only those of Robin Hood – are characterised by violence and bloodthirstiness: in *Robin Hood and the Monk* Little John kills the monk out of hand and Much slays his little page 'for fear that he should tell': in *Robin Hood and Guy of Gisborne* Robin beheads Guy and cuts his face 'with an Irish knife' so that no one can recognise the corpse. This violence reflects the real world of the medieval outlaw, just as the frequent appeals to Our Lady reflect medieval popular religion. As the stories of Robin Hood found their way into print, the audience gradually changed, as did attitudes to the hero himself. The outlaw of uncertain origins became a yeoman, his behaviour modified, becoming less violent. There is less bloodshed in the later 16th-century ballads, and even Robin's most villainous opponents escape with their lives. Another new development is the idea of Robin Hood meeting his match. In the early stories, there are hints of this, as in *Robin Hood and the Monk*, where Little John beats Robin at archery, but in *Robin Hood and the Potter* and *Robin Hood and the Curtal Friar*, the outlaw loses and has to persuade his opponent to join his men.

At the same time, the ballad-makers took the opportunity of filling the gaps in what had come to be the accepted story. Thus we get the ballad of *Robin Hood and Little John*, which tells how Little John joined Robin Hood's band, and which is a straightforward variation on *Robin Hood and the Potter*. Little John challenges Robin to a bout with staves on a narrow bridge, and finally knocks him into the stream; at which Robin's men want to deal with him, but Robin stops them and invites Little John to become a member of his band. (An American version has them celebrating Little John's acceptance in 'rum and all liquors likewise'!)

But who was Robin Hood? What were the original stories about him, and why did they last so long and make such an impression when other famous outlaws like Adam Bell are long since forgotten?

The first problem that we come up against in our search for Robin Hood is the kind of evidence that survives. We have a handful of literary references and popular proverbs – without any real details – relating to a well-known character, apparently an outlaw, of that name, between roughly 1380 and 1500. Three Scottish historians – but no English ones – give some account of him in the 15th and early 16th centuries. Then, at some time in the first thirty years of the 16th century, we have the printed version of *A Gest of Robyn Hode*, followed by nearly forty other ballads by 1700. Only one medieval manuscript, dating from about 1450, actually contains a poem about Robin Hood. So the earliest stories that we have about Robin Hood are at least 100 to 150 years later than the date at which they could have occurred. We are dealing not with one coherent story but with layer upon layer of additions and alterations.

What are the main points of the legend in these early ballads? Robin Hood is an outlaw, who lives in the greenwood or royal forest, an area jealously guarded by the medieval kings and subject to its own special laws of 'vert and venison', aimed at protecting the deer which provided both sport for the king and food for his court. Outlawry means that he had either committed some crime for which the sentence was that he should be deprived of the law's protection – outlawed – or had taken to a lawless brigand's existence. But he is a brigand who has not only been rejected by society, but questions the ideas on which that society is based: he robs the rich and helps those in need (though he never specifically gives the money to the poor), challenging the justice of society, the very justice which has condemned him.

The details of the stories offer some possible clues as to Robin Hood's historical origins. There are the long-running feud with the Sheriff of Nottingham, the many specific place-names mentioned, his death by treachery at Kirklees Priory; there are the 'Merry Men', Little John, Much, Scarlet, Gilbert 'Withondes', and, in later ballads, Friar Tuck, Alan a Dale and Maid Marian. There is the Bishop of Hereford, and the abbey of St Mary's at York. And there is Robin's own skill with the longbow and his livery of Lincoln green. If we can pin down any one of these details, we might begin to discover the 'true history' of Robin Hood.

Let us begin with the physical setting, the 'greenwood'. In *A Gest of Robyn Hode*, the poet immediately tells us that the scene is 'Bernesdale', an area between Pontefract and

Doncaster in south Yorkshire; but a fragment of doggerel from about 1400 opens 'Robin Hood in Sherwood stood', referring to the great royal forest of Sherwood to the north of Nottingham. The insistence of several of the ballads that Barnsdale is Robin Hood's true home is curious, to say the least: it was never a forest, either literally or in the legal sense of being subject to forest law. But it was on a busy route, the old Roman road to the north, and was known as a danger spot for travellers because of the robbers who haunted it: two bishops and an abbot travelling north at the end of Edward I's reign were given an extra escort of twenty archers 'on account of Barnsdale'.

The idea of an outlaw who robbed the rich to do charitable deeds is altogether more unusual. Outlaws generally reacted to their fate by abandoning all respect for law; yet this was not always the case, and there are historical examples of men who took a different view, regarding law as something sacrosanct, and blaming their fate on corrupt administrators of it. From such a viewpoint it was only a short step to setting matters to rights oneself. That such threats could be converted into action is witnessed by the deeds of the Folville brothers and their associates from 1326 to 1346, in the course of which they murdered an important government official, Roger Bellers, and held to ransom Richard Willoughby, one of the king's justices in 1332; they carried him 'from wood to wood' until 1,300 marks were paid for his release. Much of their activity was purely criminal, but in these two cases they were taking revenge on unpopular officials. The parallels with the Robin Hood stories are obvious, and the Sheriff of Nottingham was among those who pursued the Folvilles.

Yet for the central theme of the Robin Hood stories, the robbing of the rich for altruistic reasons, it is difficult to find an exact parallel. Respect for property ran deep in medieval attitudes, and the appeal of the ballads is not to the peasants, but to the knight and yeoman, to William Langland's parish priest in the 1370s who could not read Mass but knew the 'rhymes of Robin Hood and of Randolf earl of Chester'. For them, such activities would have little appeal in themselves: and if we look closely at the poems, the reason for this altruistic crime becomes clear. The original ballads probably celebrated a rather wilder figure, whose robberies were part of his way of life as an outlaw, like the gratuitous violence which lingers on in the poems. But this did not appeal to those who saw in Robin Hood a righter of wrongs, and so a good reason was found for excusing his robberies and making them part of his campaign against corruption. It is for the same reason that Robin Hood is portrayed as a yeoman who had all the manners of a hero of romance, and is eventually said to be the dispossessed Earl of Huntingdon. Even as early as the 1530s the antiquary John Leland reported that 'Robin Hood the noble outlaw' was buried at Kirklees Priory. But this development is really false to the spirit of the legend; the Huntingdon story may have arisen out of some association with Randolf Earl of Chester – about whose legend we know nothing – whose heir was the Earl of Huntingdon. The true Robin Hood is a yeoman, and he expresses many of the attitudes of the medieval yeoman. Furthermore, although his courtesy is emphasised, he has an easygoing attitude to his fellows, whom he treats as equals in the way that a noble, or a hero meant to appeal to noble audiences, would not.

His other great attribute, skill at archery, is also typical of a yeoman, and it is this which serves to date the stories most closely. The longbow was borrowed by the English from the Welsh after Edward I's campaign in Wales at the end of the 13th century, and gradually came into general use throughout England during the 14th century. The first great victory won with the longbow was against the Scots at Halidon Hill in 1333, soon followed by the even more spectacular triumphs over the supposedly invincible knights of France at Crécy in 1346 and at Poitiers ten years later. So by the middle of the 14th century the archer was something of a national hero. Archery was popular, and from the end of the 13th century everyone who was not a knight or wealthy enough to have more elaborate weapons had to possess a bow, though this need not have been a longbow. Archery practice was a common recreation on holidays.

One other aspect of the stories also rings true for this period. Archers in the royal armies were often violent and lawless men, who enlisted in order to earn pardons for their crimes. At the end of a campaign, the king's clerks would make out huge lists of those who had been rewarded in this way; it was cheaper than paying the bonuses which other soldiers expected at such a time, and the ease with which Robin Hood gains a pardon because of his skill in archery when he meets the king may be a memory of this practice.

All we can say about Robin Hood himself is that the details of his character are 14th-century, and must be earlier than 1377, but that this does not exclude the possibility that someone reworked older traditions, perhaps from the 13th century, and added contemporary details. The next stage in the development of the stories was the addition of other tales that had once been quite separate. The most important – and most ingenious – addition was that of the Sheriff of Nottingham, who may have been a comic figure with his own cycle of tales, perhaps as a popular retaliation to an official who was disliked. The Sheriff of Nottingham represented bad justice in a position of authority; Robin Hood was his complete opposite, a naturally just man deprived of justice. The sheriff was the perfect foil to Robin Hood, and quickly became a central part of his legend. Again, if we want to look for historical figures, there is little to go on, but two candidates have been suggested: Philip Mark, who was actually both sheriff and custodian of Sherwood Forest from 1210 to 1217, and Brian de Lisle, Sheriff of Yorkshire (not Nottingham), who had been chief justice of Sherwood Forest from 1221 to 1224. But the character of the sheriff in the ballads has developed to meet the requirements of the poets: so the sheriff is at first foolish and easily tricked, and then suddenly – because the story requires it – cruel and cunning.

Robin Hood's 'Merry Men', however, unlike several of the knights of King Arthur's court, have no independent existence that can be traced. However, Friar Tuck and Maid Marian have a different origin. In the traditional French pastoral poems of the 13th century, and in Adam de la Halle's play of c.1275 based on these poems, a shepherd called Robin appears with his lady-love Marian. Later, popular versions of the story were probably brought to England, where 'Robin' was quickly identified with Robin Hood. Another stock character of these popular plays, performed as part of the May-time celebrations, was a fat and jovial friar: he, like Marian, made his way into the ballads, where he was identified with Friar Tuck, apparently already one of Robin Hood's followers. There is a reference to the leader of a band of robbers calling himself 'Friar Tuck' as early as 1417, and the first known Robin Hood play of about 1470 portrays him as simply one of the outlaws, 'plucking his bow' with the rest in a fight against the sheriff. Friars were often the butt of satire, and the idea of a renegade friar among Robin Hood's men belongs to the same vein of satire as the scenes with the Sheriff of Nottingham. His character in the May Day plays, however, was much more that of a jovial buffoon and glutton; and so we get the well-loved figure of later stories, a pleasant companion and mighty trencherman who can none the less stand up for himself in a fight. The story of how a friar became a member of Robin Hood's men seems to have other, older traditions in it: the friar and Robin Hood each carry the other across a stream, before the friar throws Robin in, in a parody of the legend of St Christopher. Then Robin summons his men with three blasts of his horn, but the friar whistles up a pack of savage dogs, and Robin admits that he has met his match.

So, in our search for Robin Hood and his men in their historical setting, we are left with elusive shadows. All that we can say is that the stories as we have them are the debris of two, perhaps three centuries of medieval stories about famous outlaws and their adventures. When the stories were put into print, they were already old and had been reworked many times. Yet the legend is none the less fairly coherent.

At the end of the 15th century, Robin Hood appears in another form of popular entertainment, the plays performed at festivals such as May Day and Christmas, which
survived into the early 20th century as mummers' plays. A fragment of such a play
dating from around 1475 survives, and is closely related to the events in the ballad
Robin Hood and Guy of Gisborne, and to *A Gest of Robyn Hode*. The text is extremely
brief, consisting of forty-two lines, and clearly the mock combats which the words imply
formed most of the action. At about the same time, Sir John Paston of Norfolk wrote to
his brother on 16 April 1473 that one of his servants, W. Wood, had just left him; Sir
John complains that 'I have kept him these three years to play St George and Robin
Hood and the Sheriff of Nottingham, and now when I would have good horse he is
gone into Barnsdale and I without a keeper.' Wood's duties were evidently more than
acting in plays; Sir John seems to mean by 'good horse' a good retinue of horsemen,
because he was just off to Calais. The reference to 'going into Barnsdale' is of course
another reference to the Robin Hood story: Wood had simply disappeared. The manuscript of the play may come from the Paston archives, and could be the actual text used
by Wood and his fellow actors.

Within twenty years of Sir John Paston's letter we have numerous references to
Robin Hood in May Day games organised by the local towns and villages. He seems to
have been a popular figure in the west country: as early as 1476, the churchwardens of
Croscombe, just outside Wells in Somerset, were paying actors who played the part of
Robin Hood; while in 1498 the corporation of Wells footed the bill for 'Robin Hood's
time'. In Worcestershire, Prior William More recorded payments to players in May, June
and July who acted Robin Hood and his men: in late June 1519, he paid 'rewards to
Robin Hood and his men for gathering at Tewkesbury bridge', while at the end of July
1513, there was a play of 'Robin Hood, Maid Marian and others'. May Day is hence a
misnomer: these were plays performed as and when a suitable occasion arose, chiefly a
summer, out-of-doors, activity. Elsewhere, as at Kingston-on-Thames, Robin Hood
appears with the morris-dancers.

Robin Hood only achieves dramatic respectability at the end of the 16th century.
Anthony Munday was the author of two plays in 1598 which were published in 1601.
The Downfall of Robert, Earl of Huntingdon was responsible for establishing several of the
popular traditions about Robin Hood. Robert, Earl of Huntingdon is in love with
Matilda, daughter of Lord Fitzwater. Richard I is on the throne, but it is during his
absence on crusade, and Prince John desires Matilda as his mistress. He contrives to
outlaw Robert, who takes the name of Robin Hood; complicated plots ensue, involving
Robert's uncle, the Prior of York, and the Sheriff of Nottingham, but all is resolved in
the end by Richard's return. The second play, *The Death of Robert, Earl of Huntingdon*,
has little to do with Robin Hood; Robert/Robin dies at the end of the first act, and the
main theme is Prince John's pursuit of Matilda and her tragic death at the hands of his
henchman. It is from these plays that the idea of Robin Hood as a contemporary of
Richard I became firmly established: Munday himself took the idea from an existing
tradition reported by the Scottish historian John Major, whose *History of Greater Britain*
appeared in 1521.

As the distance of time lent enchantment to the legends, so Robin Hood's life in the
forest became a kind of pastoral ideal. In *As You Like It*, Shakespeare echoes this vision
of Robin Hood, when Charles says of the banished Duke: '… he is already in the forest
of Arden, and a many merry men with him; and there they live like the old Robin
Hood of England; they say many young gentlemen flock to him every day, and fleet the
time carelessly, as they did in the golden world'.

By the beginning of the seventeenth century, Robin Hood was firmly established as
one of the great traditional literary heroes. As with other such heroes, his popularity
was to be seen in place-names, and a rash of Robin Hood's Wells or Robin Hood's
Stones appeared on the maps. By far the most interesting is Robin Hood's Well in

Barnsdale, near the site of a Robin Hood's Stone, which is recorded as early as 1422 in the charters of Monkbretton Priory and which links in the sites mentioned in the *Gest*. This may be a genuine tradition, if we accept the Barnsdale outlaw as the 'original' Robin Hood, though the transfer of the name from stone to well is unclear. The many other sites reflect the later popularity of the ballads just as Arthurian place-names followed the popularity of Arthurian romance. One peculiar name, however, is Robin Hood's Butts, found as a field-name in Cumberland, a name for two round hills in Herefordshire, and for three different groups of tumuli in the North Riding.

Most famous of all, however, is the mysterious site of Robin Hood's grave at Kirklees Priory. This tradition goes back to John Leland's reference to Kirklees in the 1530s as the site of Robin Hood's burial. Richard Grafton in 1569 is more explicit, attributing the setting up of the tomb to the Prioress of Kirklees, describing it as having a cross of stone at either end. By the early seventeenth century, the inscription was 'scarce legible' and in the 18th century there seems to have been some confusion. In 1730, the tombstone was said to have an effigy on it; by the 1780s it was said to be a plain stone with a cross on it. At the beginning of the century, this latter tomb had been excavated, but the ground below showed no signs of having been disturbed. Furthermore, at some time in the early 18th century one of the two brothers and antiquaries, Roger and Samuel Gale (which of them is not clear), had collected an epitaph said to have been inscribed on his grave; although this is composed in mock-medieval English – or perhaps Scottish – it does seem to have been engraved on a stone somewhere, at some time, before Gale recorded it. The whole thing looks like an amateur antiquarian effort based on the epitaph found in the chapbooks, and was probably written in the early 18th century.

How has the legend of Robin Hood survived so strongly into modern times? There have been no great literary works written about him, and although Keats devoted a poem to him and one of Tennyson's last works was a play entitled *The Foresters*, neither can be called works of genius. The real survival was at the level of popular retellings of the stories; just as the chapbooks and books of ballads called 'garlands' had kept his name alive in the 18th century, so versions for children such as Pierce Egan's *Robin Hood and Little John*, first published in 1840 and frequently reprinted, kept his name alive in later years. Indeed, it is primarily as a children's storybook hero that he has lived on in literature. It is difficult to find a single example of a serious adult novel or play of any merit about him in the whole of the 19th or 20th centuries, whereas Howard Pyle, Henry Gilbert, Carola Oman, and more recently Antonia Fraser and Roger Lancelyn Green have all produced children's versions which proved extremely popular.

To some extent, adult interest has been focused on the original ballads and on the scholarly arguments as to who Robin Hood might have been. Joseph Ritson's *Robin Hood: A collection of all the ancient poems, songs and ballads*, first published in 1795, was the first scholarly attempt to explore the legend, though Ritson also has a strong political agenda: for him Robin Hood was 'a man who, in a barbarous age, and under a complicated tyranny, displayed a spirit of freedom and independence, which has endeared him to the common people', whose memory monkish chroniclers had tried to suppress. Ritson's polemical edition was followed by F.J. Child's impartial work in his *The English and Scottish Popular Ballads* (1882–98). Since then the quest for the 'real' Robin Hood has aroused considerable interest; distinguished works on the subject include Maurice Keen's *The Outlaws of Medieval Legend*, and, most recently, R.B. Dobson and J. Taylor's *Rymes of Robyn Hood*, an invaluable survey of the whole legend.

The other way in which the legend has been kept alive has been in films and on television. Even before the First World War, there were half a dozen silent versions, and Douglas Fairbanks made a classic version in 1922, in the most opulent Hollywood style. For the film versions, Robin Hood was always presented as the erstwhile Earl of Huntingdon, Prince John as the villain, and Richard I as the absent king, while Maid

Marian played a more important role than ever before, to provide a suitable part for a Hollywood leading lady. Fairbanks insisted on collected a huge library to ensure that historical details were correct, yet critics complained that his treatment did not follow 'the book'. Fairbanks quite rightly replied: 'If they know what book they're talking about, they have a distinct advantage over me.' The Fairbanks film was, of course, silent, and in black and white; so with the advent of sound and Technicolor, there was an obvious market for a new version, which was provided by United Artists in 1938 with Erroll Flynn as Robin Hood and Olivia de Havilland as Maid Marian; Flynn made a superb Robin Hood, handling the fights with great style. Of the post-war versions, the best was THE STORY OF ROBIN HOOD AND HIS MERRIE MEN produced by Walt Disney in 1952 and starring Richard Todd. The most recent example is Kevin Costner's ROBIN HOOD – PRINCE OF THIEVES (1991). There have also been television versions for the BBC and ATV.

And so this mysterious, romantic hero continues to fire men's imaginations. The Robin Hood we know today is a far cry from the violent outlaw who once stalked some northern forest; but the same independent spirit and the same protest against the injustices that any human society contains still lie at the heart of his story, and appeal to us today as strongly as they did to the 'good yeomen' of Tudor days or their medieval forebears.

RICHARD BARBER

Editions: Ritson 1795; Dobson and Taylor 1976; Wiles 1981.
Studies: Holt 1990; Knight 1994.

ROLAND (in Old French also Rollant) appears in the Carolingian epics as the nephew of → Charlemagne and stepson of Ganelon. The greatest of the twelve *pairs*, or paladins, and commander of the Frankish army, Roland is the leading character in the *Chanson de Roland*, a *chanson de geste*, the oldest extant form of which, the Oxford Version, was written around 1100 in an Anglo-Norman dialect. This text consists of *laisses* (stanzas of varying length with assonant ten-syllable lines) and has come down to us in a simple (storyteller's?) manuscript of the 12th century (Bodleian Library, Oxford). The content can be divided into four episodes.

The first of these contains the 'prologue'. After a seven-year campaign Charlemagne has brought almost all of Spain under his sway. Only the Saracen king Marsile still holds out in the city of Saragossa, but his army is too weak to take on the Franks. He therefore sends Blancadrin to Charlemagne with an offer to negotiate. In Charlemagne's council Roland warns that the Saracens are not to be trusted. His advice is to continue the war, but Ganelon thinks it more prudent to accept the offer. At Roland's suggestion his stepfather is then entrusted with the dangerous task of negotiating in Saragossa. Ganelon sets out under protest, saying that he means to have his revenge. The Saracens have little difficulty in inducing him to betray his people. It is arranged that Marsile will pretend to accept the Frankish conditions, while Ganelon ensures that Charlemagne and his army march for home over the Pyrenees, leaving a small rearguard under Roland's command to cover their retreat. The heathen will attack this rearguard and kill Roland, thus breaking Charlemagne's power for good. Ganelon's news of the so-called peace is received with joy in the Frankish camp. Despite two ominous dreams Charlemagne sets out with the main force, leaving his leading nobles, the *pairs*, and Bishop → Turpin behind with a smallish rearguard commanded by Roland and Oliver.

The second episode tells of the fateful battle at Roncevaux. Marsile surrounds the Frankish rearguard with a huge army and when Oliver learns of this vastly superior

son ause car la guerre dura depuis longuement·

Coment le duc rolant fist dresser vne quintaine deuãt
la cite de biene et coment oliuer la boutta par tie pui

Roland amuses himself at the quintain during the siege of Vienne. Grisaille, 1458, by Jean le Tavernier in a manuscript of David Aubert's *Croniques et Conquestes de Charlemagne*. Brussels, Koninklijke Bibliotheek.

hostile force he advises Roland to blow his horn Olifant. But Roland indignantly rejects the suggestion: it is a question of his honour, and his family's, and France's. He exhorts the Franks to fight bravely and Bishop Turpin gives them absolution. Shouting their warcry 'Monjoie' they charge the enemy. The first encounter consists of twelve lance duels between the *pairs* and a dozen Saracen commanders. All the heathen are defeated. Then the battle becomes general. Meanwhile, in France, a thunderstorm and an eclipse of the sun herald Roland's death. When there are only sixty Franks still alive on the battlefield Roland suggests blowing his horn. Now, however, Oliver strongly objects: it is too late. Turpin intervenes in the argument. He acknowledges that Oliver is right, but still thinks that Charlemagne should be warned; if the army turns back, at least their deaths can be avenged. Roland blows Olifant, Charlemagne hears it and gives the order to return to Roncevaux. On the battlefield, meanwhile, Roland has come face to face with the Saracen king Marsile. He cuts off his right hand and kills his son. Oliver is wounded in the back and strikes out wildly. He hits Roland. Roland bids his loyal comrade-in-arms a moving farewell. Then a bugle call announces the approach of the main Frankish force. The surviving Saracens take to their heels. The battle is over; only Roland and Turpin are still alive, but exhausted. Roland searches the battlefield for the bodies of the *pairs* and brings them to the bishop for his blessing. When Turpin gets up to bring Roland some water the effort proves too much for him, and he too dies. Left alone, Roland prepares for death. He tries to break his sword on a rock to prevent it falling into enemy hands, but Durendal remains intact; the rock splits in two. As he dies Roland thinks of his victories, his fatherland, his sword, his family and his lord, Charlemagne. Angels bear his soul to Paradise.

The third episode deals with Charlemagne's revenge. When the main Frankish army reaches the battlefield he grieves for the fallen, and above all for the loss of Roland. But soon he is told of the approach of a mighty Saracen army commanded by the powerful Emir of Babylon, Baligant. The two armies meet and a great battle ensues. It reaches its climax towards evening when the two princes face each other. Charlemagne staggers once under a powerful blow from Baligant, but then succeeds in despatching his opponent with the aid of the angel Gabriel. The Saracens flee and the Franks capture Saragossa. Marsile dies of chagrin at this decisive defeat. His wife Bramimonde returns to France with the Franks and voluntarily converts to Christianity. On the way Roland, Oliver and Turpin are buried in the church of St Romain at Blaye.

The fourth episode rounds off the story. On his return to Aachen Charlemagne tells the beautiful Aude that Roland, her betrothed, has fallen. On hearing the news the lady faints and dies. Ganelon is accused of high treason and a trial by ordeal proves his guilt. The traitor is quartered. When Bramimonde has been baptised and Charlemagne is hoping for a quiet night's sleep at last, he is sent a vision in which the angel Gabriel commands him to muster his armies again next day to do battle with the heathen.

The historical nucleus of the *Chanson de Roland* is to be found in the humiliating events of 15 August 778, when the rearguard of the Frankish army was ambushed and totally wiped out while crossing the Pyrenees. It was the end of an unsuccessful expedition which Charlemagne had mounted in the spring at the request of some local Saracen rulers who had sought his help against their lord Abd al-Rahman I, Emir of Cordoba. Following a long and unsuccessful siege of Saragossa Charlemagne suddenly changed his plans and returned to France without achieving his objective. In his *Vita Karoli Magni* (c.830) Charlemagne's biographer Einhart relates how the rearguard was suddenly attacked in the narrow mountain pass near Roncevaux by a band of mountain men, probably Basques. He names three of the Franks who died; one of them is Hruodlandus, Margrave of Brittany. Is this Roland?

Exactly how the story evolved from these historical facts has for a long time been the subject of bitter scholarly dispute. The so-called 'traditionalists' assumed a long chain of lost transitional stages, beginning with eye-witness accounts and ending with the writing of the Oxford Version. The 'individualists', on the other hand, take the view that the *Chanson de Roland* was created in one go around 1100 by a great artist who based his work on brief data in chronicles and a handful of local legends. Nowadays this distinction/ dispute seems somewhat dated. Most scholars now assume an oral preliminary stage in the story's development and a writer who composed the extant text making use of the oral material. This explains both the well-thought-out structure of the work and the text's oral characteristics. Indicative of such an oral stage prior to the writing of the Oxford Version are the fact that parents in France used the names Roland and Olivier for brothers as early as the beginning of the 11th century, and the *Nota Emilianense*, a brief Latin resumé of the Roland story included in a Spanish manuscript around 1070.

Comparing the Oxford Version with the historical facts, it is clear that during the part of the epic's development that is hidden from us many elements were added to the story. Ganelon's treachery was of course added to provide some excuse for the humiliating defeat. The band of Basque irregulars was replaced by an overwhelming force of Saracens for the same reason. But this latter change also brought the story into line with 12th-century reality, when the Christians were making every effort to reconquer the

Spanish peninsula from the Moors. For had not Charlemagne done exactly the same thing, and wasn't Roland a shining example of the *miles christianus*, the warrior for Christ? The *Chanson de Roland* breathes the spirit of the Reconquista; it may even have served as propaganda for the crusades to the Holy Land, though nowhere in the text is there explicit mention of this. The third episode with the battle with Emir Baligant is another epic addition to the history; its purpose was undoubtedly to conclude the story of the defeat with a victory. Finally, the narrative is expanded by the inclusion of Oliver, the only major character among the Franks who is not historical. His function in the epic is to counterbalance the hero, as is indicated in the text by the constantly recurring line 'Roland is valiant, Oliver is wise.' The two friends thus embody the twin concepts so beloved of the 12th century: *fortitudo et sapientia*, valour and wisdom. A true hero should possess both qualities, in equal measure. This idea is given expression in the two passages about the horn. It seems as though Oliver was added in order to provide an alternative to a Roland who relies overmuch on his prowess. The eponymous hero is indeed worthy of emulation for his valour; but his recklessness, which leads to his destruction and that of the Frankish rearguard, is condemned. In the end it is Oliver who gains Bishop Turpin's approval: the Church rejects the heroic ideal that seeks exclusively personal honour and sets in its place a hero who fights for God and uses his head.

The epic tale of Roland and Roncevaux was a great favourite in France. Alongside an oral tradition which was probably extensive but is now beyond our reach there developed in the 12th century also a written tradition. The famous Oxford Version is the oldest known representative of this, but already by the end of the 12th century it had been rewritten and the assonant rhymes replaced by pure rhyme. At the same time the narrative's content was considerably expanded, with some entire episodes being added, so that the number of lines was more than doubled.

The *Chanson de Roland* was also translated into other languages during the medieval period, and invariably adapted in accordance with the views of the translators and their patrons. About 1172 a priest in Bavaria, Pfaffe Konrad, produced the *Ruolandes liet*, a very free translation in Middle High German rhyming couplets. In this work the Christian element is greatly strengthened; the Frankish expedition is presented as primarily a religious campaign by the Christians against the infidel. The *Ruolandes liet* was in turn included in modified form in two later German cycles of Frankish epic: Der Stricker's *Karl der Grosse* (c.1230) and the *Karlmeinet* compilation of the early 14th century. Still very close to the French tradition is a translation/adaptation in Franco-Italian, a remarkable literary hybrid language in which certain Old French *chansons de geste* were made accessible in the 13th century to a North Italian public. Also in the 13th century, during the reign of the Norwegian king Hákon Hákonarson (1217–63), various Carolingian epics were translated into Old Norse prose. These translations were brought together to form the extensive cycle known as the *Karlamagnús saga*, and a translation of the *Chanson de Roland* forms the eighth section of this. Through this saga the story spread across Northern Europe; translations of (parts of) it are known in Swedish and Danish, and there are ballads about Roland and his defeat at Roncevaux which date from the late Middle Ages. In Welsh, too, a Carolingian prose cycle has been preserved. It dates from the first half of the 13th century; the section on Roland, called *Cân Rolant*, goes back to an Anglo-Norman version of the *Chanson de Roland*.

The Middle Dutch *Roelantslied* was probably translated from the Old French early in the 13th century. The text survives only in fragmentary form on small pieces of four parchment manuscripts, one rather larger remnant (557 lines) of a paper manuscript of c.1500 and in the rhymed passages in two prints of the chapbook *Den droefliken strijt van Roncevale* (Willem Vorsterman, Antwerp c.1520 and Jan van Ghelen, Antwerp 1576); the text of the chapbook is partly in verse and partly in prose. Together these survivals form a heterogeneous, but almost complete, Roncevaux episode (the second episode) from the *Chanson de Roland*.

The works mentioned thus far belong to the tradition of the *Chanson de Roland* in its strict sense; all are versions of the same story, even though some of them have been radically reworked. In addition to these, the figure of Roland also appears many times in other medieval works. In the story of → *Renaut de Montauban* from the late 12th century he provides the loyal counterpart to the rebellious hero of the title. Roland and Renaut, both of them nephews of Charlemagne, are admirably fitted to embody the feud between Charlemagne and Renaut's family in a duel which in any case ends inconclusively. Roland also represents the king in a duel in → *Girart de Vienne* (late 12th century); this time his opponent is Olivier, nephew of the rebellious Girart, and this duel too ends without a decision. It is presented as the beginning of the close comradeship in arms of Roland and Olivier, and this is reinforced by the proposed marriage of Roland and Olivier's sister Aude. The *Chanson d'Aspremont* (last quarter of the 12th century) recounts Roland's early heroic exploits: how he saved Charlemagne's life on the battlefield when the latter was nearly killed by the heathen prince Eaumont; how he acquired Eaumont's sword Durendal, was knighted by Charlemagne, etc. Two Occitanian texts about Roland date from the 13th century. *Roland à Saragosse* tells of the love between Roland and the beautiful Bramimonde, wife of the Saracen king Marsile. *Ronsasvals* takes an individual approach to the Roncevaux episode from the *Chanson de Roland*. An unusual feature here is the theme of Charlemagne's incest: he is said to have begotten Roland on his own sister.

Of the greatest importance for the dissemination of the Roland material was the *Historia Karoli Magni et Rotholandi*, usually known as the 'Chronicle of pseudo-Turpin' (→ Turpin). Chapters 21–30 of this Latin prose chronicle from the first half of the 12th century give a strongly clericalised version of the story of Roncevaux; the content, however, broadly conforms with that of the *Chanson de Roland*. This chronicle was thought in the Middle Ages to have been written by Bishop Turpin, who had himself been involved in the war; it was enormously popular, particularly among scholars. It became even more so when Vincent of Beauvais included it in his *Speculum Historiale*, and through the many translations of this in various vernaculars its influence reached well beyond scholarly circles.

In Italy the Roland material underwent a quite distinct development. There, in 1482, the Florentine poet Luigi Pulci published *Il Morgante*, a long poem in 23 cantos; it is a parody on the older, epic versions of the story. From the same period dates an unfinished poem on Roland in love, *Orlando innamorato* by Matteo Maria Boiardo. The highpoint of this Italian branch of the tradition is the *Orlando furioso* (1516, revised version 1532) by Ludovico Ariosto. This too takes an ironic approach, parodying the old heroic knights. While it retains the original setting of the conflict between Christians and Saracens, the main theme is the love between Roland and the heathen Angelica. Ariosto's *Orlando* had a considerable influence. It provided the model for, among others, *La belleza de Angelica* (1602) by the Spanish dramatist Lope de Vega and the operas *Roland* by Quinault/Lully (1685) and *Orlando* by Braccioli/Handel (1733). In 1778 Niccolo Piccini used a version of Quinault's libretto by Marmontel for the text of his Roland opera. Haydn's *Orlando paladino* of 1782 enjoyed great popularity. Reminiscent of Ariosto's masterpiece is a Dutch expression, 'een razende Roelant' (a raving Roland). The French tradition gave rise to the opera *Roland à Roncevaux* by Auguste Mermet, premièred in Paris in 1864 in the presence of Emperor Napoleon III.

Even today, the material of the *Chanson de Roland* is being retold and reworked in many ways. For example, it has been adapted for young readers and has appeared in strip-cartoon books. One striking instance, from the Basque publisher Ikusager Ediciones, is a strip cartoon by the Spanish strip-cartoonist and -writer Antonio Hernandez Palacios which gives the Basque side of events.

Scholarly study of the *Chanson de Roland* began in the 19th century. In France the great revival of interest in the Middle Ages at that time led to the rediscovery of the *chansons de geste*. In 1835 Francisque Michel excitedly announced his finding of the Oxford Version in the Bodleian. Scholarship worked hand in hand with pride in the country's culture to make the *Chanson de Roland* the national epic of France. From that time on there has been a never-ending stream of editions and studies of this and the other Carolingian epics; every year the *Bulletin bibliographique de la Société Rencesvals*, the international association of researchers in Carolingian epic, lists approximately three hundred titles.

Roland has left many traces in the visual arts of the Middle Ages. In particular, many illustrations have been preserved in manuscripts and old prints of works from the Roland tradition. But other portrayals too have survived: the hero appears in stained glass windows, capitals, frescos, woodcuts and tapestries; we find statues of him, he even turns up on playing-cards. Rita Lejeune and Jacques Stiennon have produced a detailed study of this iconography; what follows is a brief selection from their survey.

The earliest depictions they discuss are three capitals of c.1100 in the Romanesque abbey church at Conques. These show mounted knights in combat and men blowing horns. While it is difficult to prove that these are representations of Roland, we can assume that in the Middle Ages they were taken for scenes from the *Chanson de Roland*. Flanking the entrance to the cathedral in Verona are statues of Roland and Oliver. Dating from 1139, they were probably intended to remind contemporaries of the Carolingian empire, in which the two heroes were both protectors of the faith and exemplary subjects of their lord.

The Heidelberg manuscript of the *Ruolandes liet* (in the University Library), which dates from the last quarter of the 12th century, contains a brilliant series of 39 pen drawings illustrating the narrative. As in Verona, Roland is depicted as the sword-bearer, i.e. the Emperor's right-hand man. The same motif appears in a stained-glass window in Strassburg Cathedral. Made at the end of the 12th century, it shows an anonymous holy Emperor with two figures behind his throne. The Emperor almost certainly represents Charlemagne, who had recently (1165) been proclaimed a saint in the German empire, and the figures with him would then be the swordbearer Roland and his comrade-in-arms Oliver. In a sumptuous late-13th-century manuscript of Der Stricker's *Karl der Grosse* (Stadtbibliothek, St Gallen) the account of Roncevaux is illustrated with eleven large miniatures. They are among the most splendid achievements of medieval book illumination and were certainly commissioned by a secular ruler from Southern Germany.

Also worthy of mention are the miniatures in a manuscript containing Jacob van Maerlant's *Spiegel historiael*, from the second quarter of the 14th century, and the grisailles by Jean le Tavernier in David Aubert's *Croniques et conquestes de Charlemaine* (1458, Koninklijke Bibliotheek, Brussels). One of these grisailles illustrates a passage from *Girart de Vienne*: during a truce in the siege of Vienne Roland amuses himself at the quintain, a wooden figure with a huge club in its hand which rotated on a vertical axis. Knights used the quintain to practise the use of their lances; the trick was to strike the figure without being hit by the swinging club. Tilting at the quintain was a very popular sport in medieval times, at first for the aristocracy and later for the citizenry as well. The *Magdeburger Schöppenchronik* (1270–80) tells us that the sons of wealthy citizens engaged in this sport at Whitsuntide. They called the quintain 'Spielroland'; the name suggests a probable connection between the game and the gigantic statues erected from the 13th century on in many cities in Germany and elsewhere, for example in Halle (1240–45), Hamburg (before 1342), Bremen (before 1366), Prague (1352–1400) and Dubrovnik (1420). The origin of these so-called 'Rolandstatuen', often several metres in height, is contested. They are thought to symbolise the judicial power of the Emperor or, alternatively, the commercial privileges enjoyed by the citizens of the German towns.

In the 16th century we find some very striking portrayals of Roland. A manuscript of

1514 (Österreichische Nationalbibliothek, Vienna) depicts a Saint Roland. Since Charlemagne and other epic heroes were also represented as saints, this can be explained as an analogous phenomenon; but the veneration of Roland as a saint never attained any great significance. In a pack of cards preserved in the Archives départementales de la Seine-Maritime Roland features as the Jack of Diamonds. A very rare application is the use of the figure of Roland as a printer's mark by the Antwerp printer Roland van den Dorpe, to be seen for example in his *Die alder excellenste cronyke van Brabant* (Antwerp 1497).

H. VAN DIJK

Editions: Moignet 1969; Brault 1978; Van Dijk 1981; Segre 1989.
Translation: Sayers 1957.
Studies: Lejeune/Stiennon 1971; Owen 1973; Van Dijk 1981.

R OLLO (d. c.928) was a Norseman who settled in the valley of the Seine. He was given Rouen and the surrounding area in fee by the French king Charles III, the Simple, and became the ancestor of the Dukes of Normandy. What follows, though not always historically reliable, is the oldest and most influential version of his biography.

A rich king in Denmark (Dacia) has two sons, Rollo and Gurim. After their father's death they support the nobles in rebelling against the man who has set himself up as the new king; Gurim is killed in the struggle. Rollo leaves the country with six ships, sails first to the island of Scanza and then to England, where he makes a pact with King Athelstan. After narrowly avoiding shipwreck he and his men land on the coast of Walcheren, where he defeats Duke Reinier of Lorraine and Prince Radbout of Friesland, thanks in part to extra supplies sent him by Athelstan. He then sails south to the Seine estuary. On reaching there he does battle with and defeats the Franks at Pont-de-l'Arche, Meulan, Paris, Bayeux and Evreux. In Bayeux he marries Popa, daughter of Berengar; she gives him a son, William, and a daughter. During all this he also finds time for a second visit to King Athelstan in England. After a number of forays into the French interior the tide turns and he is defeated by the Franks near Chartres. King Charles offers him his daughter Gisela and a peace treaty in return for his conversion to Christianity. The treaty, concluded in Saint-Clair-sur-Epte, specifies that Rollo shall hold all the land between the coast and the Epte, i.e. Normany and Brittany, as an allodium or independent fiefdom. On this occasion the king demands that Rollo should kiss his foot in homage, but Rollo refuses. Soon afterwards Rollo is baptised and takes the name Robert. He makes gifts to seven churches, divides the land among his followers, and promulgates laws. When his wife Gisela dies childless he recalls Popa to his side and names William as his heir and successor. Weary with age and battle, he dies.

The historical Rollo was very probably the Norwegian Hrolf or Ganger-Rolf, son of Rögnvald, Count of Möre (Norway). Known for his affrays in the Orkneys, in Scotland and on the coast of France, he had established himself in the Seine valley before March 918, the date of an authentic document of Charles III the Simple which states that the king has given land to 'the Norsemen of the Seine, namely Rollo and his companions, for the defence of the [Frankish] realm'. This territory slowly but surely expanded, until by the time Rollo's grandson Richard I died in 996 it was roughly the size of the present region of Normandy. A Latin lament for Rollo's son William, written between 943 and 962, describes Rollo as a heathen who came from across the sea and married a Christian lady. There is no evidence for Rollo's marriage to a daughter of the French king, nor for Gisela's existence.

The tale of Rollo's adventures and his eventual settling in Normandy, as recounted here, comes from the Frank, Dudo of Saint Quentin, who was chaplain and chancellor to the ducal court. His history of the Dukes of Normandy was commissioned by Duke

Richard I (943–96) and his son Richard II (996–1026), while Count Rodulf of Ivry, half-brother to Richard I, is thought to have been Dudo's main source of information. Dudo devotes as much attention to Rollo's activities as the pagan commander of the Norsemen as to his leadership in Normandy.

The account of Rollo's sea-going adventures needs to be taken with a sizeable pinch of salt. This was certainly the view of Dudo's successor William, a monk of Jumièges, who reworked Dudo's chronicle about 1060 and added a continuation. William gives a drastically abridged account of Rollo's career: he appears on the scene only when the Danes arrive in Rouen. For him Rollo is a Christian ruler, not a reformed adventurer.

After William's death the chronicle of the Dukes of Normandy was again reworked by various historiographers. The most widely circulated version was that by Robert of Torigni (d. 1186), later Abbot of Mont-Saint-Michel, which was written c.1139. He restored all the material on Rollo omitted by William of Jumièges, thus more or less recreating Dudo's original narrative. Both versions are also found in the vernacular. The poet Wace reworked William of Jumièges' version c.1170 in his famous *Roman de Rou*, while his successor and rival Benoît de Sainte Maure produced an almost literal translation of Robert of Torigni's – and thus Dudo's – account. The *Chroniques de Normandie*, for instance, written in the 14th or 15th century, contain the same version of Rollo's heroic deeds as we find in Dudo.

In England and France Rollo has always been overshadowed by the most famous of his descendants, William the Conqueror. We catch a glimpse of his renown in 1617, when the dramatist John Fletcher (1579–1625) reworks the classical story of Bassianus and Geta and sets it in medieval Normandy under the title *The Bloody Brother or Rollo duke of Normandy*. In Falaise, birthplace of William the Conqueror, a statue of William was erected in 1851; a small figure of Rollo was added to it a quarter of a century later. But Rollo has on occasion improved on this subordinate position; as in the rebuilding of Caen in the 1970s, when he was granted an equal place with Richard I and William the Conqueror on the facade of the new university building.

E.M.C. VAN HOUTS

Edition: Van Houts 1992–95.
Study: Douglas 1942.

ROTHER, King of Bari, ruler of the Western Roman Empire, travels to Constantinople not once but twice to win the daughter of King Constantine. Rother is prosperous, he lacks for nothing, only – he has no consort. His counsellors advise him to take a wife so that he can produce an heir and ensure the succession. A much-travelled vassal recommends that he marry the beautiful daughter of Constantine of Constantinople; an undertaking not devoid of risk, since so far every suitor for the hand of Constantine's daughter has been ruthlessly killed by her evil-natured father. Luppolt, one of Rother's trusted vassals, takes on the task of delivering Rother's request. The king arranges a signal with Luppolt and his eleven companions: when they hear three songs sung to a harp accompaniment, Rother himself will be close at hand.

Luppolt and his friends reach Constantinople; when the king learns why they have come he has them seized and thrown into prison. Rother now decides to go to Constantinople himself under a false name (he chooses the pseudonym Dietrich). On arriving he claims to be a hero driven into exile (by Rother!) and enters Constantine's service. He hopes to meet Constantine's beautiful daughter and tell her of his intentions. But how is he to gain entry to her heavily guarded quarters? Rother/Dietrich devises a stratagem. He orders two pairs of splendid and costly shoes to be made, one of silver and one of gold. He has one silver and one gold shoe – not a pair – delivered to the princess. When she puts them on she notices the 'mistake'. The damsel, who of course would like nothing better than to possess the complete pairs, then invites the generous donor to her room; whereupon Rother gives her the missing shoes, reveals his identity and confesses his love for her. As he fits the shoes on her he takes the young woman's leg on his lap, and thus secretly performs an old folk betrothal custom. At his daughter's urging Constantine releases the imprisoned ambassadors, who recognise Rother when they hear him sing the pre-arranged songs.

The outbreak of war with the heathen king Ymelot throws Constantine's realm into confusion, and Rother takes advantage of this to remove his young bride from the city. When the couple reach Bari the girl turns out to be pregnant. Constantine is furious at her abduction. How is he to recover his daughter? On the advice of an old minstrel he fits out a ship laden with costly merchandise. In Bari Rother's wife, attracted by the precious wares, goes on board. The ship suddenly puts to sea and the lady is carried off against her will.

Of course Rother doesn't take this lying down. He gathers a great army and marches on Constantinople. He himself with a few trusty comrades secretly enters the city. Here he discovers that the heathen foe Ymelot has defeated his father-in-law Constantine. Ymelot's son Basilistius is celebrating his imminent marriage to Constantine's daughter – who is, of course, Rother's wife. Without being observed Rother and his men crawl under a table. He surreptitiously slips a ring on his wife's finger and she recognises him. However, he is discovered and taken captive. He is to be hanged. A signal from Luppolt alerts Rother's army in time; without difficulty they rescue the hero and defeat the heathen. Rother forgives his father-in-law Constantine and restores him to power. He then returns to Bari with his wife. Here is born his son Pepin, later to be ruler of the Western Roman Empire and father of → Charlemagne.

König Rother is a Middle High German 'Spielmannslied' probably composed in the middle years of the 12th century. The unknown poet came from the southern Rhineland, possibly from the Mainz area. The fact that the author appears to be familiar with Bavarian noble houses (he extols the Tengeling family from Chiemsee) suggests that we have here a travelling poet who had also spent time in Bavaria. With its unsophisticated form, in which assonances, irregular lines etc. are still quite happily used, the work belongs to an ancient, still pre-courtly narrative tradition.

The author of *König Rother* may well have been inspired by the adventures of the Sicilian king Roger II, who married a Byzantine princess and mounted various campaigns against Constantinople between 1143 and 1149.

The poem, devised according to the traditional narrative scheme of the 'bride-seeker' (→ Salman and Morolf), is strongly didactic in tone. The work demonstrates, certainly to the satisfaction of its aristocratic audience, the great superiority, both intellectual and moral, of Western chivalry to Byzantine society as represented by the malevolent Constantine. This theme is illustrated by engaging, humorous incidents. A prime example: among Rother/Dietrich's vassals is a genuine giant called Asprian. Constantine, seeking to intimidate his guest, has a monstrous lion roaming loose in the dining hall, pestering the guests and eating their bread, to the great irritation of Asprian. He seizes the brute nonchalantly in one hand and smashes it against the wall of the hall, breaking its back and ribs.

The high point of the first part of the romance is the mysterious stratagem of the shoes, by which Rother/Dietrich manages to win the princess for himself. A particular significance has always been attached to the giving and trying on of shoes in an amorous context, as we know from a late instance, the fairy-tale of Cinderella. The giving of shoes, originally a betrothal custom, later came to be seen as a courtly gesture, a sign of subjection to the lady (along the same lines, in Dutch a henpecked husband is known as a 'pantoffelheld', a slipper hero). Rother/Dietrich officially betrothes himself to his beloved princess and thus becomes, paradoxical though it may sound, a 'legitimate' abductor of his bride.

The epic's second part repeats the first with variations: if the first cycle centres on Rother's intellectual ability (the stratagem motif!), the second cycle emphasises his courage, with his military might bringing the final victory.

To judge by the many references to it in other works, the Rother material remained extremely popular throughout the Middle Ages. A similar betrothal-scene (with the trying-on of shoes) appears in the Scandinavian *Osantrix* saga which forms part of the extensive *Thidrekssaga* (composed around 1250).

In the 19th and 20th centuries the Rother story provided inspiration for many poets, among them G.L. Klee (1880), E. Taubert (1883) and H. Zimmer (1924). Ludwig Tieck produced one of the earliest translations, entitled *König Rother zieht einer Jungfrau die Schuhe an* (1808). A readable translation in modern prose is that by G. Kramer (1961).

J.H. WINKELMAN

Editions: Pörnbacher/Pörnbacher 1984.
Translation (in German): Kramer 1961.
Studies: Frings/Kuhnt 1968; Grosse/Rautenberg 1989.

R UODLIEB is the eponymous hero of a romance from the early courtly period, probably written around the middle of the 11th century in Southern Germany, of which only fragments survive. The young knight Ruodlieb leaves the familiar environment of his own country, much to his mother's sorrow, and takes service with the King of 'Africa'. His remarkable skill at, among other things, fishing wins him the confidence of the king. Ruodlieb uses an unusual bait, the so-called 'buglossa' plant. When this herb is worked into pills and scattered on the water, the fish eat it and are then unable to submerge; splashing about on the surface, they are easy prey for the fishermen. The 'great king' gladly takes the clever Ruodlieb into his service, even appointing him commander of his troops. In a border conflict Ruodlieb defeats his patron's enemy. With chivalrous courtesy he brings about a lasting peace with the defeated foe, the 'little king'. It is not vengeance but forgiveness of the enemy that characterises the admirable behaviour of the courtly prince.

Then Ruodlieb receives a letter from his mother which compels him to terminate his service and return to his own country. On his departure the 'great king' of Africa, highly satisfied with the young knight's heroic exploits, gives him both tangible and intangible gifts. First he receives two 'loaves'; he is to cut the first only after he arrives home, the second after his wedding day. The loaves turn out to contain costly silver dishes, packed full of gold and precious stones. In addition the king gives his protegé twelve 'golden' pieces of advice for his future life. The first three are: 1. Ruodlieb is advised not to trust a redhead, because such a one, carried away by anger, will forget all civil behaviour; 2. he should never, however difficult the road, ride through the farmers' standing crops; 3. on his journey he should avoid lodging with an old man married to a young wife, since the old one might well become jealous.

These three admonitions prove crucially important to the young knight's journey. He constantly finds himself in testing situations which enable him to put his patron's advice into practice. For example, along the way he encounters a red-headed fellow who promptly rides through the standing crops, occasioning great unpleasantness with the farmers. The redhead then finds lodging with an old man who has a young wife. Here, too, trouble is inevitable. The young woman makes up to the redhead in full view of her aged husband. When that night the old man catches his wife in bed with the red-haired one the result is a fatal struggle in which the interloper kills the old man.

Ruodlieb wisely steers clear of such problems, stays out of the farmer's field, and spends the night with a young farmer who is happily married to an older woman. He is courteously received by this seemingly ill-matched pair; their shared evening meal even has elements of the sacramental. The red-headed murderer, however, is made to stand trial. He tries to put the whole blame on the young woman and also attempts to involve his companion Ruodlieb in the case. While the fragmentary nature of the text makes it impossible to give an exact account of what follows, it is clear that the redhead does not escape his due punishment.

Great is the joy at Ruodlieb's homecoming. The valuable contents of the loaf given him as reward by the 'great king' are revealed. Ruodlieb's mother presses him to look for a suitable bride, so that heirs shall be born to complete their happiness. One of their advisers recommends a young woman; but Ruodlieb has secretly discovered that she is the mistress of a priest. As proof of this illicit relationship he manages to get hold of her headdress and garters, which she had left at her lover's house. Ruodlieb gives a package containing the incriminating articles to the unsuspecting messenger who, at the request of the family council, is to convey his offer of marriage to her; they are his gift to her. Recognising them, the unchaste woman naturally declines the proposal, flattering though it is – to the astonishment of the messenger. When he hears of her refusal Ruodlieb bursts out laughing.

Ruodlieb decides to go in search of a bride worthy of him. In her dreams his mother sees a white dove with a crown on its head. She interprets this as a sign of the future happiness in store for Ruodlieb.

The anonymous author, who may have been a cleric from the Benedictine monastery at Tegernsee, composed his narrative in Latin. Only fragments of Ruodlieb's story survive; almost half of it has been lost. Despite this, the content of the work is highly significant. With its exploration and idealisation of courtly chivalry it marks the beginning of courtly romance in Germany.

As we have already indicated, the first three pieces of advice given by the 'great king' have a concrete narrative function. Ruodlieb follows the advice, and this leads to positive results; the negative results are demonstrated by the contrasting figure of the redhead, who because he ignores the advice invariably runs into trouble. This section of the *Ruodlieb* follows the structural scheme of an ancient folktale, the so-called 'Ratschlagmärchen', also characterised by three pieces of advice which prove important to the fairy-tale hero at a later stage in his life. The 'great king's' other nine bits of advice have little influence on the subsequent course of events. They are items of general worldly wisdom whose validity needs no testing. In this second part Ruodlieb loses the character of the romantic hero on whom fortune smiles. He now becomes much more the Christian knight who in his striving for justice and order, his exposure of deceit, his protecting of the poor, widows and orphans, performs work pleasing to God. In this way the romance takes on elements of a legend. In this respect it is typical that it is not his love for a chosen lady that motivates Ruodlieb. On the contrary, the feminine element is far more a threat to the attainment of the masculine ideal.

The *Ruodlieb* failed to spark the interest of later generations. The work thus remains a unique specimen in the evolution of courtly romance. Various translations of it exist both in German (Langosch 1956 and Knapp 1977) and in English (Zeydel 1959 and Ford 1965).

J.H. WINKELMAN

Translations: Zeydel 1959; Ford 1965; (German) Langosch 1956; Knapp 1977.
Study: Haug 1974.

S ALMAN AND MOROLF are the main characters in a Middle High German
'Spielmannslied'. King Salman (a variant of Solomon) of Jerusalem is the ruler of
the whole Christian world. The wily Morolf (or Marcolf) is his (half-)brother. Against
her father's wishes Salman marries the pagan princess Salme (derived from Sulamit?)
from 'India' and has her baptised. However, the pagan king Fore is also interested in the
beautiful Salme. In his efforts to gain her for himself he can of course count on the help
of her father, who had never agreed to his daughter marrying Salman. King Fore heads
for Jerusalem and demands that Salman should hand Salme over to him. It goes without
saying that Salman, supported by his brother Morolf, rejects this demand.

This leads to a battle; Salman wins and Fore is captured. Princess Salme is entrusted
with guarding him, to Morolf's displeasure. Fore manages to gain power over Salme by
giving her a magic ring: she suddenly falls violently in love with him. With her aid Fore
escapes from his prison. Six months later Fore sends a minstrel to Salme with a magic
herb; after eating it she appears to be dead. Morolf is suspicious and, to establish the
truth, pours molten gold through her hand. But Salme, enchanted as she is, notices
nothing. She is laid in a golden coffin, but after three days, with the minstrel's help,
escapes alive and well.

Morolf disguises himself by assuming the skin of a Jew and – now totally unrecognisable – travels to Fore's kingdom, where Salme is living with her new lover. After much
wandering he locates the queen and challenges her to a game of chess. He is, he says, in
need of money and is prepared to stake his life against thirty marks in gold. But actually,
he admits, he is hoping that victory will win him the most beautiful lady at court. During
the game he notices how the sunlight falls through the hole in the queen's hand, despite
the fact that she is wearing a glove. Morolf is now certain that his opponent is the long-
sought Salme. While they are playing he manages by means of a splendid ring to spoil
her concentration to such an extent that she forgets all about the game. But Morolf is
betrayed by his very craftiness. Salme recognises her cunning opponent as her former
brother-in-law. Morolf is arrested, but escapes and returns to Jerusalem.

Salman now decides to recover his wife by force. He equips a great army and
marches to Fore's country. The soldiers conceal themselves in the woods; Salman
disguises himself as a pilgrim on Morolf's advice and goes to the enemy court. But
Salme recognises the pious pilgrim as her husband Salman. Fore's beautiful sister offers
to rescue Salman, but he declines. He is condemned to die on the gallows. Before it
comes to this, however, he gives a pre-arranged signal on his horn, whereupon Morolf
and his men come to his aid. Fore is hanged and Salme is taken back to Jerusalem.

For seven years Salman lives happily with his wife, who gives him a son. Then King
Princian appears at court in the guise of a pilgrim. He drops a magic ring into the wine
in Salme's goblet. Salme drinks the wine; she is now passionately in love with Princian
and runs away with him. Again Morolf sets out – this time disguised as a cripple – to
track down his faithless sister-in-law. He finds her in Akko with her new lover. Morolf
informs his brother Salman of this and then returns to Princian's realm with a mighty
army. At this time Salme is living on a rock in the sea. A mermaid offers to help Morolf
destroy the underground passage leading to Salme's dwelling. And so it befalls. Princian
is driven out. Morolf has no intention of entrusting the faithless Salme to his brother
yet again. He kills her in her bath to prevent her causing any more trouble in the future.
Salman marries Fore's likable sister and lives happily with her for another thirty years.

We know the narrative summarised above, the stanzaic 'Spielmannslied' *Salman und
Morolf*, only from late manuscripts, though the earliest forms of it probably date from
the late 12th century (1190?). Moreover, the German version is not the oldest
treatment of the material; this is to be found in two Anglo-Saxon redactions of about
1100. The starting-point for the story of Salman, which became extremely popular in
the Middle Ages, was the biblical tale of the Queen of Sheba who sought to test the

legendary wisdom of Solomon by asking him riddles (I Kings 10, 1–4). From Jewish tradition, which credited the king's opponent with superhuman, sometimes even devilish qualities, and possibly by way of Russian intermediaries, the story became known in the West. Already in the oriental-Byzantine tradition the god Mercury (his selection influenced by the Hebrew idol Marcolis?) sometimes featured as Salman/Solomon's 'demonic' opponent. The name is still recognisable, if in much altered form, in the medieval variants Marcoli/Marcolfus/Morolf.

The German poem still contains reminiscences of the old oriental legend of Solomon as handed down in talmudic, cabbalistic and oriental writings. At the same time, details from the Old Testament seem to have been worked into the narrative: Solomon was the lover of pagan women, his principal wife was Pharaoh's daughter. The name Fore in the German poem was probably derived from 'pharaoh'. That Salman eventually marries Fore's sister again seems to be a reference to the biblical account.

The epic principle of repetition determines the structure of the story to a marked degree. After Salman has abducted his pagan wife Salme she leaves him, albeit under magical compulsion, for another lover. Salme appears to be the prototype of the faithless, demonic wife who easily gets the better of the 'wise' Salman and whom only the subtle Morolf is able to deal with. The story, with its many humorous elements, remained very popular. In late-medieval Germany Matthis Hüpfuff of Strassburg produced a printed prose version of it (1499).

In the 12th century (or around 1200?) there appeared a Latin prose work entitled *Dialogus Salomonis et Marcolfi*, which is only indirectly related to the narrative summarised above. In this version Marcolf is a boorish fellow who turns up at Solomon's court with his ugly wife and is challenged to a debate. Among the topics the two of them discuss is the position of women; Solomon defends the fair sex, while Marcolf ridicules it with obscene jokes. Solomon's biblical sayings appear to provide the ancient nucleus of the debate. The oldest Dutch work in this tradition dates from 1501; it was printed in Antwerp by Henrick Eckert van Homberch with the title *Dat dyalogus of twisprake tusschen den wisen conick Salomon ende Marcolphus*. The Latin version had already been printed by Geraert Leeu in Antwerp around 1490. Short farces on the subject were also produced in the German language area, the most famous of them by Hans Folz (1513) and Hans Sachs (1550). In 1685 Christian Weise made a comedy out of it: *Comödie vom König Salomo*. The material retained its fascination down to the 20th century. In 1924 A. Paquet wrote a play, based on the chapbook, entitled *Marcolph oder König Salomo und der Bauer, ein heiteres Spiel*.

J.H. WINKELMAN

Editions: Schröder 1976; Hecht/Hecht 1977; Karnein 1979.
Study: Hartmann 1934.

SEVEN SAGES OF ROME save the life of a prince who is under sentence of death: each of them tells a story and thus wins one day's stay of execution. The outline that follows is that of the most widely disseminated version of the tale.

Following the death of his wife, the Emperor summons seven wise men to supervise the upbringing of the prince, his only child. They all accept the task and the seven-year-old boy is entrusted to their joint care. They retire with him to a country house near Rome, where he proves an apt pupil. Some time later the Emperor remarries, but this marriage remains childless. After sixteen years with the Sages his stepmother has the prince called home. The Sages and their pupil read in the stars that their lives will be in danger unless the prince maintains absolute silence for seven days after returning home; they agree that he shall do this, and so he does. At home, when all attempts to get him to speak have failed, the stepmother offers to take him into her care and cure him. But her efforts meet with no greater success. She tries to seduce him, and when he rejects her she stages an attempted rape. The court believes her. The death sentence is now a foregone conclusion, but the trial is postponed to the following day.

So that her husband shall see his son as a dangerous rival the stepmother tells the *arbor* story (the splendid tree cut back again and again to make room for a younger one, until at last it succumbs completely). Next morning sentence is passed. When it is about to be carried out the first Sage appears and as a warning against over-hasty action tells the *canis* story (a dog covered in the blood of a serpent is killed because it is thought to have devoured a baby; then the child is found unharmed beneath the overturned cradle). The execution is put off. That evening the stepmother tells the *aper* story (a shepherd kills a wild boar by using his cunning). Next morning preparations for the execution are resumed, but the second Sage appears and again persuades the Emperor to postpone matters. And so it goes on until the prince is free to speak again. Then the stepmother's deceit is exposed and the prince relates the final story, *vaticinium* (a son survives attempts to kill him by his parents, who want to prevent the fulfilment of a prophecy which says that they will serve him; he becomes a mighty prince, visits them, reveals his identity after they have humbly made him welcome and forgives them). In the framework story the prince forgives only his father; his stepmother goes to the stake. After the Emperor's death his son rules with great wisdom.

The framework story – the prince's upbringing by the Sages, the ban on speaking imposed on him when he returns home, which he obeys even when falsely accused of sexual assault by his father's wife (the Potiphar motif), his conviction, the repeated postponement of his execution and the happy ending when he is able to speak again and the truth comes to light – is oriental in origin. Scholars distinguish between an Eastern and a Western tradition, known respectively as *The Book of Sindbad* and *The Seven Sages of Rome*. Exactly where the story originated is uncertain, as is the relationship between the *Book of Sindbad* and the tale of the *Seven Sages*. India has long been regarded as the birthplace of the *Book of Sindbad*, but arguments for its Persian origin have also been adduced. Opinions also differ as to the route by which the material reached Western Europe, and the part played in this by oral tradition carried by crusaders or merchants.

Information on *The Book of Sindbad* (in Arabic sources) goes back to around the year 800. The oldest of the eight extant versions is the Syrian *Sindban* (10th–11th century). The Hebrew *Mishle Sendebar* may already have been in circulation in the 10th century, though the extant redaction dates from the 12th–13th century. In the oriental tradition one of the Sages, Sindbad, is charged with the prince's upbringing. Each of the Sages tells two stories (one about the dangers of acting hastily and one about the wiles of women). Each time the female complainant parries with a single exemplum to bolster the ruler's resolve to bring his son to justice. The prince relates one closing story.

About forty redactions of the Western narrative of the *Seven Sages of Rome* are known, grouped into eight versions by Gaston Paris (1876). There are considerable differences between some of these versions and redactions, and the relationships between versions are not always clear. The exempla are often changed and replaced by others, so that all the redactions together contain about a hundred different tales.

The *Book of Sindbad* and *The Seven Sages of Rome* have only four stories in common: *canis*, *aper*, *senescalcus* (a steward sends his own wife when his lord is looking for paid companionship) and *avis* (a lady disposes of a talking bird which betrays her infidelity to her husband). The great majority of the exempla in the *Seven Sages* are of Western origin. Some of them are taken from antiquity, such as *vidua* (the widow of Ephesus), *inclusa* (a lover abducts his sweetheart with her husband's co-operation, cf. Plautus'

Miles gloriosus) and *gaza* (a father and son seek to plunder the king's treasury for a second time, cf. the Rhampsinitos story in Herodotus). Others belong to the medieval 'matière de Rome', e.g. *Roma* (besiegers flee in panic from a faked apparition) and *Virgilius* (magical images produced by the poet-magus, the archer with the inscription 'Hic percute' and the 'Salvatio Romae'). The 'matière de Bretagne' is represented by *sapientes* (the child Merlin cures a king of blindness inflicted by seven magicians).

Because of the common features it is plausible to assume that the entire Western tradition of the *Seven Sages* is descended from a single predecessor (the non-extant 'proto-version' V). The oldest extant version (K) was written around 1155 and the proto-version V must therefore date from before the mid-12th century.

Versions K, D, A and M make up a first group in the Western tradition, and of these A is the most important. It comprises the prose *Roman des sept sages de Rome* (c.1200) and its six continuations: *Roman de Marques de Rome* (pre-1277) followed by *Laurin* (used c.1530 by Claude Patin for his *Hystoire de Giglan*), *Cassidorus, Pelyarmenus, Helcanus* and *Kanor*. Version A was reworked about 1300 as *Li Ystoire de la male marastre* (M; possibly intended as an introduction to the *Marques de Rome*, it shares only nine exempla with A). The French Version A was translated in the 13th century into Middle English, Middle Scots and Italian, in the 14th century into Swedish, Welsh (*Seith Doethon Rufein*, prose) and Middle Dutch (*Van den VII vroeden van binnen Rome*).

The most widespread version was H, the Latin *Historia septem sapientum* (c.1330). Between the 14th century and the 17th it was translated successively into German, Dutch, French, Latin, Spanish, English, Hungarian, Polish, Russian, Danish, Swedish, Icelandic, Bohemian, Armenian and Hebrew. The last quarter of the 15th century saw some ten printed editions of the Latin text (including those by R. Paffroet, Deventer c.1476 and G.Leeu, Gouda c.1479–81). A German version appeared in 1473 (Augsburg, Johann Bämler), quickly followed by the Dutch *Die historie van die seuen wijze mannen van romen* (G. Leeu, Gouda 1479, thirteen prints up to 1819). Most of these and other vernacular versions of H (such as the South Hessian *Von den syben weisen Maister*, late 14th century, and an unpublished Middle Dutch prose version in an eastern dialect) go back to the *Historia septem sapientum* itself, of which there are about thirty known manuscripts. There were two Latin reworkings of this, the *Historia calumniae novercalis* (printed by G. Leeu, Antwerp 1490) and the *Pontianus* (printed in Strassburg c.1510); the *Pontianus* was translated into Hungarian (and thence into Polish and Russian) and Hebrew. In 1412 the Alsatian Hans von Bühel adapted an existing German prose translation of H as *Dioclecianus Leben*. The 16th century produced a prose version by William Copland (c.1548–61, based on Wynkyn de Worde's print of c.1515), the *Ludus septem sapientum* by Franciscus Modius (c.1560, from German) and the Scottish metrical version of an earlier prose text by John Rolland (c.1575–78).

In the standard version of H the Emperor is called Pontianus and the prince Diocletianus. Much attention is paid to the moral of each exemplum; they also display characteristic features. Thus, *vaticinium* becomes a framework story for the → Amys-and-Amelis motif. The son who escapes death is called Alexander; in Egypt he wins the hand of the princess and a prospect of the throne, but first he visits Rome to improve himself at the court of Emperor Titus. There he meets his double Ludovicus, son of the King of Israel (in Middle Dutch, France), whom he helps to win the heart of Princess Florentina; with Ludovicus he then undergoes the same adventures as Amys and Amelis, from the duel to the curing of his leprosy. After this he visits his parents, as in *vaticinium*.

A striking version of the story which cannot be assigned to any of the versions mentioned is the Latin *Dolopathos* (prose, c.1190) by the Cistercian monk Johannes of Alta Silva (Haute Seille in Lorraine). Here the story-line of the *Seven Sages* is interwoven with the medieval Virgil legend, and after the prince has been saved from death the framework story continues with an account of his conversion to Christianity which is strongly reminiscent of → Barlaam and Josaphat. In the *Dolopathos* the framework narrative occupies roughly half the work, partly due to the detailed accounts of many of the events; it has outgrown its original primary function as the framework for a large number of exempla.

The action is set in Sicily in the reigns of the Emperors Augustus and Tiberius. Lucinius is the long-awaited son of the good, though pagan, King Dolopathus and his wife, a kinswoman of Augustus. Just before his birth it is foretold that he will reign in great wisdom and serve the highest god. At the age of seven he is entrusted by his parents to a single tutor, the poet, magus and astrologer Vergilius (Virgil). After spending seven years with Vergilius in Rome he reads in the stars that his mother has died and his father remarried. Recalled to Palermo, before he leaves he has to promise Vergilius that he will not speak until they meet again. At home they think that he has been struck dumb by grief at his mother's death and try to cheer him up with music, beautiful women and other diversions. In the process his stepmother falls victim to her own zeal, with the usual result. After Lucinius has been condemned the (unnamed) Sages appear and each relates one exemplum. Soon after the happy outcome Dolopathos and Vergilius both die, and Lucinius reigns as a philosopher-king. Towards the end of Tiberius' reign a Roman citizen of Jewish origins enters the country and preaches about Christ. Lucinius summons him, receives private instruction and becomes a Christian after this catechesis has been crowned by the raising from the dead of a young man. Given the name of Priscus at his baptism, he abdicates his throne and departs with his new teacher for Jerusalem. Since then there has been no trace of him.

The *Dolopathos* shares only one exemplum (*canis*) with the *Book of Sindbad* and three with the *Seven Sages* (*canis*, *gaza* and *puteus*: a woman thrown out of her house by her husband for infidelity turns the tables on him by pretending to jump into a well). Of the remaining five stories, three are making their first appearance in the Seven Sages story: *senex* (during a famine a son saves just one person, his old father, and prospers by his advice), *viduae filius* (an Emperor gives his son to a widow whose only son he has killed – the early-medieval Trajan legend) and *latronis filii* (an old bandit buys his sons' freedom by telling a queen three of his own adventures, including his escape from the lair of a man-eating giant – the Polyphemus motif). For two exempla the *Dolopathos* is the oldest dated source. In *creditor* we find the pound-of-flesh motif, most familiar from Shakespeare's *Merchant of Venice*: a girl sets her suitors a test, charging them a fee, but magics them to sleep before they complete it; until one of them proves too crafty for her and so wins her hand. But he forgets that he has pledged his flesh and bones to raise the necessary cash; she saves him by dressing as a man and insisting that his creditor shall spill no drop of blood. *Cygni* relates the early history of the → Swan Knight: a knight marries a fairy and they have seven children, six boys and a girl, each of them born with a golden collar. The jealous mother-in-law waylays the fairy and her children; all except the girl lose their collars and turn into swans, but in the end all recover them save for one boy who remains a swan. In the first quarter of the 13th century the French poet Herbert produced a free translation of the *Dolopathos* (*Li romans de Dolopathos*) and fragments of a German version also survive.

Complete versions of *The Seven Sages of Rome* were incorporated very early into the *Gesta Romanorum*. The oldest dated manuscript (1342) of the Latin *Gesta* places the *Seven Sages* after the collection of exempla (though a single index covers both); in other redactions of the *Gesta* they are inserted – with or without moralisations – at various points in the collection. Individual exempla from *The Seven Sages* also found their way into the *Gesta Romanorum*.

Stories similar to those in *The Seven Sages* are often found elsewhere in literature, and the widespread reception of the very popular framework story certainly played a part in this. But most of the exempla were incorporated into the cycle only in the West, and continued to circulate independently of it (e.g. *puteus*, which appears in Petrus Alfonsi's *Disciplina clericalis* as early as the beginning of the 12th century); consequently, in the absence of named sources, salient details or other indications it is hard to prove that any specific instance is taken from *The Seven Sages*.

Motifs from the *Seven Sages* appear only rarely in works for the stage. Lope de Vega reworked *vaticinium* in *El pronostico cumplido*, in March 1599 (or 1600) a play based on *The Seven Sages* (by Dekker, Haughton, Chattle and Day) was performed in London, and in 1825 *inclusa* inspired A. von Platen to write *Der Thurm mit sieben Pforten*.

Until well into the 18th century the *Seven Sages* retained a place in French salon literature. A century later their principal domain was the folk-tale, particularly in Eastern Europe; as late as 1860 a Gaelic version attributed to the bard Neil Currie was recorded in Stoneybridge, South Uist.

The tale of *The Seven Sages* is rarely illustrated in manuscripts. Old prints and chapbooks contain the usual woodcuts, sometimes just the one title print showing the main characters of the framework narrative around the deathbed of Diocletianus' mother, sometimes complete series of some forty to fifty illustrations (Augsburg prints of 1480 and 1481 and a Strassburg print of the *Gesta Romanorum* version of c.1484). In the 15th century the tale was used as a subject for wall-hangings. Illustrations of individual exempla (such as that of *canis* in a 1835 etching by Codomi-Aîmé) are not necessarily based on *The Seven Sages*; Eugène Delacroix, for example, derived his *La justice de Trajan* (1840) from the account in Dante's *Purgatorio*.

L.J. ENGELS

Editions: Oesterley 1872; Campbell 1907; Epstein 1967; Weiske 1992.
Studies: Spargo 1934; Schmitz 1974.

S IBILLA, beautiful wife of → Charlemagne, becomes the object of a dwarf's amorous passion. This dwarf eventually tricks his way into her bed, where he falls asleep. In this situation they are discovered by Charlemagne. His intention is to have both of them burnt at the stake, but because Sibilla is pregnant her penalty is reduced to banishment.

Auberijn de Mondiser is charged with escorting her to the borders of the realm. Macharijs, whose idea it had been to banish her, scents his chance to rape her and rides after them. When he attacks her Auberijn manages to resist long enough for Sibilla to escape. In the woods she meets a farmer, Baroquel, who is willing to accompany her (as her 'husband') on her journey to her family in Constantinople. In Hungary she gives birth to a son; the country's king, Loys, stands godfather to the boy, who is named after him. Sibilla is bedridden for twelve years. The dead Auberijn's dog manages to make Charlemagne understand that something has happened to his master and that Macharijs is responsible. The dog defeats Macharijs in a duel.

Loys receives a knightly education at the Hungarian court. Some years later the journey to Constantinople can be resumed. Sibilla accuses Charlemagne before the Pope and eventually she and Loys invade France with a large Greek army, occasioning Charlemagne great losses. Two of the traitors are arrested, identified by Sibilla and hanged by Loys. Loys and the Pope call upon Charlemagne to restore his wife to favour, and this he does.

When Albericus Trium Fontium wrote his *Chronicon* (c.1240), a Latin history of the world, he also incorporated into it summaries of Old French *chansons de geste*, including this tale of the repudiated queen. In fact, in his fairly detailed summary he created what is in effect the oldest version of the story, since of the *chanson* itself only 13th-century fragments survive, in total a mere 500 out of an estimated 3700 lines. According to Albericus it was the French singers who named the queen Sibilla, while in reality the episode concerned Charlemagne's first wife, the daughter of King Desiderius of the Lombards, whom he discarded after only a year in favour of Hildegard. Here Albericus too was in error, for Desiderius' daughter was actually the second wife to be repudiated by Charlemagne; Himiltrude had already preceded her. For this reason one is inclined not to link this story directly to Charlemagne's life, particularly since Sibilla, unlike the two historical wives, is later restored to her rightful place. The theme of the queen unjustly accused of adultery features in many songs and stories from quite an early date. The tale of Queen Sibilla will have resulted from linking this theme to the Carolingian cycle.

The *Chanson de Sebile* was evidently very popular, for the fragments come from different regions of France. Of great importance is a faithful Spanish prose translation of the *Chanson* dating from the early 14th century: *Noble cuento del enperador carlos maynes de rroma e de la buene enperatris seuilla su mugier* (The fine story of Emperor Charlemagne of Rome and the good Empress Sevilla his wife). This Spanish version was printed around 1500 in much abridged form as the *Hystoria de la reyna Sevilla*. The Dutch version, *Historie van Sibilla* (Antwerp c.1538), on which the summary above is based, goes back to one of the reprints and differs at several points from the *Chanson de Sebile*. The unknown translator followed his Spanish source closely until the middle of the story, but from then on shortened it more and more.

A related version is to be found in *Macaire*, a verse romance from the first half of the 14th century. It is assumed that *Macaire* and the *Chanson* developed independently of each other from a 12th-century version of the narrative, since *Macaire* differs from the *Chanson* on some fundamental points. One striking instance is the different, probably authentic beginning of the story: at first Macaire tries to seduce the queen (Blanchefleur) himself; when he fails he incites the dwarf to the action that proves so disastrous for Blanchefleur. To dispose of the only witness he personally throws the dwarf in the fire.

At the beginning of the 14th century the story also reached Germany: *Die unschuldige Königin von Frankreich*, a verse romance which in a version by Schondoch has been preserved in thirteen manuscripts. The narrative shows correspondences with *Macaire*, but also contains many elements borrowed from other works. The queen does not travel to Constantinople, but takes up residence in a forest, a motif possibly taken from the → *Berte* legend. Around 1440 a cleric reworked this German version as the story of *Genoveva*. Also close to the *Königin von Frankreich* is the Italian version of the Sibilla story in the 14th-century *Storie Nerbonesi*.

The story's popularity is attested by the prose versions of it which appeared over the course of time. The *Noble cuento* is followed by the shortened version produced after 1430 by Countess Elisabeth von Nassau-Saarbrücken and based on the *Chanson*. In France a compiler added the narrative around 1450 to a prose cycle about Garin de Monglane. In connection with the story's popularity we should also mention Jean d'Outremeuse. In his *Ly Myreur des Histors* (c.1395) this Liège historiographer included a detailed summary of the story of Sibilla in his coverage of the years 818–831.

The post-medieval distribution and influence of the tale are in stark contrast to its earlier popularity. In the Low Countries it was not reprinted. One suspects that there it remained a 'foreign' work, soon overshadowed by other works with the same or related themes. There were other stories around, and in print, about the trials of ladies unjustly accused; among them *Helena van Constantinopel*, *Alexander van Metz*, *Griseldis*, *Frederick van Jenuen* and the already-mentioned *Genoveva*. It was above all in the version by the French Jesuit René de Cerisiers (1638) that this last work made its mark (first Dutch translation 1645), and its connection with Brabant – here the French queen is ruler of Brabant – meant that it took root in Dutch soil more readily than the Sibilla story. In Germany it also appeared as a narrative song and inspired visual artists, as witness two tapestries of c.1460 and 1472, one of which once hung in a court-room. Hans Sachs used the material for his *Comedi die Königin aus Frankreich mit dem falschen Marschalk* (1549).

In later times it was the episode of the dog which made the greatest impression, as can be seen from the fairy play *Le chien de Montargis ou la forêt de Bondi* by the Frenchman Pixerécourt, in which Charlemagne no longer appears. A year later the piece was translated by Castellis as *Der Hund des Aubry*. It enjoyed great success in Germany, largely due to the performance of the peripatetic Viennese actor Karsten and his performing dog. It was Karsten's appearance at Weimar that prompted Goethe to relinquish the management of the theatre there in 1817.

   R.J. RESOORT

Edition: Besamusca/Kuiper/Resoort 1988.
Study: Chicoy-Dalbán 1974.

SIEGFRIED is one of the principal characters in the Middle High German heroic epic *Nibelungenlied*, which was put into written form around 1200. In this epic Siegfried is the son of King Siegmund and Queen Sieglinde of Xanten on the Lower Rhine, and for this reason he is also called Siegfried 'von Niederland'.

   After a courtly upbringing Siegfried becomes a knight. He then decides to visit Worms, intending to ask for the hand of the lovely Kriemhild, sister of the Burgundian kings Gunther, Gernot and Giselher. His parents make every effort to dissuade him, but he refuses to listen to them. When he reaches Worms it turns out that Hagen, Gunther's chief vassal, already knows him. He relates a number of Siegfried's heroic exploits to his lord, exploits of which the reader of the epic was not previously aware. He tells of Siegfried's encounter with the brothers Schilbung and Nibelung, who once asked him to divide a treasure between them. In return for his trouble they gave him the sword Balmung, with which he then killed them both. Thus he gained possession of the treasure of the Nibelungs. From then on the name 'Nibelung' is consistently used for whoever controls the treasure. Hagen also tells how Siegfried succeeded in killing the powerful dwarf-king Alberich and by this feat acquired a helmet or cloak that conferred invisibility on its wearer. Lastly, Hagen tells how by killing a dragon and bathing in its blood Siegfried became invulnerable.

   After this brief summary of Siegfried's past history Hagen advises his lord to receive him with a great show of honour. After the formal welcome, however, Siegfried does not ask for Kriemhild's hand; instead he challenges Gunther to a duel for his kingship. Gunther and most of the Burgundians are outraged; but Hagen and Gernot manage to prevent the situation escalating, and Siegfried then decides to remain in Worms. When the Burgundian realm is attacked by the Danes and Saxons he fights alongside the Burgundians and ensures victory. After a whole year in Worms he has still not set eyes on Kriemhild.

   Then Gunther decides to propose marriage to the Queen of Iceland, Brünhild. It is known that she requires of each of her suitors that he should beat her in three trials of strength: he must be able to throw a boulder further than she can, jump further while wearing full armour, and throw a spear more powerfully. If the suitor loses he is killed. Gunther asks Siegfried to go with him. If their enterprise is successful he will be given the king's sister for his wife. On their arrival in Iceland it becomes apparent that Brünhild is already acquainted with Siegfried, and thinks he has come for her. Siegfried tells her that it is not he but Gunther who wishes to marry her and adds, falsely, that he is only Gunther's vassal. It is then Siegfried who, with the help of his helmet of invisibility, completes the three prescribed tasks, while Gunther merely goes through the motions.

   This deception initiates a train of events which cannot now be halted and which eventually leads to the deaths of all the main characters. They return to Worms and a double wedding. But Brünhild, believing Siegfried to be merely one of Gunther's vassals, finds it intolerable that Kriemhild should marry so far beneath her station. Her questions elicit no acceptable explanation. In bed at night she overpowers Gunther, binds him hand and foot and hangs him from a hook on the wall. From this it is evident that she has seen through the deception. The following night Siegfried comes to Gunther's aid, wearing his helmet of invisibility, and subdues Brünhild. He takes from her a ring and a magic girdle, the source of her supernatural strength, and gives them to his own wife. He and Kriemhild then return to Xanten.

Ten years later, during a family gathering in Worms, Kriemhild and Brünhild quarrel about their husbands' status. Kriemhild, who knows what happened that night, shows Brünhild the ring and girdle that Siegfried had taken from her and suggests that that was not all that happened. When she abuses Brünhild, calling her a concubine, Brünhild has had enough. Deeply wounded, she resolves that Siegfried must die.

The loyal vassal Hagen takes it upon himself to carry out her plan. He asks Kriemhild to show him on Siegfried's clothing the one spot

Brünhild, having overpowered Gunther in her bedchamber, has hung him on a hook. Drawing by Johann Heinrich Fuseli, 1807. Nottingham, City Museum and Art Gallery.

where he is vulnerable, claiming that he will then be better able to protect him in an imminent war. Only now does the reader learn that while he was bathing in the dragon's blood a linden leaf had landed between Siegfried's shoulders, so that in that one place he can be wounded. The unsuspecting Kriemhild does as Hagen asks. The war does not take place; a hunt is organised instead. When Siegfried, feeling thirsty, bends over a spring to drink Hagen runs him through from behind with his spear, hitting the spot indicated by Kriemhild. The body is taken to Worms and laid before the door of Kriemhild's bedchamber; when she emerges they tell her that Siegfried has been killed by bandits. But when Hagen walks past Siegfried's bier in church the wounds begin to bleed again, proving that he is the murderer. Kriemhild now has control of the Nibelungs' treasure and is thus in a position to make many friends. At Hagen's suggestion the Burgundians confiscate the treasure and throw it in the Rhine. With this the first part of the story ends.

Thirteen years after Siegfried's death emissaries arrive from the King of the Huns, → Attila, bearing the message that their lord wishes to marry Kriemhild. Among them is Margrave Rüdiger. Initially they have little success; again it is mainly Hagen who tries to prevent an alliance with Attila. Kriemhild herself shows little interest at first, until Rüdiger promises to serve her and avenge any injury that may be done her. Then Kriemhild consents and leaves for the land of the Huns.

After another thirteen years have passed she invites her family to visit Attila's court, insisting that Hagen shall be of the party. The Burgundians set out; just before they cross the Danube it is foretold that not one of them will return, but despite this they continue their journey. At the border of the Hunnish realm they stumble on the sleeping border guard Eckewart, who takes them to Rüdiger. They stay with him for some time, become friends and celebrate Giselher's betrothal to Rüdiger's daughter. Rüdiger then escorts his guests to King Attila's court. There a quarrel soon breaks out and escalates into a bloody conflict. The dilemma now confronting Rüdiger is described at length: he is bound to Attila by his feudal oath, to Kriemhild by his promise, but as the Burgundians' escort and Giselher's future father-in-law he also has obligations to the other party. He is the only one for whom the situation involves a conflict of loyalties. With the good of his soul in mind Rüdiger distances himself from Kriemhild, but his feudal oath to Attila is binding. He therefore has no choice but to take the field against the Burgundians, his kinsmen and friends, and is slain. Among all the other characters who blindly submit to the iron laws of fate, Rüdiger is the only one whose thoughts and actions reflect the spirit of the new age. At last only Hagen and Gunther are left alive; they are captured by → Theodoric the Great, who happens to be in exile at Attila's court. Kriemhild now demands that Hagen return to her the treasure of the Nibelungs, symbol of all he has stolen from her, but Hagen refuses to comply while his lord, Gunther, is still alive. So Kriemhild has her brother killed. When Hagen, loyal to his lord even after his death, still refuses she decapitates him with her own hands. Dietrich's old instructor in swordsmanship, Hildebrand, then kills the 'she-devil' Kriemhild. Siegfried's death has now been avenged, at the cost of countless human lives.

Siegfried also features in other works from the 13th century. In the epic *Rabenschlacht* he appears with Gunther as an ally of Ermrik (→ Ermanaric) and enemy of Theodoric the Great. He is defeated, but not killed, by Theodoric. No details about him are given, however, apart from his exceptional strength and horny skin. The epic *Rosengarten*, of which several versions have been preserved, tells that Kriemhild has a rose-garden in Worms, defended by twelve brave heroes one of whom is Siegfried. To test her husband's invincibility she invites Theodoric the Great to come and fight him in the garden. Theodoric wins and threatens to kill Siegfried, but Kriemhild manages to save her husband. *Biterolf* (of which only an early 16th-century manuscript survives) also tells of Theodoric defeating Siegfried in Worms. The so-called *Anhang zum Heldenbuch*, a prose summary of the heroic epics in the *Strassburger Heldenbuch* (c.1480–1590) which contains details not found in the epics themselves, explains the strife at King Attila's court as Kriemhild's revenge on Theodoric, who had supposedly killed Siegfried in the Worms rose-garden.

Siegfried's adventures before his arrival in Worms, related in the *Nibelungenlied* by Hagen, form the subject of numerous Old Norse poems and prose narratives and of a late-medieval German poem, the *Lied vom Hürnen Seyfrid*. From the various Old Norse sources, the most important of which are the old *Edda* songs ('Sigurðarkviða', 'Sigrdrífomál', 'Fáfnismál', 'Reginsmál' etc.), it is possible to reconstruct the following account. Sigurd (Sigurðr), as Siegfried is known in Old Norse, is born at the court of King Hjálprekr of Denmark and raised by the smith Reginn. From the broken pieces of the sword left to Sigurd by his father Sigmundr Reginn forges a new sword, Gramr, with which Sigurd cleaves his anvil in two. Reginn tells Sigurd to kill the dragon Fáfnir, Reginn's brother and the guardian of a treasure. Next Reginn tells him to boil the dragon's heart. When he burns his finger in the process and licks it, Sigurd is able to understand the language of the birds. He hears two birds talking about Reginn's plan to kill him and so get his hands on the treasure. Sigurd then kills Reginn as well, loads the treasure on his horse Grani and leaves. In Hindarfjall in Frakland he finds a girl asleep on a mountain-top surrounded by a wall of flames. In some sources she is called Sigrdrífa, in others Brynhildr. They swear to be true to each other and exchange rings.

Later he marries Guðrún, daughter of Gjúki, and swears fealty to her brothers Gunnarr and Högni. He changes appearances with Gunnarr and rides through the wall of flame for a second time to win Brynhildr for Gunnarr. Later Brynhildr and Guðrún quarrel about the qualities of their respective husbands. When Brynhildr then sees Guðrún wearing the ring she had given Sigurd, she resolves that he must die. Gutthormr, Guðrún's brother, kills Sigurd in his bed. The *Völsungasaga*, an Icelandic prose work of the 13th century, combines the Sigurd songs from the *Edda* into a continuous narrative. The so-called *Snorra-Edda*, a kind of manual for skalds (court poets), also contains retellings of Sigurd's adventures.

The German *Lied vom Hürnen Seyfrid*, preserved only in 16th-century editions, again recounts the youthful adventures of Siegfried, here called Seyfrid. He is the son of King Sigmund 'von Niederland'. After running away from home he stays with a smith, whose anvil he smashes into the ground. After this the smith sends him to a place inhabited by a dragon, hoping in this way to be rid of him. But Seyfrid kills the dragon, burns it and rubs himself with the dragon's melted skin, thus becoming invulnerable. In this text the daughter of the King of Worms, Kriemhild, has been abducted by another dragon. Seyfrid rescues her with the help of a dwarf-king.

The extensive Old Norse compilation of ancient tales called the *Thidrekssaga* (→ Theodoric the Great) combined all these elements, together with the deaths of Gunnarr and Högni at the court of Attila preserved in other *Edda* songs, into one coherent narrative. So great is the degree of correspondence between the content of this work and of the *Nibelungenlied* that one must assume that the German epic was among the compiler's sources. Siegfried is also the hero of more recent ballads in various Scandinavian languages. All these ballads deal with elements drawn from the same narrative material.

In the past, research into the figure of Siegfried concentrated first and foremost on the question of his origins. Because the most important events in the epic, as well as a number of personal and place names, appear to be based on historical fact, a historical model was sought for Siegfried as well. The historical event which certainly lies behind the account in the *Nibelungenlied* is the devastating defeat inflicted by the Huns on the Burgundians in 436 or 437 somewhere near Worms. According to tradition over twenty thousand people, including the entire royal family, lost their lives. The remnants of the Burgundians were resettled in Savoy. A Burgundian law-book of 513, the *Lex Burgundionum*, mentions various names: a King Gundovech, who died in 468, and his ancestors Gibica, Godomar, Gislahari (Giselher!) and Gundahari (Gunther!). The last-named is also mentioned in other sources as the king who suffered the great defeat of 437. However, at this time Attila was not yet leader of the Huns. According to a somewhat speculative hypothesis the name Gundovech, combining a typical Burgundian element (*Gund*) with a typical Frankish element (*vech*), would indicate that this king was the offspring of a mixed Burgundian-Frankish royal couple. Gundovech would have survived the 437 disaster because at the time he was still very young. It then seemed permissible to conclude that Gundovech's mother was a Burgundian princess (Kriemhild!), and the sister of King Gundahari to boot, while his father must have been a Frankish prince, Siegfried! The sources, alas, are silent on the matter.

A second historical model, according to other researchers, could have been Sigibert I of Austrasia. The Frankish king Chlotarius I had four sons, who after his death divided the kingdom among them. Sigibert received Austrasia and married the Visigoth princess Brunichild. Chilperik I, who had received Neustria, married Brunichild's sister Galswintha, having first divested himself of his concubines. One of them, however, Fredegund, worked on him so effectively that he had his wife murdered and married her. Brunichild then goaded her husband into making war on his brother to avenge Galswintha's death. In 575 Sigibert was assassinated. Brunichild now sought to avenge the death of her husband also; it would seem that she succeeded, for in 584 Chilperik was murdered while out hunting. These events too show a number of startling parallels, including various names and details, though some names seem to have been changed around: Fredegund plays Brünhild's role, Brunichild that of Kriemhild. Moreover, these events took place a century after the fall of the Burgundian realm and the period of Attila's greatest power.

A third suggested historical model for Siegfried is Arminius, the Germanic general who in AD 9 inflicted a crushing defeat on the Romans in the Teutoburger Wald. Arminius belonged to the tribe of the Cherusci, a word derived from the Germanic *herut* (hart, deer), and some have thought they could discern deer symbols connected with Siegfried in the texts. The dragon would then symbolise the Roman legions winding their way through the landscape, the horny skin would be Roman armour worn by Arminius. This hypothesis is not very convincing, however; though Tacitus does tell us that Arminius was later murdered by his own kin.

Scholars have sought the origins of the Siegfried figure not only in history but also in myth. The radiant young hero who comes into possession of a treasure belonging to spirits of the Underworld, who kills a dragon and in the end dies young: all this has led to Siegfried being equated with the god Balder. Elements from the Old Norse tradition of the story, in particular (the girl behind the flame-wall), provide material for this mythic interpretation.

Finally, there have also been attempts to explain Siegfried as a fairy-tale figure. It turns out that Europe abounds with fairy-tales about a man who seeks the hand of a woman on another's behalf, and one cannot deny that the account of the bedroom struggle between Gunther and Brünhild suggests a fairy-tale rather than a heroic epic.

The question of Siegfried's origin, however, is closely linked to that of the origins of the *Nibelungenlied*. And this is a very difficult problem to solve, not least because of the quite marked differences not only between the manuscripts, which date from the mid-13th century on, but also and above all between the various forms in which the story has come down to us, as the above summaries show.

Ever since the beginning of the 19th century scholarly circles have been engaged in a non-stop debate as to how the epic came into existence. The original view, influenced by research into Homer, was that the *Nibelungenlied* was the result of conflating a number of old songs drawn from oral tradition. The creator of the text as we know it would thus not be the original poet, but only the compiler and adaptor of older songs. When this 'song theory' was convincingly refuted, there were attempts to show that the text had developed by 'expansion' from two older songs. But this theory too proved untenable. The next, and almost universal, view was that the epic was composed around 1200 by a learned poet, probably a cleric, based on written sources. The text itself shows considerable local knowledge of the Danube valley between Passau and Vienna, while Bishop Pilgrim of Passau appears several times without really being integrated into the narrative. Since in addition most of the manuscripts are in Bavarian dialect, it is highly likely that it was in Passau that the work acquired its definitive form. It may have been commissioned by Bishop Wolfger of Passau (1191–1204), named in a legal document as patron of the minnesinger Walther von der Vogelweide. Attempts to discover the poet's name, though, have remained extremely speculative. Scholars have tried to establish what sources he had at his disposal; but even attempts to demonstrate the influence of certain French *chansons de geste* such as → *Renaut de Montauban* and of the Latin epic *Waltharius* have produced no convincing results. The remarkable fact is that no written source for the nucleus of the story has ever been found, even though it must have been widely known throughout the whole 12th century – a conclusion supported by the many and various quotations and allusions.

More likely, therefore, is that the *Nibelungenlied* was transmitted orally for centuries before being written down c.1200. If this is so, then the dearth of information about the poet and his sources is only to be expected. The text does in fact show certain characteristics of oral literature, such as its simple coordinative sentence-structure, restricted vocabulary, limited number of rhyme-words and abundance of epic formulae. But analysis of all these aspects has also failed to yield any generally accepted conclusions. The extant manuscripts do indeed differ from each other, but not so greatly that they can be regarded as the fixed forms of different oral renderings. Probably all of them go back to a single written text, expanded and adapted several times in accordance with the then still flourishing oral tradition. That same oral tradition will also have given rise to the other versions of the story, the *Edda* songs, the *Lied vom Hürnen Seyfrid* and the *Thidrekssaga*, while the many surviving representations of scenes from the Siegfried stories produced in Scandinavia and England from the 8th to the 14th century also attest to an uninterrupted oral transmission. For this reason it is quite impossible to determine the links between the various versions more precisely; we simply do not know when these versions became fixed in written form, nor whether any possible influences took effect before or after they were written down. In this the *Nibelungenlied* differs fundamentally from the courtly romances also written down around 1200, whose poets invariably tell us their names and often, in prologues or epilogues, their sources and their aims as well.

In interpreting the figure of Siegfried some scholars have started from the story's great age, some from the fact that the text was not written down until c.1200, depending on what they wanted to prove. For example, it is particularly difficult to explain Siegfried's behaviour on his arrival in Worms. His upbringing in Xanten and his decision to go in search of a wife can be seen as typically courtly, as can the fact that he spends a whole year in Worms without meeting Kriemhild. On the other hand, his challenging of King Gunther to a duel for land and people is frequently described as a typical archaic relic. It was therefore thought possible to distinguish the different layers from which the work was built up, namely a Germanic-pagan layer and a courtly-Christian one, and also different characters, with different norms and values. Nevertheless, the *Nibelungenlied* remained extremely popular for three hundred years after the time it was written down at the beginning of the 13th century; this is clear from the many quotations and allusions in other works and from the relatively large number of manuscripts (about 35) that have survived. All this certainly does not suggest that it was regarded as outdated or ambiguous. Siegfried's behaviour on his first appearance at Worms is certainly no relic from a heroic past; it is far more reminiscent of how knights behaved in Arthurian romances ($\rightarrow$ Yvain). But whereas in Arthurian romance the challenge to a duel for land and people is set in a fictional world, in Worms Siegfried finds himself in a real world. Unlike Arthurian romance, the *Nibelungenlied* gives the impression of describing historical events (as in fact it does), not least through its highly realistic treatment of time and space. Siegfried's conduct at the Worms court is thus not so much a survival from a past age, far more a demonstration of what happens when the knightly way of life is put into actual practice.

Quotations or references from the 12th century, e.g. in the *History of the Danes* by Saxo Grammaticus, which links Kriemhild's revenge with an incident in 1131, or in Heinrich der Glîchezâre's *Reinhart Fuchs* (c.1190; $\rightarrow$ Reynard), which mentions the Nibelungs' treasure, most likely relate to an oral *Nibelungenlied*. All later references probably relate to the *Nibelungenlied* as it was written down around 1200. This goes for Wolfram von Eschenbach's *Parzival* (c.1210), for *Dietrichs Flucht* and the *Eckenlied*, two heroic epics from the 13th century, and for many other works. In nearly all the manuscripts the text of the *Nibelungenlied* is followed by an account of events after the battle at Attila's court, describing the identification and burial of the bodies and the laments for the dead. This continuation is entitled *Die Klage* and it was probably also composed around 1200, making it the oldest extensive document from the reception of the *Nibelungenlied*. Two passages from the *Nibelungenlied*, Siegfried's catching of a bear during the hunt and the laments for the murdered Siegfried (here called Zegefrit) have also survived in a 13th-century Middle Dutch translation (*Nevelingenlied*). Whether these are fragments of a complete translation or merely of an episode is not known.

The tales of Siegfried's youth as recounted in the *Lied vom Hürnen Seyfrid* were later adapted by Hans Sachs (1494–1576) as the play *Vom hürnen Seufried* (1557), in which Siegfried appears as the prototypical ham-fisted, useless apprentice blacksmith. Until well into the 18th century a prose chapbook was also available (*Vom gehörnten Siegfried*, earliest extant print 1726). Siegfried's youthful adventures therefore continued in circulation without a break, in contrast to the *Nibelungenlied* which links the tales surrounding Siegfried's death with the fall of the Burgundians; after 1500 the latter fell into oblivion.

Following the rediscovery in 1755 of the first of the three oldest manuscripts of the *Nibelungenlied*, the last section of the *Nibelungenlied* and *Die Klage* were published by Jacob Bodmer (*Chriemhilden Rache und die Klage*, 1757). The first complete edition, based through an error on two different manuscripts, did not appear until 1782, and it was to be some decades yet before the work attracted the attention of a wider public. The first reactions, by the poet Goethe and the Prussian king Frederick the Great, were somewhat negative. But increased interest in the Middle Ages in general, and the reflection on the national past provoked by French domination under Napoleon in particular, have led since the beginning of the 19th century to innumerable editions and translations, complete, shortened or adapted. Of these Karl Simrock's somewhat archaistic verse translation (1827) merits special mention because it still remains in print. The content of the *Nibelungenlied*, summarised or retold, for adults or children, has also featured in numerous collections of heroic legends, books for young people and readers for school use. Under the headword 'Nibelungenlied' the bibliography by S. Grosse and U. Rautenberg lists exactly 500 titles, a large part of them relating explicitly to Siegfried.

The present-day Nibelung reception, however, begins with *Der Held des Nordens*, a drama in three parts by F. de la Motte Fouqué. As is clear from the titles of the separate parts, *Sigurd der Schlangentöter* (1808), *Sigurds Rache* (1809) and *Aslauga* (1810), the poet was influenced mainly by various versions from the Old Norse tradition, notably the *Völsungasaga* and the *Snorra-Edda*. In keeping with the taste of the time, the heroic element consists above all in the hero's defiance of Fate. The Nibelung material has been adapted for the stage more than a hundred times since then, but few of these treatments have stood the test of time. Those few certainly do not include the drama *Der Nibelungen Hort* by Ernst Raupach (1828). We must still mention it, however, not only as the first stage adaptation of the version preserved in the German *Nibelungenlied* but also for its influence on Friedrich Hebbel, the most important dramatist of the second half of the 19th century. Raupach reworked the adventures of Siegfried's youth, briefly summarised in the *Nibelungenlied* by Hagen, as a prologue to the drama proper. He also modifies the characters to fit his own time, and reduces the near-mythic events of the epic to commonplaces by supplying human motivations for them. Thus, Siegfried becomes a victim of political intrigue and the machinations of jealous women. Friedrich Hebbel's dramatic trilogy *Die Nibelungen* appeared in 1862. Hebbel (whose actress wife had played Kriemhild in Raupach's play) omits the earlier encounter between Siegfried and Brunhild, in Raupach one of the causes of the conflict. Instead, in Hebbel's drama Siegfried and Brunhild are destined for each other by Fate. When Siegfried then relinquishes Brunhild to Gunther he assumes a burden of guilt. Brunhild feels spurned and demands Siegfried's death. But in Hebbel's version Siegfried is already guilty because of his excessive excellence. As in so many of Hebbel's dramas, every man who raises himself above the mean must be destroyed; and this includes Siegfried. Also derived from Raupach is Heinrich Dorn's opera *Die Nibelungen*, to a libretto by Eduard Gerber, which had its première in Weimar in 1854 with Franz Liszt conducting. The influence of Meyerbeer and Wagner is unmistakable.

The most important 19th-century treatment of the Nibelung material is Richard Wagner's opera cycle *Der Ring des Nibelungen* (first complete production Bayreuth 1876). The third of the four operas in the cycle is devoted to Siegfried. The first, *Das Rheingold* (première Munich 1869), begins with the theft of a golden treasure by Alberich, a fabulous being who has abjured love and from the treasure forges a ring which gives its owner immense power. The god Wotan has a castle built for him by giants, but on its completion refuses to pay, whereupon the giants kidnap the goddess Freia. The only ransom they will accept is Alberich's ring. Wotan steals the ring and hands it over to the giants. Now they hold the power, the god has forfeited his freedom. Only a successor from the race of men can win back that freedom. In Part II, *Die Walküre* (première Munich 1870), Wotan begets twins, Siegmund and Sieglinde, on a human woman. He himself raises Siegmund to be a rebel with no respect for the laws of gods or men. Sieglinde is abducted and compelled against her will to marry her abductor. One day the fugitive Siegmund comes to Sieglinde's cottage and begets a child on his sister. Wotan now instructs the valkyrie Brünnhilde to withdraw her protection from Siegmund so that he shall die soon. Sieglinde gives birth to a son – Siegfried. The third part, *Siegfried* (première Bayreuth 1876), begins with Siegfried being raised by the smith Mime. One of the giants, Fafner, the possessor of the ring, has assumed the shape of a dragon. Siegfried kills the dragon and thus acquires the ring and a helmet which makes its wearer invisible. Warned by a bird, he kills Mime and leaves. He then encounters Brünnhilde the valkyrie, whom he finds sleeping behind a wall of flame. They declare their love for each other and Siegfried gives her the ring. In Part IV, *Götterdämmerung* (première Bayreuth 1876), Siegfried comes to the court of the Gibichungs on the Rhine where he meets Gunther, Hagen and Gutrune (the Kriemhild of the *Nibelungenlied*). It turns out that Gunther has set his heart on Brünnhilde and he promises Siegfried the hand of his sister Gutrune in return for his help. Siegfried assumes Gunther's form, overpowers Brünnhilde and recovers the ring from her. When Brünnhilde discovers the deception Siegfried has to die. When his body is burned the whole palace goes up in flames. Wagner's Siegfried has no notion of historical connections or hierarchical systems, of human or divine law. He has no reverence for power or possessions and detests everything old. He is, according to Wagner, 'the new man'. Wagner's Siegfried has been seen as personifying the romantic idea of the free man who breaks the power of capital, the wish-fulfilment of Rousseau's child of nature, bound by no historical or cultural ties, the unrestrained individualist who acts with ruthless freedom. Wagner's Siegfried very largely determined Siegfried's image both in Germany and elsewhere. For the scenes with the smith and the fight with the dragon Wagner drew on de la Motte Fouqué, as he did also for the gold-curse motif, which derives from the *Edda*. But not when it came to the question of guilt: Wagner's Siegfried is quite unconscious of guilt; he dies for the gods whose guilt he has taken upon himself.

Wagner also wrote a *Siegfried Idyll* for his wife Cosima, daughter of Liszt and previously married to the conductor Hans von Bülow, on the occasion of her 33rd birthday at Christmas 1870. Not only Wagner but many other composers have drawn inspiration from the *Nibelungenlied*. There are operas by M. Maretzek (1841), N. Gade (1852), E.L. Gerber (1857), H. Grimm (1891 and 1894) and M.J. Kunkel (1909), operettas by J. Piber (1889) and O. Straus (1904) and a musical play by K. Pottgiesser (1892 and 1893).

A curiosity are the fragments of a tragicomedy entitled *Der gehörnte Siegfried* by Friedrich Engels (1844). Poets such as Emanuel Geibel (*Brunhild*, 1857) and Gerhart Hauptmann (unpublished fragments from his literary estate, 1899 and 1933) also tried their hands at the Nibelung material. More recent are the stage versions by Paul Ernst (*Brunhild*, 1909, and *Kriemhild*, 1918), Max Mell (*Der Nibelunge Not*, 1942–51) and Reinhold Schneider (*Die Tarnkappe*, 1951). The last two treat the material from a Christian standpoint. Finally, in recent years elements of the Nibelung story have again been worked into plays, if with quite a different approach: F. Kuhn's *Kredit bei den Nibelungen* (1960), a piece in which the material is used rather unsubtly to draw attention to the threat posed by resurgent fascism in West Germany, Heiner Müller's *Germania Tod in Berlin* (1976) and Volker Braun's *Siegfried Frauenprotokolle Deutscher Furor* (1986). The last two authors see German history, which clearly includes the figure of Siegfried, as a succession of miseries which can only be overcome when people finally accept that the barbaric legacy no longer has any meaning for the present day.

Since the mid-19th century a great many parodies have been produced, among them Fritz Oliven's *Die lustigen Nibelungen* (with music by Oscar Straus, 1904). Here the Burgundian kings appear as wealthy businessmen in turn-of-the-century Berlin. The subject-matter of *Die Nibelungen im Frack* (1843) by A. Grün has nothing to do with the *Nibelungenlied*; the title refers only to the form in which this verse epic is written, the Nibelung stanza. Even more numerous, however, are the plays, serious in intent, which were (and are) performed by amateurs all over Germany and Austria. One such is *Die Nibelungen in Plattling*, performed for the first time in 1990. This Bavarian village receives only one passing mention in the *Nibelungenlied*, but this was enough to persuade its inhabitants to learn a play lasting four days, to be performed each year from then on.

There have also been many lyrical versions of scenes from the *Nibelungenlied*. Running an eye down the list of names and titles two things become clear: firstly, that more famous poets have been inspired to write poems by the *Nibelungenlied* than have sought to recreate the material in dramatic form; secondly, that Siegfried features far less strongly in the lyric. The lyric poets include the romantics Ludwig Tieck (*Siegfried*, 1804) and Ludwig Uhland (*Siegfrieds Schwert*, 1812), a century later Ernst von Wildenbruch (*Siegfrieds Blut*, 1909) and finally even Bertolt Brecht (*Siegfried hatte ein rotes Haar*, 1922).

Novelists too drew inspiration from Siegfried, among them Heinrich Lersch (*Siegfried*, 1926) who, like Richard Wagner, thought he could discern in Siegfried the New Man who would come to save Germany. It was not in the Nazi period, therefore, but much earlier that a view of Siegfried developed which saw in this fictional character the new man, Germanic man, the ideal German. As a result, extreme nationalist sentiments are detectable in many versions of the story. Since World War II most treatments of the Nibelung material have been satirical: A. Schmidt, *KAFF auch Mare Crisium* (1960), J. Fernau, *Disteln für Hagen* (1966) and A. Plogstedt, *Die Nibelungen* (1975). This is not the case, however, with the very popular version for young people by the conservative Austrian authoress Auguste Lechner (1960). A more recent version is Jürgen Hodlmann's *Siegfried* (1986).

The first half of the 19th century saw the production of innumerable drawings, prints and paintings depicting scenes or characters from the *Nibelungenlied*. Among the characters Siegfried is prominently represented. Along with scenes from his youth, such as at the anvil in the smithy or fighting the dragon, the most favoured subjects were the murder scene and Kriemhild grieving over Siegfried's corpse. This last was first rendered by J.H. Füssli (1805, Kunsthaus, Zürich) in classicist style. Füssli is also the author of *Chriemhilds Klage um Sivrit* (i.e. Siegfried). The Nibelung story was to prove a constant source of inspiration for Füssli. Of his paintings and graphic work we will here mention: 'Kriemhilde sees the dead Siegfried in her dream' (1805–10, private collection, Zürich), 'Siegfried bathing in the dragon's blood' (1806, pencil and pen with wash, City of Auckland Art Gallery, New Zealand) and 'Kriemhilde throws herself on Siegfried's corpse' (1817, Kunsthaus, Zürich). The relationship between Siegfried and Kriemhilde, especially, proved an inexhaustible source. Many prints were produced as book-illustrations and became well-known in this way. Peter Cornelius produced a series of seven drawings (now in the Städelsches Kunstinstitut, Frankfurt a.M.) for an edition published in Berlin in 1817. Particularly worthy of mention is the edition illustrated by Alfred Rethel which was published in Leipzig in 1840.

Scenes from the *Nibelungenlied* were also much favoured for decorating walls in palaces and public buildings. The Königsbau in the Residenz in Munich contains a number of Nibelung rooms with frescos by Julius Schnorr von Carolsfeld (painted between 1828 and 1867). The pen drawings for the designs of these have been preserved in the Kupferstich-Kabinett in Dresden. From 1843 dates a series of woodcuts based on these designs, prepared by Eugen Neureuther for the book *Der Nibelungen Noth* (Stuttgart-Tübingen, 1843). Also well known are the wall-paintings by W. Hauschild in Neuschwanstein Castle, built between 1869 and 1886 for King Ludwig II of Bavaria, those by Franz Kirchbach in Drachenburg Castle near Königswinter on the Rhine (built between 1882 and 1884 by a successful speculator) and those in Passau Town Hall painted between 1888 and 1894 by Ferdinand Wagner, to name only a few. The last great cycle of *Nibelungen* murals was that in the Cornelianum in Worms; it comprised seven monumental paintings, the work of Karl Schmoll von Eisenwerth (1910–13). The building was destroyed by bombing in 1945. As well as the mourning scene by Siegfried's body this cycle also included Siegfried's fight with the bear. Later a pen drawing of this scene was printed in a paper produced for the troops. With his aversion to naturalism and historicism Schmoll is part of the beginning of a new movement in the German visual arts, the so-called 'Flächenkunst'. Since that time there have been very few monumental murals of any importance. Around 1900 there appeared in Vienna a much abridged retelling of the *Nibelungenlied* by Franz Keim, published and illustrated by Carl Otto Czeschka, a typical representative of the Viennese Jugendstil, using very unusual typography. In this little book the text is entirely subordinated to the typography and illustrations. There are two known drawings of Siegfried by Aubrey Beardsley, inspired by Wagner's opera (1892, Victoria and Albert Museum, London; 1895, Princeton University Library). From shortly after 1922 date seventeen charcoal drawings by Ernst Barlach, strongly anti-heroic testimony to the artist's disillusionment; they were followed by another series of seven in 1935. They are in marked contrast to the portrayals of energetic heroes so beloved during the

Kriemhild (Margaret Schon) accuses Hagen (Hans Adelbert von Schlettow) of murdering Siegfried (Paul Richter) in Fritz Lang's 1924 film DIE NIBELUNGEN.

rise of National Socialism. It is notable that the somewhat casual Siegfried is now pushed out of first place by the much harder, ruthless figure of Hagen, who is hailed as the model of Germanic loyalty: Hans Gross, Nibelung frescoes (1939).The first decades after 1945 saw only very few portrayals of scenes or characters from the *Nibelungenlied*. An exception is Max Beckmann, who in 1949 took a number of scenes from the epic as subjects for his drawings. It is striking to see how disrespectfully post-war artists treat this material, which until 1945 had seemed so exalted. Nowadays the *Nibelungenlied* is no longer the subject of illustrations but of caricatures in drawing, painting and sculpture. Examples are K.H. Hansen-Bahia (1963), E. Kienholz (1973), A. Kiefer ('Notung', 1973, Boymans-van Beuningen Museum, Rotterdam), R. Hartmetz (1975) and Salomé ('Siegfrieds Tod', 1987).

Although innumerable monuments to historical and legendary personages were erected in Germany between 1815 and 1914, the number of Siegfried monuments is limited. One well-known example was the Siegfried Fountain in Worms (Adolf van Hildebrand, 1905). The Nibelung Monument in Pöchlarn on the Danube in Austria, unveiled in 1987, confines itself to municipal coats of arms; Siegfried is represented by the arms of Xanten.

The *Nibelungenlied* has been filmed several times, each time with a comparatively large measure of attention devoted to Siegfried's youthful exploits. This is true not only of Fritz Lang's DIE NIBELUNGEN (1923–24), with a scenario by Thea von Harbou (and influenced by Czeschka's graphics), but also of H. Reinl's filmed version (1966–67) and even Curt Linda's 24-part film cartoon series DIE NIBELUNGEN ODER WAS RICHARD WAGNER NICHT WUSSTE (ZDF, 1976). In the film SIEGFRIED UND DAS SAGENHAFTE LIEBESLEBEN DER NIBELUNGEN (director Adrian Hoven, 1970) the Nibelung material merely provides a pretext for filming pornographic scenes.

In the mid-1950s Sigurd became the hero of a series of strip cartoon stories as the unconquerable blond hero of a medieval Germanic fantasy world, a sort of German Tarzan or Superman (*Sigurd, der ritterliche Held*).

N.TH.J. VOORWINDEN

Editions: Translation: Hatto 1965; Brackert 1970; Wunderlich 1977.
Studies: Hoffmann 1979; Grosse/Rautenberg 1989; Thomas 1995.

SWAN KNIGHT is the name by which the hero is known in the first three branches of the Old French 'Cycle de la Croisade', which was written between 1100 and 1300 in Northern France and in Brabant. A great part of the cycle is devoted to the First Crusade (1096–99), with → Godfrey of Bouillon playing a leading role. The branches relating to the Swan Knight were added to this vernacular account of the Crusade to furnish Godfrey with a suitably impressive genealogy: the Swan Knight is his legendary grandfather.

The first branch, *La Naissance du Chevalier au Cygne*, reveals how the Swan Knight came by his name. The story begins some considerable time after the wedding of King Oriant of Illefort and the beautiful Beatrix. The couple are still childless when one day from the castle tower they see a woman with twins, whereupon Beatrix remarks sadly and rather enviously that a multiple birth is a sign of adultery. Unfortunately, that same night Beatrix conceives septuplets – six boys and a girl – who are all born with silver chains round their necks. Immediately after the birth Oriant's vicious mother Matabrune, who has no love for her daughter-in-law, removes the children and replaces them with seven puppies. She then commands her servant Marcon to take the children into the woods and kill them. Marcon is moved by compassion and so leaves them still living in the woods, where they are found by a hermit who takes their care on himself. Meanwhile, Matabrune tells Oriant that Beatrix has given birth to seven puppies and so merits the death penalty. But Oriant refuses to kill his beloved wife, though he does agree to her incarceration.

A few years later Malquarés, another of Matabrune's servants, comes upon the hermitage in the woods and recognises the children by their necklets. When Matabrune is told of this, she tells him to take the necklets. The hermit is away with one of the boys, so Maquarés manages to get hold of only six of them. The six children immediately turn into swans and fly to a lake near the castle of their father Oriant. Matabrune decides to have the necklets melted down and made into a goblet. But the goldsmith realises that one necklet is enough to make two goblets; he therefore keeps one goblet and the five remaining necklets for himself.

Some fifteen years go by, and at last Matabrune manages to convince Oriant of the necessity of putting Beatrix to death. She is condemned to die at the stake unless some champion turns up and fights successfully in her defence. Now an angel appears to the

The story of the Swan Knight. Clockwise from bottom left: Matabrune with the chalice; the Swan Knight with his brothers and sisters in swan form; the hermit tells the Swan Knight to go to Oriant's court to defend his mother; the Swan Knight after his victory at the court. Tapestry from Doornik, c.1460; last heard of in the Katharina church in Krakow.

hermit, explains the situation and instructs the remaining boy to set out next day to defend his mother. The boy, who (like Perceval) has been raised far from the court and knows nothing of knightly combat and customs (thus stressing that victory depends on trust and faith in God), goes to the town and is baptised, receiving the name Elias. He defeats Matabrune's champion, frees his mother and enables his sister and four of his brothers to regain their human form. The brother whose necklet was melted down has to remain a swan. After her champion's defeat Matabrune flees to her castle, where she is promptly besieged by Elias. Again he is victorious, and Matabrune ends up on the pyre intended for Beatrix. Elias then leaves, on the orders of an angel, in a small boat drawn by his swan-brother. While at sea he fights another battle and also has to deal with Matabrune's vengeful brother, but eventually he reaches Nijmegen.

In the second branch, *Le Chevalier au Cygne*, we see the Swan Knight arriving at Emperor Otto's court in Nijmegen. There he enters the lists on behalf of the Duchess of Bouillon, whose inheritance has been usurped by Duke Reinier of Saxony. After a violent struggle in which Fortune favours first one then the other the duke is defeated and beheaded by Elias. The Saxon party leaves court, burning for revenge. When she hears of the Swan Knight's victory the Duchess of Bouillon asks Emperor Otto for permission to take the veil and entrust her daughter and her inheritance to the Swan Knight.

After their marriage Elias and his bride Beatrix receive the bishop's blessing. When they are in bed together the Swan Knight asks her to be a good wife and never to ask him his true identity. While Elias is sleeping an angel appears to Beatrix and tells her that she will bear a daughter who on her marriage will become Countess of Boulogne and will in her turn bear three sons: a king, a duke and a count (the later King Baldwin I of Jerusalem, Duke Godfrey of Bouillon and Count Eustace III of Boulogne).

The newlyweds are escorted on their journey from Nijmegen to the fortress of Bouillon in the Ardennes by a detachment of imperial troops commanded by the Emperor's nephew Galien. The Saxons learn of their departure from their spies and with the aid of the traitor Asselin, Provost of Coblenz, they prepare an ambush. A bolting Saxon horse warns the Swan Knight of the imminent attack. A mighty battle ensues, and Elias and his men are in danger of being defeated. Galien is killed and as the tide of battle swings to and fro Beatrix is first captured and then rescued by the Swan Knight. A skylark urges the Swan Knight to attack once more and so the imperial troops triumph over the Saxons. The company can then resume its journey to Bouillon. Once there, Elias takes up the reins of government in exemplary fashion and his fame soon spreads throughout Christendom. Beatrix gives birth to a daughter who is christened Ida. The Swan Knight is warned in a dream of a new Saxon attack, and soon afterwards war duly breaks out. In the course of it the Swan Knight is wounded and the town of Bouillon besieged. When the situation begins to look hopeless for the besieged they call on Emperor Otto for aid and he swears to avenge his nephew Galien's death. The war ends with a further heavy defeat for the Saxons. In the newly established peace Ida grows up into a beautiful and intelligent girl. An angel prophesies to her that she will have three children who will found a kingdom in the Holy Land, but that she herself will lose her father. On her seventh wedding anniversary Beatrix resolves to ask the Swan Knight once more about his identity, thus disobeying his express command. Next morning the Swan Knight makes ready and leaves. He goes to Nijmegen and asks Emperor Otto to relieve him of his duties. His swan-brother takes him away in the little boat and he vanishes, never to return.

What happens to the Swan Knight after he leaves Bouillon is related in the third branch, *La Fin d'Elias*. It turns out that Elias has returned to his mother in Illefort, the home of his youth. At the family reunion they grieve over the one child who has remained a swan. Through the intervention of a white-clad figure a letter is delivered which tells the story of the swan-children, but also how the last swan-child can recover his human form. To achieve this, the two chalices made from his necklet must be placed on an altar with a bed between them, and the swan must lie on that bed while the Eucharist is celebrated.

We are then told of the recovery of the chalices and the ritual of transformation. Shortly before the death of his father Oriant Elias takes over the kingship. After a prosperous and peaceful reign – during which he builds a castle, named Bouillon in memory of his wife, in an area which he then calls 'the Ardennes' – Elias abdicates in favour of his eldest brother, also called Oriant, and becomes a monk.

The narrative then focuses on Elias' standard-bearer Pons (from the *Chevalier au Cygne*). Overcome by consciousness of his sinfulness as a man and a soldier he goes to Abbot Gerard of St Truiden. To gain absolution Pons decides to make a pilgrimage with the abbot. They travel via Rome to the Holy Land, where they are the guests of the Saracen Cornumarant in Jerusalem. Later this will enable Abbot Gerard to recognise Cornumarant when he visits the West on an intelligence-gathering mission. Having completed their pilgrimage Gerard and Pons return to the West. They are driven off course by a storm and find themselves in the mysterious land of the Swan Knight. They recognise nobody in 'new' Bouillon, but once apprised of the facts they realise that they have discovered the Swan Knight's true identity.

A meeting then takes place between Elias, Abbot Gerard and Pons, at which Elias asks them to bring Beatrix and Ida to Illefort for a reunion with him. At this reunion Elias tells them that he will die soon. He also prophesies that before long Ida will marry and bear three sons, one of whom will be King of Jerusalem. Elias gives Ida his riches and his arms, which she is to pass on to Godfrey.

On the journey back to 'old' Bouillon a dove brings the news of Elias' death. Beatrix devotes the remainder of her life to works of Christian charity. Ida is now thirteen, a beautiful, well-brought-up young lady receiving her first suitors. The early years of her son Godfrey provide the subject-matter of the next branch, *Les Enfances Godefroi*, which thus forms the bridge to the Crusade part of the cycle.

The story of the Swan Knight circulated extremely widely in the Middle Ages. The version given here is that which became part of the Old French 'Cycle de la Croisade' between 1170 and 1220 as three separate branches by one or more anonymous poets. The probable source of *La Naissance du Chevalier au Cygne* is a tale in the *Dolopathos, sive de Rege et Septem Sapientibus* (c.1190) by Johannes de Alta Silva (→ Seven Sages). It seems a reasonable assumption, though, that it was also influenced by stories current in the oral tradition. *Le Chevalier au Cygne* is certainly the oldest of the three branches and has its basis in a (possibly oral) tradition current in Boulogne and Bouillon which represents the Swan Knight as the grandfather of Godfrey of Bouillon, probably with the aim of providing the famous crusader with a supernatural or divine origin. The other two branches were undoubtedly written as continuations of this oldest branch: as *La Naissance du Chevalier au Cygne* explains the Swan Knight's origins, *La Fin d'Elias* tells what happened to him after the central episode.

The linking of these three branches with the crusade cycle is remarkable. The patron responsible is probably Duke Henry I of Brabant (d. 1235), who had acquired Boulogne and Bouillon by his marriage to Mathilde of Boulogne (d. 1211). Throughout the crusade cycle Godfrey of Bouillon is retrospectively made a Brabanter – in a document of 1289 Jan I of Brabant would refer to him as 'our forefather of old' – thus enabling Henry I to present himself as Godfrey's heir, both in his capacity as crusader *par excellence* and in his efforts to restore the Lotharingian realm. It would seem that over time some confusion crept into the Brabant image of the Swan Knight. Critical remarks by such writers as Jacob van Maerlant and Jan van Boendale show that it was not the Swan *Knight* who was regarded as the ancestor of the Brabanters, but a *swan*. Since humans cannot be descended from animals, in the late 13th century some people rejected the story. It was probably this controversy which led to the development after 1325 of a 'second' Brabant Swan Knight tradition. In this version the hero Brabon Silvius marries a lady called Swane, and it is from this union that the Brabant ducal house descends.

But it was the old French tradition, with Elias as the Swan Knight, that scored such a hit throughout Western Europe. Via the Spanish translation of the crusade cycle, *La Gran Conquista de Ultramar*, the legend spread to the Iberian peninsula. Extant fragments point to a similar process in the Dutch language-area. In English there survives a *Romance of the Chevalere Assigne* in alliterative verse.

Remarkably enough, in the German-speaking part of Europe we find two distinct Swan Knight traditions. On the one hand traces of the French-language tradition are clearly discernible: Konrad von Würzburg (d. 1287) evidently builds on the legend of the Swan Knight as linked to the 'Cycle de la Croisade'. On the other hand, and even before Konrad, Wolfram von Eschenbach's *Parzival* (c.1210, → Perceval) shows a different reception of the Swan Knight legend. Wolfram linked the Swan Knight story to that of the Grail, though without completely eliminating the Brabant element: Parzival sends his son Loherangrin in a boat drawn by a swan to a Brabant princess whom he is to marry. She too has to promise not to ask about her husband's identity; when she eventually does so Loherangrin returns to the Grail castle. Between 1275 and 1290 this story was expanded into an independent epic of 767 stanzas, the *Lohengrin*, which became the basis for a quite distinct German Swan Knight tradition.

The French-language Brabant tradition had a long, but far from uneventful life. Around 1350 the Old French crusade cycle was reworked by an anonymous (Hainault?) poet. This work, entitled *Le Chevalier au Cygne et Godefroid de Bouillon*, gives a shortened version of the original story and stresses the Flemish and Lorraine connections; for instance, the Duchess of Bouillon's troubles come not from the Duke of Saxony but the Count of Blancquebourc. Towards the end of the Middle Ages, between 1465 and 1473, Berthault de Villebresmes wrote a prose version of the Swan Knight branches of the crusade cycle for Maria of Cleves, widow of Charles of Orleans. The House of Cleves saw itself as the successor to the extinct House of Boulogne-Bouillon and incorporated the Swan Knight into its genealogy. Elias was thus able to visit Cleves rather than Nijmegen.

The Swan Knight's post-medieval career is documented in the many printed versions of the story in various European languages. In the Netherlands alone, the story was printed more than 25 times between 1500 and 1900. Via a French prose printed text by Pierre Desrey, *La généalogie avecques les gestes et nobles faictes d'armes du très preux et renommé prince Godefroid de Bouillon* etc. (first edition 1500), these Dutch printed texts go back to *Le chevalier au Cygne et Godefroid de Bouillon*. Remarkably, where the French prose text keeps the connection between the Swan Knight story and the crusades, Dutch printed versions break this link. Increasingly, the tale of the Swan Knight becomes detached from the history of the crusades and acquires its own message of edification and entertainment.

This edifying element in the chapbook tradition is very far removed from the three-volume novel *Chevaliers du Cygne ou la Cour de Charlemagne* published in Paris in 1787 by Madame de Genlis. Elaborating on the Cleves Swan Knight tradition, she weaves a kind of horror story around the legend. This was the last literary treatment of the material until 1848, when Richard Wagner completed his opera *Lohengrin* (first performed in Weimar in 1850). Wagner harked back to medieval epics for other of his operas; here his principal source was the stanzaic poem *Lohengrin* mentioned above. From our own century there is an illustrated reworking of the tale in Dutch entitled *Een schoone en wonderlijke historie van den Zwaanridder* which follows the Dutch chapbook tradition (Joh. Vorrink 's-Gravenhage 1930).

The Swan Knight was also a frequent choice as a subject for tapestries. A tapestry produced in Doornik c.1460 is now in St Catherine's Church in Krakow, while two others in the Hermitage in St Petersburg were made in Brussels in the early 16th century. They represent 'The marriage of Beatrix' and 'The triumph of Beatrix'.

G.H.M. CLAASSENS

Editions: Cramer 1971; Nelson 1985.
Studies: Jaffray 1910; Claassens 1993.

T ANNHÄUSER is the hero of a medieval German folksong of which several variants from the 15th and 16th centuries have been preserved. These songs tell of the knight Tannhäuser (Tanhuser, Danhuser) who lives for seven years with Lady Venus in her mountain and then repents. He travels to Rome and begs the Pope to absolve him of his sins. But the Pope offers him only the prospect of eternal damnation; he gives him a withered rose branch and tells him that when that branch blooms again his sins will be forgiven. Three days after Tannhäuser has returned to the Venusberg in despair the dry branch indeed begins to bloom. But too late.

It is likely that the miracle of the blooming rose-branch was added later, though still before the Reformation, as an indictment of the popes' excessive strictness. The Dutch version in the Antwerp Songbook of 1544 (where the hero is called Daniel or Danielken) makes its anti-papal sentiments very clear: the Pope fails in his duty by being much too harsh, it is his fault that a sinner is damned despite repenting of his sins: 'Accursed may they be, those popes who drive us down to Hell.' The ballad in this form is regarded as a typical product of the Reformation, but there are other versions which hint at Tannhäuser's possible salvation by having him die after a second expression of repentance, but before he returns to Venus.

The verse romance *Die Mörin* (1453) by Hermann von Sachsenheim speaks of Tannhäuser as Lady Venus' husband. The oldest extant Tannhäuser songs date from about the same period.

It is not known whether the hero of the Tannhäuser legend and the historical Tannhäuser, a knightly poet and minnesinger (c.1200–1270), are one and the same. Sixteen songs by this poet are recorded in the famous Manesse manuscript of c.1300. The little we know of the poet's person and origins rests solely on what he himself tells us in his poems. His description of a sea voyage to Palestine suggests that he may have taken part in the crusade led by Emperor Frederick II (1228–29). This has not been established with certainty, though a miniature in the same manuscript shows him as a crusader with a cross on his right shoulder. From a panegyric for Duke Frederick II of Babenberg we know that Tannhäuser had possessions somewhere in the Vienna area and that the Duke's death in 1246 must have marked the beginning of a period of poverty and rootlessness for him. That he had links with the house of Hohenstaufen is clear from a poem in which he commemorates Frederick II, Henry VII and Conrad IV. The last datable reference points to the year 1266. A manuscript of c.1350 from Jena includes under his name not only the sixteen songs but also a penitential song in which the knight of Venus appears as a repentant sinner. If this song really is by the minnesinger Tannhäuser, then there is indeed a direct link between the historical Tannhäuser and the legend. If it was attributed to him at a later date, it at least proves that when the Jena manuscript was written the Tannhäuser legend was already known by that name.

The starting-point for the modern versions of the Tannhäuser story is Ludwig Tieck's novella *Der getreue Eckart und der Tannenhäuser* (1800). Tieck introduces a second female character: the lady who was Tannhäuser's first love and whom he later deserted in favour of Lady Venus. After his disappearance she marries Tannhäuser's friend, but after Tannhäuser's fruitless journey to the Pope – and before his return to the Venusberg – he murders this first love.

Following the publication of a version of the old Tannhäuser ballad in *Des Knaben Wunderhorn*, a collection of old German folksongs published in 1806 by Achim von Arnim and Clemens Brentano, the material was used by several romantic poets, among them Heinrich Heine (1836) and Brentano himself (1852). The Tannhäuser story by itself, however, provided insufficient material for a stage play or opera. For this reason when E. Duller wrote his libretto for the opera *Tannhäuser* by C.L.A. Mangold (1846) he combined it with the tale of the Pied Piper of Hamelin, while Richard Wagner in his opera *Tannhäuser und der Sängerkrieg auf Wartburg* (première Dresden 1845) tied it in with the legend of the song contest at Wartburg (the castle of Count Hermann of Thuringia), giving Tannhäuser elements of the legendary minnesinger Heinrich von Ofterdingen. Wagner also added St Elisabeth of Thuringia (1207–31) to the story to represent divine love and counterbalance Lady Venus.

This Wagnerian form of the Tannhäuser story has been repeatedly reworked as drama, novel and verse epic, treated seriously or parodied. The stage versions, however, failed to cause any great stir, particularly since no outstanding writers ventured to treat the material. The original tale of Tannhäuser and Lady Venus has appeared in many collections of German folktales, including some for young people. In the 20th century Tannhäuser's name tends to be used merely as a symbol of lust. In the years 1894–96 Aubrey Beardsley wrote the parody *Under the Hill or the Story of Venus and Tannhäuser*, only a few fragments from which were published in his lifetime. In 1959 John Glassco published the work, completed by himself and with Beardsley's own illustrations.

Since the Romantic era the visual arts too have frequently drawn inspiration from the Tannhäuser legend, particularly for the adornment of public places. Well known are J. Aigner's wall-paintings of scenes from Wagner's opera in King Ludwig II of Bavaria's study in Neuschwanstein Castle (built between 1869 and 1886). Linderhof Castle, west of Oberammergau, has a Grotto of Venus constructed for Ludwig II, in which the lake with the gilded ship against a painted background of the Venusberg episode unmistakably derives from Wagner's *Tannhäuser*.

N.TH.J. VOORWINDEN

Edition: Thomas 1974.
Studies: Thomas 1974; Clifton-Everest 1979.

THEODORIC THE GREAT (Dietrich von Bern) is the main character of several 13th-century German heroic epics, the so-called Dietrich epics, and of the Old Norse *Thidrekssaga* of c.1250; he also features less prominently in a number of other literary works. The Dietrich epics are divided into historical and adventure narratives. The former category contains four works: *Dietrichs Flucht*, *Rabenschlacht*, *Alpharts Tod* and *Dietrich und Wenezlan*. From these four texts we can construct the following biography of Dietrich.

Ermrich (→ Ermanaric), King of Rome, tries to take over Dietrich's lands in Northern Italy. In the resulting battle Ermrich is defeated. But when some of Dietrich's men fall into enemy hands he decides to surrender his country in exchange for the freeing of the prisoners. He travels to the court of the King of the Huns, Etzel (→ Attila), where he is made welcome and spends a number of years in exile. In an attempt to recover his lands he again defeats Ermrich. He appoints a deserter, Witege, as castellan of 'Raben' (Middle High German for Ravenna); but after returning to Etzel's court to prepare for his marriage to Etzel's niece he learns that Witege has handed the city over to the enemy. For a third time Dietrich has to do battle with Ermrich; again he is victorious, but his losses are such as to make his position untenable; again he returns to Etzel's court. When he finally takes the field for the fourth time, supported by Etzel's troops, he is accompanied by Etzel's two young sons, Scharpfe and Orte, and his own youngest brother Diether. He is responsible for the boys' safety, having promised Etzel that they will not be allowed to take part in the battle; they are left in 'Bern' (Middle High German for Verona) in the care of the elderly Elsan. They are resourceful youngsters, however, and prevail upon Elsan to let them go out riding. In open country they encounter the traitor Witege. He has no wish to fight the children, but they attack him. He is forced to defend himself, with the result that the three boys are killed. Dietrich is in despair when he hears the news. He pursues Witege, but his quarry escapes by riding into the sea, where he is carried off by a supernatural being, Frau Wachilt. Dietrich's friend Rüdiger manages to convince Etzel and his wife Helche that Dietrich is not to blame and they forgive him. However, he has still not succeeded in recovering his kingdom.

In two later manuscripts this tale is preceded by an account of Dietrich's ancestors. They begin with a lengthy history of the great Dietwart, ruler of the Roman Empire, who is shipwrecked on an island on his way to his bride and has to kill a dragon before he can celebrate his marriage in Rome. He lives to the age of 400 and has 44 children, only one of whom, Sigeher, survives. Sigeher also lives to be 400; he has 31 children, of whom only one son and one daughter survive. The daughter is Sigelint, who later becomes the mother of → Siegfried. The son, Otnid (or Ortnit), is killed fighting a dragon. His wife Liebgart subsequently marries Wolfdietrich, the hero who kills the dragon. Since Otnid had died childless, it is this Wolfdietrich who is the actual founder of Dietrich's line. Wolfdietrich lives to be 503 and his son Hugdietrich 450. Thus, by the time Dietrich's grandfather Amelunc is born we have moved on five generations and more than a thousand years! The author not only worked all kinds of literary sources into this fantastic pre-history, including the saga of Otnit and Wolfdietrich; he also drew inspiration from the Old Testament, as witness the lifespan and numbers of children of the various ancestors. With Amelunc we return to historical times. On his death Amelunc, King of Rome, leaves his realm to his three sons: Ermrich inherits Apulia, Calabria and the Marches, Dieter receives Breisach and Bavaria, two territories north of the Alps, and the third son, Dietmar, is given Lombardy, Rome, Istria, Friuli and the Inn valley. When Dietmar dies his son, Dietrich von Bern, inherits these lands, but his uncle Ermrich tries to wrest them from him.

This is the situation at the opening of the current Dietrich biography. The oldest literary text to mention Dietrich, the Old High German *Hildebrandslied* (→ Attila), assumes this state of affairs; it says that Dietrich had been forced to leave his country thirty years earlier; not by Ermrich, though, but by Odoacer, who had made himself master of large areas of Italy. The third historical Dietrich epic, *Alpharts Tod*, of which only a fragment survives, describes a single battle during one of Dietrich's attempts to reconquer his lands, followed by the tragic death of a young hero. It therefore adds nothing to Dietrich's biography, unlike the – also fragmentary – *Dietrich und Wenezlan*, in which we learn that two of Dietrich's men have been captured and can be released only if Dietrich enters the lists against the Slavic prince Wenezlan. Dietrich marches against the enemy, a Slavic tribe, with Etzel and a large army. The two main characters engage in single combat. Dietrich is on the point of defeat when Wolfhart, a young hero from Dietrich's own circle, reminds him that this would leave the Roman Empire without an heir. Thereupon Dietrich attacks his opponent so violently that the latter is forced to flee. The story is set in the period when according to the other narratives Dietrich is living as an exile at Etzel's court, but is clearly later in origin than the stories concerning Italy. The same initial situation is also assumed in the *Nibelungenlied* and

Die Klage. In these works, too, Dietrich is living at Etzel's court and enjoying his full confidence. He tries to warn the Burgundians of impending danger and attempts to prevent an open conflict. When war eventually breaks out he refuses to take part. At the end, when all the Burgundians have been killed save for Gunther and Hagen, the brothers-in-law of Etzel's wife Kriemhild, he takes the two of them prisoner and delivers them to Kriemhild, urging in vain that their lives should be spared. Dietrich's role in the *Nibelungenlied* has often been interpreted as the one Christian note in an otherwise non-Christian story. He is indeed the only one to doubt the value of force as a means of solving conflicts.

The so-called 'adventurous' Dietrich epics have a number of features in common. In all of them Dietrich has to fight heathens, giants, dwarves or dragons, often at the request of a young lady or to rescue a damsel in distress. All of them are set in the valley of the Etsch (Adige) in South Tyrol. This is so in the epic *Virginal* (also entitled *Dietrichs erste Ausfahrt*) which tells of a heathen who invades the lands of Queen Virginal at a time when the young Dietrich blushingly has to admit that he has yet to experience an adventure. Together with his fencing master, old Hildebrand, he sets out, defeats the heathen and frees Virginal, eventually returning to Bern after numerous adventures. In *Sigenot*, of which two versions are known, Dietrich is captured by a giant but freed by Hildebrand. In the *Eckenlied* Dietrich again has to fight a giant. He defeats, but is at first reluctant to kill him; only at the giant's own request does he decapitate him. *König Laurin* concerns a battle with dwarves in the mountains of the Tyrol, with Dietrich again the victor. There is an extant sequel to this story, entitled *Walberan*. In a fragment of another epic, *Goldemar*, Dietrich is again engaged with giants and dwarves. In *Der Wunderer* a lady appears at the court of King Etzel and asks Dietrich to fight a giant for her. He defeats the giant, emitting fiery breath from his mouth as he does so. This narrative differs in several ways from the other adventurous Dietrich epics. Firstly, its setting is not South Tyrol but Etzel's court; secondly, there is a hint of the supernatural about Dietrich with his fiery breath; and lastly, the text contains a prediction of Dietrich's end: later he will have to do battle with dragons in the wilderness until the Day of Judgment. In all the other adventurous Dietrich epics he returns to Bern after successfully completing the adventure. And finally, it is a striking fact that in the Middle Ages the adventurous Dietrich epics enjoyed far greater popularity than the historical epics – at least, to judge by the far larger number of manuscripts and prints of them that were produced.

There is a third type of Dietrich epic, to which *Rosengarten* and *Biterolf* belong. In the former, Dietrich and his men are invited to fight the supposedly invincible Siegfried in a rose-garden in Worms; Dietrich wins and the Burgundians become his vassals. This story, too, mentions flames shooting from Dietrich's mouth; it is because of them that Siegfried has to throw in the towel. *Biterolf*, too, involves a battle between the heroes associated with Siegfried and Gunther in Worms and those who follow Dietrich. Unlike the adventurous Dietrich epics and *Rosengarten*, however, the action in *Biterolf* seems to cover the whole of Europe. Biterolf is a king of Toledo who has left Spain in search of adventures. He goes first to Worms to the Burgundian court, then travels on to Etzel's court in Hungary and campaigns with him against the Poles. Finally he accompanies Etzel on his march to the Burgundian realm on the Rhine, where there is not only a battle but also a series of knightly duels in which every hero in the literature seems to be involved. The story ends, however, with a general reconciliation. This fantastic narrative has survived only in a single manuscript of the early 16th century.

A complete biography of Dietrich can also be found in the Old Norse *Thidrekssaga*, a sizeable prose work produced in Bergen (Norway) around 1250 which incorporates material not only from the *Nibelungenlied* but from many other sources as well. In this text Thidrek, whose seat is in Bern, is the ruler of Amlungaland. Brought up by Hildebrand, in his youth he managed to acquire a helmet and two swords: the helmet

Hildigrímur, which originally belonged to the giants Hilldur and Grímur, and the swords Naglring, taken from the dwarf Alfrik (Alberich), and Ekkisax, which he won from the giant Ekka. Many heroes join his following, including Heimir, Vidga, Fasold, Thetleif and Sintram, who also appear in the German Dietrich epics (Heime, Witege, Fasold, Dietleip and Sintram). Dietrich undertakes a military expedition to Bertangaland, where his men engage in single combat with the followers of King Isung. In the last of these contests Thidrek kills Sigurd with Vidga's sword Mimung. Erminrik then forces Thidrek to leave his lands and take refuge at King Attila's court at Susat. On his way there he is made welcome by Rodingeirr at Bakalar. While in Attila's service he campaigns against Osanctrix and Valldemarr of Holmgard. He kills Valldemarr and his son. After twenty years in exile Thidrek returns to Amlungaland with an army provided by Attila. At the battle of Gronsport Attila's sons and Thidrek's younger brother Thether are killed by Vidga, who has defected to Erminrik. Vidga escapes Thidrek's vengeance by riding into the River Moselle. Rodingeirr takes the news to Attila and his wife Erka; he convinces them that Thidrek is not to blame and they forgive him. Next, a conflict with the Niflungar arises at Attila's court, but Thidrek takes no part in it until Rodingeirr is killed. He then kills Folker and captures Högni with the aid of his fiery breath. Finally he cuts Grimilld in two when he sees her thrust burning torches into the mouths of her wounded brothers Gisler and Gernoz. After serving Attila for 32 years Thidrek returns to Amlungaland with his wife Herrad and Hildebrand. On the way they have to defeat Elsung; they then come up against Sifka, who had seized power after Erminrik's death. After defeating him at the battle of Ran Thidrek now reigns over his country in peace and erects many fine buildings. On the death of Attila he acquires Húnaland also. After Herrad's death he kills a dragon to avenge King Hertnid, marries Hertnid's widow Isollde and does battle with bandits who are threatening her country. One day he sees a golden hart. Leaping onto a black horse that happens to be standing ready, he sets off in pursuit. Too late he realises that he is being carried off by the Devil. He pleads with God and the Virgin Mary to save him.

Finally, Dietrich von Bern also features in songs and ballads in various languages and from various periods. These include the already mentioned *Hildebrantslied* in which Hildebrant, in Dietrich's service, encounters his own son in single combat and has to kill him, the song *Van den ouden Hillebrant* from the Antwerps Liedboek, in which the same combat ends in recognition and reconciliation, the song of *Koninc Ermenrikes Dot*, a number of Danish and Faroese ballads and one of the Old Norse *Edda* songs. His name occurs without further details in three Old English poems: → *Widsith*, → *Deor* and the *Waldere* fragments (→ Waltharius).

Dietrich von Bern was the Ostrogoth king Theodoric the Great, born in 454. He belonged to the Amal family, as did King Ermanaric, who in the mid-4th century ruled an enormous empire extending from the Baltic to the Crimea, and who committed suicide after his army was defeated by the Huns in 375. Ermanaric's brother Wultwulf was an ancestor of Wandalar, who died young but fathered three sons, Walamer, Widimer and Theodemer, the last of whom was the father of Theodoric. His mother Ereleuva was a Catholic, unlike his father's family who in common with most of the Goths were followers of Arianism, a divergent form of Christianity which was condemned as heresy by the Council of Constantinople in 381. Walamer and his people settled in Pannonia (Hungary) and made a treaty with the Eastern Roman Emperor Marcianus; the Emperor paid the Goths a certain sum each year to defend his borders. When his successor Leo refused to pay, the Goths invaded and plundered his lands until Leo was prepared to negotiate. Walamer renewed the treaty and sent his eight-year-old nephew Theodoric to Constantinople as surety. There he received a good education and became a person of importance. Ten years later he returned to his people. When Walamer was killed fighting the Suevi and Sciri, Theodemer was elected king. He defeated an army of Germanic tribes led by Edica, whose son Odoacer later, in 476, deposed the last emperor of the Western Roman Empire, Romulus Augustulus, and made himself King of Italy. After Theodemer's death Theodoric became King of the Ostrogoths. Under his leadership they left Pannonia and settled in Macedonia. After numerous complications Emperor Zeno commissioned him to lead a campaign against Odoacer. He crossed the Balkans with an army of (it is claimed) 100,000 men, consisting of Goths, Rugians and Romans. He defeated Odoacer for the first time at the Isonzo; Odoacer then fell back on Verona. There a second battle took place in 489, in which Theodoric was again victorious. Odoacer retreated to Ravenna and Theodoric was recognised as the Emperor's viceroy in Northern Italy. One of Odoacer's commanders, Tufa, then joined Theodoric, but when the latter sent him to Odoacer with some of his men Tufa went over to the enemy and had the Goths accompanying him murdered. In 490 Theodoric and Odoacer fought a third battle, after which Odoacer took refuge within the walls of Ravenna. In 493, after a three-year siege of the city, Theodoric reached an agreement with Odoacer by which they were to rule jointly. As soon as he was admitted to the city, however, he killed Odoacer with his own hands, thus becoming sole King of Italy. In 497 he was recognised as such by the Eastern Roman Emperor. He ruled Italy until 526 and was greatly esteemed by his subjects, both Goths and Romans, who praised him as a just ruler. His reign was a period of peace and prosperity. His foreign policy was aimed at ensuring peace with his Germanic neighbours, the Franks and Visigoths. To this end he married Audefleda, a sister of the Frankish king Clovis, but this did not prevent Clovis from pursuing his policy of expansion. When he threatened the Visigoths' territory in Southern France Theodoric came to their aid. However, they were forced to retreat over the Pyrenees into Spain and Provence was added to Theodoric's realm. Towards the end of his life he came into conflict with the Church. He had Boëthius and Symmachus imprisoned and executed for alleged high treason. Later, when Pope John I, who had been negotiating on Theodoric's behalf in Constantinople, died suddenly soon after his return, Theodoric was accused of being involved in this also. Not long after this he became unwell during a banquet, thinking he recognised Symmachus in the fish set before him which stared at him with big eyes and gaping mouth, and died shortly afterwards; his death was seen as a punishment from God. He was buried in a mausoleum in Ravenna which still exists, though his body was removed from it as early as the middle of the 6th century because of his heresy. Gothic rule in Italy came to an end in 561/62 when Eastern Roman forces inflicted a crushing defeat on the Goths.

We are relatively well informed about Theodoric's life because the first biography of him appeared soon after his death. Theodoric himself had commissioned Cassiodorus, a prominent Roman of his court, to write a *Historia Gothica* which was to demonstrate that the Goths were no barbarians but a race equal to the Greeks and Romans. Of this work, which must have been written between 526 and 533, only a summary made by Jordanes in 551 survives. The development of a strongly positive image of Theodoric is due not only to this text, but also to all those later chroniclers who included or quoted from it. However, right from the start there were also biographies of Theodoric in circulation which labelled him the bastard son of a king or the son of Macedonian slaves, portrayed him as an Arian heretic and expatiated above all on his crimes against the Church. He was described as the murderer of holy men who at the end of his life was carried off by the Devil in the shape of a wild horse. The *Dialogues* of Pope Gregory the Great relate that Pope John I and Symmachus threw him into Mount Etna. These negative accounts of Theodoric originated in religious circles and have been handed down, as *Gesta Theoderici*, in various Frankish chronicles. This is hardly surprising; not only were the Merovingian Franks political opponents of the Goths, they were also Catholics. The label of bastardy may be due to the fact that his mother was Catholic and his father Arian – according to the Church, a marriage between a Catholic and a heretic is invalid.

Later authors tried to combine the two biographies, with sometimes remarkable results. Thus, Otto von Friesing in his *Chronica sive historia de duabus civitatibus* (c.1150) speaks very positively of Theodoric's noble birth, his youth in Constantinople, his conquest of Italy on Emperor Zeno's orders and his murder of Odoacer. But then he wonders in astonishment how any people can sink so low as to abandon one tyrant, Odoacer, only to replace him with another, Theodoric. There then follows a detailed account of his crimes against Pope John, Boëthius and Symmachus, finishing with two versions of his death. The first vernacular chronicle, the *Kaiserchronik*, written around 1150 by a cleric, also shows this strange fault-line in Theodoric's biography: after telling how, as vassal to the Eastern Roman Emperor, he destroyed the usurper Odoacer and brought peace and prosperity to the land, suddenly he becomes a barbarian who kills Boëthius, Pope John and Seneca (!) and is hurled into the volcano to burn there until the Last Judgment.

Alongside these positive, negative and mixed biographies of Theodoric there is one other, far more positive than the tradition based on Cassiodorus. That is the biography which can be reconstructed from the vernacular literary texts. This biography makes no mention of his Arian faith nor of his death. Nor is there a word about his attitude to the Pope or to other senior churchmen. Nothing can be said with certainty of the origins of this last version, but it most likely developed out of oral tradition. Throughout the Germanic language area, historical events and important personages were commemorated in songs passed down by word of mouth. Jordanes speaks of these as early as the mid-6th century and the oldest extant literary text to mention Theodoric, the *Hildebrandslied*, probably originated in the 7th century. Later centuries, too, provide plenty of indications of a continuous oral tradition. Otto von Freising comments in his *Chronica*, mentioned above, that the common people say of Theodoric that he was a contemporary of → Attila, which is historically incorrect.

Since a common function of heroic literature is to legitimise the rule of a particular dynasty over a particular area, it is quite possible that even the oldest heroic works already presented the conquest of Italy as a reconquest and Odoacer's murder as legitimate action against a usurper. Moreover, it is only in the *Hildebrantslied* that Theodoric's opponent is Odoacer; in all other works the enemy is Theodoric's own uncle Ermrich (Ermenrik, Ermanaric), thus making the political history into an issue of inheritance within the family. Remarkably, not only those who recorded the Dietrich epics in later centuries, but also their patrons, were certainly aware of the biography of Theodoric as it appeared in the Latin chronicles. This means that from time to time people commissioned biographies of Theodoric which they knew contained errors of fact. It happened around 800, when the *Hildebrandslied* was written down in the monastery of Fulda, much favoured by the Carolingians, again in the 12th and 13th centuries when the *Nibelungenlied*, *Dietrichs Flucht* and *Rabenschlacht* were committed to parchment, and finally around 1500 when Emperor Maximilian I had all these tales written down yet again in a so-called 'Heldenbuch'. In other words: when Charlemagne had himself crowned King of the Langobards, when Hohenstaufen attempts to establish themselves in Italy were at their height and, finally, when Emperor Maximilian was in conflict with King Francis I of France over the Anjou possessions in Italy. It seems not inconceivable that those seeking to justify claims to Italian territory routinely resurrected the old tales about Theodoric, the biography which proved that Italy was unjustly taken from him. That is why these stories from the oral tradition do not mention Theodoric's death, and why he never succeeds in recovering his lands. That is how this King of the Goths, whose people wandered all over Europe but who never lived in the later German language area and who was himself King of Italy, could become the most popular hero of the German Middle Ages, more popular than Siegfried, whom in various epics he actually defeats either in battle or in single combat.

Theodoric remained the most famous hero of German history and literature until the end of the Middle Ages. Charlemagne had a mounted statue of him brought to

Aachen from Ravenna. Various castles in South Tyrol still contain frescoes of scenes from stories about him (Runkelstein and Lichtenberg Castles). Emperor Maximilian commissioned a statue of Theodoric by Peter Vischer the Elder, to a design by Albrecht Dürer, for his tomb in the royal chapel at Innsbruck. In the 15th and 16th centuries prose versions of the Theodoric stories were printed in so-called 'Heldenbücher', but they quickly came to be regarded as 'bad' reading (Luther) or, at the best, 'children's books' (Leibniz). When medieval literature was rediscovered in the Romantic period all attention focused on the *Nibelungenlied*. There Theodoric plays the part of the humane Christian knight who just happens to be at Etzel's court, without a word as to his previous history or his later efforts to recover his lands. Among the romantic poets only Ludwig Tieck concerned himself with Theodoric, in 1808–16 (published only in 1980!). Karl Simrock, the *Nibelungenlied*'s most famous translator, adapted the entire Theodoric material as a Modern German verse epic under the title *Amelungenlied* (1843–49). There are later reworkings of the complete material by E. König (1917–21) and W. Jansen (*Das Buch Leidenschaft*, 1920). The tales have also been retold in some dozens of collections of heroic sagas, in full or greatly abridged, for adults or the young. Certain episodes were used by G. Kinkel (*Der von Berne*, 1843) and E. von Wildenbruch (*König Laurin*, 1902); some others were adapted for the stage, but with limited success and by poets now forgotten. A version for young people was produced by the Austrian writer Auguste Lechner (*Herr Dietrich reitet*, 1953). Greater success was enjoyed by Felix Dahn, who gave an account of Theodoric the Great in his lengthy historical novel *Ein Kampf um Rom* (1876). The historical Theodoric was the subject of a drama by E. Kunow (1886) and a novel by W. Schäfer (1939). Composers who derived inspiration from Theodoric were G. Henschel (*Jung-Dietrich-Ballade*, 1892) and F. Draeseke (opera, 1900). Felix Dahn's book was filmed by Robert Siodmak (KAMPF UM ROM, 1968) with Orson Welles and Laurence Harvey.

N.TH.J. VOORWINDEN

Studies: Zink 1950; Ensslin 1959[2]; Wisniewski 1986.

TOREC is the son of King Ydor of the Baser Rivire and his wife Tristoise, whose mother is Queen Mariole. The governing factor in his life is a golden diadem which belongs to Mariole but has been stolen by the knight Bruant. At the urging of Tristoise Torec sets out to avenge this theft. He finds and defeats Bruant, who tells him that the diadem is now in the possession of his sister-in-law Miraude, a damsel who has sworn that she will only marry the knight who can defeat all the knights of King → Arthur's Round Table. During his search for Miraude Torec encounters all kinds of adventures. His experiences, both amorous and knightly, are interwoven with those of Melions, a knight with whom he becomes friendly following a fight. Torec does combat with many knights, among them Ywein (→ Yvain), spends three days on board the flying Ship of Adventure, where in the Chamber of Wisdom he listens to wise men and ladies debating on virtue, courage and love, and eventually reaches Miraude's castle. To fulfil Miraude's terms for marriage the knights of the Round Table are invited there and – with one interruption when Miraude is abducted and rescued by the now besotted Torec – defeated. Finally, the marriage takes place at Arthur's court in the presence of Torec's parents. With Miraude the diadem returns to the family of Tristoise and Torec. On the death of Ydor and Tristoise Torec and Miraude become king and queen.

In the prologue to his *Historie van Troyen* (c.1264) the Dutch poet Jacob van Maerlant lists earlier works of his, including 'Merlijn' and 'Toerecke'. In view of this it is likely that the *Torec* is Maerlant's work. As with his *Historie van den Grale* and *Merlijn*, he would have translated the work from Old French. Since there is no extant Old French original, it was long thought that the work was a product of Maerlant's own brain. However, it turns out that there actually was an Old French romance of 'Torrez chevalier au cercle d'or'. It is possible that Maerlant translated the work around 1262 at the behest of the court at Voorne for use in the education there of the later Count Floris V of Holland. If so, the work can be seen as a 'Mirror for Princes' in romance form; one reason being that the topics discussed in the Chamber of Wisdom include the cardinal and chivalric virtues.

The *Torec* has been preserved only in the so-called → Lancelot-compilation (early 14th century). The question is, how far this text agrees with that of the original version; and this has stimulated research into the sources of specific episodes and narrative strands (for instance, the treatment of Melions), including the possibility that some of the material was drawn from folklore. Contrasting with this quest for what might have existed are recent studies which, taking the *Torec* as a 'princely narrative', seek to interpret it in the best way possible in the form in which it has come down to us.

Neither the lost Old French *Torrez* nor the Middle Dutch *Torec* was able to ensure their hero's continued existence after the end of the Middle Ages.

FRANK BRANDSMA

Edition: Hogenhout/Hogenhout 1978.

TRISTAN AND ISEULT: a prince and princess whose story has come down to us in a variety of forms, but with a fairly consistent nucleus. The King of Loonnois, Rivalen, aids King Mark of Cornwall in his war against the Scots and in return receives Mark's sister Blanchefleur as his bride. Sadly, she dies immediately after giving birth to a son. The boy is named Tristan to commemorate this tragic fact and entrusted to the care of the courtier Gorneval. The youthful Tristan comes to the court of his uncle King Mark, where he is much admired for his exceptional qualities. Despite his lack of experience he succeeds in defeating Morholt, the King of Ireland's brother, in a duel, and so frees Cornwall of the obligation of sending a tribute of young people to Ireland.

Morholt dies, but he has dealt Tristan an incurable poisoned wound. Desperate with the unbearable pain, Tristan puts to sea in a little boat and by chance comes ashore in Ireland, where – incognito: he calls himself Tantris – he is cared for and cured by the king's daughter, Iseult of the Fair Hair.

Seeking a bride for King Mark, Tristan pays a second visit to Ireland. Here he kills a dragon which has been plaguing the country, but almost succumbs to his wounds. The reward for disposing of the monster is Iseult's hand, but the prize is claimed, falsely, by a powerful court official who had found the dead dragon and now produces its head as proof of his heroic deed. Luckily Tristan, who has again been cured by the princess, appears at court in the nick of time; he proves that he is the real dragon-slayer by producing the beast's tongue. Meanwhile, Iseult has discovered that it was Tristan who killed her uncle; but she suppresses her desire for revenge and agrees to accompany him to Cornwall as King Mark's bride. Once aboard ship, Tristan and Iseult accidentally drink the love potion which her mother had prepared for the royal couple. Now desperately in love with each other, they abandon themselves to their passion.

To prevent the king finding out that his bride is no longer a virgin, on the wedding night Iseult's maid Brangien takes her mistress' place in Mark's bed. Fearing discovery, Iseult decides to have Brangien killed in the forest. The murderers spare her, though, when she insists that she is being unjustly punished for lending her undamaged shift to a lady whose shift was torn. Iseult later regrets her action and is reconciled with Brangien.

HOW KING
MARKE FOVND
SIR TRISTRAM

King Mark comes upon the sleeping Tristan. Illustration by Aubrey Beardsley for an 1894 edition of Malory's *Morte d'Arthur*.

Tristan and Iseult devise all kinds of ways of meeting each other in secret. They are constantly watched by jealous barons and by a dwarf who can read the future in the stars. The latter tells Mark of the lovers' forthcoming rendezvous in an orchard. Just in time Tristan spots the head of the watching Mark reflected in the water of a fountain; he warns Iseult and they carry on an innocent conversation.

On another occasion the dwarf sprinkles flour on the floor of the royal bedchamber. Having discovered this trap also, Tristan jumps from his own bed into Iseult's. Unfortunately in doing so he reopens an old wound, so that the sheets are stained with blood. Thus Tristan and Iseult are caught in the act and condemned to die at the stake. While being taken to his execution Tristan manages to escape by jumping out of the window of a chapel. He then rescues Iseult, who has been handed over to a band of lepers, and they flee together into the forest.

One day King Mark finds the lovers lying asleep with Tristan's sword between them. Instead of killing them as he had intended, Mark exchanges his own sword for Tristan's and his ring for Iseult's. He also leaves his glove there. On the intercession of the hermit Ogrin Iseult eventually returns to court. The barons insist on the queen proving her innocence, so she agrees to undergo a trial by ordeal. She arranges a meeting with Tristan who, disguised as a pilgrim (or a leper), carries her across a puddle to the place where she is to take the oath. Iseult then serenely swears that no man has ever held her in his arms save for her husband and the pilgrim.

The exiled Tristan makes himself useful at the court of the King of Brittany, and becomes friendly with the king's son Kaherdin. Hoping to forget his beloved he marries the king's daughter, Iseult of the White Hands. But the marriage remains unconsummated, a fact revealed when the young bride tells Kaherdin one day that the water splashing her thighs is bolder than her husband. Tristan then admits to Kaherdin that he is in love with another woman. The two of them leave for Cornwall, where Kaherdin sees for himself Iseult's beauty and her love for Tristan. Tristan visits Cornwall several more times, each time in a different disguise.

Eventually, in Brittany, he suffers a mortal wound. He sends a messenger to Iseult of the Fair Hair, who alone is able to cure him. The arrangement is that on its return the ship will carry a white sail if she is on board, a black one if she has failed to come. Although Tristan's beloved is in fact on board, his wife tells him that the ship, which is prevented from entering harbour by a bad storm, is carrying a black sail. On hearing this Tristan dies. When she learns that she has come too late Iseult of Ireland promptly follows him in death. They are buried together in Cornwall; the branches of the plants on their grave intertwine.

The origin of the name Tristan must probably be sought among the Picts, the pre-Celtic people of Northern Scotland. Around 780 they had a king called Drust, son of Talorc. As early as the 9th century Drust was linked with a hero who frees a distant land of a tribute of slaves and is rewarded with the hand of a princess. The various Celtic peoples of Ireland, Wales, Cornwall and Brittany then contributed to the complex evolution of the Tristan legend. Drystan or Trystan features in a number of Welsh triads (short verses which invariably mention three persons or things) as the lover of Essylt, wife of March son of Meirchiawn.

The Tristan story may have been based on an Irish *aithed* ($\rightarrow$ Lancelot) such as that of Gráinne and Diarmaid. Gráinne is the wife of the Irish clan chief Finn; she uses a *geis* (a magical command) to make his nephew Diarmaid run away with her into the woods. There they live together, hunted by the king, but only become lovers when Gráinne remarks that the water splashing her thighs is bolder than Diarmaid. In a variant on this legend, the Welsh story-tellers would then have given the Pictish hero Drust/Tristan a leading role. It is likely that the Bretons in their turn are responsible for Tristan's fight with the dragon and his marriage to Iseult of the White Hands. The legend, further embellished with a variety of folk-tale motifs, circulated at first only in the oral tradition of professional story-tellers like 'La Chievre' and the legendary Bleheri. Not until the second half of the 12th century do we find the first evidence of a written tradition, in which the myth of doomed love (Eros) becomes linked with death (Thanatos). Tristan now becomes the melancholy hero who never laughs and his name is associated with sadness.

The legend has come down to us in the first place in a number of fragmentary French verse narratives produced for the originally Norman aristocracy of the English courts. One version, dating from 1172–75, is attributed to the French poet Thomas, probably a cleric in the service of Henry Plantagenet. The Norman Béroul, active at a noble court in Cornwall, will have written his first version in the 1180s or a little earlier. There are several short verse narratives on the subject of Tristan's return, disguised or not, to Cornwall. Between 1155 and 1189 Marie de France wrote a short story in rhyme – a *lai* – entitled *Chievrefoil*. In this Tristan himself expresses the strength of his and Iseult's love emblematically in the image of the honeysuckle whose stems are inextricably entwined with the hazel tree. Two short verse texts, the Berne *Folie* and the Oxford *Folie* (late 12th/early 13th century), tell how Tristan, disguised as a fool, tries to make contact with Iseult but is mocked by her until she discovers his true identity. Tales of clandestine meetings between the lovers are incorporated in the Anglo-Norman *Donnei des Amanz* (13th century) and the *Continuation de Perceval* by Gerbert de Montreuil (c.1230). The episode in the former is called 'Tristan rossignol' and tells how Tristan alerts Iseult to his presence in the garden by imitating the song of the nightingale. In the episode in the latter, 'Tristan ménestrel', the hero appears at a tournament disguised as a minstrel.

Alongside these French texts, in the 12th and 13th centuries versions also appeared in other languages. Between 1170 and 1190 Eilhart of Oberg wrote his *Tristant*, the sole complete form of the legend, at the court of Henry the Lion, Duke of Saxony; this work, in the form of a biography, is probably closest to the archtype. In the 14th century Eilhart's text was translated into Czech as *Tristram Welikyrék*, in a version from which all offensive passages have been deleted. Thomas's romance was the source for the version by Gottfried von Strassburg, written between 1200 and 1220. This version, unfinished though it is, is considered to be the most successful because of its great stylistic quality and subtle characterisation. Ulrich von Türheim (1235) and Heinrich von Freiberg (1285–90) completed Gottfried's work with the aid of Eilhart's version. Both continuators distance themselves from the extramarital nature of the relationship between Tristan and Iseult and defend the Christian marriage ethic. Also from the German language area is the verse novella *Tristan als Mönch* (1250), in which Tristan returns to Cornwall in the guise of a monk. A Lower Franconian fragment (c.1250) with an episode taken from Thomas shows that the legend was also known in the area north-east of Nijmegen. The Middle English translation *Sir Tristrem* (13th century), halfway between a romance and a ballad in form, also follows Thomas. This, together with the Norse translation *Tristrams saga ok Isöndar* (1226) by Brother Robert, is used to reconstruct Thomas' fragmentary version. The Norse saga has been considerably modified to fit the Christian milieu of King Hákon Hákonarson. A number of Norse and Icelandic ballads are based on this version, as is the parodic Icelandic *Saga af Tristram ok Isold*. *Geiterlauf*, a Norse translation of *Chievrefoil*, dates from 1250.

Gripped by an overwhelming fatal passion, once they have drunk the love potion Tristan and Iseult are driven to transgress all rational, moral and social laws. The successive versions of the Tristan story thus give expression to the burning medieval issues of courtly love versus Christian morality, chivalry versus feudality, the individual versus society. The poets themselves are conscious of the provocative nature of their material. They transform the love potion into a pure symbol (Thomas) or allow its effect to wear off either partially (Béroul) or totally (Eilhart) after a period of years. Reacting against this destructive passion Chrétien de Troyes wrote his courtly romances

→ *Cligès* and *Chevalier de la Charrette* (→ Lancelot), designed as anti-Tristan and neo-Tristan respectively. In the prologue to *Cligès* he also reminds his readers of a tale he had written about Mark and Iseult, a work which has not survived.

The Tristan story owes its enormous success in the Middle Ages to the prose version *L'Estoire de Monseigneur Tristan*, also known as the *Tristan en prose*, a real bestseller written about 1230 and translated into many European languages. Its author, who gives his name as Luce del Gat, does his best to gloss over the story's subversive nature. The dramatic conflict between Tristan and Mark is transformed from a feudal quarrel between vassal and overlord into a less threatening encounter between a gallant courtly hero and a treacherous coward who brings about his death. Tristan's love-life is supplemented and camouflaged with an almost endless succession of chivalrous adventures. As in most courtly romances, Tristan's courage is enhanced by his love for Iseult. The image of the hero alienated and isolated from society is replaced by that of a knight who wins himself a place among the companions of King → Arthur. Tristan's existence is less clouded by sorrow, he enjoys long periods of pleasure and delight, as during his sojourn with Iseult in Joyeuse Garde. A later editor who gives his name as Hélie de Boron appends the tale of the Grail Quest and gives a detailed family tree for Tristan, beginning with Sador, son of Bron and nephew of → Joseph of Arimathea.

The large number of surviving manuscripts (over eighty) is a significant indicator of the popularity of this prose text, which quite overshadowed the Tristan texts in verse. Translations of it appeared in Italian, among them the *Tristano Riccardiano* (late 13th century) and the *Tavola Ritonda*. The latter also included a number of episodes taken directly from Thomas. Episodes from the prose version, particularly those relating to the final stage of Tristan's life, provided material for the *Cantari*, popular stories in rhyme recited by professional storytellers in the Italian city-states. Tristan is held up to the citizens as a model *condottiere* and diplomat, a combination of valour and cunning. The *Tristano Riccardiano* may have been a source for the Spanish translations *El Cuento de Tristán de Léonis* (14th–15th century) and *Libro del muy esforçado cauallero Don Tristán de Leonís* (16th century). A ballad which derives from this, *Herida está don Tristán*, takes as its subject the final moments of the lovers' lives in Brittany. The Belorussian translation (16th century) also made use of an Italian text. In 1485 Caxton published Malory's *Morte d'Arthur*, in which the *Book of Sir Tristram de Lyones* has a central position. In this *summa* of chivalrous ideals Tristan appears as an exemplary knight, his serene love for Iseult purged of all ethical problems. Malory's treatment of the *Tristan en prose* can be seen as an expression of aristocratic life-skills which was also of interest to the urban citizen. Still unresolved is the question of the relationship between Malory and the Italian and Spanish translations. It seems likely that in his work he drew on a source which has not been preserved, different to and possibly also older than the extant French manuscripts.

During the first half of the present century research into the Tristan legend was dominated by attempts at reconstructing the archetype. Such scholars as Joseph Bédier and Gertrude Schoepperle were convinced that the medieval narratives could be traced back to a single source, the *Estoire*, Celtic or French in origin and dating from the second half of the 12th century. Since that time scholars have preferred to assume that there were a number of different traditions of the legend, oral and written, in circulation at the same time. Thomas and Béroul themselves refer in their works to the diversity of their sources. In recent years much attention has been devoted to the influence of folk-tale motifs, classical legends (Theseus and Ariadne, Paris and Oenone, Perseus and Andromeda) and oriental, particularly Arabic, sources. Another current area of study is the influence on the Tristan stories of the medieval humanism of Abélard and Bernard of Clairvaux.

The dating and authorship of the Thomas and Béroul versions are still subjects of dispute. Some researchers have wondered whether these authors ever actually intended to produce complete accounts, and consequently whether it makes sense to reconstruct their work. After all, it is clear from other fragmentary works that the medieval audience was used to stories beginning *in medias res*, in the middle of the action, with references to previous events to ensure coherence.

The ideological differences between Béroul and Thomas have led to a distinction being made between the first, 'popular, general' version and the second, 'courtly' version. According to Jean Frappier, the dividing line is marked by the significance of the love potion, which in Thomas is still symbolic since the pair are already in love before they take the fatal drink. Béroul's version is usually regarded as epic and critical of society, Thomas' as realistic and lyrical. One difference between the two versions is in their account of the lovers' sojourn in the forest: in Béroul a harsh and laborious existence, in Thomas it is idyllic. The German versions, too, differ in emphasis: while Eilhart dilates at length on Tristan's heroic exploits in Brittany, Gottfried shows a marked aversion to violence. Gottfried's version, in particular, is subject to widely differing interpretations, largely because of the paradoxical nature of his view of love, which he depicts both as Fall and as salvation. In this connection attention has focused mainly on the symbolic or allegorical significance of the grotto to which Tristan and Iseult retreat after their flight; Gottfried transforms this idyllic spot into a real temple of love.

Various aspects of Tristan have received particular scrutiny. Thus, his role as poet and musician in Thomas and Gottfried is compared with that of David at the court of King Saul and with Orpheus. Tristan also has qualities which typify him as *homo sylvester* (man of the woods, wild man): his skill with bow and arrow, his mimicry of birdsong, his habit of taking enormous leaps. In marrying Iseult of the White Hands Tristan embodies the motif, so beloved of 12th- and 13th-century literature, of the man between two women. His desire for a purely physical relationship with his wife is frustrated by the memory of his mistress, which makes him impotent. The exaggerated roleplay of his many disguises could indicate an identity problem, but it is at the same time an intellectual form of combat and a means of communication. By disguising himself as a leper – a symbol of sexual deviation – or a fool he accepts society's view of him, at the same time setting himself against the prevailing order as an outlaw. The ambiguous use of language makes him a subversive hero by casting doubt upon the evidence of things at a time when word and object were still believed to be identical. Semiotic studies have pointed to the significance of the descriptive elements, such as the weapons Tristan uses to avenge himself on his enemies: sword, bow and arrow, lance and javelin. Various explanations have been given of Mark's behaviour in the forest: the items he leaves there could be tokens of forgiveness, of a rite of investiture or of a wilful denial of reality. The difficult relationship between Mark and Tristan could indicate that the alliance between king and vassal, *the* great ideal of the 12th century, was doomed to failure.

Despite the prose romance's great popularity in medieval times, for many years this particular version was neglected by scholars studying the Tristan texts. From 1890 they had to make do with a summary of the text; since 1963 a critical edition has started to become available completed in 1997. Now we have an overview of the manuscripts and the various versions of the prose romance, and an insight into its typical narrative structure.

In the prose romance Iseult's lover personifies the ideal knight of the Round Table, though the refractory nature of the legend's material makes it impossible to force him intact into the straitjacket of the Arthurian hero. Tristan is the new hero, attempting to supplant the established hero → Lancelot. By introducing the new terms *joie* and *bone aventure* the prose author, who describes himself as *amerus* and *envoisiez* (in love and merry) opens new horizons for the reader, who is after all used to associating Tristan with sorrow. The account of Tristan's ancestors was long regarded as a tedious and unnecessary addition by the prose author; research has now demonstrated that in it he has brilliantly sown the seeds of his hero's moral weakness.

The enormous popularity of the Tristan stories during the Middle Ages is evidenced not only by the many Tristan texts but also by the numerous literary allusions by troubadours – such as Cercamon and Bernart de Ventadorn – and their successors in Italy, Spain and Germany. In their poems Tristan personifies the martyr for love or the ideal courtly lover; though the poet Hendrik van Veldeke reckons himself a greater lover than Tristan because he had fallen in love freely, without compulsion (c.1175). Notable is the negative judgment of Dante: he awards Tristan a place in Hell, and specifically among the sinners of the flesh.

Of particular interest are the iconographic witnesses to the Tristan story, providing as they do an idea of its visual transmission. What we find here are primarily domestic objects, often with an amorous context: jewel-boxes in wood or ivory, mirror-cases, combs, small leather containers, writing implements, slippers given by a bridegroom to his bride, silver-mounted crystal goblets, silver salt-cellars and the like. Sometimes several successive scenes are depicted, sometimes just one typical episode, with the orchard scene as the clear favourite. The earliest representation is on an ivory jewel-box of the Cologne school which dates from before 1200. Depicted on this are the love potion scene, the duel with Morholt, the marriage of Mark and Iseult, Iseult's abduction and the rendezvous in the orchard. This last is also often found in a religious context. The Tristan story was evidently a favourite subject for tapestries; we will mention here the four earliest examples. The oldest is a fragment from the beginning of the 14th century, preserved in the Lüneburg museum; then a tapestry from the first half of the 14th century in the monastery of Wienhausen über Celle; one from the second half of the 14th century, part of a series which includes one of Parzival, originally in the Heilig Kreuz monastery in Brunswick, now in the Herzog Anton Ulrich Museum there; and finally a mid-14th-century tapestry from a monastery in Würzburg, now in the Dom Museum in Erfurt. The orchard scene also appears on a corbel in Chester Cathedral (1380) and as an illustration in an English didactic monastic book (early 14th century). In this context it was probably intended as a warning against the dangers of lasciviousness, or as an ironic-parodic play on a familiar motif. This same orchard scene is also found on a chimney-piece in the Hôtel de Jacques Coeur in Bourges (1443–50). From the first half of the 15th century dates a slipper from the Southern Netherlands which bears a legend and the orchard scene. Here Tristan and Iseult are playing chess, in accordance with the traditional portrayal of lovers in a garden of love. Unusually, Isoude is drawing Tristan's attention to Mark's presence by showing her a strange fish in the water. Precisely the same scene appears in Dirk Potter's *Der Minnen Loep* (1411–12).

The oldest series of representations, based on Thomas, is to be found in the tiles, made c.1270 and comprising 35 scenes, from Chertsey Abbey (now in the Victoria and Albert Museum in London). Two embroidered bedspreads from Sicily made for the Guicciardini family in Florence (1395) show Tristan bearing the arms of this noble house. Runkelstein Castle near Bolzano in South Tyrol has frescoes after Gottfried (shortly after 1385), with fourteen compositions in all; these are badly damaged, but still well-known from a series of drawings made by Ignaz Seelos in 1857. The wooden ceiling of Palazzo Chiaramonte in Palermo (c.1380) is adorned with, among other things, the rendezvous in the orchard.

Luxury manuscripts of the prose romance are illuminated, particularly during the period 1340–1500, with splendid miniatures. French-language manuscripts were also copied and illustrated in Italy, notably in Lombardy, Genoa and Naples. After the rise of printing the books are illustrated with woodcuts or engravings.

In the 16th century, too, Tristan remained fashionable. The prose romance was reprinted many times between 1489 and 1533. In 1554 Jean Maugin produced a version adapted to Renaissance taste with his *Le Premier Livre du nouveau Tristan de Leonnois, Chevalier de la Table Ronde et d'Yseulte Princesse d'Yrlande, Royne de Cornouaille*. Pierre Sala's *Tristan* (1525–29) is a real adventure story. In Germany the prose adaptation of

Eilhart's *Tristrant*, the so-called *Volksbuch* (15th century), was dramatised by Hans Sachs: *Von dem strengen Lieb Herr Tristrant mit der schönen Königin Isalden* (1533). This is a moralistic play, designed to alert a general audience to the dangers of adultery. In Spain there was a new edition of the prose translation containing new material on Tristan's son. This Tristan the Younger is an improved edition of his father, a Tristan who has no love potion in his blood. The romance was translated into Italian as *L'opere magnanime dei due Tristani, cavalieri della Tavola Ritonda* (1555). The same language produced two bad imitations of the *Cantari*: *La Battaglia de Tristan e Lancelotto e della Reina Isotta* (1492), telling how → Galahad and → Lancelot rescue Tristan from the clutches of a giant, and *L'innamoramento di messer Tristano e madonna Isotta* (1520), in which Iseult serves the love potion deliberately.

After the end of the 16th century enthusiasm for the Tristan story waned – apart from the Count of La Vergne de Tressan's *Tristan de Leonois* (1780) – and was not rekindled until the time of the Romantics. Then the Middle English *Sir Tristrem* was published for the first time by Sir Walter Scott. Tristan motifs can be detected in all Scott's novels, most notably in *The Betrothed* (1824), the tale of a fatal love with a happy ending. During the Victorian age English writers were fascinated by the story. In his poem *Tristram and Iseult* (1852) Matthew Arnold puts the main stress on the hero's decline: in Brittany, dangerously wounded, he thinks back to the happier days of yore. In *The Last Tournament* (1871), set against the background of the destruction of King Arthur's realm, Tennyson tells of Tristan's return to Cornwall, where he tries to calm his jealous beloved with harp music. When he adorns Iseult with the necklace he had won in a tournament the barbarous King Mark smashes in his skull. In *Tristram of Lyonesse* (1882) Algernon Swinburne sketches a dignified pair of lovers who, tyrannised by fate, resign themselves to the love and death that spring from the magic potion. A new edition of Malory (1893–94) was illustrated by Aubrey Beardsley. Other Pre-Raphaelite painters, too, were drawn to the forbidden sensual love of Tristan and Iseult. A well-known example is the series of Tristan windows known as the Dunlop Windows (1862), produced under the direction of William Morris for Harden Grange near Bingley in Yorkshire and now in Bradford City Art Gallery. A cartoon for 'The Death of Sir Tristram' by Ford Madox Ford is now in the Fitzwilliam Museum in Cambridge; an 1864 painting on the same subject hangs in the City of Birmingham Museums and Art Gallery. Of the work of Dante Gabriel Rossetti, 'Sir Tristram and La Belle Yseult Drinking the Love Potion' (1867), in the Cecil Higgins Art Gallery, Bedford, deserves a mention. The same motif can be found in a drawing by Julius Schnorr von Carolsfeld, 'Der Liebestrank Tristans und Isoldes', demonstrating the interaction between the English Pre-Raphaelites and the German Nazarenes. Melchior Lechter created 'Tristan und Isolde' (1896), a pair of stained glass window panels, for his bedroom in Berlin; they are now in the Deutsches Glasmalerei Museum at Linnich near Bonn.

In Germany, both August Willem Schlegel (1800) and Karl Immermann (1831) began writing poetic epics on Tristan inspired by Gottfried's version; neither work was completed. In the latter, the power of the love potion is broken by divine intervention and the lovers then renounce each other. In the opera *Tristan* (completed 1859, first performance Munich 1865) Richard Wagner gives a highly personal interpretation of Gottfried, clearly showing the influence of the ideas of Schopenhauer and Buddhism. The drama restricts itself to three acts: the love potion, life in the forest and the lovers' death. In Wagner's vision of events, Isolde deliberately tries to poison herself because she does not wish to marry Mark; the poison is accidentally exchanged for the love potion. In the end Tristan and Isolde consciously choose death because only in the destruction of their bodies can they find release.

Wagner's interpretation of the legend exercised a powerful influence on the 20th-century Tristan reception. The history of this *Nachleben* in literature, ballets, music and films has yet to be written; a general survey and a few outstanding examples must suffice here. Joseph Bédier's novel *Tristan et Iseut* (1900) provided a reconstruction of the *Estoire* adapted to its new audience. He has a clear preference for Thomas, but is not insensitive to the lovers' Wagnerian death-wish. In 1928 he wrote a stage play of the same name which scored major triumphs in Paris and Dublin. The composer Frank Martin then drew on Bédier's novel for his oratorio *Le vin herbé*. A concert performance of this took place in Zürich in 1942; but its première as an opera was in Salzburg in 1948 under the title *Der Zaubertrank*, with Julius Patzak as Tristan and Maria Cebotari as Isolde. 1944 saw the performance of the ballet *Tristan fou*, to music by Wagner; the sets and costumes were designed by Salvador Dalí. In 1965 *Tristan*, a ballet in seven scenes with choreography by Tatjana Gsovsky to music by Boris Blacher, had its first performance in Berlin. Originally intended for a ballet was the orchestral work *Tristan. Prelude für Klavier, Tönbander und Orchester* (1973) by Hans Werner Henze, with quotations from Wagner's opera. Armin Schibler's *La Folie de Tristan, mystère musical* (1976–79) was performed in Montreux in 1981. Gillian Whitehead and Timothy Porter adapted the material for their operas, *Tristan and Isolt* (1978) and *Trystan and Essylt* (1980) respectively. Wagner's interpretation provides the background for Thomas Mann's novella *Tristan* (1903), which deals with the conflict between the rapture of art and the banality of existence. Also in Germany, Eduard Stucken's drama *Tristram und Yseult* appeared in 1916. Here, with strongly religious symbolism, Isolde's poison is replaced not with a love potion but with wine. Although the lovers do their utmost to resist their passion, here too they find release only in death.

Of 20th-century versions for the stage we will mention (the list is not exhaustive) the dramas by Louis K. Anspacher (1904), J. Comyns Carr (1906), Ernst Hardt (*Tantris der Narr*, 1907), Emil Ludwig (1909), Michael Field (1911), Martha Kinross (1913), Arthur Symons (1917), Thomas Hardy (*Famous Tragedy of the Queen of Cornwall at Tintagel in Lyonesse*, 1923), on which was based Rutland Boughton's opera *The Queen of Cornwall* (first performed at the 1924 Glastonbury Festival), John Masefield (1927) and John Todhunter (also 1927).

Novelists who have treated the subject in this century include John Erskine (1932), Hannah Closs (1940), Albert Cohen (*Belle du Seigneur*, 1968), Ruth Schirmer-Imhoff (1969), Rosemary Sutcliff (1971), Maria Kuncewiczowa (1967), Günter de Bruyn (1975), D.M. Meany (*Iseult. Dreams that are done*, 1985), and Diana L. Paxton (*The White Raven*, 1988). There are poems by Friedrich Rückert (published anonymously in 1839), Martha W. Austin (1905), Albert Rausch (1909), Laurence Binyon in his *Odes* (1913), E.A. Robinson (1927), Frank Kendon (1934), Florence M. Pomeroy (1958), M. Beheim-Schwarzbach (1975), Ken Smith (1978) and Brian Fawcett (1981).

In his book *L'amour et l'occident* (1939) Denis de Rougemont mounts a fierce attack on the Tristan myth and the concept of transcendent passion, which he regards as heretical in origin and incompatible with the Christian concept of love. The writer is of the opinion that adultery and unhappy love, combined with a powerful death-wish, form a dangerous leitmotiv in European literature. Probably the Tristan portrayed by John Updike in

Tristan and Iseult on a medallion by Salvador Dalí, date unknown. Collection of Dalí's heirs.

Four Sides of One Story (1965) is intended as a parody of the type of lover defined by De Rougemont as narcissistic and egotistical. Living in an American suburb, married and the father of three children, Tristan forcibly keeps his distance from Iseult so that he can continue to adore her. Denis de Rougemont has rightly remarked that the Tristan myth occupies an important place in the European history of ideas. In the 20th century one can detect the Tristan material in the underlying structure of many literary works. We may mention here, among others, the drama *Partage du Midi* (1905) by Paul Claudel, *Sparkenbroke* (1936) by Charles Morgan, *Finnegan's Wake* (1939) by James Joyce, *Spätestens in November* (1955) by H.E. Nossack, *The Serpent and the Rope* (1960) by the Indian writer Raja Rao and *Zoeken naar Eileen W.* (1981) by Leon de Winter. In this novel, set in Ireland, Fate takes the form of the unwanted pregnancy of the Catholic Eileen; her love for the Protestant Kevin is impossible by reason of the irreconcilable conflict of religion.

The writers Simone de Beauvoir (*Les Mandarins*, 1954) and Ingeborg Bachmann (*Der gute Gott von Manhattan*, 1958, and *Malina*, 1971) take issue with Wagner's interpretation of the myth. Love is seen as the way to perfection and the effects of the love potion are therapeutic. It is only woman who dares to rebel against the social order, in the end man prefers to conform to it – there are no Tristans any more. That the avant-garde also has something to say on the subject can be seen from Pierre Garnier's expansive poem *Tristan et Iseult* (1990), which also keeps Wagner's division of the narrative into three. The poet feels a particular kinship with Tristan, since the avant-garde writer's place in society is equally marginal. A postmodernist version of the Tristan story is Paul Griffiths' *The Lay of Sir Tristram* (1991), in which medieval characters appear alongside Richard Wagner and contemporaries from his circle.

Films which hark back to the Tristan myth have not proved particularly successful. L'ÉTERNEL RETOUR (1943), by Jean Delannoy in collaboration with Jean Cocteau, moves the legend to the modern age with the hero riding a four-cylinder motor-bike instead of a horse. The whole thing now seems very dated. A rather inaccessible film with a great deal of symbolism is Yvan Lagrange's TRISTAN ET ISEULT (1972). The starting-point here is the primeval instinct to survive and reproduce. The bellicose Tristan is consistently associated with animals such as the falcon, wolf and horse until he is domesticated by Iseult. In FEUER UND SCHWERT (1982) Veith von Fürstenberg shows a world which is apocalyptically destroyed in consequence of the individual's revolt against the established order. Here Tristan, as a naive robber knight, has only a subsidiary role; all attention is focused on Iseult, the magical catalyst of the story. Connections with the Tristan material are also present in François Truffaut's film FEMME D'À CÔTÉ (1981), about the amorous obsession of two people not married to each other which leads in the end to murder and suicide.

In contrast to these modern visual interpretations, the legend still lives on in oral form in the ballad of Tristram and Isin sung in the Faeroes during the long winter evenings.

M.-J. HEIJKANT

Editions: Curtis 1985; Ménard 1987–97; Lacroix/Walter 1989; Spiewok 1989.
Translation: Buschinger/Spiewok 1986.
Studies: Loomis/Hibbard-Loomis 1938; Fouquet 1971; Verbeke/Janssens/Smeyers 1971; Ferrante 1973; Baumgartner 1975; Stein 1983; Baumgartner 1987 and 1990; Marchello-Nizia 1995; Cocheyras 1996.

TROILUS is the youngest son of King Priam and Queen Hecuba of Troy. Ancient accounts of him are inconsistent in many respects; but the authors are agreed on one thing, that he was slain by Achilles while still young ('mors immatura' motif). According to Homer (*Iliad*) and Virgil (*Aeneid*) this happened on the battlefield fairly early in the Trojan War. Dictys says that it was only later, after the death of his brother → Hector, that Troilus was captured in battle and subsequently killed on the orders of Achilles, who was angry at having heard nothing from Priam about Polyxena (→ Hector). Servius however, in his commentary on Virgil, mentions a tradition according to which Achilles killed the youth for not returning his love – an interpretation documented in antique vase-paintings.

In Dares (5th–6th century, → Hector) the youthful, but strong, brave and warlike Troilus is involved in the fighting, but no feats of arms are mentioned until Hector has been disposed of. Troilus then develops into a leader of men, slaying many Greeks and even penetrating the Greek camp. His opponents, weakened by Achilles' refusal to fight (→ Hector), fear him as much as they had Hector. He wreaks terrible slaughter among the Myrmidons and this induces Achilles to rejoin the fray. Troilus lies in wait for him and wounds him. On the seventh day of the battle Achilles, recovered, returns to the field. Again Troilus seeks him out. This time, following a pre-arranged plan, all the Myrmidons fall on him together. They take heavy casualties. Troilus' horse is wounded and brings his rider down with him. Achilles charges up and kills him as he lies on the ground.

Centuries later, in Benoît's *Roman de Troie* (c.1165), Troilus is portrayed at length as Troy's most handsome hero (his appearance is described to the last detail) and, after Hector, the most chivalrous. He loved and was loved, and learned what it is to be unhappy in love. As in Dares, here too Troilus grows into his role as leader, but in this case right from the beginning. Hector urges prudence on him, but Troilus is heedless of danger and is captured. After being released he wounds Ulixes (Odysseus) when the latter is pressing Paris hard. In the third great battle there is a terrible encounter with Diomedes. It ends indecisively, but henceforth Diomedes and Troilus are sworn rivals. Later they will also be rivals in love.

The seer Calchas, in Dares not a Greek but a Trojan who joined the Greeks on Apollo's orders, is concerned about the fate of his daughter Briseida back in Troy; after all, he already knows how the war will end. He manages to arrange for her to join him in the Greek camp. Briseida's name is reminiscent of Homer's Briseis, in the *Iliad* the cause of Achilles' rancour, but in fact she was created by Benoît, who thus resolves a puzzle in Dares' work. For the last in Dares' series of portraits of Greek participants is a Briseida who plays no further part in his story. She is very beautiful, but her eyebrows meet in the middle. Benoît's Briseida meets this description – an ominous sign. She too loved and was loved, but she was not steadfast in love.

Briseida is the beloved of Troilus. She has no desire to leave him and Troy; but she goes, after much lamenting and a last night full of sighs, tears and promises. Troilus escorts her to the waiting Greek delegation. Even before they get there Benoît warns us of her inconstancy in a long tirade on the fickleness of women. It is Diomedes who then brings Briseida to Calchas; he comforts her and, instantly smitten, offers her his love. She is distant with him, but he can tell from her words that there is hope and when they part he covertly filches her glove. Briseida heaps reproaches on her father and again the author closes the episode with an allusion to her faithlessness, soon to become apparent.

Diomedes and Troilus now become arch-rivals. Diomedes captures Troilus' horse and presents it to Briseida. Troilus' increasingly evident failure in love runs parallel with his characterisation as the greatest Trojan hero since the death of Hector. Knowing that he has lost Briseida, and angrily congratulating his rival on his success, he deals Diomedes such a wound that he is taken for dead and carried to his tent. In a monologue full of inner conflict and self-reproach Briseida resolves to give her heart to the Greek. With

Troilus (left) has handed Briseida over to the Greeks. Illustration from a manuscript of
Benoît de Sainte-Maure's *Roman de Troie* produced in Italy in the second half of the 14th
century. Venice, Biblioteca Marciana.

the last word of her soliloquy, and without any comment from Benoît, she disappears
from the *Roman de Troie*.

Troilus eventually dies a hero's death by Achilles' hand without again encountering
Diomedes on the field of battle. The manner of his end earns Achilles the label 'reneié',
renegade, from the author of the *Roman*: he has denied his knighthood by an act of
'grant felenie'. This continues to be the attitude of the Trojan romances. Maerlant
(*Historie van Troyen*, 1261–66) limits himself to a single outburst, but Guido de
Columpnis (*Historia destructionis Troiae*, 1272–87) is less restrained. After Troilus' death
his invective is first directed against Homer. Homer has sung Achilles' praises, while the
true history of Troy shows beyond the shadow of a doubt that he was an unprincipled
scoundrel who had to make use of ambushes (as witness Hector) and who at most
possessed the strength to push someone already half-dead over the edge (Troilus). He
returns to the theme after the death of Memnon. And before her duel with Pyrrhus
Penthesileia mocks Achilles' son by reminding him of his father's unheroic deeds.
Mourning for Troilus and distaste for Achilles continue, greatly reinforced, into the
next phase in the reception of the *Roman de Troie*.

Troilus and Briseida function in Trojan romance as a mirror image of Achilles and
Polyxena (→ Hector). Since Benoît it is Troilus and Polyxena who receive sympathy,
while Briseida and Achilles typify incorrect forms of love. Benoît's technique attracted
imitators: it is customary to comment adversely on Briseida's behaviour. Guido – who
adds to her portrait that she flits from one lover to another – cannot even wait until she
has left Troy; he explodes as soon as he has described the farewell night. Of course later
writers modified all kinds of details in Benoît's narrative: in the Italian *Istorietta Trojana*
(prose, late 13th/early 14th century) Briseida gives Diomedes a ring and Troilus has a
spy monitoring her activities.

The story undergoes major changes from the first half of the 14th century, when the lovers are developed as an independent theme. Briseida is given a new name, Criseida, reminiscent of the Homeric Chryseis. In Boccaccio's short epic *Il Filostrato* (c.1335) she is a young widow and 'Troiolo' her naive, plaintive adorer. Criseida promises Troiolo that she will return to him, and he clings to this hope while all around him, and not only Cassandra, keep telling him what they have long known – that she is amusing herself with Diomedes. When he finally sees the truth with his own eyes Troiolo loses all desire for life and seeks death on the battlefield. The *Filostrato* was translated into French by one of the De Beauveaus, chamberlains to the Anjous (probably Louis, c.1417–62, *Roman de Troyle*). Chaucer reworked Boccaccio's version in *Troylus and Criseyde* (c.1385), a complex work which made a deep impression on his contemporaries. His analysis of the character of the fickle Criseyde, especially, is far superior to the conventional judgment on her behaviour. As a result of Chaucer's great influence Troilus and Criseida lived on for a long time and in many, mostly English, authors. John Lydgate's *Troy Book* (c.1420) clearly shows how that influence served to correct Guido de Columpnis' harsh judgment of Criseida.

And what happened to Briseida/Criseida in the end? The answer to that question had to wait for Robert Henryson's *The testament of Cresseid* (c.1485). It is, for moralists, a happy ending. Diomedes tires of her, she falls into prostitution, contracts leprosy and is reduced to begging her bread. Troilus gives her alms without recognising her. She then writes him a farewell letter in which she acknowledges her guilt and returns him the ring he had given her. William Fowler, too, has her ask Troilus' forgiveness on her deathbed (*The Last Epistle of Creseyd to Troylus*, c.1604).

From then on Criseida's image, and with it that of Troilus, begins to crumble. Shakespeare's *Troilus and Cressida* (c.1600) is a pot-pourri of traditions: Homer (in Chapman's 1598 translation), Chaucer, Lydgate and Guido de Columpnis (in Caxton's translation of Lefèvre's *Recueil* [→ Hector]). His Troilus is as blind to the disaster that Helen is bringing on Troy as he is to the cold calculation of the wanton Cressida, whose name has by now become a generic. Thomas Heywood (who also wrote an imaginative version of Caxton's *Recuyell* in poetic form: *Troia Britanica*, 1609) has Sinon bet Diomedes in Criseyde's hearing that he can seduce her; he wins the bet under Diomedes' supervision (*The Iron Age*, stage spectacle, 1632). John Dryden (*Truth Found Too Late*, 1679) reworks Shakespeare's *Troilus and Cressida* in French classicist style and attempts to rehabilitate Criseyde.

Medieval representations of Troilus (and Briseida) have been preserved mainly in 14th- and 15th-century manuscripts of the *Roman de Troie* and the *Historia destructionis Troiae*.

The modern reception has been largely determined by Shakespeare: three operas (Vidal 1910, Wolf 1951, Zillig 1954) and a literary work (Morley, *The Troyan Horse*, 1937). Walton's opera *Troilus and Cressida* (1954, libretto by Hassall) follows Chaucer, while the lovers who appear in Christa Wolf's *Kassandra* (1983) seem from the name Briseida to come from the tradition of Benoît and Guido.

L.J. ENGELS

Studies: Scherer 1963; Buchthal 1971; Hansen 1971; Martin 1972; Havely 1980; Boitani 1989; Hanly 1990; Benson 1991.

TURPIN (Latin: Turpinus) appears in Carolingian epic as an archbishop and a warrior in the Frankish army at the time of → Charlemagne. He has been identified with the historical Archbishop of Rheims who lived in the second half of the 8th century. There is no narrative in which Turpin has the leading role, but he is an important secondary figure in many *chansons de geste*.

In the *Chanson de Roland* (c.1100) Turpin, with → Roland and Oliver, is part of the Frankish rearguard which is treacherously ambushed by the Saracens. He fights valiantly and kills many of the infidel; but at the same time he carries out his duty as spiritual leader of the Christians. He gives them absolution before the battle, intervenes in the argument between Roland and Oliver as to whether Charlemagne should be summoned back, and blesses the fallen. Wearied to the point of death, he still attempts to fetch water for Roland; but this act of Christian charity proves too much for him and he dies with all his comrades on the field of Roncevaux. With his dual role as priest and warrior Turpin symbolises the Church's approval of the war against the infidel.

In other *chansons de geste*, too, Turpin represents the Church in Charlemagne's entourage. In *La Chevalerie d'Ogier* he shows himself wily as well as compassionate when by his guile he saves the captive → Ogier, for whom he is responsible, from starvation by ensuring him a plentiful supply of food. In *Le Pèlerinage de Charlemagne à Jérusalem* he exuberantly claims to be able to ride three horses at once, juggling four apples the while.

Turpin achieved fame in the Middle Ages as the author of a Latin chronicle entitled *Historia Karoli Magni et Rotholandi*, a detailed account of Charlemagne's campaigns against the infidel in Spain. Only towards the end of the 15th century did humanist scholars discover that the bishop could not possibly have been the author of this work. Nowadays it is accepted that the text evolved in France, possibly at the Abbey of Saint-Denis, where it went through a number of stages during the first half of the 12th century.

The chronicle proper is preceded by a fictional letter in which (pseudo-)Turpin dedicates his work to Leoprandus, Dean of Aachen. From this we learn that the bishop wrote his chronicle while recuperating from his wounds in Vienne after fourteen years spent marching round Spain with Charlemagne and his armies. In this version of events, therefore, Turpin did not perish with the rearguard at Roncevaux; he survived the battle because he was with the Emperor in the main army. In this letter the chronicle is expressly presented as an eye-witness account of Charlemagne's military exploits.

The first chapter of the chronicle tells how St James the Greater, disciple of Christ and brother of St John the Evangelist, had preached the Gospel in Galicia. After his death in Palestine his corpse miraculously returned to Galicia and was buried there. By Charlemagne's time, however, his grave has been forgotten and so James appears to the great Emperor in dreams no less than three times, instructing him to fight the infidels in Spain and thus make it possible for pilgrims to visit his grave.

Charlemagne obediently marches for Spain with a large army. For three months he besieges Pamplona, but fails to take the city because of its strong walls. So he prays to Christ and St James, and the walls collapse. Pamplona is captured and the infidels either baptised or slaughtered. Charlemagne then brings the whole of Spain under his sway. After three years of campaigning he returns to France, where he builds many churches and monasteries with the plundered gold from the war.

Then the infidel king Aigolant from Africa invades Spain. Charlemagne marches against him and a lengthy war ensues. On two separate occasions the Christians discover on the morning of a battle that the lances of some of their number have grown bark and leaves – a sign from God that the owners will die a martyr's death that day. During a truce Charlemagne and Aigolant meet. They debate as to which of their two religions is the better, Christianity or Islam. When a trial by ordeal decides the issue in favour of Christianity Aigolant promises to convert. He changes his mind, however, when he discovers that at Charlemagne's court the poor, whom the Christians call 'children of God', receive much less respect than eminent churchmen. In the battle that follows Aigolant is killed. Soon afterwards Ferracutus, a giant descended from Goliath, appears and challenges Charlemagne's knights to duel with him. The Saracen easily defeats many of the Christians, but then finds a worthy opponent in Roland (Rotholandus). This battle lasts two whole days. During a break Ferracutus interrogates Roland about the mysteries of Christianity and proposes that their duel shall serve as a divine judgment: if Christianity is indeed the true faith, Roland will be victorious. With God's help he manages to strike Ferracutus' weak spot (his navel) and victory thus goes to the Christians.

The twentieth chapter consists of a description of Charlemagne, his appearance, his strength and his daily life, on the lines of Einhart's *Vita Karoli Magni*. This chapter, in which the action pauses for a while, provides the transition to the account of Charlemagne's last Spanish battle, that of Roncevaux. This version of the story of the annihilation of Charlemagne's rearguard corresponds closely with that in the *Chanson de Roland*. Here too the defeat is due to the treachery of Ganelon; here too the enemy are Saracens and not, as in Einhart, Basques; and here too the main army later takes its revenge on the infidel. There then follows an account, much more detailed than in the *Chanson de Roland*, of how and where the fallen are buried. At the end of the chronicle (pesudo-)Turpin tells of a vision he had of Charlemagne's death while celebrating Mass at Vienne. At the intercession of St James, for whom he had built so many churches, the Emperor was admitted into Heaven.

The *Historia Karoli Magni et Rotholandi* takes narrative material, much of it drawn from *chansons de geste*, casts it in chronicle form and lards it with exempla and moralisations. The history of Charlemagne thus created is presented as a lesson: Charlemagne is a king with biblical characteristics, a new David, an exemplar in the battle against the infidel and false religion. With this version the material of the *chansons de geste* became suitable matter for sermons; the *Historia* shows the lessons to be learned by Christians from the heroic deeds of Charlemagne and his knights. The major role played by St James suggests that the chronicle was originally intended as propaganda for the pilgrimage to the saint's grave in Santiago de Compostela.

The 'Chronicle of pseudo-Turpin' was extremely influential in the Middle Ages. The text has been preserved in numerous manuscripts and printed redactions. It was soon incorporated in the Codex Calixtinus (mid-12th century), a compilation closely linked to the veneration of St James at Santiago. The text also made a major contribution to the *Vita Sancti Karoli*, composed on the initiative of the Emperor Frederick I Barbarossa to mark Charlemagne's canonisation in 1165. The *Historia* was translated many times into various vernaculars; in French alone we know of fifteen independent translations. In the mid-13th century the learned Dominican Vincent de Beauvais included the work in his *Speculum historiale*, a world history compiled for his brothers in the Order on the orders of the French king, the saintly Louis IX. Some decades later Jacob van Maerlant produced a verse translation of this important compilation; it was probably this that introduced the chronicle to a Dutch public.

Many depictions of Charlemagne and his history are based on the 'pseudo-Turpin Chronicle'. One example is the famous metal reliquary (c.1200–1215) in the cathedral at Aachen, in which the remains of the great Emperor are preserved. Eight gilt reliefs on its exterior depict scenes from the *Historia*. One side shows Charlemagne enthroned between the standing, proportionately smaller figures of Pope Leo III and Turpin. In Rome, a series of frescos of scenes from Charlemagne's life in Santa Maria at Cosmedin, painted for Pope Calixtus II in the first half of the 12th century, also show correspondences with the 'pseudo-Turpin Chronicle'. The Middle Dutch rhymed translation of the Chronicle in Maerlant's *Spiegel historiael* is splendidly illustrated with eight miniatures in a mid-14th-century hand (Koninklijke Bibliotheek, The Hague).

A representation of the fight between Turpin and the infidel Abîme can be seen on an architrave in Saint-Pierre Cathedral in Angoulême; it dates from shortly after 1118. In Saint-Faron Abbey in Meaux a statue of Turpin once formed part of a monumental tomb of → Ogier (pre-1180) which is no longer in existence.

H. VAN DIJK

Edition: Klein 1986.
Study: Lejeune/Stiennon 1971.

WALTHARIUS is the eponymous hero of a Latin epic probably written in the 10th century in St Gallen (Switzerland). The story, in Latin hexameters, is based on a much older Germanic heroic legend.

The Huns under King → Attila are marching west. When they are approaching Worms, capital of the Frankish realm, King Gibicho decides to offer no resistance. He agrees to pay tribute and supply hostages as security. Since the king's son, Gunthari, is too young they choose Hagano, scion of a very eminent family. The Huns then move farther west and invade the land of the Burgundians. Their king, Heriricus, whose court is at Châlon-sur-Saône, opts for the same solution and and gives as hostage his only child, his daughter Hiltgunt. Finally, King Alphere of Aquitaine is also forced to submit; he hands over his only son, Waltharius, to the Huns. Alphere and Heriricus had long ago made a formal pact providing for a future marriage between their two children.

The Huns now take the three children to King Attila's court in Pannonia. There they are carefully and lovingly brought up, the two boys in the king's immediate circle, Hiltgunt by his wife Ospirin. In time they achieve important positions at court: Waltharius becomes a valued general and Hiltgunt is given charge of the treasury.

Many years later, King Gibicho dies and is succeeded by his son Gunthari, who revokes the treaty with the Huns and refuses to pay further tribute. As soon as Hagano hears this he makes his escape. When Ospirin now tries to bind Waltharius more closely to the court, suggesting that he should marry a girl from a noble family, he too decides it is time to leave. He and Hiltgunt plan their escape carefully. After winning a victory for Attila Waltharius gives a great feast, at which the wine flows so freely that all the Huns sleep till noon next day. He then leaves the court with Hiltgunt, on foot and in full armour, his horse laden with two coffers which Hiltgunt has filled as arranged with gold arm-rings from Attila's treasury. They travel at night, hiding in the woods by day and feeding on birds and fish caught along the way. After forty days they reach the Rhine, where they pay the ferryman with fish they have caught. When he later sells the fish at court, it is seen to be of a kind not found in the Rhine. The ferryman is questioned; from his description of the couple with the jingling coffers, coupled with the fact that they were carrying fish from the Danube, Hagano concludes that the fugitives must be Waltharius and Hiltgunt, heading for home with treasure stolen from Attila.

Gunthari promptly selects twelve of his men to help him track down the two fugitives and relieve them of the treasure; he considers he has a right to it because of the tribute his father had paid to Attila in the past. Hagano, who has no wish to fight his old friend and comrade in misfortune, tries to persuade him against this. When he fails he warns Gunthari of Waltharius' exceptional strength and great combat experience, but Gunthari refuses to listen and gives the order to set out on their trail.

Somewhere in the Vosges, in a secure place accessible only through a cleft in the rocks, Waltharius and Hiltgunt are resting. Here the pursuers find them. Camalo, Gunthari's first messenger to Waltharius, demands of him both the treasure and the girl. Waltharius asks derisively by what right he demands them, but nevertheless offers him a hundred gold arm-rings to leave them in peace. Hagano advises Gunthari to accept the offer, whereupon Gunthari accuses him of cowardice. Camalo then fights Waltharius and is slain. The same fate befalls ten others; because of Waltharius' ideal defensive position, they can only attack him one at a time. Among the fallen is Patavrid, Hagano's nephew. The pre-combat exchanges become shorter and shorter, the means employed ever more varied. In one of the last fights they even try to pull Waltharius off his feet with a rope attached to a spear stuck in his shield, but without success. Finally only Gunthari remains. He retreats and rejoins Hagano, who thus far has kept out of the affair. Waltharius and Hiltgunt now leave their refuge and travel on, but are soon overtaken by Gunthari and Hagano, who has a duty to avenge his nephew Patavrid. In one last battle Waltharius now confronts two enemies who fall on him together. The fight ends when Gunthari has lost a leg, Waltharius a hand and Hagano an eye and six teeth. Hiltgunt binds up their wounds and the men make peace. Waltharius returns to his own country, marries Hiltgunt and rules his people well for another thirty years.

In the first line of his work the poet addresses his audience as *fratres*, and in the last four lines he apologises for his youthful inexperience. Taking this in conjunction with the text's numerous borrowings from classical and early-Christian authors such as Virgil (twelve lines are taken word for word from the *Aeneid*), Statius and Prudentius, who were read mainly in monastery schools, it is a reasonable assumption that the composer of the epic was a young monk. His purpose remains a riddle, though, for the text contains no trace of any Christian teaching – unless one interprets the highly negative figure of King Gunthari as personifying the cardinal sins of *superbia* (pride) and *avaritia* (avarice) and Waltharius as the model of a Christian king. Only in the last line is there an explicitly Christian thought: *Haec est Waltharii poesis. Vos salvet Iesus* (This is the poem about Waltharius. May Jesus save you).

Although the epic thus seems to have no theological or didactic function it was remarkably popular in its own time, at least among audiences familiar with Latin; no fewer than twelve manuscripts of it survive, and the evidence suggests that there must have been many more. Its distribution is also remarkable: we know of manuscripts from Flanders, France, Swabia, Bavaria and Austria. In several manuscripts the text is preceded by a brief dedication to a Bishop Erchambald by someone who calls himself Geraldus. This, together with the fact that in his *Casus Sancti Galli* Ekkehard IV relates that Ekkehard I (who died in 973) had in his youth written a *Vita Waltharii manu fortis* which he, Ekkehard IV, had revised, has led to the view that the *Waltharius* must have been written at St Gallen in the first half of the 10th century by Ekkehard I and entered general circulation between 965 (when Erchambald became Bishop of Strassburg) and 970 (the probable year of Geraldus' death). All this is far from certain, however; both Ekkehard's authorship and the date and place of origin are still matters of dispute.

The epic is also of importance as the only complete version of the story of Waltharius of Aquitaine. We do, however, have fragments of two other works on the same subject. The earlier of the two is the Old English *Waldere*, of which two fragments survive (of 31 and 34 long lines respectively, with caesura and alliteration). In the first of these Hiltgunt (whose name does not appear in the fragment) is exhorting someone described as the son of Ælfhere (Alphere) and a general in the army of Ætla (Attila) to destroy the arrogance of Gudhere (Gunthari), who has refused the arm-rings offered to him. The second fragment contains a dialogue between (probably) Hagena (Hagano) and Waldhere before the last fight. The date and place of origin of this text too are unknown. It is uncertain whether this is a version which predates the Latin *Waltharius*, bearing witness to an oral tradition, or whether the Old English text owes its existence to the influence of the *Waltharius* tradition. The only manuscript (Copenhagen) dates from the 10th century.

The second work that tells the story of Waltharius is a Middle High German heroic epic of the 13th century. Again only two fragments of it survive (of twenty and nineteen stanzas respectively, each of four long lines with end-rhyme); they describe Walther's homecoming in Langres (Champagne) and his marriage to Hildegunde. Again it is unclear whether these are the remnants of an independent epic transmitted (orally or in writing) in the vernacular or of a translation of the Latin *Waltharius*. If the latter, what we have here would be a rather long-winded ending, decked out with borrowings from all manner of other works, added by the translator himself; the Latin epic gives no account of Waltharius' homecoming.

Waltharius (Walther) appears in many works of the 12th and 13th centuries; some merely mention his name, in others he plays a modest part. The German *Rolandslied* (c.1173) has a 'Walthere der wîgant', the French *Chanson de Roland* a Gualter de l'Hum. In the *Nibelungenlied* (→ Siegfried) Etzel (Attila) recalls an earlier stay of Hagen and Walther at his court. The same work also contains a reference to Hagen's reluctance when he had once had to fight Walther. In the epics *Dietrichs Flucht*, *Rabenschlacht* and *Alpharts Tod* Walther is one of the heroes who support Dietrich von Bern (→ Theodoric the Great) in his war against Ermenrich (→ Ermanaric), while the various versions of the epic *Rosengarten* place him among the heroes at the Burgundian court in Worms. Only in *Biterolf* do we see him in his original role: Biterolf meets Walther when the latter is on his way back from the Hunnish realm to his own country. Later in this text we again find Walther at King Gunther's court in Worms. An interesting point is that in the *Waltharius* the Gunthari residing in Worms is King of the Franks; in all the other narratives Worms is the seat of the Burgundian court and Gunthari (Gunther) a Burgundian king. Finally, the minnesinger Walter von der Vogelweide, in a reference to the Waltharius story, calls the lady whose praises he sings his 'Hildegunde'.

Variants of the tale of Waltharius and Hiltgunt are known from other countries in Europe. The 11th-century *Chronicon Novaliciense* relates Waltharius' story as it appears in the Latin epic, but ends with the information that Waltharius eventually entered the monastery of Novalese in Piedmont, which he subsequently defended against bandits.

In the Old Norse *Thidrekssaga* (→ Theodoric the Great) Waltharius, here called Valtari or Vaskasteini, is a nephew of King Erminrikr (→ Ermanaric), who sends him as a hostage to King Attila's court. He manages to escape from there, together with Hilldigundr, daughter of the Greek king Ilias, during a feast. Attila sends Högni (Hagano) and eleven other warriors to track him down. Valtari kills all the eleven and Högni then takes to his heels. However, he returns by night and attacks the fugitives. During the fight Valtari puts out his eye with the haunch of a wild boar. Valtari then returns with Hilldigundr to King Erminrikr, whose standard-bearer he becomes. Later he loses a leg in battle and dies.

In a Polish version from the late 14th century, the Chronicle of Boguphalus, Walczerz wins the love of Helgunda, a Frankish princess, with his beautiful singing. A German rival sets guards on all the Rhine crossings and a ferryman refuses to carry them across. Walczerz then swims his horse across the Rhine with Helgunda. When his rival overtakes them Walczerz kills him, after which he returns with Helgunda to his castle near Krakow. Helgunda is later unfaithful to Walczerz and he kills her and her lover.

It is interesting to note the range of places credited with being Waltharius/Walther's homeland. In addition to Aquitaine, German texts also mention Spain, Kerlingen (France), Aragon, Navarre and Lengers (Langres). His name is also given as Walther von dem Wasgenstein, from the scene of his greatest feat of arms. According to the *Waltharius*, the fight with Gunthari and Hagano took place when Waltharius was travelling *in saltum Vosagum*, which is usually taken to mean the Vosges. However, this conflicts with the fact that he is supposed to have crossed the Rhine near Worms. It is therefore thought that the *Waltharius* poet made a mistake, and the actual site was a mountain known in the Middle Ages as Wasichenstein, near Obersteinbach on the border of Alsace and the Palatinate. But it is also possible that the mountain took its name from the legend, in which case *wasgen* may be derived from *wasconoland*, a name used as early as the 8th century for Aquitaine: Basqueland. If this is so, it is very likely that Walther of Aquitaine, Basqueland or Spain was originally a Visigoth hero. According to some, he lives on in the 16th-century Spanish ballads of Don Gaiferos, a hero who escapes with his beloved from Moorish captivity.

Although every narrative about Waltharius/Walther of Aquitaine presents him as an unconquerable hero who is also a model of righteousness and loyalty, after the 13th century he virtually lost his power to inspire. His only later appearance is in a historical novel written in 1855 by J.V. von Scheffel about the writing of the *Waltharius*: *Ekkehard. Eine Geschichte aus dem 10. Jahrhundert*, which includes a complete translation of the Latin epic.

N.TH.J. VOORWINDEN

Edition: Langosch 1956.
Translation (German): Genzmer 1966.
Studies: Gillespie 1973; Langosch 1973.

WELAND (Wayland) the Smith has the leading role in one of the oldest Germanic heroic tales. The earliest complete version of the story is to be found in the 'Volundarkvida' (Song of Weland) in the *Edda*. It tells how Weland and his brothers Egil and Slagfidr meet and marry three swan-maidens. Some time later the three girls run away and two of the brothers go in search of them. Weland, however, stays behind in the Ulfdalir (Wolfdales), creating all manner of splendid objects in his smithy. King Nidud's men come to his house in his absence and steal a ring. When Weland returns and notices the missing ring he thinks that his wife has come back; but that night he is attacked and taken captive. On the advice of Nidud's queen his Achilles tendons are cut to prevent him escaping. Weland is now forced to make ornaments for Nidud. In revenge he lures the king's two sons to his smithy, murders them and makes splendid objects from their body parts. Nidud's daughter Bodvild comes to the smithy with the stolen ring, which is broken. Weland drugs and then rapes her. He then informs the king of what he has done and makes his escape.

This story also appears in the *Thidrekssaga* (c.1250), though without the episode of the swan-maidens. Here Weland acquires a genealogy: his father is the giant Vadi from Sjaeland (Denmark). Weland enters the service of King Nidung of Jutland. Later they quarrel and Weland seeks revenge, but is captured and maimed. The account of the murder of Nidung's sons and the rape of his daughter is much the same as in the 'Volundarkvida', but in the saga Weland is helped by his brother Egil. After Nidung's death Weland marries his daughter. Their son is Vidga, one of the heroes in the epic tales connected with → Theodoric the Great.

The story falls into two parts: the swan-maidens and Weland's revenge. It is far from certain, however, that the swan-maiden episode was part of the original Weland story. Rather, it seems to be a folktale motif which is also found elsewhere, but never outside Scandinavia in connection with the Weland story.

Although the history of Weland has survived in complete form only in Scandinavia, the tale of his vengeance was known also to other Germanic tribes. In the Old English → *Deor* there are allusions to a story of 'Welund' and 'Beadohild'. Names from the story also occur in English place-names, for example 'Weland's smithy' in a document of 955. In his translation of Boethius' *The Consolation of Philosophy* Alfred the Great (871–899) renders the Latin 'Ubi nunc fidelis ossa Fabricii manent?' (Where now rest the bones of

Fabricius?) into Old English as 'Where now are the bones of the wise and famous goldsmith Weland?' Evidently the Latin *faber* (smith) led to the name Fabricius being linked with the smith Weland.

That the story was also known on the Continent is clear, if only from the fact that the *Thidrekssaga* was translated from the German, though the original has not survived; and Weland is mentioned as the father of Witege (Vidga) in, for instance, the Middle High German *Virginal* (c.1300). In German heroic epic (e.g. in the → *Waltharius*), and also in French (where Weland appears under the name of Galand) various weapons are said, as a kind of hallmark, to be of Weland's making. Weland's fame as a smith was evidently so widespread that the Icelandic monk Gunnlaug could use his name as a generic for 'smith' in his *Merlinuspá* (c.1200). He is also mentioned in late-medieval ballads from Germany and Scandinavia.

Pictorial representations also attest to the story's popularity in North-Western Europe. Best-known is that on the left front panel of the Auzon rune-casket (c.700), also called 'Frank's Casket' after a previous owner. It shows the moment when Bodvild arrives at the smithy. The right-hand scene on the lid includes an archer named in a runic inscription as Aegili. Whether this is the same person as Weland's brother Egil is uncertain. A picture-stone from Gotland also bears a scene from the Weland legend; this too shows the smithy.

The background to the Weland legend is obscure. The character of Weland is an uncommon one in heroic epic: not a hero in the usual sense, but a craftsman. Probably he was not a historical figure, unlike many heroes in the oldest epics. More likely is a link with the role of the smith at a time when smiths were widely regarded as uncanny individuals with supernatural powers, like the god Hephaistos/Vulcan in antiquity. Weland does indeed seem to possess supernatural powers; in the *Edda* he is called an 'elf'. Whether there is any connection between the Weland legend and the Greek myth of Daedalus is unclear, but there are some striking similarities.

With the end of the Middle Ages Weland vanishes from sight until the Romantic era, when the revival of interest in the Middle Ages also led to renewed interest in the figure of the master-smith. After the rediscovery of the *Edda* the Danish poet Adam G. Oehlenschläger retold the story in *Vaulundurs saga* (1804), at the end of which Weland is reunited with the swan-maiden Alvilde. The German translator and poet Karl Simrock developed the motif of the ring in his 1835 version. This magic ring attracts

Weland holding a beaker made from the skull of one of Nidud's sons. Left-hand front panel of a casket from Northumbria known as Frank's casket, made from walrus ivory in the first quarter of the 8th century. London, British Museum.

love to its wearer and also confers the power of flight. Weland's love for Nidung's daughter evaporates when he recovers the ring and has his wife's image again before his eyes.

This version by Simrock is the source of most of the stage versions produced in the 19th century, the most important of which is the drama planned by Richard Wagner in 1849. After he abandoned the project in 1850 – having tried to hawk it to Liszt – it was reworked as a play by Oskar Schlemm in 1880. The opera *Kovac Wieland* by the Slovak composer J.L. Bella, composed in 1881–90 and first performed in 1926, also goes back to Wagner. Vladimir Roy's libretto for this opera, with its allusions to Slovak nationalism – a live issue then as now – was based on Schlemm's play.

At the end of the 19th century the Neo-Romantics took up the material again. The Danish poet Holger Drachmann followed in the footsteps of his compatriot Oehlenschläger with his drama *Veland Smed* (1904); he linked Weland's revenge with the Twilight of the Gods, after which Weland is reunited with Alvilde in a world at peace. Others who made use of the material were the Frenchman Francis Viélé-Griffin (*La légende ailée de Wieland le forgeron*, 1899) and the German Friedrich Lienhard (*Wieland der Schmied*, 1905). Kipling's short story 'Weland's Sword' in his children's book *Puck of Pook's Hill* (1906) paints a touching picture of an old god fallen on hard times, but with his smithing skills intact. The last full-scale version is Gerhard Hauptmann's play *Veland* (1925), in which Weland's fierce thirst for vengeance alienates him from the swan-maiden Herware. Set against this is the Christian world, symbolised by the shepherd Ketill. During the Third Reich Weland was used as the symbol of aviation.

A. QUAK

Editions: Bertelsen 1908–11; Malone 1977.
Studies: Ellis Davidson 1958; Burson 1983; Nedoma 1988.

WIDSITH is the title of the longest (143 lines) and most likely the oldest (probably second half 7th century) of a group of early Old English poems in the tradition of the Germanic hero-song. These poems echo a way of life going back to the time of the *Völkerwanderung*, which the Angles and Saxons brought with them to their new homes in Britain. Consequently, they show no Christian or Latin influences, but form a direct link between Anglo-Saxon culture and its Germanic origins.

Some of these poems concern the life and art of the Old English bard; in the case of *Widsith*, of the poet of that name (literally: 'he who travels far'), of whom we are given an idealised portrait. He boasts of having visited the distant places he speaks of and served the mighty kings and princes he names. This is clearly a fictional account, for history tells us that the royal masters whom Widsith delighted with his art are separated in some cases by two hundred years; for instance, Eormanric ($\rightarrow$ Ermanaric) ruled over the Goths around 375, while Aelfwine (= Alboin), King of the Lombards, was murdered in 573. The *Widsith* is of little interest as poetry; rather, it is a survey of historical and legendary figures and events in which the poet provides a splendid encyclopedic review of the kings and kingdoms of the Germanic heroic age.

Widsith is also of interest for the poet's enormous pride in his skills of poetry and performance: each time he takes up his harp and begins to sing, his patrons remark that they have never heard finer poetry. But he can never rely on this, and his future is always uncertain. Wearily the minstrel wanders wherever his fate takes him, always seeking a lord who will protect him until all things pass away, both life and death.

The poem's structure is simple: a prologue and epilogue, each of nine lines, frame the poem proper; this consists of three parts, the three lists or *thulas* (from Icelandic *thula*, metrical list of names) of Germanic heroes, each of them constructed to a specific formula and concluding with a story or comment in which the poet extols his distant travels and his service to those rulers. The formula of the first list is 'Attila ruled over the Huns, Eormenric over the Goths'; of the second, 'I lived with the Huns, with the mighty Goths, with the Swedes, with the Geats and the South Danes'; of the third, 'I visited Wulfhere and Wyrmhere.' It is noticeable that the formulae become more and more personal: in the first list the poet does not appear in his own persona, in the second he lives among Germanic tribes, in the third he visits named Germanic rulers.

Among those mentioned in the first *thula* are King Offa of the Angles, who is greatly praised, and the neighbouring Danish kings Hrothgar (→ Beowulf) and Hrothwulf. Writing of Hrothgar, he tells us in five lines of his feud with → Ingeld of the Heathobards, of which we know the details from *Beowulf*. Strikingly, all the tribes named in the first thula save for the Huns, Goths and Burgundians lived along the North Sea and Baltic coasts.

At the start of the second *thula* Widsith again tells of how he learned his art. Then comes the survey of the many peoples among whom he claims to have lived; again he begins with the Huns and the Goths, and again they are mainly tribes from north-western Europe. This time Guthhere of the Burgundians and Aelfwine of Lombardy are singled out for lavish praise. The second *thula* concludes with a passage in which Widsith describes how he and a colleague performed at Eormanric's court and received the highest praise.

The third *thula* contains famous names from the history of the Goths and ends with references to the enmity between Goths and Huns, to the Gothic heroes Wulfhere and Wyrmhere who fought the invading Huns, and to Wudga (Widia) and Hama, two Gothic exiles.

In the epilogue the poet returns to the theme of his prologue: that a bard can exist only through the generosity of his hosts, without ever being able to rely on it. A lord should behave as a hero not only on the battlefield but also in his hall, rewarding his followers for their courage and loyalty by distributing gifts, in which case the bard would ensure that his fame was spread far and wide. The references in the poem to → Alexander the Great, the Greeks and the Persians are generally regarded as later additions.

HENK AERTSEN

Edition: Malone 1962.

W IDUKIND (or Wittekind, French Guiteclin or Guitechin), leader of Saxon resistance to the Franks under → Charlemagne, is best known as the protagonist in *Les Saisnes* (The Saxons), a *chanson de geste* written around 1200 by the Arras poet Jehan Bodel. In fact, in two manuscripts the epic is called 'the romance of Guiteclin'. There are marked variations in the text of the four extant manuscripts of *Les Saisnes*. Probably only the first three thousand lines are Bodel's own work; the rest betrays the hand of several adaptors. The epic centres on Charlemagne's war against the Saxon king Widukind, but has a courtly love-affair woven into it. So what does the story say?

Years earlier, Clovis' son Floovant had married his daughter to the Saxon king Brunamont, and their descendants are now claiming the Frankish throne. When Pepin the Short kills the Saxon Justamont a feud begins. In the first Saxon War Justamont's son Guitechin (in other manuscripts Guiteclin), having learned of Charlemagne's defeat at Roncevaux, captures Cologne. Charlemagne wants to move against the Saxons, but first he has to arrange the tribute to be paid by a conquered people, the 'Hurepois'; he remits this in exchange for their support. There follows a battle with Guitechin on the banks of the Rune (Rhine). Sebile, wife of the Saxon king, falls in love with Baudouin, → Roland's brother and Charlemagne's nephew, and betrays Guitechin's plans to cross the Rune to Charlemagne. Then the Hurepois arrive, cross the Rune and put the Saxons to flight. However, the Rune still forms the frontier, crossed covertly on a number of occasions by heroic warriors and amorous knights. Eventually it is decided to construct a bridge. This makes it possible to fight a great battle, in which Charlemagne meets Guitechin in hand-to-hand combat and kills him. Sebile is baptised in Dortmund and marries Baudouin, who becomes King of the Saxons. A second war follows, between Guitechin's descendants and Charlemagne; after Charlemagne has again been victorious one of them is baptised as 'Guiteclin the Convert'.

Bodel suggests the existence of an older version of this tale when he tells us that there are *jongleurs* singing of Guitechin who do not know his 'rich new verses' (fine alexandrines as opposed to the old decameters?). Additionally, references to the tale of Guiteclin can be found in texts dating from before Bodel's time.

The story was known in Spain in the 13th century: in the *Gran Conquista de Ultramar* Geteclin, King of the Saxons, lays siege to Cologne with his Moors, kills its ruler Adelantado and carries off his wife and daughter. Charlemagne kills Geteclin and marries the widow to his nephew Baldeovin. This version thus accords with the account in Bodel. Later Spanish romances of the 16th and 17th centuries make Sebile Geteclin's daughter, not his wife, and focus on the adventures of Sebile and Baldovinos.

The first branch of the Norse *Karlamagnús saga* (late 13th century) tells of Vitakind (Germanic form), King of Saxony, burning Mutersborg (Münster) to the ground and wounding its bishop. Charlemagne takes the field and calls Roland and Oliver to his aid; they pursue Vitakind to Dortmund and there kill him. Charlemagne then goes campaigning in Spain and sends Roland and Oliver to Nobilis. The

Widukind's grave-stone, 12th century, in St Dionysius Church, Enger.

fifth branch of the saga, *Saga af Guitalin saxa* (romance form!) begins with Charlemagne in Nobilis. Guitalin has taken Cologne and Charlemagne marches against him. Here too the bridge-building episode and the love of Baldvini and Sibilia are central. The Danish *Keyser Magnus Krønicke*, a translation of the first branche of the Norse saga, says nothing of the Saxon war, but does include – after Roncevaux – part of Baudouin's love-affair: Baldewin, Wdger and Namlun do battle with Sybilia, Queen of Saxony, and her son Justam[ont]. In the 17th century this chronicle was 're'-translated from Danish into Icelandic.

All these diverse items and episodes from the Saxon war fail to provide a satisfactory overall picture of the tradition; what is clear is that Bodel puts the material into a more logical form, and also that he does his best to reflect the topography accurately.

In all the narratives, the sections concerning Widukind have a clear historical basis (unlike the love story of Baudouin and Sebile). In 778 the Annals tell us that the Saxons, incited by one 'Widochind', are once again in revolt. In fact Widukind had been at odds with Charlemagne ever since 772. In 778 he devastated the area around Coblenz, but following an offensive by Charlemagne in 783 and 784 the Saxons were finally defeated in 785 (though Widukind was never captured!). The historical Widukind, who had been baptised in the meantime, died in 807 while on another military expedition. He was beatified by the Church, which honours his memory on 7 January.

Strikingly, in the Middle Ages German literature has no Widukind tradition, apart from a number of mentions in chronicles. The later German tradition is linked to the emergence of nationalism and the search for a historical identity. In the 17th century the character reappears in Moscherosch and in Johann Rist's 1647 play *Das friedewünschende Deutschland*. No longer the pagan foe, Widukind is now the glorious ancestor, and naturally his conversion becomes a favourite theme. In 1662 he is the subject of a musical play, *Die Wittekinden*. This tradition remained very much alive in the 18th and 19th centuries, with epic poems, ballads, novels and plays about Widukind; there were even several operas and oratorios devoted to him, all highly nationalistic in tone. More and more new folkloristic elements were added to the story. As one example we will mention Joh. Chr. Lobe, whose *Wittekind* had its première in Weimar in 1821.

A distinct chapter in Widukind's history is his annexation by the Nazis. Charlemagne, seen as a Frenchman and a tool of the Pope, suddenly becomes the 'Saksenschlachter', and there develops an idealised image of Widukind as the ancestor of the Germanic race. In the 1930s this image became hugely important in Germany; in June 1934 a wreath was laid at Widukind's tomb in the Stiftskirche Sankt Dionysius in Enger (North Rhine-Westphalia) – which also has a Widukind Museum – and 60,000 members of Fascist organisations were treated to an address on the Saxon War. Not far away, in Herford, is the only monument to Wittekind, an equestrian statue. In 1933 there were three Widukind dramas. The craze reached its peak in 1935: SA-leader Hans Sponholz published his lyrical pamphlet *Widukind erwache*, Edmund Kiss made a novel and a tragedy out of the material, and Berthold von Biedermann's *Widukind* had its première. Numerous pamphlets and 'scholarly' articles on Widukind appeared during those years, and were quickly reflected in National Socialist educational material.

J. KOOPMANS

Editions: Skårup 1980; Brasseur 1989.
Studies: Wenzel 1931; Brasseur 1990.

WIGALOIS, Knight of the Round Table, is the hero of the Middle High German Arthurian romance of that name written in the early 13th century (c.1210/15?) by Wirnt von Gravenberc (or Grafenberg). The name Wigalois sounds French, but no Old French work which could have been Wirnt's source has ever been found. The content of *Wigalois* does show a number of parallels with French medieval literature, however, especially with the verse romance *Le Bel Inconnu*. The fantastic story of the Arthurian knight Wigalois, which falls into two parts, can be summarised as follows.

The first part, an epic introduction, tells of the adventures of Wigalois' father, the renowned Gawein (→ Gawain). An unknown king called Joram appears at King → Arthur's court and offers a girdle to Arthur's consort, the lovely Guinevere. On Gawein's advice the queen refuses the gift; whereupon, to the shame of the court, Gawein – the bravest and noblest of all Arthur's company – is defeated by the unknown prince. As a result Gawein is obliged to follow Joram to his marvellous realm. The king is well-disposed towards him and gives him a wonderful girdle which, it turns out, confers magic powers. While in Joram's kingdom Gawein marries the lady Florie, the king's niece. He leaves his pregnant wife to visit Arthur's court but, fatefully, forgets to take the magic girdle; without it he is unable to find his way back to Joram's magic land. Meanwhile, his son Wigalois grows into a handsome youth with one burning ambition: to become one of Arthur's knights. Taking the girdle, he sets out for Arthur's court to find his father. Wigalois' exceptional virtue becomes apparent to all when without difficulty he seats himself on the 'stone of virtue', an honour previously reserved for Arthur himself.

The second and main part of the story tells of Wigalois' adventures. A female messenger comes to Arthur's court to ask Gawein's support for her beleaguered mistress, the Lady of Korntin. To the lady's displeasure it is Wigalois, in her eyes a callow stripling, who is charged with the task. All kinds of adventures befall Wigalois on his way to Korntin, enabling him to prove his valour. Our hero now meets the Lady of Korntin and falls head over heels in love with her. But he will not be allowed to marry Larie (such is the lovely lady's name) until he has dealt with the demonic Roaz who has occupied her land.

New adventures await Wigalois. Fortunately, magical aids are available to him in his struggle with his enemies, who prove to possess supernatural, even demonic powers. Not only has a priest attached a lucky note to his sword, but Larie has provided him with a loaf which gives him miraculous powers. When the King of Korntin then presents him with a flowering branch which affords protection against the poisonous breath of dragons, Arthur's knight would seem to be armoured against all possible foes.

But appearances are deceptive. Along the way the estimable Wigalois meets the evil dragon Pfetan and gets the worst of the encounter. Only divine intervention saves the hero's life. In later battles too his opponents prove extremely dangerous. A second time he seems about to be worsted, now by the demonic hag Rual, but again a prayer for God's help works wonders. Wigalois' adventures culminate in his duel with the invader Ruaz himself. Wigalois is victorious and thus succeeds in freeing the land of Korntin from demonic rule. He then marries Larie, heiress to Korntin, finds his father again at Arthur's court and lives 'happily ever after'.

Wigalois belongs to the continental Arthurian tradition, of which Chrétien de Troyes (active in the third quarter of the 12th century) was the great initiator. Early romances in this genre (e.g. → *Erec* and → *Yvain*) were characterised by a strict two-part structure. In a variation on the religious theme of sin and penance, the author relates how after initial failure (his personal 'crisis') the hero redeems himself through a series of adventures and eventually returns covered with glory to Arthur's court, from which he had set out at the start of the romance.

Compared with this scheme, *Wigalois* is notably lacking in any such 'crisis'; here the hero is perfect from the start. This is apparent from the 'stone of virtue' test, which Wigalois passes with flying colours. In Chrétien the epic tension derives from the discrepancy between the sought-after Arthurian ideal and the evident fallibility of the Arthurian knight; here it lies in the opposition between Christian values, represented by the Arthurian knight, and an Otherworld governed by devilish forces. For the perfect Christian knight Wigalois is in himself, and despite his (three!) magical aids, no match for the superior forces of Hell. Salvation comes from prayer to God, which repeatedly saves him in desperate situations (even his manacles break at the divine command). With God's help Wigalois proves capable of overcoming foes stronger than himself.

King Arthur's Round Table with ten figures around it, including Arthur and
Guinevere, most of them dressed in red and white. The five standing young women
are waiting on them. On the table are dishes, six large knives and a horn. Illustration
by the Cistercian monk John of Brunswick in the 1372 manuscript of *Wigalois*.
Leiden, Universiteitsbibliotheek.

The *Wigalois* poet has been criticised for his love of the fantastic and consequent lack of depth. Yet there is a clear message in his work: it shows the limitations of the human individual – without God's help even the most perfect of knights cannot withstand the Devil's power. The element of the marvellous, already so beloved of Arthurian romance, is used here to illustrate the work's supra-rational religious dimension. Given the romance's strong Christianising tendencies, Max Wehrli's observation that in the late Arthurian tradition the genre is 'baptised' certainly applies to *Wigalois*. The high-point of the story is the freeing of Korntin from demonic tyranny. The Arthurian knight Wigalois becomes (in imitation of Christ) the 'redeemer' and 'bringer of salvation'.

Wigalois was at first very popular (as the 13 extant manuscripts and 23 fragments prove), but in the late Middle Ages it met with only a limited response. Ulrich Fuetrer reworked the narrative in his *Buch der Abenteuer*, a compilation commissioned by Albrecht III of Bavaria around 1475 in which he incorporated a number of 13th-century texts. Printers, too, took an interest in the Wigalois story. A prose version was published in 1493 by Johan Schönsperger in Augsburg and in 1519 by Johannes Knoblauch in Strassburg under the title *Wigaleis vom Rade*, a reference to the Wheel of Fortune that the fortunate hero always carried with him. Four other prints were produced in the 16th century, including one by the Frankfurt publisher Sigmund Feyerabend in the *Buch der Liebe* (1587). The Hamburg print of 1611 became the source for an Icelandic chapbook (1683) and two Danish prose versions (1656, 1732). In the printed version, however, the original issues were greatly simplified, with the main emphasis on the duality of 'good' and 'evil'. The Wigalois material also forms part of the Yiddish narrative tradition, especially through the print by Josel Witzenhausen (1610–86), printer and publisher of Amsterdam, which is known by the strange title *Widuwilt* (or: *Kinig Artus Hauf*). When Gawein is about to leave, his pregnant wife asks what she shall call the child and he tells her: *wie du wilt* (Whatever you like). The lady takes him literally; hence the hero's name. The story also turns up in visual art of the late Middle Ages. Among the numerous frescos in the 'Sommerhaus' of Runkelstein Castle in South Tyrol, painted around 1385, are two strips with 22 (mostly badly damaged) scenes from Wirnt von Gravenberc's *Wigalois*.

Versions of the Wigalois story have also been produced in modern times, particularly in the 19th century.

J.H. WINKELMAN

Editions: Kapteyn 1926; Melzer 1973.
Translation: Thomas 1977.
Studies: Haug 1980; Gottzmann 1989.

Y DER, son of Nuc or Nut, is the hero of the early 13th-century Old French romance that bears his name. Because of its negative portrayal of King → Arthur, *Yder* is sometimes called an 'anti-Arthur romance'.

According to the romance Yder was born at Cardoil to a noblewoman whose lover had abandoned her even before his birth. With a half ring as a means of recognition, Yder sets out to find his father. On the way he falls in love with Queen Guenloie; but to be worthy of her he has to prove himself as a knight. During his search he meets King Arthur and helps him to fight two knights. After killing both of them he hopes that Arthur will dub him knight. But Arthur forgets about him and Yder leaves his court disappointed. He then meets King Ivenant, who promises to knight him if he can withstand his wife's efforts to seduce him. Yder's success and consequent knighting are described with a great deal of humour.

He travels on with his squire Luguain and comes to Castle Rougemont, where the rebellious vassal Talac is being besieged by King Arthur. Yder decides to help Talac. In the lists he proves more than a match for Arthur's knights; he unhorses them all, defeating Kei (Kay) no less than three times. Unknown to Yder, Guenloie is close by and watching the combat; but she fails to recognise him. Each is tormented by desire for the other. The following day Yder, with Talac and six other knights, is again victorious. At one stage Kei treacherously sends thirty men together against them; even these are defeated. By now Yder's fame has reached → Gawain's ears and he resolves to enter the lists against him. Yder knocks him out of the saddle and is about to take his horse as prize when Arthur intervenes. While they are arguing over the horse, Kei runs Yder through the back with his sword and brings him down. So appalled are both sides by this outrageous act and the gravity of Yder's wound that Arthur and Talac make peace. Luguain takes Yder away on a litter and no one expects him to recover. On the way he meets Guenloie, who recognises Yder, skilfully draws the sword from his wound and binds it up. She shows Luguain a monastery where Yder can be cared for. When the court learns that he is not dead, but recuperating in a monastery, Gawain decides to visit him. Queen Guenevere wants to go too, which makes Arthur jealous; but he too joins the company. Eventually Yder is persuaded to come to court.

One day when Arthur is away Yder rescues Guenevere from a bear. Meanwhile Talac's castle is under siege, but Arthur refuses to go to his vassal's aid. Gawain and → Yvain set out for Rougemont. Fearing that Yder's wound is not yet properly healed, they do not invite him to accompany them. Yder feels that his friends have deserted him and slips away from Arthur's court unnoticed. Two days later he reaches Rougemont, intending to help Talac, but finds that the siege has been broken. Only one tent remains; in it is a damsel who asks him to discover the identity of a knight who calls on her every day. When this knight refuses to give his name there is a terrible fight which threatens to prove fatal to both combatants. In the struggle Yder drops the ring by which he can recognise his father and risks his life to recover it. The unknown knight is so astonished that he breaks off the fight. Yder tells him about his search for his father. The knight then reveals his identity: his name is Nuc, and he is in fact Yder's father. Nuc at once decides to find Yder's mother and marry her. Yder sends a message to Guenloie and sets out with his father for Arthur's court at Caerleon. Arthur is (unjustly) so jealous of Yder that he decides to dispose of him at the first opportunity; he knows he will have Kei's support in this. Arthur takes to the road with Gawain, Yvain, Kei and Yder in search of adventure. They encounter Guenloie, who is on her way to court to meet Yder. They recognise each other, but do not speak. Guenloie asks for Arthur's help in finding a husband and suggests that she should marry whoever brings her a knife belonging to two giants who are making the Malvern woods unsafe. Yder kills both giants single-handed (Arthur prevents the others from helping him) and so wins the knife. After the fight Kei volunteers to bring the thirsty Yder some water; he takes it from a poisoned spring. Next day Yder is, to all appearances, dead. Kei suggests that the poison came from the giants. Arthur and his three knights move off, leaving the seemingly dead Yder behind. He is found by the two sons of the King of Ireland, who know of an antidote to the poison and cure him. They journey together to court, where they find Gawain and Yvain grieving over Yder's death while Arthur and Kei are in high spirits. When Gawain and Nuc find out who poisoned Yder Kei is forced to flee to escape their wrath. Yder arrives just in time to calm them down. Arthur crowns Yder king and gives him Guenloie as his wife; Luguain becomes a knight. Nuc marries Yder's mother and everybody is reconciled with everybody else.

This starring role is not Yder's only appearance in Arthurian literature; he also turns up in episodes of other romances. The first to give Yder a place among Arthur's knights was Chrétien de Troyes in his *Erec et Enide*. One day → Erec, almost unarmed, is escorting the queen and her waiting-woman through the woods when they encounter a fully-armed knight accompanied by a lady and a dwarf. The dwarf strikes first the waiting-woman, then Erec. Erec goes after the three of them, bent on taking revenge as soon as he can get hold of some arms and armour. They come to a small town where Erec finds lodging with a man who has a very pretty daughter, Enide. Erec's host provides him with arms and he fights the knight and defeats him. The loser introduces himself as Yder and promises Erec that he will go to Arthur's court with the lady and the dwarf and there surrender to the queen. When he turns out to be a very good knight Arthur asks him to join his household. Yder agrees and becomes a knight of the Round Table. He plays no further part in the story.

Some elements from *Yder* are regularly found in other works in which Yder appears: the fact that he is in some way connected with the queen (and so arouses Arthur's jealousy) and his fight with a bear. In several narratives Yder is not originally a member of the Round Table, but becomes one of Arthur's knights on merit in the course of the story; for instance, in the Middle Dutch *Wrake van Ragisel* (a translation of the Old French *Vengeance Raguidel*, c.1220–30), in which he, with Walewein (Gawain), is the predestined avenger of Ragisel. This Scots knight has been slain by the giant Gygantioen, whose daughter Belinette Yder loves. But he will only be able to marry her when Gygantioen has been killed. Not an easy task, for the giant has magic armour and is always accompanied by a trained fighting bear. As soon as Walewein arrives in Scotland to avenge Ragisel Yder joins forces with him. Walewein slays Gygantioen in single combat and Yder kills the bear. Yder and Belinette are married and Yder follows Walewein back to King Arthur's court, where he tells how they exacted vengeance for Ragisel. He becomes a knight of the Round Table and then returns to Scotland.

In the Old French romance *Durmart le Galois*, written in the first quarter of the 13th century, Yder plays a less glorious role. Out hunting, he and Queen Guenièvre have become separated from the rest of the party. Then Brun de Morois suddenly appears; he carries off the queen and Yder is powerless to prevent him, for he is unarmed. While trying to find some arms and armour he meets Durmart, who kills Brun and rescues the queen, thus saving Yder an ignominious return to court.

Yder (Isdernus), Arthur (left) and Gawain and Kay (right) head for Mardoc's moated castle to rescue Winlogee. Archivolt over the north door, 1120–40, of Modena Cathedral.

Although Yder is the leading character in one romance, his fame was too small to inspire later writers or visual artists. The only time he may have been immortalised is on the famous archivolt (1120–40) at Modena, which shows a knight called Isdernus in a scene with King Arthur (Artus de Bretania), the captive queen Guinloie or Guenevere (Winlogee) and possibly Durmart (Burmaltus).

ADA POSTMA

Edition: Adams 1983.
Studies: Gildea 1965–66; Schmolke-Hasselmann 1980; Adams 1988.

YONEC is the hero of the *lai* by Marie de France that bears his name. There once lived in Britain an old and extremely wealthy man who, being in need of children to whom he could leave his riches, had married a young wife. The wife is very attractive, so he keeps her locked up in a tower with his sister, an old maid, as companion. For seven years the lady lives confined in the tower, but she bears no children. Slowly but surely she begins to pine away.

At the beginning of April the lady gives vent to a bitter complaint: why doesn't some gallant and adventurous knight come and rescue her? At that moment a hawk flies into her chamber, lands at her feet and promptly turns into a knight. This knight had long been in love with her, but could not come to her until she voiced her complaint. He becomes her lover and promises that whenever she wishes he will be with her within an hour. As a result of her love-affair the lady completely recovers her spirits, as her husband does not fail to notice.

Then his sister discovers the secret of the hawk-knight. As soon as the husband hears about it, he has a grille with razor-sharp spikes fixed across the window. Arriving for the next rendezvous, the hawk-knight is mortally wounded. He tells his mistress that she is pregnant by him; their son, whom she is to name Yonec, must avenge his death. Then he leaves his lady; she follows the trail of blood to a splendid city, where she finds her beloved on his deathbed. He commands her to go back and gives her a ring (so long as she wears it her husband will remember nothing) and a sword (with which their son is to exact vengeance).

As her lover had foretold, the lady gives birth to a son. As soon as Yonec is ready for knighthood the lady accompanies her husband and son to an abbey in Caerleon, where they find a magnificent tomb. The lady realises that this is where her lover lies; she tells her son the whole story and then departs this life. Yonec draws his sword and strikes off his stepfather's head; he then succeeds his father as the country's king.

The earliest version of *Yonec* – of which there are four extant manuscripts – is a *lai* of 562 lines attributed to Marie de France. Of this 12th-century poet practically nothing is known. In addition to writing about a dozen *lais* (→ Lanval and → Eliduc) she translated *L'Espurgatoire saint Patrice* (St Patrick's Purgatory) and a collection of Aesop's fables from Latin. According to herself, she recorded the content of tales made into *lais* by travelling Breton minstrels. Whether these Breton *lais* were lyrical songs or musical compositions is unknown. What we now mean by a *lai* is a narrative in rhyming couplets.

During the reign of the Norwegian king Hákon Hákonarson (1217–63) the *lais* of Marie de France (with the exception of *Eliduc*), together with ten others, were translated into Norwegian as *Strengleikar*, songs sung to the accompaniment of stringed instruments.

Yonec is quite clearly a rationalised folktale: before the lady will accept the hawk-knight's love he has to prove that he is a Christian; also, the lady betrays herself (thus, unlike → Lanval, she breaks no ban). Yonec is the male counterpart of the fairy mistress (cf. → Lanval and *Tydorel*). *Yonec* contains a number of traditional motifs: the old, jealous husband who locks up his young wife (cf. Marie de France's *Guigamar*), the discovery of the affaire (cf. → Tristan and → Cligès), the transformation from beast to man and the death of the wicked stepfather.

LUDO JONGEN

Translations: Burgess/Busby 1986.

YSENGRIMUS is the Latin name of the most important wolf in Western European beast epic; in the various vernaculars he is known by such variants as Ysengrin, Ysengrijn, Ysegrim and Insingrine. He is the eponymous main character in a Latin epic which is made up of a number of episodes, linked partly by recurring characters and themes and partly by the chronological structure. In imitation of classical epic, the story begins *in medias res*.

Ysengrimus catches the fox Reinardus (→ Reynard), with whom he is permanently at odds, and proposes to eat him. Reinardus manages to avoid this fate by offering Ysengrimus a share of the ham which a passing farmer is carrying; he wants to keep some of it for himself, though. Ysengrimus agrees. Reinardus then pretends to be so exhausted that he can hardly walk. The farmer wants to catch him so he puts the ham down. Ysengrimus runs off with it, devours the lot and offers Reinardus as his share the string used to hang it.

By way of revenge, that winter the fox persuades the wolf to use his tail to fish through a hole in the ice. While he sits there waiting for a bite Reinardus steals a chicken from the village priest. Carrying his prey, and pursued by the priest and other villagers, he returns to the wolf, whose tail is by now frozen into the ice. The villagers lay into the wolf; an old woman accidently cuts off his tail and so enables him to escape in the nick of time.

Reinardus makes amends for this by introducing the wolf to a flock of sheep. The wolf is to divide their field into equal sections, and in return will be allowed to eat any sheep that stray outside their patch. The sheep appear to agree, but the field is divided in such a way that Ysengrimus gets butted by four rams at once.

The scene now moves to a meeting of the court. King Lion is ill and summons the animals' chief representatives to his court to advise him. Only Reinardus fails to appear. However, he eventually turns up and cures the king by wrapping him in a wolfskin, which – after lengthy debate – is taken from Ysengrimus. The king notices the hostility between wolf and fox and enquires how it came about. The story now continues with the explanation given to the king; the events related here thus took place before the ham-sharing incident.

A number of animals, among them Reinardus, once went on a pilgrimage. They were harassed by Ysengrimus, and later by a pack of twelve wolves, but managed to frighten them off. The incident of the fox and the cock also took place during this journey. Two of the pilgrims, the cock and the goose, deserted the company. Reinardus went after them. He plied the cock with flattery until he agreed to crow with his eyes shut; whereupon Reinardus seized him and ran off, pursued by a large crowd. The cock talked the fox into telling the pursuers that he was only taking his lawful prey. To do this the fox had to open his jaws and the cock promptly flew up into a tree. Reinardus tried to dupe him again by claiming that a piece of bark was a proclamation of universal peace, but the cock drove him away by describing the (imaginary?) approach of a hunter and his dogs.

The fox persuaded Ysengrimus to enter a monastery because he would eat so well there. While Ysengrimus was there the fox went to the wolf's lair and urinated on his cubs. The she-wolf chased him back to his own den, but got stuck in the entrance. Reinardus emerged through another exit and raped her. The wolf fared just as badly in his monastery: his behaviour was so appalling that the monks beat him and threw him out. Ever since then there has been enmity between wolf and fox – so concludes the account of earlier events given to the king. The story proper now continues.

The wolf, left without a skin by the events at court, tries to get hold of another, first from a stallion and then from a ram. Both pretend to co-operate, but then escape leaving the wolf with even more injuries. After a while, though, the wolf's skin grows back. Reinardus arranges for the lion to dine with Ysengrimus. He helps the wolf to catch some game and the lion asks Ysengrimus to share it out. Ysengrimus makes three equal portions, one for each of them. The enraged lion tears off Ysengrimus' new skin. Now Reinardus has to divide the prey. He makes three portions of differing quality: the best is for the king, the second for the queen, and the last is for their cubs. Delighted, the king asks who taught him to share things out so skilfully. 'The wolf', he replies.

So Ysengrimus is again in need of a skin; this time he demands it from the donkey, who supposedly owes him a skin. The donkey makes him swear to this on 'relics' which prove to conceal a trap. The wolf, caught, has to bite off his paw to escape.

Finally, the wolf meets Salaura the sow and offers her the kiss of peace. She thinks that they should hear Mass first and calls her relatives to sing the hymns. The pigs then kill Ysengrimus. There follows a lament for the times, and the end of the world is proclaimed. With this the story ends.

Ever since research into *Ysengrimus* began the author's name has been given as Nivardus, since this name appears in a late copy of excerpts from the text. Recently, however, new manuscripts containing excerpts have come to light, with different names for the author; so that we actually know nothing with any certainty about the writer of the work. However, a whole string of historical references makes it almost certain that it was written around 1150. It also contains so many references to Ghent and the surrounding district, and especially to religious houses in that area, that one may reasonably assume that it was written by a cleric from Ghent.

Ysengrimus takes its material from Aesop's fables, some short animal poems from Carolingian times, and probably also from vernacular tales of the oral tradition. But this material is changed and modified and for the first time set in a broad epic context. *Ysengrimus* is the first European narrative in which the fox and the wolf bear the names which later became so well-known, and the first in which their enmity provides the mainspring of the plot.

Constantly recurring themes are those of Fortune, the deceiver who is himself deceived and the misuse of language. These themes are used as the vehicle for extremely sharp criticism of contemporary abuses; at times this is so detailed that some scholars have sought to read the work as a *roman à clef*. The latest studies, however, have reverted to the view that the text's intention is more general. Scholars are agreed that the criticism relates almost exclusively to spiritual and clerical matters, and that the audience for the work should be sought within the Church, probably in monastic circles.

The work is written in elegiac couplets which demonstrate the author's mastery of his craft. Striking features are the concise style, the sometimes very witty dialogue, the many ironic metaphors and the abundance of proverbs. The characters' own words predominate over the action, and are clearly treated with greater attention and inventivity. A good example of this is the flaying of the wolf during the court session. The actual process occupies only twelve lines, but the whole passage is very long; there are endless debates as to whether Ysengrimus' skin is really suitable, and many interpretations of the flaying itself. For instance, the fox congratulates the wolf before he is flayed on the honour his family will derive from his having been permitted to lend his skin to the lion; afterwards he expresses his amazement at the splendid scarlet cloak the wolf had concealed under his shaggy fur. Some regard this dominance of the spoken word as a fault. On the other hand, it has recently been argued that it is a deliberate device intended to bring out as strongly as possible one of the work's main themes, the contrast between 'rhetoric' and 'reality'.

Ysengrimus has come down to us, in whole or in part, in 17 manuscripts, indicating that this – rather difficult – text enjoyed a reasonable distribution. The court and pilgrimage episodes were reworked into a new text, the so-called *Ysengrimus abbreviatus*. A number of manuscripts have also survived which contain collections of proverbs garnered from *Ysengrimus*. *Ysengrimus* was thus not without influence in the field of Latin literature. But this pales into insignificance beside the work's enormous impact in the various vernaculars. Without *Ysengrimus* the → Reynard stories would be inconceivable. They repeatedly make use of themes and motifs from it, and constantly elaborate on the idea of the epic world of the animal realm and the eternal conflict between fox and wolf. Because of the change of protagonist that takes place with the transition from Latin to the vernacular, the rest of the story is to be found under → Reynard.

P. WACKERS

Edition: Mann 1987.
Study: Jauss 1959.

YVAIN, son of King Urien, is the hero of Chrétien de Troyes' romance *Le chevalier au lion* (c.1180). The twin themes of the romance are on the one hand the conflict between love and marital fidelity, on the other the rootless existence led by knights seeking adventures to bring them renown. Calogrenant, Yvain's cousin, tells Arthur's court of an adventure that had befallen him seven years before. He was in the forest of Broceliande when a monstrous giant directed him to a fountain. Beside it he saw a rock set with precious gems and a tree with a golden cup hanging from it. By pouring water from the cup on to the stone he caused a tremendous thunderstorm which tore all the leaves from the trees. Suddenly the storm died down and a host of birds descended on the bare branches, singing beautifully. But then, just as suddenly, an armed knight appeared and challenged him to a duel. Calogrenant lost the fight and could count himself lucky to escape with his life.

Arthur is keen to try this adventure with his knights, but Yvain secretly leaves before them so that he can be the first to make the attempt. Everything happens as Calogrenant had said, but Yvain successfully defeats the Knight of the Fountain who, mortally wounded, flees the field with Yvain in hot pursuit. As the knight gallops through the gates of his castle the portcullises fall. The outer one slices through Yvain's horse just behind the saddle, the inner one bars his way; Yvain is trapped. Fortunately he is spotted by Lunete, lady-in-waiting to Laudine, the mistress of the castle. Recognising Yvain, to whom she is indebted for a past service he had done her, she conceals him in the castle. From his hiding-place Yvain sees the distraught Laudine grieving by the bier of her now dead husband and instantly falls in love with her. With Lunete's help the widow is persuaded to accept Yvain as guardian of the fountain and her new husband.

A few days later Arthur and his knights reach the fountain. Yvain appears as Knight of the Fountain, defeats Keu (→ Kay) and reveals his identity. After being royally entertained at Laudine's castle Arthur and his men prepare to leave. Gauvain (→ Gawain) tells Yvain not to let himself sink into easy-going domesticity; he should return to his old life on the tournament circuit. Laudine grants Yvain a year's leave of absence.

Yvain overstays his time, whereupon Laudine sends one of her ladies to tell him that his wife will no longer receive him and wants her ring back. Mad with grief, he wanders into the forest and lives there for some time as a wild man, catching game for a hermit who gives him bread and water. Eventually he is found sleeping by the lady of a castle, who recognises him by a scar he has and cures him with a magic ointment.

From now on Yvain devotes his knighthood to the service of the weak and imperilled: first he helps the lady against a troublesome count who wants her to marry him, then he rescues a lion attacked by a serpent. The grateful lion provides Yvain with game and becomes his companion. Ashamed of the way he had treated his wife, Yvain conceals his identity and calls himself 'the Knight of the Lion'. Yvain meets Lunete again; she has been arrested for helping Yvain and is to be burned at the stake next day for treason to her lady. Yvain promises to fight her accusers. He spends the night at a nearby castle, where he runs into a second adventure in the form of a giant. Next morning he has to overcome the giant before he can go to Lunete's aid. In both encounters, with the giant and with Lunete's three accusers, the odds are equalised when the lion joins in on Yvain's side.

Having recovered from the wounds suffered in these fights, Yvain undertakes to defend the rights of a lady robbed of her inheritance against her elder sister's champion, unaware that the champion concerned is Gauvain. On his way to this judicial duel Yvain passes the castle of 'Pesme Aventure' (Worst Adventure) where three hundred ladies are held captive in wretched conditions and forced to weave textiles. They are guarded by two powerful devils, but Yvain and his lion overcome them and the ladies are freed. Then comes the duel between Yvain, this time without the lion's help, and Gauvain. It is a long and violent struggle, which ends without a result: during a pause for breath the two friends recognise each other's voices. The dispute between the two sisters is decided by Arthur.

In the end Laudine accepts Yvain back at Lunete's intercession. By putting his knighthood at the service of the weak rather than of personal glory Yvain has succeeded in reconciling love and chivalry.

Yvain is the only knight of the Round Table whose historical antecedents are known for certain. Owain (the British-Celtic form of his name) was a son of King Urien of Rheged and lived in the second half of the 6th century. The Celtic kingdom of Rheged lay at the western end of the English-Scottish border, around present-day Carlisle. In Urien's time it was involved in wars against the Picts to the north and possibly also against the Anglo-Saxons. The Celtic poet Taliesin spent some time at Urien's court and celebrated the heroic deeds of both Urien and Owain in his poetry.

In Geoffrey of Monmouth's *Historia regum Britannie* and Wace's French version of it, the *Roman de Brut*, Yvain is the son of one of Arthur's sisters. Marie de France also mentions their kinship in her *Lai de* → *Lanval*. Chrétien de Troyes, though, says nothing about him being Arthur's nephew.

In the course of the Middle Ages Chrétien's Yvain story was translated and adapted many times. Hartmann von Aue's *Iwein* dates from before 1204; he stresses the tale's courtly elements, which were evidently new to his German audience and needed explanation, but without changing the general outline of the narrative. In the late 15th century Hartmann's text was reworked in stanzaic form by Ulrich Fuetrer as *Iban* and included in the *Buch der Abenteuer*, Fuetrer's Arthurian cycle. The 14th-century Middle English *Ywain and Gawain* is a greatly abridged version which puts the emphasis on the action, omitting the courtly elements such as reflections on love and descriptions of the luxury and leisure activities of the court. *Ivens saga*, the Old Norse prose version of the *Chevalier au lion*, was produced for King Hákon Hákonarson in the second quarter of the 13th century. The poet of *Herr Ivan Lejonriddaren* (1303, extant in Swedish and Danish manuscripts) drew on both Chrétien and the Norse saga. The saga gave rise to ballads which live on both in the Faroes and in Norwegian folk tradition.

A special problem is posed by the Welsh version, one of the collection of tales known as the *Mabinogion* of which the oldest manuscript dates from the 13th century. The story's title, *Iarlles y ffynnawn* (The Lady of the Fountain), puts the emphasis on the first part, and in fact the three visits to the fountain and Owain's sojourn in the castle prior to his marriage are described in far more detail than in the French version. In this text the great duel with Gwalchmei (→ Gawain) takes place much earlier, at the point where Arthur and his followers reach the fountain; there is no mention of the dispute between the two sisters; the episode that corresponds to the 'Pesme Aventure' seems to have been at first forgotten and later put in at the end of the narrative. The Welsh tale is not a translation of the French romance. While it does seem to have been influenced by Chrétien's work, it also contains elements which suggest that its author had knowledge of a different tradition. For instance, he mentions 'Owain's ravens', which also appear in 'The Dream of Rhonabwy', another story in the *Mabinogion*.

In the *Queste del Saint Graal*, which forms the central section of the → *Lancelot en prose* cycle (1215–35), we are told that Yvain joins the search for the Grail but is not among those chosen to succeed. After the *Queste* he makes no further appearance in the trilogy; the impression is that he failed to return from the Grail Quest. In a work of c.1230, Huon de Méry's *Tournoi d'Antichrist*, Yvain's shield is described during the review of combatants as symbolising his valour (*prouesse*) and liberality (*largesse*). Later heraldic listings give him a blue shield with a lion statant in gold ('Azure, a lion Or').

From the 14th century there is an as yet unpublished French prose *Yvain*, the opening of which is derived from Chrétien's romance. Also unpublished is Pierre Sala's verse adaptation (c.1515), which made Chrétien's text accessible to 16th-century readers.

In considering pictorial representations of Yvain the German *Iwein* tradition is important, especially for the eleven depictions of episodes from the romance to be found on the walls of Rodeneck Castle in South Tyrol; based on Hartmann's work, they were made soon after its completion (between 1200 and 1250). Also of importance are the frescos at Schmalkalden in Thuringia (mid-13th century) which show the events of the Iwein story in great detail and something like strip-cartoon form. About 1310–20 the Malterer family donated an embroidered wall-hanging (68 × 490cm) to St Catherine's Convent in Freiburg, where Anna Malterer was a nun. Among other things, the hanging shows Iwein and Lunete before the seated Laudine (now in the Augustinermuseum, Freiburg im Breisgau). One of the frescos (soon after 1385) on the balcony of Runkelstein Castle near Bolzano in the Italian Tyrol depicts Yvain, Gauvain and Perceval as the three greatest knights. In England, misericords (mostly 15th-century) in Chester and Lincoln Cathedrals and New College Oxford, among other places, show the rear end of a horse protruding from a gate or portcullis – a reference to the episode in which Yvain's horse is cut in half.

Although he is among the most famous and respected of Arthur's knights and has a secondary role in countless romances – often in Gawain's shadow – Yvain lacks the eminence and exemplary qualities of Gawain, Lancelot, Perceval or Galahad. He has no reason to complain, though, at the familiarity of his name in the Low Countries: from 1114 on the names Iwein and Iwa(i)nus appear more than eighty times in Flemish legal documents of the 12th and 13th centuries. In Wales, of course, the name Owain, or Owen, is still current.

Chrétien's romance and its various reworkings are the only medieval texts in which Yvain has the leading role, something he never achieved again in later times (partly because in Malory's *Morte d'Arthur* he appears only in Book IV, and neither Tennyson nor the Pre-Raphaelites took any interest in him).

C. HOGETOORN

Editions: Foerster 1884.
Translations: Jones/Jones 1949; Kibler 1991.
Studies: Loomis 1959; Whitaker 1990.

BIBLIOGRAPHY

This bibliography includes all editions, translations and studies referred to under the entries. They are listed under the heading *Editions and Studies*. It was not possible to include the very extensive *nachleben* in this bibliography.

The bibliography begins with a list of general works, providing an overview of the reference works consulted in the making of this book: histories of literature, lexicons, repertories, encyclopedias and some more general studies concerned with the border area between literature and the visual arts.

Editions and translations are given as follows: Barron 1988] *Sir Gawain and the Green Knight*. Ed., with an introduction, prose translation and notes by W.R.J. Barron. Manchester Medieval Classics, New York 1988, original edition 1974. Unless – as here – a later edition has been used, the details given are always those of the first edition. Thus, J.J. Mak's edition of *Floris ende Blancefloer* is given as Mak 1965] and the edition of the *Walewein* by G.A. van Es as Es, van, 1957], although later editions of both works are mentioned in the description. Names of scholarly series are given in as complete a form as possible.

GENERAL WORKS

Aarne, Antti, & Stith Thompson, *The Types of the Folk-Tale. A Classification and Bibliography*. Antti Aarne's Verzeichnis der Märchentypen. FF Communications 3, translated and enlarged (Helsinki 1973[3]).

Altick, Richard D., *Paintings from Books. Art and Literature in Britain, 1760–1900* (Columbus, Ohio n.d. [1985]).

Boor, H. de, & R. Newald, *Geschichte der deutschen Literatur von den Anfängen bis zur Gegenwart* II. Revised by U. Hennig (Munich 1991[11]).

Bumke, J., *Geschichte der deutschen Literatur im hohen Mittelalter* (Munich 1990).

Debaene, L., *De Nederlandse Volksboeken. Ontstaan en geschiedenis van de vaderlandse prozaromans gedrukt tussen 1475 en 1540* (Antwerpen 1951, reprint Hulst 1977).

Doutrepont, G., *Les mises en prose des épopées et des romans chevaleresques du XIVe au XVIe siècle* (Brussel 1939).

Encyclopaedia of Islam, The (London/Leiden 1954–   ).

Enzyklopädie des Märchens. Ed. K. Rank (Berlin/New York 1977–   ).

Frenzel, E., *Stoffe der Weltliteratur. Ein Lexikon dichtungsgeschichtlicher Längsschnitte* (Stuttgart 1992[8]).

Gillespie, G.T., *A Catalogue of Persons named in German Heroic Literature* (Oxford 1973).

Grosse, Siegfried, & Ursula Rautenberg, *Die Rezeption mittelalterlicher deutscher Dichtung*. Eine Bibliographie ihrer Übersetzungen und Bearbeitungen seit der Mitte des 18. Jahrhunderts (Tübingen 1989).

Grundriss der romanischen Literaturen des Mittelalters. Deel IV, 1 en 2. *Le roman jusqu'à la fin du XIIIe siècle* (Heidelberg 1978, reprint 1984).

Kienhorst, H., *De handschriften van de Middelnederlandse ridderepiek. Een codicologische beschrijving* (Deventer 1988, 2 vols.).

Lacy, Norris J., & G. Ashe, *The Arthurian Handbook* (New York/London 1988).

———, & others (eds.), *The New Arthurian Encyclopedia*. Garland Reference Library of the Humanities 931 (New York/London 1996).

Lexikon der christlichen Ikonographie. Ed. E. Kirschbaum and W. Braunfels (Rome etc. 1968–1976, 8 vols. reprint 1990).

Lexikon des Mittelalters (Zürich/Munich 1977–   ).

Loomis, Roger S. (ed.), *Arthurian Literature in the Middle Ages. A Collaborative History* (Oxford 1959).

——— , & Laura A. Hibbard Loomis, *Arthurian Legends in Medieval Art* (New York 1938).

Lottes, Wolfgang, *'Wie ein goldener Traum'. Die Rezeption des Mittelalters in der Kunst der Preraffaeliten* (Munich 1984).

Mancoff, D.N., *The Arthurian Revival in Victorian Art* (New York/London 1990).

Mehl, D., *The Middle English Romances of the Thirteenth and Fourteenth Centuries* (London 1968).

Mertens, V., & U. Müller, *Epische Stoffe des Mittelalters* (Stuttgart [1984]).

Pipers Enzyklopädie des Musiktheaters. Oper, Operette, Musical, Ballett. Ed. C. Dahlhaus & S. Döhring (Munich/Zürich 1986–1997, 6 vols.).

Rahner, H., *Griechische Mythen in christlicher Deutung.* Gesammelte Aufsätze (Zürich 1945, reprint 1957).

Reallexicon für Antike und Christentum (Stuttgart 1950–).

Scherer, M.R., *The Legends of Troy in Art and Literature* (New York/London 1963).

Thompson, S., *Motif-Index of Folk-Literature* (Copenhagen 1955, 1958², 6 vols.).

Tubach, F.C., *Index exemplorum. A Handbook of Medieval Religious Tales.* (Helsinki 1969).

Whitaker, Muriel, *The Legends of King Arthur in Art.* (Arthurian Studies XXII, Cambridge 1990).

EDITIONS, TRANSLATIONS AND STUDIES

Adams 1983] *The Romance of Yder.* Ed. and transl. Alison Adams (Arthurian Studies VIII, Cambridge 1983).

Adams, Alison, 'The *Roman d'Yder*: The Individual and Society', in: Norris J. Lacy, Douglas Kelly & Keith Busby (eds.), *The legacy of Chrétien de Troyes* II (Amsterdam 1988), pp. 71–77.

Aerts, W.J., J.M.M. Hermans & E. Visser (eds.), *Alexander the Great in the Middle Ages. Ten Studies on the Last Days of Alexander in Literary and Historical Writing* (Mediaevalia Groningana 1, Nijmegen 1978).

——— , E.R. Smits & J.B. Voorbij (eds.), *Vincent of Beauvais and Alexander the Great. Studies on the Speculum maius and its translations into medieval vernaculars* (Mediaevalia Groningana 7, Groningen 1986).

Aertsen 1988] '*Havelok the Dane*: A Non-Courtly Romance', in: N.H.G.E. Veldhoen and H. Aertsen (eds.), *Companion to Early Middle English Literature* (Amsterdam 1988), pp. 31–52.

Aguirre, R.A., *Barlaam e Josafat en la narrativa medieval.* Colección Ñova Scholar (Madrid 1988).

Alexander 1973] *Beowulf.* Transl. M. Alexander (London 1973)

Anderson, A.R., *Alexander's Gate, God and Magog and the Inclosed Nations* (Cambridge 1932).

Anderssohn, J.C., *The Ancestry and Life of Godfrey of Bouillon* (Bloomington 1947).

Archibald, E., '*Apollonius of Tyre*' in the Middle Ages and the Renaissance (New Haven 1984).

——— , *Apollonius of Tyre. Medieval and Renaissance Themes and Variations.* Including a text and translation of the *Historia Apollonii Regis Tyri* (Cambridge 1991).

Ashe, Geoffrey, *King Arthur. The dream of a golden age* (London 1990).

Barber, Richard, *King Arthur. Hero and Legend* (Cambridge 1990).

Barron 1988] *Sir Gawain and the Green Knight.* Ed. and transl. W.R.J. Barron (Manchester Medieval Classics, Manchester 1988).

Baumgartner, Emmanuèle, *Le 'Tristan en prose'. Essai d'interpretation d'un roman médiéval* (Genève 1975).

——— , *Tristan et Iseut. De la légende aux récits en vers* (Paris 1987).

——— , *La harpe et l'épée. Tradition et renouvellement dans le Tristan en prose* (Paris 1990).

Bayot 1914] *Gormont et Isembart, fragment de chanson de geste du XIIe siècle.* Ed. Alphonse Bayot. Classiques Français du Moyen Age (Paris 1914).

Beckett, L., *Richard Wagner. Parsifal* (Cambridge 1981).

Bédier, J., *Les légendes épiques* (Paris 1908–1913, 4 vols.)

Bender, K.H., *König und Vasall. Untersuchungen zur Chanson de geste des XII. Jahrhunderts.* Studia Romanica 13 (Heidelberg 1967).

Benson, C.D., *The History of Troy in Middle English Literature: Guido delle Colonne's Historia destructionis Troiae in Medieval England* (Cambridge 1980).

——— (ed.), *Critical essays on Chaucer's 'Troilus and Criseyde' and his major early poems* (Buckingham 1991).

Berger/Suard 1986] *Histoire de Raoul de Cambrai et de Bernier, le bon chevalier.* Transl. R. Berger & F. Suard, historical introd. by M. Rouche (Troesnes 1986).

Bertelsen, H., *Thidreks saga af Bern* (Copenhagen 1908–1911).

Besamusca/Kuiper/Resoort 1988] *Sibilla, een zestiende-eeuwse Karelroman in proza.* Ed. B. Besamusca, W. Kuiper & R. Resoort (Muiderberg 1988).

Besamusca 1991] *Lanceloet. De Middelnederlandse vertaling van de Lancelot en prose overgeleverd in de Lancelotcompilatie. Pars 2 (vs. 5531–10740).* Ed. B. Besamusca. Middelnederlandse Lancelotromans V (Assen/Maastricht 1991).

Besamusca, Bart, 'The Influence of the *Lancelot en prose* on the Middle Dutch *Moriaen*', in: W. van Hoecke, G. Tournoy en W. Verbeke (eds.), *Arturus Rex.* Vol. II, *Acta conventus Lovaniensis* (Louvain 1991), pp. 352–360.

Besamusca/Postma 1997] Lanceloet. *De Middelnederlandse vertaling van de Lancelot en prose overgeleverdin de Lancelotcompilatie. Pars 1 (vs. 1–5530), voorafgegaan door de verzen van het Brusselse fragment.* Ed. Bart Besamusca and Ada Postma (Middelnederlandse Lancelot romans 4, Hilversum 1997).

Blake 1970] *The history of Reynard the Fox.* Ed. N.F. Blake, transl. from the Dutch original by William Caxton (London etc. 1970).

Boeckler, A., Heinrich von Veldeke, *Eneide.* Die Bilder der Berliner Handschrift (Leipzig 1939).

Boer, R.C., *Die Sagen von Ermanarich und Dietrich* (Halle 1910).

Boitani, P. (ed.), *The European Tragedy of Troilus* (Oxford 1989).

Boor, H. de, *Das Attilabild in Geschichte, Legende und heroischer Dichtung* (Bern 1932, reprint Darmstadt 1963).

Bouwman, A., *Reinaert en Renart.* Het dierenepos *Van den vos Reynaerde* vergeleken met de Oudfranse *Roman de Renart* (2 vols., Amsterdam 1991).

Brackert 1970] *Das Nibelungenlied.* Ed. and transl. H. Brackert (2 vols., Frankfurt 1970).

Brackert/Frey/Seitz 1972] Wernher der Gartenaere, *Helmbrecht.* Ed. and transl. H. Brackert, W. Frey & D. Seitz (Frankfurt a.M. 1972, reprint 1980).

Brady, Caroline, *The Legends of Ermanaric* (Berkeley/Los Angeles 1943).

Brandsma 1992] *Lanceloet. De Middelnederlandse vertaling van de Lancelot en prose overgeleverd in de Lancelotcompilatie. Pars 3 (vs. 10741–16263).* Ed. F. Brandsma (Middelnederlandse Lancelotromans VI, Assen/Maastricht 1992).

Brasseur 1989] Jehan Bodel, *Les Saisnes.* Ed. A. Brasseur (Genève 1989).

Brasseur, A., *Etude sur la chanson des Saisnes de Jehan Bodel* (Genève 1990).

Brault 1978] *The Song of Roland.* Ed. G.J. Brault (2 vols., London 1978).

Brugger-Hackett, Silvia, *Merlin in der europäischen Literatur des Mittelalters* (Stuttgart 1991).

Brewer, Derek, and Jonathan Gibson (eds), *A Companion to the 'Gawain'-Poet* (Cambridge 1997).

Bryant 1982] Chrétien de Troyes, *Perceval. The Story of the Grail.* Transl. Nigel Bryant (Woodbridge 1992; repr. 1996).

Brummack, J., *Die Darstellung des Orients in den deutschen Alexandergeschichten des Mittelalters* (Berlin 1966).

Buchthal, H., *Historia Troiana. Studies in the History of Mediaeval Secular Illustration* (Studies of the Warburg Institute 32, London/Leiden 1971).

Bumke, J., *Die romanisch-deutsche Literaturbeziehungen im Mittelalter. Ein Überblick* (Heidelberg 1967).

——— , *Wolfram von Eschenbach* (Stuttgart 1991⁶).

Buntz, H., *Die deutsche Alexanderdichtung des Mittelalters* (Stuttgart 1973).

Burgess/Busby 1986] *The Lais of Marie de France*. Transl. Glyn S. Burgess and Keith Busby (Harmondsworth, 1986).

Burson, A.C., 'Swan Maidens and Smiths', in: *Scandinavian Studies* 55 (1983), pp. 1–19.

Busby, K., *Gauvain in old French Literature* (Amsterdam 1980).

Busby, K.] Chrétien de Troyes, *Le Roman de Perceval ou Le Conte du Graal*. Ed. Keith Busby (Tübingen/London 1993).

Buschinger/Spiewok 1986] Eilhart von Oberg, *Tristant und Isalde*. Transl. Danielle Buschinger and Wolfgang Spiewok (Göppinger Arbeiten zur Germanistik 436, Göppingen 1986).

Bzdyl 1989] *Layamon's Brut. A History of the Britons*. Transl. Donald G. Bzdyl (Medieval and Renaissance Texts and Studies 65, Binghamton, NY 1989).

Cable 1971] *The Death of King Arthur*. Transl. J. Cable (Harmondsworth 1971).

Calin, William C., *The old French epic of revolt: Raoul de Cambrai, Renaud de Montauban, Gormond et Isembard* (Genève/Paris 1962).

—————, *The Epic Quest* (Baltimore 1966).

Callen King, K., *Achilles: Paradigms of the War Hero from Homer to the Middle Ages* (Berkeley 1987).

Campbell 1907] *The Seven Sages of Rome*. Ed K. Campbell (Boston 1907, reprint Genève 1975).

Cary, G., *The medieval Alexander* (Cambridge 1956, reprint 1967).

Castets 1909] *La Chanson des Quatre fils Aymon*. Ed. F. Castets (Montpellier 1909, reprint Genève 1974).

Cerquiglini 1981] Robert de Boron, *Le roman du Graal (Manuscrit de Modène)* Ed. and transl. Bernard Cerquiglini (Paris 1981).

Chambers, R.W., *Beowulf. An Introduction to the Study of the Poem*. Revised by C.L. Wrenn (Cambridge 1921, 1959[3]).

Chicoy-Dalbán, J.I., *A study of the Spanish 'Queen Seuilla' and related themes in European Medieval and Renaissance periods* (Toronto 1974).

Claassens, Geert H.M., *De Middelnederlandse Kruisvaartromans* (Amsterdam 1993).

Clarke 1973] Geoffrey of Monmouth, *Life of Merlin*. Ed. Basil Clarke (Cardiff 1973).

Clifton-Everest, J.M., *The Tragedy of Knighthood. Origins of the Tannhäuser-legend* (Oxford 1979).

Cocheyras, J., *Tristan et Iseut. Genèse d'un mythe littéraire* (Paris 1996).

Colliot, R., Adenet le Roi, *Berte aus grans piés* (2 vols., Paris 1970).

Comparetti, D., *Virgilio nel medioevo*. Ed. G. Pasquali (2 vols., Florence 1981[3]).

Cook, R.F., *'Chanson d'Antioche', chanson de geste. Le Cycle de la croisade est-il épique?* (Amsterdam 1980).

Cormier, R.J., *One Heart, One Mind. The Rebirth of Vergil's Hero in Medieval French Romance* (Jackson, Missouri 1973).

Cowen 1969] Sir Thomas Malory, *Le Morte d'Arthur*. Ed. Janet Cowen (2 vols., Harmondsworth 1969).

Cramer 1971] *Lohengrin. Edition und Untersuchungen*. Ed. Thomas Cramer, (Munich 1971).

Cramer 1972] Hartmann von Aue, *Erec*. Transl. Thomas Cramer (Frankfurt a.M. 1972).

Crossley-Holland 1987] *Beowulf*. Transl. and introd. by Kevin Crossley-Holland (Woodbridge 1987).

Curschmann, Michael, *Spielmannsepik. Wege und Ergebnisse der Forschung von 1907 bis 1965* (Stuttgart 1968).

Curtis 1985] *Le roman de Tristan en prose*. Ed. Renée L. Curtis (3 vols., Cambridge 1985).

Dembowski 1969] *La Chanson d'Ami et Amiles*. Ed. P.F. Dembowski (Paris 1969).

Dijk, van, 1981] *Het Roelantslied*. Ed. H. van Dijk (2 vols., Utrecht 1981).

Dobson, R.B., and J. Taylor, *Rymes of Robin Hood: an introduction to the English Outlaw* (London 1976).

Dougherty/Barnes 1966] *La Geste de Monglane*. Vol. I, *Hernaut de Beaulande*, vol. II, *Renier de Gennes*, vol. III, *Girart de Vienne*. Ed. by D.M. Dougherty and E.B. Barnes (Eugene 1966).

Douglas, D.C., 'Rollo of Normandy', in: *English Historical Review* LVII (1942), pp. 417–436.

Doutrepont, G., *La Littérature française à la Cour des Ducs de Bourgogne*. La Bibliothèque du XVe siècle, vol. VIII (Paris 1909).

Draak, Maartje, & Frida de Jong, *Het feestgelag van Bricriu* (Amsterdam 1986).

Dufournet and Dulac 1994] *La Châtelaine de Vergy*. Edited by Jean Dufournet and Liliane Dulac (Paris 1994).

Dufournet/Méline 1985] *Le Roman de Renart*. Ed. and transl. J. Dufournet & A. Méline (2 vols., Paris 1985).

Duijvestijn 1989] *Madelgijs*. Ed. B.W.Th. Duijvestijn (Brussels 1989).

Dunn 1903] *La Chançun de Willame*. Ed. G. Dunn (London 1903).

Duparc-Quioc, S., *La Chanson d'Antioche* (2 vols., Paris 1976/1978).

Edel, D., *Helden auf Freiersfüssen. 'Tochman Emire' und 'Mal y kavas Kulhwch Olwen'. Studien zur frühen inselkeltischen Erzähltradition* (Verhandelingen Kon. Ned. Akademie van Wetenschappen, afd. Letterkunde. N.R. 107, Amsterdam etc. 1980).

Ehrhart, M.J., *The Judgement of the Trojan Prince Paris in Medieval Literature* (Philadelphia 1987).

Einhorn, J, *Spiritalis unicornis. Das Einhorn als Bedeutungsträger in Literatur und Kunst des Mittelalters* (Munich 1976).

Eisenhut 1958] *Dictys Cretensis Ephemeridos belli Troiani libri a Lucio Septimio ex Graeco in Latinum sermonem translati*. Ed. W. Eisenhut (Leipzig 1958, 1973²).

Eisenhut, W., 'Spätantike Troja-Erzählungen mit einem Ausblick auf die mittelalterliche Troja-Literatur', in: *Mittellateinisches Jahrbuch* 18 (1983), pp. 1–28.

Ellis Davidson, Hilda R., 'Wieland the Smith', in: *Folklore* 69 (1958), pp. 145–159.

Emden 1977] Bertrand de Bar-sur-Aube, *Girart de Vienne*. Ed. W. van Emden (Paris 1977).

Ensslin, W., *Theoderich der Grosse* (Munich 1959²).

Epstein 1967] *Tales of Sendebar, Mishle Sendebar*. Ed. and transl. M. Epstein (Judaica, 1st Series, Nr. 2, Philadelphia 1967).

Erichsen 1967] *Die Geschichte Thidreks von Bern*. Transl. Fine Erichsen. (Sammlung Thule 22, Düsseldorf/Cologne 1967).

Es, van, 1957] *De jeeste van Walewein en het schaakbord van Penninc en Pieter Vostaert*. Ed. G.A. van Es (Zwolle 1957, reprint Culemborg 1976).

Esty, Najaria Hurst, *Wace's 'Roman de Brut' and the fifteenth century 'Prose Brute Chronicle'. A comparative study* (Columbus, Ohio 1978).

Eusebi 1962] *La Chevalerie d'Ogier de Danemarche*. Ed. M. Eusebi (Testi e documenti di letteratura moderne 6, Milan 1962).

Ferrante, Joan Marguerite, *The Conflict of Love and Horror. The Medieval Tristan Legend in France, Germany and Italy* (The Hague/Paris 1973).

Fisher/Davidson 1978] *Saxo Grammaticus: The History of the Danes, vol. I: Text; vol. II: Commentary*. Edited by Hilda Ellis Davidson; transl. Peter Fisher (Cambridge, 1978, 1979, reprinted in one volume 1996).

Flinn, J., *Le Roman de Renart dans la littérature française et dans les littératures étrangères au Moyen Age* (Paris 1963).

Foerster 1884] Cristian van Troyes, *Sämtliche erhaltene Werke*. Vol. I, *Cligès*, vol. II, *Der Löwenritter (Yvain)*, vol. III, *Erec und Enide*. Ed. Wendelin Foerster (Halle 1884, 1887, 1890, reprint Amsterdam 1965).

Ford 1965] *The Ruodlieb. The First Medieval Epic of Chivalry from Eleventh-Century Germany*. Transl. G.B. Ford jr. (Leiden 1965).

Fouquet, Doris, *Wort und Bild in der mittelalterlichen Tristantradition* (Berlin 1971).

Frappier, Jean, *Les chansons de geste du Cycle de Guillaume d'Orange*. Vol. I, *La Chanson de Guillaume, Aliscans, La Chevalerie Vivien* (Paris 1955).

———, *Chrétien de Troyes* (Paris 1968).

———, *Chrétien de Troyes et le mythe du graal. Etude sur 'Perceval' ou le 'Conte du Graal'* (Paris 1979).

Frescoln 1983] Guillaume le Clerc, *The Romance of Fergus*. Ed. W. Frescoln (Philadelphia 1983).

Frings, Th., & J. Kuhnt, *König Rother*. Rev. I. Köppe-Benath (Bonn/Leipzig 1922, reprint 1968).

Frugoni, C., *La fortuna di Alessandro Magno dall'antichità al Medioevo* (Florence 1978).

Gamerschlag, Kurt (Hrsg.), *Moderne Artus-Rezeption 18.–20. Jahrhundert* (Göppinger Arbeiten zur Germanistik 548, Göppingen 1991).

Geck, E., *Herzog Ernst*. Facsimile of the ed. Anton Sorg, Augsburg ca. 1476 (Wiesbaden 1969).
Geith, K.–E., *Carolus Magnus. Studien zur Darstellung Karls des Grossen in der deutschen Literatur des 12. und 13. Jahrhunderts* (Bern/Munich 1977).
Genzmer 1966] *Das Waltharilied und die Waldere-Bruchstücke*. Transl. and introd. F. Genzmer (Stuttgart 1966).
Gerritsen 1963] *Die Wrake van Ragisel. Onderzoekingen over de Middelnederlandse bewerkingen van de Vengeance Raguidel, gevolgd door een uitgave van de Wrake-teksten*. Ed. and study W.P. Gerritsen (2 vols., Assen 1963).
Gerritsen 1987] *Lantsloot vander Haghedochte. Fragmenten van een Middelnederlandse bewerking van de Lancelot en prose*. Ed. and introd. W.P. Gerritsen (Middelnederlandse Lancelotromans II, Amsterdam/Oxford/New York 1987).
Gibbs/Johnson 1984] Wolfram von Eschenbach, *Willehalm*. Transl. Marion E. Gibbs and Sidney M. Johnson (Harmondsworth 1984).
Gildea 1965–66] *Durmart le Galois. Roman arthurien du treizième siècle*. Ed. Joseph Gildea (2 vols., Villanova 1965–1966).
Goossens 1983] *Reynaerts Historie. Reynke de Vos*. Gegenüberstellung einer Auswahl aus den niederländischen Fassungen und des niederdeutschen Textes von 1498. Ed. by J. Goossens (Darmstadt 1983).
Goossens, J., *Die Reynaert-ikonographie* (Darmstadt 1983).
——— , & T. Sodmann (eds.), *Reynart Reynard Reynke. Studien zu einem mittelalterlichen Tierepos* (Cologne/ Vienna 1980).
Gorra 1887] *Testi inedita di storia trojana, preceduti da uno studio sulla leggenda trojana in Italia* (Turin 1887).
Göttert 1980] Heinrich der Glîchezâre, *Reinhart Fuchs*. Ed. and transl. K.–H. Göttert (Stuttgart 1980).
Gottzmann, C.L., *Artusdichtung* (Sammlung Metzler 249, Stuttgart 1989).
Gowans, Linda M., *Cei and the Arthurian Legend* (Cambridge 1988).
Green 1939] *Anseijs de Mes, according to Ms N*. Ed. H.J. Green (Paris, 1939).
Grieve, Patricia E., *Flore and Blancheflor and the European Romance* (Cambridge Studies in Medieval Literature 32, Cambridge 1997).
Grillo, P.R., *The Jerusalem-continuations* (2 vols., Tuscaloosa 1984–1987).
Guerrand/Thomas/Zink 1990] *Girart de Roussillon ou l'épopée de Bourgogne, Le manuscrit de Vienne, Codex 2549*. Ed. R.–H. Guerrand, M. Thomas & M. Zink (Paris 1990).
Guessard/Grandmaison 1860] *Huon de Bordeaux*. Ed. F. Guessard and Ch. Grandmaison, Paris 1860).
Guidot 1986] *Garin le Lorrain*. Transl. B. Guidot (Nancy 1986).
Guidot 1988] *Gerbert*. Transl. B. Guidot (Nancy 1988).
Guiette 1940–51] [David Aubert] *Croniques et conquestes de Charlemaine*. Ed. R. Guiette (3 vols., Brussels 1940–1951).
Gysseling 1980] *Corpus van Middelnederlandse teksten (tot en met het jaar 1300)*. Ed. M. Gysseling with W. Pijnenburg. Series II, *Literaire handschriften*. Vol. I, *Fragmenten* (The Hague, 1980).
Haan, de, 1974] *Ferguut and Galiene*. A facsimile of the only extant Middle Dutch manuscript (Leiden, University Library, Ms. Letterkunde 191). Ed. M.J.M. de Haan (Leiden 1974).
Hackett 1953–55] *Girart de Roussillon*. Ed. W. Mary Hackett (3 vols., Paris 1953–1955).
Ham 1939] *Girart de Roussillon. Poème bourguignon du XIVme siècle*. Ed. E.B. Ham (New Haven, Conn. 1939).
Hamilton/Perry 1975] *The Poem of the Cid*. Ed. by Ian Michael together with a new prose transl. by Rita Hamilton and Janet Perry (Manchester 1975).
Hanly, M.G., *Boccaccio, Beauveau, Chaucer: Troilus and Criseyde: Four perspectives on influence* (Norman, Oklah. 1990).
Hanning, R.W., '*Havelok the Dane*: Structure, Symbols, Meaning', in: *Studies in Philology* 64 (1967), pp. 586–605.
Hansen, I., *Zwischen Epos und höfischem Roman. Die Frauengestalten im Trojaroman des Benoît de Sainte Maure* (Munich 1971).

Hartmann, W., *Die deutschen Dichtungen von Salomon und Markolf*. Vol. II, *Das Spruchgedicht von Salomon und Markolf* (Halle 1934).

Hatto 1965] *The Nibelungenlied*. Transl. A.T. Hatto (Harmondsworth 1965).

Hatto 1986] Wolfram von Eschenbach, *Parzival*. Transl. A.T. Hatto (Harmondsworth 1986).

Haug, W., 'Einleitung', in: *Ruodlieb Faksimile-Ausgabe des Codex Latinus Monacensis 19486 der bayrischen Staatsbibliothek München und der Fragmente von St. Florian.* Vol. I (Wiesbaden 1974).

———— , '*Das land, von welchem niemand wiederkehrt.*' *Mythos, Fiktion und Wahrheit in Chrétiens 'Chevalier de la Charrete', im 'Lanzelet' Ulrichs von Zatzikhoven und im 'Lancelot' Prosaroman* (Tübingen 1978).

———— , '"Paradigmatische Poesie". Der spätere deutsche Artusroman auf dem Weg zu einer "nachklassischen" Ästhetik', in: *Deutsche Vierteljahresschrift* 54 (1980), pp. 204–231.

Have, J.B. van der, *Roman der Lorreinen: de fragmenten en het geheel* (Schiedam 1990).

Havely, N.R. (ed.), *Chaucer's Boccaccio: Sources of Troilus and the Knight's and Franklin's Tales* (Chaucer Studies 5, Cambridge 1980, reprint 1992).

Hecht/Hecht 1977] 'Salman und Morolf'. Ed. G. Hecht and W. Hecht, in: *Deutsche Spielmannserzählungen des Mittelalters* (Leipzig 1977).

Hellinga 1952] *Van den vos Reynaerde*. Vol. I, *Teksten*. Diplomatic ed. W.G. Hellinga (Zwolle 1952).

Henry, A., *Les oevres d'Adenet le Roi* (4 vols., Bruges/Brussels, 1951–1963).

Hieatt 1975–80] *Karlamagnús saga. The Saga of Charlemagne and his heroes*. Transl. C.B. Hieatt (3 vols., Toronto 1975–1980).

Hirsch 1986] *Barlaam and Josaphat. A Middle English Life of Buddha*. Ed. J.C. Hirsch (Early English Text Society 290, London etc. 1986).

Hoffmann, W., *Das Siegfriedbild in der Forschung* (Darmstadt 1979).

Hogenhout/Hogenhout 1978] *Torec*. Ed. Jan and Maaike Hogenhout (Abcoude 1978).

Holt, J.C., *Robin Hood* (London 1990).

Houts, van, 1992–95] *The Gesta Normannorum Ducum of William of Jumièges, Orderic Vitalis and Robert of Torigni*. Vol. I, *Introductory and Books I–IV*. Ed. and transl. E.M.C. van Houts (Oxford 1992). Vol II *Books II–VIII* (Oxford 1995).

Hubert/Porter 1962] *The Romance of Flamenca. A Provencal Poem of the XIIIth Century*. English verse transl. M.J. Hubert; ed. M.E. Porter (Princeton 1962).

Iseley 1961] *La Chançun de Willame*. Ed. N.V. Iseley, with an etymological glossary by G. Piffard (Chapel Hill 1961).

Jaffray, R., *The two knights of the Swan, Lohengrin and Helias* (London/New York 1910).

Jauss, H.R., *Untersuchungen zur mittelalterlichen Tierdichtung* (Tübingen 1959).

Johnson 1992] Penninc and Pieter Vostaert, *Roman van Walewein*. Ed. and transl. D. F. Johnson (New York 1992).

Jones/Jones 1949] *The Mabinogion*. Transl. Gwyn and Thomas Jones (London 1949, revised ed. Gwyn and Mair Jones, 1974).

Jones, T., 'The early evolution of the legend of Arthur', in: *Nottingham Mediaeval Studies* (1964), pp. 3–21.

Kapteyn 1926] *Wigalois. Der Ritter mit dem Rade*. Ed. J.M.N. Kapteyn (Bonn 1926).

Karl der Grosse. Werk und Wirkung. Catalogue (Aachen 1965).

Karnein 1979] *Salman und Morolf*. Ed. A. Karnein (Altdeutsche Textbibliothek 85, Tübingen 1979).

Kay 1992] *Raoul de Cambrai*. Ed. and transl. Sarah Kay (Oxford 1992).

Kennedy, E., *Lancelot and the Grail. A study of the Prose Lancelot* (Oxford 1986).

Kibler 1991] Chrétien de Troyes, *Arthurian romances*. Transl. W.W. Kibler; *Eric and Enide* transl. by C.C. Carroll (Harmondsworth 1991).

Kippenberg, B., *Gregorius, der gute Sünder*. Ed. F. Neumann, transl. B. Kippenberg (Stuttgart 1959).

Klaeber 1922] *Beowulf and the Fight at Finnsburg*. Ed. F. Klaeber (Boston 1922, 1953³).

Klein 1986] *Die Chronik von Karl dem Grossen und Roland. Der lateinische Pseudo-Turpin in den Handschriften aus Aachen und Andernach*. Ed. and transl. H.W. Klein (Beiträge zur romanischen Philologie des Mittelalters 13, Munich 1986).

Klooke, K., *Joseph Bédiers Theorie über den Ursprung der Chansons de geste und die daran anschliessende Diskussion zwischen 1908 und 1968* (Göppingen 1972).

Knapp 1977] *Ruodlieb.* Ed. and transl. G.P. Knapp (Stuttgart 1977).

Knapp, G.P., *Hector und Achill: Die Rezeption des Trojastoffes im deutschen Mittelalter* (Bern/Frankfurt a.M. 1974).

Knight, Stephen, *Arthurian Literature and Society* (London/Basingstoke 1983).

——— , *Robin Hood: A Complete Study of the English Outlaw* (Oxford 1994).

Kölbing 1884] *Amis and Amiloun.* Ed. E. Kölbing (Heilbronn 1884).

Kortekaas 1984] *Historia Apollonii regis Tyri.* Ed. G.A.A. Kortekaas (Mediaevalia Groningana 3, Groningen 1984).

Kramer 1961] *König Rother.* Transl. G. Kramer (Berlin 1961).

Kroeber/Servois 1860] *Fierabras, chanson de geste.* Ed. A. Kroeber and G. Servois (Paris 1860).

Kühn and Nellmann 1995] *Parzival.* Transl. Dieter Kühn. Ed. Eberhard Nellmann. Bibliothek des Mittelalters (Frankfurt 1995).

Kuiper, W., *Die riddere metten witten scilde.* Oorsprong, overlevering en auteurschap van de Middelnederlandse *Ferguut.* Ed. and study (Amsterdam 1989).

Labande, E.R., *Étude sur Baudouin de Sebourc, chanson de geste. Légende poétique de Baudouin II du Bourg, roi de Jérusalem* (Paris 1940).

Lacroix/Walter 1989] *Tristan et Iseut. Les Poèmes français. La Saga norroise.* Ed. and transl. Daniel Lacroix & Philippe Walter (Paris 1989).

Lacy 1992–96] *Lancelot-Grail: The Vulgate and Post Vulgate in Translation.* Ed. N.J. Lacy (5 vols. Hamden 1992–96).

Langosch 1956] *Waltharius, Ruodlieb, Märchenepen. Lateinische Epik des Mittelalters mit deutschen Versen.* Ed. K. Langosch (Darmstadt 1956, 1967³).

Langosch, K., *Waltharius. Die Dichtung und die Forschung.* Erträge der Forschung 21 (Darmstadt 1973).

Lavaud/Nelli 1960] *Les Troubadours. Jaufre. Flamenca. Barlaam et Josaphat.* Ed. and transl. René Lavaud and René Nelli (Bruges 1960).

Leclanche 1986] *Le conte de Floire et Blanchefleur.* Transl. J.–J. Leclanche (Paris 1986).

Lejeune, R., & J. Stiennon, *The legend of Roland in the Middle Ages* (2 vols., London 1971).

Lepage 1978] *Les rédactions en vers du Couronnement de Louis.* Ed. Y. Lepage (Geneva 1978).

Leube, E., *Fortuna in Karthago. Die Aeneas-Dido-Mythe Vergils in den romanischen Literaturen vom 14. bis zum 16. Jahrhundert* (Heidelberg 1969).

Lida de Malkiel, M.R., *Dido en la literatura española. Su retrato y defensa* (London 1974).

Lie 1987] *The Middle Dutch Prose Lancelot.* A study of the Rotterdam Fragments and their place in the French, German, and Dutch *Lancelot en prose* tradition. Ed. O.S.H. Lie (Middelnederlandse Lancelotromans III, Amsterdam/Oxford/New York 1987).

Lindner 1971] *Kudrun.* Transl. J. Lindner (Berlin 1971).

Lot, Ferdinand, *Etude sur le Lancelot en prose* (Paris 1918, enlarged ed. 1954).

Lot-Borodine, Myrrha, 'Christ-chevalier: Galaad', in: M. Lot-Borodine, *De l'amour profane à l'amour sacré. Etudes de psychologie sentimentale au Moyen Age* (Paris 1979), pp. 159–185.

Louis, R., *Girart, comte de Vienne, dans les chansons de geste: Girart de Vienne, Girart de Fraite, Girart de Roussillon* (2 vols., Auxerre 1947).

Lulofs 1983] *Van den vos Reynaerde.* Ed. F. Lulofs (Groningen 1983).

MacLeach 1937] *Amis and Amiloun.* Ed. Edward MacLeach (London 1937).

MacMillan 1949–50] *La Chanson de Guillaume.* Ed. D. MacMillan (Paris 1949–1950).

Mak 1954] *Amijs ende Amelis.* Ed. J.J. Mak (Zwolle 1954).

Mak 1965] Diederic van Assenede, *Floris ende Blancefloer.* Ed. J.J. Mak (Zwolle 1965, Den Haag 1980⁴).

Malone 1962] *Widsith.* Ed. Kemp Malone (Anglistica XIII, Copenhagen 1962).

Malone 1977] *Deor.* Ed. Kemp Malone (Rev. ed. 1977, reprint 1979).

Mann 1987] *Ysengrimus.* Ed. and transl. J. Mann (Mittellaiteinische Studien und Texte 12, Leiden etc. 1987).

Marchello-Nizia, C., *Tristan et Iseut. Les premières versions européens* (Paris 1995).

Martin, J.H., *Love's Fools: Aucassin, Troilus, Calisto and the Parody of the Courtly Lover* (London 1972).

Matarasso 1969] *The Quest of the Holy Grail* (*La Queste del Saint Graal*). Transl. P.M. Matarasso (Harmondsworth 1969, reprint 1981).

Melzer 1973] *Wigalois*. Ed. H. Melzer. Deutsche Volksbücher in Faksimiledrucken, Reihe A, Bd. 10 (Hildesheim/New York 1973).

Ménard 1987–97] *Le roman de Tristan en prose*. Ed. Philippe Ménard and others (9 vols. Genève 1987–1997).

Mertens, V., *Gregorius Eremita. Eine Lebensform des Adels bei Hartmann von Aue in ihrer Problematik und ihrer Wandlung in der Rezeption* (Zürich/Munich 1978).

Micha 1978–83] *Lancelot. Roman du XIIIe siècle*. Trans. A. Micha (9 vols., Paris 1978–1983).

Micha 1979] Robert de Boron, *Merlin*. Ed. Alexandre Micha (Genève 1979).

Michel jr., Emanuel J., *Les Enfances Godefroi* (Tuscaloosa 1993).

———— , & Jan A. Nelson, *La Naissance du Chevalier au Cygne* (Tuscaloosa 1977).

Mitchneck 1935] *Yon or la Venjance Fromondin. A thirteenth-century chanson de geste of the Lorraine cycle*. Ed. S.R. Mitchneck (New York 1935).

Moignet 1969] *La Chanson de Roland*. Ed. and transl. G. Moignet (Paris etc. 1969).

Morris, Rosemary, *The Character of King Arthur in Medieval Literature* (Cambridge 1982).

Müller/Wapnewski 1986] *Richard Wagner-Handbuch*. Ed. U. Müller & P. Wapnewski (Stuttgart 1986).

Nedoma, Robert, *Die bildlichen und schriftlichen Denkmäler der Wielandsage* (Göppinger Arbeiten zur Germanistik 490, Göppingen 1988).

Nelson, Jan A., *Le Chevalier au Cygne and La Fin d'Elias* (Tuscaloosa 1985).

Neumann 1958] Hartmann von Aue, *Gregorius Der 'gute Sünder'*. Ed. Fr. Neumann (Wiesbaden 1958).

Newton, Sam, *The Origins of 'Beowulf' and the Pre-Viking Kingdom of East Anglia* (Cambridge 1993).

Ninck 1962] Wernher der Gärtner, *Meier Helmbrecht*. Transl. J. Ninck (Stuttgart 1962).

Normand/Raynaud 1877] *Aiol. Chanson de geste publiée d'après le manuscrit unique de Paris*. Ed. J. Normand & G. Raynaud (Paris 1877).

O'Gorman 1995] Robert de Boron, *Joseph d'Arimathie*. A critical edition of the verse and prose versions by R. O'Gorman (Toronto 1995).

Oesterley 1872] *Gesta Romanorum*. Ed. H. Oesterley (Berlin 1872, reprint Hildesheim 1963).

Ohly, F., *Der Verfluchte und der Erwählte. Vom Leben mit der Schuld.* (Opladen 1976).

Oostrom, F.P. van, *Lantsloot vander Haghedochte. Onderzoekingen over een Middelnederlandse bewerking van de 'Lancelot en prose'* (Middelnederlandse Lancelotromans I, Amsterdam/Oxford/New York 1981).

Overdiep 1931] *De Historie van den vier Heemskinderen*. Ed. G.S. Overdiep (Groningen etc. 1931).

Overdiep 1939] *Een fragment van den roman der Lorreinen*. Ed. G.S. Overdiep (Assen 1939).

Owen 1991] Guillaume le Clerc, *Fergus of Galloway. Knight of King Arthur*. Transl. D.D.R. Owen (London 1991).

Owen, D.D.R., *The Legend of Roland. A Pageant of the Middle Ages* (London 1973).

Paardekooper-van Buuren/Gysseling 1971] *Moriaen*. Ed. H. Paardekooper-Van Buuren and M. Gysseling (Zutphen [1971]).

Panzer/Ruh 1968] Wernher der Gartenaere, *Helmbrecht*. Ed. Fr. Panzer and K. Ruh (Tübingen 1968[8]).

Pörnbacher, H., & I. Pörnbacher, 'König Rother', in: W.J. Schröder (ed.), *Spielmannsepen*. Vol.I, *König Rother. Herzog Ernst*. Ed. and transl. (Darmstadt 1984), pp. 161–222.

Radin, A.P., *The Romance of Achilles. From Homer to Benoît de Sainte-Maure* (Berkeley 1981).

Resoort 1980] *Robrecht de duyvel*. Ed. Rob Resoort (Muiderberg 1980).

Resoort, R.J., *Een schoone historie vander borchgravinne van Vergi. Onderzoek naar de intentie en gebruikssfeer van een zestiende-eeuwse prozaroman* (Hilversum 1988).

Rey, A., & A. García Solalinde, *Ensayo de una bibliografía de las Leyendas Troyanas en la literatura española* (Bloomington, Ind. 1942).

Riquer, M. de, *Les chansons de geste françaises*. Transl. by I. Cluzel. (2nd revised ed., Paris 1956[2]).

Ritson 1795] *Robin Hood: A Collection of all the ancient poems, songs and ballads*, ed. Joseph Ritson (London 1995).

Roach 1959] Chrétien de Troyes, *Le Roman de Perceval ou Le Conte du Graal*. Ed. W. Roach (Genève/Paris 1959).

Roberts-Baytop, A., *Dido, Queen of Infinite Literary Variety. The English Renaissance borrowings and influences* (Salzburg Studies in English Literature 25, Salzburg 1974).

Rombauts/De Paepe/De Haan 1982] *Ferguut*. Ed. E. Rombauts, N. de Paepe and M.J.M. de Haan (The Hague 1982²).

Rombauts, E., & A. Welkenhuysen (eds.), *Aspects of the medieval animal epic* (Louvain/The Hague 1975).

Rosenberg/Danon 1996] *Ami and Amile. A Medieval Tale of Friendship*. Transl. Samuel N. Rosenberg and Samuel Danon (1981; rpt Ann Arbor 1996).

Ross, D.J.A, *Alexander historiatus. A Guide to Medieval Illustrated Alexander Literature* (Warburg Institute Surveys 1, London 1963; Beiträge zur klassischen Philologie 186, Frankfurt a.M. 1988²).

——, *Illustrated Medieval Alexander-Books in Germany and the Netherlands. A Study in Comparative Iconology* (Cambridge 1971).

——, *Studies in the Alexander Romance* (London 1985).

Rossi, M., *Huon de Bordeaux et l'évolution du genre épique au XIIIe siècle* (Paris 1975).

Rübesamen 1962] *Gesta Romanorum. Die Taten der Römer*. Revised ed. of Grässe's translation (Munich 1962).

Ruelle 1960] *Huon de Bordeaux*. Ed. P. Ruelle (Brussels/Paris 1960).

Ryan, W.F., & Ch.B. Schmitt (eds.), *Pseudo Aristotle, The Secret of Secrets. Sources and Influences* (Warburg Institute Surveys 11, London 1982).

Sayers 1957] *The Chanson de Roland*. Transl. Dorothy Sayers (Harmondsworth 1957).

Sandkühler, K., *Die Geschichte des heiligen Graals* (Stuttgart 1958).

Scheidegger, J., *Le Roman de Renart ou le texte de la dérision* (Genève 1989).

Schmelter, H.U., *Alexander der Grosse in der Dichtung und bildenden Kunst des Mittelalters. Die Nektanebos-Sage* (Bonn 1977).

Schmitt, C.B., & D. Knox, *Pseudo-Aristoteles Latinus. A Guide to Latin Works Falsely Attributed to Aristotle Before 1500* (Warburg Institute Surveys and Texts 12, London 1985).

Schmitt, L.E., & R. Noll-Wiemann, *Deutsche Volksbücher in Faksimile-Drucken. A.2, Apollonius von Tyrus* (Hildesheim/New York 1975).

Schmitz, G., *Deutsche Volksbücher in Faksimiledrucken. A.7, Die sieben weisen Meister* (Hildesheim/New York 1974).

Schmolke-Hasselmann, Beate, *Der arthurische Versroman von Chrestien bis Froissart. Zur Geschichte einer Gattung* (Tübingen 1980).

Schröder 1976] *Spielmannsepen*. Vol. II, *Sankt Oswald. Orendel. Salman und Morolf*. Ed. and transl. W.J. Schröder (Darmstadt 1976).

Schroeder, H., *Der Topos der Nine Worthies in Literatur und bildender Kunst* (Göttingen 1971).

Segre 1989] *La Chanson de Roland*. Ed. C. Segre. revised ed., transl. from the Italian by M. Tyssens (Textes littéraires français 368, 2 vols., Genève 1989).

Severin, Tim, *The Brendan Voyage* (London 1978).

Short/Merrilees 1984] Benedeit, *Le voyage de Saint Brandan*. Ed. and transl. I. Short. Introd. and notes B. Merrilees (Paris 1984).

Simpson, Roger, *Camelot Regained. The Arthurian Revival and Tennyson 1800–1849* (Arthurian Studies 21, Cambridge 1990).

Simrock 1978] *Kudrun (Gudrun)*. Ed. K. Simrock (Stuttgart 1978).

Skårup 1980] *Karlamagnússaga*. Ed. P. Skårup (Copenhagen 1980).

Smithers 1987] *Havelock*. Ed. G.V. Smithers (Oxford 1987).

Sodmann 1980] Jacob van Maerlant, *Historie van den Grale* und *Boek van Merline*. Ed. T. Sodmann (Niederdeutsche Studien 26, Cologne/Vienna, 1980).

Sollbach 1987] *St. Brandans wundersame Seefahrt*. Ed. and transl. G.E. Sollbach (Frankfurt a.M. 1987).

Sonet, J., *Le roman de Barlaam et Josaphat* (3 vols., Namur 1949–1952).

Sowinski 1970] *Herzog Ernst. Ein mittelalterliches Abenteuerbuch*. Ed. and transl. B. Sowinski (Stuttgart 1970, 1980⁴).

Spargo, J.W., *Virgil the Necromancer. Studies in Virgilian Legends* (Harvard Studies in Comparative Literature 10, Cambridge, Mass. 1934).

Spiewok 1989] *Das Tristan-Epos Gottfrieds von Strassburg. Mit der Fortsetzung des Ulrich von Türheim*. Ed. W. Spiewok (Berlin 1989).

Spijker, I., *Aymijns kinderen hoog te paard. Een studie over 'Renout van Montalbaen' en de Franse 'Renaut'-traditie* (Hilversum 1990).

Stein, Peter K., *Tristan in den Literaturen des Europäischen Mittelalters* (Salzburg 1983).

Stimming 1899] *Der anglonormannische Boeve de Haumtone*. Ed. A. Stimming (Halle 1899).

Strijbosch, Clara, 'The Saint and the World: the Middle Dutch Voyage of Saint Brendan' in: *Medieval Dutch Literature in its European Context*. Ed. Erik Kooper (Cambridge Studies in Medieval Literature 21, Cambridge 1994), pp. 191–207.

––––––– , *De bronnen van de Reis van Sint Brandaan* (Middeleeuwse studies en bronnen XLIV, Hilversum 1995).

Stuip 1985] *La Châtelaine de Vergy*. Ed. R. Stuip (Paris, 1985).

Suard 1992] *La Geste des Lorrains*. Études présentées et réunies par F. Suard (Paris 1992).

Suard, François, *Guillaume d'Orange. Étude du roman en prose* (Paris 1979).

––––––– , *La Chanson de Guillaume* (Paris 1991).

Suerbaum, W., *Vergils Aeneis. Beiträge zu ihrer Rezeption in Geschichte und Gegenwart* (Bamberg 1981).

Symons/Boesch 1964⁴] *Kudrun*. Ed. B. Symons & B. Boesch (Altdeutsche Textbibliothek 5, Tübingen 1954³).

Taylor, Beverly, & Elisabeth Brewer, *The Return of King Arthur. British and American Arthurian Literature since 1900* (Arthurian Studies 9, Cambridge 1983).

Thiel, van, 1974] *Leben und Taten Alexanders von Makedonien. Der griechische Alexanderroman*. Ed. H. van Thiel (Darmstadt 1974).

Thomas 1977] Wirnt von Grafenberg, *Wigalois, the Knight of Fortune's Wheel*. Ed. J.W. Thomas (Lincoln 1977).

Thomas 1989] *Renaut de Montauban*. Ed. J. Thomas (Textes littéraires français 371, Genève 1989).

Thomas, J.W., *Tannhäuser: Poet and Legend. With Texts and Translations of his Works* (Chapel Hill 1974).

Thomas, Neil, *Reading the Nibelungenlied* (Durham 1995).

Thompson, Raymond H., *The Return from Avalon. A Study of the Arthurian Legend in Modern Fiction* (Westport/London 1985).

Thorp, N.R., *La Conquête de Jérusalem* (Tuscaloosa 1992).

Thorpe 1966] Geoffrey of Monmouth, *The History of the Kings of Britain*. Transl. Lewis Thorpe (Harmondsworth 1966).

Thurneysen, R., *Die irische Helden- und Königsage bis zum siebzehnten Jahrhundert* (Halle a.S. 1921).

Togeby, K., *Ogier le Danois dans les littératures européennes* (Copenhagen 1969).

Tolkien, J.R.R., 'Beowulf: the Monsters and the Critics', in: *Proceedings of the British Academy* 22 (1936), pp. 245–295.

Tolstoy, Nikolai, *The Quest for Merlin* (1985; rpt London 1990).

Topsfield, L.T., *Chrétien de Troyes. A Study of the Arthurian Romances* (Cambridge 1981).

Treharne, R.F. *The Glastonbury Legends* (London 1967).

Tyler 1919] *La Chançun de Willame*. Ed. E.S. Tyler (New York 1919).

Tyssens, M., *La geste de Guillaume d'Orange dans les manuscripts cycliques* (Paris 1967).

Uri 1962] *De historie van Partinoples, grave van Bleys*. Ed. S.P. Uri. (Nederlandse Volksboeken XIV, Leiden 1962).

Vallerie 1947] *Garin le Loheren, according to manuscript A*. Ed. J.E. Vallerie (Ann Arbor 1947).

Van den vos reynaerde. Het Comburgse handschrift (Louvain 1991).

Varty, K., *Reynard the fox* (Leicester 1967).

––––––– (ed.), *A la Recherche du Roman de Renart* (2 vols., New Alyth 1988–1991).

––––––– *Reynard, Renart, Reinaert and Other Foxes in Medieval England. The Iconographic Evidence*. (Amsterdam 1999).

Verbeke, Werner, Jozef Janssens en Maurits Smeyers, *Wort und Bild in der mittelalterlichen Tristantradition* (Berlin 1971).

Vermeer-Meyer 1982] Marie de France, *De lais*. Transl. Anneli Vermeer-Meyer (Utrecht/Antwerp 1982).

Vielhauer 1979] *Amis und Amiles*. Ed. I. Vielhauer (Amsterdam 1979).

Vielhauer 1985] *Das Leben des Zauberers Merlin* [Geoffrey of Monmouth's 'Vita Merlini']. Ed. Inge Vielhauer (Amsterdam 1985).

Wackers, P., *De waarheid als leugen. Een interpretatie van 'Reynaerts historie'* (Utrecht 1986).

Walter 1984] *Hervis de Metz*. Transl. Ph. Walter (Nancy 1984).

Wathelet-Willem, J., *Recherches sur la Chanson de Guillaume. Etudes accompagnées d'une édition* (Paris 1975).

Weber 1977] Wolfram von Eschenbach, *Parzival*. Ed. and transl. G. Weber (Darmstadt 1977).

Weiske 1992] *Gesta Romanorum*. Ed. B Weiske (2 vols., Tübingen 1992).

Weitzmann, K., *Ancient Book Illumination*. Martin Classical Lectures 16 (Cambridge, Mass. 1959).

Wenzel, W., *Wittekind in der deutschen Literatur* (Münster 1931).

Wiles, David, *The Early Plays of Robin Hood* (Cambridge 1981).

Williams-Krapp, W., *Die deutschen und niederländischen Legendare des Mittelalters. Studien zu ihrer Überlieferungs-, Text- und Wirkungsgeschichte*. Texte und Textgeschichte (Würzburger Forschungen 20, Tübingen 1986).

Winkelman, J.H., *Die Brückenpächter- und die Turmwächterszene im 'Trierer Floyris' und in der 'Version Aristocratique' des altfranzösischen Florisromans* (Leiden 1977).

Wisniewski, Roswitha, *Kudrun* (Stuttgart 1969²).

———— , *Mittelalterliche Dietrich-Dichtung* (Stuttgart 1986).

Wolf, A., *Gregorius bei Hartmann von Aue und Thomas Mann* (Munich 1967).

Wolf-Bonvin 1990] *La chevalerie des sots. Le roman de Fergus – Trubert, fabliau XIIIe siècle*. Transl. Romaine Wolf-Bonvin (Paris 1990).

Wunderlich 1977] *Der Schatz des Drachentöters. Materialien zur Wirkungsgeschichte des Nibelungenliedes*. Ed. W. Wunderlich (Stuttgart 1977).

Wynn, M., *Wolfram's Parzival. On the Genesis of its Poetry* (Frankfurt a.M. 1984).

Zemel, R.M.T., *Op zoek naar Galiene. Over de Oudfranse Fergus en de Middelnederlandse Ferguut* (Amsterdam 1991).

Zeydel 1959] *Ruodlieb. The Earliest Courtly Novel*. Transl. E.H. Zeydel (Chapel Hill 1959, 1969³).

Zink, G., *Les légendes héroiques de Dietrich et d'Ermerich dans les littératures germaniques* (Lyon 1950).

Zumthor, Paul, *Merlin le Prophète. Un thème de littérature, polémique, de l'historiographie et des romans* (Lausanne 1943, reprint 1973).

INDEX OF LITERARY AND HISTORICAL FIGURES

* Raoul de Cambrai
Aalart * Renaut de Montauban
Abd al-Rahman I * Roland
Abel * Gregorius
Abenner* Barlaam & Josaphat
Abime * Turpin
Acelin * Louis the Pious
Acglavael * Moriaen
Achilles* Aeneas, Alexander the Great, Cú
    Chulainn, Hector, Lancelot, Troilus
Acopart = Escopart * Bevis of Hampton
Adarn * Gregorius, Hector, Lancelot
Adelaide = Berte aux Grands Pieds
Adelaide of Champagne * Barlaam & Josaphat
Adelantado * Widukind
Ælfhere = Alphere * Waltharius
Ætla = Attila * Waltharius
Aegili * Weland
Aelfwine = Alboin * Widsith
Ælis * Girart de Roussillon
Aeneas = Aeneas * Hector
Aetius * Attila
Agamemnon * Aeneas, Hector
Agravain * Arthur, Lancelot
Agulandus/Agulant * Charlemagne, Lorraine,
    Turpin
Aife * Cú Chulainn
Aigolant = Agulandus
Ailbe * Brendan
Ailill * Cú Chulainn
AIOL
Ajax * Hector
Alain * Joseph of Arimathea
Alan a Dale * Robin Hood
Alane * Guillaume d'Orange
Albanac* Brut
Alberich * Siegfried, Theodoric the Great
Alboin * Widsith
Albrecht III of Bavaria* Wigalois
Alexander, brother of Baudouin * Baudouin de
    Sebourc
Alexander, son of an emperor * Seven Sages of
    Rome
Alexander the Great * Godfrey of Bouillon,
    Hector, Widsith
Alfonso, son of Fernando I * Cid
Alfonso el Sabío * Cid
Alfonso II d'Este * Renaut de Montauban
Alfrik = Alberich * Theodoric the Great
Alice * Robert the Devil
Alis, son of the emperor of Greece * Cligès
Alis, maid * Flamenca
Alise * Berte aux Grands Pieds
Aliste * Berte aux Grands Pieds
Alixandre * Cligès

Alkmene * Merlin
Alphere of Aquitaine * Waltharius
Alvar Fáñez * Cid
Alvilde * Weland
Amadis * Gawain
Amans * Apollonius
Amata* Aeneas
Amauride Viés Mes * Huon
Ambrosius = Merlin * Merlin
Ambrosius Aurelius * Arthur, Lancelot, Merlin
AMELIS * Amys & Amelis, Seven Sages of Rome
Amelunc * Theodoric the Great
Amfortas = Anfortas * Perceval
Ami = Amys
AMYS * Amys & Amelis, Seven Sages of Rome
Amiles = Amelis * Amys & Amelis
Amlethus = Hamlet * Orendel
Ammius* Ermanaric
Ammon * Alexander the Great
Amoraen/Amorijs * Gawain
Amphitryon * Merlin
Anchises * Aeneas, Hector
Andri * Berte aux Grands Pieds
Andromache * Hector
Andromeda * Tristan & Iseult
Anfortas * Perceval
Angelica * Roland
Angrès of Windsor * Cligès
Anna, Saint * Brendan
Anna, sister of Arthur * Arthur, Merlin
Anna Malterer, nun * Yvain
Antenor, Trojan * Aeneas, Hector
Anterior, Spanish king * Maugis
Antiochus * Apollonius
Antor, Auctor = Ector * Kay, Merlin
Apollo * Hector
APOLLONIUS OF TYRE
Araches * Barlaam & Josaphat
Archambaut of Bourbon * Flamenca
Archistrates * Apollonius
Ardericus/Arderik * Amys & Amelis
Ariadne * Tristan & Iseult
Aristotle * Alexander the Great, Merlin
Armida * Renaut de Montauban
Arminius * Siegfried
Aron * Oswald
Arondel, horse * Bevis of Hampton
Arondele * Fergus
Artofilaus * Fergus
Artorius = Arthur * Yder
ARTHUR * Brut, Cligès, Culhwch & Olwen, Erec
    & Enide, Fergus, Galahad, Gawain, Godfrey
    of Bouillon, Hector, Kay, Lancelot, Lanval,
    Merlin, Moriaen, Parthonopeus, Perceval,
    Torec, Tristan, Wigalois, Yder, Yvain

Macaire = Macharijs * Sibilla
Madelgijs = Maugis
Madul * Charlemagne
Mæhild * Deor
Maid Marian * Robin Hood
Maid of Escalot * Lancelot
Maél Duin * Brendan
Magog * Apollonius, Alexander the Great
Mainet (alias of Charlemagne) * Berte aux
    Grands Pieds
Makaris of Lausanne * Aiol
Malebron * Fluon
Malegijs = Maugis * Renaut de Montauban
Mallart * Louis the Pious
Malquarés * Swan Knight
Manannán Cú Chulainn
Manegeel = Lunete * Yvain
Manesier * Aiol
March = Mark * Tristan & Iseult
Marcianus * Theodoric the Great
Marcilijs * Lorraine
Marco Polo * Barlaam & Josaphat
Marcolf/Marcolfus/Marcoli=Morolf * Salman &
    Morolf
Marcolis * Salman & Morolf
Marcon * Swan Knight
Mardochaeus * Alexander the Great
Margarijs * Parthonopeus
Margiste * Berte aux Grands Pieds
Marguerite * Flamenca
Marguerite de Joinville * Louis the Pious
Maria, sister of Martha and Lazarus * Joseph of
    Arimathea
Maria * Cid
Maria Magdalena * Girart de Rousillon
Maria of Brabant* Ogier
Maria of Cleves * Swan Knight
Marie * Baudouin de Sebourc
Marie de Champagne* Girart de Vienne,
    Lancelot
Mariole * Torec
Mark * Tristan & Iseult
Marsile * Roland
Martha *Joseph of Arimathea
Matabrune * Swan Knight
Mathilde of Boulogne * Swan Knight
MAUGIS * Renaut de Montauban
Maximilian I* Arthur, Gawain, Kudrun,
    Helmbrecht, Theodoric the Great
Mechthild * Renaut de Montauban
Medb * Cú Chulainn
Medea * Hector
Medraut = Mordred * Arthur
Meier Helmbrecht * Helmbrecht
Meirchiawn * Tristan & Isoude
Meleagant * Arthur, Kay, Lancelot
Melions * Torec
Melior * Parthonopeus
Melwas * Arthur
Memnon * Troilus
Menelaos * Hector
Menfloers * Hector

Mennoen * Hector
Menw * Culhwch & Olwen
Mercurius * Salman & Morolf
MERLIN /Merlin/Merlinus * Arthur, Gawain,
    Hector, Kay, Lancelot, Seven Sages of Rome
Mibrien * Aiol
Michaël * Brendan, Ogier
Milo * Charlemagne
Milon, father of Roland * Fierabras,
    Charlemagne
Milon de Pouille * Girart de Vienne
Mio Cid = Cid
Mirabel * Aiol
Miraude * Torec
Montaigne * Amys and Amelis
Montesinos * Aiol
Morant * Berte aux Grands Pieds
Mordred * Arthur, Gawain, Lancelot
Morgan la Fay = Morgaine * Arthur, Gawain,
    Lancelot
Morgawse * Gawain
Morholt * Tristan & Iseult
MORIAEN * Perceval
MOROLF * Salman & Morolf
Mosollamus * Alexander the Great
Moyses * Joseph of Arimathea
Mozes * Gregorius
Much = Robin Hood
Mundzucus = Botelunc * Attila
Myrddin * Merlin

Nachor* Barlaam & Josaphat
Namlun * Widukind
Napoleon I * Charlemagne, Siegfried
Napoleon III * Merlin, Roland
Nascien * Galaad
Nectanabus * Alexander the Great
Nero * Alexander the Great
Nibelung * Siegfried
Nicodemus * Joseph of Arimathea
Nidud * Weland
Nidung * Weland
Nimue/Niniane/Nivienne * Merlin
Nine Worthies = Neuf Preux * Alexander,
    Arthur, Charlemagne, Godfrey of Bouillon,
    Guillaume d'Orange, Hector,
Noah * Brendan
Nobel/Noble, lion * Reynard the Fox
Nuc/Nut * Yder
Nymenche * Merlin

Oberon = Auberon * Huon
Ocise = Crisea * Erec & Enide
Odoakar * Ermanaric, Theodoric the Great
Oede * Huon
Oedipus * Alexander the Great, Gregorius
Oenone * Tristan & Iseult
Offa * Widsith
OGIER VAN DENMARK * Amys & Amelis,
    Charlemagne, Girart de Vienne, Turpin
Ogier le Danois = Ogier of Denmark
Ogrin * Tristan & Iseult

William the Silent * Guillaume d'Orange
William of Dampierre, count of Flanders *
    Reynard the Fox
William of Orange = Guillaume d'Orange *
    Charlemagne
William III of Angoulême * Amys & Amelis
William V of Aquitaine * Amys & Amelis
Winlogee = Guinevere * Arthur, Yder
Witburgis = Guibourc, Guillaume d'Orange
Witege = Vidga * Theodoric the Great, Weland
Witiza = Benoit * Guillaume d'Orange
Wittekind = Widukind
Wolfdietrich * Deor, Theodoric the Great
Wolfger, bishop of Passau * Siegfried
Wolfhart * Theodoric the Great
Wonder, king * Gawain
Wudga = Widia * Widsith
Wulfhere * Widsith
Wultwulf * Theodoric the Great
Wyrmhere * Widsith

Ximena = Jimena * Cid

Ybert de Ribemont * Raoul de Cambrai
Yblis * Lancelot
Ydain * Gawain

YDER * Erec & Enide, Kay
Ydor vander Baser Rivire * Torec
Ygerna * Arthur, Merlin
Ymelot * Rother
Yoen of Gascony* Lorraine
Yon of Gascony * Renaut de Montauban
YONEC * Lanval
Yrene * Lorraine
Ysabele * Gawain
Ysbaddaden Pennkawr * Culhwch & Olwen
YSENGRIMUS /Ysegrim/Ysemgrimus/Ysengrijn/
    Ysengrin/Insingrine * Reynard the Fox
Ysoré (Issoire) de Coninbre * Guillaume
    d'Orange
Yúsuf * Cid
YVAIN * Arthur, Fergus, Torec, Gawain, Yder
Yvon * Godfrey of Bouillon
Yvonet * Perceval
Yvori of Montbrant * Bevis of Hampton
Yvorijn = Sorgalant * Maugis
Ywein = Yvain * Torec, Gawain

Zegevrit = Siegfried
Zeno * Theodoric the Great
Zeus * Alexander the Great, Merlin

CONTRIBUTORS

DR H. AERTSEN (1943) teaches Old and Middle English language and literature at the Free University in Amsterdam. He has published on Chaucer, *Sir Gawain and the Green Knight*, *Havelok* and on philological subjects.

DR RICHARD BARBER (1941) is a historian and a publisher. His interests cover a wide range of subjects, particularly in areas where myth and history are combined. He has written several books about English medieval history; the Arthurian legends have also been a major area of his research. He is currently working on a study of the Holy Grail from its medieval origins to modern interpretations.

DR A.A.M. BESAMUSCA (1955) lectures on medieval Dutch literature at the University of Utrecht. His main field of interest is the Middle Dutch chivalric romance.

DR F.P.C. BRANDSMA (1960) lectures on comparative literature at the University of Utrecht. He is engaged in research into narrative technique in the medieval romance.

DRS TH.J.A. BROERS (1946), graduated from Leiden University with a study of *Willem van Oringen*.

PROF. DR G.H.M. CLAASSENS (1960), professor of medieval Dutch literature at the Catholic University of Louvain, has as his area of research the literature and historiography of the Middle Ages. He gained his doctorate with a study of the Middle Dutch crusade romances.

PROF. DR H. VAN DIJK (1939) is Professor of Older Dutch Literature at the University of Groningen.

DR B.W.TH. DUIJVESTIJN (1940), lecturer at the Gelderland College of Higher Education, was awarded his doctorate for a study of the *Madelgijs* and its German translation. His field of research is Dutch-German literary relations.

PROF. DR DORIS R. EDEL (1936) is Professor of Celtic Languages and Culture at the University of Utrecht. Her research is concerned with Celtic literature and its relationship with the society that produced it.

PROF. DR L.J. ENGELS (1932) is Emeritus Professor of Medieval Latin Language and Literature at the University of Groningen.

DR BAUKJE FINET-VAN DER SCHAAF (1935) is attached as *maître de conférences* to the University of Metz, where she teaches Dutch language and culture.

PROF. DR W.P. GERRITSEN (1935) is Professor of Medieval Literature at the University of Utrecht.

DR ANNELIES VAN GIJSEN (1953) received her doctorate for a study of Colijn van Rijssele's *Spiegel der Minnen*. She is attached to the UFSIA in Antwerp and is investigating the relationships between astrology and alchemy and texts of Middle Dutch literature.

DR J.B. VAN DER HAVE (1941), lecturer at the Rotterdam College of Higher Education, published mainly on the *Roman der Lorreinen*.

DR M. JOSÉE HEIJKANT (1952) lectures on Italian literature at the University of Leiden. Her doctoral thesis was on the *Tristano Riccardiano*, an Italian translation of the Prose Tristan.

DRS CORRIE HOGETOORN (1934) is engaged in research on French and Provençal literature of the Middle Ages.

DR E.M.C. VAN HOUTS (1952) is a fellow of Newnham College, University of Cambridge. She specialises in the Latin literature and historiography of the Anglo-Norman period.

DR L. JONGEN (1948), teaches Middle Dutch literature at the University of Leiden; he has translated a number of Middle Dutch works into modern prose.

DR J. KOOPMANS (1959), of the Department of French and Romanian at the University of Amsterdam, published editions of texts and studies in the field of late-medieval popular and stage literature.

DR W.TH.J.M. KUIPER (1948) is a lecturer in the Dutch Department of the University of Amsterdam. His main interest is in epic works of the manuscript period.

DRS MIEKE J. LENS (1960), until recently an assistant at the University of Groningen, has published on the Middle Dutch *Huge van Bordeeus* tradition and is preparing a thesis on the subject.

DRS A.G. VAN MELLE is a former lecturer on historical and modern Dutch literature at the Central College of Higher Education at Utrecht.

DRS G. ADA POSTMA (1951) recently co-edited a Middle Dutch Lancelot romance at the University of Utrecht. She is also preparing a dissertation on the *Rijmbijbel* of Jacob van Maerlant.

DR A. QUAK (1946) is a senior lecturer in Old Germanic language and literature at the University of Amsterdam.

DR R.J. RESOORT (1944) is a lecturer in the Department of Historical Literature in the Dutch Department of the University of Amsterdam. He specialises in the late Middle Ages.

PROF. DR F. VAN DER RHEE (1912) is Emeritus Professor of Old Germanic. His publications, mainly linguistic in nature, concern Longobardian, Germanic-Romance contacts and Early Germanic phonology and morphology.

DR IRENE SPIJKER (1956) is engaged in research on Middle Dutch and Old French Carolingian epic. She received her doctorate for a study of the relationship between *Renout van Montalbaen* and *Renaud de Montauban*.

DRS R.D.H. STUFKENS (1946) lectures on historical literature at the Middelburg branch of the Rotterdam College of Higher Education; his field of research is Arthurian romance.

DR R.E.V. STUIP (1942), senior lecturer in Medieval French Literature at the University of Utrecht, publishes on 12th- and 13th-century works and 15th-century prose romances.

DRS VEERLE UYTTERSPROT (1963) studied Germanic philology at the Catholic University of Brussels and currently lectures on historical literature at the same university.

W.M. VERBAAL (1960), licentiate in classical philology, teaches post-classical Latin at the University of Ghent.

DR N.TH.J. VOORWINDEN (1934), formerly a senior lecturer at the University of Leiden, teaches German language and literature of the medieval period. His publications relate mainly to German heroic epic.

DR H. DE VRIES (1932) is engaged in research on Spanish literature in the Middle Ages and the Renaissance.

DR P.W.M. WACKERS (1950) lectures on Medieval Dutch literature at the Catholic University in Nijmegen.

DR J.H. WINKELMAN (1940), senior lecturer at the University of Amsterdam, specialises in the medieval literature and culture of Germany and the Low Countries.

DR R.M.T. ZEMEL (1949), lecturer in medieval literature at the Free University in Amsterdam, received his doctorate for a comparative study of the Old French *Fergus* and the Middle Dutch *Ferguut*.